dBASE IV™ Handbook

3rd Edition

George Tsu-der Chou
with W. Edward Tiley

QUE®
CORPORATION
LEADING COMPUTER KNOWLEDGE

dBASE IV™ Handbook

3rd Edition

Copyright © 1989 by Que® Corporation.

Library of Congress Catalog No.: LC 88-61115
ISBN 0-88022-380-4

92 91 90 89   8 7 6 5 4 3 2 1

Interpretation of the printing code: The rightmost double-digit number is the year of the book's printing; the rightmost single-digit number, the number of the book's printing. For example, a printing code of 89-4 shows that the fourth printing of the book occurred in 1989.

The *dBASE IV Handbook,* 3rd Edition, is based on dBASE IV.

DEDICATION

Dedicated to my wife, Jane-Wen
and our children, Doris, Tina, and Tom

Publishing Director

David P. Ewing

Acquisitions Editor

Terrie Lynn Solomon

Editors

Kathie-Jo Arnoff
Mary Bednarek
Shelley O'Hara
Katherine Murray
Rebecca Whitney

Technical Editor

Jeff Booher
Timothy S. Stanley
W. E. Winston

Book Design and Production

Dan Armstrong
Brad Chinn
Cheryl English
Lori A. Lyons
Jennifer Matthews
Cindy L. Phipps
Joe Ramon
Dennis Sheehan
Louise Shinault
Carolyn A. Spitler
Peter J. Tocco

Composed in Garamond and American Typewriter
by Que Corporation

Screen reproductions in this book were created by
means of the InSet program from INSET Systems Inc.,
Danbury, CT

ABOUT THE AUTHOR

George Tsu-der Chou

George Tsu-der Chou, of Vancouver, Washington, is a consultant in the field of database design and development. He has developed database management systems for a large number of clients, such as Gregory Government Securities, Morley Capital Management, Hi-Tech Electronics, West Coast Lumber Inspection Bureau, NERCO, Inc., and others. These systems include analytical managerial database systems and administrative database management programs that deal with inventory and accounting functions.

The author earned his Ph.D. in Quantitative Methods, with supporting studies in Computer Science, Economics, and Econometrics, from the University of Washington. He is currently a full professor at the University of Portland in Oregon, where he teaches courses in business data processing and data management, quantitative methods, operations research, business forecasting, and other subjects. He has taught computer programming in FORTRAN, COBOL, BASIC, and IBM Assembler.

Dr. Chou wrote the popular *dBASE III Handbook* and *Using Paradox*, both published by Que Corporation. He is also the author of *Microcomputer Programming in BASIC* and *Computer Programming in BASIC*, both published by Harper & Row. The former has been translated into Spanish and published in Mexico; reprints of that book have also been distributed in the Philippines.

Dr. Chou has also written a financial analytical modeling program, COMPASS (Computer Assisted Portfolio Planning Management System). Combining database and analytical tools, this software represents the first major effort in the computerization of portfolio management. COMPASS, marketed by Morley & Associates, has now been adopted by many major banks and financial institutions in the United States and Canada.

CONTENTS AT A GLANCE

TABLE OF CONTENTS

11   Conditional Branching and Program Loops ... 451

III   Advanced dBASE IV Programming

12   Modular Programming 479

IV   Command Summary and Functions Summary

ACKNOWLEDGMENTS

First, we thank Kathy Murray, Kathie-Jo Arnoff, Mary Bednarek, Shelley O'Hara, and Rebecca Whitney for their excellent editing of the original manuscript for this book.

Second, we thank Terrie Lynn Solomon for managing many of the stages of developing and editing this book.

Third, we thank the staff members at Ashton-Tate who updated us on the development of dBASE IV and provided technical support.

Last but not least—many thanks to all of the members of the production staff who gave extra time and effort to completing the final production stages of this book.

TRADEMARK ACKNOWLEDGMENTS

Q ue Corporation has made every attempt to supply trademark information about company names, products, and services mentioned in this book. The trademarks indicated below were derived from various sources. Que Corporation cannot attest to the accuracy of this information.

Ashton-Tate, dBASE II, dBASE III Plus, and Framework are registered trademarks and dBASE IV is a trademark of Ashton-Tate Company.

COMPAQ is a registered trademark of COMPAQ Computer Corporation.

EPSON is a registered trademark and MX-100 is a trademark of EPSON America, Inc.

Hewlett-Packard is a registered trademark and LaserJet is a trademark of Hewlett-Packard Corporation.

IBM is a registered trademark and IBM PC XT, Personal Computer AT, OS/2, and Personal System/2 are trademarks of International Business Machines Corp.

Lotus 1-2-3 is a registered trademark of Lotus Development Corporation.

MS-DOS is a registered trademark of Microsoft Corporation.

VisiCalc is a registered trademark of VisiCorp, Inc.

CONVENTIONS USED IN THIS BOOK

In the *dBASE IV Handbook*, 3rd Edition, certain conventions were used to help make learning and using dBASE IV as easy as possible. These conventions include the following:

- ❏ The names of Control Center menus are capitalized (such as Organize menu, Append menu, etc.).

- ❏ Options selected from the Control Center menus appear in boldface type (as in "Select the **Print database structure** option from the Layout menu.").

- ❏ dBASE IV commands entered at the dot prompt and all program listings appear in a special typeface (such as "At the dot prompt, enter USE EMPLOYEE").

- ❏ In the dBASE IV command lines that are used to show the syntax of the command, the brackets and italicized information indicate that you should enter your own information at that point. For example, the command line

    . SAVE TO *<name of memory file>*

    indicates that after you type the . SAVE TO portion of the command, you should enter the name of the memory file to which you want to save the variables.

- ❏ This book includes numerous margin notes that provide important information about tips, cautions, and commands.

Introduction

Welcome to the wonderful world of dBASE IV™. Just a few years ago, only users of large, expensive computer systems could enjoy the power of database management. The introduction of dBASE II® changed the way data was organized and manipulated on small, yet powerful microcomputers. As a result, individuals and small businesses can benefit from database management programs.

dBASE IV has evolved from several versions, starting with dBASE II. dBASE II offered database management capabilities, but this program, designed for the early generations of microcomputers, had limited memory capacity and computational power and was not considered user-friendly. dBASE III®, a drastically different program that evolved from dBASE II, attempted to solve some of these problems.

Although dBASE III's data-storage capacity and computational speed were increased and dBASE III was easy to use, there was a demand for a friendlier, more powerful program. Ashton-Tate, Inc., the developer of dBASE III, responded with dBASE III® Plus. This version provided not only additional data-processing commands but also a pull-down Assistant menu that made selecting menu options easy.

To maintain the lead in database software, Ashton-Tate, Inc. released dBASE IV. This program is heralded to be the most powerful and yet user-friendly database management system for microcomputers. In addition to new commands, dBASE IV has made many significant improvements over earlier versions of the dBASE systems.

1

The improvements, among others, include the following:

❏ A versatile Control Center from which you easily can perform most dBASE IV and DOS operations

❏ Powerful query by example (QBE) operations

❏ Multiple index tags you can set up that are updated automatically as data records change

❏ Powerful and flexible report, label, and data form generators

❏ Structured Query Language (SQL) to provide effective links between dBASE IV and other database systems

With these new improvements and added features, dBASE IV has established its leadership and again defined the industry standard in database management systems.

How Do You Use dBASE IV?

As a database management tool, dBASE IV has two processing modes: interactive and batch-processing. In interactive mode, you can create and manipulate data files by selecting the appropriate menu option or by typing easy-to-use, English-like commands directly from the keyboard. Because the computer responds instantly, you can monitor the input and output.

The other mode, batch-processing mode, is one of the most important capabilities provided by a dBASE system. Batch processing offers all the power and flexibility necessary for designing an integrated menu-driven database management system. Depending on your needs and experience, you can use both modes to manage your database.

A primary objective of the *dBASE IV Handbook*, 3rd Edition, is to demonstrate how you can use dBASE IV commands for effective database management. For purposes of clarity, the examples in this book have been kept simple and concise. To maintain continuity among the examples, the same database is used to illustrate as many different commands as possible. Simple examples give you a better understanding of the underlying principles. Once you fully understand the principles of database management and the correct uses of the dBASE IV commands, you can easily design a more sophisticated database system of your own.

Who Should Use This Book?

If you own dBASE IV, you should use this book. *dBASE IV Handbook*, 3rd Edition, is intended not as a substitute for the dBASE IV manual but rather as a user's guide that goes beyond the basics presented in the manual. Think of the dBASE IV manual as a dictionary that lists and describes the commands and vocabulary. Think of this book as a handbook that shows you how to compose with these commands and vocabulary items.

Beginning users will find this book especially useful. From the easy-to-follow examples, you can learn to design and create a database for your own data management needs. By duplicating the examples, you see firsthand the commands you use to perform various functions. In seven of the beginning chapters, a QuickStart section is included. These sections provide simple exercises you can use to review the material covered in the chapter and to practice the dBASE IV procedures. When it comes to mastering the dBASE IV commands and operations, no approach is better than doing it yourself.

Experienced users who upgrade to dBASE IV also will have many uses for this book. The book teaches you how to use the new Control Center and highlights commands new to dBASE IV. Because the dBASE IV commands are grouped by functions, you can use *dBASE IV Handbook*, 3rd Edition, as a comprehensive reference manual. (If you have not upgraded to dBASE IV, you can use this book to learn about the new features before you decide whether to switch to the latest version.)

If you do not own dBASE IV but are considering purchasing the program, this book is for you also. The opening chapters introduce the concepts of a database, show you how a database can answer your data management needs, and provide an overview of dBASE IV and its functions. Examples in subsequent chapters demonstrate the powerful utilities offered by dBASE IV.

One of the significant features offered by dBASE III Plus and dBASE IV is its networking capability. Because of the vast variations in setting up a particular network, the discussion of that topic is beyond the scope of this book. However, the principles and operations of using dBASE IV are virtually the same. You can use this book to learn the basic and advanced features of dBASE IV for a network version as well.

How Is This Book Organized?

This book is divided into four major parts. Part I, "Introduction to dBASE IV," includes Chapters 1–8. This part covers the dBASE IV procedures for performing database management tasks, including creating a database; entering, editing, and displaying records; sorting, indexing, and summarizing data; and creating reports and labels. Both Control Center menu options and dot prompt commands are explained.

Part II, "Command-File Programming," consists of Chapters 9–11. This part introduces the fundamentals of command-file programming and shows you how to create dBASE IV programs to facilitate database management tasks.

Part III, "Advanced dBASE IV Programming," covers Chapters 12–14. These chapters discuss the advanced features of the program, including modular programming and Structured Query Language (SQL). You learn how to design a multiple-level, menu-driven application.

Part IV, "Command Summary and Functions Summary," describes and lists all the dBASE IV commands and functions.

Read the following paragraphs for a chapter-by-chapter breakdown of the book's contents.

Chapter 1, "Introduction to Databases and dBASE IV," discusses the basic concepts of database management. This chapter introduces the most commonly used relational database model and the basic features of dBASE IV.

Chapter 2, "Getting Started," shows you how to start your dBASE IV program and organize your disk files by using directories. In this chapter, you also are introduced to the powerful Control Center menu system. A QuickStart teaches you to start the program, exit to the dot prompt, get help, and exit dBASE.

Chapter 3, "Creating and Entering Data," begins a discussion of the dBASE IV commands and menu options you can use to perform basic database management functions. This chapter explains the steps for defining a data structure and creating a database file. The chapter describes the menu options and dot-prompt commands you use to enter data. Creating and using a custom data entry form is presented also.

Chapter 4, "Displaying Data," teaches you how to display and print the structure and contents of a database file. In addition, this chapter shows you how to use the powerful query by example (QBE) operations to select records.

Chapter 5, "Editing Data," covers how to modify the contents of a database file. You learn to change the database structure and the data records from both the Control Center and the dot prompt. In the QuickStart, exercises teach you to change the database structure, edit and add data records, and modify a query design.

Chapter 6, "Sorting, Indexing, and Summarizing Data," demonstrates the procedure for rearranging the data records in a database file. This chapter describes the methods you use to sort data records and index files. Examples illustrate these operations and highlight the advantages of sorting versus indexing.

Chapter 7, "Memory Variables, Expressions, and Functions," explains storing data in temporary memory locations called variables and illustrates the usefulness of expressions in data manipulation. This chapter shows how you can perform sophisticated mathematical operations and how you can use dBASE IV's built-in functions to convert data from one type to another.

Chapter 8, "Generating Labels and Reports," teaches you how to use dBASE's built-in label and report generators to create labels and reports. Examples present the available options you can use to design, edit, and use custom labels and reports.

Chapter 9, "Fundamentals of Command-File Programming," introduces the use of batch-processing mode. This chapter shows you how to assemble dBASE IV commands into a program file. The instructions in this file are then carried out by the computer in batch-processing mode. Through the use of numerous examples, this chapter illustrates the power and flexibility of batch mode.

Chapter 10, "Programming Input and Output Operations," focuses on the ways you can perform input and output operations in a program file. The chapter demonstrates how to use input commands to enter and modify data and output commands to place data on-screen and on the printed page.

Chapter 11, "Conditional Branching and Program Loops," offers ways to change the normal processing sequence by using conditional branching and program loops. This chapter covers using the DO WHILE command and other commands to perform database management functions that require repetitive operations.

Chapter 12, "Modular Programming," centers on the concept of structured programming. In this chapter, you learn how to divide a database management system into several small, easy-to-manage subsystems or procedures that you then link through a multilevel menu. You also learn how to design a database management program that uses several different database files.

Chapter 13, "An Integrated Database System," presents a model that illustrates a complete database management system for a small business. This chapter spotlights a multiple-level, menu-driven application that consists of modules for billing, controlling inventory, and maintaining customers' accounts. From the example, you see how to design and integrate various data management functions in a menu-driven dBASE program.

Chapter 14, "The Introduction of SQL in dBASE IV," describes the powerful Structured Query Language commands. You learn ways to perform database management operations with these commands and ways to integrate SQL into your dBASE IV programs. The goal of this chapter is to introduce you to dBASE IV SQL so that you understand the concepts involved.

The dBASE IV Command Summary provides the syntax and examples for dBASE IV commands. The dBASE IV Functions Summary lists dBASE IV's built-in functions.

The *dBASE IV Handbook*, 3rd Edition, contains four useful appendixes. Appendix A includes the standard ASCII character codes. Appendix B summarizes the differences between dBASE III Plus and dBASE IV. Appendix C describes the procedure for installing and configuring the dBASE IV program, and Appendix D lists a summary structure of the dBASE IV menu options.

Part I

▼

Introduction to dBASE IV

Includes

Introduction to Databases and dBASE IV

Getting Started

Creating and Entering Data

Displaying Data

Editing Data

Sorting, Indexing, and Summarizing Data

Memory Variables, Expressions, and Functions

Generating Labels and Reports

1

Introduction to Databases and dBASE IV

Database management systems (DBMS) have long been used to organize and manipulate large collections of business data. The central instrument of a DBMS is the database. Depending on the design you choose, a database may appear in different forms. Because dBASE IV is a relational database management system, relational models are the only form of database discussed in this book.

The beginning of this chapter explains the basic design of a relational database. A database example describing the organization structure of a typical firm is used to explain the design philosophy of a relational database. Later in the chapter, you will see how dBASE IV can be used to implement such an application as a relational database management system. Discussions on the operations and procedures for creating and using a database with dBASE IV are given in the forthcoming chapters. This chapter provides you with your first glance of the program.

What Is a Database Management System?

The term *database management system* refers to the systematic organization and management of a large collection of information in a large computer system. Although used for some time by data-processing personnel, the term has become more generally known since the introduction of such microcomputer programs as dBASE II®.

A *database* is a collection of useful information organized in a specific manner. For instance, you can view a personal telephone directory as a database (see fig.1.1).

Fig. 1.1.

A Telephone database.

```
James C. Smith        (206) 123-4567
Albert K. Zeller      (212) 457-9801
Doris A. Gregory      (503) 204-8567
Harry M. Nelson       (315) 576-0235
Tina B. Baker         (415) 787-3154
Kirk D. Chapman       (618) 625-7843
Barry W. Thompson     (213) 432-6782
Charles N. Duff       (206) 456-9873
Winston E. Lee        (503) 365-8512
Thomas T. Hanson      (206) 573-5085
```

This telephone directory is a listing of names and telephone numbers arranged randomly—arranged, that is, in the order in which they were entered. However, you can organize these telephone numbers in a specific order or form according to your preference. For example, you can group the entries by area codes and alphabetically by last name within each area code group (see fig. 1.2).

```
                    Charles N. Duff           (206) 456-9873
                    Thomas T. Hanson          (206) 573-5085
                    James C. Smith            (206) 123-4567
                    Albert K. Zeller          (212) 457-9801
                    Barry W. Thompson         (213) 432-6782
                    Harry M. Nelson           (315) 476-0235
                    Tina B. Baker             (415) 787-3154
                    Doris A. Gregory          (503) 204-8567
                    Winston E. Lee            (503) 365-8512
                    Kirk D. Chapman           (618) 625-7845
```

Fig. 1.2.

Ordered data entries in the Telephone database.

In addition to rearranging the phone numbers by the last names of their owners, you can add new entries to the list, modify the existing entries, or delete unwanted entries from the list.

The telephone database is a very simple one. Each entry stands alone and does not relate to another entry. A more complex database might involve relations among entries. The organization structure of a firm such as that shown in figure 1.3, for example, shows a database in which the entries are related.

In the database shown in figure 1.3, information about each of the employees and their positions in the firm must be saved as data entries and arranged in a certain manner. In addition, information regarding the relations among these employees and positions needs to be stored as data entries in the database as well. The manner in which these data entries are to be organized and stored in a database depends on the design you choose to adopt.

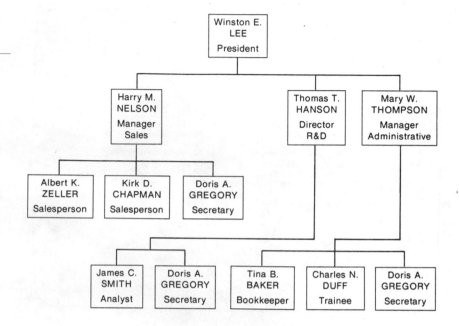

Relational Databases

Information stored in a database can be organized or viewed in a number of ways, depending on the model you choose. These database models include hierarchical, network, and relational databases. Because dBASE IV is a relational database system, this book is limited to covering the concepts and applications of relational databases.

Data Tables

A relational model organizes data elements in one or more two-dimensional data tables, each of which consists of a number of rows and columns. Each row contains information belonging to one entry in the database. Data within a row is divided into several items, each item occupying one column in the table.

For example, the telephone directory example mentioned in the last section can be organized in such a data table (see fig. 1.4).

```
Data Table: Phone
================================================================
  Last Name    First Name    Area Code    Phone Number
----------------------------------------------------------------
  Smith        James C.       206          123-4567
  Zeller       Albert K.      212          457-9801
  Gregory      Doris A.       503          204-8567
  Nelson       Harry M.       315          576-0235
  Baker        Tina B.        415          787-3154
  Chapman      Kirk D.        618          625-7843
  Thompson     Barry W.       213          432-6782
  Duff         Charles N.     206          456-9873
  Lee          Winston E.     503          365-8512
  Hanson       Thomas T.      206          573-5085
----------------------------------------------------------------
```

Fig. 1.4.

The Phone data table.

The information contained in figure 1.4 represents a data table, which may be assigned a name such as Phone. Each row of the data table contains information about a unique telephone number and its owner, while each column contains a value describing the information in the row.

Once the data table is filled with the necessary data, you can display selective entries from the table by specifying certain filter conditions. For example, if you need to know all the phone numbers with a given area code (such as 206), you can ask to display those rows that have area code 206 in one of their columns.

Single-Table Databases

A simple telephone database may contain a single data table like the Phone example shown above. Likewise, information in the organization structure in figure 1.3 can also be organized in a single data table named Employee (see fig. 1.5).

Fig. 1.5

*A single-table
database for the
organization.*

```
Data Table: Employee
================================================================
Name                Position     Department  Supervisor
----------------------------------------------------------------
Winston E. Lee      President
Harry M. Nelson     Manager      Sales       Winston E. Lee
Thomas T. Hanson    Director     R&D         Winston E. Lee
Mary W. Thompson    Manager      Admin.      Winston E. Lee
Albert K. Zeller    Salesperson  Sales       Harry M. Nelson
Kirk D. Baker       Salesperson  Sales       Harry M. Nelson
Doris A. Chapman    Secretary    Admin.      Harry M. Nelson
Doris A. Chapman    Secretary    Admin.      Thomas T. Hanson
Doris A. Chapman    Secretary    Admin.      Mary W. Thompson
James C. Smith      Analyst      R&D         Thomas T. Hanson
Tina B. Baker       Bookkeeper   Admin.      Mary W. Thompson
Charles N. Duff     Trainee      Admin.      Mary W. Thompson
```

In the Employee data table, twelve rows and four columns are used to store information about the firm's organizational structure. The first three columns describe respectively the name of the employee, the employee's position, and the department in which the employee works. The last column identifies the employee's supervising manager.

You may think it seems more concise and simple to design your database as a single-table database. However, a single-table database does have its problems.

One of the problems is that in a single-table database, redundant data entries are needed to fill the data entry when describing multiple relationships among the data entries. In figure 1.5, for example, three entries are needed for defining the relationship between Doris and her three managers: Harry, Thomas, and Mary. Of course, these multiple relations must be defined. However, it is redundant to repeat Doris's personal information three different times. With a relational database, this redundancy is eliminated.

In the Employee data table, most rows are filled with values in their columns. One exception is the first row for the president of the firm, who does not belong to a given department and has no supervising manager. As a result, the last two columns in the first row are left blank or are entered as null values. Null values should be avoided in a data table because they may cause problems in data manipulation operations and therefore are not allowed in some database systems.

In a single-table database, null values are often unavoidable. For example, if one of the managers quits and a new replacement has not been found, all the employees supervised by this manager will have null values in the supervisor columns.

Therefore, you should design your database so that it uses a number of data tables for storing information. For example, a database system for handling the information of the organization structure in figure 1.1 could use three data tables: one for storing the information about the managers, one to store information about the subordinates, and another to describe the relations between the managers and their subordinates. The data table for storing information about the managers and their subordinates could be constructed as shown in figure 1.6.

```
    Data Table: Manager
    =================================================================
    M_ID            M_Name              M_Position  M_Department
    -----------------------------------------------------------------
    123-45-6789     Winston E. Lee      President
    412-63-3218     Harry M. Nelson     Manager     Sales
    205-33-9860     Thomas T. Hanson    Director    R&D
    621-45-3425     Mary W. Thompson    Manager     Admin.
    -----------------------------------------------------------------

    Data Table: Staff
    ================================================
    S_ID            S_Name              S_Position
    ------------------------------------------------
    732-07-8219     Albert K. Zeller    Salesperson
    356-87-4231     Kirk D. Baker       Salesperson
    124-76-0234     Doris A. Chapman    Secretary
    972-45-8123     James C. Smith      Analyst
    865-34-5670     Tina B. Baker       Bookkeeper
    555-23-4572     Charles N. Duff     Trainee
    ------------------------------------------------
```

Fig. 1.6

The manager and staff data tables.

The relations between managers and their subordinates can also be defined as *records* in a data table. For example, as shown in figure 1.7, the data table named Supervise is set up for storing the relation between the managers and their subordinates.

Fig. 1.7

A relation data table.

```
          Data Table: Supervise
==========================================
  M_Name                 S_Name
------------------------------------------
  Harry M. Nelson        Albert K. Zeller
  Harry M. Nelson        Kirk D. Chapman
  Harry M. Nelson        Doris A. Gregory
  Thomas T. Hanson       James C. Smith
  Thomas T. Hanson       Doris A. Gregory
  Mary W. Thompson       Tina B. Baker
  Mary W. Thompson       Charles N. Duff
  Mary W. Thompson       Doris A. Gregory
------------------------------------------
```

In summary, the Manager and Staff data tables can be linked together with the Supervise relation table in an ER-diagram (Entity-Relation diagram). An ER-diagram describes the relation between two entities—in this case, the managers and the staff (see fig. 1.8).

In the Supervise relation data table, each row describes the name of the manager (M_Name) and the name of the subordinate (S_Name) the manager supervises. From the relation data table, you may notice that the names of the managers and one of their subordinates (such as Doris A. Gregory) appear several times in the table, while the names of some subordinates appear only once in the table. This happens because there are different types of relationships that exist among these managers and their subordinates.

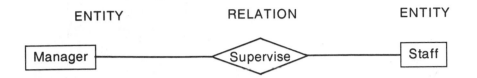

ENTITY   RELATION   ENTITY

| Manager | Supervise | Staff |

Fig. 1.8

An Entity-Relation (ER) diagram.

Relationships

A *relationship* is a link, an association, or a connection between two or more entities. An *entity* can be defined as an object of interest in the database management application. In our example, the managers or the subordinates in the firm can be considered as entities. A relationship is used to define the supervision association between a manager and the manager's subordinates.

Basically, three types of relationships can exist between two entities: one-to-one, n-to-one, and m-to-n relations.

In a one-to-one relation database model, only one entry in the first entity associates with one entry in the second entity. An organization structure that can be defined as a one-to-one relational model requires that one manager supervise only one subordinate and each subordinate be supervised by only one manager. Assuming that the firm has only six employees (Harry, Thomas, Mary, Albert, James, and Tina), an example of a one-to-one relation database model is illustrated in figure 1.9.

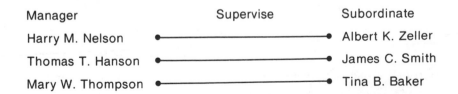

Manager	Supervise	Subordinate
Harry M. Nelson	•————————•	Albert K. Zeller
Thomas T. Hanson	•————————•	James C. Smith
Mary W. Thompson	•————————•	Tina B. Baker

Fig. 1.9.

A one-to-one relation database model.

When you have a one-to-one relation model, each relation can be defined as a single entry in the Supervise relation data table (see fig. 1.10).

In an n-to-one relation model, one entry in the entity associates with n (one or more) entries in the other entity. In the organization structure example, this means that one manager may supervise one or more

Fig. 1.10.

Describing one-to-one relations.

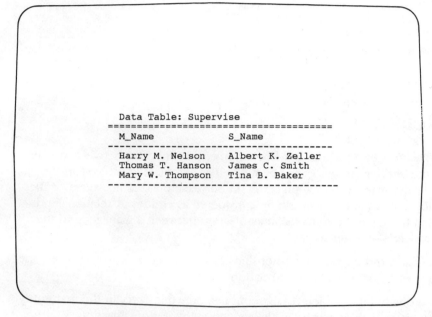

```
            Data Table: Supervise
============================================
   M_Name                S_Name
--------------------------------------------
   Harry M. Nelson       Albert K. Zeller
   Thomas T. Hanson      James C. Smith
   Mary W. Thompson      Tina B. Baker
--------------------------------------------
```

subordinates, but that each subordinate can only be supervised by one manager. Similarly, although uncommon, you may have an organization structure in which one subordinate is supervised by one or more managers; but each manager supervises only one subordinate.

As an example, the organization structure shown earlier in figure 1.3 can be revised to conform an n-to-one relation model (see fig. 1.11).

Fig. 1.11.

N-to-one relations.

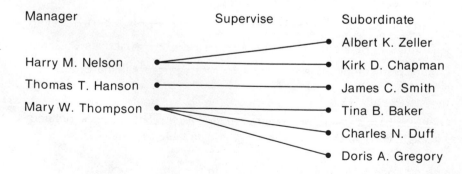

Manager   Supervise   Subordinate

Harry M. Nelson   Albert K. Zeller

                                    Kirk D. Chapman

Thomas T. Hanson   James C. Smith

Mary W. Thompson   Tina B. Baker

                                    Charles N. Duff

                                    Doris A. Gregory

From figure 1.11, you can see that manager Harry supervises two subordinates, Albert and Kirk, while each of these subordinates is supervised only by one manager. Similar relations existed between Mary and three of her subordinates (Tina, Charles, and Doris). When you have an n-to-one (or one-to-n) relation model, you need more than one entry in the data table to describe their relations. For example, three entries are required in the Supervise relation data table to describe the relations between Mary and her subordinates (see fig. 1.12).

```
        Data Table: Supervise
    =========================================
        M_Name              S_Name
    -----------------------------------------
        Mary W. Thompson    Tina B. Baker
        Mary W. Thompson    Charles N. Duff
        Mary W. Thompson    Doris A. Gregory
    -----------------------------------------
```

Fig. 1.12.

Describing n-to-one relations.

The most common relation model is that of an m-to-n model in which one entry in an entity associates with one or more entries in the other entity and vice versa. The organization structure originally defined in figure 1.3 assumes such an m-to-n relation model. That is, one or more of the managers in the firm supervises one or more subordinates, and some subordinates are supervised by one or more managers (see fig. 1.13).

As in an n-to-one relation model, you need multiple entries in a data table for describing these m-to-n relations. The entries for defining the relations described in figure 1.11 are shown earlier in the Supervise data table (refer to fig. 1.7).

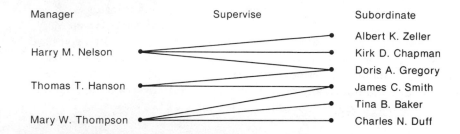

Fig. 1.13.

M-to-n relations.

Components of Relational Database Files

As shown in earlier examples, data tables represent the backbone of a relational database. A data table contains a given number of rows and columns. Each row is called a *data record* and each column is called a *data field*. The data table is assigned a name and saved as a database file with that name.

Although a database can contain several data tables, you can also have a very simple database that has only one data table like that of the Employee data table. The data fields of such a data table, which are specified in a dBASE IV database structure, become an integral part of the database file (see fig. 1.14).

In addition to the database structure, a database file stores the data records containing information about the employees (see fig. 1.15).

Database Structure

A database structure contains detailed descriptions of each field in a data record. These details include the following items:

Description	Information Entered
Field name:	Name or identification of the data field
Field type:	Kind of data field
Field width:	Dimension of the data field

```
Layout   Organize   Append   Go To   Exit                    9:31:07 am
                                              Bytes remaining:    3950
 ┌─────┬────────────┬────────────┬───────┬─────┬───────┐
 │ Num │ Field Name │ Field Type │ Width │ Dec │ Index │
 ├─────┼────────────┼────────────┼───────┼─────┼───────┤
 │  1  │ FIRST_NAME │ Character  │  12   │     │   N   │
 │  2  │ LAST_NAME  │ Character  │  10   │     │   Y   │
 │  3  │ AREA_CODE  │ Character  │   3   │     │   Y   │
 │  4  │ PHONE_NO   │ Character  │   8   │     │   N   │
 │  5  │ MALE       │ Logical    │   1   │     │   N   │
 │  6  │ BIRTH_DATE │ Date       │   8   │     │   Y   │
 │  7  │ ANNUAL_PAY │ Numeric    │   8   │  2  │   N   │
 └─────┴────────────┴────────────┴───────┴─────┴───────┘

 Database C:\...dbdata\EMPLOYEE   Field 1/7                    Caps
        Enter the field name. Insert/Delete field:Ctrl-N/Ctrl-U
 Field names begin with a letter and may contain letters, digits and underscores
```

Fig. 1.14.

A dBASE IV database structure.

```
Records    Fields    Go To    Exit                          11:47:02 am
┌────────────┬───────────┬───────────┬──────────┬────┬────────────┬────────────┐
│ FIRST_NAME │ LAST_NAME │ AREA_CODE │ PHONE_NO │MALE│ BIRTH_DATE │ ANNUAL_PAY │
├────────────┼───────────┼───────────┼──────────┼────┼────────────┼────────────┤
│ James C.   │ Smith     │   206     │ 123-4567 │ T  │  07/04/60  │  22000.00  │
│ Albert K.  │ Zeller    │   212     │ 457-9801 │ T  │  09/20/59  │  27900.00  │
│ Doris A.   │ Gregory   │   503     │ 204-8567 │ F  │  07/04/62  │  16900.00  │
│ Harry M.   │ Nelson    │   315     │ 576-0235 │ T  │  02/15/58  │  29000.00  │
│ Tina B.    │ Baker     │   415     │ 787-3154 │ F  │  10/12/56  │  25900.00  │
│ Kirk D.    │ Chapman   │   618     │ 625-7845 │ T  │  08/04/61  │  19750.00  │
│ Mary W.    │ Thompson  │   213     │ 432-6783 │ F  │  06/18/55  │  24500.00  │
│ Charles N. │ Duff      │   206     │ 456-9873 │ T  │  07/22/64  │  13500.00  │
│ Winston E. │ Lee       │   503     │ 365-8512 │ T  │  05/14/39  │  34900.00  │
│ Thomas T.  │ Hanson    │   206     │ 573-5085 │ T  │  12/24/45  │  28950.00  │
└────────────┴───────────┴───────────┴──────────┴────┴────────────┴────────────┘

 Browse  C:\...dbdata\EMPLOYEE   Rec 1/10        File          Caps
                        View and edit fields
```

Fig. 1.15.

Listing of data records in dBASE IV.

In dBASE IV, you can also specify which data fields you would like to index. *Indexing* is a process with which you can arrange the data records in a given data table so that information can be retrieved or presented in a certain order.

Defining the structure serves several purposes. When you manipulate data, you can use the field names specified in the structure to recall and refer to data stored in those fields. For instance, you can use the field name LAST NAME throughout a database application to locate all the information associated with a particular last name.

Specification of the data type dictates how the information is to be used. If you define a data field as numeric, items stored in the field can be included in formulas. But data stored in a field defined as character can be used only as a label or as the object in a search operation; a character string can never be included in a formula, even if the character string consists only of numbers.

Because dBASE IV assumes that data fields are of a fixed length, the dimension of a data field is defined as the number of characters to be used by the largest data item that will be entered in the field. By declaring the dimension of a data field, you reserve the necessary storage space for anticipated data items. If the longest last name in your database has 10 characters, you must declare the dimension of the field LAST NAME as 10, even though some last names require fewer than 10 letters.

Data Records

As mentioned earlier, contents of a database file are organized into data records and fields. A *data record* holds the data items for a single entry. In the Employee database file, for example, information about an employee makes up a data record.

Data records in a database file are usually arranged in the order in which they are entered. Each data record is assigned a sequential record number when the record is added to the database. Users can subsequently identify these data records by their record numbers.

Data Fields

A *data field* is a storage unit holding a single data item within a data record. Each data field is given a name by which it is identified in the database. A field name contains a fixed number of characters, which may be a combination of letters, numbers, and certain symbols.

The contents of a data field may be a character string or a numeric value. A character string may be as short as a single letter or as long as a paragraph. A numeric value can be either an integer or a number with a decimal point. The number of characters reserved for character strings and the number of digits reserved for numeric values must be clearly defined in the database structure before the data field is used.

In dBASE IV, other types of data fields can also be defined. These field types are date, memo, and logical fields. Some of these fields are special kinds of character fields, and others are reserved for holding data in special formats.

Relational Database Functions

As the preceding examples illustrate, a relational database provides an effective means for maintaining and manipulating a large amount of information. Some useful functions you can perform on a relational database include

- ❏ Maintaining and updating the contents of the database

- ❏ Locating and retrieving data that meets a given set of specifications

- ❏ Sorting or rearranging a set of data items into a predetermined sequence or order

- ❏ Linking data items in different database files to have indirect indexing on the data items

Data maintenance operations include adding data to the database, changing part or all of its contents, and deleting items from it. New data records can be inserted in a relational database, and any part of an item can be modified or deleted. In the telephone database, for example, a new telephone number can be added to the database by appending a new record to the end of the file. Any item in the database, such as an area code or a local number, can be modified or replaced. This data maintenance capability is a useful tool for inventory management, as well.

Another important function in database management is being able to locate and retrieve data in the database by referring to the item's record number and field name. In a relational database, finding a record that contains a specific item in one field is a fairly simple task.

The ability to sort, or rearrange, the data records in a database is another valuable feature in a relational database management system. For instance, in a mailing-label application, having all the names and addresses in descending or ascending order by ZIP code is often desirable; and telephone numbers are usually sorted alphabetically by the person's last name.

Linking data elements in different database files is yet another powerful feature in a data management system. For instance, by using the account number as a data field in several files, you can link all the records containing a given account number in those files.

These functions are discussed more fully in later chapters of this book.

What Is dBASE IV?

dBASE IV is a relational database management system. The program runs on IBM ® Personal Computers and compatible machines, and is designed for creating, maintaining, and manipulating relational databases.

dBASE IV stores data in a database file in the form of a relational data table. Information in the database can be processed two ways: through interactive command processing, or through batch command processing.

With *interactive command processing*, you manipulate information in the database by selecting the appropriate options from the menu or by using commands entered interactively from the keyboard. As these menu options or commands are interpreted and performed by dBASE IV, results are displayed on an output device such as a monitor or a printer.

One of the powerful tools provided by dBASE IV for assisting the interactive command processing is the Control Center interface. With the menu options provided by the Control Center, you can develop your data management system and effortlessly carry out the data manipulation operations. These operations can also be performed by entering the appropriate commands from the keyboard at the dot prompt. The power and advantage of command processing at the dot prompt will be discussed in later chapters.

With *batch command processing*, data manipulation tasks are defined in a set of command procedures. The collection of commands is stored in a command file, which can be considered a computer program. These commands are then executed in a batch. With a batch command file, a processing menu can be designed so that users can select specific tasks while the program is being executed.

dBASE IV Files

In dBASE IV, in addition to database files, information related to the database files are stored in various different disk files. Because different types of information are used in a database application, different kinds of data structures are defined in disk files. Each dBASE IV disk file must be assigned a two-part file identification: a file name, and an extension. A unique file name is assigned by the user. The extension consists of a period (.) and three letters that indicate the file's type. The sections that follow explain this concept more fully.

File Name

A dBASE IV file name consists of a string containing no more than eight characters, not counting the file extension. These characters can be letters, numbers, or the underscore character (_). No blank spaces are allowed in a file name. The following strings of characters are acceptable file names:

EMPLOYEE.dbf
PHONES.dbf
Accounts.dbf
PAYCHECK.fmt
ID_NO.dbf
LETTERS.dbt
ADDRESS.dbf
mailing.lbl
ATABLE.txt
Billing.prg

A file name, together with its file extension (for example, .dbf or .prg), constitutes a symbolic name for the disk file. The file name and extension provide a unique reference for the disk file. As a matter of convention, file extensions usually designate the type of file or its purpose.

File Types

Types of disk files (with their default file extensions) that can be set up in dBASE IV for storing and processing information related to a database are

Disk File Type	Extension
Catalog files	.cat
Database files	.dbf
Database memo files	.dbt
Format files	.fmt, .fmo
Index files	.ndx, .mdx
Label files	.lbl, .lbo
Memory files	.mem
Program or command files	.prg
Query files	.qbe, .qbo
Report form files	.frm, fro
Screen files	.scr
Text output files	.txt
View files	.vue

In the preceding section, you have learned the structure and contents of a database file. Description of other dBASE IV files are made in the following sections.

Catalog Files

A *catalog file* is used by dBASE IV for grouping all disk files that are related to a given application. A catalog file holds the names of a set of related database files and their related operational files (such as format, report form, and label files).

Database Memo Files

A *database memo file*, which is similar to a database file, is used to store large blocks of text called *memos*. A database memo file provides supplementary storage space for a database file. The memo text can be defined as a data field in a database file, but the contents of the memo field are stored in a memo file that is separate from the database file itself. Unlike character fields, memo fields can vary in length from record to record.

Format Files

In dBASE IV, in addition to a standard form provided for entering data records to a database file, you can also design a custom form for the data-entry operation. A *format file* stores all the information about such a custom data-entry form.

Index Files

Arranging data into the desired order is an important function in database management. dBASE IV indexes the contents of a database file according to the contents of a specified field; this operation achieves the effect of sorting. An *index file* provides the necessary working space for indexing. With an index file, a set of data can be viewed or processed in a logical order rather than the order in which the records were entered in the database.

In dBASE III Plus® and its predecessors, individual index (.ndx) files are used to store the information about how the records in a database file are arranged according to the values in indexing keys. dBASE IV uses a different method of indexing: With a single multiple index (.mdx) file, dBASE IV keeps track of the information needed for arranging the records in a database file with several different index tags. An index tag works just like an individual index file, except that all the index tags you set up will be automatically updated and maintained. They can be used for ordering the records at any time.

Label Files

Label files contain information used for printing labels with the LABEL command. A label file, which is similar to a format file, stores the specifications for printed labels. The specifications can include the width and the height of a label, the spacing between labels, and so forth. The specifications also spell out which fields are to be printed and where and in what format this information will be displayed on the label.

Memory Files

A *memory file* stores the contents of active memory variables. There are four types of memory variables: numeric, character, date, and logical variables. Numeric memory variables represent temporary memory locations that can hold the results of computations. The results stored in memory variables can be used again in subsequent processing. A character memory variable is used to hold a character string. Date and logical variables are used to store date values or logical values, respectively. Values of these memory variables are saved in a memory file with the SAVE command; the RESTORE command is used to "read" the values from disk and store them in memory variables. Memory variables play an important role in data manipulation. For example, they can be used to keep track of the last invoice number issued.

Program or Command Files

A *program file* stores a collection of dBASE IV commands that are to be processed in batch mode. Because the set of instructions is often called a program (or procedure), a command file is sometimes called a *command program file* or *procedure file*. A command file can be created either with the text-editing program that is a part of dBASE IV or with a word-processing program in nondocument mode.

Query Files

Query files contain information for finding and viewing selective records in a database file. In a query design, filter conditions are used for searching selective records. Records found are then displayed in a query view. Those records can be saved as a separate database file. A query file can also be used to update the data records in that database file.

Report Form Files

Report form files contain information used for generating reports with the REPORT command. Information in a report form file specifies the contents of reports and their format, such as the information which is to appear in the report heading and the data items that are to be used in the report.

Screen Files

Screen files contain information related to the screen layout of a custom data-entry form. Such screen files are created when you use the form generator provided by dBASE IV for designing your custom data-entry forms.

Text Output Files

A *text output file* stores text that can be "shared" with other computer programs. For instance, a table of data created with dBASE IV can be written to a text output file. After you have exited dBASE IV, that file can be read by other software, such as a word-processing program or another database management program. A text output file provides the link for information exchange among different computer programs.

View Files

View files store information about the records generated by a query operation. For example, when you displaying selective data records for a given set of data fields produced by a query, these records will be saved in a view file. In addition, when you merge or link data records from more than one database file with a query operation, view file will be used to save the resulting records.

dBASE IV Data Fields

A *data field* is a division of a data record. Data fields within a record are used to stored different types of data in the database. Depending upon the nature of the data elements, five different types of data fields can be used in dBASE IV:

Character (or text) fields
Memo field
Numeric fields
Logical fields
Date fields

Each type of data field is used to store one type of data. The type of the data field governs the form in which the data must be entered and the way in which the data can be used.

Character and Memo Fields

Character fields and memo fields store text, which can include letters, numerals, special symbols, and blank spaces. Most characters defined in the American Standard Code for Information Interchange (ASCII) can be text characters. (A list of the ASCII characters is given in Appendix A at the end of this book.) However, character fields and memo fields are different. A character field can store a short block of text, but only a memo field can store a large block of text. In addition, the text stored in these two fields is used differently. Details of these differences are the subjects of later chapters.

Numeric Fields

Any values or numbers in a database can be stored in a numeric field, whose contents are used for computational applications. Numeric fields are of two types: integer and decimal. The sign (positive or negative) associated with a number or value is considered a part of the field contents. Values can be stored in a fixed number or a floating number internally. When values are stored in a floating number format, they have greater precision than those stored in the fixed point format.

Date Fields

A date field is used to store dates, which can be represented in various forms. A common format for a date is mm/dd/yy, where mm, dd, and yy represent numeric codes for the month, day, and year, respectively. A date in dBASE IV is treated differently from text or a number. Date values must be used only as dates in data manipulation; they cannot be treated as normal character strings. Date values can, however, be used in date arithmetic.

Logical Fields

Logical fields hold a single character that represents a true (.T.) or false (.F.) condition. A logical field can therefore divide the contents of a database file into two groups: one for which the condition is true, and another for which the condition is false. For example, a database consisting of a set of student records can include a logical field to identify the sex of a student. A .T. entered in the logical field MALE indicates that the student is male, whereas an .F. indicates that the student is female.

System Requirements

dBASE IV is designed to run on the IBM Personal Computer, PC XT™, Personal Computer AT™, and 100 percent compatible computers. The program can also be run on IBM Personal System/2™ Models 30, 50, 60, and 80 as well as the COMPAQ® Portable I, II, III, and Deskpro 286 and 386 machines.

Disk Operating Systems

dBASE IV requires MS-DOS® or PC DOS version 2.0 or later (including 2.00 and 2.10). The program can also be run under PC DOS versions 3.00, 3.10, 3.20, and 3.30; and under OS/2 version 1.00 in DOS compatibility mode. Although Ashton-Tate® will soon release dBASE IV for the OS/2™ operating system, only the DOS version of the program is discussed in this book.

Memory Requirements

The minimum amount of computer memory (RAM) required is 640K (kilobytes). The first release of dBASE IV does not support the Expanded and Extended memory.

Disk Capacity

Because of the amount of the disk space required for storing the program files, a hard disk is required to run dBASE IV. If you have a hard disk, you still need a floppy disk drive in order to install the dBASE IV program files. You can use either a 5 1/4-inch, 360K (or 1.2M) disk drive or a 3 1/2-inch, 720K disk drive.

Output Devices

Output from the dBASE IV program can be displayed on a monitor or a printer. The program supports an IBM monochrome or a CGA, EGA, or VGA color graphics monitor. dBASE IV can display printed output on a wide range of printers, including most popular laser printers.

System Limitations

The type of processor used in the microcomputer and the amount of available memory limit the size of the database. The available storage space on the floppy disk or hard disk determines the number of files that can be stored. Furthermore, both dBASE IV and the disk operating system limit the number of files that can be created and that can be open at one time. A maximum of 10 database (.DBF) files can be active at one time, and 47 individual index tags (the equivalent of 47 index or .NDX files in dBASE III Plus) can be created, maintained, and stored in a multiple index (.MDX) file. Only one format file can be specified for each database file. Still, a total of 99 different files of all types can be active at one time during processing. Note, however, that a database file containing a memo field is counted as two files.

A database (.DBF) file can contain a maximum of one billion data records, each of which can hold up to 4,000 characters and can be divided into as many as 256 data fields. However, each data record in a database memo (.DBT) file can store up to 512,000 characters of text.

A character field can store as many as 254 characters of information, whereas a memo field can hold only 4,096 characters. A numeric field can store up to 19 characters, which can include digits, decimal points, and the sign of a value (a + or −), but no commas. Smaller yet, a date field holds a string of eight characters (mm/dd/yy), and a logical field can contain only one character (T or F, Y or N).

Chapter Summary

This chapter introduced you to the fundamental concepts of data management. In this chapter, you learned how databases store and process data, which types of files are used for storing various types of information, and which data field types are used to store specific data values. Additionally, this chapter explained the two ways in which data is processed in dBASE IV: through interactive command processing or through batch command processing. In the next chapter, you get started using the program by organizing the directories on the hard disk and installing and starting dBASE IV.

2

Getting Started

B ecause dBASE IV is specifically designed to run on an IBM Personal
Computer or compatible machine, a thorough understanding of the
computer system is vital for effective use of the program. If you are not
familiar with the basic components of the IBM PC and its disk operating
system (DOS), you should read the system manuals for reference.

Before you use dBASE IV, however, the program must be installed on
your computer system. Furthermore, the disk you will use to start the
program must be prepared so that the system will accommodate the
maximum number of database files and data buffers you will need. This
operation is called *configuring the system*. The procedures for installing
dBASE IV and setting up the system configuration are explained in
Appendix F, and you may want to work through those procedures before
you proceed to the rest of the book.

One of the new, user-friendly features offered by dBASE IV is the
interactive mode of processing available with the Control Center menu.
The menu's components and the layout of the Control Center are
discussed in this chapter, as is dBASE IV's interactive processing mode,
which involves entering commands at the dot prompt.

Because of the size of the dBASE IV program, a hard disk is needed in
order to process the program and the data files efficiently. As a result, a
thorough understanding of the use of disk directories for organizing your
disk files is vital to an effective utilization of your storage resources. In
this chapter, you will learn how to manage and organize your disk files
on a hard disk.

The special terms and operations introduced in this chapter include the
following:

☐ Disk file directories
☐ Creating a new directory
☐ Switching between directories
☐ Installing the dBASE IV program
☐ The Control Center
☐ The dot prompt

Organizing dBASE IV Disk Files

The most important storage medium used in a microcomputer system is
its disk unit. When the first generation of personal computers was
introduced, the floppy disk drive became the primary memory device for
storing information because of its data needs and low cost. At that time,
most application programs were relatively small and required only a
moderate amount of disk space.

Early database application programs could accommodate only a limited
number of data files of moderate sizes. For these applications, the amount
of storage space in a floppy disk seemed to be adequate. In addition, the
early version of the disk operation system (DOS) was designed around
floppy disk applications.

However, recent advancement in the database management programs has
drastically changed the storage requirement. Like dBASE IV, most
database management programs are now rather large and require
substantial amounts of disk storage space. As a result, you need a hard
disk for storing the program files and the data files you will create for the
data management operations within dBASE IV.

As the number of disk files increases, the task of organizing these disk
files becomes increasingly important. A properly managed disk file not
only allows quick access during data processing but also enables you to
update and maintain files easily.

In response to the need for an efficient way for organizing disk files,
recent versions of disk operation systems (PC DOS 2.0 or MS-DOS 2.0
and later versions) provide the means for grouping related disk files in a

given file directory. In addition, multiple levels of subdirectories can be structured within a directory for storing those groups of dBASE IV files that are related to different applications.

As you will learn later, the only efficient way to manage your dBASE IV files is to create a common directory for storing all the files related to the dBASE IV operations. Within that directory, you will create separate subdirectories: one for holding all the system files supplied by dBASE IV, and others for saving all the data files (including the database files and their related files) for different applications.

In the following section, you will learn how to manage your disk files by using file directories.

Structure of File Directories

The disk space on a hard disk is divided into a number of directories, each of which is used to store related disk files (see fig. 2.1). The main, or top level, directory is called the *root directory*. Below the root directory, you can have a number of directories in the second level. In turn, directories can be created within each of these second-level directories. Each of one of these directories created can be considered as a subdirectory of the second-level directory.

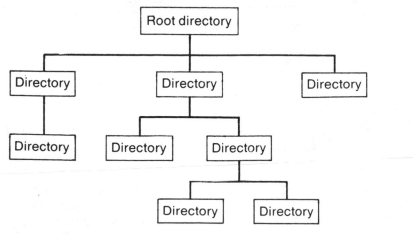

Fig. 2.1.

The structure of the disk file directory.

The Root Directory

When you first turn the computer on, the current directory is the *root directory*, which contains the system files, such as COMMAND.COM and CONFIG.SYS. These system files are normally used for DOS operations and for defining the system configuration.

In the root directory, you also store a number of batch files such as AUTOEXEC.BAT and DBASE.BAT, each of which may be used for processing a batch of DOS commands in a certain sequence. When the root directory is the current directory, a backslash appears alone after the DOS prompt. For example, if you start your computer from the hard disk (which is commonly designed as drive C), a listing of the files in the root directory may look like that in figure 2.2.

```
C:\>DIR

    Volume in drive C is DBASE
    Directory of  C:\

COMMAND  COM    23868   7-30-86   2:35p
CONFIG   SYS      133   6-08-88   8:05a
AUTOEXEC BAT       35   8-15-88   8:30a
DBASE    BAT       56   6-18-88   8:22p
DBASE          <DIR>    6-08-88   8:25a
        5 File(s)  12738560 bytes free

C:\>
```

Fig. 2.2.
A sample listing of files in the root directory.

In figure 2.2, the DOS command Dir (or DIR) is used to display the current active directory. The name of the disk volume (for example, DBASE) is assigned when the disk is formatted. Depending on the type of hard disk you use, the format of the volume label may look different. The hard disk used in figure 2.2 is a 20M Bernoulli hard disk cartridge by

Iomega. The name of the current directory is C:\. The backslash (\) is used to identify the root directory.

Making a Directory

Your computer system may be used to perform various data processing needs. You may use it to process your accounting data with the accounting software. You may perform your sales forecasts with a spreadsheet program. Still, you would like to use a database management program such as the dBASE IV to manage all the important data. Because when you are in a given application, you'll need only those disk files related to the application, you should group the related files in a particular directory so that you can find the files for that application easily. For example, when you use dBASE IV, the program uses a directory named DBASE for holding all of those program files provided by dBASE IV.

Although during the dBASE IV installation process, the program will create the DBASE directory, you may create it yourself before the installation process by entering the name of the directory (such as DBASE) after the DOS command MD (for Make Directory) after the DOS prompt (C>), such as

Command:
MD *(Make Directory) Make a file directory.*

    MD DBASE

In response to the command, a new directory of the name specified will be created. If you would like to verify the existence of the directory just created, display the root directory by using the DIR (Directory) command after the DOS prompt (C>), such as

    DIR

The directory then will be displayed as

Command:
DIR *(Directory) Display the current file directory.*

    DBASE   <DIR>   6-Ø8-88 8:25a

The \DBASE directory is now considered as a subdirectory under the root directory. It is important to remember that even after you have created a new directory, the root directory remains the current directory until you switch to a different directory.

Changing Directories

Command:
CD (Change Directory) Change the current file directory.

If you would like to switch to a directory that is different from the current active directory, you can issue the DOS command CD (for Change Directory) at the DOS prompt, followed by the name of the directory to which you want to switch. To switch from a given directory to one of its subdirectories, you can enter the DOS command CD followed by the name of the subdirectory. For example, if you would like to switch from the current directory (that is, the root directory) to the DBASE directory, you could enter CD DBASE after the DOS prompt (C>) in the following form:

    CD \ DBASE

Tip:
Use PROMPT to monitor the current file directory.

In response to the CD DBASE command, the DOS prompt (C>) will be returned. At this point, you are in the DBASE directory. However, unless you tell DOS to display the current directory name, you will not know where you are in the directory structure. If you would like to know at all times the name of the active directory, you can issue the PROMPT PG command after the DOS prompt (C>), such as

    PROMPT PG

The name of the current directory then is displayed as part of the DOS prompt. For example, if the DBASE directory is the current directory, the DOS prompt appears as follows:

    C:\DBASE>

To cancel the display of the current directory, you can issue the PROMPT command without the PG clauses after the DOS prompt (C>), such as

    PROMPT

This causes the DOS prompt to appear again as

    C>

Creating a Subdirectory

During the dBASE IV installation, all the program files will be saved in the \DBASE directory. For better organization of your data files, you may want to create a subdirectory within the \DBASE directory.

To create a directory within another directory, you can use the MD commands as illustrated earlier. For example, if you would like to create within the DBASE directory a directory (you also can call this a *subdirectory*) named DBDATA, make sure that DBASE is the current directory, and then enter MD DBDATA at the DOS prompt. If you have used the PROMPT command to display the name of the current directory, the prompt and MD command would look like this:

```
C:\DBASE>MD DBDATA
```

To display the contents of the newly created DBDATA subdirectory, first change to the subdirectory by typing CD DBDATA after the DOS prompt; then use the DIR command to display the files in that directory, such as

```
C:\DBASE>CD DBDATA
```

After you press Enter, the prompt changes to C:\DBASE\DBDATA>. Then, to display the contents of the DBDATA subdirectory, you type DIR after the prompt, such as

```
C:\DBASE\DBDATA>DIR
```

After you press Enter, the following is displayed (the creation dates and times shown in the two left columns on your screen will vary from the ones shown here):

```
Volume in drive C is DBASE
Directory of  C:\DBASE\DBDATA

.              <DIR>      8-18-88   8:35a
..             <DIR>      8-10-88   8:35a
        2 File(s)   12728320 bytes free
```

```
C:\DBASE\DBDATA>
```

Notice that you do not include a backslash (\) in the CD DBDATA command because the DBDATA is not at the root directory. However, from the example, you can see the listing of the directory (C:\DBASE\DBDATA). The two backslashes indicate how the current directory DBDATA can be traced back to the root directory; that is, the directory DBDATA is a subdirectory of the DBASE directory (DBASE\) which, in turn, is a subdirectory of the root directory (\). Hence, the description of \DBASE\DBDATA is called a *directory path*, which leads from the current active directory back to the root directory.

When you change from one directory to directory at a different level, you must include the backslash (\) in the directory path. For example, if you are currently in the DBDATA directory and would like to switch to the directory within which the current directory is located, you can use the following DOS command after the C> prompt:

CD \DBASE

Otherwise, if you enter the DOS command CD DBASE at this point, you would get an error message of Invalid directory. When you switch from one directory to another within the same disk drive (for example, C:) you do not have to include the disk drive in the CD command. You could switch to a directory in another disk drive by specifying the drive in the CD command, such as

CD D:\LOTUS\COSTS

Tip:
Use .. to move to the parent directory.

However, you can use a double period (..) command to switch to the immediate parent directory from a given subdirectory. For example, if you are in DBDATA, which is under the \DBASE directory, you can switch to the \DBASE directory by issuing the .. command after the C> prompt (assuming that the PROMPT PG command has already been issued). For this operation, the prompt and command entered appear as

C:\DBASE\DBDATA>CD ..
C:\DBASE>

Displaying Directories

When you are at the DOS prompt, as illustrated earlier, you can get a listing of the directory. The DOS command DIR, when used without any directory path, will display a listing of the files in the current active directory.

You can also display the files of a directory other than the current directory. For example, if C:\DBASE\DBDATA is the current directory, you still can display the files in the DBASE directory. To do that, you can first switch to the DBASE directory by using the CD \DBASE command; then issue the DIR command. However, when you do this, you will be switched to the DBASE directory. If you would like to remain in the current directory while displaying the files in the DBASE directory, you can use the DIR .. command.

The double periods (. .) instruct DOS to display the directory one level up from the current directory. In this case, because the current directory DBDATA is the immediate subdirectory of the DBASE directory, the double period command displays the files in the DBASE directory.

Similarly, regardless where you are in the directory structure, you may display the files in the root directory without leaving the current directory by using the DIR \ command. Using the backslash without specifying any directory path in the DIR command instructs DOS to display the directory at the root level.

When you are in a given directory, you can display a selective group of disk files by using the asterisk (*) or the question mark (?) as a masking character. The asterisk designates that any character string can be used in its place. For example, if you would like to display all the database files in the directory, you could use the DIR *.DBF command. The command DIR *.PRG displays all the command program files. The question mark designates that a single character can be used in its place. If you would like to list all the disk files whose names begin with DB, you can enter the DIR DB??????.* command at the DOS prompt, whereas the command DIR DB???.DBF will display all the database files whose names begin with DB followed by any three other characters.

The double periods (. .) and backslash (\) can also be used in a CD command to switch from the current directory to the immediately preceding directory and to the root directory, respectively. For example, when you are in DBDATA (C:\DBASE\DBDATA), issuing the command CD .. would make the DBASE directory the current directory. (*Note:* Be sure that you insert a space between the CD command and the double periods.) Similarly, by issuing the CD \ command, you will be returned to the root directory, regardless where you are in the directory structure.

Installing the dBASE IV Program

Before you start dBASE IV, you need to install the program on your computer system. Installation involves copying the program files to the appropriate subdirectories of the hard disk and setting up the proper configuration for your system.

dBASE IV is available in two disk formats: 3 1/2-inch microfloppy disks and 5 1/4-inch floppy disks. To run dBASE IV, you need a hard disk

system. The procedure for installing dBASE IV onto your hard disk is
explained in Appendix D.

Starting the dBASE IV Program

After you have successfully installed dBASE IV on your computer system,
you are ready to start using dBASE IV. However, for a better organization
of your data, you may want to create a subdirectory (named DBDATA)
within the \DBASE directory. You could use the DBDATA subdirectory to
store your data files, which will help you keep the data separate from the
dBASE IV program files already in the \DBASE directory. The section
"Creating a Subdirectory," earlier in this chapter, explains the procedure
necessary for creating the DBDATA subdirectory.

After you've created the data subdirectory, you can start the dBASE IV
program from this subdirectory by using the following steps:

1. Start the computer system with either a cold boot or a
   warm boot, and issue the PROMPT PG command so that you can
   monitor the current directory:

   ```
   C>PROMPT $P$G
   ```

2. Move to the \DBASE\DBDATA subdirectory by typing CD
   command at the C> prompt:

   ```
   C:\>CD \DBASE\DBDATA
   ```

3. Then set the path to \DBASE at the prompt so that the computer
   will be able to find all the necessary program files in that
   directory:

   ```
   C:\DBASE\DBDATA>PATH=\DBASE
   ```

4. Then issue the DBASE command at the returned prompt:

   ```
   C:\DBASE\DBDATA>DBASE
   ```

5. Soon, the first dBASE IV message screen will appear (see fig. 2.3).
   Press Enter to continue.

6. In response to the Enter keystroke, the opening Control
   Center screen menu is displayed (see fig. 2.4). You are now ready
   to use dBASE IV.

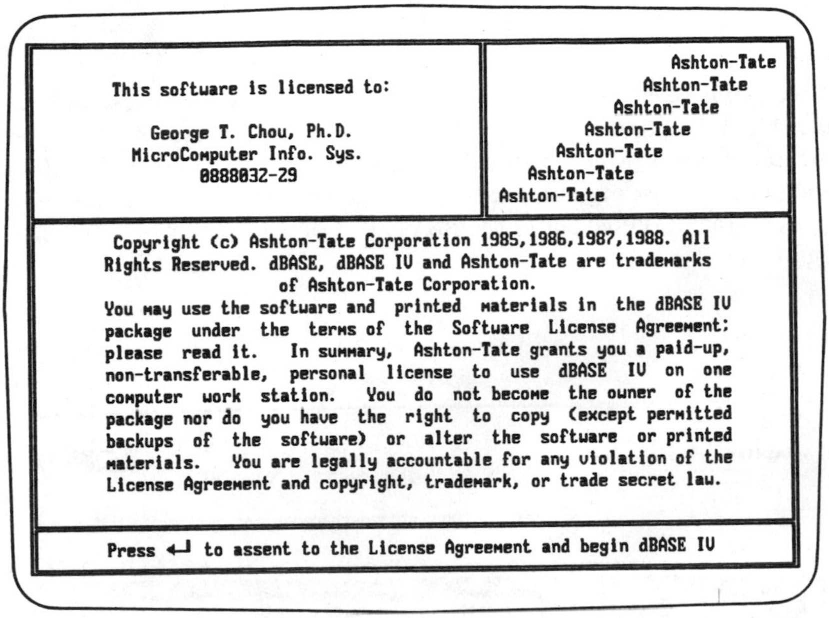

Fig. 2.3.

dBASE IV's initial logon screen.

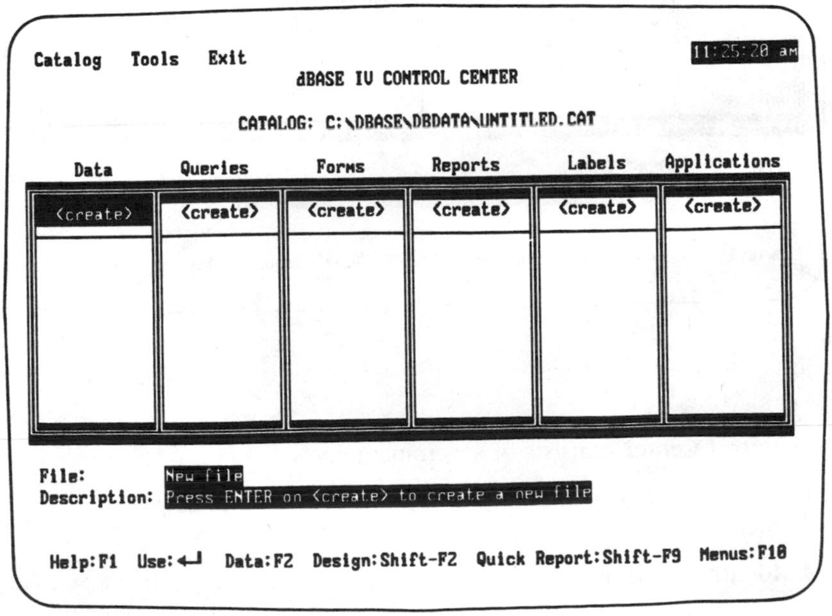

```
┌─────────────────────────────────┬─────────────────────┐
│                                 │        Ashton-Tate  │
│   This software is licensed to: │       Ashton-Tate   │
│                                 │      Ashton-Tate    │
│      George T. Chou, Ph.D.      │     Ashton-Tate     │
│      MicroComputer Info. Sys.   │    Ashton-Tate      │
│          0888032-29             │   Ashton-Tate       │
│                                 │  Ashton-Tate        │
├─────────────────────────────────┴─────────────────────┤
│   Copyright (c) Ashton-Tate Corporation 1985,1986,1987,1988. All
│  Rights Reserved. dBASE, dBASE IV and Ashton-Tate are trademarks
│                    of Ashton-Tate Corporation.
│  You may use the software and  printed materials in  the dBASE IV
│  package  under  the  terms of  the  Software License Agreement;
│  please  read it.   In summary,  Ashton-Tate grants you a paid-up,
│  non-transferable,  personal  license  to  use  dBASE  IV  on one
│  computer  work  station.   You  do  not become  the  owner of the
│  package nor do  you have  the  right  to  copy  (except permitted
│  backups  of  the  software)  or  alter  the  software or printed
│  materials.   You are legally accountable for any violation of the
│  License Agreement and copyright, trademark, or trade secret law.
├───────────────────────────────────────────────────────┤
│   Press ◄┘ to assent to the License Agreement and begin dBASE IV
└───────────────────────────────────────────────────────┘
```

Fig. 2.4.

The opening Control Center screen.

```
Catalog  Tools  Exit                              11:25:20 am
                   dBASE IV CONTROL CENTER

             CATALOG: C:\DBASE\DBDATA\UNTITLED.CAT

    Data     Queries    Forms     Reports    Labels   Applications
 ┌─────────┬─────────┬─────────┬─────────┬─────────┬─────────┐
 │<create> │<create> │<create> │<create> │<create> │<create> │
 │         │         │         │         │         │         │
 │         │         │         │         │         │         │
 │         │         │         │         │         │         │
 │         │         │         │         │         │         │
 │         │         │         │         │         │         │
 └─────────┴─────────┴─────────┴─────────┴─────────┴─────────┘

 File:        New file
 Description: Press ENTER on <create> to create a new file

  Help:F1  Use:◄┘  Data:F2  Design:Shift-F2  Quick Report:Shift-F9  Menus:F10
```

The Control Center

After you have successfully entered dBASE IV, you will be presented with the dBASE IV Control Center, a friendly user-interface system. With the menu options provided by the Control Center, you will be able to design and process most of your database management tasks without writing any programs. The layout of the dBASE IV Control Center is shown in figure 2.5.

Fig. 2.5.

Layout of the Control Center.

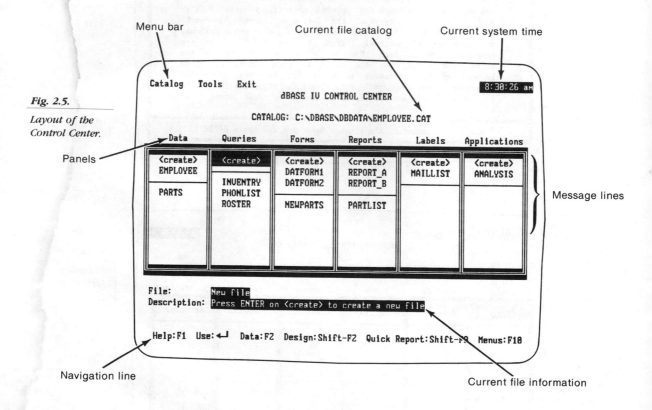

The Control Center consists of seven main parts:

1. The menu bar, which displays all the current available menu options

2. Identification of the current catalog

3. Panels showing the files in each of the database management operations

4. Information on the file being used

5. Navigation line showing the navigation keystrokes

6. Message lines displaying the information about the current menu option selected and its use

7. The current system time

The Menu Bar

All the menu options appear on the top left corner of the Control Center. There are multiple levels of menu options. The main or top level of main options are shown on the Control Center as Catalog, Tools, and Exit. Below each of these main menu options are a number of submenu options that become available when the main menu option is selected.

To select one of these main menu options from the Control Center, you need to hold down the Alt key and press the key corresponding to the first letter of the menu option. For example, press Alt-C to bring up the Catalog menu options and Alt-T to display the Tools options.

The Catalog Menu Options

A catalog is used in dBASE IV for saving a group of disk files that are related to a given application. The Catalog menu provides the means by which you can efficiently manage your disk files in the current catalog. As an illustration, you can bring up the Catalog menu by pressing Alt-C. The Catalog menu options are displayed in figure 2.6.

Tip:
Use Alt-C to invoke the Catalog menu.

From figure 2.6, you can see that the Catalog menu allows you to create a new catalog and change from one catalog to another. This menu also lets you enter information describing a given catalog. From this menu, you also can change the contents of the current catalog—adding new files to or removing existing files from the current catalog, changing the description of a given file. The structure of the Catalog menu can be described in a diagram as shown in figure 2.7.

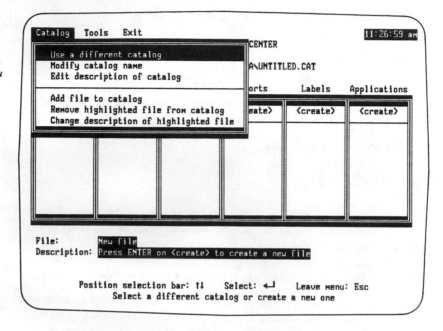

Fig. 2.6.

The Catalog menu options.

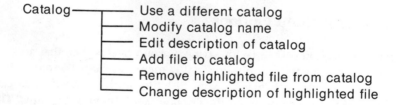

Fig. 2.7.

The structure of the Catalog menu.

To select an option from the menu, use the cursor or the up-arrow (↑) and down-arrow (↓) keys to highlight the option; then press the Enter key. In response to the option selection, another level of menu options is presented. For example, if you choose the **Use a different catalog** option from the Catalog menu, you will be presented with a list of options that allow you to create a new catalog or to select an existing catalog. Details on how to create and select a catalog are discussed in subsequent chapters.

The Tools Menu Options

The Tools menu, which you invoke by pressing Alt-T, provides a list of options with which you can perform a number of important operations, as shown in figure 2.8.

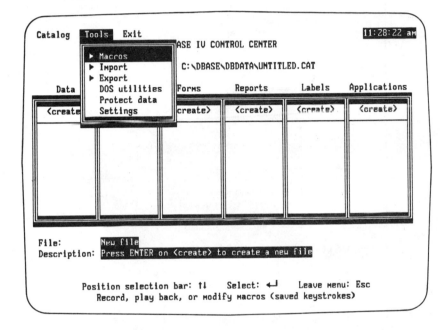

For each option within the Tools menu, there are a number of submenu options. The menu structure of the Tools menu is shown in figure 2.9.

In this menu, you can save a series of keystrokes as a macro script. You can then play the script and execute the series of keystrokes by pressing the macro key you specify. By using the Macros submenu options, you can modify, copy, delete, or append these macro key scripts.

From the Tools menu, you can also use one of the tools options to import or export files between dBASE IV and other computer programs. The **Import** and **Export** options allow you to modify the file format to conform with the format of other application software files.

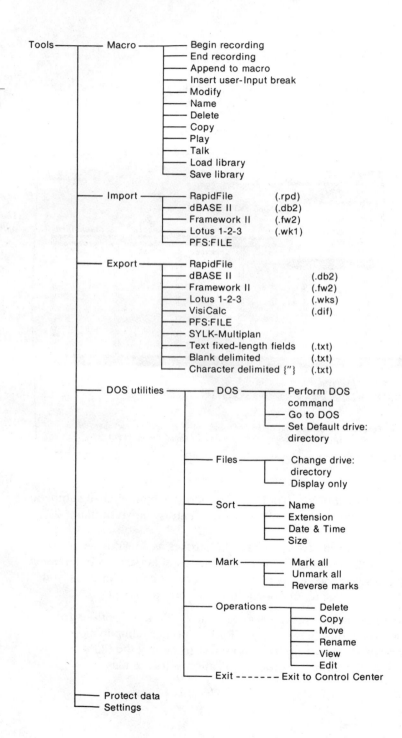

Fig. 2.9.

*The structure of
the Tools menu.*

The DOS utilities provided by the Tools menu allow you execute any DOS command from within the dBASE IV. You can also perform a number of file management operations with the Tools options. For example, you can copy, delete, sort, and mark the disk files. You can manage the files in the current file directory or in another directory by changing your directory from the DOS submenu.

Tip:
Execute DOS operations from the Tools menu.

By choosing the **Protect data** option from the Tools menu, you can assign a password that allows only authorized persons to have access to a given set of data files. You also can define default settings for dBASE IV by selecting the **Setting** option from the Tools menu. These settings allow you to define the desired environment when you are in dBASE IV. For example, you can use this option to have the bell sound when you have filled a data field or to set the number of decimal places for values in numeric fields.

The Exit Menu Option

The Exit menu enables you to exit dBASE IV and return to DOS or transfers you to the dBASE IV dot prompt mode. Do not press Esc to exit from the Control Center, however: If you do, you may lose valuable data during some operations.

Caution:
Do not press Esc to exit from the Control Center.

From dot prompt mode, you can enter dBASE IV commands to perform database management operations. Dot prompt mode is discussed later in this chapter.

The Current System Time

In the upper right corner of the Control Center, the current system time is displayed. The system time is updated continuously. You can set the system time before you enter dBASE IV by issuing the TIME command at the DOS prompt, such as

```
C>TIME
Current time is 17:30:50:89
Enter new time: 18:00

C>DATE
Current date is 12-07-88
Enter new date (mm-dd-yy): 12-08-88
```

Tip:

*Use Alt-D to
perform DOS
operation within
the Tools menu.*

You can change the system date and time while you are in dBASE IV by
using the **DOS utilities** option from the Tools menu. To do that, first
select the Tools menu by pressing Alt-T. When the Tools menu appears,
choose the **DOS utilities** option. You then choose the DOS menu option
by pressing Alt-D. From the submenu displayed, you select the **Perform
DOS** command option. In return, you will be asked to enter the DOS
command for setting the system as though you were at the normal DOS
prompt (see fig. 2.10).

Fig. 2.10.

*Setting system
time within
dBASE IV.*

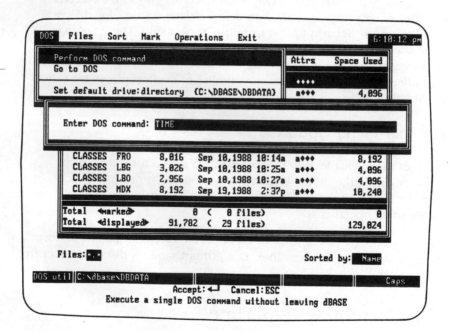

After entering the correct system time, you can press any key to return to
dBASE IV.

The Current Catalog

In dBASE IV, catalogs are used to save a set of related disk files. The most
effective way to organize your disk files is to group all files related to a
given application and store them in a named catalog. Details on how to
create and use a catalog are discussed in the next chapter. In the Control
Center, the name of the current catalog is displayed at the center below
the menu bar.

Changing the Current Catalog

In addition to creating a new catalog, you can switch from the current catalog to another existing catalog by pressing Alt-C to choose the Catalog menu. You then select the **Use a different catalog** option from the Catalog menu. In response to the menu selection, a list of the existing catalogs in the default disk drive and subdirectory are displayed. You can then use the up- or down-arrow keys to highlight the catalog you want, and then you select the catalog by pressing Enter. As you move among the existing catalogs, a description of the highlighted catalog is shown in the window on the lower portion of the screen (see fig. 2.11).

Tip:

Use Alt-C to invoke the Catalog Menu for changing current catalog

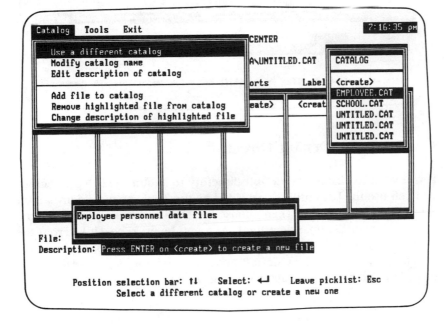

Fig. 2.11.

Changing the current catalog.

After you have changed the catalog, the new catalog is displayed in the catalog name on the Control Center. Along with the catalog name, you also will see the current default data directory, such as C:\DBASE\DBDATA, as shown in figure 2.12.

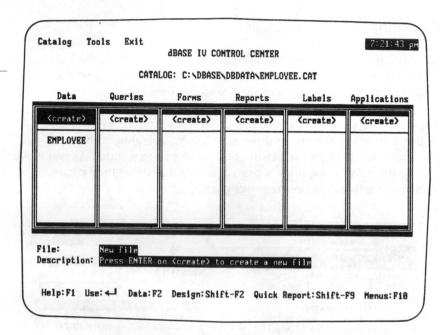

Fig. 2.12.

Showing the new catalog in the Control Center.

Changing the Default Directory

Tip:

Use Alt-T to invoke the Tools menu to change default file directory.

If you want to change the default directory to another existing directory, you can use the DOS utilities provided by the Tools menu. To invoke the Tools menu, press Alt-T. Then choose the **DOS utilities** option from the displayed menu. Again, select the DOS menu by pressing Alt-D. From the DOS submenu, choose the **Set default drive:directory** option, and press Enter. Then enter the new default drive and directory in the space provided, and press Enter again (see fig. 2.13).

The Control Center Panels

There are six panels in the Control Center. These panels appear on the top of the double-line box in the center of the screen. These panels are used to identify the disk files in the current catalog, which are grouped in various database management operations. The names and functions of these panels are as follows:

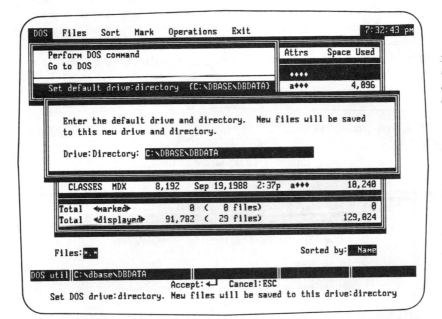

Fig. 2.13.

Changing the default drive and directory.

Panel	Description
Data panel	For displaying all the database files
Queries panel	For showing the Query By Example (QBE) files
Forms panel	For listing the custom data-entry forms
Reports panel	For identifying the custom report forms
Labels panel	For showing the custom label forms
Applications panel	For grouping the application programs and scripts, etc.

To select a given type of database management operation, you can move along the panels by using the left- (←) or right-arrow (→) keys.

Each panel in the Control Center uses a vertical column to display the disk files for a given database management operation. Each column is further divided into two sections separated by a horizontal line. Above the horizontal line, the Control Center displays the current file. Other existing files are shown in the column below the line. Any one of these files can be used or opened. To use one of these files, you simply press the up- (↑) or down-arrow (↓) keys to highlight the file; and then press Enter to select it. In response to the selection, the submenu shown in figure 2.14 is displayed.

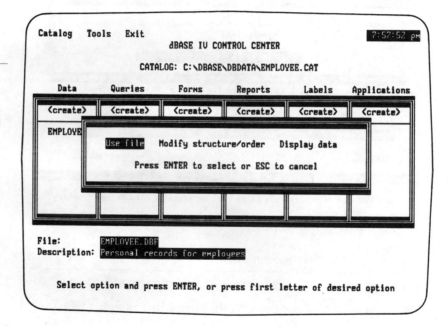

Fig. 2.14.

Open a disk file for use in dBASE IV.

You then can select the **Use file** option from the submenu. As a result, the file you selected will be moved to the top of the column below the **<create>** row. At the same time, the name and description of the file are displayed at the lower portion of the screen (see fig. 2.15).

If you would like to create a new file in a given panel, you can select **<create>** as the option. You then are given the screen for entering the appropriate information for the mew file. Discussions on creating new files in various database management operations are included in later chapters.

Tip:

Select <create> from the panel to create new file.

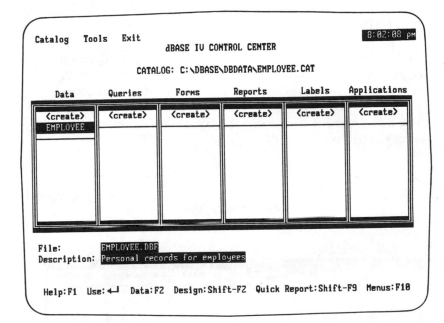

```
 Catalog  Tools  Exit                              8:02:08 PM
                    dBASE IV CONTROL CENTER

                CATALOG: C:\DBASE\DBDATA\EMPLOYEE.CAT

    Data      Queries     Forms      Reports     Labels    Applications

  <create>   <create>   <create>   <create>   <create>    <create>
  EMPLOYEE



  File:        EMPLOYEE.DBF
  Description: Personal records for employees


  Help:F1  Use:↵  Data:F2  Design:Shift-F2  Quick Report:Shift-F9  Menus:F10
```

Fig. 2.15.

*Displaying the
disk file being
used.*

Navigation Line

At the bottom of the Control Center screen, you will see the navigation
line on which information about the use of function keys is displayed.
The navigation line shows you how to move between menu or submenu
options. The contents of the navigation line change as you select a
different menu.

Message Lines

During processing of a given database management operation or task,
monitoring or error messages are often displayed at the bottom of the
Control Center, informing you of the current status of the operation. The
actual position and length of the messages vary among different
operations.

Aborting a Menu Selection

If you have made a mistake or have decided to abort the operation while selecting menu and submenu options, use the Esc key to undo the selection. Each time you press Esc, the previous submenu choice is displayed. However, if you are at the main menu when you press Esc, you will be asked whether to abandon the current operation and leave the Control Center (see fig. 2.16).

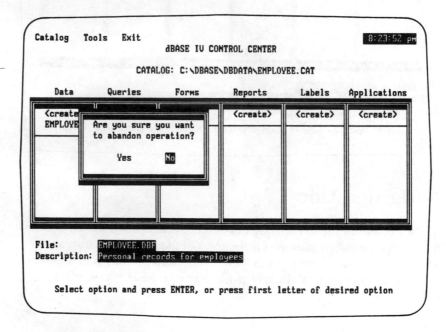

By selecting the default **No** option you will be returned to the Control Center; otherwise, you will be transferred to the dot prompt.

If you have accidentally entered dot prompt mode, however, you can return easily to the Control Center. Simply type ASSIST at the dot prompt and press Enter, such as

    .ASSIST

The Dot Prompt

In interactive processing mode, you can manipulate data not only by using the menu options provided by the Control Center but also by entering dBASE IV commands at the dot prompt. For example, you can display all the records in the active database file by entering the command DISPLAY ALL (see fig. 2.17).

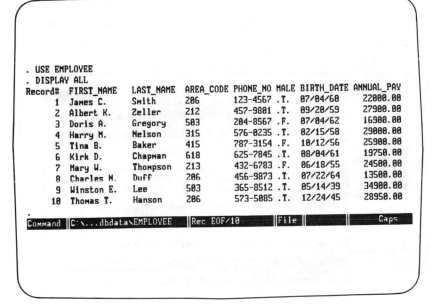

Fig. 2.17.

Issuing dBASE IV commands at the dot prompt.

Entering dBASE III commands at the dot prompt is a quick, efficient way to manipulate data. For beginning users of dBASE IV, the Control Center menu seems an easy, natural way of manipulating the information in a database. After you have learned the basics of dBASE IV, however, you may find that entering the dBASE IV commands at the dot prompt is the more efficient way in some applications. By selecting options from the menu and submenu in the Control Center, you are in effect building a set of dBASE IV commands. You can achieve the same effect by entering the dBASE IV commands at the dot prompt. Whichever method you use, you can enjoy the tremendous processing power of the dBASE IV program.

Getting Help

Tip:

Press F1 to get help.

Help is available not only from the comprehensive dBASE IV user's manual but also from the program's built-in message system. If you have questions about the function of a specific command or menu option while you are processing data in dBASE IV, you can ask for help by pressing the HELP function key, F1. Whenever you press the F1 key, a message screen describing the current command or submenu option is displayed. For example, if you press F1 while the <**create**> option of the Data panel in the Control Center is highlighted, information on how to create a database file will be displayed in the help message box, as shown in figure 2.18.

Fig. 2.18.

A sample help screen.

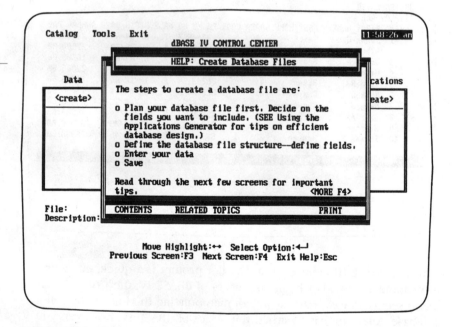

Additional screens of help messages can be displayed by selecting the appropriate option displayed. After you have read the help message, you can return to the Control Center by pressing Esc.

Whenever you make a mistake in entering a command in dot prompt mode (such as misspelling DISPLAY ALL as DISPLAY AL), dBASE IV will ask

    Do you want some help? (Y/N)

When you are in dot prompt mode, if you misspell a key word in a dBASE IV command, an error message box will be displayed (see fig. 2.19).

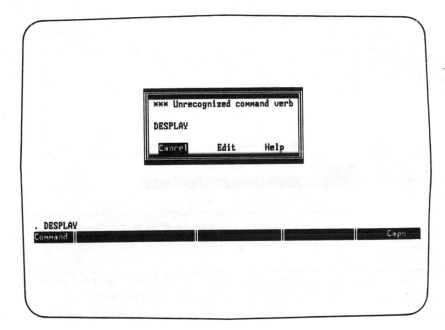

Fig. 2.19.

A sample error message.

You then are asked to select either the **Cancel**, **Edit**, or **Help** option. If you choose the **Help** option, information about the suspected command is displayed.

Leaving dBASE IV

When you have finished using dBASE IV, you can exit the program by using Alt-E to choose the Exit menu from the Control Center. When the options of the Exit menu appear, choose the **Quit to DOS** option to return to the DOS prompt (see fig. 2.20).

If you are in dot prompt mode, you would exit dBASE IV and return to the DOS prompt by issuing the QUIT command and pressing Enter, such as

. QUIT

Tip:
Always use Alt-E to invoke the Exit menu to leave dBASE IV.

Tip:
Issue QUIT at the dot prompt to exit dBASE IV.

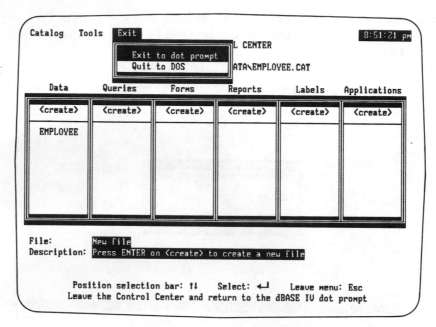

Fig. 2.20.

*Quitting dBASE IV
from the Control
Center.*

Remember that you must use the Exit menu from the Control Center or
the **Quit** command at the dot prompt in order to leave dBASE IV.
Information in your database files may be lost if you attempt to exit the
program by any other means.

A dBASE IV QuickStart

At the end of several chapters in this book, you will find a QuickStart
section like this one, presenting an example that you can follow quickly
to apply the concepts and procedures discussed in the chapter. In this
section, for example, you will follow the procedures necessary for getting
you started using the dBASE IV program.

Setting up DBDATA Directory

You can set up the DBDATA directory for saving your data files in the DBASE directory before or after installing the dBASE IV program onto your hard disk (usually drive C:). To set up the DBDATA directory before the installation process, follow these steps:

1. Change your disk drive to the data drive you want (for example, C:).

2. When the C> prompt appears, type PROMPT PG so that the name of the current directory will be displayed as part of the prompt. After the C>, type the following command and press Enter:

   PROMPT PG

   As a result, the current directory (in this case, the root directory) is displayed as part of the prompt:

   C:\>

3. At the root directory, type MD DBASE and press Enter. (This creates the DBASE directory.)

4. Change the directory to DBASE by typing CD DBASE after the C> prompt and pressing Enter, such as

   C:\>CD DBASE
   C:\DBASE>

5. Create the DBDATA subdirectory by typing MD DBDATA after the C> prompt and pressing Enter, such as

   C:\DBASE>MD DBDATA
   C:\DBASE>

6. Return to the root directory by typing CD \ after the C> prompt, such as

   C:\DBASE>CD \
   C:\>

Now you can install dBASE IV onto your hard disk.

If you choose to install the program first, you can create the DBDATA directory after the installation process by following Steps 3 through 6 (be sure that you are at the root directory before beginning with Step 3).

Because the DBASE directory will be created during the installation, all you need to do is to create the DBDATA directory in the DBASE directory.

Installing dBASE IV

The steps for installing dBASE IV programs onto your hard disk are as follows:

1. You should be at the root directory of your data disk (C:\>), if not, use the CD command to change the directory.

2. Change the current disk drive to your floppy drive (A:), such as

   ```
   C:\>A:
   A:\>
   ```

3. Put the installation disk in your floppy drive (A:) and then type INSTALL, such as

   ```
   A:\>INSTALL
   ```

Starting dBASE IV

After installing the program, you can start dBASE IV by following these steps:

1. Move to the DBDATA directory by typing CD \DBASE\DBDATA, as in

   ```
   C:\>CD \DBASE\DBDATA
   C:\DBASE\DBDATA>
   ```

2. Set directory path for dBASE IV programs by typing PATH=\DBASE, such as

   ```
   C:\DBASE\DBDATA>PATH=\DBASE
   ```

3. Issue the DBASE command to start the program:

   ```
   C:\DBASE\DBDATA>DBASE
   ```

Switching to Dot Prompt Mode

You are now in the Control Center. To switch from the Control Center to the dot prompt:

1. Select the Exit menu by pressing Alt-E.

2. Choose the **Exit to dot prompt** option and press Enter. You then see a dot at the bottom of the screen, indicating that you are in the dot prompt mode.

Getting Help in Dot Prompt Mode

When you are in dot prompt mode and you need help with an operation, type HELP, such as

. HELP

A table of contents of the help messages then is presented. You can select the subject with which you need help. After viewing the messages, press Esc to exit each level of messages.

Returning to the Control Center

To switch from dot prompt mode back to the Control Center, type ASSIST at the dot prompt, such as

. ASSIST

Getting Help in the Control Center

The help system provided by dBASE IV is context sensitive; that is, by pressing F1, you can get help on menu option you are currently using. To see how the help messages work, highlight the <**create**> option in the Data panel, and then press F1.

Leaving dBASE IV

To exit from dBASE IV and return to the DOS prompt when you are using the Control Center, follow these steps:

1. Invoke the Exit menu by pressing Alt-E.

2. Choose the **Quit to DOS** option from the menu and press Enter.

If you are using dot prompt mode, type QUIT at the dot prompt to leave dBASE IV, such as

```
. QUIT
```

Chapter Summary

This chapter introduced you to the important concepts of creating and using directories on your hard disk. You also learned about installing dBASE IV on your system, explored the organization and features of the Control Center, and learned to access the dot prompt mode of dBASE IV. This chapter concluded with a quickstart section designed to help you learn quickly the procedures for installing, starting, and exiting dBASE IV. In the next chapter, you will learn how to create and enter data in dBASE IV.

3

Creating and
Entering Data

This chapter explains how to design and create a database file. You can use a database file to store data elements as simple as employee information or as complicated as an accounting system. In this chapter, you also learn how to create a new file catalog for grouping and storing the data files that are related to a given application. After learning how to create a database file, you are shown how to enter data into the file. In addition to using the default form for data entry, you also learn how to design and use a custom data-entry form by using the powerful dBASE IV form generator.

The chapter highlights how simple database management can be when you use the menu from the Control Center and the dBASE IV commands. If you are a beginning dBASE IV user, you may prefer the menu options, because most data-manipulation operations can be performed by selecting a sequence of menu and submenu options. However, processing data by entering dBASE IV commands at the dot prompt may prove a shortcut for many of these operations. In this chapter, you will see how data-manipulation operations can be performed with either of these methods. You can choose whichever mode of processing best suits you.

The chapter explains how to

❑ Create a new file catalog
❑ Create a new database file

❑ Define the structure of a database file
❑ Enter data in a newly created database file
❑ Add or append new records to an existing database file
❑ Display the database file directory
❑ Display the structure and contents of a database file

The following dBASE IV commands are introduced in this chapter:

Command	Function
SET CATALOG TO	Create a file catalog
CREATE	Creates a database file
USE	Activates a database file
APPEND	Adds records to a database file
DISPLAY, LIST	Displays data
DIR	Displays a file directory

What Is a File Catalog?

The basic unit of a database management system is a database file. A database file is similar to a data table, which was described in Chapter 1. A data table consists of a number of rows (records) and columns (data fields). You can create a data table by choosing the appropriate menu option from the Data panel in the Control Center or by entering CREATE at the dot prompt. For managing your database files efficiently, you should group all the files related to a given application in a file catalog. A *file catalog* is a database file that is used to store information about those files included in the catalog.

Creating a New File Catalog

If you would like to create your new database file from the Control Center, you need to create a new file catalog before you begin the file creation operation. By using the catalog, you can then group and save all the database files you create later for a given application. You can create a file catalog one of two ways: by using the Control Center or by using dot prompt mode. The sections that follow explain each method of creating a file catalog.

Creating a Catalog from the Control Center

When you are in the Control Center, you use the Catalog menu to set up a new catalog for grouping your disk files. Display the Catalog menu by pressing Alt-C. When the Catalog menu appears on the screen, you select the **Use a different catalog** option. In return, any existing catalogs will be displayed in the catalog box in the upper right corner of the Control Center.

Tip:
Use Alt-C to invoke the Catalog menu.

If you would like to set up an existing catalog that you have previously created, you simply use the up- (↑) or down-arrow (↓) key to highlight the catalog file, and then select it by pressing Enter. If you have not created a catalog, you will see two items in the catalog box: **<create>** and UNTITLED.CAT (see fig. 3.1). The second item, UNTITLED.CAT, is set up by dBASE IV automatically as a default catalog. The file extension .CAT indicates that the file is a catalog file.

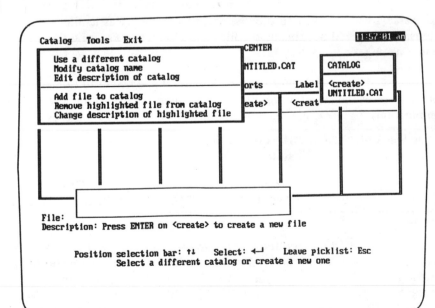

Fig. 3.1.

Creating a new file catalog from within the Control Center.

Tip:
To set up a new
file catalog,
*select <**create**>*
from the Catalog
menu.

To set up a new file catalog, you need to select the <**create**> option from the catalog menu. In response to your selection, you are then asked to assign a name to the new catalog to be created.

File Catalog Name

Caution:
Do not use the
same name for
more than one
file catalog in
the same
directory.

The name of a catalog can include up to eight characters, which can be letters, numeric digits, or the underscore (_). You should use unique and descriptive names for file catalogs. You cannot use the same name for more than one file catalog in the same file directory. A few acceptable database catalog names are

> EMPLOYEE
> BILLINGS
> GROUP_A
> ACCOUNTS
> BRANCH1

Each catalog will be saved on the disk as a file with .CAT as its file extension. You need not specify the file extension when entering the catalog name (see fig. 3.2).

In summary, the procedure for creating a new catalog from the Control Center involves the selection of the following menu options (the key combinations for invoking the menu are described in the parentheses):

> Catalog(Alt-C)/**Use a different catalog**/<**create**>/
> **Enter name for new catalog**

After you have entered the name for the new catalog and pressed Enter, a catalog with that name is created and displayed at the top of the Control Center screen (see fig. 3.3).

A catalog file is used to keep track of the information on the disk files that are to be included in the catalog. In addition to assigning a name to a catalog file, you can also include descriptive information about the catalog for later reference. For example, in addition to naming EMPLOYEE.CAT for the catalog file, you can also enter a description of the catalog file after the file is created.

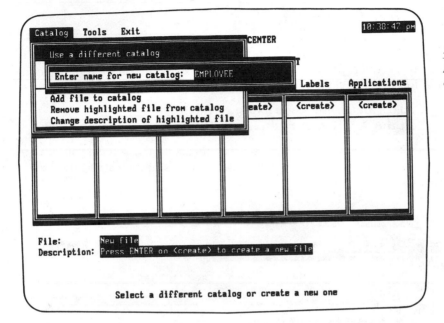

Fig. 3.2.

Naming a new file catalog.

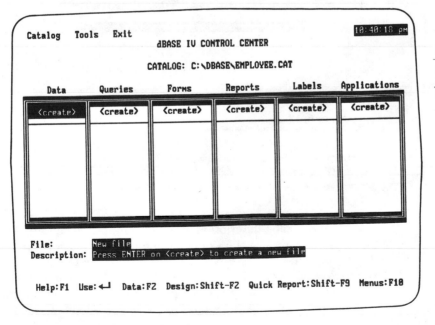

Fig. 3.3.

Showing the new file catalog in the Control Center.

Catalog Description

When a catalog is being used and its name shown at the top of the
Control Center, you can enter or edit the catalog description by selecting
the following menu options:

Catalog(Alt-C)/**Edit description of catalog/**
Edit the description of this .cata file

When the catalog file description box appears on the screen, you can
type in the text that best describes the contents of the catalog file (see
fig. 3.4).

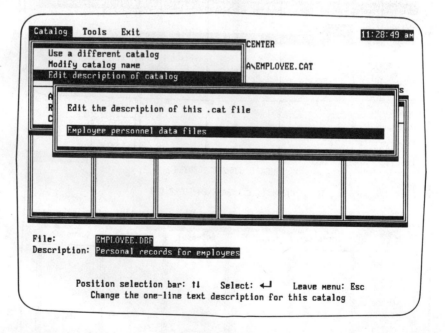

Fig. 3.4.

*Entering a file
catalog
description.*

After you enter the catalog description, it is saved in the catalog file. The
description will not appear in the Control Center until it is later
highlighted again in the catalog box when you choose the **Use a
different catalog** option from the Catalog menu. At that point, the
catalog description appears in a file description box at the lower portion
of the Control Center (see fig. 3.5). Although it is a good idea to include

descriptions in a catalog file, catalog description is optional. If you do not include a catalog description, the file description box will be blank when you highlight a catalog file in the catalog box.

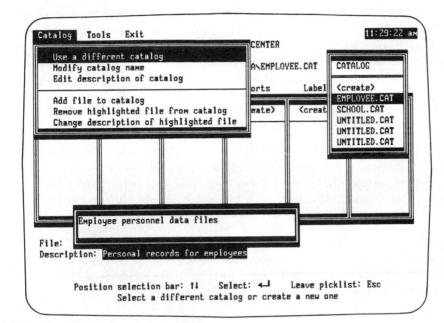

Fig. 3.5.

Showing the file catalog description.

Master Catalog

When you are using DOS utilities or are looking at the files in the directory, you may see a file named CATALOG.CAT. Like a catalog file you create, CATALOG.CAT works as a master catalog. This file is created automatically by dBASE IV to keep track of all the catalog files. Every time you create a new catalog, the name and description of the new catalog is added to the master catalog. When an existing catalog is deleted, its information is automatically removed from the master catalog.

In order to preserve the contents of the master catalog, it is important that you name your own catalog something other than CATALOG.CAT. Similarly, you should not delete the CATALOG.CAT file. However, if you accidentally delete CATALOG.CAT, do not panic: dBASE IV automatically re-creates the master catalog file when you enter the program again. You can then set up your own catalogs.

Caution:
Do not name your own catalog CATALOG.CAT.

Creating a Catalog
from the Dot Prompt

If you want to create a new catalog from the Control Center, you can follow the procedures explained in the preceding section and skip this section, if you wish. If you choose to create a catalog by using the dot prompt method, you can use the commands explained in this section. However, if you have already followed the instructions in the preceding section and have created the EMPLOYEE.CAT file, you will need to delete that catalog file before following those steps in this section. (Instructions for deleting catalog files are included later in this chapter.)

Tip:
Use the Exit menu (not the Esc key) to move from the Control Center to the dot prompt.

From the Control Center, you can enter dot prompt mode by pressing Alt-E to invoke the Exit menu and selecting the **Exit to dot prompt** option. Although pressing the Esc key may allow you to leave the Control Center, try to avoid using Esc because it may cause data loss in certain cases.

When dot prompt mode is active, you will see a dot appear at the bottom of the screen. At this point, you can start issuing dBASE IV commands. You can return to the Control Center at any time by issuing the ASSIST command, such as

Command:
ASSIST *Changes from dot prompt mode to the Control Center.*

. ASSIST

The command for creating a new catalog at the dot prompt is SET CATALOG TO, followed by the name of the new catalog, such as

. SET CATALOG TO <*name of the catalog*>

The less-than (<) and greater-than (>) symbols signify the name of the file catalog that is to be created. These symbols are not part of the command and should not be entered. If the catalog name specified in the command already exists, the existing file catalog is invoked and no new catalog will be created.

Command:
SET CATALOG TO
Create or select a file catalog.

An example of SET CATALOG TO might be

. SET CATALOG TO EMPLOYEE

If the catalog name you enter has not been used before, you will be asked whether you want to Create new file catalog?. If you answer Yes, you then will be asked to enter the description of the catalog. After typing in the catalog description, a new catalog will be created and set to use (see fig. 3.6).

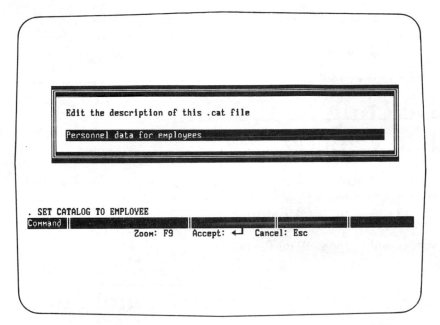

Fig. 3.6.

Entering a file catalog description at the dot prompt.

After the new catalog is created, the message File catalog empty is displayed.

The text you entered at the dot prompt SET CATALOG TO EMPLOYEE represents a dot prompt command in dBASE IV command language. In addition to the object of the command—in this case, the name of the catalog EMPLOYEE—the command contains the SET CATALOG TO command key words. As a shortcut, you need only the first four characters to identify a key word. That is, you can use CATA in the place of CATALOG in the dot prompt command, such as

. SET CATA TO EMPLOYEE

Each time you enter a command, a dot will reappear after the command is carried out. As a result, you can perform a task by issuing a set of consecutive commands.

Another shortcut worth mentioning here is that you can repeat a command that you have issued earlier. Because dBASE IV retains the most recent commands, you can recall each of the commands by pressing the up-arrow (↑) or down-arrow (↓) keys. Each time you press one of the arrow keys, a previously entered command is displayed. When you find

Tip:
Use the up-arrow (↑) and down-arrow (↓) keys to display previously entered commands.

the one you would like to repeat, press Enter after it appears at the dot prompt. Of course, you can use the arrow keys to move your cursor around and edit the command before accepting it, if you wish.

Deleting an Existing File Catalog

Tip:

Use the DOS command ERASE *to delete unwanted file catalogs.*

If you accidentally create an unwanted catalog, you can remove it one of two ways: by using the Tools menu to delete the catalog's corresponding file or by using the ERASE command at the DOS prompt before or after entering dBASE IV. An easy way to delete a disk file is to use the DOS utilities within dBASE IV for the task.

Deleting Files from the Control Center

When you are in the Control Center, the steps for deleting a disk file (which may be a catalog or another type of file) are

1. Invoke the Tools menu from Control Center menu bar by pressing Alt-T, and select the **DOS utilities** option from the menu box.

2. Choose the DOS option from the menu bar by pressing Alt-D.

3. Use the up-arrow (↑) or down-arrow (↓) keys to highlight the file to be deleted and mark it by pressing Enter. (You also can press Enter to unmark a file you marked accidentally.)

4. Select the Operations menu from the menu bar by pressing Alt-O.

5. Choose the **Delete** option from the menu, and select the **Single file** option to delete the marked file.

The menu selection sequence can be described as follows:

> **Tools**(Alt-T)/**DOS utilities**/DOS(Alt-D)/(highlight and mark the file to be deleted)/Operations(Alt-O)/**Delete/Single file**

If you press Enter at this point, the EMPLOYEE.CAT file will be permanently removed. Otherwise, you can abandon the deletion process by pressing Esc.

Before you carry out the deletion operation, be sure that the file you are about to erase is the correct one. Once the file is deleted, it will be lost and cannot be recovered within dBASE IV.

However, it is important to note that deleting an existing catalog does not automatically erase the disk files included in the catalog. Removing the catalog file will simply exclude the disk files from the deleted catalog files. The disk files will still be retained in the disk directory. They can be added to another catalog later.

Caution:
Deleting a file catalog does not erase the files in it.

Deleting Files from the Dot Prompt

If the program is in dot prompt mode, you use the ERASE command to remove an existing catalog from disk, such as

. ERASE *<name of the catalog file>*

Command:
ERASE *Deletes a disk file.*

An example of the ERASE command might be

. ERASE EMPLOYEE.CAT

However, you cannot erase a catalog when it is open. An error message will appear if you try to erase an open catalog file (see fig. 3.7).

Caution:
You cannot erase an open catalog; close the catalog before erasing it.

When this error message is displayed, you need to abort the operation by choosing the **Cancel** option from the error message box and closing the catalog file. You can then try to erase the file again. To close the catalog file, you will issue the SET CATALOG (or SET CATA TO) command without the file name, such as

. SET CATALOG TO

Tip:
Use SET CATALOG TO *to close an open catalog.*

After the catalog is closed, you can issue the ERASE command to delete the catalog file (see fig. 3.8).

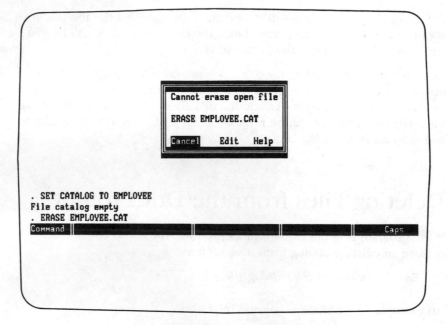

Fig. 3.7.

An error message for attempting to erase an open file.

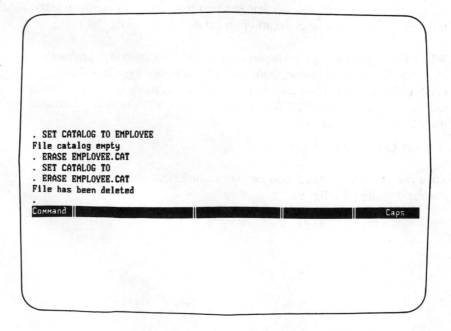

Fig. 3.8.

Dot prompt commands for erasing a file catalog.

Creating a Database File

Like creating a new file catalog, you can also create a new database file either by selecting the appropriate menu options from the Control Center or by issuing the dBASE IV commands at the dot prompt. Creation of a new database file involves two tasks: (1) assigning a unique name to the database file, and (2) defining the database structure of the file.

The file name is used for identifying the database file later, and the database structure of a database file specifies the attributes of the data table. Such file attributes include the name, type, and length of each of the data fields. In the database structure, you also can tell dBASE IV which data field(s), if any, you would like to use for arranging your records—a process called *indexing*.

The sequence for performing these two tasks varies depending upon whether you are using the Control Center menu options or dot prompt commands. When you are creating a new database file from within the Control Center, you will be asked first to define the structure and then to name the database file name before saving the file on disk.

If you are using dBASE IV commands at the dot prompt, you need to give a name to the database file before you will be provided the necessary form on the screen for defining the database structure. However, the procedure for defining the database structure is identical in either case once you are presented with the structure definition form. It is advisable to learn how to create a database file via the Control Center menu options and then use the dot prompt commands as a shortcut.

Creating the Database File from the Control Center

If you would like to create a new database file from the Control Center, you need to use the left-arrow (←) or right-arrow (→) keys to highlight the <**create**> option in the Data panel (see fig. 3.9).

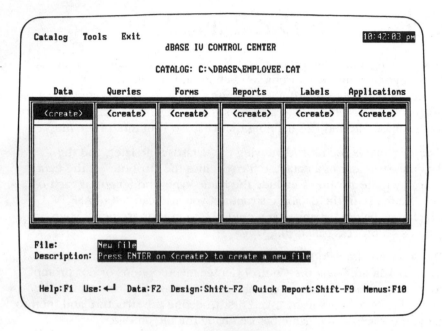

Fig. 3.9.

Selecting the **<create>** *option in the Data panel.*

Defining the Database Structure

After you select the **<create>** option from the Data panel, a blank structure definition form will appear on the screen (see fig. 3.10). On the top of the form, a menu bar is displayed. The menu options on the menu bar are for performing various data manipulation operations which will be discussed later. The main body of the form provides space for defining the specifications of each data field, such as its record number, field name, field type, and field width (this may include the number of decimal points for numeric fields). The last column in the form is used for identifying the data fields with which dBASE IV builds an index. The important use of such an index field will be discussed a little later in this chapter.

Displayed at the bottom of the screen is a summary of all the valid keystrokes you can use during this operation, with instructions on how to enter information on the highlighted data field. The upper right corner of the screen shows the amount of available memory. The current field is shown in the status bar as Field 1/1. Information in the status bar is

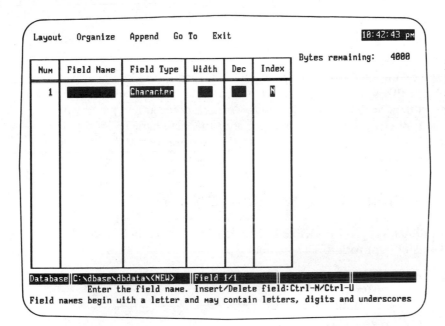

Fig. 3.10.

The database structure definition form.

updated as new fields are defined and added to the database structure. On the status bar, the current data disk and directory (for example, C:\dbase\dbdata\<NEW>) are also displayed.

Entering the Data Field Name

After you begin creating a database file, the cursor appears at the beginning of a data field on the field definition form. You then can enter the name of the data field. A data field name can contain up to 10 characters, the first of which must be a letter. The remaining characters may be letters, numerals, or underscores. As in database file names, no blank spaces are allowed. Underscores often are used to separate words in a field name. Some examples of acceptable data field names are

FIRST_NAME
LAST_NAME
MIDDLE_INT
AREA_CODE
PHONE_NO
ACCOUNT_NO

GROSS_WAGE
BIRTH_DATE
ANNUAL_PAY

The definition form provides space for 10 characters in a field name. When that space is filled, the cursor automatically moves to the form's next data field and a beep sounds. You can enter a field name with fewer than 10 characters. Pressing Enter after the last character of the field name causes the cursor to move to the next item on the form, and no beep is sounded.

Entering the Data Field Type

In dBASE IV, you can define five types of data fields that store different kinds of information. The six field types are

C	Character/text fields
N	Numeric fields
F	Floating value fields
D	Date fields
L	Logical fields
M	Memo fields

To define the field type, enter one of the five letters (C, N, D, F, L, or M) when the cursor is in the field type. The default field type is a character/ text field; you can select it by pressing Enter. By pressing the space bar, you can choose a field type other than the one displayed. Each time you press the space bar, a different field type appears in the Type column. When the appropriate type appears, press Enter to select it.

Entering the Data Field Width

The width of a data field is the maximum number of characters allowed in the field. In character/text or memo fields, the field width determines the length of the text that can be entered in the field. All letters, numeric digits, symbols, and spaces are considered part of the text. A memo field, like a character field, is used to hold alphanumeric data. Although you cannot sort the information in a memo field, you may want to use a memo field to store a large section of text that you do not plan to manipulate later. The contents of a memo field are saved in a separate file on the disk, thus conserving memory space.

A date field is always eight characters wide and stores the numeric codes for the month, the day, the year, and the slashes that separate the codes. The standard date format is mm/dd/yy.

Because a logical field accepts only one character indicating a true/false value, the width of the logical field is always one character.

The width of a numeric or a floating value field is defined in two ways. First, you define the maximum number of digits allowed in the value, including the sign and the decimal point, if those are to be used. Then you determine the number of digits to appear to the right of the decimal point. For example, to store values up to 9999.99, you set the width of the field to seven and define two decimal places. An integer value does not require decimal places defined in the field width. Commas or dollar signs (such as $9,999.99) cannot be entered as part of the value.

The difference between a numeric field and a floating value field lies in the degree of precision that dBASE IV allows. For most applications, a numeric field will be sufficient. If you need a high degree of precision demanding a large number of significant digits for the values, you may use the floating value field. Unless it is necessary (like for calculating financial values involving high-order exponents in a formula), try to use numeric fields over floating value fields because floating value fields require the most memory space.

Tip:
For most values, use numeric instead of floating value data fields.

A Sample Database Structure

To illustrate the process of defining the database structure, we have created a database file to store information about a firm's employees. Employee information is stored in each data record in the file. Each item shown in figure 3.11 can be defined as a data field.

The data fields FIRST_NAME, LAST_NAME, AREA_CODE, and PHONE_ NO are defined as character/text fields. These store the employee's name and phone number. The width of these fields is set to accommodate the maximum number of characters to be entered in the fields.

The logical field MALE identifies the sex of the employee, and accepts only a single character: T for true, or F for false. Alternatively, you could define a character/text field named SEX to store a variable for male or female. However, a logical field can be searched more efficiently than a character/text field.

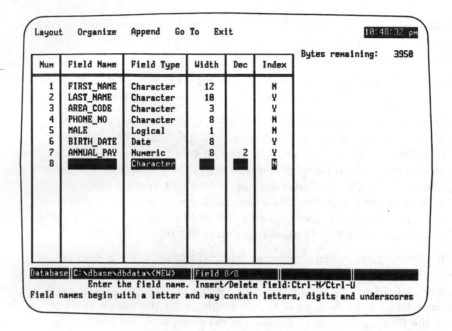

Fig. 3.11.

A sample
database
structure.

The date field BIRTH_DATE is defined to store an employee's birth date
in the form dd/mm/yy. Remember that a date field is not a character/text
field, although the date field may contain a string of alphanumeric
characters. The contents of a date field can be manipulated only with
date operators.

The numeric field ANNUAL_PAY is used to store the employee's annual
salary. Because the maximum length of the numeric field is eight
characters, you can enter values up to 99999.99.

In the last column of the structure definition form, you notice that a
number of data fields are indexed (signified with Y in the Index
column). This tells dBASE IV that in later data manipulation operations,
you may need to arrange the records in this file according to the values
in one or more of these indexed data fields.

Indexing is an efficient method for arranging the data records according
to the value of the indexed field. By selecting an index field, dBASE IV
automatically builds an index tag that will help maintain the records in a
certain order. Using an index field and speeding up the data search
process are discussed later. At this point in the discussion, you do not
need to be concerned with that aspect of creating the database structure.

After all the fields are defined, you terminate the process by pressing Enter or Ctrl-End. (To use Ctrl-End, simply press and hold down the Ctrl key while you press also the End key.) By pressing those keystrokes, you tell dBASE IV to save the database structure in a database file. As a result, you will be prompted to assign a name to the database file (see fig. 3.12).

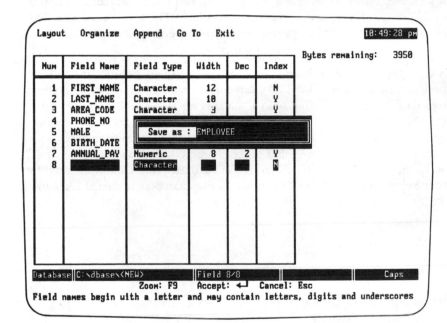

Fig. 3.12.

Naming the database file created.

As soon as you enter the name of the database file and press Enter, the database structure is saved to the disk.

Naming a Database File

The name of a database file can include up to eight characters, which can be a combination of letters, numeric digits, or the underscore (_). A few acceptable database file names are

EMPLOYEE
Directory
PHONES

INVENTRY
Accounts
ADDRESS
COURSES
ITEMSOLD

When naming a file, you can enter the name in either upper- or lowercase letters. To access a file, you also can enter the name in upper- or lowercase. For example, the database file EMPLOYEE can be recalled by typing *Employee* or *employee*. When the directory is displayed, however, all file names appear in uppercase.

Caution:

Do not use blank spaces, periods, slashes, colons, or semi-colons in a file name.

A database file name cannot contain spaces or symbols other than the underscore. Because dBASE IV interprets a space as a separator between two data items, a file name with a space is not acceptable. The period (.), the slash (/), the colon (:), and the semicolon (;) are reserved for special functions in dBASE IV and should not be used in file names. In addition, the backslash (\) and other characters such as | <> + = , [ ] " and single characters a thru j are reserved aliases that cannot be used by themselves as single-letter file names. Some examples of illegal file names are

PHONE NO
PART1;35
BUS/101
MODEL:A

If you enter an illegal file name, a syntax error message will inform you that an item violates the syntax rules for a dBASE IV command. If you enter CREATE PHONE NO, for example, dBASE IV "reads" your input as two separate file names and displays an error message.

No warning message is displayed if a database file name has more than eight characters, but only the first eight characters are saved. For example, when PARTS_RCAVCRS is entered as a file name, only the first eight characters (PARTS_RC) will be recognized and used.

Entering Data into a Database File

After the database structure is saved, the following prompt appears at the bottom of the screen:

Input data records now? (Y/N)

If you press Y, the program displays the data-entry form for the file you have just defined. For example, after you have defined the EMPLOYEE database file structure, dBASE IV displays the first data-entry form for that file. You then position the cursor in the desired field and enter data in the space provided on the entry form. When the field is full, the cursor moves to the next field. If your data item does not fill the field, you can move the cursor to the next field by pressing Enter after you enter the last character of the data item. After you have entered the information to the data field for the first record, the screen will look like figure 3.13.

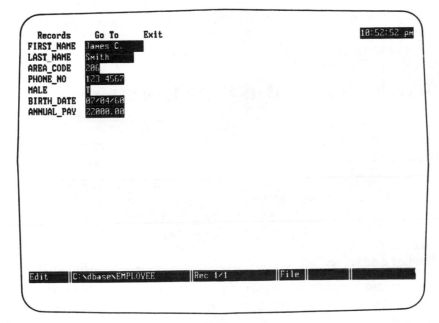

Fig. 3.13.

A default data-entry form.

As soon as the last data field is filled, a new data-entry form is displayed. You can continue entering data for all the records you need. During data entry, each data record you enter is assigned a record number. In figure 3.13, for example, the record indicator in the status bar shows Rec: 1/1. The first part of the indicator shows the current record's position in the database file (in this instance, it is the first record in the file). The number after the slash (/1) indicates the total number of records in the database file.

Using the blank form, you can enter the next record to the database file. For this example, four data records have been entered:

Field	Record 1	Record 2	Record 3	Record 4
FIRST_NAME	James C.	Albert K.	Doris A.	Harry M.
LAST_NAME	Smith	Zeller	Gregory	Nelson
AREA_CODE	206	212	503	315
PHONE_NO	123-4567	457-9801	204-8567	576-0235
MALE	T	T	F	T
BIRTH_DATE	07/04/60	09/20/59	07/04/62	02/15/58
ANNUAL_PAY	22000.00	27900.00	16900.00	29000.00

During data entry, you can use the PgUp and PgDn keys to move between data records. Press the PgUp key to return to the previous record; to proceed to the next record, press the PgDn key.

Terminating the Data-Entry Process

Data entered in a database file is saved record by record. As soon as the last field of a data record has been completed, that record is added to the database file. Then you can terminate the data-entry process.

To terminate data entry, you can press Enter when the cursor is on the first field of a new data-entry form. For example, when you have entered data in the last field of data record 4, the form for record 5 is displayed. At this point, the data from record 4 has already been added to the database file. Pressing Enter now will terminate the data-entry procedure. The last data record added to the database file would be record 4.

Tip:
Always use Ctrl-End to save entered data records.

You can also use the Ctrl-End key combination to end the data-entry process. Ctrl-End saves the displayed data record and returns the program to the dot prompt or the Control Center menu. The Ctrl-End combination can be entered at any time, regardless of the cursor's position on the entry form. If Ctrl-End is pressed before all data fields are filled, the empty data fields are filled with blank spaces. If you press Ctrl-End when all the fields in the entry form are blanks, however, a new empty record will be added to the database. For now, do not worry if this happens. You will learn later how to delete an unwanted record.

The Esc key can be used in dBASE IV to stop any function in progress and return to the Control Center menu or the dot prompt. However, that method should be used with care. Improper use of Esc can cause you to lose data.

When you press the Esc key, the computer "forgets" the most recent operation. What constitutes the most recent operation may vary from one type of procedure to another. For example, if you press the Esc key while entering data, any data entered to the current record is discarded. Data entered to the preceding record is not affected, however, because that data was saved before the current record was displayed.

Caution:
Pressing the Esc key during data entry causes dBASE IV to ignore the record being entered.

After you have successfully saved the records in the newly created database file, you will be returned to the Control Center. At this point, the name of the new database file will be displayed and highlighted in the Data panel as the current file appearing above the horizontal line in the column (see fig. 3.14). At the same time, the file name together with the file directory path are shown in the lower portion of the Control Center. However, the space reserved for file description remains blank until you enter a descriptive text for the file.

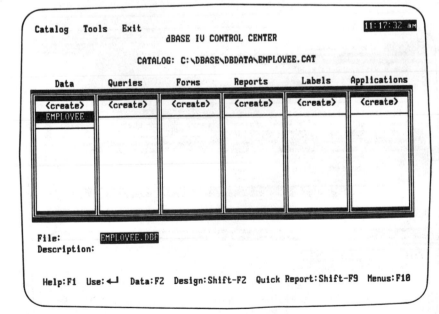

Fig. 3.14.

Showing the new database in the data panel.

Adding the File Description
to the File Catalog

When you create a new database file from within the Control Center, the new file is automatically added to the current file catalog. As a part of the information for each file in the catalog, you need to enter a description for the file.

To add a description to the highlighted file, you may invoke the Catalog menu by pressing Alt-C, and then select the following menu options in this sequence:

Catalog(Alt-C)/**Change description of highlighted file/**
Edit the description of this .dbf file

At this point, you then can enter the descriptive text for the database file (see fig. 3.15).

Fig. 3.15.

*Adding a
database file
description to the
file catalog.*

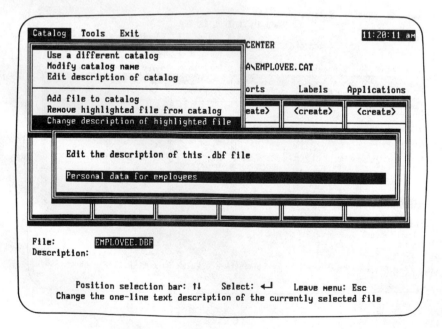

After entering the file description, pressing Enter will return you to the Control Center. The file description then appears as a part of the file information displayed at the bottom of the Control Center screen.

Creating a Database from the Dot Prompt

If you want to create a new database file by entering commands from the dot prompt, all you have to do is enter the CREATE command that includes the name of the database file:

. CREATE   *<name of the database file>*

An example of the CREATE command might be

. CREATE EMPLOYEE

As a shortcut, you can abbreviate CREATE by using the first four letters, CREA, as in

. CREA EMPLOYEE

After you issue the command, a structure definition form like that shown earlier in figure 3.10 will appear. From this point on, you can follow the procedure discussed in the preceding section for defining the database structure and entering the first batch of data records.

When you are in dot prompt mode, after creating a new database and saving the database structure and data records, you will be prompted to enter a file description once you have set up a file catalog by issuing the SET CATALOG TO command earlier. If you have not set up a file catalog, you will not be asked to supply a file description because the file description is needed for a file catalog only.

Command:
CREATE
Create a new database file.

Appending Data to a Database File

New data records can be added to the database file in one of two ways. One way is to append a new data record to the end of the file, and the other way is to insert a data record within the database file.

Appending Data from the Control Center

If you want to use the Control Center menu to add new records to the end of an existing database file, you first need to highlight the database file in the Data panel. Then, bring up the database structure of the database file by pressing Shift-F2. In return, in addition to the database structure, a menu bar will appear on the screen. For example, after highlighting the database file in the Data panel of the Control Center, you can press Shift-F2 to display a copy of the database structure (see fig. 3.16).

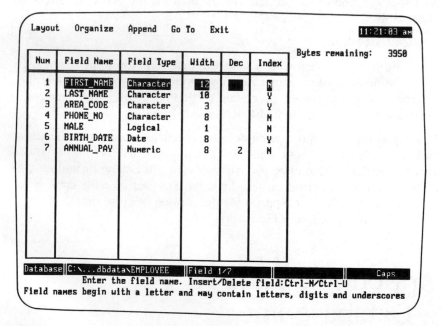

Fig. 3.16.

The database structure screen invoked with Shift-F2.

Notice that in figure 3.16, the menu bar shows four menu options: Layout, Organize, Append, Go To, and Exit. To add records to the database file, you choose the Append menu by pressing Alt-A. In response to the keystrokes, a list of options for the append operation will be displayed. You can append data records by entering them from the keyboard or by copying records from other dBASE IV or non-dBASE IV file records.

By choosing the **Enter records from keyboard** option, you can add
data records to the end of the current database file. After making the
menu selection, a new data record form will be provided for data entry.
At this point, you can start entering the information to the data fields of
the new record. After you finish one record, another new record form
will be displayed. You can continue adding records to the database file
until you press the Ctrl-End keystrokes combination to terminate the
data-entry operation. By pressing the Ctrl-End keystrokes, all the records
you have entered will be added automatically to the database file, and
you will be returned to the Control Center.

Now, using the procedure described earlier, you can enter the remaining
data records to the database file. For this example, the following records
have been appended to the existing Employee database file:

Field	Record 5	Record 6	Record 7	Record 8	Record 9
FIRST_NAME	Tina B.	Kirk D.	Mary W.	Charles N.	Winston E.
LAST_NAME	Baker	Chapman	Thompson	Duff	Lee
AREA_CODE	415	618	213	206	503
PHONE_NO	787-3154	625-7845	432-6782	456-9873	365-8512
MALE	F	T	F	T	T
BIRTH_DATE	10/12/56	08/04/61	06/18/55	07/22/64	05/14/39
ANNUAL_PAY	25900.00	19750.00	24500.00	1350.00	34900.00

Appending Data from the Dot Prompt

For adding new records to the end of the database file, all you need to
do is issue the APPEND (or APPE) command after selecting the database
file to which the new records will be appended. For example, to add
new records to the end of the Employee database file, issue the following
commands at the dot prompt (assuming that the database file is currently
active and is being used):

Command:
APPEND *Add new
records to an
existing
database file.*

    . APPEND

In response to the APPEND command, a new data record form will be
presented for data entry. You then can enter the data in the same manner
as described above. Again, to terminate the data-entry operation, press
the Ctrl-End keystrokes combination.

Using an Existing Database File

Database files are usually saved in auxiliary storage, such as a floppy disk or a hard disk. To conserve memory, only active database files are stored in random-access memory (RAM), where the data can be quickly accessed. Although several database files may remain active simultaneously, only one file can be active in a work area.

As demonstrated in the previous example, data records are added to the end of the currently active database file (the one whose name appears in the status bar) when you use the append operation. In the example, EMPLOYEE was the last database file activated, and that file remains active. If you now apply the append operation, data recorded will be added to the end of the EMPLOYEE file. If another file, such as PAYROLL, had been created after EMPLOYEE, PAYROLL would be the active file to which the APPEND command would add data.

If PAYROLL is the active file but you want to enter new data to the EMPLOYEE file, EMPLOYEE must be reactivated or put to use before you can apply the append operation.

Using a Database from the Control Center

You can put an existing database file to use from the Control Center menu by first highlighting the file in the Data panel, and then pressing Enter. You may recall that the file currently being used is shown above the horizontal line, while all the other existing files are displayed below the horizontal line in the Data panel.

After selecting the database file to be used, you will be given a set of options to choose from. At this point, you will choose the **Use file** option. For example, after highlighting the EMPLOYEE file in the Data panel (below the horizontal line) and pressing Enter, you will see the options as shown in figure 3.17.

At this point, you can select the **Use file** option from the menu box. As a result, the EMPLOYEE database file will be put to use and its name will be switched to the position above the horizontal line in the Data panel.

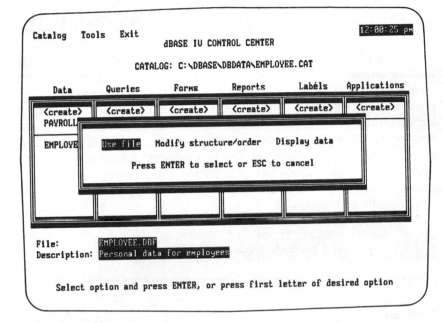

Fig. 3.17.

Selecting the database file to be used.

Using a Database from the Dot Prompt

The operation of selecting an existing database file can also be accomplished by issuing the USE command from the dot prompt, such as

. USE <*name of the database file*>

For example, you could issue the USE command as follows:

. USE EMPLOYEE

Because only database files can be accessed with USE, you do not need to enter the extension .DBF. After you enter USE, the contents of the database file are copied from the disk to RAM, and a dot prompt appears on the screen. Then you can enter other dBASE IV commands, such as APPEND.

Command:

USE
Select and activate an existing database file.

Closing an Active Database File

When a database file is being used, the file is considered to be open. You can manipulate the contents of the database file with most of the dBASE IV database management operations when the file is being used or remains open. However, some disk handling operations cannot be carried out on an open file whether you are in the Control Center or at the dot prompt. For example, you may not be able to delete an open database file when you are at the dot prompt. In order to carry out the file delete operation, you need to first close the database file. The operation of closing an active file can be performed from within the Control Center and from dot prompt mode.

Closing a Database File from the Control Center

There are two ways to close an open database file from within the Control Center. After you finish using one database file, you can close it by putting another database file in use. For example, if you are done with the EMPLOYEE database file and would like to use another database file such as PAYROLL, you can close the former by highlighting the latter database and pressing Enter.

The second way to close an active database file is to press Enter while the file is being used and the file name is highlighted above the horizontal line in the Data panel. In response to the keystroke, you will be presented with a menu box (see fig. 3.18). From the menu, you then can choose the **Close file** option.

Closing a Database File from the Dot Prompt

Tip:

Issue the USE *command to close the current database file without opening another one.*

When you are in dot prompt mode, you can close a database file by issuing the USE command without specifying a database file name or by using another database file with the USE command. For example, if you would like to close the EMPLOYEE file, you can issue one of the following two commands:

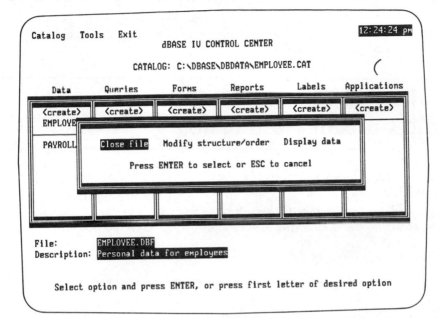

Fig. 3.18.

Closing the database file in use.

. USE

or

. USE PAYROLL

As you will learn in later chapters, you may need to keep a number of database files active and open. You can close all active database files with the following command:

. CLOSE DATABASES

Similarly, the CLOSE ALL command will enable you to close all files of all types in dBASE IV.

Command:
CLOSE DATABASES
Close all open database files.

Organizing Database Files

Database files created in dBASE IV can be renamed, duplicated, copied to files with different names, or erased. They can also be included in different file catalogs. Database files that are currently in a catalog can be

Command:
CLOSE ALL
Close all open files.

removed from the catalog. In dBASE IV, you may change your current disk drive and directory to another directory in another disk drive without leaving the program.

Adding a Database File to the Current File Catalog

All the database files created in dBASE IV can be saved to disk within a chosen directory such as DBDATA. They can be accessed when you are in that directory. If you would like to get files from another directory, you need to first change the default drive and directory. The procedures for changing the default disk drive and directory were discussed in Chapter 2.

Adding a Database from the Control Center

To add an existing database file to the current catalog from within the Control Center, you need to invoke the Catalog menu by pressing Alt-C. From the menu, you then choose the **Add file to catalog** option. You then select the database to be added to the catalog from the file box on the screen.

For example, if you would like add the PAYROLL database file from the disk to the current catalog, you can select the menu options in the following sequence (see fig. 3.19):

Catalog(Alt-C)/**Add file to catalog**/<**PAYROLL.DBF**>

After selecting the PAYROLL database file, before adding it to the catalog, you will be asked to enter a file description. The file description you enter is saved in the catalog for later references to the file.

Adding a Database from the Dot Prompt

When you are in dot prompt mode, any database file that is set to use after you have set up a file catalog with the SET CATALOG command will be automatically included in that catalog. For example, if you would like to add the database file PAYROLL to the EMPLOYEE catalog, all you need

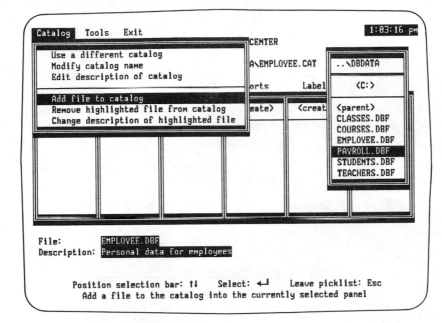

Fig. 3.19.

Adding an existing database file to the current catalog.

to do is issue the USE PAYROLL command once when the catalog is active, such as

. SET CATALOG TO EMPLOYEE
. USE PAYROLL

Removing a Database File from the Current File Catalog

All the database files that have been included previously in a file catalog will be displayed in the Data panel of the Control Center when you select the catalog for use. Any of these files can be removed from the current catalog and can also be permanently deleted from the disk. Although you may remove an existing file from the current catalog by using dBASE commands issued at the dot prompt, it is a lot easier to do it from within the Control Center.

Removing Files from within the Control Center

To remove a dBASE file from the current catalog, you first need to highlight the database file in the Data panel of the Control Center. After that, you can invoke the Catalog by pressing Alt-C, and then select the **Remove highlighted file from catalog** menu option.

For example, if you would like remove the PAYROLL database file from the file catalog, you can select the menu options in the following sequence after highlighting the file in the Data panel (see fig. 3.20):

Catalog(Alt-C)/**Remove highlighted file from catalog**

Fig. 3.20.

Removing a database file from the current file catalog.

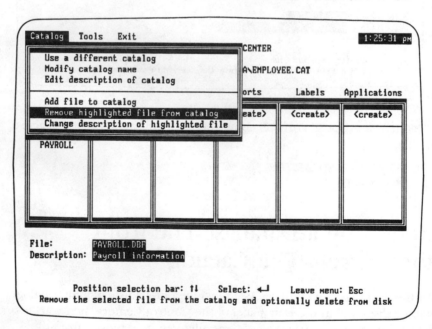

When you press Enter, you will be asked to confirm your action, such as

```
Are you sure you want to remove
this file from the catalog?

    Yes    No
```

If you answer Yes, the file is excluded from the file catalog. But it will still be retained in the disk and can be later added back to the catalog, unless you instruct dBASE IV to permanently delete it by answering Yes to the forthcoming prompt:

```
Do you also want to delete
this file from the disk?

    Yes    No
```

Be careful not to answer Yes if you think you might need to use the database file in later applications. Otherwise, a Yes answer will delete the disk file from the disk. Once the file is deleted, it cannot be recovered.

Deleting a File from the Dot Prompt

There is no dBASE IV command that allows you to remove the file only from the catalog and not permanently from the disk. After setting up the file catalog, you can delete a file from the catalog *and* from the disk in dot prompt mode by using the ERASE command:

```
. ERASE  <name of the database file>
```

However, this practice of removing a file from the file catalog is not recommended if you need to reuse the file later because the ERASE operation removes the file permanently from the disk. Once the file is erased, it cannot be recovered. Therefore, try to use the procedure discussed above—removing the file from the catalog—from within the Control Center.

Performing File Operations

Database files created in dBASE III or dBASE IV can be renamed, duplicated, copied to files with different names, or erased. Most of these file handling operations can be performed either by issuing the dBASE IV commands from the dot prompt or by using the DOS utilities options from the Tools menu within the Control Center.

File Operations from the Control Center

▶

Tip:

*Perform DOS
operations from
the Tools menu.*

The three most commonly used DOS operations for managing your disk
files are: delete, copy, and rename. The procedures for performing these
operations are very similar. They all begin with choosing the **DOS
utilities** option from the Tools menu (which you invoke by pressing
Alt-T). When the DOS utilities menu appears, you then can choose one of
the options from the Operations menu. The Operation menu is invoked
by pressing the Alt-O keystrokes combination. The options provided by
the Operations menu include **Delete**, **Copy**, **Move**, **Rename**, **View**, and
Edit (see fig. 3.21).

Fig. 3.21.

*Options provided
by the DOS
utilities
operations.*

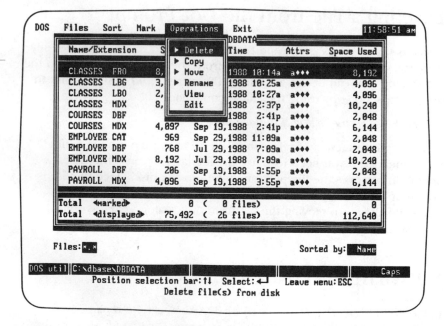

Before you perform one of these operations on the files, you need to
highlight the file by using the up-arrow (↑) or down-arrow (↓) key;
then mark it by pressing Enter. A file that has been marked has a small
triangle appearing in the margin just before the name. After you have
marked the file, you can activate one of the **Delete**, **Copy**, and **Rename**
operations from the Operation menu.

The menu options for deleting, copying, and renaming a database file
from within the Control Center can be summarized as follows:

Operation	Menu options
Delete	Tools (Alt-T)/**DOS utilities**/<*mark the file to be deleted*>/Operations (Alt-O)/**Delete**
Copy	Tools (Alt-T)/**DOS utilities**/<*mark the file to be copied*>/Operations (Alt-O)/**Copy**
Rename	Tools (Alt-T)/**DOS utilities**/<*mark the file to be renamed*>/Operations (Alt-O)/**Rename**

Each of these operation can be carried out on a single or a set of marked files. There are two ways to mark your files to be operated on. The first method involves marking the files one at a time by using the up-arrow (↑) and down-arrow (↓) keys to highlight the file, then press the Enter key. If you accidentally mark a file by mistake, you can remove the marking with the same procedure—by first highlighting the file with the arrow keys and by then pressing Enter.

Another method for marking the files is to use the **Mark all** option provided by the Mark menu (invoked by pressing Alt-M) within the DOS utilities. Similarly, you can choose the **Unmark all** to remove all the file marks or choose the **Reverse marks** to unmark all the marked files and mark all the unmarked files.

Except for those cases in which you need to delete a group of files at a time, for most applications, you probably would not try to copy a group of files to another file. Similarly, you would not rename a group of files to the same file name.

File Operations from the Dot Prompt

From the dot prompt, all DOS commands can be executed directly by preceding them with the command RUN or !. For example, each of the following commands displays in DOS format a directory of the files in the directory:

```
. ! DIR
. RUN DIR
```

This command is analogous to the Tools section of the Control Center. The command is even more important when considering program or command files.

▶

Command:
COPY FILE ... TO
... *Copy a file.*

▶

Command:
RENAME ... TO ...
Rename a file.

When you are in dot prompt mode, each of the file operations can be carried out with a dBASE IV command. The commands for the delete, copy, and rename operations are

Operation	dBASE IV Dot Prompt Command
Delete	. ERASE *<name of the database file>*
Copy	. COPY FILE *<source file>* TO *<destination file>*
Rename	. RENAME *<old file name>* TO *<new file name>*

Some examples of file operation commands include

```
. ERASE EMPLOYEE.DBF
. COPY FILE PAYROLL.DBF TO BACKUP.DBF
. RENAME EMPLOYEE.DBF TO STAFF.DBF
```

▶

Caution:
*Be sure to close
an open
database file
before applying
the delete, copy,
and rename
operations.*

Remember that before you apply these operations to a database file, you must make sure that the file is closed. You cannot delete the file being used. Otherwise, an error message File already open will appear. Likewise, you must close the database file if you want to copy its contents to another file or rename the database file. In addition, the file extension .DBF must be included as the file identification when you issue these commands.

Customizing a Data-Entry Form

During the data-entry process described earlier, dBASE IV provides a standard form for entry of values to the data fields. An example of standard form is shown in figure 3.22.

In the standard data-entry form, all data fields in the database structure are listed in sequence. The space provided for the field contents is shown in a reverse-video box. Such a standard form should be sufficient for most data-entry operations. However, dBASE IV also allows you to design a custom data-entry form. For example, figure 3.23 shows a custom data-entry form that you can use for entering information to data records in the EMPLOYEE database file.

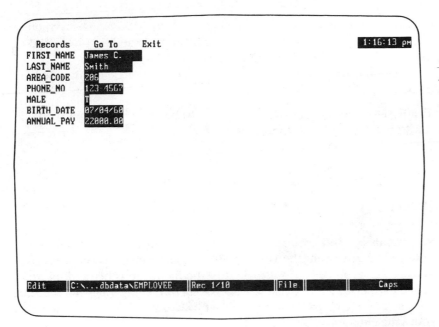

Fig. 3.22.

A standard data-entry form set up by dBASE IV.

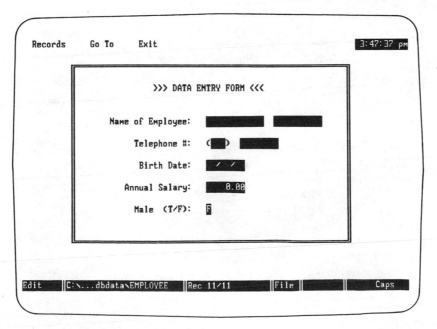

Fig. 3.23.

A custom designed data-entry form.

On the custom data-entry form, you can place the data fields anywhere on the screen and provide your own field labels. In addition to including instructional messages for the data-entry procedure (or other information), you can add graphic designs such as single- or double-line boxes.

The design of a custom data-entry form can be done both from within the Control Center and from the dot prompt.

Designing Custom Forms from the Control Center

Tip:
Select <create> from the Forms panel to create a new data form.

You can design and create a custom data-entry form by choosing the <**create**> option from the Forms panel in the Control Center after putting the database file in use (that is, the file name is being displayed above the horizontal line in the Data panel). After selecting the <**create**> option, you will be presented with a set of layout options for designing your data-entry form (see fig. 3.24)

Fig. 3.24.

Options of the layout menu in form design.

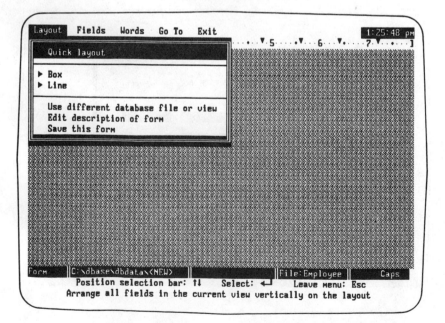

```
 Layout   Fields   Words   Go To   Exit                     1:25:48 pm
┌─────────────────────────┐ ...·▼.5..·▼.....▼.6..▼.....7.▼.....]
│  Quick layout           │
│                         │
│  ▶ Box                  │
│  ▶ Line                 │
│                         │
│    Use different database file or view │
│    Edit description of form            │
│    Save this form                      │
└─────────────────────────┘



 Form   │C:\dbase\dbdata\<NEW>│          │File:Employee│    Caps
         Position selection bar: ↑↓    Select: ↵    Leave menu: Esc
         Arrange all fields in the current view vertically on the layout
```

From figure 3.24, you will note that the name of the database file (EMPLOYEE) is shown in the status bar at the bottom of the screen. From the layout options, you are given the choice of a quick layout. From the quick layout, you can add the necessary form tile and field labels, etc. You can also use the **Box** or **Line** option to add a box or line in your form design. In addition, you can switch to a different database file to edit the description of the form.

Using the Quick Layout

To design the data-entry form as shown in figure 3.23, you select the **Quick layout** option from the Layout menu to create a form skeleton. Selecting the **Quick layout** option causes all the fields in the database file to be displayed on the form screen (see fig. 3.25).

Tip:

Use the quick layout to set up a basic design, and then modify it, if necessary.

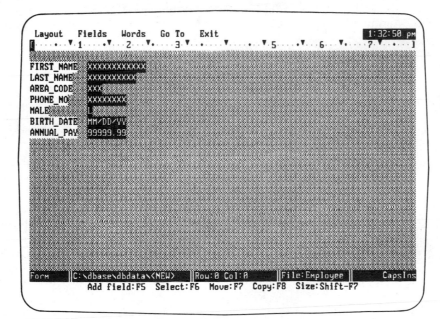

Fig. 3.25.

A quick layout for the data-entry form.

Modifying the Quick Layout

If you would like to beautify the data-entry form, you may want to

1. Reposition the data fields on the form.
2. Insert space between fields, if desired.
3. Edit the field labels.
4. Add boxes or lines around the data fields.
5. Add headings or a form title.

Repositioning Data Fields

The form painter provided by dBASE IV makes it easy to rearrange any portion of the form on the screen. You can reposition a data field on the screen by following these steps:

1. Position the cursor (which appears as a blinking dash) to the beginning of the data field. Then press F6 and Enter.

2. Move the cursor to the position where you would like to place the data field, and press the F7 function key. Then press Enter.

You can move the FIRST_NAME data field from the upper left corner of the form to the center by following these steps:

1. Position the cursor at the beginning character of the field (which is depicted as XXXXXXXXXXX). Press F6 and Enter.

2. Move the cursor to the middle of the screen, and press F7 and Enter.

After such a move, the screen may look like the one shown in figure 3.26.

You can use the same procedure to rearrange all the data fields so that the form looks like the one shown in figure 3.27.

Editing Texts

From figure 3.27, you may notice that all the labels for the data fields have not been moved. You can delete or edit these labels by first positioning the cursor on the text to be deleted or edited. You can then

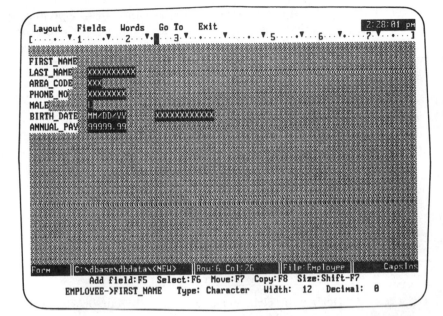

Fig. 3.26.

Moving the FIRST_NAME to the center of the form.

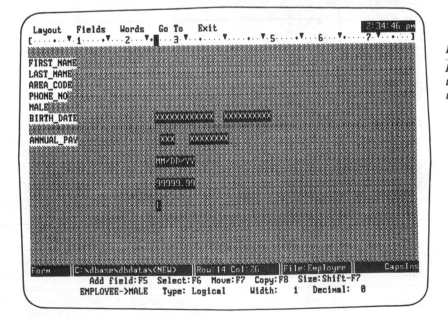

Fig. 3.27.

Repositioning all the data fields on the form.

use the Del key to erase the text one character at a time or to type in a new label. When you are typing text, if the Ins key has been pressed (Ins will appear at the right corner of the status bar) the text will be inserted into the existing text. Otherwise, the text you type will overwrite the existing text.

If you would like to open a blank line between two existing lines, move the cursor to the beginning of the second line; then press Ins and Enter. To delete an existing line from the form, place the cursor at the beginning of that line and then press Ctrl-Y.

The keystrokes used to edit the texts on a form are summarized in table 3.1.

Table 3.1
Keys for Editing Screens

Key	Function
Ins	Switches between insert and overwrite modes.
Del	Deletes the character of a label at the cursor. Deletes the data field at the cursor.
Backspace	Erases the character to the left of the cursor.
Ctrl-Y	Deletes the line at the cursor.
Ctrl-T	Deletes the word of a label at the cursor. Deletes the data field at the cursor.
Cursor key	Moves the cursor one character in the indicated direction.
Home	Moves the cursor to the beginning of the current word, or to the beginning of the previous word.
End	Moves the cursor to the beginning of the next word.
Ctrl-Z	Moves the cursor to the beginning of the line.
Ctrl-B	Moves the cursor to the end of the line.
Ctrl ←	Moves the cursor to the beginning of the previous word of a label.
Ctrl →	Moves the cursor to the beginning of the next.
PgUp	Move the cursor to the top of the form.
PgDn	Move the cursor to the bottom of the form.

With these operations, you can redesign the form and make it look like the one in figure 3.28.

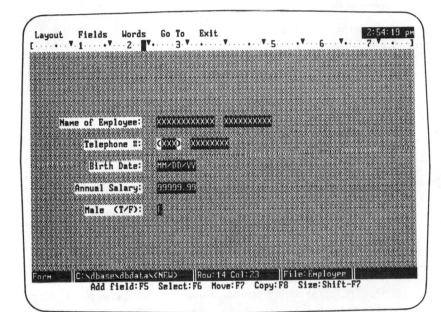

Fig. 3.28.

Adding new labels for the data fields.

Moving Portions of the Form

By examining the entry form in figure 3.28, you may notice that the labels and data fields are not quite centered in the form. You can reposition the labels and data fields by using the area move operation provided by dBASE IV.

To move a section of the form, follow these steps:

1. Use the arrow keys to position the cursor (which appears as a blinking dash) in the upper left corner of the area to be moved.

2. Press F6 to begin highlighting the area.

3. Use the right-arrow (→) key to move the cursor to the right until it passes the rightmost position of the area; then use the down-arrow (↓) key to move the cursor so that the whole area to be moved is highlighted. Press the Enter key to fix the area.

4. Move the cursor to the upper left corner of the new area, and then press the F7 function key. At this point, you can either press Enter to complete the move or use the arrow keys to adjust the position of the area.

You can follow these steps to move the labels and data fields to the center of the form:

1. Position the cursor at the beginning of the first field label (in this case, "Name of Employee") and press the F6 function key.

2. Use the right-arrow (→) key to move the cursor to the end of the rightmost data field (in this case, LAST_NAME), and use the down-arrow (↓) key to move the cursor to the lower right corner of the form until all the data fields and labels are highlighted. Then press Enter to fix the highlighted area.

3. Move the cursor to the upper left corner of the area to which you would like to reposition the labels and data fields; then press the F7 function key. Because the new area covers part of the old area, you will be prompted:

   ```
   Delete covered text and fields (Y/N)
   ```

   After you respond with Y to the prompt, all the highlighted labels and data fields will be repositioned to the designated area (see fig. 3.29). To eliminate the highlighting shade from the area after the move, press the Esc key once.

Adding Borders to the Form

After you have placed the data fields at the desired locations on the form, you now can add other graphic design features such as a box for the border and a form title. To add a title, you can move the cursor to the desired position and type in the text. To place a box (single- or double-line), you can select the **Box** option from the Layout menu (which is invoked by pressing Alt-L). Then select either the **Single line** or **Double line** option from the Box submenu to place the box on the form (see fig. 3.30).

After selecting **Double line** option, for example, you then move the cursor to the upper left corner of the box, and press Enter to anchor it. Then use the right-arrow (→) key and the down-arrow (↓) key to move

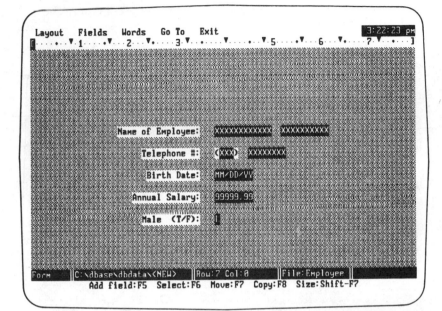

Fig. 3.29.

Moving all the data fields and their labels.

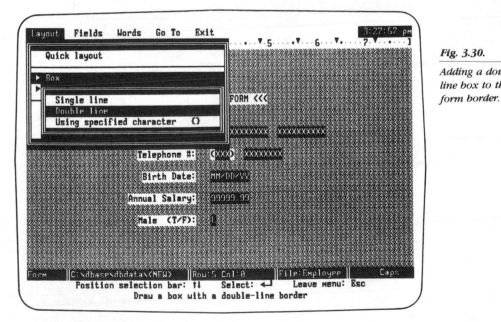

Fig. 3.30.

Adding a double-line box to the form border.

the cursor to the lower right corner of the box and press Enter. The completed form is shown in figure 3.31.

Fig. 3.31.

A finished custom data-entry form.

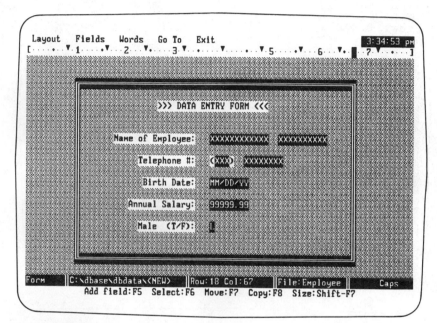

Saving the Data-Entry Form

Once you are satisfied with the form you have designed, you can save it for later data-entry operation by selecting the **Save changes and Exit** options from the Exit menu (invoked with Alt-E). When you save the form, you need to assign the form a name, such as EMPLOYEE. This form design then is saved under the name you specify, and it is given .SCR as the file extension. It is often a good idea to assign the same name to the form as the database file because you can easily relate the data-entry form with the database file. Once the form is saved, it will be displayed in the Form panel in the Control Center. You can later add a description to the form file in the same manner you add a description to a database file, as discussed earlier.

When you save a data-entry form, the information about how the form looks on the screen is saved in a screen file with a .SCR file extension (such as EMPLOYEE.SCR). In addition, the information about all the data fields and their corresponding labels and headings are saved in a format file that will be saved under the same name with a .FMT file extension (such as EMPLOYEE.FMT). Although you can modify the contents of the format file (using a text editor) to alter the form format, it is important to remember that any changes you made directly in the format file will not be reflected in the screen file.

Caution:
Any changes made in the format file will not change the data-entry form on the screen.

Modifying the Data-Entry Form

To modify an existing data-entry form, use the cursor to highlight the form to be modified in the Forms panel of the Control Center. In return, you will be prompted

        Display data   Modify layout

        Press ENTER to select or ESC to cancel

At this point, select the **Modify layout** option. When you select the option, the existing form layout is displayed on the screen (see fig. 3.32).

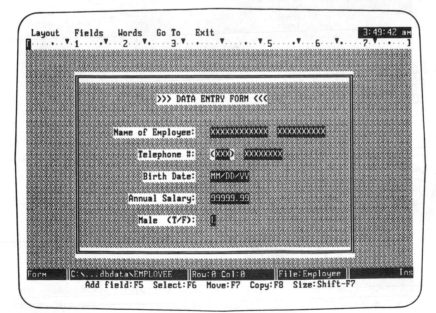

Fig. 3.32.

Displaying an existing form for modifications.

You can modify any part of the form by following the previously described procedures for designing a data-entry form. After you have completed the modifications, you can save the modified form by choosing the **Exit/Save** options. If you find that you have made a mistake and you want to abort the modification process, you can do so by pressing Esc.

In addition to those mentioned earlier, there are a number of operations you can use to modify the data-entry form. These operations include removing an existing data field from the form, placing another data field on the form, modifying a data fields on the form, and specifying the data format for a data field. Any one of these operations can be carried out while you are in the form modification process by selecting one of the options provided by the Fields menu, which you display by pressing Alt-F (see fig. 3.33).

Fig. 3.33.

Options of the Fields menu.

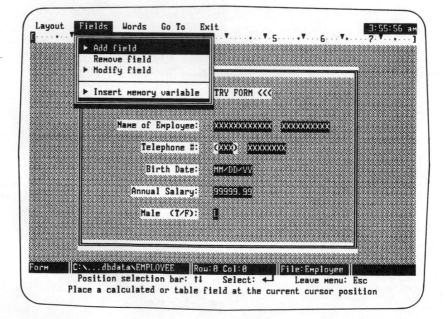

Removing a Data Field

Any data field which has been placed on the form can be removed in one of two ways. The simplest way to remove it is to first move the cursor to the data field (anywhere in the field), and then press the Del key.

Another way is to select **Remove field** from the Fields menu after positioning your cursor at the field to be removed. For example, if you would like to remove the FIRST_NAME field from the form, move the cursor to the template of that field (in the form of XXXXXXXXXXX), and then press Enter.

Adding a Data Field

Any data fields that are in the database file can be placed on the form. However, you are not required to show every data field on the form. For example, you can design multiple forms, each of which is used for entering data to certain data fields in the database file. Or, if you mistakenly remove a field from the form, you can add it back to the form at any time.

To place a field on the form, first position your cursor at the beginning of the field location, and then press F5. Or you could place the field by choosing the **Add** option from the Fields menu (invoked by pressing Alt-F). After pressing F5 or selecting the menu option, a field box showing all the existing data fields in the database file will appear. For example, if you would like to add the FIRST_NAME field back to the form after it has been removed, you could set the FIRST_NAME field from the field box after choosing the **Add field** menu option (see fig. 3.34).

After choosing the field to be added to the form, you need to specify the field attributes. (When you use the quick form to place all the data fields on the form, default settings are used for defining the field attributes.) In addition to the name, type, length, and decimals of the field, you need to define the field template, picture functions, editing options, and other display attributes (see fig. 3.35).

Specifying Field Templates

A *field template* specifies the format of how the data item should be entered and displayed in the data fields on the form. A template is made of a series of symbols that dictate the type of character that should be included in the field value. The legal template symbols for a character field are

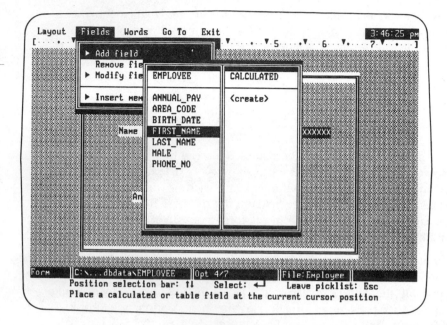

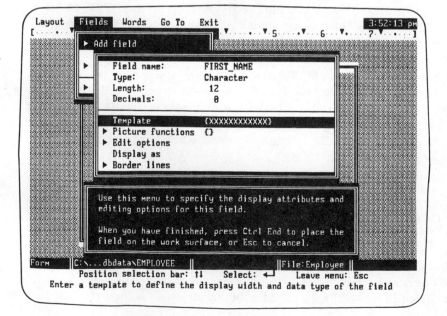

X	for an character of any type
A	for an alphabetic letter (a-z, A-Z)
#	for an numeric digit (0-9)
N	for an alphabetic letter, a numeric digit, or an underscore (_)
Y	for accepting Y (for yes) or N (for no)
L	for accepting T (for true), F (false), Y (for yes), and N (for no)
!	for converting the entering character to uppercase

For example, the default template for character fields is represented with a string of Xs such as XXXXXXXXXXXX for the FIRST_NAME data field. Each X indicates that any type of text character can be entered in its place in the field. If you want to allow only a special type of characters in the field, you need to use different template symbols for specifying the template. For example, if you want to capitalize the first character of the FIRST_NAME field, you could use !XXXXXXXXXX for the template in which the symbol ! will automatically convert the first character entered to uppercase, regardless of whether the character is entered in lowercase or uppercase. Do not use !AAAAAAAAAA for the FIRST_NAME field template, because it does not allow a blank space in the field to accept a first name like "James C."

Caution:
Do not use a series of A's in the template for a character string that includes blank spaces.

The # allows you to accept a numeric digit in a character field value. For example, a model number RCA-100 can be entered to the field whose template is defined as !!!X###. The N template symbol enables you to enter an alphabetic letter, a numeric digit, and an underscore (_) in a field string.

The Y and L template symbols are used for designing logical questions by using a character data field that anticipates True/False or Yes/No answers.

The template symbols for numeric fields are

9	for a numeric digit and a sign (+ or –) only
#	for a numeric digit, space, and sign
*	display leading zeros as asterisks
$	display leading zeros as $
,	for display a comma in common business form
.	for showing a decimal point

The template symbol 9 allows only numeric digit and sign (+ or –) to be entered in this place. No blank spaces are allowed. For example, if you specify 9999 as the field template, you can enter only a value in four numeric digits to its field. You may not enter a value in less than four digits such as 245 to the field. Therefore, if the values to be entered to the numeric fields vary in number of digits, do not use 9 as the template symbol. Instead, you should use # as the template symbol. Because the # allows a blank space to be entered in its place, you can specify, for example, #### as a template that will allow values such as 2345 or 234 to be entered to the field.

The * and $ symbols, when they are specified as a part of the template, will fill in the leading zeros with these symbols. For example, if you specify *#### or $#### as the field template, the field value of 234 will be displayed as *234 or $234 respectively after it is entered.

The comma (,) allows you to display a field in the common business form. That is, a ##,###,### will display the value of 12345 in the form of 12,345 after it is entered from the keyboard.

Similarly, the decimal point (.) enables you to specify the decimal point in the field value. For example, if you specify the field template as ##,###.###, the field value of 1234.5678 will be displayed as 1,234.568. Because only three places after the decimal point were specified in the template, the fourth digit after the decimal point will be rounded up or down by using the conventional rule.

Caution:
Be sure to save the field template by pressing Ctrl-End.

When you are using date and logical fields, their templates are pre-determined by dBASE IV. A template of MM/DD/YY is assumed for all date fields, while all logical fields will be assigned a template of L. The L symbols allows only T or F to be entered in its place.

After you have specified the field template, press Ctrl-End to save it.

Defining [Field] Picture Functions

While a template dictates the form in which the data can be entered in a field, a field picture regulates how field values are displayed on the form.

To define the field picture, you first position the cursor at the field; then select **Modify field** from the Fields menu and **Picture functions** from the options displayed. For example, after you place the cursor at the

beginning of the FIRST_NAME field and select the **Picture functions**
option, the option for defining its field picture is displayed in a box (see
fig. 3.36).

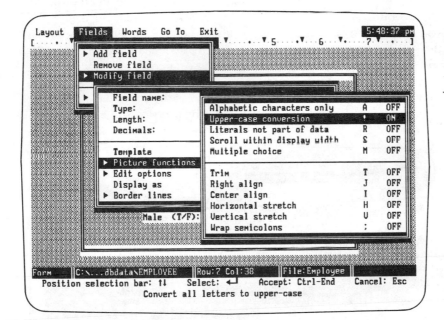

Fig. 3.36.

*Defining a picture
function.*

When you are defining a picture function, you specify how the field value
is to be displayed in the form. For example, you could specify that only
alphabetic characters should be displayed, whether or not to convert all
the characters to uppercase, etc. In addition, you can specify a limited a
set of values that can be entered in the field. You execute the functions
by pressing Enter to toggle the ON/OFF switch. For example, if you
would like to display the value in the FIRST_NAME field all in capital
letters, highlight the **Upper-case conversion** option and press Enter.
The status of the item (shown on the right side of the box) is switched
from OFF to ON. To save the picture function, press Ctrl-End.

Caution:

*Be sure to save
the picture
function by
pressing Ctrl-
End.*

It is important to note that the picture function only governs how the
field value is to be displayed; the function does not override the field
template defined in the **Template** operation. For example, the template
defined for the FIRST_NAME field, !XXXXXXXXXX, still accepts characters
of any type for the field values (such as "James C."). Even though all the

characters will be displayed as uppercase letters (as "JAMES C.") after you used the {!} picture function, the data values stored in the database file remains as entered ("James C.").

One of the powerful picture function is the **Multiple choice** option that allows you to specify a multiple field values for the field. For example, you can use the **Multiple choice** option to define the possible values for the AREA_CODE field by specifying the two acceptable area codes, 206 and 503 (see fig. 3.37). As a result, during data entry only one of these two values will be a valid entry. Instead of entering one of these two values to the AREA_CODE field, you can press the space bar to display these values, and select the one you want by pressing the Enter key.

Fig. 3.37.

Defining multiple choice field values.

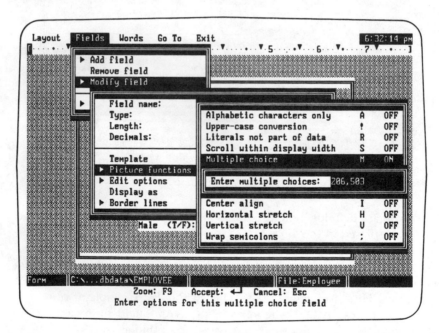

When entering the multiple choice values to the picture function, you need to separate multiple values with commas (as shown in fig. 3.37). However, if the field value itself contains a comma, be sure to enclose the value in quotation marks to avoid confusion.

A modified data-entry form that includes the field template and picture functions is presented in figure 3.38.

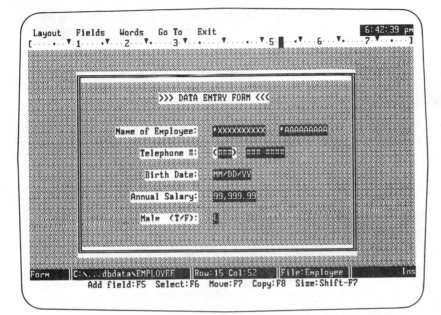

Fig. 3.38.

A modified data-entry form.

From the modified form, you will notice that the template for the
LAST_NAME field (!AAAAAAAAA) indicates that it will accept only
alphabetical letters and the first letter will always be in uppercase. The
AREA_CODE (###) and PHONE_NO (###-####) fields accept only
numeric digits (a minus sign is automatically inserted in the phone
number). The numeric field, ANNUAL_PAY, accepts a values in a
common business format (99,999.99). The BIRTH_DATE and MALE
fields are assigned predetermined field templates for a data field
(MM/DD/YY) and a logical field (L).

Using the Data-Entry Form

The data-entry form, which has been saved in a screen file named
EMPLOYEE.SCR, can now be used for appending or editing records in the
database file. Before using an existing data-entry form, however, you must
set up the form. You can design more than one form to be used for the
data in a database file.

To select the data-entry form to be used for data entry or data editing, you first highlight the form in the Form panel of the Control Center, and then press Enter.

In return, the custom data-entry form will be used to display the existing records. To add new records to the database file, you need to go to the last record and then append new records to the file.

For example, if you need to add data records to the EMPLOYEE database file by using the custom data-entry form created earlier (EMPLOYEE), follow these steps:

1. In the Control Center, highlight EMPLOYEE in the Data panel.

2. Highlight EMPLOYEE in the Form panel and press Enter.

3. Select the **Display data** option

When the first record of the EMPLOYEE database is displayed on the custom data-entry form,

1. Invoke the Go To menu by pressing Alt-G and select the **Last record** option (see fig. 3.39).

Fig. 3.39.

Selecting the **Last record** *option.*

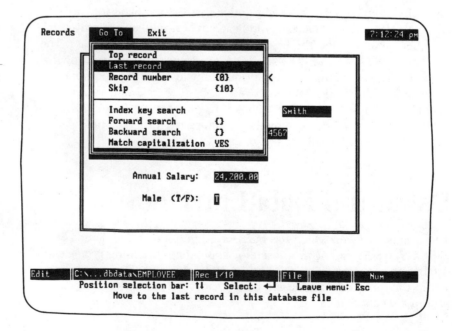

2. When the last record is displayed (Rec 10/10), press PgDn.

3. Answer Y to the prompt Add new records? (Y/N).

As a result, you are given a blank data-entry form for entering data to the new record (see fig. 3.40).

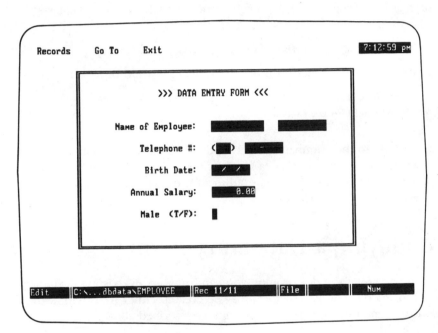

Fig. 3.40.

Using the modified data-entry form.

Using the Data-Entry Form from the Dot Prompt

The procedures described in the preceding section for creating, modifying, and using a custom data-entry form can also be used at the dot prompt once the data-entry form is invoked and displayed on the screen by issuing the appropriate commands.

Designing a Data-Entry Form

Command:

CREATE SCREEN
*Design a new
data-entry form.*

When you create a custom data-entry form, all the information related to the form is saved in a screen file with .SCR file extension. To design a new data-entry form at the dot prompt, you can use the CREATE SCREEN command to bring up the data-entry form after selecting the database file to be used:

   . CREATE SCREEN *<name of the data-entry form>*

For example, the correct form of this command would be

   . USE EMPLOYEE
   . CREATE SCREEN EMPLOYEE

In response to the commands entered, the data-entry form similar to that shown earlier (refer to fig. 3.24) will be displayed. From this point on, you can follow the same steps as outlined in the last section for designing and saving the data-entry form.

Modifying a Data-Entry Form

Command:

MODIFY SCREEN
*Changing a
custom data-
entry form.*

When you are at the dot prompt, you can bring up an existing data-entry form for modifications. The form may be created either from within the Control Center or from the dot prompt as described above.

The command for bringing up an existing data-entry form from the dot prompt is MODIFY SCREEN, and you use it in the following form:

   . MODIFY SCREEN *<name of the data-entry form>*

For example, the command is issued as in the following:

   . USE EMPLOYEE
   . MODIFY SCREEN EMPLOYEE

In return, the form named EMPLOYEE.SCR is displayed on the screen. You then can use the procedures described in the last section to make the necessary modifications.

Invoking the Format File for the Data-Entry Form

Every time you save a screen file (such as EMPLOYEE.SCR), a format file with the same name with .FMT file extension (such as EMPLOYEE.FMT) will be created. The format file holds the information about the format for the data fields and their corresponding labels (and form title). This format file needs to be invoked before you use the form for the data-entry operations.

To invoke an existing data-entry form for data-entry operation from the dot prompt, you need to issue the SET FORMAT TO command as follows:

> . SET FORMAT TO *<name of the data-entry form>*

Command:
SET FORMAT TO
Select a data-entry form.

For example, if you would like to use the custom data-entry form EMPLOYEE.FMT (created after you saved the form in EMPLOYEE.SCR) for editing a data record you can issue the following commands at the dot prompt:

> . USE EMPLOYEE
> . SET FORMAT TO EMPLOYEE
> . EDIT

Chapter 3 QuickStart

In this chapter, you have learned the procedures for creating a new database file and entering data into its records. Before creating the database file, you created a new file catalog for holding the database file. In addition, you have seen how to design and save custom data-entry forms for input operations. In this section, you will use a simple database to review and practice these procedures.

Setting Up a File Catalog

First, you need to create a file catalog to store the databases and related files. For this example, the name of the catalog file is QIKSTART.CAT (of course, you can choose a different file name if you wish). The file name must use no more than eight characters (alphabetic and underscore are acceptable).

To create the QIKSTART file catalog,

1. After you enter dBASE IV, the current file catalog and the directory path are displayed at the top of the Control Center screen. The path may look like

   C:\DBASE\DBDATA\UNTITLED.CAT or
   C:\DBASE\DBDATA\EMPLOYEE.CAT, etc.

2. Invoke the Catalog menu by pressing Alt-C.

3. Choose the **Use a different catalog** option from the menu.

4. Select the **<create>** option from the Catalog box.

5. At the Enter name for new catalog: prompt, enter QIKSTART and press Enter.

6. When you return to the Control Center, QIKSTART should appear on the screen.

Adding the File Catalog Description

To add the description of the QIKSTART.CAT catalog file, follow these steps:

1. Invoke the Catalog menu by pressing Alt-C.

2. Choose the **Edit description of catalog** option from the menu.

3. Enter the description Files for QuickStart exercises at the prompt.

4. When you return to the Control Center, the file description will not appear on the screen. It will be displayed only when you later select the catalog.

The ADDRESS Database

The database you may use to practice the procedures in this section consists of a single Address data table (see fig. 3.41).

```
LAST NAME FIRST NAME ADDRESS              CITY        STATE ZIP
--------- ---------- -------------------- ----------  ----- -----
Taylor    George F.  123 Main Street      New York    NY    10021
Peters    Cathy K.   3467 First Avenue    Los Angles  CA    94321
Bush      Alfred G.  13456 N. 95th Street Seattle     WA    98185
Johnson   Robert J.  3245 Oak Street      Portland    OR    97203
Morrow    Peter T.   2046 Skyline Drive   Fremont     CA    94538
Harvey    Jane W.    9709 Broadway        Vancouver   WA    98665
King      Steven W.  2771 Plaza Drive     Pittsburgh  PA    15230
Morgan    Albert C.  1354 S. 78th Avenue  Portland    OR    97202
Peterson  Janet      3098 Oceanview Road  San Diego   CA    92121
Ball      Thomas     9440 Rockcreek Road  Beaverton   OR    97201
```

Fig. 3.41.

Contents of the ADDRESS data table.

Defining the Database Structure

To create the ADDRESS.DBF database file, you need to define all the field attributes in the database structure. The database structure may look like that shown in figure 3.42.

First, you may try to create the database structure yourself without reading the following section. If you encounter some difficulty, here are the steps for creating the ADDRESS.DBF database structure:

1. At the Control Center, select <**create**> option from the Data panel and press Enter.

2. When the database structure design form appears, enter the attributes for the first data field, LAST_NAME. After entering one field attribute (such as Field Name, File Type, etc.) press Enter to move on to the next field attribute.

3. Enter Y in the Index column for the LAST_NAME, STATE, and ZIP fields because you will want to arrange the records in later practices.

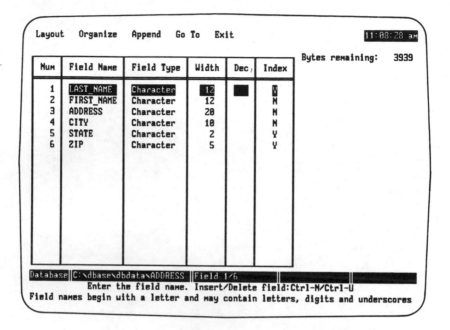

Fig. 3.42.

Database structure for the ADDRESS.DBF.

4. After defining all the field attributes, save the database structure in the ADDRESS.DBF file by pressing Ctrl-End.

5. Select the **Save changes and exit** option from the Exit menu; enter name of the database file, ADDRESS, at the prompt Save as:, and press Enter.

6. When asked Input data records now? (Y/N), answer N because you want to design a data-entry form for the input operation.

7. After you return to the Control Center, you should see the database file ADDRESS in the Data panel.

Adding the Database File to the File Catalog

To add a description of the ADDRESS.DBF file to the QIKSTART.CAT file catalog, follow these steps:

1. When ADDRESS is highlighted in the Data panel as the active file, invoke the Catalog menu by pressing Alt-C.

2. Choose the **Edit description of highlighted file** option from the menu.

3. Enter the description Address file for friends at the prompt.

4. When you return to the Control Center, the file description should appear on the screen.

Designing a Custom Data-Entry Form

In the following section, you will practice creating a data-entry form named ADDRESS.SCR for entering data into the ADDRESS.DBF (see fig. 3.43).

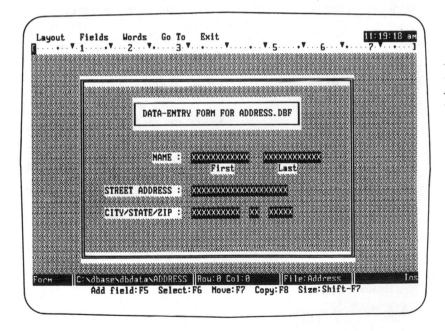

Fig. 3.43.

Data-entry form for the ADDRESS.DBF.

To create the ADDRESS.SCR data-entry form, follow these steps (if you make a mistake and would like to start over, press Esc to abort the operation):

1. Select ADDRESS in the Data panel as the active database file.

2. Select the <**select**> option from the Forms panel and press Enter.

3. Choose **Quick layout** from the Layout menu.

4. Reposition all the fields and their labels; position the cursor at the beginning of the first field label (that is, LAST_NAME) and the use the → key to shade the field until it goes beyond the last character of the longest field (that is, the ADDRESS field). Then use the ↓ key to move the cursor down so that the shaded area covers all the fields in the block to be moved. Press Enter to fix the area.

5. Use ↑ to position the cursor to the position corresponding to the upper left corner of the new position for the block, and then press F7.

6. When the shaded block appears on the screen, you can use the arrow keys to move it around. When the block is positioned at the location on the screen you want, press Enter to fix its location.

7. When the prompt Delete covered text and fields? (Y/N) appears, enter Y.

8. Edit the field labels and move the fields around until you are satisfied with their appearance on the form. Add the form title ''DATA-ENTRY FORM FOR ADDRESS.DBF''.

9. To place a double-line box around the form, position the cursor to the upper left corner of the box, and then invoke the Layout menu by pressing Alt-L.

10. Choose the **Box** option from the Layout menu, and then select the **Double line** option.

11. When the = symbol appears on the corner, press Enter to anchor it.

12. Use the → and the ↓ keys to draw the double box. You may use the arrow keys to change the box. When you are done drawing the box, press Enter.

13. Use the same procedure to draw a single-line box around the form title.

14. Add all the necessary notes and labels you need.

15. Save the form by pressing Ctrl-End, and then enter ADDRESS as the name of the form to be saved.

16. When you return to the Control Center, the data-entry form named ADDRESS should appear in the Forms panel.

Entering Data

Now that the data-entry form is created, you can use it to enter data to the ADDRESS.DBF:

1. Use the cursor key to highlight ADDRESS in the Forms panel if it is not already being highlighted (the ADDRESS should also be highlighted in the Data panel).

2. Press Enter and select the **Display data** option from the menu.

3. As the data-entry form appears, enter the values to the data fields—you may use the contents of the data table shown in figure 3.41.

4. After entering all the data, press Alt-E to invoke the Exit menu and select the Exit option to return to the Control Center.

Chapter Summary

In this chapter, you learned to create database files from the Control Center and from the dot prompt. Additionally, you learned how to create and use file catalogs and how to define the database structure for the new database file. This chapter also introduced the concept of adding data records to the database file and showed you how to manage your database files. Lastly, this chapter illustrated how to use the default data-entry form that is automatically set up by dBASE IV and explained how to create and use a custom data-entry form created with the form generator. In the next chapter, you will learn various methods of displaying selected data.

4

Displaying Data

In the last chapter, you learned how to create a database file and enter data into its records. In the process of creating a database file, the database structure was defined. The database structure and records are stored in a database file. This chapter teaches you how to display the structure and data records of the database file. These procedures involve selecting menu options from the Control Center and entering appropriate commands at the dot prompt.

In this chapter, the powerful function of the Query By Example (QBE) operation is introduced. By using the QBE operation, you are able to find and display the set of records whose field values match the values specified in the query fields and the records that meet a certain set of predefined filter conditions. These filter conditions can also be incorporated in the dBASE IV dot prompt commands when they are used for displaying selective data records.

As mentioned in Chapter 2, the only efficient way to manage your dBASE IV files is to organize them in various levels of directories. For that reason, this chapter also discusses the menu options and dBASE IV commands for listing the contents of various file directories.

Displaying File Directories

After you create database files and their related disk files, you save the files in a file directory. At any time during processing, you can display the contents of a given file directory. You can do this either by selecting the appropriate menu options from within the Control Center or by issuing dBASE IV commands at the dot prompt. The sections that follow explain each of these methods.

Displaying Directories from the Control Center

When you are in the Control Center, the files in the current file catalog are displayed in the panels. If the file you are looking for is in another catalog, you can simply switch to that catalog by selecting the Catalog menu from the Control Center. The procedures for working with file catalogs are discussed in Chapter 3.

Listing Files in the Current Directory

If you would like to display all the disk files in a given directory, you can use the **DOS utilities** option provided by the Tools menu (invoked by pressing Alt-T) from within the Control Center. For example, when you are in the DBDATA directory (within the \DBASE directory), select the menu options, and the contents of the directory are displayed (see fig. 4.1).

In figure 4.1, you can see that the attributes of each file are shown on one line of the screen. The attributes displayed include the file's name and extension, the file size (in bytes), the date and time the file was created, and the memory space it occupies. Because of the screen size, only eleven files are listed at a time, and the other files are hidden from view.

You can use the up-arrow (↑) and down-arrow (↓) keys to scroll up and down the screen to view the hidden files. You can also use the PgUp and PgDn keys to scroll the display one screenful at a time.

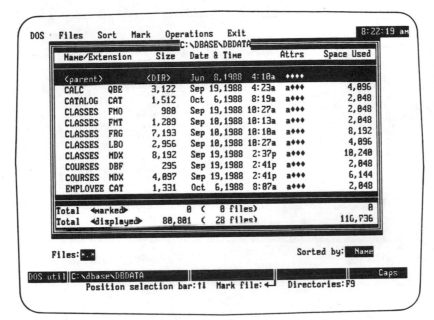

Fig. 4.1.

Displaying the contents of the file directory.

By default, the files in the directory are displayed alphabetically by file name. You can also sort them by file extension (such as .DBF, .MDX, FMT, etc.), by the data and time, and by file size.

If you would like to display in one group all files of the same type, you can sort them by their file extensions. To do that, you first need to press Alt-S to invoke the Sort menu in the DOS utilities menu bar; then choose the **Extension** option and press Enter (see fig. 4.2).

After you select the **Extension** option, the files are arranged in the order of their extensions. As a result, files of the same type will be displayed as a group.

Similarly, you can select the **Date & Time** or the **Size** options from the DOS utilities menu bar to arrange the files according to the order in which they were created or the size of the disk files (from the smallest to the largest).

Fig. 4.2.

*Sorting files by
their extensions.*

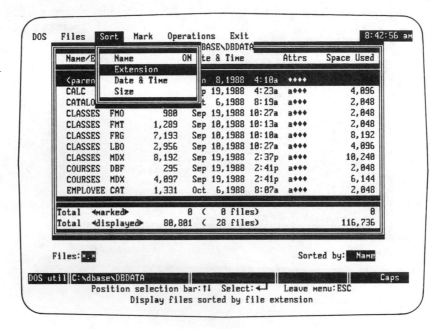

Listing Files in Another Directory

If the file you are searching for is in another directory, you need to
change the directory when you are using the DOS utilities. To display
files in the directory other than the default directory, you need to invoke
the Files menu from the DOS utilities by pressing Alt-F; then type the
path of the other directory (see fig. 4.3).

Caution:

*Use the Files
menu (Alt-F)
from **DOS
utilities** only for
viewing files in
another file
directory.*

It is important to note that changing the directory by using the Files
menu from the DOS utilities does not change the current directory used
in the Control Center. The directory change allows you to view (but not
access) files in another directory. When you exit from DOS utilities and
return to the Control Center, the original directory becomes the current
directory. If you want to change the default directory, you need to use
the DOS menu (Alt-D) from **DOS utilities**, and then select the **Set
default drive:directory** option accordingly (see fig. 4.4). A discussion
on changing the default data disk drive and directory was included
Chapter 3.

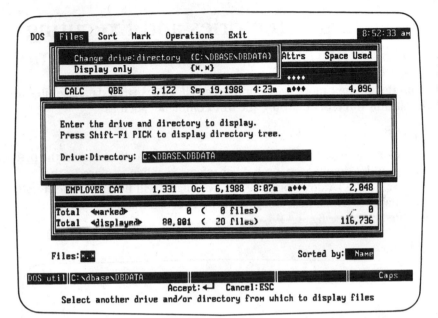

Fig. 4.3.

Changing the current file directory.

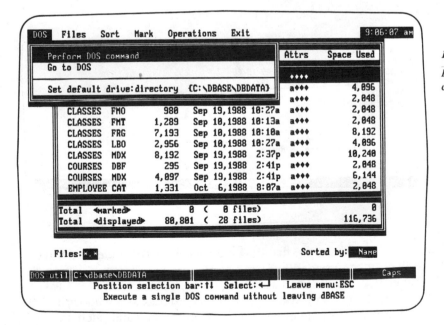

Fig. 4.4.

Performing a DOS command.

Displaying Directories and Executing DOS Commands from the Dot Prompt

From dot prompt mode, you can display all the existing database files in the default directory by using the DIR command, such as

. DIR

Tip:

At the dot prompt, use F4 for DIR *operation.*

As a shortcut, when you are in dot prompt mode, you can issue the DIR command by simply pressing F4. For example, when you are in the \DBASE\DBDATA directory, the DIR command will list the names of all the database (.DBF) files along with their record numbers, update dates, and file sizes (see fig. 4.5).

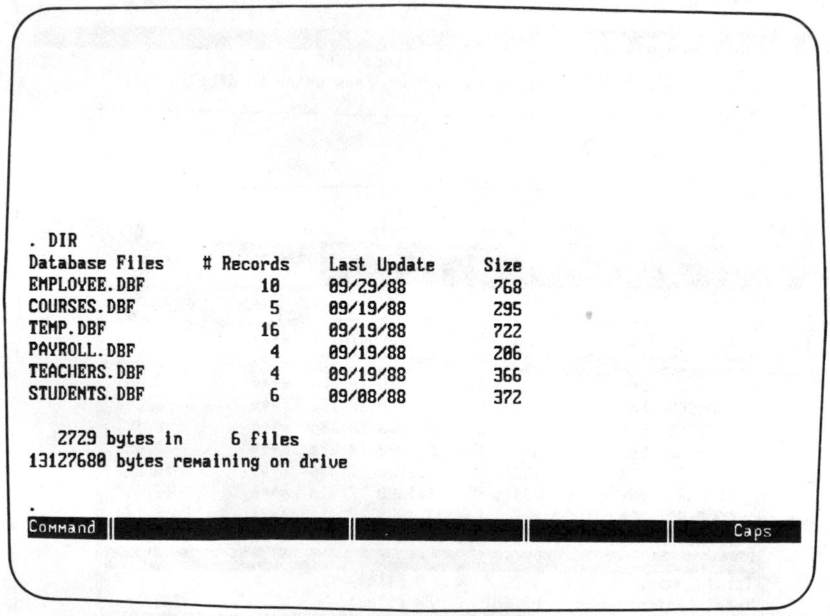

Fig. 4.5.

Listing files in current directory.

```
. DIR
Database Files    # Records    Last Update    Size
EMPLOYEE.DBF         10         09/29/88       768
COURSES.DBF           5         09/19/88       295
TEMP.DBF             16         09/19/88       722
PAYROLL.DBF           4         09/19/88       206
TEACHERS.DBF          4         09/19/88       366
STUDENTS.DBF          6         09/08/88       372

   2729 bytes in      6 files
13127680 bytes remaining on drive
.
```

```
Command                                                                Caps
```

Tip:

Use the asterisk (*) as a wild card character for displaying files of all types.

In figure 4.5, you can see that only the database (.DBF) files are listed with the DIR command; other types of files are not shown. If you need to list other types of files such as catalog files (.CAT), format files (.FMT), and index files (.MDX), you need to use an asterisk as a wild card character along with file extensions in the DIR command, such as

. DIR *.CAT

Figure 4.6 shows examples of using these commands.

The asterisk instructs dBASE IV to list all the files name in its place. You can also use the asterisk in the place of the file extension to include files of all types in the DIR command (see fig. 4.7):

. DIR EMPLOYEE.*

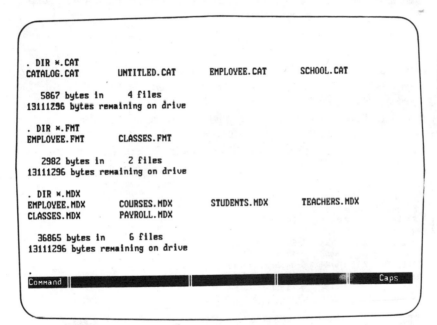

```
. DIR *.CAT
CATALOG.CAT        UNTITLED.CAT      EMPLOYEE.CAT        SCHOOL.CAT

    5867 bytes in     4 files
13111296 bytes remaining on drive

. DIR *.FMT
EMPLOYEE.FMT       CLASSES.FMT

    2982 bytes in     2 files
13111296 bytes remaining on drive

. DIR *.MDX
EMPLOYEE.MDX       COURSES.MDX       STUDENTS.MDX        TEACHERS.MDX
CLASSES.MDX        PAYROLL.MDX

   36865 bytes in     6 files
13111296 bytes remaining on drive

.
Command                                                         Caps
```

Fig. 4.6.

Listing files by their types.

When the asterisk is used as a wild card character, it tells dBASE IV to perform the specified operation on files that have any characters in place of the * and that match the other criteria. For example, DIR *.CAT will cause dBASE IV to display all files that have the extension .CAT, no matter what the name of the file might be. This command would display EMPLOYEE.CAT as well as PHONE.CAT, because all files with the .CAT extension will be displayed.

Furthermore, you can use DIR *.* to list all files in the current directory.

When you issue the DIR command from the dot prompt, except for the database (.DBF) files, all the other types will show only their file names. Other information such as file sizes (in number of records and bytes)

Tip:
At dot prompt, use RUN to execute DOS commands.

Fig. 4.7.

*Listing files with a
wild card (˙).*

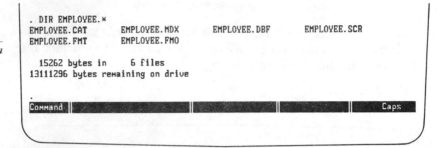

```
. DIR EMPLOYEE.*
EMPLOYEE.CAT        EMPLOYEE.MDX        EMPLOYEE.DBF        EMPLOYEE.SCR
EMPLOYEE.FMT        EMPLOYEE.FMO

   15262 bytes in      6 files
13111296 bytes remaining on drive

.
Command                                                           Caps
```

and file update dates are not displayed with the DIR command. However,
you can issue the DOS DIR command within dBASE IV by adding the RUN
keyword in front of the DIR command. Any command followed by the
RUN keyword will be executed as though you were at the DOS prompt
outside of dBASE IV. For example, if you issue RUN DIR ∗.MDX from the
dot prompt, you will get a list of all the files in the current directory (see
fig. 4.8).

Fig. 4.8.

*Executing a DOS
command at the
dot prompt.*

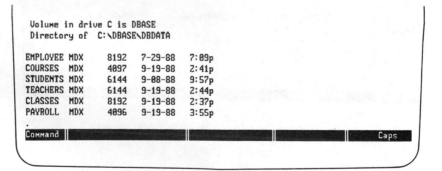

```
 Volume in drive C is DBASE
 Directory of  C:\DBASE\DBDATA

EMPLOYEE MDX      8192   7-29-88    7:09p
COURSES  MDX      4097   9-19-88    2:41p
STUDENTS MDX      6144   9-08-88    9:57p
TEACHERS MDX      6144   9-19-88    2:44p
CLASSES  MDX      8192   9-19-88    2:37p
PAYROLL  MDX      4096   9-19-88    3:55p
.
Command                                                           Caps
```

If you need to list the files in another directory, you can include the
directory path in the RUN DIR command. For example,

   . RUN DIR \DBASE\∗.EXE

Caution:
*Be sure that
COMMAND.COM
is present in the
boot disk before
you issue the
RUN command.*

However, before you issue the RUN command, the DOS COMMAND.COM
file must be present in the directory from which you boot your
computer. If you boot from the hard disk, the COMMAND.COM file must
be in the root directory. If you boot your computer from a floppy disk,
the boot disk must be in drive A before you issue the RUN command.
Otherwise, an error will occur when you issue the RUN command, and
you will need to reboot the system and risk losing your data.

You can issue any valid DOS command at the dot prompt by using the RUN keyword, such as

. RUN TIME

Care must be taken not to change the directory by using the CD (Change Directory) command at the dot prompt (such as RUN CD \DBASE), because it will change the default directory. Unless you remember to change back to the current directory before returning to the Control Center, you will no longer be working in the directory you were using before you entered dot prompt mode.

Caution:
The RUN CD *command changes the current default directory.*

Displaying and Printing the Database Structure

The database structure of an existing database file can be displayed by selecting a set of options from within the Control Center or by issuing a simple dBASE IV command at the dot prompt. Similarly, printing the database structure is a simple extension of the display procedure. Both procedures are discussed in the following sections.

Displaying the Structure from the Control Center

The procedure for bringing up the database structure of the current database file involves pressing Shift-F2 while the database file is being highlighted. For example, if you would like to examine the database structure of the EMPLOYEE database file, follow these steps:

Tip:
Use Shift-F2 to recall an existing database structure.

1. Highlight the database in the Data panel.

2. Press Shift-F2.

The database structure then is displayed on the screen, and the Organize menu is automatically opened. Press Esc to reveal the database structure (see fig. 4.9).

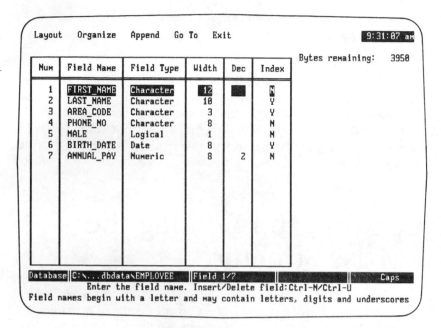

Fig. 4.9.

Displaying an existing database structure.

In addition to viewing the existing structure, you may also modify the attributes of the data fields on the same screen. The procedure for editing these field attributes will be discussed in a later section.

If, after examining the database structure, you would like to return to the Control Center without making any changes to the structure, press Alt-E to open the Exit menu and select the **Abandon changes and exit** option.

Displaying Structure from the Dot Prompt

When you are in dot prompt mode, you can display the database structure of a database one of two ways. If you intend to examine the database structure without modifying its field attributes, you can use the DISPLAY STRUCTURE (or DISP STRU) command after selecting the database file with the USE command, such as

. USE *<name of the database file>*
. DISPLAY STRUCTURE

For example,

. USE EMPLOYEE

The DISPLAY STRUCTURE command, when executed, shows the name, size, and the date of last update, together with the attributes of the existing data fields (see fig. 4.10).

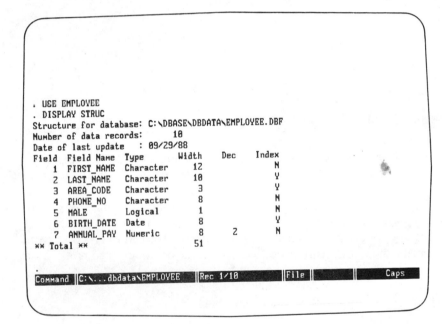

```
. USE EMPLOYEE
. DISPLAY STRUC
Structure for database: C:\DBASE\DBDATA\EMPLOYEE.DBF
Number of data records:      10
Date of last update    : 09/29/88
Field  Field Name  Type       Width   Dec   Index
    1  FIRST_NAME  Character     12            N
    2  LAST_NAME   Character     10            Y
    3  AREA_CODE   Character      3            Y
    4  PHONE_NO    Character      8            N
    5  MALE        Logical        1            N
    6  BIRTH_DATE  Date           8            Y
    7  ANNUAL_PAY  Numeric        8     2      N
** Total **                     51
```

```
Command  C:\...dbdata\EMPLOYEE    Rec 1/10       File            Caps
```

Fig. 4.10.

Displaying database structure at the dot prompt.

In dot prompt mode, as a shortcut, you can issue the DISPLAY STRUCTURE command by simply pressing F5.

Printing the Database Structure from the Control Center

To print the structure that is displayed on the screen, first open the Layout menu by pressing Alt-L, and then choose the **Print database structure** option from the Layout menu. As a shortcut, you can press Shift-F9 to print the database structure.

Tip:

From the Control Center, press Shift-F9 to print the database structure.

Printing the Database Structure from the Dot Prompt

If you are using dot prompt mode and would like to display the database structure to the printer, you can add the TO PRINT key words to the end of the DISPLAY STRUCTURE command, such as

. DISPLAY STRUCTURE TO PRINT

Displaying and Printing All Data Records

Data records that have been stored in an existing database file can be displayed in several ways. You can display some or all of the data fields in the current record, in all existing records, or in selected records. To display one or more of the records in the active database file, you select the appropriate menu options from the Control Center or issue the necessary dot prompt commands. After you've displayed the records, you can print them from either the Control Center or the dot prompt.

Displaying Records from the Control Center

Tip:
Use F2 to display records in the highlighted database.

If you need to display all the records in a database file, press F2 after highlighting the database file in the Data panel of the Control Center. In response to the keystroke, contents of the records in the highlighted database file are displayed.

However, there are two formats in which contents of the records are displayed. In one format, contents of the records are displayed one record per screen in a data edit form (see fig. 4.11).

As shown in figure 4.11, each data field is displayed in one row on the screen. A blinking cursor in the form of a dash (#) is positioned at the very beginning of the record. The status bar shown at the bottom of the

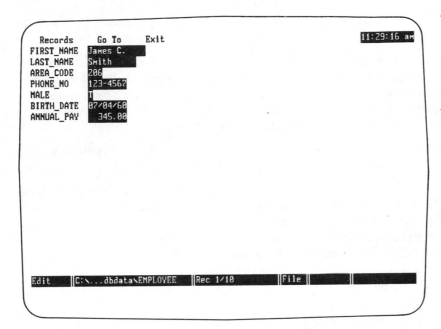

Fig. 4.11.

A data record displayed in edit format.

screen indicates the processing mode (such as Edit), the name and path of the database file (C:\...dbdata\EMPLOYEE), and the current record number and the total number of records (Rec 1/10).

To go to the next data record, press the PgDn key. Pressing the PgUp key will display the last record. If you would like to go to a specific record, press Alt-G to select the Go To menu, and then choose one of the following options:

Top record
Last record
Record number/Enter record number:
Skip/Enter number of records to skip:

The second format, called the browse form, shows the field values of each record as a line and each data field as a column (see fig. 4.12).

In a browse form, a total of 17 records can be displayed on the screen at one time. If the database file contains more than 17 records, the rest will be hidden from view. However, you can use the down-arrow key (↓) or the PgDn key to move down beyond the last record shown on the screen 'to reveal the hidden records. Similarly, press the up-arrow (↑) key or the PgUp key to move back up to reveal the hidden records.

Because of the size of the screen, only a limited number of data fields can be displayed at one time. However, if your database file has more fields than can be displayed on the same screen, you can use Tab to move to the right beyond the last displayed field to reveal the other fields. To move to the left between fields, use Shift-Tab.

When you are using browse format, you can use the Go To menu to view a specific record that will not fit into the screen display.

Tip:
Use F2 to switch between edit format and browse format.

You can switch from browse format to edit format by pressing F2. dBASE IV "remembers" the last format used and uses it to display the records the next time you press the F2 key. In addition, when you switch from edit format to browse format, sometimes the cursor will be positioned at the last record in the file. As a result, only that record will appear on the screen, making it look as though there were only one record in the database file. To reveal the rest of the records, press the PgUp key.

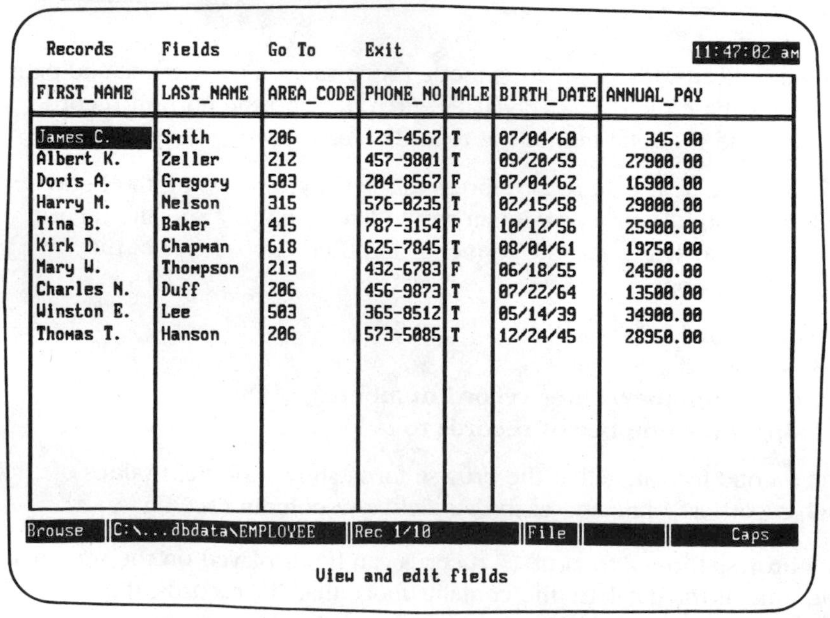

Fig. 4.12.

A data record displayed in browse format.

```
┌──────────────────────────────────────────────────────────────────────┐
│  Records     Fields     Go To     Exit                    11:47:02 am  │
│ ┌─────────────┬──────────┬──────────┬──────────┬────┬──────────┬──────────────┐ │
│ │ FIRST_NAME  │LAST_NAME │AREA_CODE │PHONE_NO  │MALE│BIRTH_DATE│ ANNUAL_PAY   │ │
│ ├─────────────┼──────────┼──────────┼──────────┼────┼──────────┼──────────────┤ │
│ │ James C.    │Smith     │206       │123-4567  │T   │07/04/60  │     345.00   │ │
│ │ Albert K.   │Zeller    │212       │457-9801  │T   │09/20/59  │   27900.00   │ │
│ │ Doris A.    │Gregory   │503       │204-8567  │F   │07/04/62  │   16900.00   │ │
│ │ Harry M.    │Nelson    │315       │576-0235  │T   │02/15/58  │   29000.00   │ │
│ │ Tina B.     │Baker     │415       │787-3154  │F   │10/12/56  │   25900.00   │ │
│ │ Kirk D.     │Chapman   │618       │625-7845  │T   │08/04/61  │   19750.00   │ │
│ │ Mary W.     │Thompson  │213       │432-6783  │F   │06/18/55  │   24500.00   │ │
│ │ Charles N.  │Duff      │206       │456-9873  │T   │07/22/64  │   13500.00   │ │
│ │ Winston E.  │Lee       │503       │365-8512  │T   │05/14/39  │   34900.00   │ │
│ │ Thomas T.   │Hanson    │206       │573-5085  │T   │12/24/45  │   28950.00   │ │
│ └─────────────┴──────────┴──────────┴──────────┴────┴──────────┴──────────────┘ │
│  Browse   C:\...dbdata\EMPLOYEE     Rec 1/10        File           Caps │
│                        View and edit fields                            │
└──────────────────────────────────────────────────────────────────────┘
```

Displaying Records from the Dot Prompt

When you are at the dot prompt, you can display the contents of all the records in the current active database by issuing the LIST command, as in

. LIST

For example, you can use the LIST command to list all the record contents of the EMPLOYEE.DBF database file (see fig. 4.13).

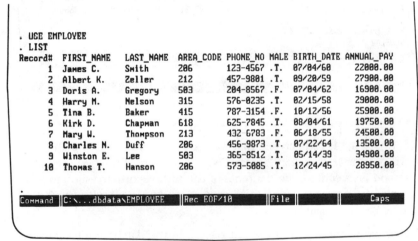

```
. USE EMPLOYEE
. LIST
Record#  FIRST_NAME   LAST_NAME   AREA_CODE  PHONE_NO   MALE  BIRTH_DATE  ANNUAL_PAY
      1  James C.     Smith       206        123-4567   .T.   07/04/60    22000.00
      2  Albert K.    Zeller      212        457-9801   .T.   09/20/59    27900.00
      3  Doris A.     Gregory     503        204-8567   .F.   07/04/62    16900.00
      4  Harry M.     Nelson      315        576-0235   .T.   02/15/58    29000.00
      5  Tina B.      Baker       415        787-3154   .F.   10/12/56    25900.00
      6  Kirk D.      Chapman     618        625-7845   .T.   08/04/61    19750.00
      7  Mary W.      Thompson    213        432 6783   .F.   06/18/55    24500.00
      8  Charles N.   Duff        206        456-9873   .T.   07/22/64    13500.00
      9  Winston E.   Lee         503        365-8512   .T.   05/14/39    34900.00
     10  Thomas T.    Hanson      206        573-5085   .T.   12/24/45    28950.00
.
Command  C:\...dbdata\EMPLOYEE      Rec EOF/10      File            Caps
```

Fig. 4.13.

Showing all records with the LIST command.

If you would like to display the contents of the current data record, you use the DISPLAY (or DISP) command, such as

. DISPLAY

When you select a database file with the USE command, the record pointer is always placed at the first record. As a result, if you issue the DISPLAY command at this point, the contents of the first record will be displayed. If you would like to go to a specific record, you can use the GOTO command to place the record pointer at a given record, such as

. GOTO   <*record #*>

Once the record pointer is placed at the desired record, you can then issue the DISPLAY command to show the record's contents (see fig. 4.14).

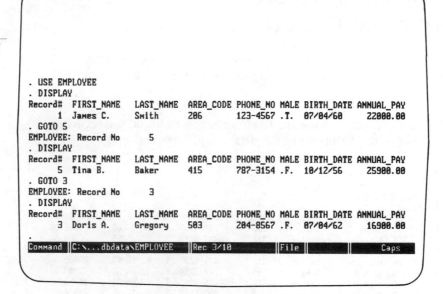

Fig. 4.14.

Viewing a record with the DISPLAY *command.*

```
. USE EMPLOYEE
. DISPLAY
Record#  FIRST_NAME  LAST_NAME  AREA_CODE PHONE_NO MALE BIRTH_DATE ANNUAL_PAY
      1  James C.    Smith      206       123-4567 .T.  07/04/60     22000.00
. GOTO 5
EMPLOYEE: Record No    5
. DISPLAY
Record#  FIRST_NAME  LAST_NAME  AREA_CODE PHONE_NO MALE BIRTH_DATE ANNUAL_PAY
      5  Tina B.     Baker      415       787-3154 .F.  10/12/56     25900.00
. GOTO 3
EMPLOYEE: Record No    3
. DISPLAY
Record#  FIRST_NAME  LAST_NAME  AREA_CODE PHONE_NO MALE BIRTH_DATE ANNUAL_PAY
      3  Doris A.    Gregory    503       204-8567 .F.  07/04/62     16900.00
.
Command ║C:\...dbdata\EMPLOYEE   ║Rec 3/10       ║File ║        ║   Caps
```

From figure 4.14, you can see that by issuing the GOTO 5 command, the record pointer is placed at "Record No. 5". As a result, when the DISPLAY command is executed, the contents of the fifth record are shown. Similarly, the contents of the third record are displayed with the GOTO 3 and DISPLAY commands.

You can go to the first and the last record in the database file by using the GO TOP and GO BOTTOM commands, respectively.

As a shortcut, when you are using dot prompt mode, you can issue the LIST command by simply pressing F3. You can also use DISPLAY ALL in place of LIST for showing all the records. When you use LIST or DISPLAY ALL, each record will be displayed in sequence. It may take more than one line to display a record that has more fields than can be listed on the same line.

If you would like to display the records in browse format, you can use the BROWSE command after putting the database file in use, such as

. BROWSE

In response to the command, data records will be displayed in the browse form, as shown in figure 4.12.

Printing Data Records from the Control Center

If you need to display all the records to the printer, you can press Shift-F9 (for instant report) while the records are being displayed on the screen. Then select **Begin printing** to start printing the records. If you prefer, you can choose the **Eject page** option to advance the paper, and then select **Begin printing** to start printing at the top of a new page. Before the actual printing process, you can preview the output by choosing the **View report on screen** option.

Printing Data Records from the Dot Prompt

To display records to the printer, add the TO PRINT key words to the LIST and DISPLAY ALL commands, such as

```
. DISPLAY TO PRINT
```

Displaying Selective Records and Fields

One of the powerful features of dBASE IV is the Query By Example (QBE) operation. With the QBE operation, you can retrieve and display a subset of the data records in the database file that meet certain search or filter conditions. These conditions can also be incorporated in dot prompt commands to display a selective set of records.

In addition to displaying selective records in a database file, a query operation also can be used for modifying contents of selective records. In the following section, you learn how to use the query operation for displaying data records.

Displaying Selective Records from the Control Center

The QBE operation can be performed by creating a query. In the query, you specify the filter conditions. dBASE IV then will display only those records in the current database file that meet these conditions.

Creating a Query

When you are in the Control Center, you can create a new query by selecting the <**create**> option from the Queries panel and pressing the Enter key after highlighting the database file to be used. In return, you will be provided a query design work surface. On the work surface, you will specify the filter conditions to be used in the query operation. The layout of a query form is shown in figure 4.15.

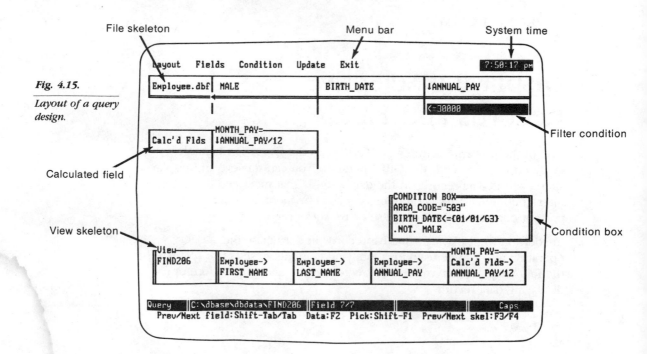

Fig. 4.15.

Layout of a query design.

The query design work surface is divided into three main sections. The upper portion of the work surface shows a file skeleton and a calculated field skeleton, and the bottom of the screen displays the view skeleton. The middle section of the work surface is for displaying the condition box.

In a file skeleton, the name of the file is displayed at the beginning of the skeleton, followed by all of its data fields. However, if there are too many data fields to be shown on the skeleton at a time, some will be hidden from view. When this happens, a left or right arrow will appear to the leftmost or rightmost data field in the skeleton, indicating the direction of the hidden fields. For instance, in figure 4.15, a left arrow appears in the MALE field, telling you that there are more fields hidden to the left of this field. Below the data fields in a file skeleton, spaces are provided for entering the filter condition (such as <=30000 in the ANNUAL_PAY field).

Below the file skeletons, you may find the calculated field skeleton. A calculated field is created with a formula that includes one or more existing fields in the database file.

In the file skeleton, you can specify multiple filter conditions in one or more data fields. These conditions are used by the query operation to screen the records in the database file. As an option, these filter conditions can also be entered in a condition box that appears in the middle section of the work surface.

At the bottom of the work surface, you will see a view skeleton. The view skeleton tells dBASE IV which data fields you want displayed by the query operation. The view skeleton may include some or all of the data fields in the database file. It may also include any calculated fields created by the query operation. A down arrow is added to the data field in the file skeleton or the calculated field, indicating that it is be included in the view skeleton. You have full control of which data fields are to be included in the view skeleton.

In some query operations, you may use more than one database file. Therefore, you may have multiple file skeletons appearing on the work surface. Use the F3 and F4 keys to move up and down through these file skeletons. With the functions keys, you can also move to the calculated field skeleton and the view skeleton.

Tip:
Use F3 and F4 to move among the file skeleton, the calculated field skeleton, the condition box, and the view skeleton.

In summary, the file skeleton and the calculated field skeleton provide the input media, and the view skeleton dictates the query output. The condition box provides an optional space for specifying all the filter conditions to be used by the query operation.

For example, if you would like to create a query for viewing the records in the EMPLOYEE.DBF database file, highlight the EMPLOYEE file in the Data panel, choose the <**create**> option from the Queries panel, and press Enter (see fig. 4.16).

Fig. 4.16.

Query design work surface.

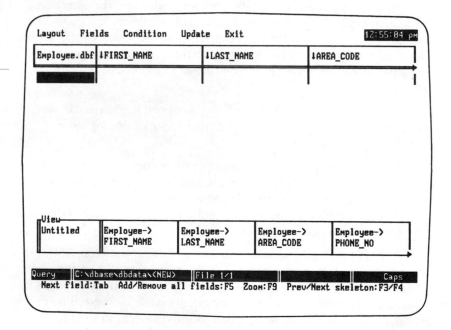

Tip:
Use Tab to move one field to the right and Shift-Tab to move one field to the left.

On the query design work surface, the name of the database file (Employee.dbf) appears in the file skeleton. By default, all the existing fields in the database file are included in the view skeleton. A right arrow appears in the AREA_CODE field in the file skeleton, indicating that there are more fields hidden from view to the right of the field. You can use the Tab key to move one field to the right and Shift-Tab to move one field to the left.

Specifying Filter Conditions

You can tell dBASE IV to display certain records that meet a set of predefined filter conditions. For example, if you need to display the employee records whose AREA_CODE fields have the value 206, you can enter the filter condition as "206" in the AREA_CODE field (see fig. 4.17).

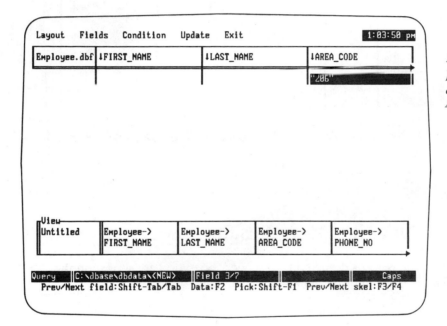

Fig. 4.17.

Entering a filter condition in AREA_CODE field.

Processing the Query

After specifying the filter condition for the AREA_CODE query field, you can begin the query operation by pressing the F2 key. dBASE IV then searches all the records in the database file for those records with field values that satisfy the filter condition. The program then displays the values of the data fields specified in the view skeleton. The result of the query condition specified in figure 4.17 is shown in figure 4.18.

From figure 4.18, you will note that only those records whose AREA_CODE fields have a value of "206" are displayed.

Tip:

Press F2 to begin a query operation.

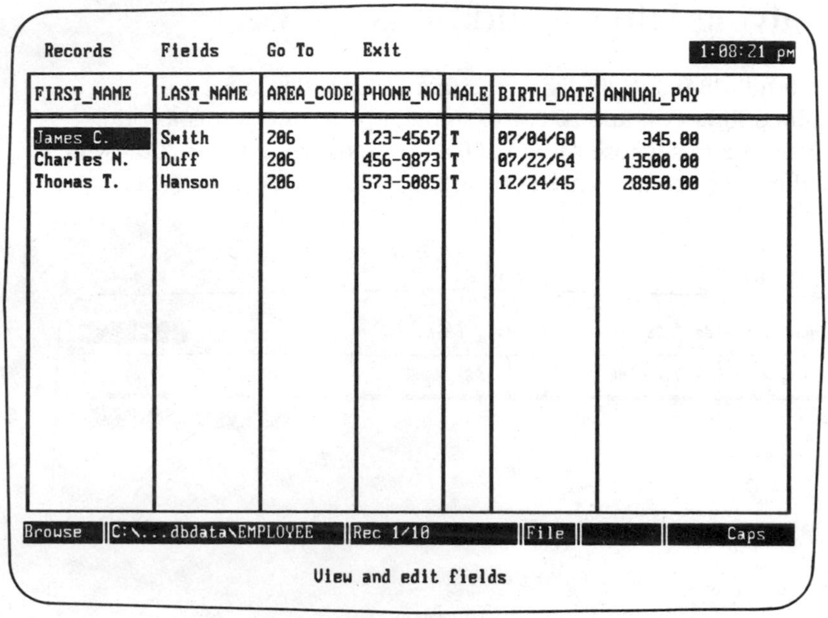

Fig. 4.18.

*Results of the
query operation.*

Printing the Query Results

Tip:
*Use Shift-F9 to
print the query
view.*

After the records displayed by the query operation are shown on the
screen, you can print them by pressing Shift-F9.

Saving the Query

After viewing the records generated by the query operation, you can
either perform another query operation by modifying the query criteria
or save the query design for future use. In either case, you first invoke
the Exit menu by pressing Alt-E. Then choose one of the following
options:

Exit
Transfer to Query Design

When you choose the **Exit** option, you will be prompted:

```
Query design has been changed.
Do you want to save it?

   Yes          No
```

If you answer No, you will be returned to the Control Center without saving the query design. When you answer Yes, you will be asked to assigned a name to the query file to be saved.

Tip:
Use the Exit menu (Alt-E) to save the query design.

If you choose the **Transfer to Query Design** option in the Exit menu, you will be returned to the query design work surface. At that point, you can modify the query design and perform another query operation.

When the query design work surface is displayed, you can also save the query design and exit to the Control Center by choosing **Exit** from the Exit menu and electing to save the changes. In turn, you will be asked to assign a name to the query file. For example, if you would like to save the query form as FIND206 you can enter the file name after the prompt, as in

```
Save as: FIND206
```

After you save the query design and return from the query operation, the name of the query file (FIND206.QBE) is displayed in the Queries panel. To add to the file catalog a description of the query file, choose the following menu options:

Catalog(Alt-C)/**Change description of highlighted file/
Edit the description of this .qbe file**

The file description you entered and the file name will be displayed in the file information area on the Control Center (see fig. 4.19).

Using an Existing Query

After a query design is saved as a query file, such as FIND206.QBE, it can be retrieved for a number of different uses. First, you can recall the query design, and then use the records produced by the query as a database file. The query design can also be recalled for making modifications. Or, you can display the records produced by the query again by repeating the query operation from the design.

Fig. 4.19.

*Entering query
description to file
catalog.*

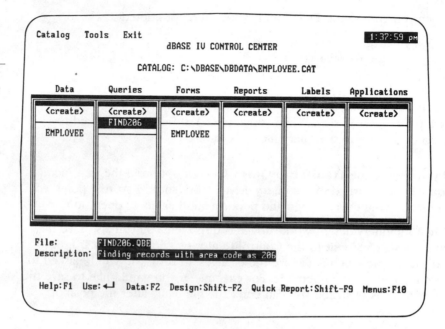

In order to recall an existing query design, you need first to highlight the query file in the Queries panel, and then press Enter. In response to the keystroke, you will be given the choice of three options: **Use view**, **Modify query**, and **Display data** (see fig. 4.20).

If you select **Use view**, dBASE IV will reactivate the query operation and create a temporary file that contains the records with the data fields specified in the view skeleton. After that, you can treat the temporary file as though it were a regular database file. However, you need to note that the temporary file created with an existing query will be valid only while the query is in use. The temporary file will be erased when you recall another query file or close the view.

Closing a Query View

After you are finished using a view produced by an existing query operation, you can close the view by highlighting the query file in the Queries panel, choosing **Close view**, and pressing Enter.

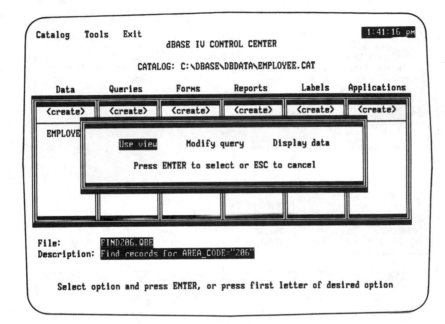

Fig. 4.20.

Using an existing query view.

Saving Query View as a Database File

If you would like to create a permanent database file from the view for later use, you can do that while you are designing the query or when you recall (use) the query design. In either case, when the query design is being displayed on the work surface, you can save the query view as a database file by choosing the **Write view as a database file** option from the Layout menu (invoked by pressing Alt-L). By default, the database file created will have the same name as the query file. Of course, you can assign another name to it, if you wish (see fig. 4.21).

Tip:

Use the Layout menu (Alt-L) for saving a query view as a database file.

If you need to redisplay the data records generated by the query, select the **Display data** option. dBASE IV will then perform the query operation again and produce the records accordingly.

To recall the existing query design for modification, you can choose the **Modify query** option. There is a shortcut for bringing up the query design, however. The shortcut will be discussed in the following section.

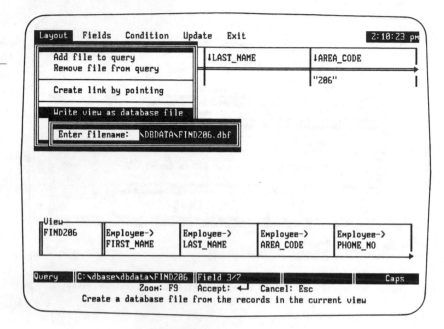

Fig. 4.21.

Saving the query view as a database file.

Displaying Selective Records from the Dot Prompt

When you are using dot prompt mode, you display selective records either by using a query or by specifying the filter conditions in DISPLAY or LIST commands.

Creating a New Query

A new query can be created from the dot prompt by issuing the CREATE QUERY command:

. CREATE QUERY *<name of query file>*

For example, if you would like to create the FIND206 query as shown in the preceding section, you would issue these commands at the dot prompt:

. USE EMPLOYEE

In response to these commands, a query design form like that shown in figure 4.16 is displayed. After that, you can specify the filter conditions on the file skeleton and choose the fields to be displayed in the view skeleton. The procedure for displaying the query results is identical to the one described in the last section.

Specifying Filter Conditions

The DISPLAY and LIST commands can also be used to display a selective sets of data records by adding the necessary filter conditions:

    . DISPLAY FOR <*filter conditions*>
    . LIST FOR <*filter conditions*>

For example,

    . USE EMPLOYEE
    . DISPLAY FOR AREA_CODE="2Ø6"
    . LIST FOR AREA_CODE="2Ø6" .OR. AREA_CODE="5Ø3"
    . DISPLAY FOR .NOT. MALE .AND. ANNUAL_PAY>=2ØØØØ

Notice that single and double quotation marks can be used interchangeably to enclose a character string and that you can use .NOT. (another relation operator) to set a filter condition.

When you use the DISPLAY and LIST commands, all the data fields of the selected records will be displayed. If you would like to display only certain data fields of the records, you can add a field list to the command:

    . DISPLAY <*field list*> FOR <*filter conditions*>
    . LIST <*field list*> FOR <*filter conditions*>

For example,

    . USE EMPLOYEE

    . LIST FIRST_NAME, LAST_NAME FOR AREA_CODE = "2Ø6"

    . DISPLAY AREA_CODE,PHONE_NO FOR LAST_NAME="Baker"

    . DISPLAY LAST_NAME, ANNUAL_PAY FOR (ANNUAL_PAY>=2ØØØØ .AND.
      ANNUAL_PAY <=3ØØØØ)

    . LIST LAST_NAME, BIRTH_DATE FOR BIRTH_DATE <={Ø1/Ø1/6Ø}

The LIST and DISPLAY commands display record contents on the screen. To display the record contents to the printer, add TO PRINT at the end of the command, such as

. DISPLAY LAST_NAME FOR AREA_CODE = "2Ø6" TO PRINT
. LIST FOR AREA_CODE="2Ø6" .OR. AREA_CODE="5Ø3" TO PRINT

By adding filter conditions in DISPLAY and LIST commands, you can find a given set of records and then display their contents. At the dot prompt, you can also use the LOCATE command to find these records before displaying them, as in

. LOCATE <filter conditions>

For instance, to find the employee record with James C. in the FIRST_NAME field, you enter

. LOCATE FOR FIRST_NAME="James C."

When the command is executed, the records are searched, and the first record with the alphanumeric string James C. in the FIRST_NAME field is located. The record pointer then is set to the number of that record. The FIRST_NAME field may contain more than the alphanumeric string James, but if the first five characters match the search string, the record is selected; the characters after the first five characters are not examined. If more than one employee in the company has the first name James (even with a different middle initial), the first record containing James is selected.

When the record is found, you can then issue the DISPLAY command to display its field values (see fig. 4.22).

Fig. 4.22.

Searching records with the LOCATE command.

```
. LOCATE FOR FIRST_NAME="James C."
Record =        1
. DISPLAY
Record# FIRST_NAME   LAST_NAME  AREA_CODE PHONE_NO MALE BIRTH_DATE ANNUAL_PAY
      1 James C.     Smith      206       123-4567 .T.  07/04/60     22000.00
.
Command  C:\...dbdata\EMPLOYEE    Rec 1/10        File              CapsIns
```

The LOCATE command finds the records whose field values match those specified in the filter condition. The string contained in the filter condition does not have to be the complete string; it may contain only the first few characters. As long as the field values match these characters, the record will be selected. As a result, the following LOCATE command finds the record of James C. Smith because EMPLOYEE.DBF has only one record with a first name beginning with J:

```
. LOCATE FOR FIRST_NAME="J"
```

By using relation operators such as .AND. or .OR. in the LOCATE command qualifier, you can specify multiple relations. Some examples are

```
. LOCATE FOR LAST_NAME="Smith" .AND. FIRST_NAME="James C."

. LOCATE FOR MALE .AND. ANNUAL_PAY>=20000 .AND.
   AREA_CODE="315"

. LOCATE FOR (AREA_CODE-"206".AND.MALE).OR.
   (ANNUAL_PAY>20000.AND.ANNUAL_PAY <=30000)
```

If more than one record is found that meets the filter condition in the LOCATE command, the record pointer will be positioned on the first of these records. At that point, you can use the CONTINUE command to move the pointer to the next record that satisfies the filter condition, and you then can display its contents, such as

```
. CONTINUE
. DISPLAY
```

For example, suppose that record 6 was found by a LOCATE command. When you enter the CONTINUE command, the record pointer moves to record 7. As a result, the contents of record 7 will be displayed.

When you use the LOCATE command to search for records, the search begins with the current record and continues to the end of the file.

Chapter 4 QuickStart

In the QuickStart in Chapter 3, you created a file catalog named QIKSTART.CAT. In this QuickStart, you practice the procedures for displaying the contents of the file catalog and its associated files.

Invoking the QIKSTART.CAT
File Catalog

First, you can bring up that file catalog and its files by following these steps:

1. Press Alt-C to invoke the Catalog menu.

2. Choose the **Use a different catalog** option.

3. Select QIKSTART.CAT and press Enter.

In the last QuickStart, you created the ADDRESS.DBF database file and entered data to its records. These files are saved in the C:\DBASE\DBDATA directory on the hard disk. In the next section, you will practice displaying the contents of the file directory and the database file.

Displaying the File Directory

To display the files in the current file directory (C:\DBASE\DBDATA), use the **DOS utilities** option provided by the Tools menu options:

1. Press Alt-T to invoke the Tools menu.

2. Choose the **DOS utilities** option from the menu.

Sorting Files in the Directory

You should now see all the files in the file directory. To view these files alphabetically,

1. Press Alt-S to invoke the Sort menu.

2. Select the **Name** option from the menu.

To sort the files according to their extensions,

1. Press Alt-S to invoke the Sort menu.

2. Select the **Extension** option from the menu.

You can also sort these files according to their sizes and the creation date and time by choosing the appropriate options from the Sort menu.

Changing File Directories

To view files in another directory (such as C:\DBASE):

1. Press Alt-F to invoke the Files menu.

2. Select the **Change drive:directory** option from the menu.

3. Change the directory to C:\DBASE (move the cursor to the beginning of the word \DBDATA and press the Del key several times to remove the current directory name).

Performing a DOS Command

To execute a DOS command that will display the system time,

1. Press Alt-D to invoke the DOS menu.

2. Choose the **Perform DOS command** option.

3. When the Enter DOS command: prompt is displayed, type TIME.

4. Press Enter to return to the DOS utilities screen.

Now, return to the Control Center by pressing the Alt-E.

Displaying Database Structure

To view the database structure of the ADDRESS.DBF, follow these steps:

1. Highlight ADDRESS in the Data panel.

2. Press Shift-F2.

3. Press the Esc key to remove the Organize menu options and reveal the database structure.

If you would like to print the database structure, make sure that the printer is ready, and then press Shift-F9 and select the **Begin printing** option.

To return to the Control Center, press Alt-E to open the Exit menu, and select the **Abandon changes and exit** option from the menu.

Displaying All Records in a Database File

To view all the records in the ADDRESS.DBF file,

1. Highlight the ADDRESS file in the Data panel.

2. Press the F2 function key.

3. Data in all the records will be displayed in either edit format (one record at a time) or in browse format (showing all the records in ADDRESS.DBF on the same screen). Press F2 to switch from one format to another.

To display all the records to the printer, press Shift-F9 and choose the **Begin printing** option. Be sure the printer is turned on before pressing the keystrokes.

Return to the Control Center by pressing Alt-E and choosing the **Exit** option from the Exit menu.

Viewing Selective Records in a Database File

Let's design a query to find all the addresses in California (STATE="CA"). Here are the steps:

1. Highlight the <**create**> option from the Queries panel and press Enter while ADDRESS database is active in the Data panel.

2. Press the Tab key several times until the STATE field appears in the file skeleton.

3. Enter "CA" in the STATE field as the filter condition (see fig. 4.23).

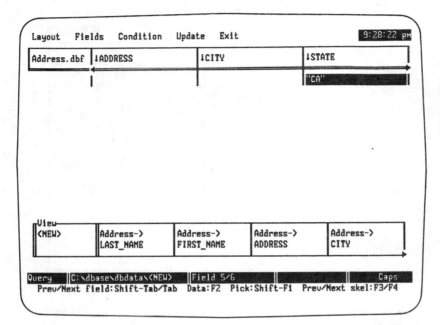

Fig. 4.23.

Enter filter condition to the STATE field.

4. Press F2 to see the records found. If the records are displayed in an edit format, press F2 to view them in browse format (see fig. 4.24).

Now, save the query as FINDCA.QBE and exit to the Control Center:

1. Press Alt-E and select the **Exit** option from the menu.

2. Answer Yes to the following prompt:

   Query design has been changed.
   Do you want to save it?

   Yes   No

3. Enter the name of the query (FINDCA) to the Save as: prompt.

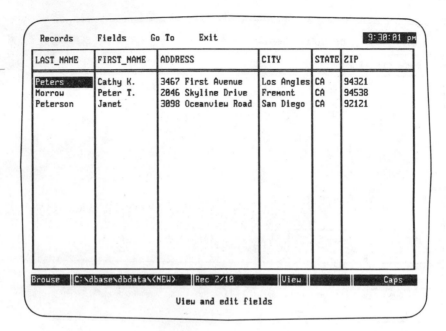

Fig. 4.24.

*Showing
California
addresses in
browse format.*

Chapter Summary

In this chapter, you added to the concepts you mastered in Chapter 3 by learning how to display database structures and data. By using the Control Center and the dot prompt methods, you learned to list the files in directories, to display and print database structures, to sort files and records, and to display selective records. You also learned the basics of using dBASE IV's powerful Query By Example (QBE) feature to locate and display specific records. In the next chapter, you will learn how to edit the data in the database.

Editing Data

After you create a database file, you often need to modify the contents of the database in order to respond to changing data requirements. For example, you may need to change a few of the field attributes in the database structure, or you might need to edit and update field values. The menu options available from the Control Center and the dot prompt commands necessary for editing the database structure and the records of an existing database file are explained in this chapter.

In the last chapter, you saw how a query could be used for displaying a selective set of records. This chapter shows you how to edit those selected records in either edit or browse format. You can also modify an existing query design for retrieving those records you would like to edit. In addition, the procedure for changing the file and view skeleton in a query is explained in this chapter. A more complex query design that involves multiple filter conditions with relational operators also is introduced.

Modifying an Existing Database Structure

When you include a database file in the current file catalog, you need to enter the database description to the catalog. In addition, because the data requirements for your database will inevitably change, you must be able to modify the database structure after you've created the database. dBASE IV makes these modifications easy.

Modifying Structure from within the Control Center

When the Control Center is displayed on the screen, highlight the database file you want in the Data panel, and press Shift-F2. For example, after you select the EMPLOYEE database file from the Data panel and press Shift-F2, the database structure is displayed on the screen (see fig. 5.1). You then can begin editing the database information, including the database file description for the file catalog and the field attributes defined in the database structure.

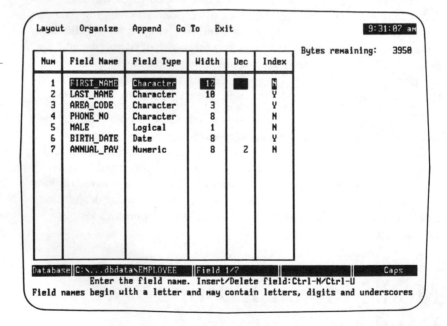

Fig. 5.1.

Recalling an existing database structure.

Editing the Database Description

When you add a database file to the file catalog, you need to enter text describing the database file. You can edit the text while you are modifying the database structure. To do that, you first invoke the Layout menu by pressing Alt-L, and then choose the **Edit database description** option. In return, the current database file description will be displayed, and you can make the necessary changes to the text (see fig. 5.2).

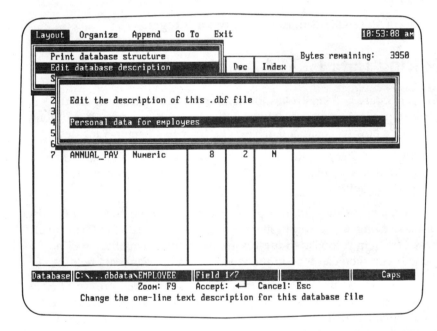

Fig. 5.2.

Editing a database description in the file catalog.

However, if you display the database structure by using the MODIFY STRUCTURE command at the dot prompt, unless you have activated the file catalog with the SET CATALOG TO command, you will not be allowed to edit the file description at this point.

Moving around Data Fields

When you are editing the attributes of the data fields, you can use the up-arrow (↑) or down-arrow (↓) keys to move between the data fields and highlight the one that you need to edit. You can press the PgUp and PgDn keys to move to the first and last fields, respectively.

To move between the attributes of a highlighted field, use the Enter key to skip to the next attribute, and use the left-arrow (←) or right-arrow (→) key to move within an attribute. Use the Home and End keys to move to the beginning and the end of the highlighted field.

When you have a very large database structure, you can move to a specific field by specifying its field number when you choose the Field option from the Go To menu (which is invoked by pressing Alt-G). The following line shows the sequence of menu options used to move to another field:

Go To(Alt-G)/**Field number/Enter an integer:**

Editing Data Field Attributes

The procedure and keystrokes for editing the field attributes are the same as those used when you are creating the database structure. If you don't remember how to create a database file, refer to Chapter 3 for details.

In addition to changing the field attributes, you can also create a new data field, delete an existing data field, or rearrange the order of the existing data fields.

To insert a new data field into the structure, move the cursor to the data field above which you would like to insert the new data field, and then press Ctrl-N. In response to the keystrokes, a new blank field will be opened. You then can type in the attributes of the new data field.

To remove an existing data field from the database structure, you first highlight the data fields by using the cursor keys, and then press Ctrl-U. If you accidentally delete a data field, do not panic. You can recover the deleted data field easily by first pressing Ctrl-N to insert a blank field to the structure, and then typing in the attributes of the deleted field. However, be careful to ensure the accuracy of the field attributes.

Before dBASE IV creates a new data field, it checks to see whether the field is the one you deleted earlier. The new field is considered a replacement of the old field only if all the field attributes you enter match those of the deleted field. Otherwise, dBASE IV considers the inserted field as a brand new field. All the values in the deleted field will be lost when you save the modified database structure.

With the steps of deleting and inserting fields, you can also rearrange the existing fields in the database structure. For instance, if you would like to move the second data field to the last field in the structure, you simply delete the second field, move the cursor to the end of the database structure, and then insert a new field with the attributes of the deleted field.

When you begin to modify the structure of the database, dBASE IV automatically creates a backup file. The backup file has the same name, structure, and contents as the original database file, but instead of having the extension .DBF, the backup file has the extension .BAK. After you have edited the structure, dBASE IV adjusts the contents of the original file to conform to the new structure.

The contents of a character/text field remain in the same field only if you choose Yes in response to the question Should data be copied from backup for all fields? (Y/N). Otherwise, the contents of the fields named differently from the original are lost. If the width of a numeric field is changed, the contents of the field are automatically adjusted to the new width. When a new field is added to the structure, blank spaces are written in the new field in all data records. When an existing data field is deleted from the structure, the contents of that field are erased automatically from the database file.

Making Mistakes in Editing

At any point during the process of editing the database structure, if you made mistakes and would like to start over, you can abort the editing process and return to the Control Center or the dot prompt by choosing the **Abandon changes and exit** option from the Exit menu (invoked by pressing Alt-E).

It is always a wise practice to leave a given process by using the Exit menu instead of pressing the Esc key. Pressing the Esc key, in most cases, allows you to interrupt what you have been doing in that operation. However, you will be less certain which tasks have been accomplished and which part of the data has been saved when you use the Esc key. In some operations, you may lose valuable data by pressing Esc.

Once you are returned to the Control Center or the dot prompt, you can bring up the database structure again for editing.

Caution:
Use the Exit menu instead of the Esc key to abort editing.

Saving the Modified Database Structure

After making the desired changes to the database structure, you can return to the Control Center or begin inputting data to the modified database structure after it has been saved. However, while the database structure is being saved to the database file with the original file name (such as EMPLOYEE.DBF), the original database structure with its data records are saved in a backup file with the .BAK file extension (such as EMPLOYEE.BAK). Data records will be copied from the backup file to the new database file for all the data fields when you answer Yes to the prompt displayed when you save the database structure:

```
Should data be COPIED from backup for all fields? (Y/N)
```

    Yes   No

To return to the Control Center or the dot prompt without inputting new records to the database file with the modified structure, choose the **Save changes and exit** option from the Edit menu (invoked by pressing Alt-E).

If you would like to continue adding records to the database file, press Ctrl-End. In response, you will be prompted at the bottom of the screen:

```
Input data records now (Y/N)
```

You then can answer Y and continue with the data-entry operation.

Modifying Structure from the Dot Prompt

Unlike the database structure that is displayed from the Control Center, the database structure displayed with the DISPLAY STRUCTURE command at the dot prompt is for viewing only. You cannot edit any information in the database structure. However, if you would like to bring up the database structure for viewing and also for possible modifications, you can use MODIFY STRUCTURE (or MODI STRU for short) in place of the DISPLAY STRUCTURE command, such as

```
MODIFY STRUCTURE
```

For example, if you would like to bring up the database structure of the EMPLOYEE.DBF database file in the same format as shown in figure 4.9, you can enter the following commands at the dot prompt:

```
. USE EMPLOYEE
. MODIFY STRUCTURE
```

Again, you can send a copy of the database structure to your printer by choosing the **Print database structure** option from the Layout menu (invoked by pressing Alt-L).

You can return to the dot prompt after examining the database structure without making any changes to the structure by selecting the **Abandon changes and exit** option from the Exit menu.

Modifying an Existing Query Design

In Chapter 4, you learned how to use a query for displaying a selective set of data records by specifying the filter conditions in the file skeleton. You can use such a query for displaying the records that need modification. If the filter conditions require changes, you can either create a new query for displaying the records or modify an existing query design.

Before you start changing the query design, you need to recall it from the query file. To bring up an existing query file for viewing or modification, you highlight the query file in the Queries panel, and then press Shift-F2. In response to the keystrokes, the query design saved earlier will be displayed. At this point, you can edit the query design accordingly.

Tip:
Use Shift-F2 to recall an existing query design.

Multiple Filter Conditions

You can specify more than one filter condition in a given query field. These filter conditions will be entered in separate lines. In doing so, you instruct dBASE IV to find those records that satisfy any one of these conditions. For example, if you would like to find records in the EMPLOYEE.DBF database file whose records have "206" or "503" in its

AREA _CODE field, you can enter these two filter conditions in the field accordingly (see fig. 5.3).

Each one of the filter conditions entered in the same field will be considered as an "OR" condition. That is, either the first ("206") OR the second ("503") field values will be used for the record search. As a result, records selected by the query operation will include those records with "206" field values or those with field value of "503" in the query field (AREA _CODE).

Fig. 5.3.

Entering multiple .OR. filter conditions.

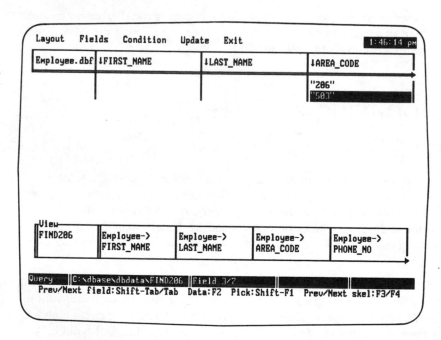

Tip:
Use down-arrow and up-arrow keys to open and close a line in the file skeleton.

To specify several filter conditions in the same query field, use the down-arrow (↓) key to open a new line in the file skeleton for entering another filter condition. To close a blank line in the file skeleton, press the up-arrow (↑) key.

If you have mistakenly entered a query criterion, use Ctrl-U to remove it.

Tip:
Use Ctrl-U to remove an unwanted filter condition.

Another form of multiple filter conditions is joint, or AND, conditions. They are entered on the same line in the query form. All the criteria entered in this way are considered jointly in searching the data records. Only those records that satisfy all of these conditions simultaneously will be selected. For example, if you would like to find those male employees whose area code is 206, you can enter the "206" in the AREA_CODE field AND the .T. in the MALE (a logical field) data field on the same line in the file skeleton (see fig. 5.4).

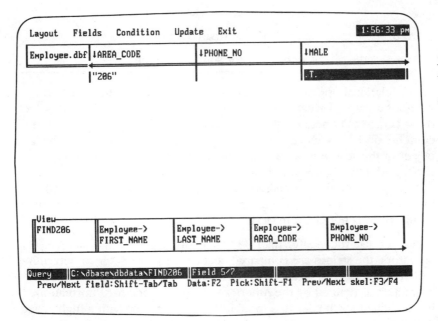

Fig. 5.4.

Entering multiple .AND. filter conditions.

Using Relational Operators

In addition to specifying the exact field value as a filter condition for the query operation, you can also use one of the following relational operators for selecting the records:

Operator	Description
=	equal to
<> (or #)	not equal to
>	greater than
>=	greater than or equal to

Operator	Description
<	less than
<=	less than or equal to
$	contains (a certain character)
Like	appears like (for pattern match)
Sounds like	sounds like (for soundex match)

These relational operators are used in a filter condition to determine whether a particular data record will be chosen for display. If you select the = (equal to) operator, the condition will be satisfied only when the contents of the search key and the search object are identical. If the object of the search is Smith, the condition will be met only if the LAST_NAME field (the search key) contains Smith. The condition will not be met if the field contains smith or SMITH. Because upper- and lowercase letters are treated as unique characters in a data record, the string Smith is not equal to smith.

When you use the greater than (>) or less than (<) relational operators, the strings are compared character by character to determine which string has the greater or lesser value. The order of alphanumeric characters as defined by the American Standard Code for Information Interchange (ASCII) is listed in table 5.1. A character with a high-order designation is greater than a character with a low-order designation.

Table 5.1
The Order of Alphanumeric Characters

Lower Order

(space) ! " # 5-$ % & ' (apostrophe) ( ) * + , (comma) - . (period)

/ Ø...9 : ; < = > ? @ A B C...X Y Z [\ ] ^ a b c...x y z

Higher Order

In keeping with the order defined in table 5.1, each of the following relations is true:

"smith" > "Smith"

"Samson" > "Sam"

"JOHN" < "john"

"ABC123" < "ABC12"

"(2Ø6)" < "2Ø6"

"Smith, James" <> "Smith,James"

Note that the string smith is greater than Smith. The first character of smith (s) has a higher order designation than does S.

When you use a relational operator to filter data records in a date field, a later calendar date is evaluated as being greater than an earlier date. For example, 01/01/60 is greater than 12/31/59. In the query form, you would enclose the date in a pair of curly brackets {} (scc fig. 5.5).

Tip:
Use { } to enclose date value in a filter condition.

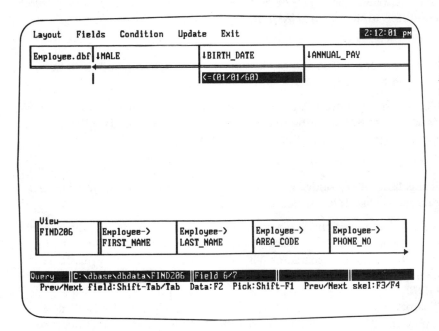

Fig. 5.5.

Entering a date value in a filter condition.

When you perform query operations on a numeric field, you will have less confusion in using the logical operators. For example, you could use any one of the following query criteria in a numeric field such as ANNUAL _ PAY:

>=22ØØØ

<29ØØØ

#2ØØØØ

The $ sign can be used in a filter condition to search data records whose query field contains a certain substring of characters. The substring may appear anywhere in the field values.

For example, if you specify $"son" as a filter condition in the LAST_NAME field, the query operation will display all the records whose value in the LAST_NAME field containing the "son" substring (such as Nelson, Thompson, and Hanson).

Sometimes, when you try to locate a record by using one of its field values as a filter condition and you do not remember exactly the field value, you can use the Like relational operator. The Like relational operator allows you find those field values that match a certain pattern in the filter condition. For example, if you do not know the exact spelling of a first name (Jane, Jan, or Janet, etc.), you may use the following filter condition in the FIRST_NAME field:

    Like "Jan*"

In return, all the first names like Jane, Jan, Janet, and Janelle will be selected by the Like "Jan*" filter condition.

The asterisk (*) used in the string for the Like operator is called a *wild-card character*, indicating that any substring in its place is acceptable. It can also appear in the front of a string, such as

    Like "*ny"

If this Like filter condition is used in a FIRST_NAME field, you may get first names like Johnny, Benny, Denny, Tony, etc.

Another wild-card character you may use in filter condition with the Like operator is the question mark (?). A question mark in the filter string indicates any single character will be considered to be acceptable. For example, Like "?a?a" specified in the filter condition for the FIRST_NAME field may yield first names like "Tara", "Sara", "Papa", "Mama", etc. Like "J???son" will find field values like "Jackson" and "Johnson". However, the filter condition will not find "Jason" because only two characters appear before the substring "son"; Like J???son requires three characters as defined in the match pattern (???).

You can combine the asterisks and questions in a filter condition. For instance, if you specify Like "?a*" as a filter condition in a query field, you will get field values like "Tara", "Barbara","Carl", and "Carrie".

While the Like operator allows you select those field values that match a certain pattern defined in the string, the Sounds like operator enables you to find data records by using a soundex function. A *soundex function* provides a phonetic match—or sound-alike match—between the filter value and the field values in the records. For example, if you specify Sounds like "Carl" as a filter condition, you may find field values like Carl, Carol, and Carrol, etc. Because the soundex rules are rather complex, you may need to experiment with different field values as filter conditions for finding the sound-alike field values.

Multiple Filter Conditions in One Field

You can specify more than one filter condition in one query field in the file skeleton. To do that, you need to separate these conditions with commas. For example, if you would like to find those employees whose annual salaries are between 20,000 and 30,000 dollars, you could specify the ">=20000, <=30000" conditions in the ANNUAL_PAY field in the file skeleton (see fig. 5.6).

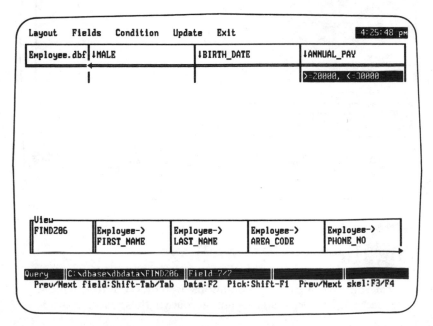

Fig. 5.6.

Entering multiple filter conditions in one field.

▶
Tip:
Use commas to separate filter conditions.

When entering your filter conditions, due to the space provided in the file skeleton under the data field, only part of the condition will be displayed, even though you are allowed to continue typing a long filter condition. If this proves to be unsatisfactory, you can open up (or zoom in on) the field by using the F9 function key when that field is the current field.

▶
Tip:
Use F9 to zoom in a field for defining filter conditions.

For example, suppose that you want to enter a set of long filter conditions in the BIRTH_DATE field in the Employee.dbf file skeleton. First, position the cursor in that field, and then press F9. In response to the keystroke, a large box appears. At the top of the box, the data field in use is displayed. You can then type in the filter conditions in the space provided (see fig. 5.7).

Fig. 5.7.

Using the zoom operation in defining filter conditions.

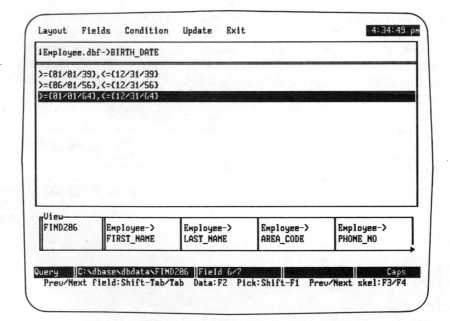

Using the Condition Box

From what you have seen, filter conditions are entered into the file skeleton under the query fields. As an alternative, these filter conditions also can be entered in a condition box. This alternative may prove to be useful when you want to group all the filter conditions together for easy viewing.

If you would like to use such a condition box, select the **Add condition box** option from the Condition menu (which you invoke by pressing Alt-C). From the same Condition menu, you can choose the **Delete condition box** option to remove an existing condition box, or the **Show condition box** option to hide or reveal an existing condition box. When a condition box is hidden from view, a marker "CONDITION BOX" will be displayed at the lower right corner, above the view skeleton.

An example of the condition box is shown in figure 5.8. To reveal the hidden portion of the box contents, you can press the F9 function key when the cursor is in the condition box. The complete contents of the condition box is revealed in figure 5.9.

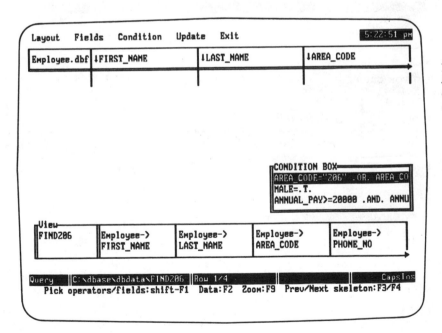

Fig. 5.8.

Defining filter conditions in the condition box.

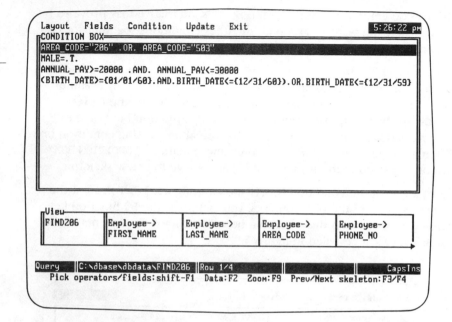

When you enter filter conditions, you can use the following keys for editing:

Key	Function
Home	Moves the cursor to the beginning of the line.
End	Moves the cursor to the end of the line.
Up arrow	Moves up one line.
Down arrow	Moves down one line.
Del	Deletes a character to the right of the cursor.
Backspace	Deletes a character to the left of the cursor.
Ctrl-T	Deletes a word to the right of the cursor.
Ctrl-Y	Deletes all the characters to the right of the cursor.

If you intend to specify multiple filter conditions on the same line in the condition box, you need to use one of the .OR. or .AND. logical operators. Here are a few examples:

```
AREA_CODE="2Ø6".OR.AREA_CODE="2Ø6"
ANNUAL_PAY>=2ØØØØ .AND. ANNUAL_PAY <=3ØØØØ
AREA_CODE="2Ø6".AND.MALE
BIRTH_DATE>={Ø1/Ø1/6Ø}.OR.MALE=.F.
```

In the above examples, MALE is a logical field. The filter condition of
MALE is equivalent to MALE=.T.. You can use the .NOT. operator to
define the false value for a logical field in a filter condition as

```
.NOT.MALE
AREA_CODE="5Ø3".OR..NOT. MALE
```

You can use nested filter conditions to define a more complex query
operation. These nested filter conditions can be grouped together with
pairs of parentheses, such as

```
(AREA_CODE="2Ø6".OR.AREA_CODE="5Ø3")
  .OR.(AREA_CODE="415".OR.AREA_CODE="212")
(ANNUAL_PAY>=2ØØØØ.AND.MALE)
  .OR.(ANNUAL_PAY>3ØØØØ.AND..NOT.MALE)
```

Modifying the View Skeleton

When you start a query operation and enter the query design work
surface, the database file in use is displayed in the file skeleton, and all of
its data fields are automatically arranged in the view skeleton in the same
order as they appear in the file skeleton. As a result, all of these fields
will be used to display the resulting records from the query operation.
However, this can be changed. That is, you may want to remove some of
these data fields from the view skeleton and retain only the data fields in
which you are interested. You also can rearrange the order in which the
data fields will be displayed.

Removing Fields from View

For changing the field composition in the view skeleton, you use the F5
function key. By toggling F5, you can remove a data field from the view
skeleton. With the same function key, you can add a field to the view
skeleton if the field is not already in the skeleton.

Tip:
Use F5 to change field composition in the view skeleton.

To remove a data field from the skeleton, first highlight the field, and then press F5. For adding a data field from the file skeleton to the view skeleton, highlight the field in the file skeleton and press F5.

Moving around View Fields

Tip:
Use F3 and F4 to move among skeletons.

Tip:
Use Tab and Shift-Tab to move among fields.

Tip:
Use the Home key to move to the first column and the End key to move to the last field.

To move around the file skeletons, use the F3 and F4 function keys. The F3 function key moves down from one skeleton to another skeleton, and F4 function key moves up between skeletons. Use Tab to move one field to the right and Shift-Tab to move one field to the left. To go to the first column of the file skeleton, press the Home key; press the End key to go to the last field.

If you would like to remove all the fields from the view skeleton instead of deleting one field at a time, you can move the cursor to the beginning of the file skeleton under the name of the database file, and press the F5 function key once or twice. If the view skeleton contains all the data fields of the database file, pressing the F5 function once will remove them all from the view skeleton. If the view skeleton contains only some of the data fields in the file skeleton, you need to press F5 twice to remove these from the view skeleton.

For example, if you would like to remove all the data fields from the view skeleton in figure 5.10, you would first highlight the first column of the file skeleton (under the name of the file Employee.dbf, as shown in the figure) and then press the F5 function key. In response to the keystroke, all the data fields in the skeleton will be erased from the screen.

Adding Fields to View

At this point, if you change your mind and would like to add all the data fields back to the view skeleton, simply press F5 again. If you would like to add, say, only the LAST_NAME, FIRST_NAME, and ANNUAL_PAY data fields to the skeleton, you can highlight each of these fields in the file skeleton and then press F5. As a result, each of these fields will be added to the view skeleton in sequence. The resulting view skeleton will look like the one shown in figure 5.11.

```
Layout   Fields   Condition   Update   Exit                    10:53:30 am

Employee.dbf ↓FIRST_NAME          ↓LAST_NAME           ↓AREA_CODE
```

Query │C:\dbase\dbdata\FIND206 │File 1/1
Next field:Tab Add/Remove all fields:F5 Zoom:F9 Prev/Next skeleton:F3/F4

Fig. 5.10.

Clearing all the fields in the view skeleton.

```
Layout   Fields   Condition   Update   Exit                    11:02:16 am

Employee.dbf │ MALE               BIRTH_DATE           ↓ANNUAL_PAY
```

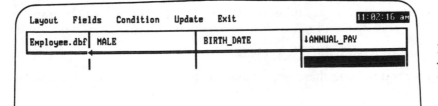

View
FIND206   │Employee->   │Employee->   │Employee->
           │LAST_NAME   │FIRST_NAME   │ANNUAL_PAY

Query │C:\dbase\dbdata\FIND206 │Field 7/7   Caps
Prev/Next field:Shift-Tab/Tab Data:F2 Pick:Shift-F1 Prev/Next skel:F3/F4

Fig. 5.11.

Adding fields to the view skeleton.

Rearranging View Fields

If you would like to rearrange the order of the data fields in the view skeleton, you can do this one of two ways: you can remove all fields from the view skeleton and add them back from the file skeleton, one at a time and in a different sequence; or you can rearrange the data fields by using the F6 and F7 function keys. The second method is the easier of the two. You use F6 to select in the view skeleton the field to be moved, and you use F7 to move the field. For example, if you would like to move the LAST_NAME field to the right of the FIRST_NAME field in the view skeleton (figure 4.30 shows the field's position before the move), follow these steps:

1. Use the F4 function key to move the cursor down to the view skeleton and highlight the field to be moved (LAST_NAME).

2. Press F6. As a result, the LAST_NAME field is enclosed in a box.

3. At this point, you can use Tab or Shift-Tab to adjust the box to enclose the field(s) to be moved.

4. After boxing the fields to be moved (in this example, just the LAST_NAME field), press F7.

5. Use the Tab key to move the field one field to the right. Press Shift-Tab to move the field one field to the left.

6. To remove the box, press Esc.

After you perform these steps, the view skeleton will appear as shown in figure 5.12.

Modifying an Existing Query

The command for modifying an existing query at the dot prompt is

. MODIFY QUERY <*name of the query file*>

For example,

. MODIFY QUERY FIND206

When the command is executed, the query named FIND206 will be displayed on the screen. At this point, you can use the same procedure described in the last section to change the file and view skeletons.

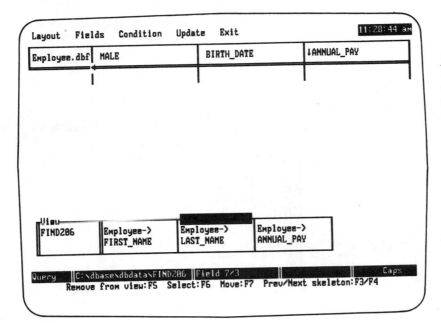

Fig. 5.12.

The view skeleton after fields are moved.

Editing Data Records

Once you've displayed the information in the data records by using any of the procedures discussed in the preceding sections, you can edit the records in the database. The sections that follow explain the methods of editing data from the Control Center and from the dot prompt.

Editing Records from within the Control Center

After you highlight a database file in the Control Center and press F2 to display the records, you can edit the information displayed on-screen. You also can edit the records that are produced and displayed with a query operation.

Regardless of how the records are retrieved, they are displayed either in edit format (one record per screen) or in browse format (one record

Tip:
Use F2 to switch from edit format to browse format.

per line, up to seventeen records per screen). You can always switch the display format from one to the other by pressing the F2 function key. For instance, the records of EMPLOYEE.DBF that are displayed when F2 is pressed are shown in figure 5.13.

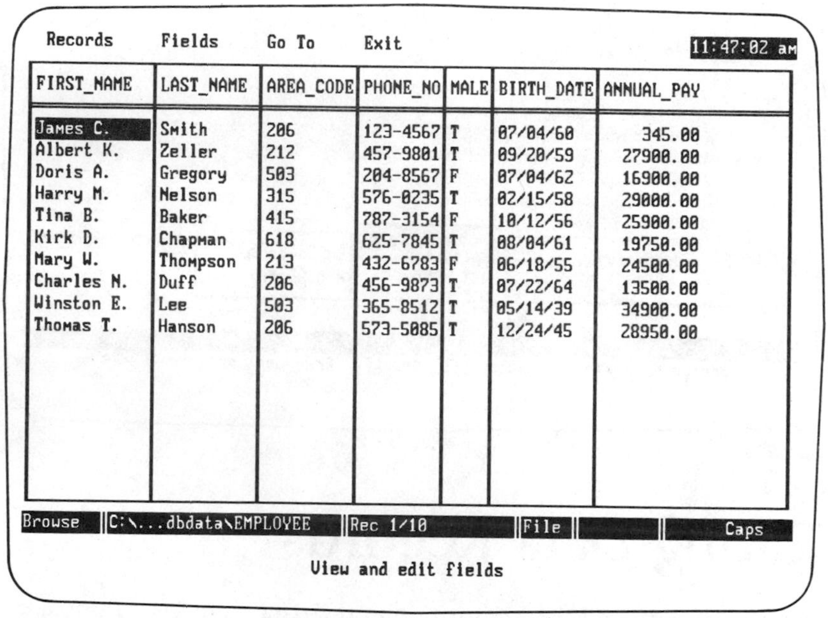
Records Fields Go To Exit 11:47:02 am
FIRST_NAME LAST_NAME AREA_CODE PHONE_NO MALE BIRTH_DATE ANNUAL_PAY
James C. Smith 206 123-4567 T 07/04/60 345.00
Albert K. Zeller 212 457-9801 T 09/20/59 27900.00
Doris A. Gregory 503 204-8567 F 07/04/62 16900.00
Harry M. Nelson 315 576-0235 T 02/15/58 29000.00
Tina B. Baker 415 787-3154 F 10/12/56 25900.00
Kirk D. Chapman 618 625-7845 T 08/04/61 19750.00
Mary W. Thompson 213 432-6783 F 06/18/55 24500.00
Charles N. Duff 206 456-9873 T 07/22/64 13500.00
Winston E. Lee 503 365-8512 T 05/14/39 34900.00
Thomas T. Hanson 206 573-5085 T 12/24/45 28950.00
Browse C:\...dbdata\EMPLOYEE Rec 1/10 File Caps
View and edit fields

Fig. 5.13.

Editing records in the browse format.

The data records shown in figure 5.13 are displayed in browse format. When you are in this mode, use the following keys to move around field attributes and edit the field values:

Key	*Editing Operation*
Up arrow (↑)	Moves up one record.
Down arrow (↓)	Moves down one record.
Left arrow (←)	Moves one character to the left.
Right arrow (→)	Moves one character to the right.
Tab	Moves one field to the right.
Shift-Tab	Moves one field to the left.
Home	Moves to the first field of the record.

End	Moves to the last field of the record.
PgUp	Moves to the first record (on the same field).
PgDn	Moves to the last record (on the same field).
Del	Deletes one character to the right.
Backspace	Deletes one character to the left.
Ctrl-Y	Deletes all the characters to the right in the field.

When data records are displayed in edit format (see fig. 5.14), use the following keys for your editing operations:

Key	Editing Operation
Up arrow (↑)	Moves up one field.
Down arrow (↓)	Moves down one record.
Left arrow (←)	Moves one character to the left.
Right arrow (→)	Moves one character to the right.
Home	Moves to the beginning of the field.
End	Moves to the end of the record.
PgUp	Moves to beginning of the previous record.
PgDn	Moves to beginning of the next record.
Ctrl-PgUp	Moves to the first record in the database file.
Ctrl-PgDn	Moves to the last record in the database file.
Del	Deletes one character to the right.
Backspace	Deletes one character to the left.
Ctrl-Y	Deletes all the characters to the right in the field.

In either edit or browse format, you can press the Ins (Insert) key to toggle between insert mode and override mode. When you are editing the data records, the current record number is monitored in the status

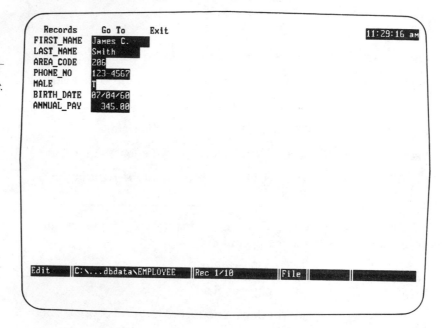

```
   Records    Go To     Exit                              11:29:16 am
   FIRST_NAME  James C.
   LAST_NAME   Smith
   AREA_CODE   206
   PHONE_NO    123-4567
   MALE        T
   BIRTH_DATE  07/04/60
   ANNUAL_PAY    345.00








  Edit    C:\...dbdata\EMPLOYEE     Rec 1/10        File
```

bar at the bottom of the screen. To go to a specific record, you can
specify its record number after selecting the **Record number** option
from the Go To menu (which you invoke by pressing Alt-G). The
selections and prompts for this operation are

   Go To(Alt-G)/**Record number/Enter record number:**

Updating Data Records

The procedure described previously allows you to edit the field values in
a given record. However, in the case that you would like to change the
field values for a set of records that satisfy certain filter conditions, you
can use the update operation provided in a query. For example, if you
would like to give every employee a pay raise of, say, 10%, you can
change all the values in the ANNUAL_PAY fields by using a formula or an
expression, such as ANNUAL_PAY*1.1. Specify such an expression in the
ANNUAL_PAY field in the file skeleton of a query design after invoking
the update operation (see fig. 5.15).

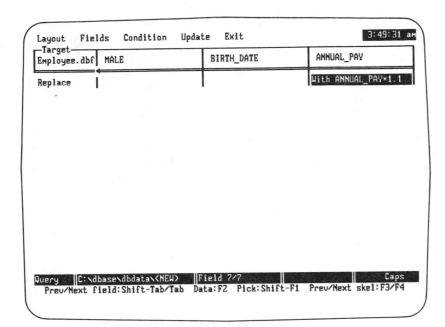

Fig. 5.15.

Replacing values in the ANNUAL_ PAY field.

The update query shown in figure 5.15 is created by

1. Bringing up the query design by highlighting the EMPLOYEE database file in the Data panel and choosing the <**create**> option from the Queries panel.

2. Placing the **Replace** operator under the file name of the file skeleton (Employee.dbf) by using these menu selections:

    Update Menu (Alt-U)/**Specify update operation**/
    Replace values in Employee.dbf

3. Specifying the cxpression (ANNUAL_PAY*1.1) with the keyword With in the ANNUAL_PAY data field.

You will notice that when you are using the query for an update operation, no data field will be displayed in the view skeleton.

To start processing the update operation, invoke the Update menu by pressing Alt-U. In turn, select the **Perform the update** option from the Update menu. As a result, a message box will appear informing you of the number of records that have been replaced (see fig. 5.16).

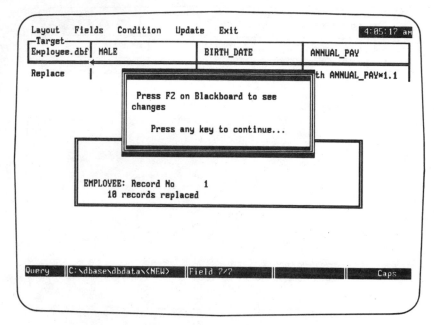

Fig. 5.16.

*Showing the
number of records
replaced.*

The update operation will not display the resulting records automatically. To see the records after the update operation, press F2.

You can save the update query by choosing the **Save changes and exit** option from the Exit menu (invoked with Alt-E). An existing update query will be displayed in the Queries panel with an asterisk appearing to the left of its file name.

In an update operation such as **Replace**, you can also specify filter conditions that allow you to update values in certain data records. The filter conditions can be specified in any of the data fields in the file skeleton. They can also be specified in the field whose values are to be updated with an expression. In this case, the filter conditions should appear before the expression for the update operation. A comma must be used to separate the filter conditions and the expression (see fig. 5.17).

From figure 5.17, you can see that the filter condition "2Ø6" appears before the update operation that begins with the keyword "With" and the expression "216". Of course, you can use an optional condition box (after you display the Condition menu by pressing Alt-C) to specify the filter conditions and define only the update operation in the data field (see fig. 5.18).

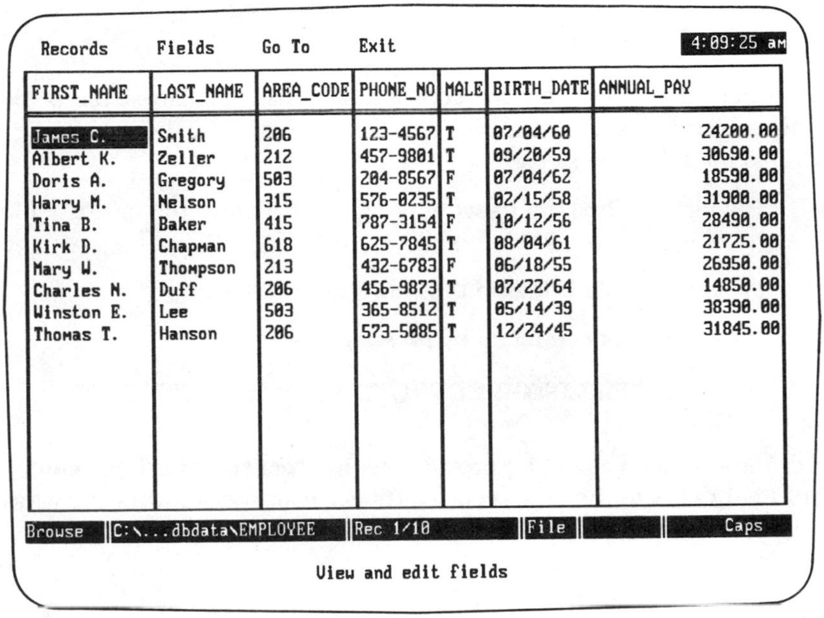

```
 Records    Fields    Go To    Exit                    4:09:25 am

 FIRST_NAME  LAST_NAME  AREA_CODE PHONE_NO MALE BIRTH_DATE ANNUAL_PAY

 James C.    Smith      206       123-4567 T    07/04/60        24200.00
 Albert K.   Zeller     212       457-9801 T    09/20/59        30690.00
 Doris A.    Gregory    503       204-8567 F    07/04/62        18590.00
 Harry M.    Nelson     315       576-0235 T    02/15/58        31900.00
 Tina B.     Baker      415       787-3154 F    10/12/56        28490.00
 Kirk D.     Chapman    618       625-7845 T    08/04/61        21725.00
 Mary W.     Thompson   213       432-6783 F    06/18/55        26950.00
 Charles N.  Duff       206       456-9873 T    07/22/64        14850.00
 Winston E.  Lee        503       365-8512 T    05/14/39        38390.00
 Thomas T.   Hanson     206       573-5085 T    12/24/45        31845.00



 Browse   C:\...dbdata\EMPLOYEE      Rec 1/10        File           Caps
                     View and edit fields
```

Fig. 5.17.

Viewing the replaced records in browse format.

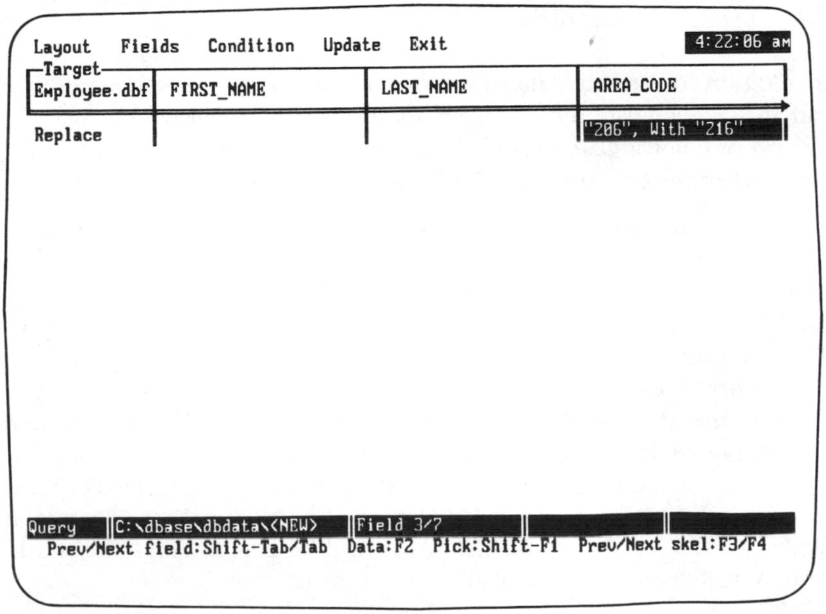

```
 Layout   Fields   Condition   Update   Exit              4:22:06 am
 ┌Target─
 Employee.dbf  FIRST_NAME      LAST_NAME          AREA_CODE

 Replace                                          "206", With "216"














 Query    C:\dbase\dbdata\<NEW>     Field 3/7
   Prev/Next field:Shift-Tab/Tab  Data:F2  Pick:Shift-F1  Prev/Next skel:F3/F4
```

Fig. 5.18.

Using a filter condition in the replace operation.

Adding Records

The procedure for adding new records to an existing database file is the same as that discussed in Chapter 3 for appending data. The procedure involves the following steps:

1. Highlight in the Data panel of the Control Center the database file to which you would like to add records.

2. Press Shift-F2 to bring up the data structure screen.

3. Invoke the Append menu by pressing Alt-A.

4. Select the **Enter records from keyboard** option and press Enter.

After these steps, you will be provided with a data-entry form for entering your field values to the new records. The standard default data-entry form will be used unless you have selected a custom form from the Control Center.

Appending Records from Another Database File

In addition to entering data to the new records from the keyboard, you can also append data records from another database file. To do that, instead of following Step 4 in the preceding procedure, you select the **Append records from dBASE file** option from the Append menu.

If the database from which you would like to append data has a database structure identical to that of the current database file, data in every field of the other database file will be copied and added to the current database file. Otherwise, only those fields that are common to the two database files will be added to the current database file. The other fields in the current database file will be left blank. For example, suppose that database file ABC.DBF has three fields—LAST_NAME, FIRST_NAME, and ADDRESS—while the database file XYZ.DBF has four fields—FIRST_NAME, LAST_NAME, PHONE_NUMBER, and BIRTH_DATE. When you append data records from XYZ.DBF to ABC.DBF, only two common fields—LAST_NAME and FIRST_NAME—will be copied over. The third field, ADDRESS, will be left blank in the new records.

Importing Data from a Non-dBASE File

Another way to add data to an existing database file is to import data from non-dBASE file. For this, you need to select the **Copy records from non-dBASE file** option from the Append menu. In response to the option selection, you will be asked to specify the format of the data file, such as

RapidFile® (.rpd)
dBASE II (.db2)
Framework® II (.fw2)
Lotus 1-2-3® (.wks)
VisiCalc® (.dif)
SYLK-Multiplan®
Fixed length text file
Text file, field values separated with blank space(s)
Text file, field values separated with quotation marks (")

Deleting an Existing Record

You can delete any record when it is being displayed and highlighted on the screen. The record may be displayed in edit or browse format. In either case, when the cursor is positioned in any field of the record, its record number will be indicated in the status bar at the bottom of the screen.

The deletion of a data record requires a two-step process. First, you mark the record, and then you erase it. To mark a data record to be deleted, press Ctrl-U when the record is being highlighted on the screen. As soon as you press the keystrokes, a "Del" mark appears in the right corner of the status bar on the screen. You may flip through all the records in the database file and mark those you would like to delete.

You can also use the update operation within a query to mark selective records. The update operation for marking records is similar to that for changing the field values described earlier. To mark selective records, you can specify the filter conditions in the file skeleton in the query design after selecting the **Mark records for deletion** from the **Specify update operation** option of the Update menu (invoked by pressing Alt-U) in the query design (see fig. 5.19).

Fig. 5.19.

Marking selective records for deletion.

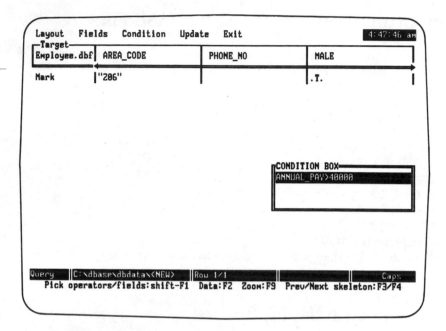

From figure 5.19, you can see that the filter conditions are specified in the AREA_CODE and MALE fields as well as in the condition box. The **Mark update operator** option appears under the file name (Employee.dbf) of the file skeleton. When the update operation is carried out in this case, no record will be marked because these filter conditions are not met.

Removing Record Deletion Marks

Marking a record for deletion does not automatically remove it from the database file. You can remove the deletion mark by pressing Ctrl-U when the marked record is being highlighted on the screen.

Erasing a Marked Record

If you want to permanently erase the marked records from the database file, you need to perform the PACK operation. The PACK operation will create the revised database file by copying those unmarked records from the original database file. To perform the PACK operation, follow these steps:

1. Highlight the database file that contains marked records to be deleted.

2. Press Shift-F2 to bring up the data structure screen.

3. Invoke the Organize menu by pressing Alt-O.

4. Select the **Erase marked records** option and press Enter.

In a while, you will see the PACK operation is being performed. The number of records being copied from the old database file to the new database file will be displayed in the process. During the PACK operation, all index files associated with the database file are automatically updated. Discussion of the functions of index files occurs later in this book.

Editing Records from the Dot Prompt

In dot prompt mode, you can edit the current record by simply entering the EDIT command, such as

. EDIT

To edit the contents of a specific record, indicate the record number in the EDIT command line, as in the following command:

. EDIT RECORD *<record number>*

For example, you enter the following command to edit the contents of record 5:

. EDIT RECORD 5

The contents of record 5 then are displayed so that you can edit the data. When you are done editing, press Ctrl-End to save the edited data.

You can also bring up the data records in browse format for viewing and editing by using the BROWSE command at the dot prompt, such as

. BROWSE

When you are using browse format, only the first 80 characters are displayed if a record contains more than 80 characters. However, you can display only selected field contents in order to keep the display within the screen size limit. To display selected data fields, specify the field names in the BROWSE FIELDS command, as in

. BROWSE FIELDS *<field name 1>*, *<field name 2>*,...

For example, if you want to display only the names and telephone numbers in the EMPLOYEE.DBF database file, you enter the BROWSE FIELDS command in the format

. GO TOP
. BROWSE FIELDS FIRST_NAME,LAST_NAME,AREA_CODE,PHONE_NO

The result of the BROWSE FIELDS command is shown in figure 5.20.

Fig. 5.20.

Showing the selective fields with the BROWSE FIELDS *command.*

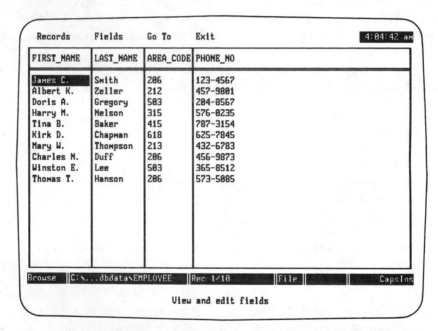

Records	Fields	Go To	Exit	4:04:42 am

FIRST_NAME	LAST_NAME	AREA_CODE	PHONE_NO
James C.	Smith	206	123-4567
Albert K.	Zeller	212	457-9801
Doris A.	Gregory	503	204-8567
Harry M.	Nelson	315	576-0235
Tina B.	Baker	415	787-3154
Kirk D.	Chapman	618	625-7845
Mary W.	Thompson	213	432-6783
Charles N.	Duff	206	456-9873
Winston E.	Lee	503	365-8512
Thomas T.	Hanson	206	573-5085

Browse	C:\...dbdata\EMPLOYEE	Rec 1/10	File		CapsIns

View and edit fields

Contents of one or more records can be modified by replacing their field values with new values. In dot prompt mode, data replacement operations can be performed with the REPLACE command also. The format for the REPLACE command is

. REPLACE *<name of field>* WITH *<new field value>*

For example, the replacement operation previously mentioned would be written in dot prompt mode as

. REPLACE AREA_CODE WITH "216"

The REPLACE command can also be used with filter conditions, as in

. REPLACE <name of field > WITH *<new field value>* FOR
<filter conditions>

Some examples of the REPLACE command used with qualifiers are

. REPLACE AREA_CODE WITH "216" FOR AREA_CODE="206"

. REPLACE ANNUAL_PAY WITH ANNUAL_PAY*1.1Ø FOR MALE

. REPLACE ANNUAL_PAY WITH ANNUAL_PAY*1.15 FOR .NOT. MALE
.AND. AREA_CODE="5Ø3"

Inserting Records

In addition to appending records at the end of a file, you can insert new
records between existing records. The Control Center does not offer the
capability of inserting records, however, so the insertion must be carried
out in dot prompt mode. The syntax for the command is

. INSERT

The INSERT command adds a new data record after the current record
and places the program in edit mode. To add a data record before the
current record, enter the following command:

. INSERT BEFORE

To add a new record between the third and fourth record of the active
file, use one of the following sets of commands:

. GOTO 3
. INSERT

. GOTO 4
. INSERT BEFORE

Both of these command sequences display the entry form for data record
4 and place dBASE IV in editing mode. New data can then be entered on
the data-entry form. After entering the data, be sure to press Ctrl-End to
save the inserted record.

Deleting Records

In dot prompt mode, you can remove records by using the DELETE command. The syntax of this command is

. DELETE RECORD <*record number*>
. DELETE ALL
. DELETE FOR <*filter conditions*>

Some examples of DELETE are

. DELETE RECORD 5
. DELETE ALL
. DELETE FOR AREA_CODE="5Ø3"
. DELETE FOR MALE
. DELETE FOR LAST_NAME="Smith".AND. ANNUAL_PAY>2ØØØØ

Removing Records Permanently

After data records have been marked for deletion, you can use the PACK operation to remove them from the database file, such as

. PACK

A word of caution: Always be sure to back up your database files before using the PACK operation. After PACK is executed, the marked records are removed permanently.

Undeleting Records

As you know, records marked for deletion are removed only when you enter PACK at the dot prompt. You can remove the deletion marks by using the RECALL command, as in

. RECALL RECORD <*record number*>
. RECALL ALL
. RECALL <*filter conditions*>

Some examples are

. RECALL RECORD 5
. RECALL ALL

```
. RECALL FOR AREA_CODE="5Ø3"
. RECALL FOR MALE
. RECALL FOR LAST_NAME="Smith".AND. ANNUAL_PAY>2ØØØØ
```

Emptying a Database File

All records can be removed from a database file with the dot prompt ZAP command. The format for the command is simply

```
. ZAP
```

When you use this command, the records are deleted but the data structure is left intact. The ZAP command achieves the same effect as a combination of the following two commands:

```
. DELETE ALL
. PACK
```

When you enter the ZAP command, dBASE IV requests confirmation. The following message is displayed:

```
ZAP C:\DBDATA\EMPLOYEE.DBF? (Y/N)
```

If you answer N, the ZAP command is aborted. Remember that once the data records are zapped, the records are erased from the file and cannot be recovered.

Chapter 5 QuickStart

In this chapter, you learned the procedures for modifying

- ☐ Field attributes in an existing database structure
- ☐ An existing query design
- ☐ Data in data records

Let's bring up the QIKSTART.CAT file catalog and files so that we can practice these procedures. If you have a problem recalling the file catalog and files, refer to the Chapter 4 QuickStart for the procedures.

Modifying Database Structure

As an exercise, let's add a new logical field named MALE and a date field named BIRTH_DATE to the ADDRESS.DBF database file. First, bring up the database structure of the database file and enter the new fields by following these steps:

1. Highlight the ADDRESS.DBF file in the Data panel.

2. Press Shift-F2.

3. Press Esc once to hide the organization menu option from the screen.

4. Use the ↓ key to move the cursor to the bottom of the database structure form.

5. Enter the logical field MALE.

6. Move down to next field and enter the BIRTH_DATE date field.

After you enter the changes as shown in figure 5.21, open the Exit menu by pressing Alt-E, and select **Save changes and exit**. Then, answer Yes to the following prompt:

```
You have made changes to the field structure
of this database file. Are you sure you want
to save these changes?
```

Editing Data Records

Because you have added two new fields to the ADDRESS.DBF database file, you need to enter values to these fields. To do that, you invoke editing mode by following these steps:

1. Highlight the ADDRESS file in the Data panel.

2. Press F2 to display the record for editing.

3. If data records are displayed in browse format, press F2 to switch to edit format.

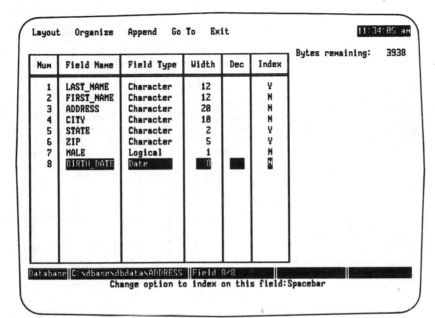

```
 Layout   Organize   Append   Go To   Exit                    11:34:05 am

                                             Bytes remaining:     3938
 ┌─────┬──────────────┬────────────┬───────┬─────┬────────┐
 │ Num │ Field Name   │ Field Type │ Width │ Dec │ Index  │
 ├─────┼──────────────┼────────────┼───────┼─────┼────────┤
 │  1  │ LAST_NAME    │ Character  │  12   │     │   Y    │
 │  2  │ FIRST_NAME   │ Character  │  12   │     │   N    │
 │  3  │ ADDRESS      │ Character  │  20   │     │   N    │
 │  4  │ CITY         │ Character  │  10   │     │   N    │
 │  5  │ STATE        │ Character  │   2   │     │   Y    │
 │  6  │ ZIP          │ Character  │   5   │     │   Y    │
 │  7  │ MALE         │ Logical    │   1   │     │   N    │
 │  8  │ BIRTH_DATE   │ Date       │   8   │     │   N    │
 │     │              │            │       │     │        │
 └─────┴──────────────┴────────────┴───────┴─────┴────────┘
 Database C:\dbase\dbdata\ADDRESS   Field 8/8
              Change option to index on this field:Spacebar
```

Fig. 5.21.

Modified database structure for ADDRESS.DBF.

4. Go to the first record in the file by pressing Alt-G to invoke the Go To menu and selecting the **Top record** option. Rec 1/10 in the status bar at the bottom of the screen indicates that the first record is displayed.

5. Enter T in the MALE file and enter the birth date (05/12/57) for George F. Taylor.

6. After finishing the first record, press F2 to switch to browse format in order to continue the data editing operation.

7. When the browse form appears, press Enter several times to move the cursor to the MALE field and enter F. Then enter a date value (03/08/61) in the BIRTH_DATE field.

8. Repeat the same process until you have filled in the values for the MALE and BIRTH_DATE fields in all the records (see fig. 5.22).

9. Now, save the edit records by pressing Alt-E and selecting the **Exit** option.

Fig. 5.22.

Contents of the edited record.

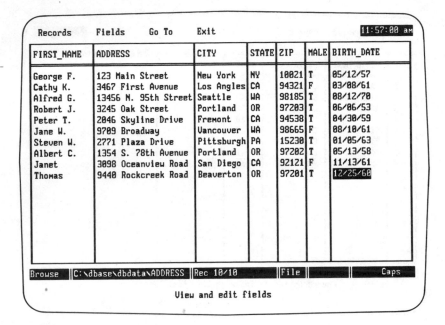

```
 Records     Fields     Go To     Exit                    11:57:00 am

 FIRST_NAME  ADDRESS               CITY       STATE ZIP   MALE BIRTH_DATE

 George F.   123 Main Street       New York   NY    10021 T    05/12/57
 Cathy K.    3467 First Avenue     Los Angles CA    94321 F    03/08/61
 Alfred G.   13456 N. 95th Street  Seattle    WA    98185 T    08/12/70
 Robert J.   3245 Oak Street       Portland   OR    97203 T    06/06/53
 Peter T.    2046 Skyline Drive    Fremont    CA    94538 T    04/30/59
 Jane W.     9709 Broadway         Vancouver  WA    98665 F    08/10/61
 Steven W.   2771 Plaza Drive      Pittsburgh PA    15230 T    01/05/63
 Albert C.   1354 S. 78th Avenue   Portland   OR    97202 T    05/13/58
 Janet       3098 Oceanview Road   San Diego  CA    92121 F    11/13/61
 Thomas      9440 Rockcreek Road   Beaverton  OR    97201 T    12/25/60




 Browse   C:\dbase\dbdata\ADDRESS  Rec 10/10         File          Caps
                        View and edit fields
```

Adding Records

Let's append one new record to the ADDRESS.DBF database file by using the standard default data-entry form:

1. Highlight ADDRESS in the Data panel and press Shift-F2 to display the database structure.

2. Press Alt-A to invoke the Append menu.

3. Select the **Enter records from keyboard** option.

4. When the data form for the new record (Rec 11/11) appears, enter all the field values accordingly (see fig. 5.23).

5. Save the new record by pressing Alt-E and selecting the **Exit** option.

6. Return to the Control Center by again pressing Alt-E and selecting the **Save changes and exit** option.

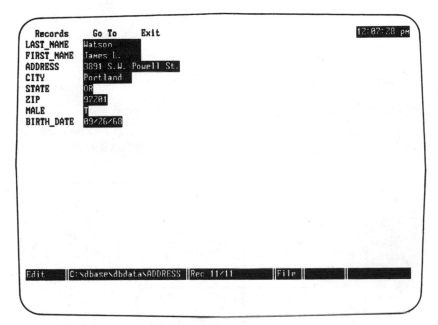

Fig. 5.23.

Contents of the first added record.

Let's append another new record to the ADDRESS.DBF database file by using the custom data-entry form ADDRESS.SCR created in the Chapter 3 QuickStart. However, first you need to add the two new fields to the custom data-entry form by following these steps:

1. Highlight ADDRESS in the Forms panel while ADDRESS is being highlighted in the Data panel. Press Enter.

2. Select the **Modify layout** option from the menu. The data-entry design form then appears, and you need to add the BIRTH_DATE and MALE fields to the form (as explained in the following steps).

3. First, place the cursor at the position where BIRTH_DATE field should appear (right below the CITY field) and press Alt-F to invoke the Fields menu.

4. Select the **Add field** option, and then select the BIRTH_DATE field options.

5. Press Ctrl-End to accept the {MM/DD/YY} template.

6. Add the label "BIRTH DATE" to the field.

7. Move the cursor to the position where the MALE field should appear (right below the end of the ZIP field), and press Alt-F.

8. Select the **Add field** option, and then select the MALE field.

9. Press Ctrl-End to accept the {L} template.

10. Enter the field label "MALE ? (T/F)" in front of the field.

11. Now, save the modified data-entry form (see fig. 5.24) by pressing Alt-E options and select the **Save changes and exit** option.

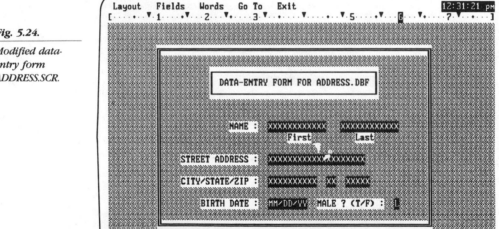

Fig. 5.24.

Modified data-entry form ADDRESS.SCR.

Now, you can add a new record by using the modified data-entry form:

1. Highlight ADDRESS in the Forms panel while ADDRESS is being highlighted in the Data panel. Press Enter.

2. Select **Display data** option from the menu.

3. Go to the end of the database file by choosing the **Last record option** from the Go To menu (invoked with Alt-G).

4. Press the PgDn key.

5. Answer Y to the prompt:

   ===> Add new records? (Y/N)

6. Now, enter values to the fields of the new record (see fig. 5.25).

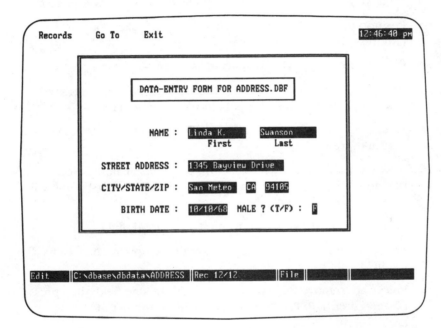

| Records | Go To | Exit | | 12:46:40 PM |

DATA-ENTRY FORM FOR ADDRESS.DBF

NAME : Linda K.   Swanson
       First   Last

STREET ADDRESS : 1345 Bayview Drive

CITY/STATE/ZIP : San Meteo CA 94105

BIRTH DATE : 10/10/68 MALE ? (T/F) : F

Edit   C:\dbase\dbdata\ADDRESS Rec 12/12   File

Fig. 5.25.

Contents of the second added record.

7. Save the record by pressing Alt-E and selecting the **Exit** option.

Modifying Query Design

In the Chapter 4 QuickStart, you created the FINDCA.QBE query design. Now let's return to the query design, press Shift-F2, and experiment with modifying the design:

1. While ADDRESS is highlighted in the Data panel, highlight FINDCA in the Queries panel and press Enter.

2. Choose the **Modify query** option from the menu.

3. Press Enter in response to the following prompt:

   WARNING: File definition has changes

   Press any key to continue...

4. Next, you need to experiment with changing the view skeleton.

5. Position the cursor under the name of the file skeleton (Address.dbf).

6. Press F5 to remove all the fields in the view skeleton.

7. Press Tab to move the cursor to the LAST_NAME field. Press F5. Now LAST_NAME should appear in the view skeleton.

8. Press the Tab key again to move the cursor to the FIRST_NAME field and press F5.

9. Now LAST_NAME and FIRST_NAME both appear in the view skeleton. You want to switch the two fields so that first name will appear before last name.

10. Press F4 to move the cursor to the LAST_NAME field.

11. Press F6 to select the field to be moved; then press Enter to fix the field.

12. Press Tab to move the cursor to the right by one field; then press F7 and Enter. FIRST_NAME now appears to the left of LAST_NAME.

13. To add the STATE field to the view skeleton, press F3 to move the cursor back up to the file skeleton.

14. Press Tab several times until the cursor appears in the STATE field.

15. Press F5 to add the STATE field to the view skeleton (see fig. 5.26).

To process the query, press F2. The results produced by the query are shown in figure 5.27. From the figure, you will notice that all the names whose addresses are in CA (California) are selected and displayed in browse format (if not, press F2 to switch from edit format to browse format).

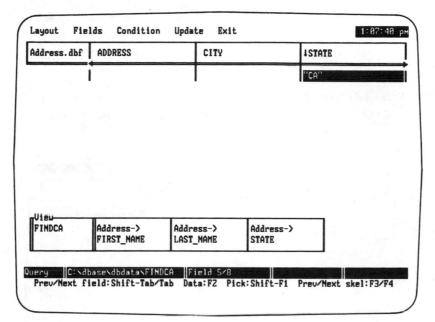

Fig. 5.26.

Modified view skeleton.

```
 Layout   Fields   Condition   Update   Exit           1:07:40 PM
┌──────────────┬────────────────────┬──────────────┬─────────────────┐
│ Address.dbf  │ ADDRESS            │ CITY         │ ↓STATE          │→
├──────────────┼────────────────────┼──────────────┼─────────────────┤
│              │  │                 │      │       │ "CA"            │→
└──────────────┴────────────────────┴──────────────┴─────────────────┘




 ┌View─────┬──────────────┬──────────────┬──────────────┐
 │ FINDCA  │ Address->    │ Address->    │ Address->    │
 │         │ FIRST_NAME   │ LAST_NAME    │ STATE        │
 └─────────┴──────────────┴──────────────┴──────────────┘
 Query   C:\dbase\dbdata\FINDCA   Field 5/8
   Prev/Next field:Shift-Tab/Tab  Data:F2  Pick:Shift-F1  Prev/Next skel:F3/F4
```

Fig. 5.27.

Showing all California address in view.

```
 Records   Fields   Go To   Exit                      1:09:48 PM
┌──────────────┬──────────────┬──────────────────────────────────────┐
│ FIRST_NAME   │ LAST_NAME    │ STATE                                │
├──────────────┼──────────────┼──────────────────────────────────────┤
│ Cathy K.     │ Peters       │ CA                                   │
│ Peter T.     │ Morrow       │ CA                                   │
│ Janet        │ Peterson     │ CA                                   │
│ Linda K.     │ Swanson      │ CA                                   │




└──────────────┴──────────────┴──────────────────────────────────────┘
 Browse   C:\dbase\dbdata\FINDCA   Rec 2/12          View
                        View and edit fields
```

Now return to the query design by pressing Shift-F2. Let's add a new filter condition to the STATE field with the following steps:

1. Use ↓ to open up a new line, and then enter the "WA" condition to the STATE field.

2. Press Tab several times to move the cursor into the MALE field and enter .T. and .F. as two separate conditions (see fig. 5.28).

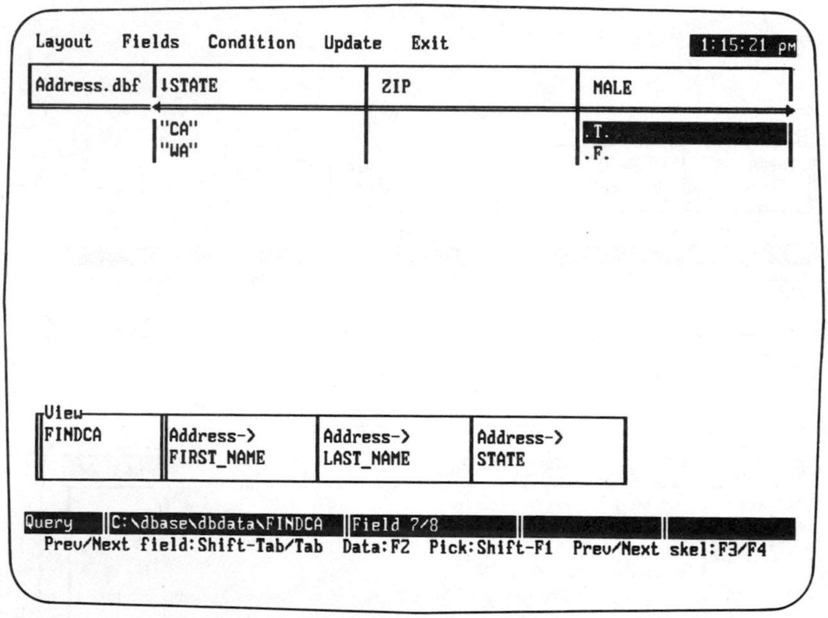

Fig. 5.28.

Entering multiple filter conditions.

3. Process the query by pressing F2. Results will show only those California males and Washington females in the records (see fig. 5.29.)

4. Save the modified query design by pressing Alt-E and selecting the **Save changes and exit** option.

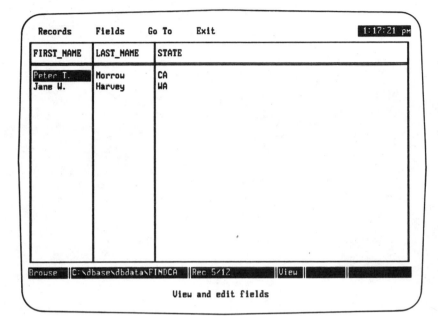

Fig. 5.29.

Showing address of California males and Washington females.

Chapter Summary

This chapter introduced you to the procedures required for editing data and modifying existing query designs. You learned to switch between the two modes for viewing data: edit format and browse format. Additionally, the procedures for building more complex queries and for using relational operators in queries were explained in detail. Also included were procedures for adding, inserting, and deleting records. In all cases, you learned to perform these operations from both the Control Center and from dot prompt mode. In the next chapter, you will learn how to sort, index, and summarize data.

6

Sorting, Indexing, and Summarizing Data

This chapter, which explains how to arrange data so that you can perform data management functions, introduces two important operations: sorting and indexing. Discussions on the strengths and weaknesses of these operations are offered in this chapter so that you will know when to use sorting versus indexing for organizing your data records.

If you choose, you can sort and index database files by selecting options from the Control Center's Organize menu. Additionally, you can use dot prompt commands to execute these operations. The following commands are explained in this chapter:

```
SORT
INDEX
USE INDEX
SET INDEX TO
REINDEX
CLOSE INDEX
FIND
SEEK
```

One of the important features provided by dBASE IV, which was not available in earlier versions of dBASE, is the capability of maintaining multiple index tags in an MDX file for a database file. As a result, you can activate any one of these index tags for retrieving data records based on the values in an indexed field. In this chapter, you will see how to set up and use these index tags.

This chapter also introduces procedures for generating summary statistics, such as computing totals and averages of values in a numeric field, counting records in any data field, and finding the maximum and minimum value in a numeric field, etc. These statistics can be generated by using a query design or by issuing the dot prompt commands TOTAL, SUM, AVERAGE, and COUNT.

Organizing Data in a Database File

The contents of a database file are organized by data fields and data records. Definitions of the data fields are specified when the file is created. Data records are stored in a file in the order in which they are entered. For example, the 10 data records stored in the EMPLOYEE database file are arranged in the order in which they were entered (see fig. 6.1). Each record is assigned a number, which you can use for later reference.

Data records organized in this way may not be suitable for your needs. Because the files are not arranged alphabetically, a listing of the records in the EMPLOYEE.DBF database file would not produce a satisfactory employee roster. As you can see, data records must often be rearranged when they are retrieved or displayed.

Sorting versus Indexing

Data records in a database file can be rearranged in one of two ways. The first way is to sort the records according to the values of one or more of the data fields. Sorted records are then saved to a new database file. If you need to view the sorted records, you then select the new database file.

```
 _____
|  Records    Fields    Go To    Exit         8:54:31 am |
| _____ |
| |FIRST_NAME |LAST_NAME |AREA_CODE|PHONE_NO|MALE|BIRTH_DATE|ANNUAL_PAY| |
| |_____|_____|_____|_____|____|_____|_____| |
| |James C.   |Smith     |216      |123-4567|T   |07/04/60  |  24200.00| |
| |Albert K.  |Zeller    |212      |457-9801|T   |09/20/59  |  30690.00| |
| |Doris A.   |Gregory   |503      |204-8567|F   |07/04/62  |  18590.00| |
| |Harry M.   |Nelson    |315      |576-0235|T   |02/15/58  |  31900.00| |
| |Tina B.    |Baker     |415      |787-3154|F   |10/12/56  |  28490.00| |
| |Kirk D.    |Chapman   |618      |625-7845|T   |08/04/61  |  21725.00| |
| |Mary W.    |Thompson  |213      |432-6783|F   |06/18/55  |  26950.00| |
| |Charles N. |Duff      |216      |456-9873|T   |07/22/64  |  14850.00| |
| |Winston E. |Lee       |503      |365-8512|T   |05/14/39  |  38390.00| |
| |Thomas T.  |Hanson    |216      |573-5085|T   |12/24/45  |  31845.00| |
|                                                          |
| |Browse||C:\...dbdata\EMPLOYEE  ||Rec 1/10    ||File||  || |
|                    View and edit fields                  |
 _____
```

Fig. 6.1.

The database structure of EMPLOYEE.DBF.

Another method of rearranging records in a database file is indexing. The indexing operation does not actually rearrange the records in the database file. Instead, it creates an index file whose records are arranged based on the values in one or more index fields. The records in an index file store the locations of the records in the actual database file. Information in these records are used to relate the actual records in the database file. The operation of indexing a database file will be discussed later in this chapter.

The advantages of using the sorting operation is that it creates permanently sorted records which can be used later without repeating the operation. However, sorting does use more storage space, unless you delete the original unsorted database file after the sort operation. Sorting also takes longer than indexing.

On the other hand, because indexing creates only an index file and not another database file, it takes less storage space. Additionally, indexing is a lot faster than sorting.

Therefore, if your database file has relatively few records and you plan to use the set of sorted records frequently, it is better to use the sorting operation. Otherwise, for most applications, the indexing operation is preferable. The next section begins the discussion of the sort operation.

Sorting Data Records

You can use a sorting operation to arrange data records in ascending or descending order according to the contents of a specified field or fields, which are called *key fields*. Before the sorting process begins, a working file is created automatically by dBASE IV; this is known as the *target file*. The records to be sorted are copied to the target file so that the original files remain intact while the sort is performed on the target file records. After you complete the sorting operation, the data records in the target file are arranged as specified in the key field(s).

You can sort records from the Control Center or from the dot prompt. The sections that follow explain each of these methods.

Sorting Records from the Control Center

Tip:
To sort records, use the **Sort** *option from the Organize menu on database structure screen.*

To sort records in the current database file, you use one of the options available in the Control Center's Organize menu from the database structure screen. To invoke an existing database structure, highlight the database file in the Data panel and press Shift-F2. Once the Organize menu appears, you can select the **Sort database on field list** option and then specify the field list as the sorting key.

Sorting Records with a Single Key Field

Tip:
Available sort orders are Asc, AscDict, Dsc, and DscDict.

Data records in a database file can be sorted according to the values in one or more key fields. For example, if you would like to rearrange the records in EMPLOYEE.DBF by the values in the LAST_NAME field, you would sort the file with a single sorting key "LAST_NAME". To do that, you first highlight EMPLOYEE in the Data panel and press Shift-F2. Then, select the **Sort database on field list** option (see fig. 6.2).

In return, you will be asked to define the field order and the type of sort desired. There are four types of sorts available: ascending (Asc), descending (Dsc), ascending dictionary (AscDict), and descending dictionary (DscDict).

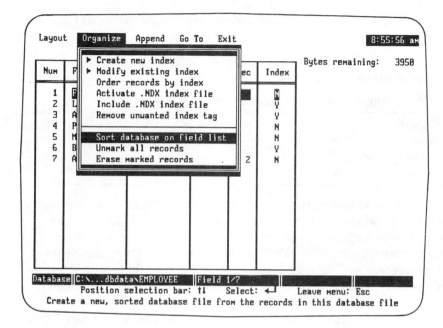

Fig. 6.2.

Sorting records in EMPLOYEE.DBF.

The ascending sorting order (the default order) is the same as the ASCII order shown in Chapter 5 (table 5.1). A list of first names sorted in ascending order might look like the following:

    ALBERT
    BOB
    Bob
    albert

In an ascending order, uppercase letters appear before lowercase letters. If you would like to ignore cases, you can use the ascending dictionary order for sorting your data elements. The list sorted in ascending dictionary order would look like

    albert
    ALBERT
    BOB
    Bob

Tip:

Use AscDict or DscDict to ignore cases.

In an ascending dictionary, the character strings are arranged as they would appear in a dictionary. Uppercase and lowercase letters are treated as the same. In the list above, entries *albert* and *ALBERT* are treated as the same order. The entry *albert* appears before *ALBERT* because that is how the items were entered in the database file.

The descending and descending dictionary orders cause the opposite results of the ascending and ascending dictionary:

Descending	*Descending Dictionary*
albert	BOB
Bob	Bob
BOB	albert
ALBERT	ALBERT

You can also sort records by using a date or numeric field as a sorting key. If you sort dates into an ascending or ascending dictionary order, records with earlier dates are placed before records with later dates. When numeric values are sorted in ascending or ascending dictionary order, records with smaller values are placed before those with larger values. You cannot sort records by using a logical field as a sorting key.

The default sort order assumed by dBASE IV is an ascending order. To change to descending order, move the cursor to the **Type of sort** column and press the space bar. The field order determines the order in which the data records will be arranged.

As an example, if you would like to sort the last names in the EMPLOYEE.DBF database file into an ascending order, in the column of the field order you would enter the name of the key field (such as LAST_NAME) to be used for the sorting operation (see fig. 6.3).

To begin sorting and save the sorted records in a new database file, press Ctrl-End and enter the name of the new database file (BYLAST.DBF) at the prompt:

    Enter name of sorted file:

Next, the sorting begins. dBASE IV monitors the progress of the sort by displaying the name of the target database file with its directory path and the sorting order (/A stands for ascending order):

    SORT TO C:\DBASE\DBDATA\BYLAST.dbf ON LAST_NAME/A

At the end of the sorting process, the message

    100% Sorted ... 10 Records sorted

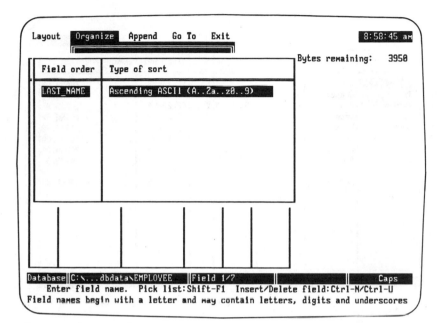

Fig. 6.3.

Defining sort order and sort type.

is displayed above the status bar at the bottom of the screen. When you see the message, you know that the sorted records have been saved in the BYLAST.DBF target file. When you return to the Control Center from the database structure screen (using Alt-E), you will see the new file is displayed in the Data panel.

Viewing the Sorted Database File

Now, you can examine the sorted database file named BYLAST by highlighting the name and pressing F2. However, before highlighting the sorted file, you need to close the current file (EMPLOYEE.DBF) by selecting the **Close file** option from the menu and pressing Enter.

Caution:
Close the current database file before using the sorted database file.

The sorted records then are displayed in response to the keystroke. Figure 6.4 shows that the last names are arranged in ascending order.

In the above examples, the character field LAST_NAME is used as a sorting key field. As you will see in later examples, you can also arrange the records chronologically by using a date field such as the

Fig. 6.4.

*Data records
sorted by last
names.*

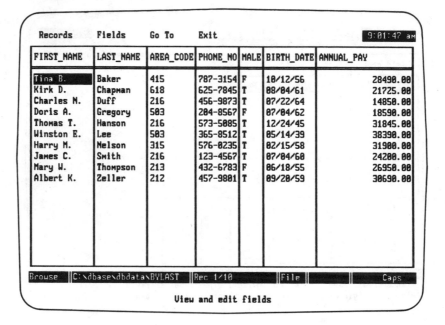

Fig. 6.4.

*Data records
sorted by last
names.*

BIRTH_DATE. Similarly, you can rank values in a numeric field by using
the field (such as ANNUAL_PAY) as a sorting key.

Sorting Records with Multiple Key Fields

You can sort the records in a database file by using more than one
sorting key fields in a given order. For example, you may want to sort the
records in the EMPLOYEE.DBF by using the AREA_CODE and
PHONE_NO fields as sorting keys. In addition, you can specify the
records will be sorted first by AREA_CODE and then by PHONE_NO.
To do that, you would specify these two key fields accordingly in the
Field order column—in an ascending order for AREA_CODE and a
descending order in PHONE_NO (see fig. 6.5). To change from
ascending to descending order in the Type of sort column, press the
space bar.

After you perform the sort, the data records in the sorted database file
(BYACPHNO.DBF) are arranged as shown in figure 6.6. In the figure,
notice that all the area codes first are arranged in an ascending order and
phone numbers of the same area code are arranged in a descending
order.

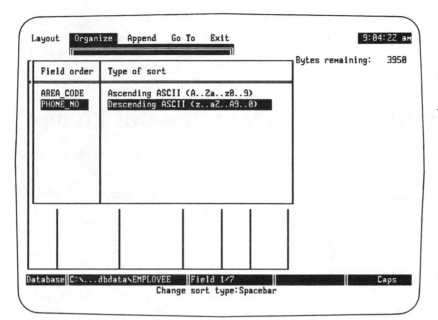

Fig. 6.5.

Sorting records with multiple key fields.

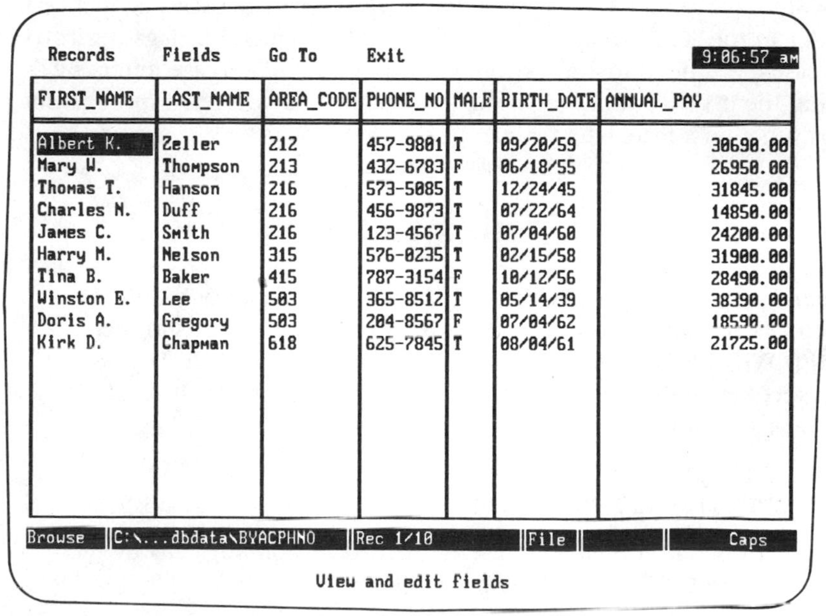

Fig. 6.6.

Data records sorted by area codes and phone numbers.

In figure 6.6, you will notice that all the area codes are arranged in an ascending order (from 212 to 618). Within the same area code (such as 216), phone numbers are arranged in a descending order (573-, 456-, 123-, etc.)

Sorting Records from the Dot Prompt

Command:
SORT TO...ON
and SORT ON...TO
Sorts records
according to a
specified key.

In dot prompt mode, you can sort the records in a database file by using the SORT command, such as

. SORT TO < *name of sorted file*> ON < *sorting key*> [/A] [/D]

or

. SORT ON < *sorting key*> TO < *name of sorted file*> [/A] [/D]

Caution:
You may not
specify
ascending
dictionary or
descending
dictionary
order in SORT
command.

In the SORT command, you can specify the name of the new database file for saving the sorted records. The sorting key in the SORT command can be defined as one or more sorting fields. The sorting order is defined in the command as either /A (for ascending ASCII) or /D (for descending ASCII). You cannot specify ascending dictionary or descending dictionary order in the SORT command. In order to sort character strings regardless of cases, you need to convert the strings into all uppercase letters by using the UPPER() function in the command. You will learn more about this function a little later.

Sorting Records with a Single Key Field

When you use a single key field for the sort, the name of the field becomes the sort key. For example, to arrange the records in the EMPLOYEE.DBF chronologically by birthdates, specify BIRTH_DATE as the sort key in the SORT command after selecting the database file for use, such as

. USE EMPLOYEE
. SORT TO BYBDATE ON BIRTH_DATE

The sort operation then arranges the records chronologically by the values in the BIRTH_DATE field (see fig. 6.7).

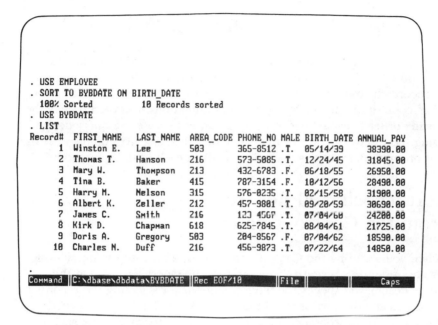

Fig. 6.7.

Sorting records by birthdates.

When you sort records, ascending order is assumed to be the default; in other words, you don't need to specify the /A. However, if you choose a descending order, you must specify /D for descending, such as

. SORT TO SORTED ON ANNUAL _ PAY/D

The sort operation then ranks the values in the ANNUAL_ PAY from the largest to the smallest.

Tip:
Add /D in the SORT command for a descending sort order.

Sorting Records with Multiple Key Fields

If you would like to sort records in a database file by using more than one field as the sort key, you could specify these fields (separated with commas) in the SORT command. The sorting order for each of these fields can be individually specified. For example,

. USE EMPLOYEE
. SORT TO TESTFILE ON AREA _ CODE,PHONE _ NO/D
. SORT ON LAST _ NAME/D,FIRST _ NAME TO TESTFILE

Tip:
Use commas to separate sorting fields.

Sorting Selected Data Records

During the sorting operation, all the records are sorted according to the contents of the key field. However, you can sort only a selected set of records by using a query design to select those records with a set of filter conditions. After defining the filter conditions, you then specify the sorting order in the sorting key fields. You can create the query design by using the Control Center or by issuing the CREATE QUERY command at the dot prompt. The sections that follow explain each of these methods.

Sorting Selected Records from the Control Center

When you are using the Control Center, you can create the query design by choosing the < **create**> option from the Queries panel. On the query design, you specify the filter conditions for selecting the records to be sorted and the sort order in the sorting key fields. As you learned previously, four sorting orders are available (Asc for ascending, AscDic for ascending dictionary, Dsc for descending, and DscDict for descending dictionary). If you need to save the sorted records to a new database file, you can save the query view as the database file after processing the query.

For example, if you would like to sort the phone numbers in those records in EMPLOYEE.DBF that belong to male employees (MALE=.T.), you can create a query design for specifying the filter condition (.T.) in the logical MALE field. Then, sort the PHONE_ NO field accordingly. Here are the steps for the sort operation:

1. Highlight EMPLOYEE.DBF in the Data panel of the Control Center and select the **Use file** option.

2. Select < **create**> from the Queries panel and press Enter.

3. On the query design form, enter .T. in the MALE field and enter Asc (for ascending order) as the sorting order in the PHONE_ NO field (see fig. 6.8).

4. To process the query, press F2. The results of the query are shown in figure 6.9 (SORTED8.SCR).

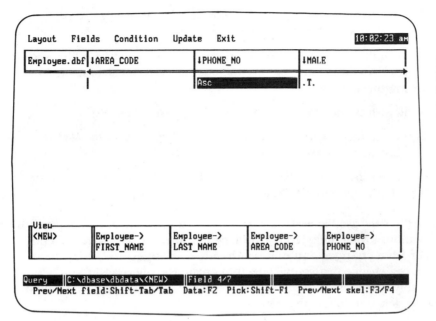

Fig. 6.8.

Sorting selective records with a query design.

```
 Layout   Fields   Condition   Update   Exit          10:02:23 aM

 Employee.dbf ↓AREA_CODE          ↓PHONE_NO           ↓MALE

                                  Asc                 .T.




 View
 <NEW>      Employee->    Employee->    Employee->    Employee->
            FIRST_NAME    LAST_NAME     AREA_CODE     PHONE_NO

 Query    C:\dbase\dbdata\<NEW>     Field 4/7
   Prev/Next field:Shift-Tab/Tab   Data:F2  Pick:Shift-F1  Prev/Next skel:F3/F4
```

Fig. 6.9.

Sorting male records by phone numbers.

```
 Records   Fields   Go To   Exit              10:03:43 aM

 FIRST_NAME LAST_NAME AREA_CODE PHONE_NO MALE BIRTH_DATE ANNUAL_PAY

 James C.   Smith     216       123-4567 T    07/04/60      24200.00
 Winston E. Lee       503       365-8512 T    05/14/39      38390.00
 Charles N. Duff      216       456-9873 T    07/22/64      14850.00
 Albert K.  Zeller    212       457-9801 T    09/20/59      30690.00
 Thomas T.  Hanson    216       573-5085 T    12/24/45      31845.00
 Harry M.   Nelson    315       576-0235 T    02/15/58      31900.00
 Kirk D.    Chapman   618       625-7845 T    08/04/61      21725.00








 Browse   C:\dbase\dbdata\<NEW>     Rec 1/7         View  ReadOnly
                       View and edit fields
```

From figure 6.9, you can see that only those records having .T. in the MALE field are sorted by their phone numbers.

If you would like to save the sorted records to a new database file (such as MALEPHNO.DBF), you can save the query view as a database file by following these steps:

Tip:
If you wish, you can save the sorted records in a query view to a separate database file.

1. Return to the query design screen by pressing Shift-F2.

2. Invoke the Layout menu by pressing Alt-L and select the **Write view as database file** option.

3. Assign the new database name (MALEPHNO.DBF) in response to the prompt Enter filename:.

After the database file is saved, you can return to the Control Center with or without saving the query by invoking Exit menu (Alt-E) and selecting either **Save changes and exit** or **Abandon changes and exit**. Unless there is a chance that you will need to create the query again, you probably should not save the query. If you've saved the query and would like to delete it, follow these steps:

1. When the query file to be deleted is highlighted in the Queries panel, press Enter and select the **Close view** option. Remember that you cannot delete a file when it is being used or open. You need to close the file before deleting it.

2. After the file is closed, it is moved below the horizontal line. Highlight the file again for removal.

3. Invoke the Catalog menu by pressing Alt-C, select the **Remove highlighted file from catalog** option, and answer Yes to the following prompt:

   Are you sure you want to remove this file from the catalog?

   Yes   No

4. Then answer Yes to the following prompt:

   Do you also want to delete this file from the disk?

   Yes   No

Caution:
Close the file before removing it from disk.

You can use multiple fields as the sorting key in the query design. In that case, you need to specify the sorting priority for each of these fields following its sorting order. For example, if you would like to first sort the AREA_ CODE field into ascending order and then sort the PHONE_ NO

field into descending order, you would enter Asc1 in the AREA_ CODE
field and Dsc2 in the PHONE_ NO field (see fig. 6.10).

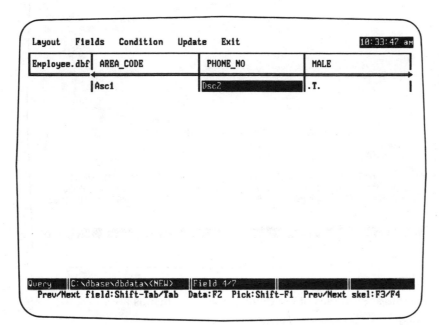

Fig. 6.10.

Sorting values in multiple fields.

Sorting Selected Records from the Dot Prompt

When you are working in dot prompt mode, you can sort selective
records by adding the filter conditions to the SORT command, such as

> . SORT TO < *sorted database file*> ON < *sorting key*>
>   FOR < *filter conditions*>

For example,

> . SORT ON ANNUAL_PAY/D TO SORTED FOR AREA_ CODE="5Ø3"

Results of the sort are shown in figure 6.11. From the figure, you can see
that only records with 503 in the AREA_ CODE field are sorted.

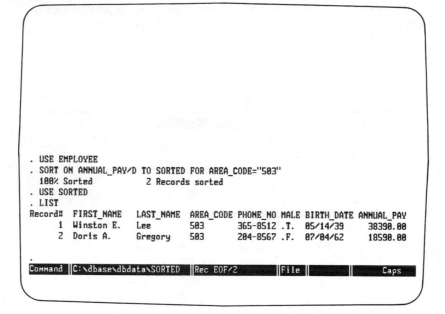

Fig. 6.11.

Using a filter condition in the SORT *command.*

```
. USE EMPLOYEE
. SORT ON ANNUAL_PAY/D TO SORTED FOR AREA_CODE="503"
  100% Sorted          2 Records sorted
. USE SORTED
. LIST
Record#  FIRST_NAME   LAST_NAME   AREA_CODE PHONE_NO MALE BIRTH_DATE ANNUAL_PAY
      1  Winston E.   Lee         503       365-8512 .T.  05/14/39    38390.00
      2  Doris A.     Gregory     503       204-8567 .F.  07/04/62    18590.00
.
Command  C:\dbase\dbdata\SORTED  Rec EOF/2     File           Caps
```

A few more examples of conditional SORT commands are

. SORT TO MALEPAY ON ANNUAL _ PAY/D FOR MALE

. SORT TO BDATE ON BIRTH _ DATE FOR BIRTH _ DATE> ={Ø1/Ø1/6Ø}

. SORT ON LAST _ NAME TO FEMALES FOR .NOT. MALE

. SORT TO FONELIST ON PHONE _ NO/D FOR AREA _ CODE="5Ø3" .OR.
  AREA _ CODE="2Ø6"

. SORT TO SORTED ON FIRST _ NAME FOR AREA _ CODE> ="212"

. SORT ON AREA _ CODE/A, PHONE _ NO/D FOR MALE
  .AND. BIRTH _ DATE> ={Ø1/Ø1/6Ø}

Indexing a Database File

Indexing is another method of arranging records in a database file. Unlike sorting, indexing does not create another database for storing the sorted data records. Instead, indexing creates an index tag that keeps track of the values of the index key and the corresponding record numbers in the original database file. All index tags are saved in a multiple index file with the .MDX file extension.

To see how the indexing operation works, let's assume the original database file (.DBF) has the following records:

Record # in .DBF File	LAST_NAME	BIRTH_DATE
1	Taylor	01/01/63
2	Faust	05/14/65
3	Johnson	06/18/61
4	Baker	07/04/62
5	Madison	11/22/64

When you want to arrange the records in the database file by indexing the LAST_NAME field, an index tag will be created in a multiple index (.MDX) file for holding values of the index field and their record numbers:

Record # in .MDX File	Value of the Indexed Field	Record # in the Original .DBF File
1	Baker	4
2	Faust	2
3	Johnson	3
4	Madison	5
5	Taylor	1

The index file is assigned a name with an .NDX extension (such as LASTNAME.NDX).

Similarly, when you arrange records chronologically by indexing the BIRTH_DATE, the following index tag in the multiple index (.MDX) file will be created:

Record # in .MDX File	Value of the Indexed Field	Record # in the Original .DBF File
1	06/18/61	3
2	07/04/62	4
3	01/01/63	1
4	11/22/64	5
5	05/14/65	2

The record numbers in the original database file provide the necessary links between the index tag and the database file. They are used for arranging the records when the index tag is activated. The sequence of records in the original database file are not physically changed when you index the file.

Because the index tag contains only a limited amount of information, it takes up a lot less storage space than the sorted database file and thus requires less time to process. Therefore, unless you need to save the sorted records, it is always a more efficient way to arrange records by using indexing than sorting.

Using index tags in a multiple index (.MDX) file is a new improved feature offered by dBASE IV. In the earlier versions of the dBASE programs (dBASE II, dBASE III, and dBASE III Plus), individual index (.NDX) files were used for indexing database files. An individual index file works the same way as an index tag for arranging data records. However, index tags are superior to index files for two important reasons.

First, index tags created by dBASE IV automatically update their contents whenever the data records are modified. Information in the index tags always match with that in the database file. On the other hand, you have to update individual index files yourself by reindexing them after data records have been changed, unless you select the existing index files to be used at the time you put the database file to use (for example, USE EMPLOYEE INDEX BYLAST, etc.). If you fail to reindex them, information in the index files will no longer match that in the database file and serious errors will result.

Second, index tags are easier to maintain and monitor. Instead of creating a set of individual index files—each of which occupies a separate disk file—all the index tags are grouped together in one file. As a result, you can effortlessly identify these index tags with a single command. You do not have to remember the names of all the individual index files. Another advantage of MDX files is that the use of a multiple index file instead of several index files reduces the number of files DOS must maintain open. This is especially important for DOS versions prior to 3.3 especially.

Tip:
Whenever possible, use index tags instead of individual index files.

Although you can still use individual index (.NDX) files in dBASE IV, it is highly recommended that you avoid using them. Instead, you should start using index tags in a multiple index (.MDX) file. However, if you have created individual index (.NDX) files in earlier versions of dBASE (dBASE II, dBASE III, and dBASE III Plus), you can still use them in dBASE IV.

Multiple Index File

When you define the database structure of a database file, you are asked to select either Y or N in the index column for each of the data fields. In the EMPLOYEE.DBF database structure, for example, the fields of LAST_ NAME, AREA_ CODE, and BIRTH_ DATE were indexed (see fig. 6.12).

```
 Layout    Organize    Append    Go To    Exit                    10:52:00 am

                                            Bytes remaining:    3950
 ┌─────┬──────────────┬──────────────┬───────┬──────┬───────┐
 │ Num │  Field Name  │  Field Type  │ Width │ Dec  │ Index │
 ├─────┼──────────────┼──────────────┼───────┼──────┼───────┤
 │  1  │ FIRST_NAME   │ Character    │  12   │      │   N   │
 │  2  │ LAST_NAME    │ Character    │  10   │      │   Y   │
 │  3  │ AREA_CODE    │ Character    │   3   │      │   Y   │
 │  4  │ PHONE_NO     │ Character    │   8   │      │   N   │
 │  5  │ MALE         │ Logical      │   1   │      │   N   │
 │  6  │ BIRTH_DATE   │ Date         │   8   │      │   Y   │
 │  7  │ ANNUAL_PAY   │ Numeric      │   8   │   2  │   N   │
 └─────┴──────────────┴──────────────┴───────┴──────┴───────┘



 Database C:\...dbdata\EMPLOYEE      Field 1/7                         Caps
          Enter the field name. Insert/Delete field:Ctrl-N/Ctrl-U
 Field names begin with a letter and may contain letters, digits and underscores
```

Fig. 6.12.

The original database structure of EMPLOYEE.DBF.

As a result, an index tag for each of these indexed fields was created at the time the database was created. For example, when the EMPLOYEE.DBF was created, you saw messages such as

    INDEX ON LAST_NAME TAG LAST_NAME
    INDEX ON AREA_CODE TAG AREA_CODE
    INDEX ON BIRTH_DATE TAG BIRTH_DATE

The index tag named LAST_ NAME was created for indexing the LAST_ NAME field. As records were entered to the EMPLOYEE.DBF database file, all the last names in the file and their corresponding record numbers were saved in the index tag. Similarly, values of the

AREA_CODE and BIRTH_DATE fields along with their record numbers in EMPLOYEE.DBF were saved in their index tags respectively. These index tags were saved in the multiple index (MDX) file (for example, EMPLOYEE.MDX). A total of up to 47 index tags can be included in a multiple index file.

However, remember that unless you invoke one of the index tags, the records in the database file will not be arranged automatically.

Using Index Tags

When you want to arrange data records by using one of the index tags you've created, you select the index tag either from the Control Center or from the dot prompt. The following sections explain each method.

Using an Index Tag from the Control Center

When you are using the Control Center, you select and use an existing index tag by using the Organize menu on the database structure screen. (You invoke this menu by pressing Shift-F2 when the database file is open.)

For example, if you would like to arrange the records in EMPLOYEE.DBF in an ascending order by area code, you can select the AREA_CODE index tag created earlier (see fig. 6.13).

After you select the AREA_CODE index tag to arrange the records in the database file, you then can display the ordered records (see fig. 6.14) by pressing F2 while the database structure screen is displayed.

Figure 6.14 shows that all the area codes then are arranged in ascending order. When an index tag is set up during the creation of the database structure, a default ascending order is assumed. If you would like to use a descending order to arrange the data records, you need to modify the index tag after it is set up (this procedure is explained later in this chapter).

After viewing the ordered records, you can invoke the Exit menu and choose one of the following options:

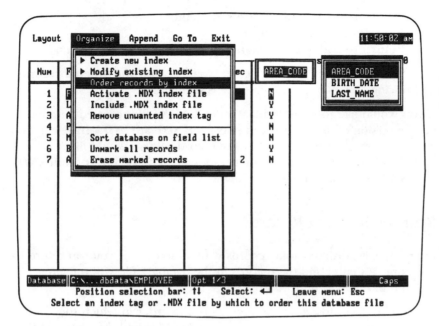

Fig. 6.13.

Ordered records with AREA_CODE index tag.

```
Layout    Organize    Append    Go To    Exit                  11:50:02 am

       ┌──────────────────────────────┐              ┌─AREA_CODE─┐  ┌─AREA_CODE──┐
 Num   F │ ▸ Create new index          │ ec          │ AREA_CODE │  │ AREA_CODE  │
       │ ▸ Modify existing index       │             └───────────┘  │ BIRTH_DATE │
       │   Order records by index      │                            │ LAST_NAME  │
   1   F │   Activate .NDX index file  │              N             └────────────┘
   2   L │   Include .NDX index file   │              Y
   3   A │   Remove unwanted index tag │              Y
   4   P │                             │              N
   5   M │   Sort database on field list│             N
   6   B │   Unmark all records        │              Y
   7   A │   Erase marked records      │    2         N
       └──────────────────────────────┘

Database │C:\...dbdata\EMPLOYEE    │Opt 1/3│                          │ Caps
          Position selection bar: ↑↓    Select: ↵    Leave menu: Esc
       Select an index tag or .NDX file by which to order this database file
```

Fig. 6.14.

Ordered records by area codes.

```
Records     Fields     Go To     Exit                          11:54:01 am
┌───────────┬───────────┬──────────┬─────────┬────┬──────────┬───────────┐
│FIRST_NAME │ LAST_NAME │ AREA_CODE│ PHONE_NO│MALE│BIRTH_DATE│ANNUAL_PAY │
├───────────┼───────────┼──────────┼─────────┼────┼──────────┼───────────┤
│Albert K.  │ Zeller    │ 212      │ 457-9801│ T  │ 09/20/59 │  30690.00 │
│Mary W.    │ Thompson  │ 213      │ 432-6783│ F  │ 06/18/55 │  26950.00 │
│James C.   │ Smith     │ 216      │ 123-4567│ T  │ 07/04/60 │  24200.00 │
│Charles N. │ Duff      │ 216      │ 456-9873│ T  │ 07/22/64 │  14850.00 │
│Thomas T.  │ Hanson    │ 216      │ 573-5085│ T  │ 12/24/45 │  31845.00 │
│Harry M.   │ Nelson    │ 315      │ 576-0235│ T  │ 02/15/58 │  31900.00 │
│Tina B.    │ Baker     │ 415      │ 787-3154│ F  │ 10/12/56 │  28490.00 │
│Doris A.   │ Gregory   │ 503      │ 204-8567│ F  │ 07/04/62 │  18590.00 │
│Winston E. │ Lee       │ 503      │ 365-8512│ T  │ 05/14/39 │  38390.00 │
│Kirk D.    │ Chapman   │ 618      │ 625-7845│ T  │ 08/04/61 │  21725.00 │
└───────────┴───────────┴──────────┴─────────┴────┴──────────┴───────────┘

Browse  │C:\...dbdata\EMPLOYEE   │Rec 2/10│       │File│          │ Caps
                              View and edit fields
```

1. **Exit** (for returning to the Control Center)
2. **Transfer to Query Design**
3. **Return to Database Design** (the database structure screen)

After returning to the Control Center, you can view the ordered records by pressing F2 while the database file is highlighted.

Tip:

Include your .NDX files as index tags in the .MDX file.

If you would like to use individual index (.NDX) files created with an earlier version of dBASE, you can select the **Activate .NDX index** option from the Organize menu to order the records. If you would like to include an .NDX file to the multiple index file, choose the **Include .NDX index file** option from the same menu.

Rearranging Data Records

After you have ordered your records with an index tag, you can return to the Control Center and the records in the database file will remain ordered in that way until you rearrange them.

Tip:

To return records to their natural order, reselect the database file.

If you would like to return the records to the order in which they originally appeared, you can close the database file and then reselect the database file by following these steps:

1. When the database file is highlighted, press Enter and select the **Close file** option.

2. Highlight the database file again.

To rearrange your records with another index tag, follow the same procedure described above. For example, to order the birth dates in EMPLOYEE.DBF chronologically with the BIRTH_ DATE index tag, follow these steps:

1. Highlight the EMPLOYEE.DBF in the Data panel and press Shift-F2.

2. Select the **Order records by index** option from the Organize menu.

3. Select the **BIRTH_ DATE** index tag.

4. To display the order records, press F2. The results are shown in figure 6.15.

```
  Records      Fields    Go To     Exit                         12:33:44 pm

  FIRST_NAME   LAST_NAME   AREA_CODE  PHONE_NO  MALE  BIRTH_DATE  ANNUAL_PAY

  Winston E.   Lee         503        365-8512  T     05/14/39       38390.00
  Thomas T.    Hanson      216        573-5085  T     12/24/45       31845.00
  Mary W.      Thompson    213        432-6783  F     06/18/55       26950.00
  Tina B.      Baker       415        787-3154  F     10/12/56       28490.00
  Harry M.     Nelson      315        576-0235  T     02/15/58       31900.00
  Albert K.    Zeller      212        457-9801  T     09/20/59       30690.00
  James C.     Smith       216        123-4567  T     07/04/60       24200.00
  Kirk D.      Chapman     618        625-7845  T     08/04/61       21725.00
  Doris A.     Gregory     503        204-8567  F     07/04/62       18590.00
  Charles N.   Duff        216        456-9873  T     07/22/64       14850.00




  Browse    C:\...dbdata\EMPLOYEE     Rec 9/10       File              Caps
                          View and edit fields
```

Fig. 6.15.

Ordered records by birthdates.

Figure 6.15 shows that all the records have been rearranged according to the values in the BIRTH_ DATE index field.

Adding a New Index Tag

When you create the database structure, index tags are set up and saved in the default multiple index (.MDX) file that shares the name of the database file. A new index tag can be added to the multiple index file in one of two ways. The first way involves changing the index column from N to Y while restructuring an existing database structure. In this way, you can create a new index tag by using the index field as the key. You can also add a new index tag by using a menu option provided by the Organize menu option. The other way involves creating a new index tag by selecting the appropriate option from the Organize menu on the database structure screen.

Adding a Single-Field Index Tag

Tip:

To add single-field index tags, restructure the database file.

If you would like to add a new index tag that uses a single field as the key to the multiple index file, the best way to do this is through the restructuring operation. For example, if you plan to create a new index tag so that you can later arrange the values in the ANNUAL_ PAY field of the EMPLOYEE.DBF, you can change the index column in its database structure from N to Y (see fig. 6.16). Then, when you save the modified database structure by selecting the **Save changes and exit** option from the Exit menu (Alt-E), the following message appears, indicating that the index tag is being created:

INDEX ON ANNUAL_PAY TAG ANNUAL_PAY

Fig. 6.16.

Modifying ANNUAL_PAY fields to set up an index tag.

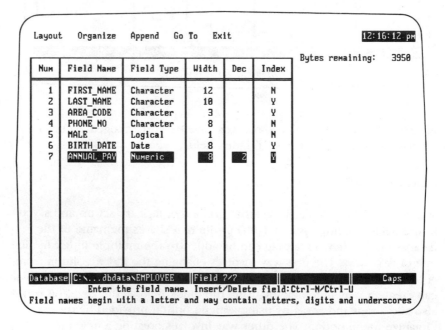

Adding a Multiple-Field Index Tag

When you add a new index tag by restructuring a database file, the new index tag must be made up with a single index field. If you want to create an index tag that requires more than one field, you have to use the **Create existing index** option from the Organize menu on the database structure screen.

For example, if you plan to arrange the records in EMPLOYEE.DBF by using the values in the AREA_ CODE and PHONE_ NO fields, you can create an index tag by choosing the **Create new index** option from the Organize menu after you have recalled the database structure of the database file.

In response to the menu option selection, you will be asked to name the index tag and then describe the fields involved as an index expression (see fig. 6.17).

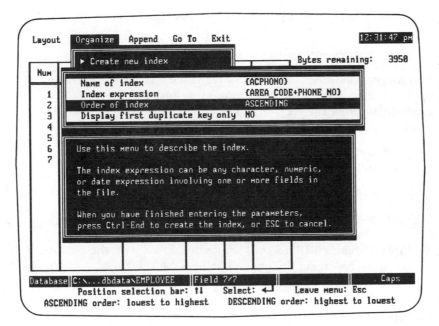

Fig. 6.17.

Creating a multiple-field index tag.

The index expression can be a single key field, a set of key fields, or an expression. An expression contains data fields, other data elements such as memory variables (explained in Chapter 7), and symbols such as the plus sign (+) that define operations performed on the data. If you use a single key field, the key field can be a character/text field, a date field, or a numeric field. Logical and memo fields cannot be used as key fields in the indexing operation.

When you specify multiple fields in an index expression, the character string made up of the expression will be used as the index key. Records will be ordered according to the character string.

In figure 6.17, you will notice that in addition to describing the name of the index tag and the index expression you can also define the order of index (use the space bar to toggle between Ascending and Descending orders). In addition, you can also specify whether you want duplicate records to be displayed by setting the **Display first duplicate key only** option to Yes or No. (Toggle between the choices by pressing the space bar.) If you select No, all the records with the same value in the index key will be displayed; otherwise, only the first record with the index key value will be shown.

When you press Ctrl-End to create the index tag, the following message appears:

```
INDEX ON AREA_CODE +PHONE_NO TAG ACPHONO
```

This message indicates that the new tag named ACPHONO is being set up. Once the tag is set up, you can use it to order the records. For example, to order the records in EMPLOYEE.DBF by using the ACPHONO index tag, follow these steps:

1. Invoke the Organize menu (Alt-O) and select the **Order records by index** option.

2. Select the **ACPHONO** index tag from the index tag box.

3. Press F2 to display the ordered records (see fig. 6.18).

As shown in figure 6.18, records are arranged first with the area codes in an ascending order and the phone numbers are similarly ordered within a given area code.

Deleting an Existing Index Tag

Regardless of how an index tag was created, you can delete the tag from the multiple index file by choosing the **Remove unwanted index tag** from the Organize menu on the database structure screen. Then highlight the index tag to be deleted from the index tag box and press Enter (see fig. 6.19).

Tip:

Removing single-field index tags will automatically restructure the database file.

If you created the tag by specifying Y in the index column of the data field in the database structure, deleting the index tag will change the index column to N automatically. You do not have to modify the database structure yourself to reflect the change of index tags.

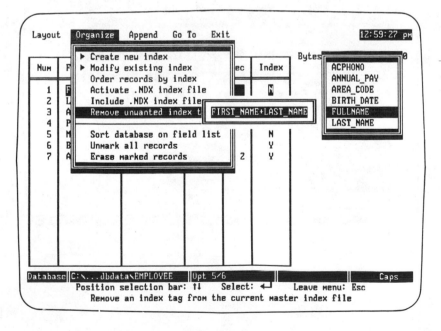

Records ordered
with a multiple-
field index tag.

Fig. 6.18.

```
 Records    Fields    Go To    Exit                      12:48:15 pm
┌──────────────┬──────────┬──────────┬──────────┬────┬──────────┬────────────┐
│ FIRST_NAME   │ LAST_NAME│ AREA_CODE│ PHONE_NO │MALE│BIRTH_DATE│ ANNUAL_PAY │
├──────────────┼──────────┼──────────┼──────────┼────┼──────────┼────────────┤
│ Albert K.    │ Zeller   │ 212      │ 457-9801 │ T  │ 09/20/59 │   30690.00 │
│ Mary W.      │ Thompson │ 213      │ 432-6783 │ F  │ 06/18/55 │   26950.00 │
│ James C.     │ Smith    │ 216      │ 123-4567 │ T  │ 07/04/60 │   24200.00 │
│ Charles N.   │ Duff     │ 216      │ 456-9873 │ T  │ 07/22/64 │   14850.00 │
│ Thomas T.    │ Hanson   │ 216      │ 573-5085 │ T  │ 12/24/45 │   31845.00 │
│ Harry M.     │ Nelson   │ 315      │ 576-0235 │ T  │ 02/15/58 │   31900.00 │
│ Tina B.      │ Baker    │ 415      │ 787-3154 │ F  │ 10/12/56 │   28490.00 │
│ Doris A.     │ Gregory  │ 503      │ 204-8567 │ F  │ 07/04/62 │   18590.00 │
│ Winston E.   │ Lee      │ 503      │ 365-8512 │ T  │ 05/14/39 │   38390.00 │
│ Kirk D.      │ Chapman  │ 618      │ 625-7845 │ T  │ 08/04/61 │   21725.00 │
└──────────────┴──────────┴──────────┴──────────┴────┴──────────┴────────────┘
 Browse   C:\...dbdata\EMPLOYEE    Rec 2/10        File          Caps
                      View and edit fields
```

Fig. 6.19.

Deleting the
FULLNAME
index tag.

```
 Layout   Organize   Append   Go To   Exit              12:59:27 pm
        ┌──────────────────────────────┐       Bytes      ┌─────────────┐
        │ ► Create new index           │                  │ ACPHONO     │
   Num  │ ► Modify existing index      │ec    Index       │ ANNUAL_PAY  │
        │   Order records by index     │                  │ AREA_CODE   │
    1   │   Activate .NDX index file   │       N          │ BIRTH_DATE  │
    2   │   Include .NDX index file    │                  │ FULLNAME    │
    3   │   Remove unwanted index t    │ FIRST_NAME+LAST_NAME │ LAST_NAME │
    4   │                              │                  └─────────────┘
    5   │   Sort database on field list│       N
    6   │   Unmark all records         │       Y
    7   │   Erase marked records       │  2    Y
        └──────────────────────────────┘
 Database  C:\...dbdata\EMPLOYEE    Opt 5/6                    Caps
           Position selection bar: ↑↓   Select: ↵   Leave menu: Esc
           Remove an index tag from the current master index file
```

Modifying an Existing Index Tag

You can also modify any index tag you created earlier by using the **Modify existing index** option from the Organize menu on the database structure screen. This option is a very useful one. As mentioned earlier, the default index order is an ascending order. You cannot specify a descending order when you set up an index tag when the database structure is being created. You can change the index order by using this option, however.

For example, when the ANNUAL_PAY index tag was added as you restructured the EMPLOYEE.DBF, the index order was assumed to be in an ascending order. You can now change it to a descending order by choosing the **Modify existing index** option from the Organize menu. When the options for modifying the index appear, highlight the **Order of index** option and press the space bar. You will see the index order change from ASCENDING to DESCENDING (see fig. 6.20).

Fig. 6.20.

Modifying the ANNUAL_PAY index tag.

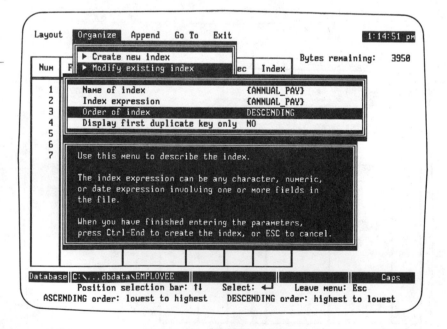

When you press Ctrl-End to process the modification, the
ANNUAL‗PAY index tag is changed as indicated by the following
message

```
INDEX ON ANNUAL‗PAY TAG ANNUAL‗PAY DESCENDING
```

Using Index Tags from the Dot Prompt

Earlier sections explained that index tags can be set up by specifying in
the database structure which fields are to be indexed. You can also
create index tags by issuing the appropriate commands at the dot
prompt. Although you can create individual index (.NDX) files at the dot
prompt, you should avoid using them because index tags in a multiple
index (.MDX) file represent a more efficient way for arranging data
records. (*Note:* The discussion in this section is limited to multiple index
files except where specific reference is made to .NDX files.)

Creating Index Tags

When you arc using dot prompt mode, you can create an index tag for
ordering records in the current database file. The command for creating
an index tag is

```
. INDEX ON < index key> TAG < name of index tag> [DESCENDING]
```

Command:
INDEX ON TAG
*Creates an
index tag.*

The name of the index tag can be a string of up to ten characters in the
form of letters, digits, and the underscore (‗). The index key can be a
single index field or an index expression that consists of multiple index
fields. The default order for the index operation is ascending. You can
add the optional clause, DESCENDING at the end of the INDEX command to
arrange the data records into a descending order. You can use the
command in the following way:

```
. INDEX ON LAST‗NAME TAG LAST‗NAME

. INDEX ON ANNUAL‗PAY TAG ANNUAL‗PAY DESCENDING

. INDEX ON AREA CODE+PHONE‗NO TAG ACPHONO
```

Although you can choose any legitimate name for the index tag, for quick
reference, you may want to name the index tag the same as the index
field when you use a single field as the index key.

Tip:
*Try to name
single-field index
tag as the field
name.*

Creating a Multiple Index File

When you create the first index tag for a database file, unless you specify otherwise, the production multiple index (.MDX) file will be set up automatically for storing the index tag. The name of the multiple index file (such as EMPLOYEE.MDX) will be set to that of the database file (EMPLOYEE.DBF). Any index tag created later will be added to the production multiple index file by default.

The total number of index tags that you can store in a multiple index (.MDX) file is 47. For most applications, you should be able to use the production multiple index file to save all the index tags needed for organizing your records. If you need more than 47 index tags for the database file, you can set up additional multiple index files. To do that, you specify the name of the multiple index file in the INDEX command, such as

. INDEX ON < *index key*> TAG < *name of index tag*>
   [OF *name of multiple index file*>] [DESCENDING]

For example,

. INDEX ON FIRST_NAME+LAST_NAME TAG FULLNAME OF MDXFILE1

The name of the multiple index file (MDXFILE1.MDX) is specified after the index tag (FULLNAME) following the key word "OF". When processing the command, dBASE IV checks to see whether a multiple index file with that name exits. If so, the index tag will be added to that file; otherwise, a new multiple index file of that name will be created to save the index tag.

Using Index Tags

Any index tag saved in the multiple index file is updated automatically when the contents of the data records in the database file are modified. These index tags remain in the background until they are called out for controlling the indexing operation. For example, the AREA_CODE, LAST_NAME, and ANNUAL_PAY index tags saved in the EMPLOYEE.MDX production multiple index file will not be used to arrange the data records in the EMPLOYEE.DBF unless you designate one of them to be the controlling index.

The command for designating an index tag as the controlling index is SET ORDER, used in the form

. SET ORDER TO < *name of the index tag*>

For example, if you would like to arrange the data records in the EMPLOYEE.DBF by the values in the AREA_ CODE fields by selecting the AREA_ CODE index tag as the controlling index, issue the following commands:

. USE EMPLOYEE
. SET ORDER TO AREA_CODE

In return, the following message appears, indicating the current controlling index:

Master Index: AREA_CODE

If you would like to change the controlling index, use the SET ORDER command to designate a different index tag as the new controlling index.

You can return to the natural order in which the records appeared originally either by issuing the SET ORDER TO command without specifying an index file, such as

. SET ORDER TO

or by reissuing the USE command, as in

. USE EMPLOYEE

Every time you issue the USE command for an existing database file, all the records are arranged in their natural order.

Adding Multiple Index Files to the Work Area

In most cases, you will be using the index tags stored in the production multiple index file. The index tags in the production multiple index file are always put in the work area whenever the database file is selected with the USE command. If you have created additional multiple index files, you can add them to the work area by using the SET INDEX TO command, as in

. SET INDEX TO < *name of .MDX file*>

Command:
SET ORDER TO
Selects the controlling index tag.

Tip:
Issue the USE *command to put records back to natural order.*

Command:
SET INDEX TO
Selects an .MDX file.

For example,

```
. SET INDEX TO MDXFILE1
```

This command puts the MDXFILE1.MDX multiple index file created earlier (containing index tag named FULLNAME) to the work area for future use. As a result, you can now designate any index tag in the MDXFILE1.MDX as the controlling index.

It is important to note that the multiple index file specified in the SET INDEX command does not replace the production multiple index file. Instead, it is added to the work area so that any one of the index tags in both multiple index files can be designated as a controlling index (see fig. 6.21).

Fig. 6.21.

Adding MDXFILE1.MDX to the work area.

```
. USE EMPLOYEE
. SET INDEX TO MDXFILE1
Database is in natural order
. SET ORDER TO FULLNAME
Master index: FULLNAME
. LIST
Record#  FIRST_NAME  LAST_NAME  AREA_CODE  PHONE_NO  MALE  BIRTH_DATE  ANNUAL_PAY
      2  Albert K.   Zeller     212        457-9801  .T.   09/20/59      30690.00
      8  Charles N.  Duff       216        456-9873  .T.   07/22/64      14850.00
      3  Doris A.    Gregory    503        204-8567  .F.   07/04/62      18590.00
      4  Harry M.    Nelson     315        576-0235  .T.   02/15/58      31900.00
      1  James C.    Smith      216        123-4567  .T.   07/04/60      24200.00
      6  Kirk D.     Chapman    618        625-7845  .T.   08/04/61      21725.00
      7  Mary W.     Thompson   213        432-6783  .F.   06/18/55      26950.00
     10  Thomas T.   Hanson     216        573-5085  .T.   12/24/45      31845.00
      5  Tina B.     Baker      415        787-3154  .F.   10/12/56      28490.00
      9  Winston E.  Lee        503        365-8512  .T.   05/14/39      38390.00

. SET ORDER TO AREA_CODE
Master index: AREA_CODE
.
Command  C:\...dbdata\EMPLOYEE    Rec EOF/10      File            NumCaps
```

```
. USE EMPLOYEE
. SET INDEX TO MDXFILE1
. SET ORDER TO FULLNAME
. SET ORDER TO AREA_CODE
```

From figure 6.21, you will note that the AREA_ CODE index tag in the production multiple index file (EMPLOYEE.MDX) is ever present in the work area, even after you add the MDXFILE1.MDX to the work area.

Listing Multiple Index Files

All existing multiple index files created for all the database files can be listed by using the DIR command with the asterisk as a wild card (see fig. 6.22):

        DIR *.MDX

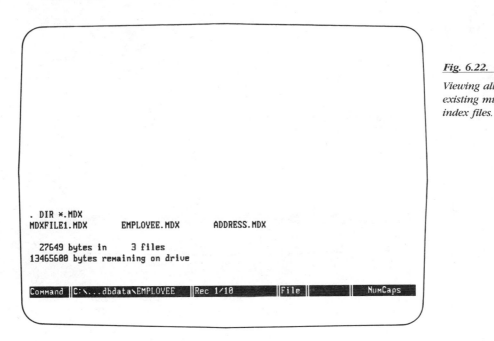

```
. DIR *.MDX
MDXFILE1.MDX        EMPLOYEE.MDX        ADDRESS.MDX

  27649 bytes in      3 files
13465600 bytes remaining on drive


Command ||C:\...dbdata\EMPLOYEE  ||Rec 1/10      ||File ||      ||    NumCaps ||
```

Fig. 6.22.

Viewing all the existing multiple index files.

However, from the list of multiple index files produced by the DIR command, you may not be able to identify which one belongs to a specific database file. For example, you do not know which multiple index file belongs to the EMPLOYEE.DBF database file.

If you would like to find the multiple index files for a particular database file, you could use the MDX( ) function, as in

    . ?MDX(< .*MDX file number* >)

Function:
?MDX(n)
Shows nth .MDX file.

MDX( ) is a dBASE IV function. The expression in parentheses is called an *argument*. In this case, the expression should be a number that corresponding the multiple index file number. The question mark is the keyword or symbol for displaying the value of the MDX( ) function.

For example, to find out the name of the multiple index files that belong to EMPLOYEE.DBF, you can issue the commands ?MDX(1) and ?MDX(2) (see fig. 6.23).

Fig. 6.23.

Viewing a multiple index file.

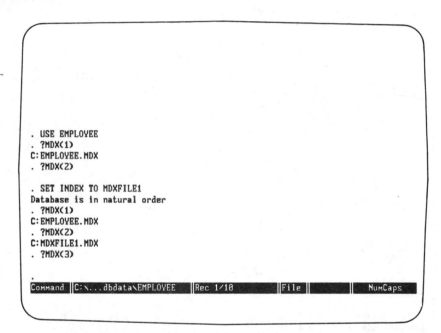

```
. USE EMPLOYEE
. ?MDX(1)
C:EMPLOYEE.MDX
. ?MDX(2)

. SET INDEX TO MDXFILE1
Database is in natural order
. ?MDX(1)
C:EMPLOYEE.MDX
. ?MDX(2)
C:MDXFILE1.MDX
. ?MDX(3)

.
Command ||C:\...dbdata\EMPLOYEE  ||Rec 1/10      ||File ||       ||   NumCaps
```

The figure shows that the name of the first multiple index file (the production file, EMPLOYEE.MDX) is displayed after the ?MDX(1) command is executed. Similarly, the value of MDX(2) is MDXFILE1.MD, indicating the second multiple index file that belongs to EMPLOYEE.DBF.

Viewing Index Tags

Function:
?TAG(n) *Shows nth index tag.*

Similar to showing names of all the multiple index files in the work area, you can also view all the index tags by using the TAG( ) function, such as

. ?TAG(< *the index tag number* >)

One way to view the names of the first index tag in the work area is to issue the ?TAG(1) command. You can also examine other index tags in the same manner (see fig. 6.24).

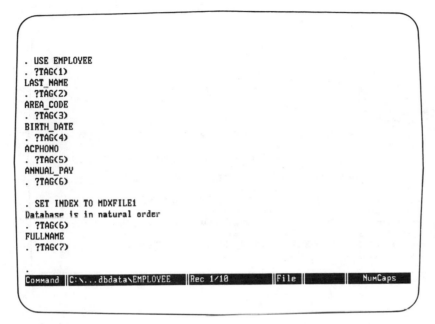

```
. USE EMPLOYEE
. ?TAG(1)
LAST_NAME
. ?TAG(2)
AREA_CODE
. ?TAG(3)
BIRTH_DATE
. ?TAG(4)
ACPHONO
. ?TAG(5)
ANNUAL_PAY
. ?TAG(6)

. SET INDEX TO MDXFILE1
Database is in natural order
. ?TAG(6)
FULLNAME
. ?TAG(7)
```

| Command | C:\...dbdata\EMPLOYEE | Rec 1/10 | File | | NumCaps |

Fig. 6.24.

Viewing an index tag.

Another way to view all the index tags in the work area is to use the REINDEX command (see fig. 6.25).

In figure 6.25, you will notice that all the current index tags in the work area will be rebuilt with the REINDEX operations.

The REINDEX command is used for rebuilding the index tags and index files. Because dBASE IV automatically rebuilds the index tags in the multiple index files when the contents of the data records are modified, it is not necessary to reindex the tags yourself. However, by issuing the REINDEX command, you will be able to see all the index tags in the work area.

Tip:
Use REINDEX to view all index tags in work area.

Deleting an Existing Tag

The command for deleting an unwanted index tag is

. DELETE TAG < *name of index tag*>

The index tag to be deleted must be one of the index tags in the production multiple index file. Otherwise, if the index tag belongs to

Command:
DELETE TAG
Removes an index tag from an .MDX file.

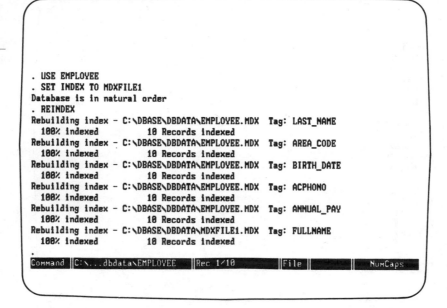

Fig. 6.25.

Using REINDEX *to view existing index tags.*

```
. USE EMPLOYEE
. SET INDEX TO MDXFILE1
Database is in natural order
. REINDEX
Rebuilding index - C:\DBASE\DBDATA\EMPLOYEE.MDX  Tag: LAST_NAME
  100% indexed            10 Records indexed
Rebuilding index - C:\DBASE\DBDATA\EMPLOYEE.MDX  Tag: AREA_CODE
  100% indexed            10 Records indexed
Rebuilding index - C:\DBASE\DBDATA\EMPLOYEE.MDX  Tag: BIRTH_DATE
  100% indexed            10 Records indexed
Rebuilding index - C:\DBASE\DBDATA\EMPLOYEE.MDX  Tag: ACPHONO
  100% indexed            10 Records indexed
Rebuilding index - C:\DBASE\DBDATA\EMPLOYEE.MDX  Tag: ANNUAL_PAY
  100% indexed            10 Records indexed
Rebuilding index - C:\DBASE\DBDATA\MDXFILE1.MDX  Tag: FULLNAME
  100% indexed            10 Records indexed
.
Command  C:\...dbdata\EMPLOYEE      Rec 1/10            File            NumCaps
```

another multiple index file, you have to put that index file into the
working area with the SET INDEX command before deleting the tag, as in

```
. USE EMPLOYEE
. SET INDEX TO MDSFILE1
. DELETE TAG FULLNAME
```

Deleting an Existing Multiple Index File

A multiple index file can be removed permanently from the disk by
issuing the ERASE command at the dot prompt, such as

```
. ERASE MDXFILE1.MDX
```

If the multiple index file is being used or is open, you need to close the
file before you can erase it. To close all index files, use the CLOSE INDEX
command.

Caution:

Do not delete the production multiple index file.

You must not delete the production multiple index file. If you delete the
production multiple index file, you will not be able to open the database
file.

Modifying an Index Tag

If you need to modify an index tag—for example, to change the index tag from ascending to descending order—you need to use the menu option from the Control Center. There is no dot prompt command for modifying an index tag quickly. However, you might want to delete the index tag first and then re-create it. Because creating an index tag is a relatively easy task, re-creating the tag may be quicker than making the necessary modifications from the Control Center.

Searching for Data in an Indexed Database File

With an indexed database, you can search quickly for records whose contents are the same as those of the index key field. For example, if the EMPLOYEE.DBF file is indexed on the AREA_CODE field, all the records with the same area code are arranged consecutively in one block. The record you are searching for will be found and be made the current record if its index field has a unique value. If the values in the index fields of several records match the search value, the record pointer will be placed at the first of these records.

Searching for Data from the Control Center

To find a specific record by the value of its index key field, use the Seek operator in the indexed field in the file skeleton of a query design. Before you can begin the SEEK operation, you must index the database file with the appropriate index tag.

Tip:
Use the SEEK *operator in a query to find indexed records.*

For example, if you want to find James C. Smith's record you must first index the EMPLOYEE.DBF file by using the LAST_NAME index tag. Here are the necessary steps:

1. Bring up the database structure screen (Shift-F2) while the database file is being highlighted.

2. Select the **Order records by index** option from the Organize menu and then select the LAST_NAME index tag as the controlling index.

After the database file has been indexed by the LAST_NAME key field, you can use a query design for finding the specific record. To bring up a query design screen, press Shift-F2.

As a query design appears, enter in the indexed field the SEEK operator and the field value you are searching for. Use a comma to separate the operator and the field value (see fig. 6.26).

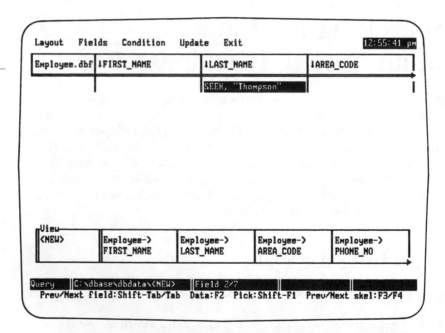

The results from processing the query are shown in figure 6.27. In the figure, you can see that the record with Thompson in the indexed field (LAST_NAME) is found and displayed in the view.

When you search the records in an indexed file, the values of the index field's records are compared with the value specified in the search expression. In other words, the indexed records are searched until a record is found that has in the index key field (LAST_NAME) a value matching the value of the search field value. The record found becomes

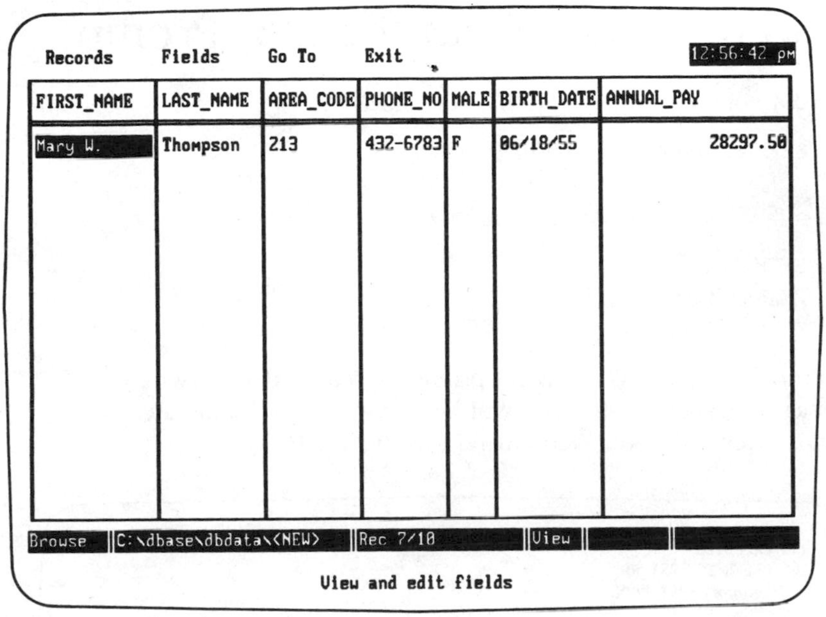

Fig. 6.27.

Record found by the SEEK *operation.*

the current record and its record number is displayed in the status bar (for example, Rec 7/1Ø for Thompson). If more than one record is found, all the records will be displayed in the view as well.

You can specify a character string, a numeric value, or a date as the search field value. When you use a character string (such as "Smith") as the search expression, the string must be enclosed in quotation marks. A record will be selected if the first part of the character string in the record's index field matches the first part of the character string in the search field value. The match need not be exact. If you specify "Sm" as the search expression, for example, records whose values in the LAST_NAME field begin with "Sm" (Smith, Smyth, Smithers, etc.) will be considered as a match.

If you use a date for the search value, you must enclose the date in a pair of curly brackets {}. For example, if you have indexed the database file by the values in the BIRTH_DATE field and you want to find the record whose value in the key field is 07/04/62, you enter {Ø7/Ø4/62} as the search field value.

When you use a numeric value or a date as a search field value, there must be an exact match between the expression and the field value for a record to be selected.

Searching Data from the Dot Prompt

Command:
SEEK
Finds indexed records.

The dot command for the SEEK operation is

. SEEK < *search field value*>

You might use, for example,

. SEEK "Smith"
. SEEK 25900
. SEEK {07/04/62}

When the record is found, a dot prompt is returned; otherwise, a message Find not successful will be displayed. To display the record found, enter the DISPLAY command (see fig. 6.28).

Fig. 6.28.

Designating a controlling index tag.

```
. USE EMPLOYEE
. SET ORDER TO LAST_NAME
Master index: LAST_NAME
. SEEK "Smith"
. DISPLAY
Record# FIRST_NAME   LAST_NAME  AREA_CODE PHONE_NO MALE BIRTH_DATE ANNUAL_PAY
      1 James C.      Smith      216       123-4567 .T.  07/04/60    24200.00
. SET ORDER TO ANNUAL_PAY
Master index: ANNUAL_PAY
. SEEK 25900
Find not successful
. SEEK 31900
. DISPLAY
Record# FIRST_NAME   LAST_NAME  AREA_CODE PHONE_NO MALE BIRTH_DATE ANNUAL_PAY
      4 Harry M.      Nelson     315       576-0235 .T.  02/15/58    31900.00
. SET ORDER TO BIRTH_DATE
Master index: BIRTH_DATE
. SEEK {07/04/62}
. DISPLAY
Record# FIRST_NAME   LAST_NAME  AREA_CODE PHONE_NO MALE BIRTH_DATE ANNUAL_PAY
      3 Doris A.      Gregory    503       204-8567 .F.  07/04/62    18590.00
Command ||C:\...dbdata\EMPLOYEE  ||Rec 3/10     ||File ||        Caps
```

Caution:
Index the records before using SEEK.

From figure 6.28, you will note that before you issue the SEEK command, the database file needs to be indexed with one of the index tags by using the SET ORDER command. Note that you need to enclose the character string in quotation marks (for example, "Smith") and the date value in curly brackets (for example, {07/04/62}) for the search field value. But, a numeric search field value should appear without any quotation marks or brackets.

Additionally, in dot prompt mode, you can use the FIND command with a character search string to search the data records in an indexed file. With FIND, the character string need not be enclosed in quotes, although it may be. The syntax of the FIND command is

. FIND < *character string*>

The FIND command searches the indexed database file for the first record with a character string that matches the contents of the key field. When a record with the specified string is found, the record pointer is set to that record. The FIND command and the SEEK command work the same way; the former, however, can be used only with character fields, whereas the latter can be used for character, numeric, and date fields.

▷ **Tip:**
Enclose date values in curly brackets; no brackets or quotation marks are necessary for numeric values.

▷ **Command:**
FIND
Finds indexed character string.

Counting and Summarizing Data Records

Summarizing data is one of dBASE IV's most important functions. For example, you may need to count the number of employees listed in EMPLOYEE.DBF whose annual salaries fall within a certain range. Or perhaps you need to find the highest, lowest, total, or average annual salary for all male employees. The dBASE IV COUNT, MAX, MIN, SUM AVERAGE, and TOTAL summary operations can help you accomplish those tasks either from within the Control Center or at the dot prompt.

Summarizing Data from the Control Center

When you are using the Control Center, you can perform some summary operations by using a query design. In the query, you can specify one of the COUNT, MAX, MIN, SUM, and AVERAGE operators in a query field in the file skeleton. In the view skeleton, you can display the query field with an alternative field label describing the summary statistics.

Counting Records

You can tally the records in a database file with a COUNT operation. For counting the records in a database file, you can use any one of the data fields in the file for the counting operation.

For example, you can count the total number of records in the EMPLOYEE.DBF by choosing the LAST_NAME field to enter the COUNT operator (see fig. 6.29).

Fig. 6.29.

Using the COUNT *operator for counting records.*

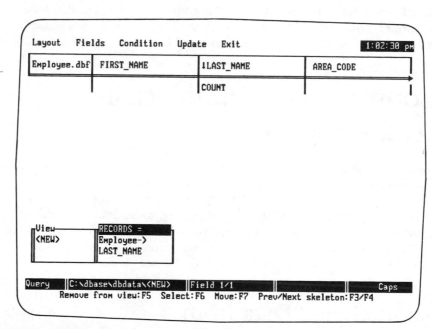

The query design in figure 6.29 was produced with the following steps:

1. Bring up a new query design by selecting < **create**> from the Queries panel.

2. Clear all the fields in the view skeleton (press F5 while the cursor is under the name of the file skeleton).

3. Enter the COUNT operator in the LAST_NAME field.

4. Press F5 to show the LAST_NAME query field in the view skeleton.

5. Move the cursor to the LAST_NAME field in the view skeleton by pressing F4 and assign an alternate field name such as "RECORDS =" (do not leave out the equal sign).

The result of the query displays the total record count in the view screen, using the alternate field name (see fig. 6.30).

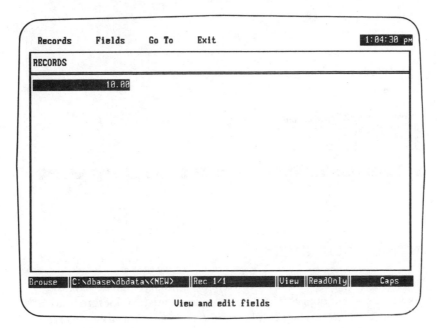

```
  Records    Fields    Go To    Exit                    1:04:30 PM

  RECORDS

              10.00
```
```
  Browse   C:\dbase\dbdata\<NEW>    Rec 1/1       View  ReadOnly     Caps
                         View and edit fields
```

Fig. 6.30.

Showing record count in the query view.

You can add filter conditions to the query field for counting selective records (see fig. 6.31).

In figure 6.31, you notice that filter conditions are specified in the logical MALE field (.T.) and the BIRTH_DATE date field (< ={12/31/59}). As a result, only those records that meet the filter conditions will be subject to the counting operation.

Of course, if you have more restrictive filter conditions, you can specify them in the condition box and then enter the COUNT operator in any of the data fields.

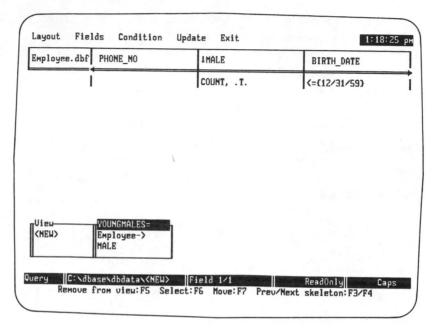

Fig. 6.31.

Counting selective records with filter conditions.

Summary Statistics

A query design can also be used to display summary statistics for the values in a numeric query field. The summary statistics operators are SUM, AVERAGE, MAX, and MIN. They can be used to produce the total, average, maximum, and minimum value in the query field. You can use one of these operators in a query field in the file skeleton with or without other filter conditions.

For example, if you would like to know the total salary paid to the employees you could enter the SUM operator in the ANNUAL_PAY query field in the query design (see fig. 6.32).

When the query is processed, the total value for the ANNUAL_PAY field will be displayed in the view (see fig. 6.33).

The AVERAGE operator can be used to calculate the average for a numeric fields with or without filter conditions. For example, figure 6.34 shows the query design that will produce the average pay for the male employees by using the AVERAGE operator in the ANNUAL_PAY field and a filter condition (.T.) in the logical MALE field.

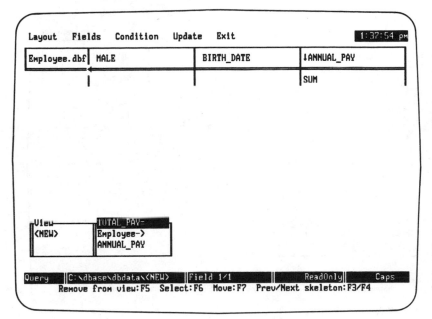

Fig. 6.32.

Summing up values in ANNUAL_PAY field.

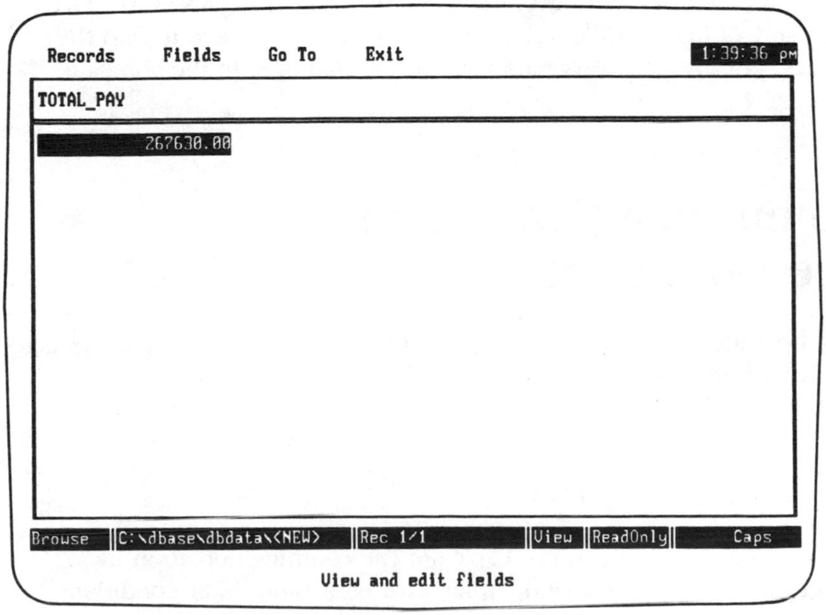

Fig. 6.33.

Showing total value in ANNUAL_PAY in the query view.

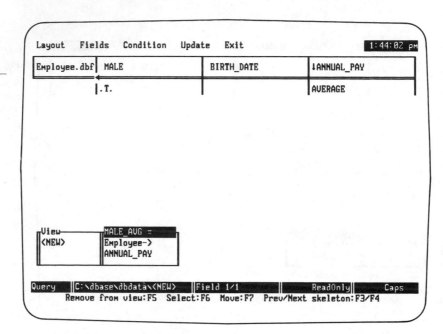

Fig. 6.34.

Computing AVERAGE *value of selective records.*

Similarly, you can use the MAX (or MIN) operator in the ANNUAL_PAY field and a filter condition (.F.) in the MALE logical field to find the highest (or lowest) salary paid to a female employee in the company (see fig. 6.35).

Summarizing Data from the Dot Prompt

The operations of counting records and providing summary statistics can easily be performed from the dot prompt with the appropriate commands.

Counting Records

Command:
COUNT
Counts records.

In dot prompt mode, you can carry out the counting operation by entering the COUNT command, either with or without filter conditions:

. COUNT [FOR < *filter conditions*>]

Figure 6.36 shows several examples of using the COUNT command.

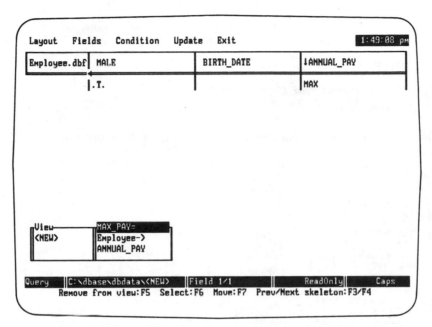

Fig. 6.35.

Finding maximum value in selective records.

Fig. 6.36.

Examples of COUNT *commands at the dot prompt.*

Summing Numeric Values

Command:

SUM
Sums numeric values.

You can perform the summing operation in dot prompt mode by entering a SUM command in one of the following formats:

. SUM [FOR < *filter conditions*>]

. SUM < *numeric field 1*>, < *numeric field 2*>, . . .
[filter conditions]

Figure 6.37 shows different examples of using the SUM command.

Fig. 6.37.

Examples of SUM *commands at the dot prompt.*

```
. USE EMPLOYEE
. SUM
      10 records summed
ANNUAL_PAY
    267630
. SUM ANNUAL_PAY FOR MALE
       7 records summed
ANNUAL_PAY
    193600
. SUM ANNUAL_PAY FOR MALE .AND. BIRTH_DATE<={12/31/59}
       4 records summed
ANNUAL_PAY
    132825
. SUM ANNUAL_PAY FOR AREA_CODE="503" .OR. AREA_CODE="216"
       5 records summed
ANNUAL_PAY
    127875
.
```

| Command | C:\...dbdata\EMPLOYEE | Rec EOF/10 | File | | | CapsIns |

From figure 6.34, you will note that if you issue the SUM without specifying any field, each of the numeric fields in the database file will the summed. If you have more than one numeric field in the database file, you can specify the fields to be summed in the command. Filter conditions can be added to the SUM command for summing the values in selective records.

Computing Averages

You can perform the averaging operation in dot prompt mode by
entering the AVERAGE command in one of the following formats:

. AVERAGE [FOR < *filter conditions*>]

. AVERAGE < *field 1*>, < *field 2*>, ...
[FOR < *filter conditions*>]

Figure 6.38 shows examples of using the AVERAGE command. Like SUM,
AVERAGE can be used to calculate the average values in all the numeric
fields in the database file. You can specify the numeric fields whose
values to be averaged. If not, all the numeric fields will be summarized.
Filter conditions can be added to the command for selecting those
records for the average operation.

Command:
AVERAGE
*Computes
numeric
averages.*

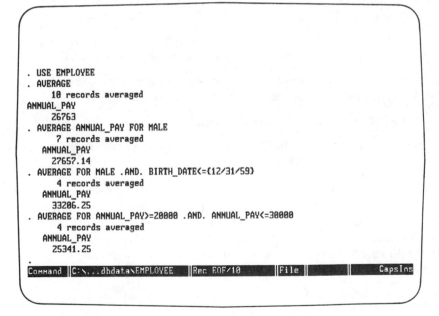

```
. USE EMPLOYEE
. AVERAGE
      18 records averaged
ANNUAL_PAY
      26763
. AVERAGE ANNUAL_PAY FOR MALE
       7 records averaged
   ANNUAL_PAY
      27657.14
. AVERAGE FOR MALE .AND. BIRTH_DATE<={12/31/59}
       4 records averaged
   ANNUAL_PAY
      33206.25
. AVERAGE FOR ANNUAL_PAY>=20000 .AND. ANNUAL_PAY<=30000
       4 records averaged
   ANNUAL_PAY
      25341.25
.
Command  C:\...dbdata\EMPLOYEE    Rec EOF/10     File             CapsIns
```

Fig. 6.38.

Examples of
AVERAGE
*commands at the
dot prompt.*

Saving Totals to a File

Records whose key fields contain the same data can be processed in
groups. Values stored in the numeric fields in those groups can be

totaled and saved as summary statistics in another database file. Because this operation is not available from the query design, you use a dot prompt command to total field values and save the totals to a file.

Before you can enter the TOTAL command, you must use a sorting or indexing command to arrange the records of the database file in ascending or descending order. The records must be sorted or indexed on the key field you will use with the TOTAL command.

Command:
TOTAL
Saves totals to a database file.

The format of the TOTAL command is

. TOTAL ON < *key field*> TO < *name of summary file*> [FOR < *filter conditions*>]

The TOTAL command sums the active database file's numeric fields and saves the results to the summary file. All the numeric fields in the database file are totaled unless you specify otherwise. The summary file's numeric fields contain totals for all the records whose key fields contain the same data. The structure of the summary file is copied from that of the database file.

If a field in the summary file is not large enough for the total, an error message is displayed and asterisks (*) are placed in the data field.

For example, you can use the TOTAL command to group the values in the ANNUAL_PAY field by area code and calculate their totals:

. TOTAL ON AREA_CODE TO TOTALS

However, before you issue the TOTAL command, the records in the database file must be indexed or sorted first (see fig. 6.39).

The index tag AREA_CODE is designated here as the controlling or master index for arranging the records by their area codes before the total operation. The results of the TOTAL command are saved in the TOTALS.DBF file having the same database structure as the EMPLOYEE.DBF, except its values in the ANNUAL_PAY field will contain the group totals.

You can also add filter conditions in the TOTAL command for computing group totals from selective records, such as

. TOTAL ON AREA_CODE TO TOTALS FOR AREA_CODE="503" .OR. AREA_CODE="216"

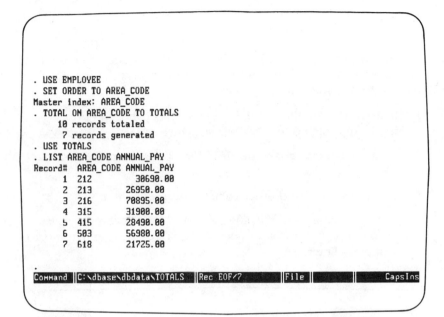

Fig. 6.39.

Saving totals to the TOTALS.DBF database file.

```
. USE EMPLOYEE
. SET ORDER TO AREA_CODE
Master index: AREA_CODE
. TOTAL ON AREA_CODE TO TOTALS
      10 records totaled
       7 records generated
. USE TOTALS
. LIST AREA_CODE ANNUAL_PAY
Record#   AREA_CODE ANNUAL_PAY
      1   212          30690.00
      2   213          26950.00
      3   216          70895.00
      4   315          31900.00
      5   415          28490.00
      6   503          56980.00
      7   618          21725.00


Command  C:\dbase\dbdata\TOTALS    Rec EOF/7      File              CapsIns
```

Chapter 6 QuickStart

In this chapter, you learned the procedures for organizing your data records by using the methods of sort and index. You also saw in this chapter how to generate summary statistics by using the COUNT, SUM, AVERAGE, MAX, and MIN operations. Let's now practice these procedures and operations with the ADDRESS.DBF created earlier in the QIKSTART.CAT for the QuickStart exercises.

First, change the current file catalog to QIKSTART.CAT from within the Control Center by using these options:

Catalog (Alt-C)**Use a different catalog**\\QIKSTART

Sorting Records

To sort the records in ADDRESS.DBF into descending order according to the values in the ZIP field and save the sorted records to a new database file named BYZIP.DBF, follow these steps:

1. Highlight the ADDRESS.DBF file in the Data panel and press Shift-F2 to bring up the database structure screen.

2. Select the **Sort database on field list** option from the Organize (Alt-O).

3. Enter ZIP to the Field order column and press Enter.

4. When the cursor is in the Type of Sort column, press the space bar to select the sort order (descending) as shown in figure 6.40. Then press Enter.

Fig. 6.40.

Sorting records by ZIP codes.

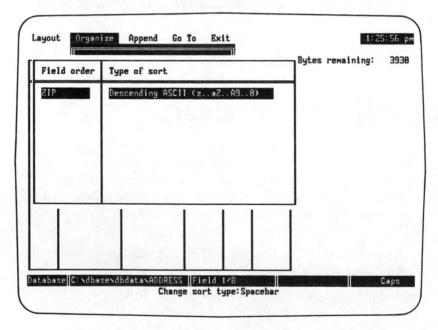

5. Press Ctrl-End to save the sorted records to BYZIP.DBF.

6. Return to the Control Center by selecting the **Save changes and exit** option from the Exit menu (Alt-E).

Viewing the Sorted Records

To view the sorted records in the BYZIP.DBF file, follow these steps:

1. When the ADDRESS.DBF file is highlighted in the Data panel, highlight the BYZIP.DBF.

2. Press F2 to display the sorted records. Use F2 to toggle between edit and browse formats (see fig. 6.41).

Records	Fields	Go To	Exit				1:39:06 PM

LAST_NAME	FIRST_NAME	ADDRESS	CITY	STATE	ZIP	MALE	BIR
Harvey	Jane W.	9709 Broadway	Vancouver	WA	98665	F	08/
Bush	Alfred G.	13456 N. 95th Street	Seattle	WA	98185	T	08/
Johnson	Robert J.	3245 Oak Street	Portland	OR	97203	T	06/
Morgan	Albert C.	1354 S. 78th Avenue	Portland	OR	97202	T	05/
Watson	James L.	3891 S.W. Powell St.	Portland	OR	97201	T	09/
Ball	Thomas	9440 Rockcreek Road	Beaverton	OR	97201	T	12/
Morrow	Peter T.	2046 Skyline Drive	Fremont	CA	94538	T	04/
Peters	Cathy K.	3467 First Avenue	Los Angles	CA	94321	F	03/
Swanson	Linda K.	1345 Bayview Drive	San Meteo	CA	94105	F	10/
Peterson	Janet	3098 Oceanview Road	San Diego	CA	92121	F	11/
King	Steven W.	2771 Plaza Drive	Pittsburgh	PA	15230	T	01/
Taylor	George F.	123 Main Street	New York	NY	10021	T	05/

Browse	C:\dbase\dbdata\BYZIP	Rec 1/12	File		Caps

View and edit fields

Fig. 6.41.

Records sorted by ZIP codes.

Using a Query for Sorting Selective Records

Let's create a new database file named CALIF.DBF for saving the records of ADDRESS.DBF that belong to residents of the state of California and that are sorted by ZIP code. To do that, specify the filter condition "CA" in the STATE query field and the sort order "Asc" in the ZIP field.

Also, you need to select the data fields (LAST_NAME, FIRST_NAME, ADDRESS, CITY, STATE, and ZIP) to be included in the view skeleton (see fig. 6.42).

Fig. 6.42.

Sorting California records by ZIP codes.

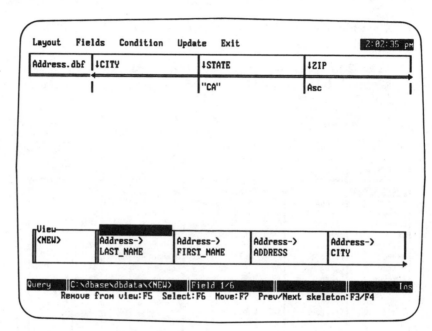

1. Highlight ADDRESS.DBF from the Data panel and press Enter.

2. Select the **Use file** option.

3. Select < **create**> from the Queries panel and press Enter.

4. When the query design form appears, enter "CA" to the STATE field and Asc to the ZIP field.

5. Remove the unwanted fields (MALE and BIRTH_DATE) from the View skeleton.

6. Invoke the Layout menu (Alt-L) and select the **Write view as database file** option and name the file CALIF.

7. To view the sorted records, press F2 (see fig. 6.43).

8. Return to the Control Center by choosing the **Exit** option from the Exit menu.

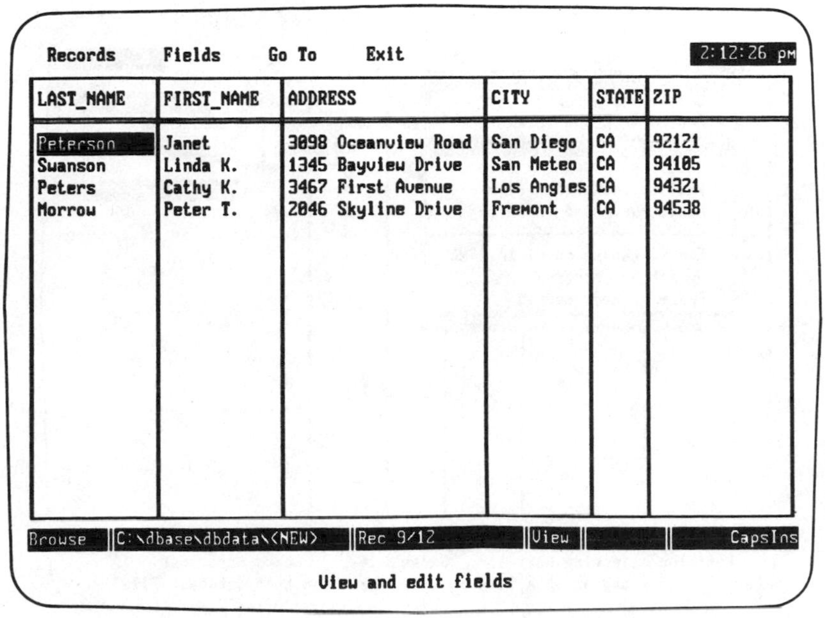

```
   Records    Fields    Go To    Exit                    2:12:26 pm

  LAST_NAME   FIRST_NAME  ADDRESS               CITY        STATE ZIP

  Peterson    Janet       3898 Oceanview Road   San Diego   CA    92121
  Swanson     Linda K.    1345 Bayview Drive    San Meteo   CA    94185
  Peters      Cathy K.    3467 First Avenue     Los Angles  CA    94321
  Morrow      Peter T.    2046 Skyline Drive    Fremont     CA    94538













  Browse   C:\dbase\dbdata\<NEW>      Rec 9/12        View              CapsIns
                          View and edit fields
```

Fig. 6.43.

California records sorted by ZIP codes.

Indexing Records

When you created the ADDRESS.DBF file, you created the index tags in the database structure by specifying Y in the Index column for the LAST_NAME, STATE, and ZIP fields. Now, practice using the STATE index tags for arranging the records in the database file by following these steps:

1. Highlight the ADDRESS.DBF in the Data panel and press Shift-F2 to bring up the database structure.

2. Select the **Order records by index** option and choose the STATE index tag (see fig. 6.44). Press Enter.

3. Press F2 to view the records that were ordered by state (see fig. 6.45).

4. Now, invoke the Exit menu (Alt-E) and select the **Return to Database Design** option.

Fig. 6.44.

*Index records
with STATE index
tag.*

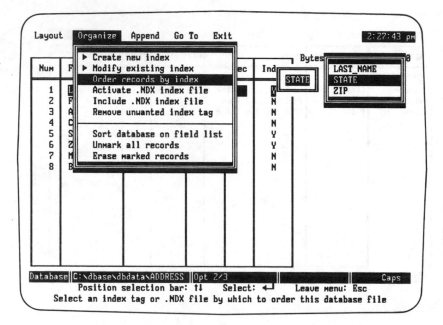

Fig. 6.45.

*Records ordered
with the STATE
index tag.*

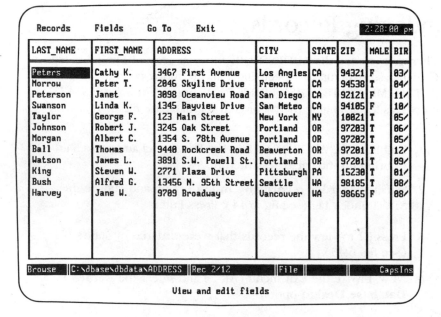

Modifying an Existing Index Tag

From figure 6.45, you will note that the state values are arranged in ascending order (the default order). You can change it to a descending order by modifying the STATE index tag:

1. On the database structure screen, select the **Modify existing index** option from the Organize menu.

2. Choose STATE index tag for modifications.

3. Move the cursor to the **Order of index** option and press the space bar to select DESCENDING order (see fig. 6.46).

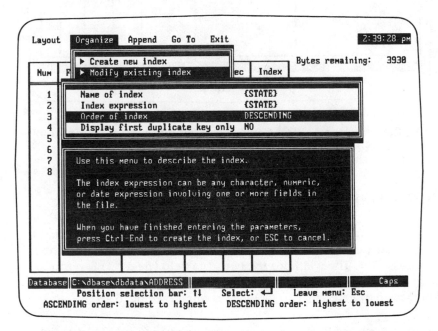

Fig. 6.46.

Modifying the STATE index tag.

4. Press Ctrl-End to save the changes.

5. Use the modified STATE index tag to arrange the records.

6. Invoke the Organize menu (Alt-O), select the **Order records by index** option, and choose the STATE index tag. Then press Enter.

7. Press F2 to view the records that have been ordered by state (see fig. 6.47).

Fig. 6.47.

Records ordered with the modified STATE index tag.

Records	Fields	Go To	Exit					2:45:09 pm

LAST_NAME	FIRST_NAME	ADDRESS	CITY	STATE	ZIP	MALE	BIR
Harvey	Jane W.	9709 Broadway	Vancouver	WA	98665	F	08/
Bush	Alfred G.	13456 N. 95th Street	Seattle	WA	98185	T	08/
King	Steven W.	2771 Plaza Drive	Pittsburgh	PA	15230	T	01/
Watson	James L.	3891 S.W. Powell St.	Portland	OR	97201	T	09/
Ball	Thomas	9440 Rockcreek Road	Beaverton	OR	97201	T	12/
Morgan	Albert C.	1354 S. 78th Avenue	Portland	OR	97202	T	05/
Johnson	Robert J.	3245 Oak Street	Portland	OR	97203	T	06/
Taylor	George F.	123 Main Street	New York	NY	10021	T	05/
Swanson	Linda K.	1345 Bayview Drive	San Mateo	CA	94105	F	10/
Peterson	Janet	3098 Oceanview Road	San Diego	CA	92121	F	11/
Morrow	Peter T.	2046 Skyline Drive	Fremont	CA	94538	T	04/
Peters	Cathy K.	3467 First Avenue	Los Angles	CA	94321	F	03/

Browse	C:\dbase\dbdata\ADDRESS	Rec 6/12		File			CapsIns

View and edit fields

8. Return to the Control Center by choosing the **Exit** option from the Exit menu.

Summarizing Records

Before you practice the procedures for producing summary statistics, let's add a numeric field named WEALTH to the database structure of the ADDRESS.DBF. The width for the new data field (field #9) is set to 6 with 0 decimal places (integer). An index tag for the new data field is also set up by entering Y to its Index column (see fig. 6.48).

As an example, you can enter a set of values to the WEALTH data field (see fig. 6.49).

If you don't remember how to enter these values added to the new data field as shown in figure 6.49, following these steps:

1. Put the records back in natural order (after the last indexing operation), close the ADDRESS.DBF file by selecting the **Close file** option after pressing ENTER while the file is being highlighted in the Data panel.

```
  Layout   Organize   Append   Go To   Exit                    3:17:27 pm

                                            Bytes remaining:    3924
  ┌─────┬─────────────┬─────────────┬───────┬──────┬────────┐
  │ Num │ Field Name  │ Field Type  │ Width │ Dec  │ Index  │
  ├─────┼─────────────┼─────────────┼───────┼──────┼────────┤
  │  1  │ LAST_NAME   │ Character   │  12   │      │   Y    │
  │  2  │ FIRST_NAME  │ Character   │  12   │      │   N    │
  │  3  │ ADDRESS     │ Character   │  20   │      │   N    │
  │  4  │ CITY        │ Character   │  10   │      │   N    │
  │  5  │ STATE       │ Character   │   2   │      │   Y    │
  │  6  │ ZIP         │ Character   │   5   │      │   Y    │
  │  7  │ MALE        │ Logical     │   1   │      │   N    │
  │  8  │ BIRTH_DATE  │ Date        │   8   │      │   N    │
  │  9  │ WEALTH      │ Numeric     │   6   │  0   │   Y    │
  │     │             │             │       │      │        │
  └─────┴─────────────┴─────────────┴───────┴──────┴────────┘

 Database C:\dbase\dbdata\ADDRESS  Field 9/9                     CapsIns
          Enter the field name. Insert/Delete field:Ctrl-N/Ctrl-U
 Field names begin with a letter and may contain letters, digits and underscores
```

Fig. 6.48.

Adding the WEALTH field to the database structure.

```
  Records     Fields    Go To    Exit                      3:20:56 pm
 ┌────────────────────┬───────────┬─────┬─────┬─────┬───────────┬────────┐
 │ ADDRESS            │ CITY      │STATE│ZIP  │MALE │BIRTH_DATE │WEALTH  │
 ├────────────────────┼───────────┼─────┼─────┼─────┼───────────┼────────┤
 │ 123 Main Street    │ New York  │ NY  │10021│ T   │ 05/12/57  │ 185000 │
 │ 3467 First Avenue  │ Los Angles│ CA  │94321│ F   │ 03/08/61  │ 125000 │
 │ 13456 N. 95th Street│ Seattle  │ WA  │98185│ T   │ 08/12/70  │  50000 │
 │ 3245 Oak Street    │ Portland  │ OR  │97203│ T   │ 06/06/53  │ 105000 │
 │ 2046 Skyline Drive │ Fremont   │ CA  │94538│ T   │ 04/30/59  │ 150000 │
 │ 9709 Broadway      │ Vancouver │ WA  │98665│ F   │ 08/10/61  │  75000 │
 │ 2771 Plaza Drive   │ Pittsburgh│ PA  │15230│ T   │ 01/05/63  │  25000 │
 │ 1354 S. 78th Avenue│ Portland  │ OR  │97202│ T   │ 05/13/58  │  90000 │
 │ 3098 Oceanview Road│ San Diego │ CA  │92121│ F   │ 11/13/61  │  82000 │
 │ 9440 Rockcreek Road│ Beaverton │ OR  │97201│ T   │ 12/25/60  │  45000 │
 │ 3891 S.W. Powell St.│ Portland │ OR  │97201│ T   │ 09/26/60  │  39000 │
 │ 1345 Bayview Drive │ San Meteo │ CA  │94105│ F   │ 10/10/60  │  65000 │
 └────────────────────┴───────────┴─────┴─────┴─────┴───────────┴────────┘

 Browse  C:\dbase\dbdata\ADDRESS  Rec 12/12          File          CapsIns
                         View and edit fields
```

Fig. 6.49.

Values entered to the WEALTH data field.

2. Display the records in browse format by pressing F2 after highlighting the ADDRESS.DBF in the Data panel.

3. Press Tab to move the cursor into the WEALTH field.

4. Invoke the Fields menu (Alt-F) and select the **Freeze field** option (for easy data entry).

5. Enter WEALTH as the field to be frozen.

6. Fill in values in the WEALTH field. After entering each value, press Enter or ↓.

7. Press Ctrl-End to save the values and return to the Control Center.

Now you can use the numeric field in the exercises. First, count the records in the ADDRESS.DBF file that belong to males by following these steps:

1. Select < **create**> option from the Queries panel.

2. Remove all the fields in the view skeleton by pressing F5 while the cursor is positioned on Address.dbf in the file skeleton.

3. Enter the COUNT operator in the MALE field, followed by a filter condition .T. in the same field.

4. Put the MALE field in the view skeleton by pressing F5.

5. Move the cursor to the view skeleton by pressing F4, type an alternate field name (MALE_COUNT) for the MALE file followed by an equal sign (see fig. 6.50).

6. Press F2. You should see the number of records counted displayed in the field labeled MALE_COUNT.

7. Return to the query design by using the Exit menu.

Next, find the average wealth for those people in California by using a query design with an AVERAGE operator (see fig. 6.51):

1. On the query design, enter "CA" in the STATE field.

2. Enter AVERAGE in the WEALTH field.

3. Put WEALTH in the View skeleton and assign an alternate name as AVG_WEALTH.

4. Press F2.

Practice using the SUM, MAX, and MIN operators in the query design.

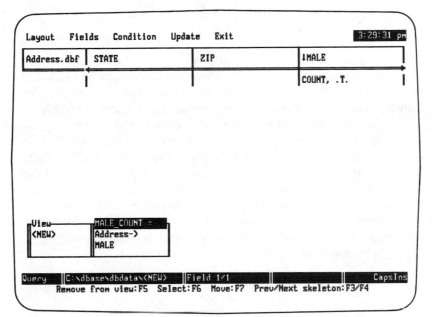

Fig. 6.50.

Counting records in the ADDRESS.DBF file.

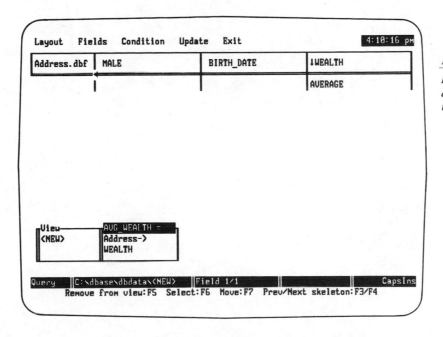

Fig. 6.51.

Finding the average value in the WEALTH field.

Chapter Summary

This chapter introduced index and sort, the two most useful operations in dBASE IV for organizing your data. These operations can be carried out from the Control Center and from the dot prompt. You can use the sort operation on an active database file to arrange data records according to the contents of one or more key fields. The result of the sorting operation is a target file that contains the ordered data records. The index option is similar to sort, but indexing is much faster than sorting. Indexing creates an index file that contains only key field values and their corresponding record numbers. The index file is used to rearrange data records in the active database file. Additionally, you learned to use multiple index files and to summarize, count, and average data by using query designs. In the next chapter, you are introduced to memory variables, expressions, and functions.

Memory Variables, Expressions, and Functions

Often, in addition to storing data in a database, you need to retain the intermediate results of data manipulation procedures so that the values can be used for further processing. Instead of storing the values as records in a file, you can save them as variables. A *memory variable* is a memory location that is set aside to store a data element. Memory variables are important in data manipulation because they take up little memory space and their contents can be recalled almost instantly. This chapter explains how memory variables are defined and used in database management.

This chapter also discusses the use of expressions and functions in data manipulation. An *expression* is a combination of data field values and memory variables that is used to define the operations performed on specified data elements. *Functions* are predefined operations whose results (such as numbers and character strings) can be used in expressions. For example, you can use a function to find the square root of a number and then use the square root for further processing.

The following commands for processing memory variables are introduced in this chapter:

Commands	Actions
STORE =	Enters data into memory variables
? DISPLAY MEMORY	Displays memory variables
SAVE TO	Saves memory variables to disk file
ERASE RELEASE	Discards memory variables. Erases or deletes memory files or disk files of memory variables.
RESTORE	Retrieves memory variables from disk file

The following are some of the commonly used built-in functions of dBASE IV:

Functions	For
CDOW, CMONTH, DATE, DAY, DMY DOW, MDY, MONTH, TIME, YEAR	Time and date processing
CTOD, DTOC, VAL, STR	Field/Variable conversion
AT, LEFT, LEN, LTRIM RIGHT, RTRIM SPACE, STUFF, SUBSTR, TRIM	Character string manipulation
ABS, EXP, INT, LOG, MAX, MIN, MOD, ROUND, SQRT	Mathematical operation
RECNO	Current record pointer
COL, PCOL, ROW, PROW	Displaying a location

Memory Variables

The term *variable* is used in algebra to mean a quantity that may assume different values. In dBASE IV, a variable is a name assigned to a memory location that can be used to hold a data element. The value stored in a memory variable can be the value in a data field or some other data item. Character strings, numeric values, and dates can be stored in memory variables.

Memory variables are stored temporarily in RAM during processing. Contents of memory variables are stored outside the structure of a database file and are not considered part of the database contents.

Memory variables are the major components of formulas. Intermediate results from computations or data manipulations are often stored in memory variables to be recalled and used in further calculations or report generation.

Determining the Type of Memory Variable

dBASE IV offers four types of memory variables: character, numeric, date, and logical. The type is determined when data is stored in the variable: if a numeric value is assigned to a variable, for example, then the type of that variable is numeric. The contents of memory variables can be used only in expressions appropriate to the type of the variable. Character variable contents can be processed only by character operators and functions, for example, and mathematical computations can be performed only on numeric values.

You can change the variable type by assigning a different kind of data. For instance, when a character string is placed in a variable, that variable becomes a character variable. If you later assign a numeric value to the same variable, it becomes a numeric variable.

Naming the Variable

A memory variable name can consists of up to 10 characters. As with field names, these 10 characters may be a combination of letters, digits, and the underscore character (_). However, the first character of a memory variable name must be a letter. The following are acceptable memory variable names:

SALES	GrossPay	DISCOUNT
SaleDate	WEEKLYHRS	PAY_ RATE
AccountNo	UnitSold	TaxRate

Caution:

Do not name a variable the same as a data field.

Do not use the command or function names and reserved words such as TOTAL, SUM, AVERAGE, COUNT, MAX, MIN, DISPLAY, LIST, etc., as memory variables. Using any of these items can confuse the program and yield unpredictable results. Also, the same name should not be used for a variable and a data field in the same application. When the same name is assigned to a variable and to a field, the name is recognized only for the field when the file containing the field is activated.

Because memory variables are often needed to retain the field contents for further computation, you may want to assign a variable name that is related to the corresponding field name. For example, if the field name contains an underscore, such as ACCOUNT_ NO, then the name without the underscore, AccountNo, can be used for the variable. If the field name does not contain an underscore, you may want to create a memory variable name consisting of the field name preceded by the letter M. For instance, you can use the name MSales for the memory variable to hold the contents of the data field SALES.

Entering Data in a Memory Variable

You can enter data in a memory variable by entering data from the keyboard, by assigning to it the contents of a data field from the active record, or by copying the contents from another memory variable.

Assigning Data to a Memory Variable with =

The equal sign (=) is a command entered from the keyboard. This command assigns a character string, a value, or a logical state (.T. or .F.) to a memory variable. Use the following form:

. < *name of memory variable*> =< *data element*>

The equal sign (=) is interpreted differently in dBASE IV than in normal mathematical use. Instead of stating that two quantities are equal, the equal sign signifies an action: The memory variable on the left side of the equal sign is assigned the value of the data element on the right. The = sign is called an assignment operator when used in this way. It "assigns" a value to the memory variable.

The data element assigned to the memory variable must be defined in a specific form, depending on the kind of data element. To avoid ambiguity, you must enclose character strings in quotation marks. Contents of a logical variable must be specified in the form .T. or .F. (or .Y. or .N.). Be sure to include the two periods. Numbers entered in numerical variables can be integers or decimal values (see fig. 7.1). A date value enclosed in curly brackets (such as {12/24/88}) can be entered in a date variable with the = command.

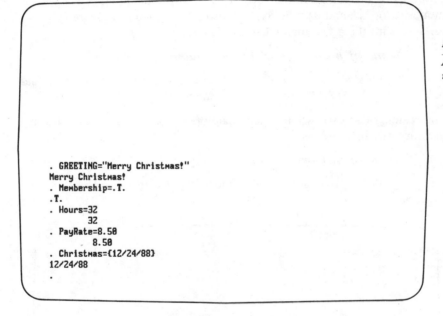

Fig. 7.1.

Assigning data to memory variables.

```
. GREETING="Merry Christmas!"
Merry Christmas!
. Membership=.T.
.T.
. Hours=32
        32
. PayRate=8.50
        8.50
. Christmas={12/24/88}
12/24/88
.
```

Note: In figure 7.1 and other figures in this chapter, you may notice that the status bar is not shown on the screen display. The status bar can be removed by entering the SET STATUS OFF dot command. To display the status bar again, enter SET STATUS ON.

If the memory variable name and the data element have been defined correctly, the data element is assigned to the variable. Unless ECHO has been turned off, the program confirms the command by echoing the contents of the variable immediately after the = command is executed. If an error is made in the = command, the error message Syntax error will be displayed. You will then be asked to choose one of the following options:

Cancel   Edit   Help

By choosing Cancel, you will be returned to the dot prompt and you must re-enter the command. The Edit option when selected will position the cursor at the end of the last command entered. You can use the arrow keys to move the cursor to the command text to make the necessary correction. If you need information about the command, choose the Help option.

Contents of a data field in the active data record (including character, numeric, logical, and date fields) can also be assigned to a memory variable with the = command. Use the following format:

. < *name of memory variable* > = < *name of data field* >

Figure 7.2 illustrates use of the = command to assign the contents of data fields in the EMPLOYEE database file to memory variables.

The results of an expression or algebraic operation can be assigned to a memory variable, such as

. < *name of memory variable* > = < *expression* >

Later sections of this chapter deal in more detail with the subject of expressions.

Fig. 7.2.

Assigning contents of data field to memory variable.

```
. USE EMPLOYEE
. GO TOP
EMPLOYEE: Record No      1
. FirstName=FIRST_NAME
James C.
. M_Male=MALE
.T.
. BirthDate=BIRTH_DATE
07/04/60
. AnnualPay=ANNUAL_PAY
      24200
.
```

Assigning Data Elements to Variables with STORE

The STORE command also assigns to a memory variable a data element or the contents of a data field of the active record. In fact, you can use the = and STORE commands interchangeably. The STORE command has the following formats:

    . STORE < *data element* > TO < *name of memory variable* >
    . STORE < *name of data field* > TO < *name of memory variable* >

The first format is used for entering data from the keyboard. This STORE command assigns character, numeric, date, and logical memory variables (see fig. 7.3).

```
. STORE "Merry Christmas!" TO Greeting
Merry Christmas!
. STORE .T. TO Membership
.T.
. STORE 32 TO Hours
        32
. STORE 8.5 TO PayRate
        8.50
  STORE {12/24/88} TO Christmas
12/24/88
.
```

Fig. 7.3.

Using the STORE *command.*

The second format of the STORE command assigns to a memory variable the content of a data field of the active record, regardless of the field type. The variable type becomes that of the data field when the STORE command is executed. The example in figure 7.4 illustrates assignment of contents of data fields in the EMPLOYEE database file to corresponding variables.

Fig. 7.4.

Using another form of the STORE *command.*

```
. USE EMPLOYEE
. LOCATE FOR FIRST_NAME="Doris"
Record =        3
. DISPLAY
Record#  FIRST_NAME    LAST_NAME  AREA_CODE PHONE_NO MALE BIRTH_DATE ANNUAL_PAY
      3  Doris A.      Gregory    503       204-8567 .F.  07/04/62      18590.00
. STORE FIRST_NAME TO FirstName
Doris A.
. STORE MALE TO M_Male
.F.
. STORE BIRTH_DATE TO BirthDate
07/04/62
. STORE ANNUAL_PAY TO AnnualPay
    18590
.
```

Displaying Memory Variables

When you enter data into memory variables, the variables are stored temporarily in RAM. You can display the contents of all the variables at any time during data manipulation.

Displaying All Variables with DISPLAY MEMORY

The DISPLAY MEMORY command can be used to display detailed information about all active memory variables. Enter the command as

    . DISPLAY MEMORY

Command:

DISPLAY MEMORY *Shows current value of the memory variable in use.*

When you enter this command, all active memory variables are displayed in the order they were last updated. DISPLAY also shows the type of data stored in each variable and the variable contents (see fig. 7.5).

```
        User Memory Variables

ANNUALPAY   pub  N        18590  (18590.00000000000000)
BIRTHDATE   pub  D  07/04/62
M_MALE      pub  L  .F.
FIRSTNAME   pub  C  "Doris A.    "
CHRISTMAS   pub  D  12/24/88
PAYRATE     pub  N         8.50  (8.50000000000000000)
HOURS       pub  N           32  (32.00000000000000000)
MEMBERSHIP  pub  L  .T.
GREETING    pub  C  "Merry Christmas!"

   9 out of 500 memvars defined (and 0 array elements)


        User MEMVAR/RTSYM Memory Usage

2800 bytes used for 1 memvar blocks (max=10)
 850 bytes used for 1 rtsym blocks (max=10)
   0 bytes used for 0 array element memvars
  28 bytes used for 2 memvar character strings

3678 bytes total
Press any key to continue...
```

Fig. 7.5.

Results of the
DISPLAY MEMORY
command.

The abbreviation *pub* after a variable name indicates that the variable is a public variable. All variables are either *public* or *private*. A private variable can be accessed only by the program module in which it is defined. The contents of a public variable can be accessed by every part of the program. This distinction, however, is useful only for batch command processing (discussed in Chapter 11). All variables defined in interactive mode are public variables.

The DISPLAY MEMORY command also displays summary statistics regarding the number of variables defined, the amount of memory used, and the numbers of variables and bytes of memory still available.

Displaying Single Variables with the ? Command

Instead of displaying all existing variables as a group, you can display a single variable by entering the ? command in the form

. ? < *name of memory variable to be displayed*>

Figure 7.6 shows how the ? command can be used to display the contents of several different types of memory variables.

Fig. 7.6.

Example using the ? command.

```
. ?Greeting
Merry Christmas!
. ?Membership
.T.
. ?Hours
        32
. ?FirstName
Doris A.
. ?BirthDate
07/04/62
. ?AnnualPay
    18590
. ?Christmas
12/24/88
.
```

Saving Memory Variables on Disk

Command:

SAVE TO
Saves memory variables to a disk file.

Memory variables are stored temporarily in RAM and can be accessed at any stage of the data manipulation process. When you leave dBASE IV, however, the variables are erased (or released) from memory. If you want to use these variables in different dBASE IV applications, you must therefore store the variables permanently. The SAVE command is used to store in a disk file the contents of the active memory variables.

The SAVE command stores all or part of the current set of memory variables to a disk file. To save all active memory variables, use the SAVE command in the following form:

. SAVE TO < *name of memory file*>

To save the active variables to a file called VARLIST, for example, you enter

. SAVE TO VARLIST

This command tells the computer to copy all the memory variables to a file named VARLIST. Unless you specify otherwise, the file extension for the memory file created by this command is .MEM; the file name therefore is VARLIST.MEM.

You can also elect to save only some of the variables. To select the variables you want to save, use a selection clause such as ALL LIKE or ALL EXCEPT:

. SAVE ALL LIKE < *variable description*> TO < *name of memory file*>

. SAVE ALL EXCEPT < *variable description*> TO < *name of memory file*>

The symbol < *variable description*> refers to the "skeleton" of a variable name. dBASE IV has two symbols (called *wild cards*) that can be substituted for the characters in a variable name. The question mark (?) substitutes for a single character, and the asterisk (*) stands for a string of characters of any length. A skeleton contains the characters and wild-card symbols necessary for specifying a set of variables. For instance, to save in the file NETVARS.MEM all the active memory variables with names beginning with the letters *NET* (NETREVENUE, NETCOST, NETPROFIT, etc.), you can use a skeleton containing the asterisk, such as

Tip:
Use * *and* ? *with* LIKE *or* EXCEPT *to save selective memory variables to a disk file.*

. SAVE ALL LIKE NET* TO NETVARS

The asterisk (*) in the variable description stands for any series of characters; the program therefore saves every variable whose name begins with NET.

The ? wild card simplifies definition of memory variable sets. Suppose, for example, that you want to save all memory variables with six-character names including RATE as the second through fifth characters (WRATE1, MRATE2, YRATE3, etc.). You can use the ? wild card as follows:

. SAVE ALL LIKE ?RATE? TO RATES

The variable-name skeleton ?RATE? instructs dBASE IV to store all variables with six-character names and RATE in the second through fifth positions, regardless of what characters occupy positions 1 and 6.

Skeletons can be used to exclude specific variables from a memory disk file. For example, if you want to exclude memory variables whose names begin with the letters NET, you can use the ALL EXCEPT clause in the SAVE command, such as

```
. SAVE ALL EXCEPT NET????? TO MEMVARS
. SAVE ALL EXCEPT NET* TO MEMVARS
```

The first command saves all memory variables that have names beginning with NET followed by any five characters. The second command saves all memory variables to the file except those that have names beginning with NET followed by any characters.

Deleting Memory Variables

▷

Tip:

Use RELEASE *to remove unwanted memory variables to conserve memory space.*

Memory variables can be deleted from the active list of memory variables. The RELEASE command permanently removes from memory some or all of the active memory variables. As with the SAVE command, the clauses ALL, ALL LIKE, and ALL EXCEPT can be used to select the memory variables to be released:

```
. RELEASE ALL
. RELEASE ALL LIKE   < variable-name description >
. RELEASE ALL EXCEPT  < variable-name description >
```

The wild cards * and ? can be used for deletion in the same way they were used with the SAVE command. Following are some examples:

```
. RELEASE ALL LIKE *NET
. RELEASE ALL LIKE ?RATE?
. RELEASE ALL EXCEPT *NET
. RELEASE ALL EXCEPT NET?????
```

▷

Tip:

Use ERASE *to delete an unwanted memory variable file.*

The RELEASE command removes the specified active memory variables from RAM, not from a memory file. To delete a memory file that has been saved on disk, use the ERASE command:

```
. ERASE  < name of memory file to be erased >
```

For instance, the following command removes the memory file MEMVAR.MEM:

```
. ERASE MEMVAR.MEM
```

Loading Memory Variables from Memory Files

Memory variables that have been saved in a memory file can be copied back to RAM. The RESTORE command retrieves all the memory variables in a memory file and places them in the computer's memory. The format for this command is

. RESTORE FROM *< name of memory file>*

The following command places in RAM the memory variables from the RATES.MEM memory file:

. RESTORE FROM RATES.MEM

When you use the RESTORE command, all memory variables currently in RAM are erased before the memory variables from RATES.MEM are restored. To retain the current memory variables, you must combine the ADDITIVE clause with the RESTORE command:

. RESTORE FROM *< name of the memory file>* ADDITIVE

For example, to retrieve all variables in VARLIST.MEM and add them to the current active memory list, you use the following command:

. RESTORE FROM VARLIST.MEM ADDITIVE

Command:

RESTORE FROM
*Reloads mem(
variables from
disk file to
memory.*

Expressions

Besides serving as temporary storage, memory variables can be used in processing operations. A memory variable can be specified in an expression in order to define a procedure, to describe a qualifier phrase in a command, or to serve as an output element.

Depending on the application, different types of expressions can be used in dBASE IV. An expression can include a data field, a memory variable, a constant, or a combination of these elements. All elements in an expression must be the same type, however. If an expression contains data elements of different types, the error message Data type mismatch is displayed.

Using Arithmetic Expressions

The most common expression is the arithmetic expression, which can contain a value, a memory variable, a numeric data field, or combinations of these joined by one or more arithmetic operators (+, −, *, /, etc.). The following are arithmetic expressions:

```
32
HOURS
ANNUAL _ PAY
HOURS*PAYRATE
ANNUAL _ PAY  + Ø.Ø5*ANNUAL _ PAY
```

HOURS and PAYRATE are names of memory variables, and * is the symbol for multiplication. The expression HOURS*PAYRATE indicates that the contents of the variable HOURS are to be multiplied by the contents of PAYRATE.

Expressions are useful for arithmetic calculations. An expression can be used to assign a value to a memory variable, for example, or to place a new value in a numeric data field. In figure 7.7, the arithmetic expressions entered at the dot prompt assign values to the memory variables whose names are entered to the left of the equal signs.

The multiplication symbol (*) in the arithmetic expression is called an *arithmetic operator*. Other arithmetic operators are +, −, /, and ^ for the operations of addition, subtraction, division, and raising the power, respectively. When more than one arithmetic operator is included in an expression, the expression is evaluated from left to right according to the following series:

Highest priority	^
Second priority	*, /
Lowest priority	+,−

This order of evaluation sometimes is called the *order of precedence*.

Tip:
Use parentheses in an arithmetic expression to define the evaluation sequence.

You can use parentheses in an arithmetic expression to define the evaluation sequence and alter the normal order of precedence. Material within parentheses is always evaluated first. When pairs of parentheses are nested in an arithmetic expression, the expression within the inner parentheses is evaluated first. Then the expressions within the outer parentheses are evaluated. Arithmetic operators within parentheses are evaluated from left to right following the normal order of precedence. For example, the arithmetic expression

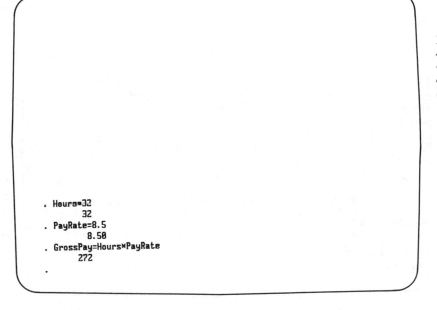

Fig. 7.7.

Arithmetic expressions assigning values to variables.

```
. Hours=32
       32
. PayRate=8.5
       8.50
. GrossPay=Hours*PayRate
      272
.
```

(QTYA+QTYB)*PRICE*((1-DISCOUNT)/100)

is evaluated as follows:

1. Evaluate (1-DISCOUNT).

2. Evaluate (QTYA+QTYB).

3. Evaluate ((1-DISCOUNT)/100). (The result of step 1 is used in place of 1-DISCOUNT.)

4. Evaluate (QTYA+QTYB)*PRICE. (The result of step 2 is used in this step.)

5. Evaluate the entire equation: (QTYA+QTYB)*PRICE*((1-DISCOUNT)/100). (This is the result of step 4 multiplied by the result of step 3.)

You can also use the contents of numeric data fields in an arithmetic expression. The values are taken from fields in the active record. Figure 7.8 shows that the numeric field ANNUAL_PAY in EMPLOYEE.DBF can be used in an arithmetic expression to compute the income tax for the employee "Smith".

```
. USE EMPLOYEE
. LOCATE FOR LAST_NAME="Smith"
Record =       1
. DISPLAY
Record# FIRST_NAME  LAST_NAME  AREA_CODE PHONE_NO MALE BIRTH_DATE ANNUAL_PAY
      1 James C.     Smith       216      123-4567 .T.  07/04/60   24200.00
. TaxRate=0.18
        0.18
. IncomeTax=TaxRate*ANNUAL_PAY
     4356
.
```

Similarly, as shown in figure 7.9, an arithmetic expression can be used
with a DISPLAY command to compute the amount of withholding tax
(ANNUAL_PAY*WithHolding) for all records of EMPLOYEE.DBF belonging to
male employees.

By using an arithmetic expression with the REPLACE command, you can
adjust the contents of the numeric fields in the active record (see fig.
7.10). To raise by 5 percent all the employees' annual salaries (in the
numeric field ANNUAL_PAY), you use the REPLACE command and
the expression ANNUAL_PAY*1.05. The command causes the value in
ANNUAL_PAY to be replaced by a value 5 percent higher. In addition,
many functions perform operations on numerical data. These may be
included in numerical expressions. More information about functions is
included later in this chapter.

Using Character Expressions

Character expressions are also used frequently in dBASE IV. A character
expression may contain a character string enclosed in quotation marks, a

Fig. 7.9.

An arithmetic expression used with DISPLAY.

```
. USE EMPLOYEE
. WithHolding=0.12
        0.12
. DISPLAY LAST_NAME, FIRST_NAME, ANNUAL_PAY×WithHolding FOR MALE
Record# LAST_NAME FIRST_NAME    ANNUAL_PAY×WithHolding
        1 Smith     James C.                      2904
        2 Zeller    Albert K.                  3682.80
        4 Nelson    Harry M.                      3828
        6 Chapman   Kirk D.                       2607
        8 Duff      Charles N.                    1782
        9 Lee       Winston E.                 4606.80
       10 Hanson    Thomas T.                  3821.40
.
```

Fig. 7.10.

An arithmetic expression with REPLACE.

```
. USE EMPLOYEE
. REPLACE ALL ANNUAL_PAY WITH ANNUAL_PAY×1.05
       10 records replaced
. LIST LAST_NAME,ANNUAL_PAY
Record# LAST_NAME ANNUAL_PAY
        1 Smith     25410.00
        2 Zeller    32224.50
        3 Gregory   19519.50
        4 Nelson    33495.00
        5 Baker     29914.50
        6 Chapman   22811.25
        7 Thompson  28297.50
        8 Duff      15592.50
        9 Lee       40309.50
       10 Hanson    33437.25
.
```

character memory variable, a character data field, or a combination of these joined by the + sign.

For example, each of the following phrases is a character expression:

```
"Employee's Name"
FIRST_NAME
LAST_NAME
"Employee's  Name"+"is"+FIRST_NAME+LAST_NAME
```

Character expressions often are used to assign a character data element to a memory variable. For instance, either of the following commands assigns the contents of the character expression to a character variable:

```
. LongString=StringA+StringB+StringC
. STORE StringA+StringB+StringC TO LongString
```

You can use a character expression to combine data fields in the records of the active database file and show the result with a DISPLAY or LIST command. For example, in figure 7.11 a character expression combines contents of two fields (FIRST_NAME and LAST_NAME). The result of the expression is a string consisting of the employee's first and last names.

Fig. 7.11.

A character expression with DISPLAY *and* LIST.

```
. USE EMPLOYEE
. DISPLAY FIRST_NAME+FIRST_NAME FOR MALE
Record#  FIRST_NAME+FIRST_NAME
       1 James C.    James C.
       2 Albert K.   Albert K.
       4 Harry M.    Harry M.
       6 Kirk D.     Kirk D.
       8 Charles N.  Charles N.
       9 Winston E.  Winston E.
      10 Thomas T.   Thomas T.
. LIST LAST_NAME+","+FIRST_NAME FOR .NOT. MALE
Record#  LAST_NAME+","+FIRST_NAME
       3 Gregory   ,Doris A.
       5 Baker     ,Tina B.
       7 Thompson  ,Mary W.
       .
```

In addition, the REPLACE command can be used to substitute the result of a character expression for the contents of a field in active records of the database. In figure 7.12, the contents of the variable NEWCODE have replaced the contents of the AREA_ CODE field in EMPLOYEE.DBF.

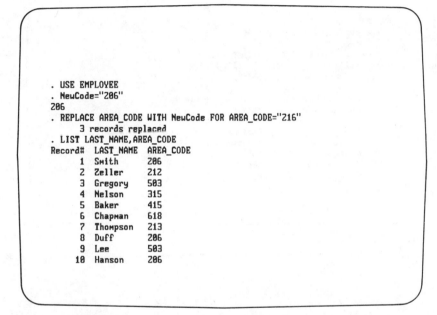

Fig. 7.12.

A character expression with REPLACE.

```
. USE EMPLOYEE
. NewCode="206"
206
. REPLACE AREA_CODE WITH NewCode FOR AREA_CODE="216"
        3 records replaced
. LIST LAST_NAME,AREA_CODE
Record#  LAST_NAME  AREA_CODE
      1  Smith      206
      2  Zeller     212
      3  Gregory    503
      4  Nelson     315
      5  Baker      415
      6  Chapman    618
      7  Thompson   213
      8  Duff       206
      9  Lee        503
     10  Hanson     206
```

There also are many functions that manipulate character variables. These functions, which are discussed later in this chapter, can be included in character expressions.

Displaying Expressions

Results of character and numeric expressions can be displayed in a number of ways. For example, a DISPLAY or a LIST command can be used with a character expression to display the contents of the variable NameLabel along with the name of an employee (see fig. 7.13).

You can also use the ? command to display the results of a character expression (see fig. 7.14). Notice that with the ? command, a comma is used to separate the character string "Income tax for the year ....." from the numeric expression ANNUAL_PAY*Ø.18. Each is considered a separate expression.

Fig. 7.13.

*Displaying
character and
numeric
expressions.*

```
. USE EMPLOYEE
. NameLabel="Employee Name ...... "
Employee Name ......
. LIST NameLabel+LAST_NAME+","+FIRST_NAME
Record#  NameLabel+LAST_NAME+","+FIRST_NAME
       1 Employee Name ...... Smith     ,James C.
       2 Employee Name ...... Zeller    ,Albert K.
       3 Employee Name ...... Gregory   ,Doris A.
       4 Employee Name ...... Nelson    ,Harry M.
       5 Employee Name ...... Baker     ,Tina B.
       6 Employee Name ...... Chapman   ,Kirk D.
       7 Employee Name ...... Thompson  ,Mary W.
       8 Employee Name ...... Duff      ,Charles N.
       9 Employee Name ...... Lee       ,Winston E.
      10 Employee Name ...... Hanson    ,Thomas T.
```

Fig. 7.14.

*Using ? to display
the results of a
character
expression.*

```
. USE EMPLOYEE
. LOCATE FOR LAST_NAME="Gregory"
Record =        3
. ?"Income tax for the year .....",ANNUAL_PAY*0.18
Income tax for the year .....     3513.51
.
```

An expression must contain only data elements of the same type. A character expression and a numeric expression cannot be joined with a plus sign, for example. The following expression will result in the error message Data type mismatch because ANNUAL_PAY*Ø.18 is a numeric expression:

    ? "Income tax for the year ....."   +ANNUAL_PAY*0.18

However, you can use the STR function, which is discussed later in this chapter, to convert the result of ANNUAL_PAY*Ø.18 to a character value. That value can then be concatenated with the character string "Income tax....."

Caution:

An expression displayed by ? must contain data elements of the same data type.

Functions

Functions in dBASE IV provide a "built-in" way of performing mathematical and string manipulations. A function takes values (called *arguments*) that are "passed" to it and performs an operation on those values. The function then "returns" the value resulting from the operation it has performed. The arguments of functions can be either the contents of data fields or the results of expressions.

Functions are divided into groups according to the types of data they return and the kinds of operations they perform. Mathematical functions can round a decimal number to the integer, compute the square root of a value, and perform many other actions. String functions can select parts of a character string for use in searching, sorting, and indexing operations. Other string functions can insert blank spaces in a character string or trim off unwanted blank spaces. Functions for data-type conversion change data elements from one type to another. These functions can convert a date to a character string, a numeric field value to a character string, or the contents of a character variable to a numeric value. The time and date functions display date and time in a number of formats that are used in business data processing applications.

Format of a Function

A function, which is designed to perform a special operation, must have a function name. The argument of the function is enclosed in parentheses. The format of a function therefore is

. < *name of function*>(< *argument*>)

In the example

. INT(3.7415)

the INT function returns the integer portion of the decimal value 3.7415, which is the argument of the function. The result of the function INT(3.7415) is the numeric value 3. As shown in figure 7.15, this function may be used as an expression in a ? command or as part of an arithmetic expression.

Fig. 7.15.

An example of using the INT *function.*

```
. ?INT(3.7415)
       3
. Answer=1200/INT(3.7415)
       400
.
```

Many functions are available for manipulating data elements of different types. These functions are summarized by their operations in the following sections.

Mathematical Functions

As stated earlier, a mathematical function performs a mathematical operation on numeric data elements that are passed to the functions. The arguments can be numeric values or the contents of numeric data fields. The results of mathematical functions are always returned as numeric data. In addition to INT (explained in the preceding section), the types of mathematical functions supported by dBASE IV are ROUND, SQRT, LOG, and EXP.

The ROUND Function

The ROUND function rounds a decimal value to the number of decimal places specified by the argument $<n>$. The decimal value argument can be the contents of a memory variable or numeric data field, or the result of a numeric expression. The format of the ROUND function is

. ROUND($<$ *numeric expression$>$,$<$ n$>$*)

Note that the result and the argument of the function always have the same number of decimal places (see fig. 7.16). The argument $<n>$ controls not the number of decimal places displayed, but the number of places to which the decimal argument is rounded. Consequently, the command

. ?ROUND(3.7415,Ø)

returns the value 4, which is 3.7415 rounded to zero places after the decimal point. The command

. ?ROUND(3.7415,3)

should return 3.742; the result is the original value rounded to three places after the decimal point. However, the number of decimal places to be used to display a value can be set by dBASE IV. By default, two decimal places are assumed. That is why the value for ?ROUND(3.7415,3) returns a value of 3.74 instead of 3.742.

You can change the number of decimal places by using the SET DECIMAL TO command. As seen in figure 7.16, after issuing the SET DECIMAL TO 4 command, the value of ?ROUND(3.7415,3) becomes 3.7420.

Function:
ROUND()
Rounds a value to a specified decimal place.

Tip:
Use SET DECIMAL TO *to display the rounded value i a specified number of decimal places.*

When you set the decimal places to less than the number of decimal places in the value, the value will be rounded for display only. For example, the answer of A*B will be rounded to two places after the decimal after issuing the SET DECIMAL TO 2 command. However, the value of a memory variable stored internally has not been rounded to 2 but still retains the number of decimals specified in the ROUND( ) operation.

Fig. 7.16.

An example of using the ROUND *function.*

```
. ?ROUND(3.7415,0)
        4
. ?ROUND(3.7415,3)
        3.74
. SET DECIMAL TO 4
. ?ROUND(3.7415,3)
        3.7420
. A=3.15
        3.1500
. B=7.135
        7.1350
. ?A*B
       22.4753
. SET DECIMAL TO 3
. ?A*B
       22.475
. SET DECIMAL TO 2
. ?A*B
       22.48
.
```

The SQRT Function

Function:
SQRT( )
Tabulates the square root of a value.

The SQRT function returns the square root of the value in the argument. The format is

. SQRT(< *numeric expression* >)

Use the SET DECIMAL command to determine the number of decimal places for the returned square root value (see fig. 7.17).

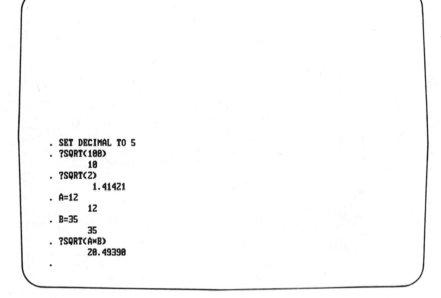

Fig. 7.17.

*An example of
using the* SQRT
function.

```
. SET DECIMAL TO 5
. ?SQRT(100)
       10
. ?SQRT(2)
       1.41421
. A=12
       12
. B=35
       35
. ?SQRT(A*B)
       20.49390
.
```

The LOG Function

Two types of logarithms are used in mathematics and statistics. One is the base-10 (or *common*) logarithm, which is denoted as *log10x*. The other type of logarithm is the base-e (or *natural* logarithm, where $e = 2.71828183...$ This logarithm is denoted by the symbol *ln x*.

Function:
LOG() *and*
LOG10()
*Computes the
natural and
common
logarithm.*

In dBASE IV, the function for the natural logarithm (ln) is

. LOG(< *numeric expression*>)

For the common logarithm (log ^{10},) use

. LOG1Ø(< *numeric expression*>)

Figure 7.18 shows a few examples of using the LOG( ) and LOG1Ø( ) function.

Fig. 7.18.

An example of using the LOG *function.*

```
. ?LOG10(100)
        2
. ?LOG10(1000)
        3
. SET DECIMAL TO 5
. ?LOG(100)
        4.60517
. E=2.718282823
        2.71828
. ?LOG(E)
        1.00000
.
```

The EXP Function

Function:

EXP()
Computes the exponents of a value.

EXP is the exponential function. When passed the argument *x*, the function returns the value e^x ("e to the x power"). The format of the EXP function is

. EXP(< *numeric expression* >)

Figure 7.19 shows some examples. The command ?EXP(1.00) causes the value of e1, 2.72, to be displayed. Because the argument of the function is displayed with two decimal places (1.00), the result returned by the function also has two decimal places. If you use more decimal places in the argument, as in the command ?EXP(1.00000000), you'll get a more accurate answer. You can also use a numeric expression as the argument for the EXP function, as shown in the third command, ?EXP(A*B).

The ABS Function

Function:

ABS()
Tabulates the absolute value.

ABS is the absolute value function. When you specify a numeric expression as an argument, the function returns the absolute value of the expression. The format is

```
. SET DECIMAL TO 18
. ?EXP(1)
        2.7182818285
. ?EXP(18)
      22826.4657948867
. A=2
        2
. B=4
        4
. ?EXP(A*B)
     2980.9579870417
.
```

Fig. 7.19.

An example of using the EXP function.

.ABS (< *numeric expression* >)

Figure 7.20 shows examples of using the ABS function. Notice that even when the value of the expression is negative, the ABS function returns a positive value.

The MAX Function

The MAX function returns the larger value of two numeric expressions that are supplied as arguments. The form of the MAX function is

. MAX(< *numeric expression 1* > , < *numeric expression 2* >)

In figure 7.21, the MAX function evaluates the two numeric expressions A+B and A*B and returns the larger of the two values.

Function:
MAX( )
*Finds the
maximum value.*

Fig. 7.20.

An example of using the ABS *function.*

```
.  SET DECIMAL TO 5
.  A=2
                2
.  B=4
                4
.  ?A-B
               -2
.  ?ABS(A-B)
                2
.  ?ABS(-3.45678)
            3.45678
.
```

Fig. 7.21.

An example of using the MAX *function.*

```
.  SET DECIMAL TO 2
.  A=10
               10
.  B=20
               20
.  ?MAX(A+B,A*B)
              200
.
```

The MIN Function

The MIN function, the opposite of MAX, evaluates the two numeric expressions supplied as arguments and returns the smaller value. The format is

Function:
MIN( )
Finds the minimum value.

. MIN(< *numeric expression 1* > , < *numeric expression 2* >)

In figure 7.22, the MIN function evaluates the two numeric expressions A+B and A*B and returns the smaller of the two values (A+B, or 30).

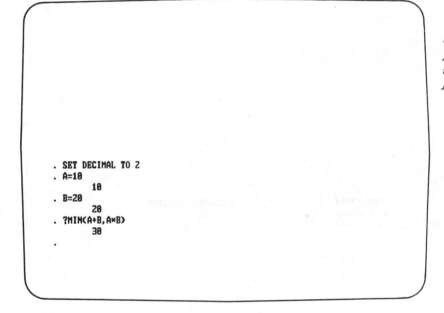

```
. SET DECIMAL TO 2
. A=10
        10
. B=20
        20
. ?MIN(A+B,A*B)
        30
.
```

Fig. 7.22.

An example of using the MIN *function.*

String Manipulation Functions

Several functions are available for manipulating character strings in various ways. For instance, characters in a string can be converted from uppercase to lowercase letters. Blank spaces in a character field can be removed or added. Any character in a character string can be isolated for displaying or for sorting and indexing operations.

The LOWER Function

Function:

LOWER( )
Converts to
lowercase the
letters of a
character string.

The LOWER function converts to lowercase characters all the capital letters in a character string. Numeric digits and other symbols are not changed, however. The argument of the LOWER function is a character expression, which can be a combination of character strings in quotation marks, character memory variables, and the contents of character data fields. The format is

. LOWER(< *character expression*>)

Figure 7.23 shows several examples of using the LOWER function.

Fig. 7.23.

An example of using the LOWER *function.*

```
. ?LOWER("THIS IS A SAMPLE PHRASE IN UPPERCASE LETTERS")
this is a sample phrase in uppercase letters
. USE EMPLOYEE
. GO TOP
EMPLOYEE: Record No      1
. ?LOWER(FIRST_NAME)
james c.
. ?LOWER(LAST_NAME)+","+FIRST_NAME
smith     ,James C.
.
```

The LOWER function is effective for searching. To locate the record containing a particular value in a character field, for example, use LOWER to convert all contents of that character field into lowercase letters. Then you can find the string by specifying the search key in all lowercase letters, regardless of whether the string was entered in the field in lowercase or uppercase letters. In figure 7.24, the LOCATE command is used with the LOWER function to find the records that contain a last name in the forms of *SMITH, Smith, smith,* or any other combination of upper- and lowercase letters.

Fig. 7.24.

Using the LOWER
function with the
LOCATE *command.*

```
. USE EMPLOYEE
. LOCATE FOR LOWER(LAST_NAME)="smith"
Record =        1
. DISPLAY LAST_NAME, FIRST_NAME
Record# LAST_NAME  FIRST_NAME
      1 Smith      James C.
```

Without the LOWER function, the following LOCATE command finds only
records with smith in the LAST_NAME field.

> . LOCATE FOR LAST_NAME="smith"

The UPPER Function

The UPPER function performs a string conversion opposite to that of the
LOWER function. UPPER converts to uppercase letters the lowercase letters
in the character string (see fig. 7.25). The format of the UPPER function is

Function:
UPPER()
*Converts to
uppercase the
letters of a
character string.*

> . UPPER(< *character expression* >)

Figure 7.25 shows that by using UPPER(LAST_NAME) in the LOCATE
command, you can convert to uppercase letters the string stored in the
LAST_NAME field. Consequently, you can use SMITH as the search key for
locating the data record.

```
. ?UPPER("This is a Character String !")
THIS IS A CHARACTER STRING !
. USE EMPLOYEE
. LOCATE FOR UPPER(LAST_NAME)="SMITH"
Record =        1
. DISPLAY UPPER(LAST_NAME)+","+FIRST_NAME
Record#  UPPER(LAST_NAME)+","+FIRST_NAME
      1  SMITH     ,James C.
.
```

The TRIM Function

The TRIM function removes any trailing spaces from a character string.
The argument of the function is a character expression, which may
contain a combination of character strings and character/text data-field
contents. The format of the TRIM function is

. TRIM(< *character expression* >)

Because the width of a character/text field is preset when the structure
is defined, trailing spaces are automatically added to the end of any
character string shorter than the field width. When the strings are
displayed together, the blank spaces may make the display too wide. For
instance, when the contents of the FIRST_ NAME and LAST_ NAME fields
are displayed on the same line, several spaces separate the characters in
the two fields (see fig. 7.26). When you use the TRIM function to remove
the trailing spaces from the first field, FIRST_ NAME, the display looks
more attractive.

Fig. 7.26.

Using the TRIM *function.*

```
. USE EMPLOYEE
. LOCATE FOR FIRST_NAME="Doris"
Record =        3
. ?FIRST_NAME+LAST_NAME
Doris A.     Gregory
. ?TRIM(FIRST_NAME)+LAST_NAME
Doris A.Gregory
. ?TRIM(FIRST_NAME)+" "+LAST_NAME
Doris A. Gregory
.
```

In figure 7.26, the TRIM function is used to remove all blank spaces in
FIRST_ NAME before it is concatenated with a single space and the
contents of LAST_ NAME.

The RTRIM Function

The RTRIM function performs an operation identical to that of the TRIM
function. RTRIM removes the trailing blanks from the right of the
character expression in the argument. The format of the function is

. RTRIM(< *character expression* >)

The TRIM and RTRIM functions can be used interchangeably to produce
the same result.

The LTRIM Function

The LTRIM function removes all the leading blanks from the left of the
character expression in the argument. The format of the function is

. LTRIM(< *character expression*>)

Figure 7.27 shows use of the LTRIM function to remove the spaces to the left of the characters in the memory variable named B.

Fig. 7.27.

Using the LTRIM *function.*

```
. A="John J. "
John J.
. B="        Smith"
         Smith
. ?A+B
John J.          Smith
. ?A+LTRIM(B)
John J. Smith
.
```

The SPACE Function

Function:
SPACE( )
Creates a
character string
of the specified
number of blank
spaces.

The SPACE function creates a character string containing the number of blank spaces specified in the argument. The format of the function is

. SPACE(< *number of blank spaces*>)

The SPACE function can be used to create a memory variable that contains a specified number of spaces. You can also use this function to insert a number of spaces between data elements that are to be displayed (see fig. 7.28).

Fig. 7.28.

Using the SPACE *function.*

```
. STORE "ABC" TO StringA
ABC
. STORE "XYZ" TO StringB
XYZ
. STORE SPACE(10) TO TenBlanks

. ?StringA+TenBlanks+StringB
ABC          XYZ
.
```

The SUBSTR Function

Function:
SUBSTR( )
Extracts a substring from a character string.

The SUBSTR (substring) function extracts a part of a character string. The arguments of the function include the character string, the starting position of the substring, and the number of characters to be extracted:

. SUBSTR(< *character expression*> ,< *starting position*> ,< *number of characters*>)

In figure 7.29, the first SUBSTR function returns the substring CD from the string ABCDEFG. The second argument gives the starting position (character 3 of the string), and the third argument specifies that two characters are to be extracted.

As shown in figure 7.30, the SUBSTR function can extract a part of a character string from a data field and assign the substring to a memory variable. The substring (the first three characters of PHONE _ NO) is stored to the memory variable Prefix, and that variable is used in a character expression with the ? command.

```
. ?SUBSTR("ABCDEFG",3,2)
CD
. ?SUBSTR("abcdefg",2,4)
bcde
.
```

```
. USE EMPLOYEE
. GOTO 5
EMPLOYEE: Record No      5
. DISPLAY PHONE_NO
Record#  PHONE_NO
      5  787-3154
. STORE SUBSTR(PHONE_NO,1,3) TO Prefix
787
. ?"The telephone prefix is "+Prefix
The telephone prefix is 787
.
```

With SUBSTR functions, you can even rearrange the characters in a character string. Figure 7.31 shows how to use SUBSTR to move the last three characters of the variable StringX to the beginning of the string. Two substrings, SUBSTR(StringX,4,3) and SUBSTR(StringX,1,3), are combined by means of a character expression, and the result is assigned back to the variable StringX.

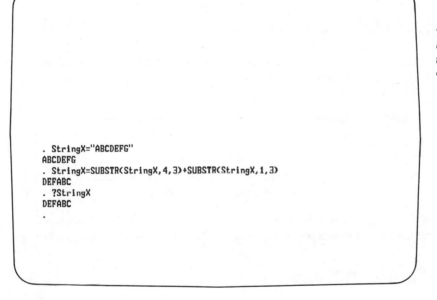

```
. StringX="ABCDEFG"
ABCDEFG
. StringX=SUBSTR(StringX,4,3)+SUBSTR(StringX,1,3)
DEFABC
. ?StringX
DEFABC
.
```

Fig. 7.31.

Using SUBSTR *to rearrange characters.*

The SUBSTR function enables you to use a part of the contents of a character data field for locating, sorting, or indexing operations. For example, the following commands illustrate the use of SUBSTR functions with the LOCATE, DISPLAY, LIST, SORT, and INDEX operations (EMPLOYEE.DBF is the active database file):

. LOCATE FOR SUBSTR(PHONE_NO,5,4)="5Ø85"

. DISPLAY LAST_NAME FOR
SUBSTR(LAST_NAME,1,1)="G"

. LIST AREA_CODE, PHONE_NO FOR
SUBSTR(PHONE_NO,1,3)="123"

```
. SORT ON SUBSTR(PHONE_NO,1,3) TO SORTPRFX

. INDEX ON SUBSTR(PHONE_NO,1,3) TO  INDXPRFX
```

In the first three commands, a substring—for example, (PHONE_NUMBER,5,4) or (LAST_NAME,1,1)—is used for specifying the condition in the qualifier clause (FOR...) of a LOCATE, DISPLAY, or LIST command. The last two commands use a substring, (PHONE_NO,1,3), as the key data field for sorting and indexing.

The LEFT Function

▷

Function:
LEFT()
Extracts a number of characters from the left.

The LEFT function allows you to extract a substring of a specified number of characters from the character expression in the argument. The format of the function is

. LEFT(< *character expression* > , < *numeric expression* >)

The value of the numeric expression determines the number of characters to be extracted from the left of the character string. The extracted substring can be displayed or assigned to another string. Figure 7.32 shows some examples of using the LEFT function.

As shown in figure 7.32, LEFT(FIRSTNAME,5) extracts five characters from the left of the character string Doris Y. The result is the substring Doris.

The RIGHT Function

▷

Function:
RIGHT()
Extracts a number of characters from the right.

Similar to the LEFT function, the RIGHT function extracts a specified number of characters from the right of the character string represented by the character expression in the argument:

. RIGHT(< *character expression* > ,< *numeric expression* >)

The value of the numeric expression determines how many characters are to be extracted from the right of the character string. The extracted substring can be displayed or assigned to another string. An example of using the RIGHT function (used with the LEFT and SUBSTR functions) is shown in figure 7.33.

```
. FirstName="Doris Y."
Doris Y.
. LastName="Taylor"
Taylor
. ?LEFT(FirstName,5)
Doris
. FullName=LastName+", "+LEFT(FirstName,5)
Taylor, Doris
. ?"The Full Name is "+FullName
The Full Name is Taylor, Doris

.
```

Fig. 7.32.

Using the LEFT *function.*

```
. FullName="Doris Y. Smith"
Doris Y. Smith
. LastName=RIGHT(FullName,5)
Smith
. FirstName=LEFT(FullName,5)
Doris
. Initial=SUBSTR(FullName,7,2)
Y.
. ?LastName+", "+FirstName+" "+Initial
Smith, Doris Y.

.
```

Fig. 7.33.

Using the RIGHT *function.*

The STUFF Function

The STUFF function can be used to replace a portion of a character string with another character string. The portion to be replaced is identified by the beginning character position and the number of characters to be replaced. The format of the STUFF function is

> . STUFF(< *1st character string>* ,< *beginning position>* ,< *number of characters to be replaced>* ,< *2nd character string>*)

Figure 7.34 shows an example of using the STUFF function. Beginning with the sixth character, four characters in the string Mary Jane Smith (represented by OLDNAME) are replaced by the string Kay (NEWINITIAL).

Fig. 7.34.

Using the STUFF
function.

```
. OldName="Mary Jane Smith"
Mary Jane Smith
. NewInitial="Kay"
Kay
. ?STUFF(OldName,6,4,NewInitial)
Mary Kay Smith
.
```

The AT Function

The AT function is used to search a character string for a specified substring. If the substring is found, the function returns a number that indicates the starting position of the substring within the string. If the character string does not contain the substring, the function returns a value of zero. The format of the AT function is

Function:
AT( )
Finds a substring from a character string.

   . AT(< *key substring*> ,< *character string*>)

In figure 7.35, the number returned by the first AT function (7) indicates that the substring M. begins at the seventh position in the character string Harry M. Nelson. Using the same logic, you can locate the names of all employees with the middle initial M (see fig. 7.36).

```
 . ?AT("M.","Harry M. Nelson")
         7
 . ?AT("son","Harry M. Nelson")
        13
 .
```

Fig. 7.35.

Using the AT *function.*

Data Type Conversion Functions

Data type conversion functions change data elements from one type to another. For instance, these functions can convert a numeric value or the contents of a numeric field to a character string. Similarly, contents of a date field can be converted to a character string, which may then be used in searching or indexing operations.

Fig. 7.36.

Using the AT
function with
LOCATE.

```
. USE EMPLOYEE
. LOCATE FOR AT("M.",FIRST_NAME)<>0
Record =        4
. DISPLAY
Record#  FIRST_NAME   LAST_NAME  AREA_CODE PHONE_NO MALE BIRTH_DATE ANNUAL_PAY
       4  Harry M.     Nelson        315     576-0235 .T.  02/15/58    33495.00
. ?"The name found is "+TRIM(FIRST_NAME)+" "+LAST_NAME
The name found is Harry M. Nelson
.
```

The VAL Function

Function:

VAL( )
Converts a
character string
to a value.

The VAL function converts a character string of digits to a numeric value.
You specify the character string of digits in the argument, and the
function returns a numeric value. If the character string contains
nonnumeric characters, however, the VAL function returns a zero. The
format of the function is

. VAL(< *character string*>)

The VAL function can be used to enter the contents of a character string
of digits in a numeric variable or expression (see fig. 7.37). If a string
containing a decimal number, such as 123.789, is converted to a value by
the VAL function, the rounded integer value of the string, such as 124, is
displayed if the number of decimal places is set to 0 by SET DECIMALS.
Otherwise, the number of decimals used to display the returned value is
determined by the SET DECIMAL command (see fig. 7.38).

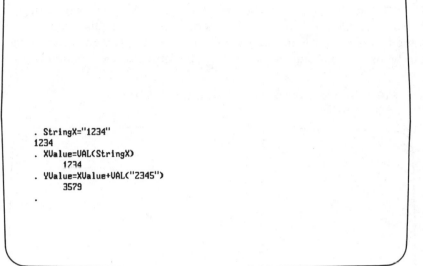

Fig. 7.37.

Using the VAL *function.*

```
. StringX="1234"
1234
. XValue=VAL(StringX)
      1234
. YValue=XValue+VAL("2345")
      3579

.
```

Fig. 7.38.

Results of using the VAL *function with decimal arguments.*

```
. SET DECIMAL TO 0
. ?VAL("123.456")
      123
. ?VAL("123.789")
      124
. SET DECIMAL TO 2
. ?VAL("123.456")
      123.46
. ?VAL("123.789")
      123.79

.
```

The STR Function

Function:
STR( )
*Converts a value
to a character
string.*

The STR function is used to convert numeric data to a character string. The STR function returns a character string representing the numeric value that is passed as the argument (see fig. 7.39). The character string can be used in a character expression. The format of the function is

. STR($<$ *numeric expression$>$ [,length], [,decimal]*)

Fig. 7.39.

Using the STR
function.

```
. ?"xxxxx"+STR(123.456)+"xxxxx"
xxxxx        123xxxxx
. ?"xxxxx"+STR(123.456,5)+"xxxxx"
xxxxx   123xxxxx
. ?"xxxxx"+STR(123.456,5,1)+"xxxxx"
xxxxx123.5xxxxx
.
```

In the argument, the length and decimal are optional. A default length of characters and zero decimal places are assumed if they are not specified.

In figure 7.39, the first STR function converts the numeric value 123.456 to the character string 10 characters long (by default) and without any decimal places. The second STR function returns a string five characters long and zero decimal places. The last STR function displays a five-character string, with one decimal place. Unlike the VAL( ) function, the STR( ) function actually rounds the value returned to the number of decimal places specified in the argument (zero is the default). You cannot restore the lost decimal places.

The contents of numeric data fields can also be used as arguments for the STR function. This function enables you to convert the results of numeric fields and then use character expressions to combine the results with the contents of character fields. The results can then be displayed with a ? command (see fig. 7.40).

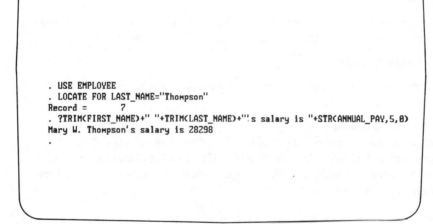

Fig. 7.40.

Displaying results of the STR *function with the* ? *command.*

```
. USE EMPLOYEE
. LOCATE FOR LAST_NAME="Thompson"
Record =        7
. ?TRIM(FIRST_NAME)+" "+TRIM(LAST_NAME)+"'s salary is "+STR(ANNUAL_PAY,5,0)
Mary W. Thompson's salary is 28298
.
```

The STR function is important in data manipulation because you cannot mix numeric and character values in commands. For example, the following command will produce an error message because ANNUAL_ PAY is a numeric field.

```
. ?TRIM(FIRST _NAME) +" " +TRIM(LAST _NAME) +"'s salary
  is " +ANNUAL _PAY
```

The error can be avoided by converting the contents of ANNUAL_ PAY to a character string before issuing the ? command.

The DTOC Function

Function:

DTOC( )
*Converts a date
to a character
string.*

Dates are stored in date fields and in date memory variables. Many restrictions apply to the use of dates in data manipulation. For example, the contents of a date field cannot be used as a key in the LOCATE FOR, DISPLAY FOR, and LIST FOR commands. You cannot mix dates or date variables with character strings for displaying. However, you can use a DTOC (date-to-character) function to convert a date into a character string. Then the string can be used to perform operations that can be carried out only with character strings. The format of the DTOC function is

. DTOC(< *date*>)

The date specified in the argument of the function must be the contents of a date variable or a date field. For instance, if you enter

. ?DTOC("Ø3/Ø8/85")

the error message Invalid function argument is displayed because the argument is a character string.

Figure 7.41 shows how to display a date along with a character string (such as a label). The contents of the date field BIRTH_DATE are first assigned to a date variable (BIRTHDATE). The contents of either the field or the variable can then be converted to a character string and included in a character expression.

After converting a date field into a character string, you can use all or a part of the character string to carry out different searching operations. For example, to search for all employees who were born in or before 1960, use the SUBSTR function to select a substring of the character string DTOC(BIRTH_DATE); then use the resulting substring as the qualifier for the LIST command (see fig. 7.42).

In figure 7.42, the DTOC function converts the contents of the date field BIRTH_DATE to a character string. The string contains the date in the form *mm/dd/yy*. The substring containing the seventh and eighth characters (yy) is extracted by the SUBSTR function and used as a qualifier for the selective LIST operation.

One of the new features in dBASE IV is that you can enclose a date in a pair of curly brackets (such as {12/31/60}). As a result, you can see from figure 7.42 that you can search all the records whose value in the BIRTH_DATE fields is   < ={12/31/6Ø} and produce the same results as that in the first part of the figure.

Fig. 7.41.

Using the DTOC
function.

```
. USE EMPLOYEE
. GO BOTTOM
EMPLOYEE: Record No      10
. STORE BIRTH_DATE TO BirthDate
12/24/45
. ?"Contents of the date field is "+DTOC(BIRTH_DATE)
Contents of the date field is 12/24/45
. ?"Contents of the date variable is "+DTOC(BirthDate)
Contents of the date variable is 12/24/45
.
```

Fig. 7.42.

Using DTOC *with*
LIST.

```
. USE EMPLOYEE
. LIST LAST_NAME, BIRTH_DATE FOR SUBSTR(DTOC(BIRTH_DATE),7,2) <="60"
Record#  LAST_NAME  BIRTH_DATE
      1  Smith      07/04/60
      2  Zeller     09/20/59
      4  Nelson     02/15/58
      5  Baker      10/12/56
      7  Thompson   06/18/55
      9  Lee        05/14/39
     10  Hanson     12/24/45

. LIST LAST_NAME, BIRTH_DATE FOR BIRTH_DATE<={12/31/60}
Record#  LAST_NAME  BIRTH_DATE
      1  Smith      07/04/60
      2  Zeller     09/20/59
      4  Nelson     02/15/58
      5  Baker      10/12/56
      7  Thompson   06/18/55
      9  Lee        05/14/39
     10  Hanson     12/24/45
.
```

The CTOD Function

Dates can be entered in a date field only with the APPEND, BROWSE, or EDIT commands. A date cannot be entered directly in a date variable with the STORE or = commands. The following commands will not assign a date to the date variable ADATE correctly. The first two commands in the list will assign a numeric value (1/25/85) to a numeric variable, while the last two commands store a character string ("01/25/85") to a character variable:

```
. STORE Ø1/25/85 TO ADATE
. ADATE=Ø1/25/85
. ADATE="Ø1/25/85"
. STORE "Ø1/25/85" TO ADATE
```

Function:

CTOD( )
Converts a character string to a date.

The commands "confuse" the program because the type of data element you intend to assign to a date variable has not been clearly identified. When you put quotation marks around the date, it is treated as a character string. On the other hand, without the quotation marks, the date will be misinterpreted as an arithmetic expression (dividing the value of 01 by 25, for instance). Fortunately, the CTOD (character-to-date) function solves some of these problems. The CTOD function converts a character string to a date. The format of a CTOD function is

```
. CTOD( < character string> )
```

For example, the following STORE command uses a CTOD function to enter a date (01/25/85) in the date variable ADATE:

```
. STORE CTOD("Ø1/25/85") TO ADATE
```

In dBASE IV, you can enclose a date value in a pair of curly brackets to assign it to a date variable or field. For example,

Tip:

Use curly brackets to enclose a date value before assigning it to a date memory variable.

```
. STORE {12/24/88} TO XmasEve
. NewYearsDay={Ø1/Ø1/89}
```

Similarly, as shown in figure 7.43, you can use the REPLACE command to replace the contents of a date field (BIRTH_DATE) with a date that is converted from a character string as CTOD("1Ø/1Ø/59" or enclosed in curly brackets as {Ø9/2Ø/59}.

Fig. 7.43.

Using CTOD *with* REPLACE.

```
. USE EMPLOYEE
. LOCATE FOR LAST_NAME="Zeller"
Record =        2
. REPLACE BIRTH_DATE WITH CTOD("10/10/59")
     1 record replaced
. DISPLAY LAST_NAME,BIRTH_DATE
Record# LAST_NAME  BIRTH_DATE
     2  Zeller      10/10/59
. REPLACE BIRTH_DATE WITH {09/20/59}
     1 record replaced
. DISPLAY LAST_NAME,BIRTH_DATE
Record# LAST_NAME  BIRTH_DATE
     2  Zeller      09/20/59
.
```

The CHR Function

Function:

CHR( )
Shows the ASCII character of a specified code.

The CHR function returns an ASCII character (see Appendix A) when that character's numeric code is specified in the argument of the function. The format of the function is

. CHR(< *numeric code of an ASCII character* >)

You can display the ASCII characters by simply specifying their numeric codes as arguments for the CHR function (see fig. 7.44).

ASCII characters include control characters, letters, numbers, and symbols. You use a control character, such as CHR(12), to send a "form feed" code to the printer so that it will eject a page. Most control characters are invisible when you enter them at the keyboard. Some require multiple keystrokes. In such cases, the ASCII numeric code for the control character can be printed with a ? command to perform the control operation. For instance, if the printer is activated, the command

. ?CHR(12)

will cause the printer to advance the paper to the top of the next page.

Fig. 7.44.

*Results of using
the CHR function.*

```
.  ?CHR(83)
S
.  ?CHR(109)
M
.  ?CHR(105)
i
.  ?CHR(116)
t
.  ?CHR(104)
h
.  ?CHR(83),CHR(109),CHR(105),CHR(116),CHR(104)
S m i t h
.  ?CHR(83)+CHR(109)+CHR(105)+CHR(116)+CHR(104)
Smith
.
```

The ASC Function

Function:
ASC( )
*Shows the ASCII
code of the
specified
character.*

The CHR function returns the ASCII character whose numeric code is provided in the argument; ASC does the reverse. When you specify an ASCII character in the argument, the ASC function returns the corresponding numeric code for the character enclosed in quotation marks (see fig. 7.45). The format of the function is

. ASC(< *ASCII character* >)

From figure 7.45, you will note that the ASC function returns a numeric value for the ASCII character code. If more than one character is included in the argument, ASC( ) returns the ASCII character code of the first character in the string.

Time/Date Functions

dBASE IV has a set of functions for processing dates and time. Some of these functions require an argument, and others do not. Although the

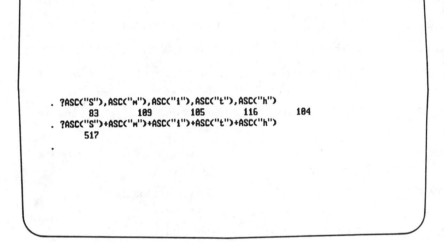

Fig. 7.45.

*Results of using
the* ASC *function.*

input data type is a date, the data elements returned by these functions can be numeric values or character strings. The date/time functions include TIME, DATE, DMY, CDOW, CMONTH, DOW, DAY, MDY, MONTH, and YEAR.

The TIME and DATE functions always use as input the current time and date stored in the internal system clock and therefore do not need arguments. Their formats are

    TIME( )
    DATE( )

The other functions require arguments, which can be the contents of date fields or of date memory variables:

    < *name of function*> (< *date field/variable*>)

Descriptions of these functions are given in table 7.1. The contents of the BIRTH_ DATE field in James C. Smith's record is used as the sample date.

Table 7.1
Descriptions of Time/Date Functions

Function	Example	Returned Data Element	Returned Data Type
TIME	. ?TIME( )	Current system time	Character
DATE	. ?DATE( )	Current system date	Character
CDOW	. ?CDOW(BirthDate)	Character date of the week	Character
CMONTH	. ?CMONTH(BirthDate)	Character month of the year	Character
DOW	. ?DOW(BirthDate)	Numeric code for day of the week	Character
DAY	. ?DAY(BirthDate)	Numeric code for day of the year	Numeric
DMY	. ?DMY(BirthDate)	A date in the form of DD Month YY	—
MDY	. ?MDY(BirthDate)	A date in the form of Month DD YY	—
MONTH	. ?MONTH(BirthDate)	Numeric code for month of the year	Numeric
YEAR	. ?YEAR(BirthDate)	Numeric code for year	Numeric

Figure 7.46 shows examples of the values returned from these date functions.

The ROW, COL, PROW, and PCOL Functions

dBASE IV has four functions that find the current cursor position on the screen and the printing position on the printer paper: ROW, COL, PROW, and PCOL. The ROW and COL functions return the row and column positions of the cursor. Similarly, the current printing position on the printer can be

```
. BirthDate={05/14/59}
05/14/59
. ?TIME()
15:58:39
. ?DATE()
11/27/88
. ?CDOW(BirthDate)
Thursday
. ?CMONTH(BirthDate)
May
. ?DOW(BirthDate)
        5
. ?DAY(BirthDate)
       14
. ?DMY(BirthDate)
14 May 59
. ?MDY(BirthDate)
May 14, 59
. ?MONTH(BirthDate)
        5
. ?YEAR(BirthDate)
     1959

.
```

Fig. 7.46.

Examples of using time and date functions.

found by using the PROW and PCOL functions. These functions are often used in batch-processing mode to controlling the output position on the screen or the printer paper; these functions therefore are discussed in later chapters.

A Summary Example

Functions play an important role in data manipulation. As a summary of the frequently used functions, figure 7.47 provides an example that calculates the ending balance on a beginning principal of $10,000.

The example computes the ending balance on 01/25/86 (Date2) of a savings account that begins with a deposit of $10,000 (Principal) on 01/25/85 (Date1). The annual interest rate (YearRate) is assumed to be 12 percent (0.12 in decimal form). Interest earned by the account is compounded daily at the rate of 0.032877 percent (DailyRate, determined by dividing the annual rate of 12 percent by 365 days). The number of days elapsed between 01/25/85 and 01/25/86 (Days) is computed by taking the difference between the two dates:

Fig. 7.47.

Using functions to calculate loan balance.

```
. Date1={01/25/85}
01/25/85
. Date2={01/25/86}
01/25/86
. Days=Date2-Date1
        365
. SET DECIMAL TO 8
. YearRate=0.12
         0.12000000
. DailyRate=YearRate/365
         0.00032877
. Principal=10000
     10000
. EndBalance=Principal*(1+DailyRate)^Days
     11274.74615639
. ?"Ending Balance = ",ROUND(EndBalance,2)
Ending Balance =        11274.75000000
.
```

Days = Date2 – Date1

The ending balance (EndBalance) is then computed with the following formula:

EndBalance = Principal × (1 + DailyRate)^Days

Chapter Summary

This chapter introduced the concept of memory variables, expressions, and functions. A memory variable is a name assigned to a memory location that is used to store a data element temporarily. Four types of memory variables can be used: character, numeric, date, and logical. Expressions in dBASE IV define the operations to be carried out on specified data elements. dBASE IV has two types of expressions: arithmetic and character expressions. This chapter also introduced all the dBASE IV functions that you use to convert data elements from one type to another, to manipulate character strings, and to perform mathematical operations. In this chapter, only those commonly used functions were discussed. For a complete list of dBASE IV built-in functions, see the dBASE IV Summary of Functions, included later in this book.

8

Generating Labels
and Reports

I n the preceding chapters, you have seen how to use dot commands to
print or display on-screen the contents of data records and memory
variables. You can develop your own programs with these commands to
generate labels and reports for your database management applications.
However, you need a fair amount of knowledge and programming
experience to produce labels and reports this way.

Instead of writing programs, you can generate reports and labels with the
user-friendly and powerful report and label generators provided with
dBASE IV. In this chapter, you explore the available features and learn
how to use these generators to produce useful reports and labels.

One of the most important database applications is to store names and
addresses in a database file. In addition to searching and displaying
selective information, you can produce mailing labels. This chapter
presents the options you can use to design your mailing labels.

In addition to creating labels, you can produce sophisticated and
complex reports without writing a program. By using the report
generator, you can choose one of three quick layouts (column, form, and
mailmerge) to present your report. Or you easily can modify one of these
layouts to suit your needs. This chapter discusses the features you can
use to create your report.

Creating Labels from the Control Center

To create a custom label, you invoke the label generator by selecting the appropriate menu option from the Control Center or by entering the appropriate command at the dot prompt. Once you select the label generator, you design your labels in the same way regardless of how the generator was invoked.

You can save the label design on disk in a label file (.LBL). The label file contains all the data fields; the contents of these fields will be used to make the labels. The file also contains specifications such as the label's width and length. After you create and save a label file, you can recall it whenever you want to create labels with the same contents.

To illustrate designing and processing mailing labels, you need to create a sample database file as an example. Create the database file ACCOUNTS.DBF with the database structure shown in figure 8.1. Address information is divided into four fields: address, city, state, and ZIP code.

Fig. 8.1.

The database structure of ACCOUNTS.DBF.

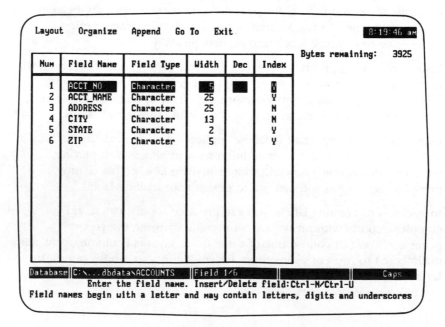

The following summarizes the information stored in ACCOUNTS.DBF:

Account #	Account Name	Address,City,State,Zip
A-101	Fairwind Travel	3256 Mountainview Drive Mesa, AZ 85201
B-101	Evergreen Florists	2658 Broadway Vancouver, WA 98664
C-101	ACME Construction	1456 S.E. 132nd Avenue Portland, OR 97204
A-201	B & J Fine Furniture	3567 S. W. Canyon Road Beaverton, OR 97203
A-301	Western Electronic	2478 University Avenue Seattle, WA 98105
C-201	Ace Secretarial Services	5214 Main Street Salem, OR 97201
C-301	Lake Grove Bookstore	3456 Boonesferry Road Lake Oswego, OR 97035
A-202	Everex Computers	13456 Market Street San Diego, CA 91355
C-202	Johnson & Associates	10345 Riverside Drive New York, NY 10038
B-201	National Data Services	3081 Columbus Avenue Santa Monica, CA 90406

To design your labels from the Control Center, highlight the database file you want to use. Then select the < **create**> option from the Labels panel and press Enter. For instance, you may want to produce mailing labels that look like the following:

A-101

Fairwind Travel
3256 Mountainview Drive
Mesa   AZ   85201

B-101

Evergreen Florists
2658 Broadway
Vancouver   WA   98664

C-101

ACME Construction
1456 S.E. 132nd Avenue
Portland   OR   97204

A-201

B & J Fine Furniture
3567 S. W. Canyon Road
Beaverton   OR   97203

	A-301				C-201		
Western Electronic				Ace Secretarial Services			
2478 University Avenue				5214 Main Street			
Seattle		WA	98105	Salem		OR	97201

	C-301				A-202		
Lake Grove Bookstore				Everex Computers			
3456 Boonesferry Road				13456 Market Street			
Lake Oswego		OR	97035	San Diego		CA	91355

	C-202				B-201		
Johnson & Associates				National Data Services			
10345 Riverside Drive				3081 Columbus Avenue			
New York		NY	10038	Santa Monica		CA	90406

To produce these mailing labels, highlight the ACCOUNTS database file from the Data panel and press Enter. Then select < **create**> from the Labels panel and press Enter. A design form for the mailing labels is displayed (see fig. 8.2).

Fig. 8.2.

A label design form.

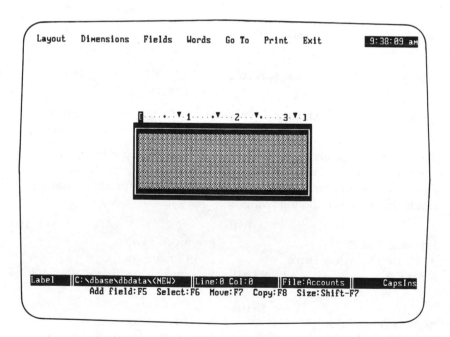

Defining Label Dimensions

To define the dimensions of the label, press Alt-D to invoke the Dimensions menu (see fig. 8.3). You must define the parameters that determine the size and dimensions of the label.

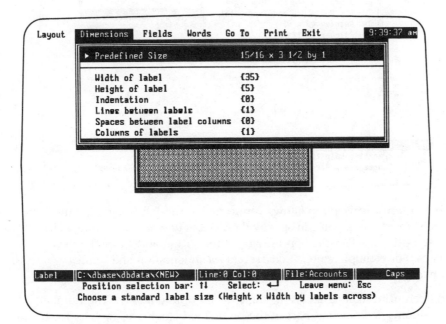

Fig. 8.3.

The Dimensions menu.

You can select the label size from the Dimensions menu. The default size is 15/16 by 3 1/2 (inches) by 1 (column). To select other sizes, highlight the **Predefined Size** option and press the Enter key (see fig. 8.4). To select any one of these label sizes, highlight the size you want and press Ctrl-End.

Next, you define the width of the label by specifying the number of characters. The default width is set to 35 characters. To change the default, highlight the **Width of label** option and press Enter. At the Enter an integer prompt:, enter the desired width. For example, you can type 30 and press Enter.

The default height is 5 lines. You can specify a different label height. For example, to specify 4 as the label height, highlight the **Height of label** option, press Enter, type 4, and press Enter again.

Fig. 8.4.

Selecting a predefined label size.

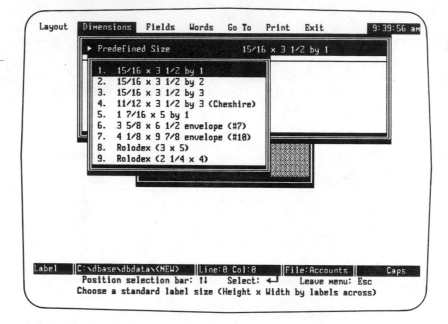

The **Indentation** option allows you to define the left margin for the labels. In addition, you can specify the lines between labels. To specify these options, select the appropriate menu option and enter the new values. For example, enter Ø characters for indentation and 2 lines between labels.

Caution:

*The **Columns of labels** option takes precedence over the label size.*

You can print mailing labels in single or multiple columns. The number of columns is defined as part of the predefined label size, such as 15/16 × 3 1/2 by 2 columns, 11/12 × 3 1/2 by 3 columns, and so on. Or you can define the number of columns by entering a number in the **Columns of labels** option. The number you enter overrides the default in the predefined size. For example, select a 2-column label format for the **Columns of labels** option and 5 for the **Spaces between the label columns** option.

After you define the label dimensions (see fig. 8.5), press Ctrl-End to continue. A label design is displayed with the dimensions you defined (see fig. 8.6).

Placing Data Fields on the Label Form

For the next step in designing labels, you place the desired data fields on the label form. To do that, position the cursor at the beginning of the

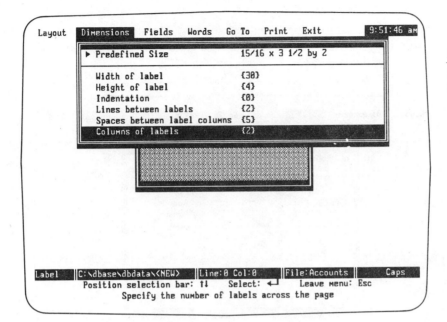

Fig. 8.5.

The label dimensions.

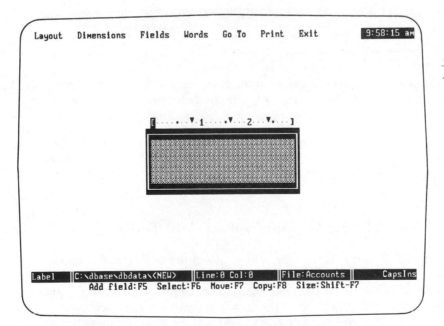

Fig. 8.6.

A label form.

data field (for example, line 0 and column 24). Then press Alt-F to invoke the Fields menu and select the **Add field** option. The fields you can place on the label are displayed (see fig. 8.7).

Fig. 8.7.

The fields for the label.

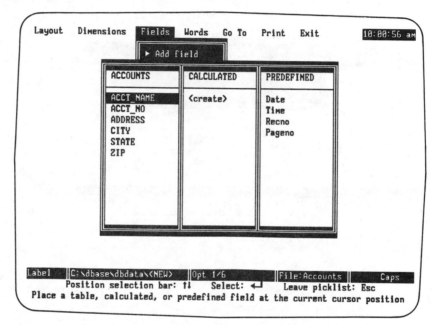

The data fields you can place on the label form include those defined in the ACCOUNTS.DBF database file and the fields predefined by dBASE IV (the system date and time, record number, and page number).

For example, you can place the ACCT_NO field on the label form by highlighting the field and pressing Enter (see fig. 8.8). A set of menu options for defining the display attributes are displayed (see fig. 8.9).

Defining the Display Field Template

In addition to the name, type, and length of the field, you can specify the field template and picture functions. The field template defines the template symbols for the field value. For example, the default template for ACCT_NO is {XXXXX}. The template symbol X represents any character. Because the ACCT_NO field is five characters long, the default is set to five X's.

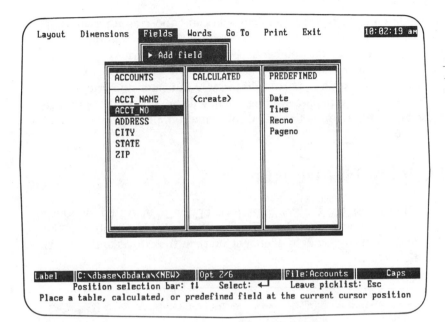

Fig. 8.8.

Adding the account number to the label.

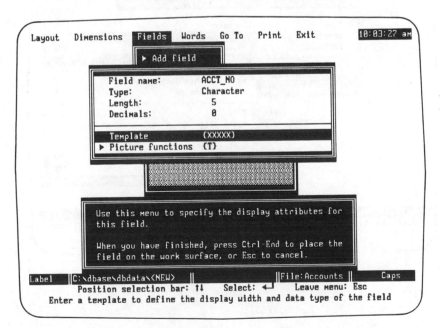

Fig. 8.9.

Defining the field template for ACCT_NO.

Depending on the type of data field, you can choose another appropriate symbol to define the field template. Suppose that, for example, you want to display your account number as a capital letter followed by a dash and then three numeric digits. You can define the field template as !-999. The ! is used to display an uppercase letter; 999 indicates numeric digits. To view a list of the template symbols, highlight the **Template** option and press Enter. After you define the display field template, press Ctrl-End to continue.

Defining Picture Functions

You also can use the **Picture functions** option to activate functions for data conversion and alignments. To view the available picture functions for the current display field, highlight **Picture functions** and press Enter (see fig. 8.10).

Fig. 8.10.

Defining the field picture for ACCT_NO.

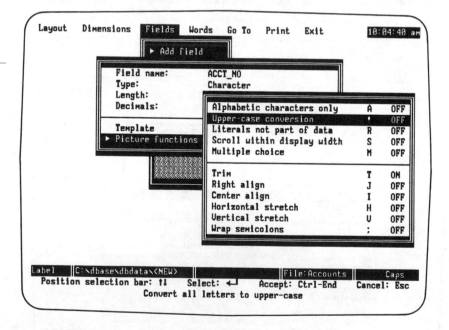

```
 Layout   Dimensions   Fields   Words   Go To   Print   Exit        10:04:40 am

                         ▶ Add field

            Field name:       ACCT_NO
            Type:             Character
            Length:
            Decimals:     ┌────────────────────────────────────────┐
                          │ Alphabetic characters only      A   OFF │
                          │ Upper-case conversion           !   OFF │
            Template      │ Literals not part of data       R   OFF │
          ▶ Picture functions│ Scroll within display width  S   OFF │
                          │ Multiple choice                 M   OFF │
                          ├────────────────────────────────────────┤
                          │ Trim                            T   ON  │
                          │ Right align                     J   OFF │
                          │ Center align                    I   OFF │
                          │ Horizontal stretch              H   OFF │
                          │ Vertical stretch                V   OFF │
                          │ Wrap semicolons                 ;   OFF │
                          └────────────────────────────────────────┘

 Label │ C:\dbase\dbdata\<NEW>                    │ File:Accounts │   Caps
      Position selection bar: ↑↓    Select: ↵    Accept: Ctrl-End   Cancel: Esc
                      Convert all letters to upper-case
```

template. For example, if you activate the **Upper-case conversion** function, all the characters in the field are displayed in uppercase letters even though you define the template differently.

The **Trim** function allows you to trim off the trailing blank spaces in the data field. If you do not use the **Trim** function, a fixed field length is used to display the field value. You can use the **Right align** and **Center align** features to align the field value in the label.

Tip:
Use the **Trim** *function to cut off trailing blank spaces in a field value.*

To save the picture, press Ctrl-End. The picture functions you selected are displayed in the **Picture functions** option—for example, {T} for the **Trim** function.

After you define all the display attributes for the data field, press Ctrl-End to place it on the label form. The field template is placed at the current cursor position (see fig. 8.11).

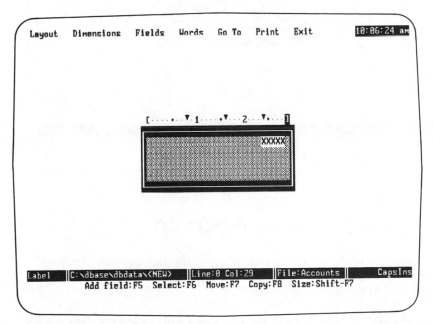

Fig. 8.11.

The ACCT_NO template.

To place other data fields (ACCT_NAME, ADDRESS, CITY, STATE, and ZIP) on the label form, move the cursor to the location you want to place the field, invoke the Fields menu (press Alt-F), and select the **Add field** option. For this example, place all the fields on the label and choose the default settings for the display attributes. Don't use the **Trim** function for the CITY field; you want the STATE and ZIP fields to print in the same locations on the labels regardless of the actual width of the CITY field.

After you place all the necessary fields on the label form (see fig. 8.12), you can view the labels on-screen to verify the layout.

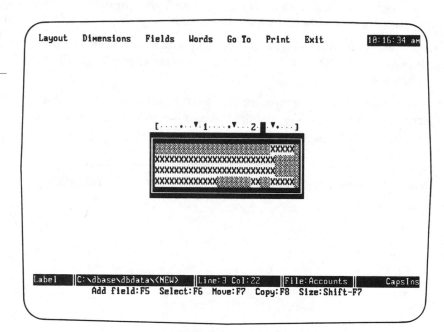

Fig. 8.12.

All the field templates on the label.

Viewing Labels On-Screen

Tip:

Preview the labels on-screen before you print them.

To view the labels on-screen before you print them, invoke the Print menu by pressing Alt-P. From this menu, choose the **View labels on screen** option (see fig. 8.13).

In addition to the label form, the program (.LBG) file for producing the label form is created automatically. When you ask dBASE IV to produce the mailing labels, dBASE converts the commands in the program (.LBG) file to an object code (.LBO) file. dBASE IV then uses this file to generate the mailing labels. (Note that an experienced programmer can modify the program file, but a beginning user need not be concerned with the .LBG and .LBO files.)

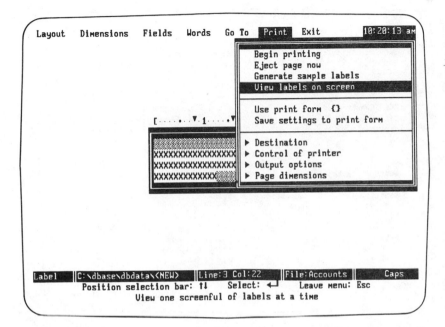

Fig. 8.13.

The Print menu.

After generating the program, dBASE IV displays the mailing labels on-screen according to the design you defined (see fig. 8.14). All the labels are displayed in sections, using one screen per section. Press the space bar to view the next section. To interrupt viewing and return to the label form design screen, press Esc.

Printing Labels

If you want to check the placement on the printed label, you can choose the **Generate sample labels** from the Print menu (see fig. 8.13). A sample label layout is printed with the field template such as the following:

```
XXXXXXXXXXXXXXXXXXXX     XXXXXXXXXXXXXXXXXXXX
XXXXXXXXXXXXXXXXXXXX     XXXXXXXXXXXXXXXXXXXX
XXXXXXXXXXXXXXXXXXXX     XXXXXXXXXXXXXXXXXXXX
XXXXXXXXXXXXXXXXXXXX     XXXXXXXXXXXXXXXXXXXX
```

If you are satisfied with the labels, you can print them. Invoke the Print menu (press Alt-P) and select the **Begin printing** option. You can interrupt printing by pressing the Esc key.

Tip:
Use the **Generate sample labels** *option to view the label placement.*

Fig. 8.14.

Previewing the mailing labels.

```
                          A-101                              B-101
        Fairwind Travel                 Evergreen Florists
        3256 Mountainview Drive         2658 Broadway
        Mesa              AZ  85201      Vancouver         WA  98664


                          C-101                              A-201
        ACME Construction               B & J Fine Furniture
        1456 S.E. 132nd Avenue          3567 S. W. Canyon Road
        Portland          OR  97204      Beaverton         OR  97203


                          A-301                              C-201
        Western Electronic              Ace Secretarial Services
        2478 University Avenue          5214 Main Street
        Seattle           WA  98105      Salem             OR  97201


                          C-301                              A-202
        Lake Grove Bookstore            Everex Computers
        3456 Boonesferry Road           13456 Market Street
        Lake Oswego       OR  97035      San Diego         CA  91355


             Cancel viewing: ESC,   Continue viewing: SPACEBAR
```

Saving a Label Design

If you save the label file, you can use it again when you need to print labels for this database. To save the file, invoke the Exit menu (press Alt-E) and select the **Save changes and exit** option. When the Save as: prompt appears, enter a name for the label design (for example, ACCOUNTS). The label form file is saved with an .LBL extension. (The .LBG and .LBO files are saved under the same name.)

Using an Existing Label Design

To use a label design again, first put the designated database file into use. Then highlight the label file in the Labels panel and press Enter. Finally, select the **Print label** option from the Labels menu. From here you can select to generate a sample, view, or print the labels.

Modifying a Label Design

To change a label design you have created and saved, you first select the database file. Then you highlight the label file in the Labels panel and press Enter.

From the Labels menu, select the **Modify layout** option and press Enter. For example, if you want to change the ACCOUNTS.LBL file, select ACCOUNTS in the Data panel and press Enter (if the database file is not already being used). Then highlight ACCOUNTS in the Labels panel and press Enter. The ACCOUNTS label design is displayed on-screen.

At this point, you follow the same procedures for creating a label. To save the modified label design, select the **Save changes and exit** option from the Exit menu.

Printing Labels on Envelopes

Instead of printing names and addresses on mailing labels, you also can use the label generator to print envelopes. Figure 8.15 shows a sample label design for printing envelopes.

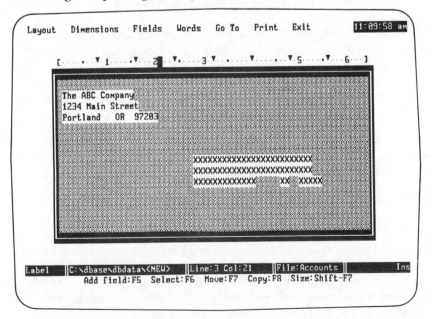

Fig. 8.15.

An envelope label design.

You can create the envelope label design by following these steps:

1. Highlight ACCOUNTS in the Data Panel.

2. Select < **create**> from the Labels panel.

3. Press Alt-D to invoke the Dimensions menu.

4. Highlight the **Predefined Size** option and press Enter.

5. Select 4 1/8 × 6 1/2 envelope (#10) for the predefined size.

6. Place the ACCT_NAME, ADDRESS, CITY, STATE, and ZIP fields on the envelope form.

7. Add the sender's address on the upper left corner of the envelope form.

When you position your data fields and text (such as sender's address), you can use the Tab and Shift-Tab (in addition to the arrow keys) to move your cursor to the preset tab positions. Use the Home key to move the cursor to the beginning of the line. Pressing the PgUp and PgDn keys positions the cursor to the top and bottom of the form respectively.

Setting Printer Control Codes

If you want to send a string of characters to set printer control codes, you must specify the starting and ending control codes on the Print menu (see fig. 8.16). You can use these control codes to advance printer paper, change type font (for italic, and so on) and pitch (characters per inches), and other options. You need to refer to your printer manual for the appropriate codes and their functions.

For example, you can use the starting printer control code shown in figure 8.16 to print condensed type on an EPSON MX-100® printer. The ending printer control code returns the printer to normal print type.

Using Selective Records

Tip:

Use a query to select records to be used for labels.

Instead of using all the records in a database file, you can use a query to select the records for which you want labels or envelopes. In the query design, you specify the filter conditions and save the query view. Finally, you create a label form or use an existing label form to produce the mailing labels for the records generated by the query.

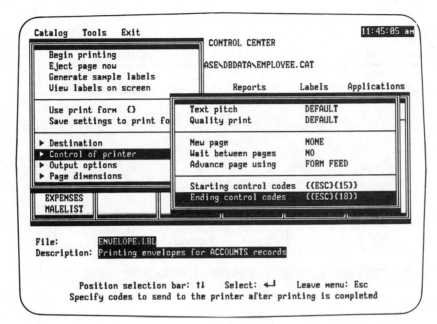

Fig. 8.16.

Setting printer control codes.

For example, if you want to print labels for just Washington and Oregon accounts (NW accounts), you must create a query to select the appropriate records. Create a query design named NWACCTS. In the NWACCTS query design, specify "WA" and "OR" filter conditions (in separate lines) in the file skeleton. Include all the fields you want printed on the ACCOUNTS label design (see fig. 8.17).

After you design the query, you can view the records included in the query by pressing F2. These records, as shown in figure 8.18, meet the filter conditions you specified (value in the STATE field equals "WA" or "OR").

To save the query and return to the Control Center, press Alt-E to invoke the Exit menu and then select the **Exit** option.

To create a new label form or use an existing label form for the query records, first select the view: highlight the query file in the Queries panel and press Enter. Then select the **Use view** option. Now you can use the label form to produce mailing labels for the records in the query view.

For example, if you want to use the records from the NWACCTS query view to generate mailing labels with the ACCOUNTS label form, follow these steps:

Fig. 8.17.

Defining filter conditions in the query.

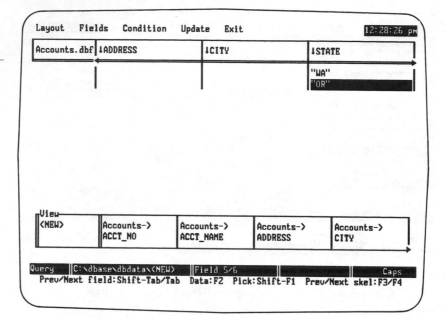

```
 Layout    Fields   Condition   Update   Exit              12:28:26 PM
┌──────────────────────────────────────────────────────────────────┐
│Accounts.dbf│↓ADDRESS          │↓CITY          │↓STATE             │
│            ◄─────────────────────────────────────────────────────►│
│            │                  │               │"WA"               │
│            │                  │               │"OR"               │
│                                                                    │
│                                                                    │
│                                                                    │
│  ┌View─────────────────────────────────────────────────────────── │
│  │<NEW>      │Accounts->  │Accounts->  │Accounts->  │Accounts->    │
│  │           │ACCT_NO     │ACCT_NAME   │ADDRESS     │CITY          │
│  │                                                              ───►│
└──────────────────────────────────────────────────────────────────┘
 Query  │C:\dbase\dbdata\<NEW>│  │Field 5/6│  │           Caps
  Prev/Next field:Shift-Tab/Tab   Data:F2  Pick:Shift-F1  Prev/Next skel:F3/F4
```

Fig. 8.18.

The records produced by the query.

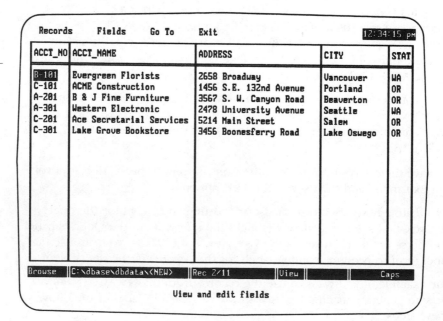

```
 Records      Fields     Go To     Exit              12:34:15 PM
┌────────┬───────────────────────┬──────────────────────┬────────────┬─────┐
│ACCT_NO │ACCT_NAME              │ADDRESS               │CITY        │STAT │
├────────┼───────────────────────┼──────────────────────┼────────────┼─────┤
│B-101   │Evergreen Florists     │2658 Broadway         │Vancouver   │WA   │
│C-101   │ACME Construction      │1456 S.E. 132nd Avenue│Portland    │OR   │
│A-201   │B & J Fine Furniture   │3567 S. W. Canyon Road│Beaverton   │OR   │
│A-301   │Western Electronic     │2478 University Avenue│Seattle     │WA   │
│C-201   │Ace Secretarial Services│5214 Main Street     │Salem       │OR   │
│C-301   │Lake Grove Bookstore   │3456 Boonesferry Road │Lake Oswego │OR   │
│        │                       │                      │            │     │
└────────┴───────────────────────┴──────────────────────┴────────────┴─────┘
 Browse │C:\dbase\dbdata\<NEW>│  │Rec 2/11│  │View│  │         Caps
                        View and edit fields
```

1. Highlight the query file NWACCTS in the Queries panel and press Enter.

2. Select the **Use view** option.

3. Highlight the label file ACCOUNTS in the Labels panel and press Enter.

4. Select the **Print label** option.

5. Select the **Current view** option.

6. To preview the mailing labels, select the **View labels on screen** option.

The mailing labels are shown in figure 8.19.

```
              B-101                        C-101

    Evergreen Florists          ACME Construction
    2658 Broadway               1456 S.E. 132nd Avenue
    Vancouver        WA  98664   Portland        OR  97204


              A-201                        A-301

    B & J Fine Furniture        Western Electronic
    3567 S. W. Canyon Road      2478 University Avenue
    Beaverton        OR  97203   Seattle         WA  98105


              C-201                        C-301

    Ace Secretarial Services    Lake Grove Bookstore
    5214 Main Street            3456 Boonesferry Road
    Salem            OR  97201   Lake Oswego     OR  97035



              Press any key to continue...
```

Fig. 8.19.

Previewing the mailing labels.

After you make sure that you are satisfied with the mailing labels, you can print them.

Sorting Records

If you want to produce mailing labels that are arranged in a certain order, you can index the records with the appropriate index tags before you use the label form. For example, if you need to order your mailing labels by ZIP code, you first index the records in the ACCOUNTS.DBF with the ZIP index tag and then use the ACCOUNTS label form. To do so, complete the following steps:

1. Highlight the ACCOUNTS database file in the Data panel and press Shift-F2 to bring up the database design.

2. Select **Order records by index** and choose the ZIP index tag as the controlling index.

3. Return to the Control Center by pressing Ctrl-End.

4. Highlight the ACCOUNTS label file in the Labels panel and press Enter.

5. Select the **Print label** option.

6. Preview the mailing labels on-screen before you print them by choosing the **View labels on screen** option.

The first set of mailing labels is shown in figure 8.20.

Notice that in figure 8.20 the ZIP codes are sorted in ascending order. You can produce mailing labels that are sorted by their account number by simply indexing the records in the ACCOUNTS database file with the ACCT_NO index tag before you use the label form.

Creating Labels at the Dot Prompt

The label generator, one of the powerful tools provided with dBASE IV, helps you manage your data. Although you can access the label generator easily from the Control Center, you also can create a new label form by issuing the CREATE LABEL command:

. CREATE LABEL < *name of the label file*>

```
                          C-202                          A-101
        Johnson & Associates          Fairwind Travel
        10345 Riverside Drive         3256 Mountainview Drive
        New York          NY  10038   Mesa              AZ  85201


                          B-201                          A-202
        National Data Services        Everex Computers
        3081 Columbus Avenue          13456 Market Street
        Santa Monica      CA  90406   San Diego         CA  91355


                          C-301                          C-201
        Lake Grove Bookstore          Ace Secretarial Services
        3456 Boonesferry Road         5214 Main Street
        Lake Oswego       OR  97035   Salem             OR  97201


                          A-201                          C-101
        B & J Fine Furniture          ACME Construction
        3567 S. W. Canyon Road        1456 S.E. 132nd Avenue
        Beaverton         OR  97203   Portland          OR  97204


        Cancel viewing: ESC,   Continue viewing: SPACEBAR
```

Fig. 8.20.

Mailing labels sorted by ZIP codes.

For example, the following commands use the ACCOUNTS database and create a label form named ACCOUNTS:

. USE ACCOUNTS
. CREATE LABEL ACCOUNTS

A label design form is displayed. You use the same procedure described earlier to design the label form.

Using an Existing Label Form at the Dot Prompt

At the dot prompt, you can use an existing label form to produce the mailing labels with the LABEL FORM command:

. LABEL FORM < *name of the label form*>
[FOR < *filter conditions*>] [TO PRINT]

Command:
LABEL FORM
Selects an existing label form to be used.

For example, the following commands specify to use the ACCOUNTS label form:

```
. USE ACCOUNTS
. LABEL FORM ACCOUNTS
```

After processing these commands, the mailing labels are displayed on-screen. If you want to print your labels, add the TO PRINT phrase at the end of the LABEL FORM command.

You can produce mailing labels with selective records from a database file by adding the necessary filter conditions in the LABEL FORM command. The following command prints mailing labels for records whose STATE field equals "CA":

```
. LABEL FORM ACCOUNTS FOR STATE="CA" TO PRINT
```

You also can arrange the records with an index tag before you use the label form:

```
. USE ACCOUNTS
. SET ORDER TO ACCT_NO
Master index: ACCT_NO
. LABEL FORM ACCOUNTS TO PRINT
```

The SET ORDER command designates ACCT_NO as the controlling index. Records in the ACCOUNTS database file are arranged in ascending order by account number. Consequently, mailing labels printed by the LABEL FORM command are arranged by account number.

Modifying a Label Form at the Dot Prompt

▶ **Command:**
MODIFY LABEL
Brings up an existing label form for modification.

You can recall a label form to make changes with the MODIFY LABEL command:

```
. MODIFY LABEL < name of label form>
```

For example, the following commands call the label form ACCOUNTS for editing:

```
. USE ACCOUNTS
. MODIFY LABEL ACCOUNTS
```

The label design saved in the label form file is displayed on-screen. You then can use the procedure described earlier to make any changes to the form.

Creating Reports from the Control Center

One of the most significant enhancements made by dBASE IV is the report generator. With the report generator, you can produce sophisticated and complex reports without writing a program. With the generator, you can choose one of three quick layouts (column, form, and mailmerge) to present your report. Or you easily can modify one of these layouts to suit your needs.

To create a report, you first invoke a report design form by selecting the appropriate menu option from the Control Center or by using the necessary command at the dot prompt. Once the report design form is displayed, you design your report form in the same way regardless of how you invoked the generator.

At the Control Center, first put the database you want into use in the Data panel. To create a new report form, select the < **create**> option from the Reports panel. The report form specifies the layout and details of the headings and their locations in the report.

To illustrate the features of the report generator, a database file named EXPENSES.DBF has been created. The database structure and contents of this database are shown in figures 8.21 and 8.22 respectively.

EXPENSES.DBF contains 17 records that represent the expense items for October 1988. Various types of summary reports will be generated with the data in these records. Note that in figure 8.21 the DATE and TYPE fields are indexed. Index tags created from these two fields will be used later to arrange records in the database file to produce summary reports.

Fig. 8.21.

The database structure of EXPENSES.DBF.

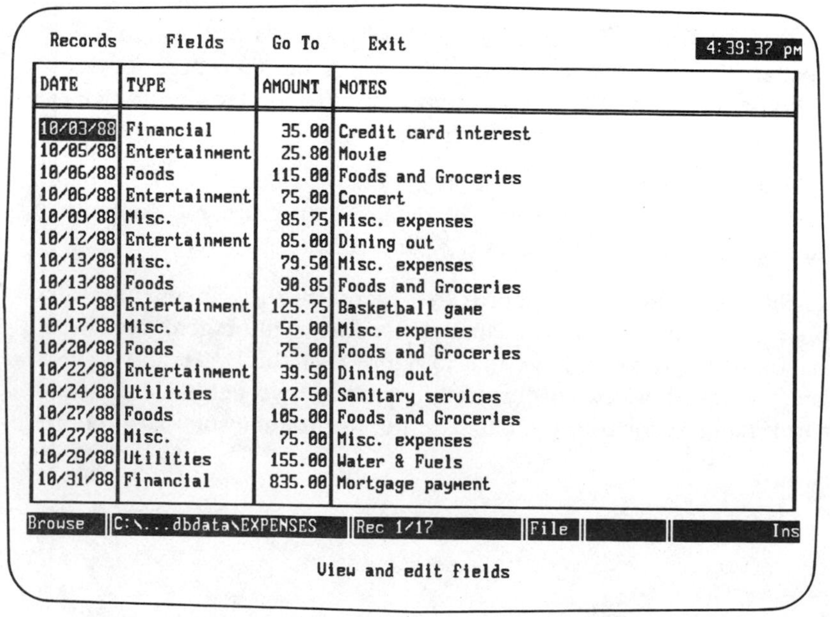

Fig. 8.22.

The records in EXPENSES.DBF.

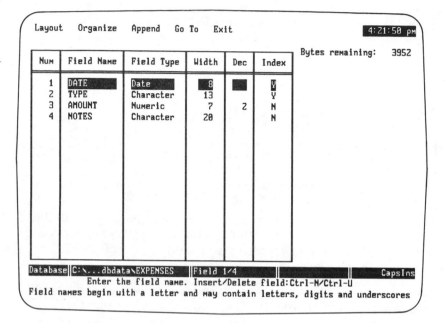

Designing a Columnar Report

The most common report form is a column layout with field values in a columnar format. For example, the expense report shown in figure 8.23 illustrates a report produced by using the field values in the EXPENSES.DBF records.

```
Page No.    1
10/31/88
                      EXPENSE REPORT

                For the Month of October 1988


Date        Expense Type  Amount      Description
----        ------------  ------      -----------
10/03/88    Financial         35.00   Credit card interest
10/05/88    Entertainment     25.80   Movie
10/06/88    Foods            115.00   Foods and Groceries
10/06/88    Entertainment     75.00   Concert
10/09/88    Misc.             85.75   Misc. expenses
10/12/88    Entertainment     85.00   Dining out
10/13/88    Misc.             79.50   Misc. expenses
10/13/88    Foods             90.85   Foods and Groceries
10/15/88    Entertainment    125.75   Basketball game
10/17/88    Misc.             55.00   Misc. expenses
10/20/88    Foods             75.00   Foods and Groceries
10/22/88    Entertainment     39.50   Dining out
10/24/88    Utilities         12.50   Sanitary services
10/27/88    Foods            105.00   Foods and Groceries
10/27/88    Misc.             75.00   Misc. expenses
10/29/88    Utilities        155.00   Water & Fuels
10/31/88    Financial        835.00   Mortgage payment
                            2069.65
```

Fig. 8.23.

An expense report.

To generate the expense report shown in figure 8.23, you first select a basic design for the report form. To do this, follow these steps:

1. Put the EXPENSES database file into use in the Data panel.

2. Select the < **create**> option from the Reports panel and press Enter.

The Layout menu is displayed. Select the **Quick layouts** option from the menu; this option automatically provides a basic design for the report form. If you choose **Quick layouts**, you are asked to select one of three layouts—column, form, and mailmerge (see fig. 8.24).

A column layout presents field values in a column format while form layout displays fields values in a horizontal format. Mailmerge layout

Fig. 8.24.

The Quick layouts menu.

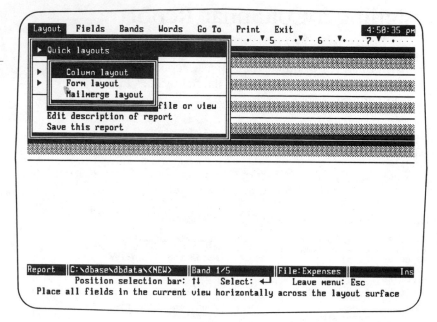

allows you to design form letters; you can insert field values into your text.

To learn how to produce a report, choose the **Column layout** option. When you select this option, a standard columnar report form is displayed (see fig. 8.25).

Note the various parts of the report layout in figure 8.25. The report is divided into different sections each of which is formed by a band.

The Page Header Band, at the top of the report, is used for entering the heading and title of the report. Information in the Page Header Band is displayed and printed at the beginning of each page of the report. Inside this band, dBASE IV adds automatically predefined fields such as the page number and system date (MM/DD/YY). You can remove these fields if you want.

In addition to the predefined fields, the names of the data fields in the database file are displayed as column labels. You also can change these labels.

The Report Intro Band appears below the Page Header Band. In the Report Intro Band, you can add field labels or other information to describe the field values.

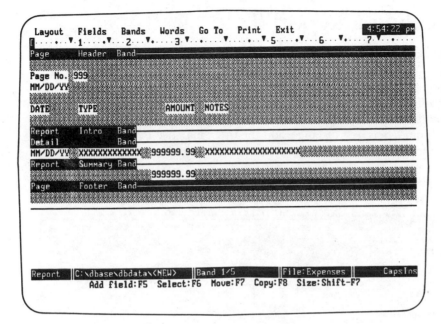

Fig. 8.25.

*A standard
columnar report
layout.*

The next band, the Detail Band, contains the values for the records in the database. You use the field template to display the field values for each of the records in the Detail Band:

MM/DD/YY XXXXXXXXXXXXX 999999.99 XXXXXXXXXXXXXXXXXXXXX

The Report Summary Band is next; use this band to present summary statistics, such as column totals. In a standard column form, values in each of the numeric fields are summed and displayed in this band.

The Page Footer Band, at the bottom of the report form, contains footers for the report. Information specified in this band is printed at the bottom of each page.

In addition to these bands, you can add different summary bands to the report. Later examples show how to include group summaries.

Adding a Report Title and Column Labels

After you view the standard column report form, you can add a report heading and change the column labels. To do that, position the cursor at the desired location on the form and add or edit the report heading and column labels. For instance, add the title "Expense Report For the Month of October 1988" and change the column labels as shown in figure 8.26.

Fig. 8.26.

Adding a report heading.

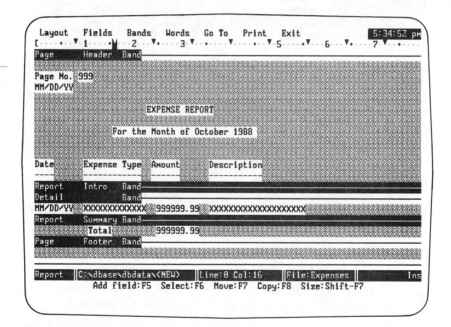

The keystrokes in table 8.1 facilitate editing operations.

Table 8.1
Editing Keystrokes

Key	Function
Home	Move to the beginning of the current line
End	Move to the end of the text line
PgUp	Move to the top of the form
PgDn	Move to the bottom of the form

Key	Function
Ctrl-Y	Delete the current line
Insert	Insert a line at the cursor (in insert mode)
Ctrl-T	Delete a word to the right of the cursor
Ctrl-G	Delete a character to the right of the cursor
Del	Delete a character to the right of the cursor
Tab	Move the cursor to the next right tab position
Shift-Tab	Move the cursor to the next left tab position

Viewing the Report On-Screen

You can preview the report on-screen before you print it. To view the report, press Alt-P to select the Print menu. From this menu, select the **View report on screen** option.

When you preview your report, a program for producing the report is generated and temporarily stored in a program (.FRG) file. In addition, an object code (.FRO) file is generated. dBASE uses this object code file to produce the report. When you save the report form, it is saved in a file with a .FRM extension along with its corresponding .FRG and .FRO files (saved under the same name as the .FRM file).

The .FRO can be read and understood only by dBASE IV. An experienced dBASE IV programmer can modify the contents of the .FRG file to change the report form. However, as a beginning user, you need not be concerned with the .FRG and .FRO files.

The column report as defined in the standard form is displayed (see fig. 8.27). Press the space bar to display the rest of the report.

Printing the Report

After you make sure that you are satisfied with the report, you can print it. Invoke the print menu (press Alt-P) and select the **Begin printing** option. The printed report looks like the one shown in figure 8.23.

Tip:
Preview the report on-screen before you print it.

Fig. 8.27.

Previewing the
report.

```
Page No.   1
10/31/88

                     EXPENSE REPORT

                 For the Month of October 1988


   Date      Expense Type  Amount     Description
   ----      ------------  ------     -----------
   10/03/88  Financial      35.00     Credit card interest
   10/05/88  Entertainment  25.80     Movie
   10/06/88  Foods         115.00     Foods and Groceries
   10/06/88  Entertainment  75.00     Concert
   10/09/88  Misc.          85.75     Misc. expenses
   10/12/88  Entertainment  85.00     Dining out
   10/13/88  Misc.          79.50     Misc. expenses
   10/13/88  Foods          90.85     Foods and Groceries
   10/15/88  Entertainment 125.75     Basketball game
   10/17/88  Misc.          55.00     Misc. expenses
   10/20/88  Foods          75.00     Foods and Groceries
   10/22/88  Entertainment  39.50     Dining out
   10/24/88  Utilities      12.50     Sanitary services
              Cancel viewing: ESC,  Continue viewing: SPACEBAR
```

Printing a Report to a DOS Text File

Tip:

Print your report
to a text file if
you need to edit
it in a word
processor.

In addition to printing a report, you also can instruct dBASE IV to write
the report to a DOS text file. This option comes in handy if you need to
merge the report to other documents; you don't have to retype the
report.

To send the report to a DOS text file, follow these steps:

1. Put the database file and report form into use.

2. Invoke the Print menu.

3. Highlight the **Destination** option and press Enter.

   You are prompted for the report destination. The default
   destination is set to PRINTER.

4. Press the space bar to change the destination to a DOS FILE.

   A default name for the DOS file is inserted in the **Name of DOS
   file** option. The default DOS file name (COLUMN01.PRT) has the
   same root name as the .FRM file, but has a .PRT extension (see
   fig. 8.28). You can change the DOS file name if you want.

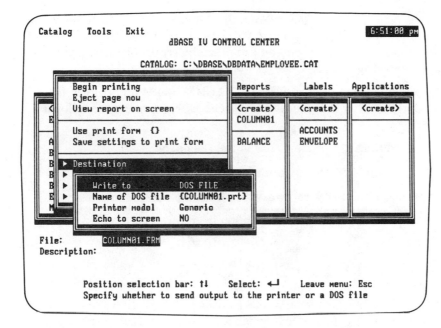

```
 Catalog  Tools  Exit                                    6:51:00 PM
                       dBASE IV CONTROL CENTER

                  CATALOG: C:\DBASE\DBDATA\EMPLOYEE.CAT

        Begin printing                  Reports    Labels      Applications
        Eject page now
        View report on screen          <create>   <create>    <create>
                                       COLUMN01
        Use print form  {}                        ACCOUNTS
        Save settings to print form    BALANCE    ENVELOPE

      ▶ Destination
      ▶
      ▶    Write to        DOS FILE
      ▶    Name of DOS file  {COLUMN01.prt}
      ▶    Printer model   Generic
      ▶    Echo to screen  NO


      File:     COLUMN01.FRM
      Description:


            Position selection bar: ↑↓    Select: ↵    Leave menu: Esc
            Specify whether to send output to the printer or a DOS file
```

Fig. 8.28.

Printing a report to a DOS text file.

5. Press Ctrl-End to return to the Print menu.

6. To write the report to the DOS file, press Ctrl-End again.

Now you can view and print the report with a text editor or word processor.

Saving the Report Form

If you want to use the report form again, press Ctrl-End and assign a name to the report form file (for example, COLUMN01.FRM) to save the form file. The report form (.FRM) file contains all the information about the report layout. When you save the file, you also create the program for producing the report form (.FRG file).

Using an Existing Report Form

You can recall a report form to use again. First, put the database file into use in the Data panel. Then highlight the name of the report form in the

Reports panel and press Enter. From the Reports menu, choose the **Print report** option. After that, you can view the report on-screen by choosing **View report on screen**. Or you can print the report by selecting the **Begin printing** option.

For example, if you want to use the COLUMN01.FRM report form to print a report with the values in EXPENSES.DBF, complete the following steps:

1. Put EXPENSES.DBF into use in the Data panel.

2. Highlight COLUMN01 in the Reports panel and press Enter.

3. Choose the **Print report** option from the Reports menu.

4. Select the **Begin printing** option from the Print menu.

Modifying a Report Form

You can recall a report form to make changes. To recall the report form, you first need to put the database file into use in the Data panel. Then highlight the report form file in the Reports panel and press Enter. From the Reports menu, select the **Modify layout** option to display the report layout.

For example, if you want to modify the COLUMN01.FRM report form, complete the following steps:

1. Put EXPENSES.DBF into use in the Data panel.

2. Highlight COLUMN01 in the Reports panel and press Enter.

3. Choose the **Modify layout** option from the Reports menu.

The existing report layout is displayed on-screen so that you can make the necessary changes.

Removing Fields

On the report layout, you can add or remove data fields from the report. To delete a field, move the cursor to the field template and press the Del key. You can use this method to delete any data field defined in the database structure or those fields predefined by dBASE (such as DATE, TIME, RECNO, PAGNO, and so on).

For example, the expense report fits on one page; therefore, you don't need to include the page number. To remove the field template (999) for the PAGENO field, follow these steps:

1. Move the cursor to the field template.

   The name of the field is displayed at the bottom of the screen so that you can verify the field name before you delete it.

2. Press the Del key.

3. To delete the Page No. label, position your cursor at the label and press Ctrl-Y.

   The rest of the form moves up one line (see fig. 8.29).

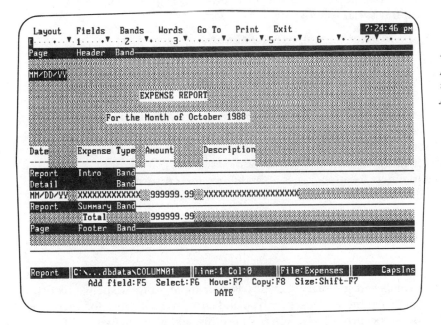

Fig. 8.29.

Deleting the page number field from the form.

Note that any field you remove from the report layout still remains in the database structure. Unless you delete the field by restructuring the database file, the field is not lost. As a result, if you accidentally remove a field from the report layout, don't panic. You can add the field to the report.

Caution:

Fields you remove from the report form still remain in the database structure.

Moving Fields

In addition to deleting fields, you also can move a field from the current position to another position in the report layout. You use the F6 key to select the field and the F7 key to move the field.

For example, if you need to move the DATE field (MM/DD/YY) from the upper left corner to the upper right corner, follow these steps:

1. Move the cursor to the DATE field template (MM/DD/YY).

2. Press F6 and then Enter to select the field.

3. Press F7 to begin moving the field.

4. Position the cursor at the spot you want to place the field. (You can use Tab to move the cursor.)

5. Press Enter to complete the move.

Moving a Section of the Report Form

You can use the preceding steps to move a section of text from one area to another in the report form. To select the section to move, position the cursor at the upper left corner of the area and then press F6. Move the cursor to the lower right corner of the area and press Enter. To move the area to a new location, press F7 and move the cursor to the upper left corner of the new location and then press Enter.

Adding a Summary Band

In a report, you often need to group data records so that you can present group totals and summary statistics. For example, in the expense report, you can group the expenses by type and show the subtotals for each type of expense occurred in October. To do this, add a summary band for group records and use the values in the TYPE field.

To add a summary band to the report layout, follow these steps:

1. Move the cursor to the line for the Report Intro Band and invoke the Bands menu (press Alt-B).

2. Select the **Add a group band** option and press Enter.

3. Select the **Field value** option and press Enter.

4. Choose the TYPE field for the group band and press Enter (see fig. 8.30).

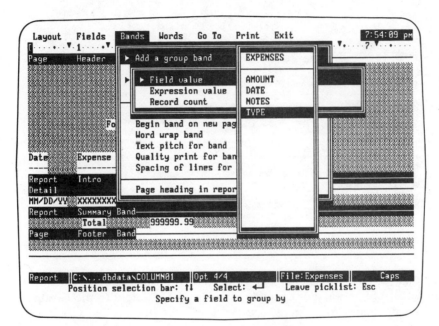

Fig. 8.30.

Adding a group band to the report form

A Group 1 Intro Band and Group 1 Summary Band are formed before and after the Detail Band. Also, the name of the field (TYPE) is indicated at the bottom of the screen (see fig. 8.31).

Adding Fields

Because the expenses are grouped by expense type, you do not need to display the expense type in a column. To remove the column from the layout, move the cursor to the field template for TYPE (XXXXXXXXXXXXX) and press Del. Then move to the column label and press Ctrl-T to delete it.

You do not need the expense type column, but you do need to describe the name of the expense type in the band. To do this, you need to add the TYPE field to the band.

Fig. 8.31.

*The summary
band on the
report form.*

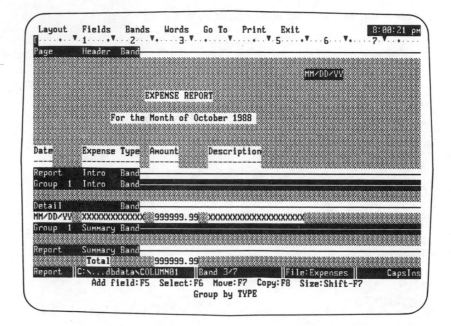

To add a field to the report form, you invoke the Fields menu and choose
the **Add field** option. For example, to add the TYPE field to the Group 1
Intro Band, follow these steps:

1. Move the cursor to the line below the Group 1 Intro Band.

2. Press Alt-F to invoke the Fields menu.

3. Choose the **Add field** option and press Enter.

4. Select the TYPE field from the field list and press Enter.

5. Define the field template (or choose the default template) and
    press Ctrl-End to return to the report layout.

The field template is added to the preselected location in the report
layout (see fig. 8.32).

Adding Summary Fields

To add a summary field with subtotals for each expense type in the
Group 1 Summary Band, follow these steps:

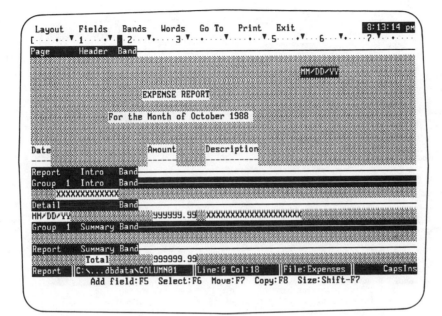

Fig. 8.32.

Adding the TYPE field to the group band.

1. Move the cursor to the line below the Group 1 Summary Band.

2. Press Alt-F to invoke the Fields menu.

3. Choose the **Add field** option, select **Sum** from the SUMMARY field list, and press Enter.

4. Define the display attributes for the summary field.

   Assign a name (for example, BY_TYPE) and description (for example, Sum expenses by type) to the field, if you want.

5. Specify the field to summarize on (for example, the AMOUNT field).

6. Define the field template (9,999.99) and picture if you do not like the default settings (see fig. 8.33).

7. Press Ctrl-End to save these display attributes and return to the report layout.

8. Add the Subtotal label to the summary field.

The report layout after adding the summary field and its label are shown in figure 8.34.

Fig. 8.33.

*Adding a
summary field to
the summary
band.*

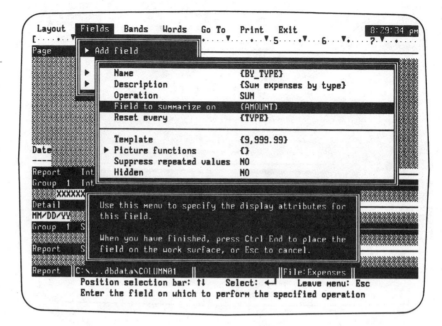

Fig. 8.34.

*The subtotal on
the report form.*

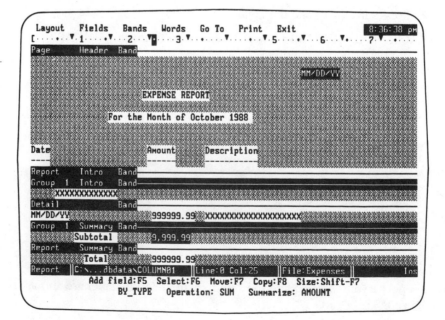

Modifying Field Display Attributes

Note that in figure 8.34 the field templates for the AMOUNT and TOTAL fields are shown as 999999.99 in default format; the summary field for the subtotal line is displayed as 9,999.99 in a business convention format. You can modify the templates for the AMOUNT and TOTAL fields to conform to a business convention format.

To modify the display attributes, invoke the Fields menu (press Alt-F) and select the **Modify field** option. For example, if you want to change the field template for the AMOUNT field, follow these steps:

1. Move the cursor to the AMOUNT field template (999999.99) and press Alt-F to invoke the Fields menu.

2. Select the **Modify field** option and press Enter.

3. Highlight the **Template** option and press Enter.

4. Edit the template (change it to 9,999.99) and press Enter.

5. Press Ctrl-End to save the modified display attributes and return to the report layout.

Use the same procedure to change the TOTAL field template to 9,999.99. You can finish editing the report layout by adding a line, "Summarized by Expense Type", to the report heading and other text (such as a dashed line above the total and subtotal values) as shown in figure 8.35. Save the modified report form by pressing Ctrl-End.

Indexing Records for the Summary Report

When you summarize values in a data field and produce summary statistics in a report, you must index on the summary data field before you use the report form. For example, the revised report form COLUMN01.FRM sums values in the AMOUNT field according to the values in the summary TYPE field. Therefore, you must index the records in EXPENSES.DBF with the TYPE index tag before you use the report form.

Caution:
Be sure to index the records before you use the summary report.

Fig. 8.35.

Adding labels and text to the report form.

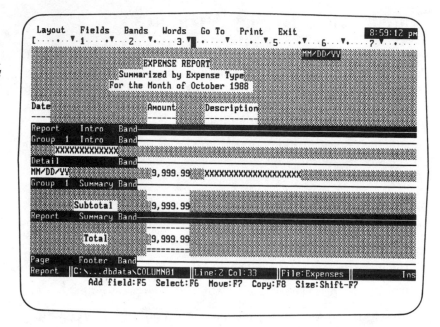

Fig. 8.35.

Adding labels and text to the report form.

Figure 8.36 shows the report produced by the modified report form COLUMN01 with the records indexed with the TYPE index tag.

Copying a Report Form To Create a New Form

Tip:

Create a new report form by making a copy of an existing one.

You can create a new report form by modifying an existing one. However, when you save the modified report file, the new report replaces the existing report, and you lose the original report layout. If you want to retain the original report layout, you can create a new report form by "borrowing" a layout from an existing .FRM report file and then modifying the layout to suit your new design.

In the previous example, the report layout was saved in COLUMN01.FRM. You can create a new report form file named COLUMN02.FRM by copying the contents of COLUMN01.FRM to COLUMN02.FRM. You don't have to copy the .FRG and .FRO files associated with the COLUMN01.FRM. The .FRG and .FRO for the new COLUMN02.FRM file are created automatically by dBASE IV later.

```
                                                    10/31/88
                         EXPENSE REPORT
                    Summarized by Expense Type
                   For the Month of October 1988

      Date                  Amount     Description
      ----                  ------     -----------
            Entertainment
      10/05/88                 25.80   Movie
      10/06/88                 75.00   Concert
      10/12/88                 85.00   Dining out
      10/15/88                125.75   Basketball game
      10/22/88                 39.50   Dining out
                            ---------
             Subtotal        351.05
            Financial
      10/03/88                 35.00   Credit card interest
      10/31/88                835.00   Mortgage payment
                            ---------
             Subtotal        870.00
            Foods
      10/06/88                115.00   Foods and Groceries
      10/13/88                 90.85   Foods and Groceries
      10/20/88                 75.00   Foods and Groceries
      10/27/88                105.00   Foods and Groceries
                            ---------
             Subtotal        385.85
            Misc.
      10/09/88                 85.75   Misc. expenses
      10/13/88                 79.50   Misc. expenses
      10/17/88                 55.00   Misc. expenses
      10/27/88                 75.00   Misc. expenses
                            ---------
             Subtotal        295.25
            Utilities
      10/24/88                 12.50   Sanitary services
      10/29/88                155.00   Water & Fuels
                            ---------
             Subtotal        167.50
                            ---------
              Total        2,069.65
                            =========
```

Fig. 8.36.

The expense report summarized by expense type.

Use the following steps to make a copy of COLUMN01.FRM and save it as COLUMN02.FRM:

1. Press Alt-T to invoke the Tools menu from the Control Center.

2. Select the **DOS utilities** option from the menu.

3. Highlight the report form file (for example, COLUMN01.FRM) and press Enter to mark it.

4. Invoke the Operations menu (press Alt-O).

5. Select the **Copy** option and then the **Single File** option.

6. Enter the name of the new report form file (for example, COLUMN02.FRM) at the Filename prompt (see fig. 8.37).

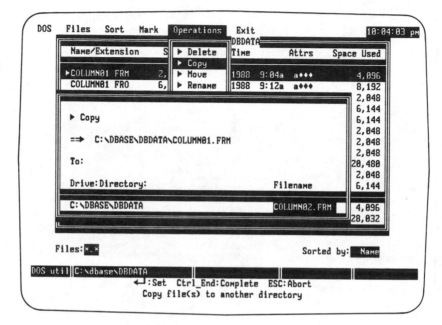

Fig. 8.37.

Making a copy of an existing report form file.

7. Press Ctrl-End to begin the copy operation.

8. Invoke the Exit menu (press Alt-E) and press Enter to return to the Control Center.

9. Move the cursor to the < **create**> option in the Reports panel and then invoke the Catalog menu (press Alt-C) to add COLUMN02.FRM to the current file.

10. From the Catalog menu, select the **Add file to catalog** option.

11. Choose COLUMN02.FRM from the file list and enter the file description.

Now, you can modify the COLUMN02 report form without losing the original COLUMN01.FRM report layout.

As an example, you can change the expense report layout to add a new column for estimating the expense items for November 1988 (add a 5 percent increase from October's expenses). And you can change the title of the report to reflect the changed contents (see fig. 8.38).

Note that in the modified report layout in figure 8.38 the November column is created by adding three fields to the report. The first

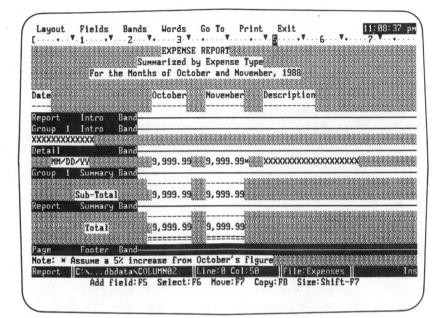

Fig. 8.38.

Adding a new column to the report.

added field, shown in figure 8.39, is a calculated field (named NOV_ AMOUNT). This field uses the value in the AMOUNT field multiplied by 1.05 (a 5 percent increase).

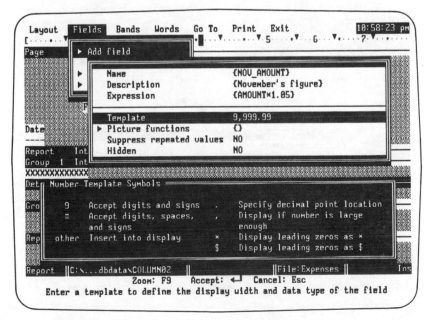

Fig. 8.39.

Defining the NOV_AMOUNT calculated field.

The other two fields are summary fields that sum the group values. The subtotal field named NOV_BYTYPE for the November column is created by summing the values in the calculated field NOV_AMOUNT (see fig. 8.40). Similarly, the total field named NOV_TOTAL is a summary field created by summing all the values in the NOV_AMOUNT field (see fig. 8.41).

The report generated with the new COLUMN02.FRM report form is shown in figure 8.42.

Using Multiple Database Files To Create a Form Report

One of the powerful capabilities of a relational database design is that you can create a database management system that consists of several database files or tables. Then you can link them for different applications. For instance, you may need to produce a report that pulls information from more than one database file.

Fig. 8.40.

Defining the NOV_BYTYPE summary field.

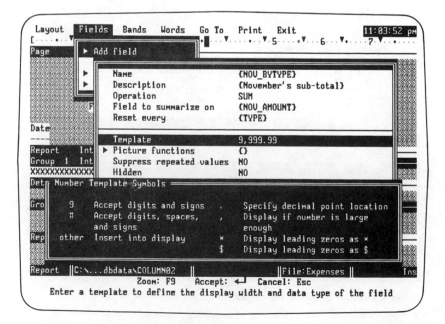

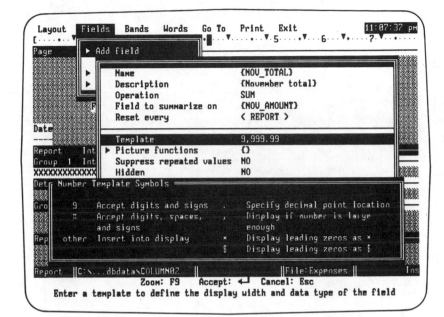

Fig. 8.41.

Defining the NOV_TOTAL summary field.

For example, the ACCOUNTS.DBF database file shown earlier contains information about the account numbers, names, and addresses of the accounts. You can save other information such as the credit limits and current balances for these accounts in a separate database file (BALANCE.DBF, for example). The database structure and contents of BALANCE.DBF are shown in figures 8.43 and 8.44 respectively.

If you need to use information in more than one database file to produce a report, you first need to link the fields. To do so, use a query.

Using a Query To Link Database Files

To link database files, you need to create a query design in which you define the linking field, and you must select the fields from the database files. Then you can use the contents of the query view to design a report.

For example, to create a query design that links the fields in ACCOUNTS.DBF and BALANCE.DBF, complete the following steps:

1. Put the first database file (for example, ACCOUNTS) into use in the Data panel.

Tip:

To use multiple database files in a report, link the files with a query.

Fig. 8.42.

A revised expense report.

```
                                                              10/31/88
                            EXPENSE REPORT
                       Summarized by Expense Type
                 For the Months of October and November 1988

Date                     October      November     Description
----                     -------      --------     -----------
Entertainment
    10/05/88                25.80        27.09*     Movie
    10/06/88                75.00        78.75*     Concert
    10/12/88                85.00        89.25*     Dining out
    10/15/88               125.75       132.04*     Basketball game
    10/22/88                39.50        41.48*     Dining out
                        ----------     --------
           Subtotal       351.05       368.60
Financial
    10/03/88                35.00        36.75*     Credit card interest
    10/31/88               835.00       876.75*     Mortgage payment
                        ----------     --------
           Subtotal       870.00       913.50
Foods
    10/06/88               115.00       120.75*     Foods and Groceries
    10/13/88                90.85        95.39*     Foods and Groceries
    10/20/88                75.00        78.75*     Foods and Groceries
    10/27/88               105.00       110.25*     Foods and Groceries
                        ----------     --------
           Subtotal       385.85       405.14
Misc.
    10/09/88                85.75        90.04*     Misc. expenses
    10/13/88                79.50        83.48*     Misc. expenses
    10/17/88                55.00        57.75*     Misc. expenses
    10/27/88                75.00        78.75*     Misc. expenses
                        ----------     --------
           Subtotal       295.25       310.01
Utilities
    10/24/88                12.50        13.13*     Sanitary services
    10/29/88               155.00       162.75*     Water & Fuels
                        ----------     --------
           Subtotal       167.50       175.88
                        ----------     --------
              Total     2,069.65     2,173.13
                        ==========     ========
```

2. Select the < **create**> option from the Queries panel and press Enter.

3. When the file skeleton for ACCOUNTS.DBF is shown in the query design, invoke the Layout menu (press Alt-L) and choose the **Add file to query** option.

4. From the file list, select the second database file (for example, BALANCE.DBF) and press Enter.

5. When the second database appears, enter the word link1 to the linking field (ACCT_NO) in both file skeletons.

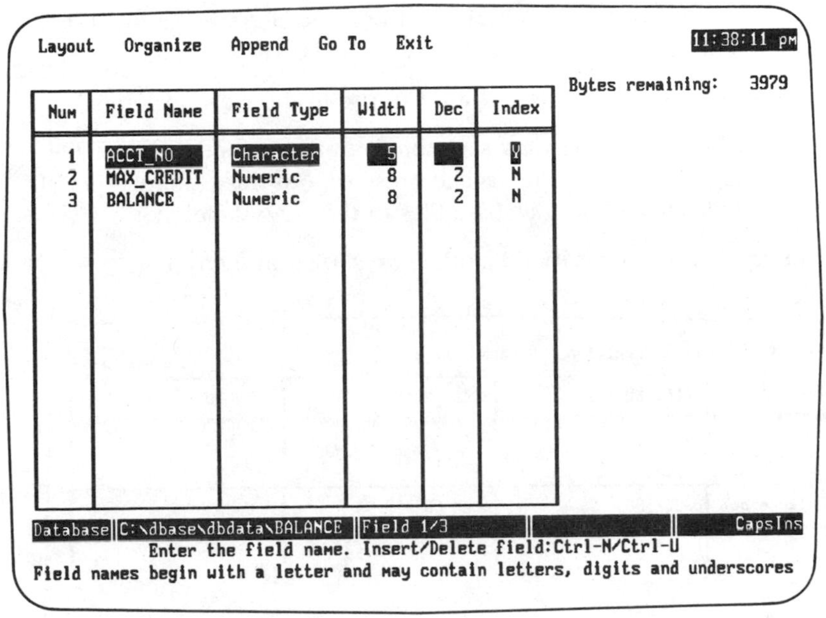

Fig. 8.43.

The database structure of BALANCE.DBF.

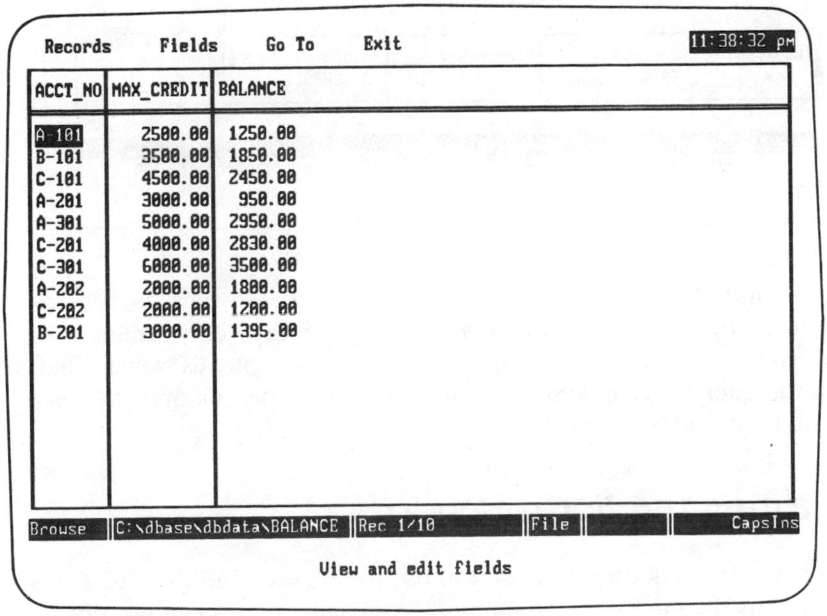

Fig. 8.44.

The records in BALANCE.DBF.

Use F3 and F4 to move between the file skeletons; use the Tab and Shift-Tab keys to move between fields.

6. Include the data fields you want to use in the view skeleton.

To add fields to the view skeleton from the second database file, highlight each of the fields and press F5. (In this example, put all the fields from both database files to the view skeleton.)

The query design should look like the one shown in figure 8.45.

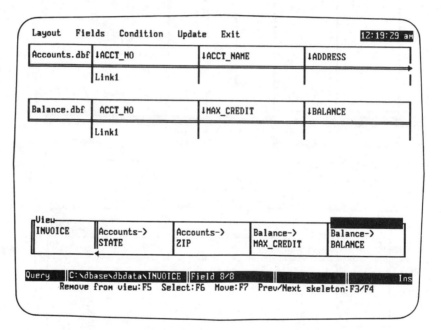

Fig. 8.45.

*Linking
ACCOUNTS.DBF
and
BALANCE.DBF
in a query.*

After you design the query file, you can process it and view the records produced by the link operation. Or you can save the query file for later use. To save the query file, assign a name (for example, INVOICE) and exit the query design. Before you save the query, the link operation is carried out, and the view is created.

Creating the Form Report

After you save a query view, you can use the records and the data fields created by the query view in a report. For example, you can use the

records produced by the INVOICE.QBF query to produce invoice
statements. To do so, complete these steps:

1. Highlight the query in the Queries panel and press Enter.

2. Select the < **create**> option from the Reports panel and press
   Enter.

3. Select the **Quick layouts** option.

4. Select the **Form layout** option to create a report with a form
   layout design.

A form layout display value appears in each field as a line. Information in
a record is displayed as a section in a detail band (see fig. 8.46).

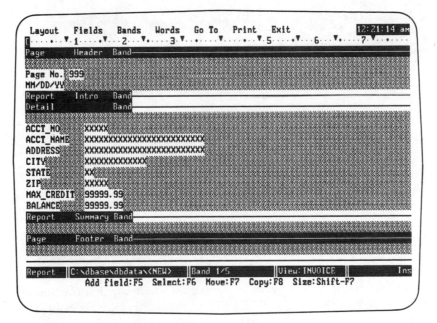

Fig. 8.46.

*A standard report
layout.*

You can modify the field labels and reposition the field template and
produce a report. The modified layout is shown in figure 8.47. In the
modified layout, a calculated field named AMOUNT_DUE is computed by
the formula BALANCE*0.2 (assuming that 20 percent of the current
balance is due). All the amounts due (in the AMOUNT_DUE calculated
field) are summed and displayed as a summary field (named TOTAL_DUE)
in the summary band.

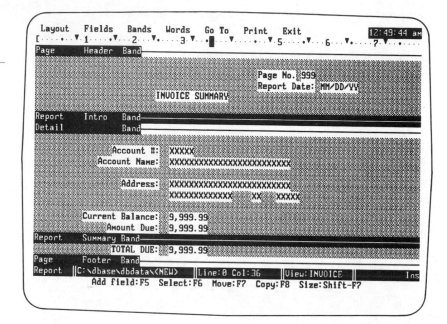

Fig. 8.47.

*The modified
report layout.*

The report form is saved as the FORMREPT.FRM report file. The report
produced by FORMREPT.FRM is shown in figure 8.48.

Using a Mailmerge Layout

Another report layout you can choose to create is the mailmerge layout.
A mailmerge layout allows you to type documents in the form of a letter
or memo; then you can insert the contents of selected data fields from
one or more database files. For example, you can write a memo to each
of the employees in the company. In the memo you merge information in
their personal data file (EMPLOYEE.DBF) to the memo (see fig. 8.49).

The memo in figure 8.49 is produced with a mailmerge report form file
named MEMOREPT.FRM. Follow these steps to create the
MEMOREPT.FRM report form:

1. Put the EMPLOYEE database file into use in the Data panel.

2. Select < **create**> from the Reports panel and press Enter.

3. Choose the **Quick layouts** option and then the **Mailmerge
   layout** option.

```
                              Page No.   1
                              Report Date: 10/31/88
        INVOICE SUMMARY


      Account #:  A-101
   Account Name:  Fairwind Travel

        Address:  3256 Mountainview Drive
                  Mesa            AZ   85201

Current Balance:  1,250.00
     Amount Due:    250.00

      Account #:  B-101
   Account Name:  Evergreen Florists

        Address:  2658 Broadway
                  Vancouver       WA   98664

Current Balance:  1,850.00
     Amount Due:    370.00

      Account #:  C-101
   Account Name:  ACME Construction

        Address:  1456 S.E. 132nd Avenue
                  Portland        OR   97204

Current Balance:  2,450.00
     Amount Due:    490.00

      Account #:  A-201
   Account Name:  B & J Fine Furniture

        Address:  3567 S. W. Canyon Road
                  Beaverton       OR   97203

Current Balance:    950.00
     Amount Due:    190.00

      Account #:  A-301
   Account Name:  Western Electronic

        Address:  2478 University Avenue
                  Seattle         WA   98105

Current Balance:  2,950.00
     Amount Due:    590.00

      Account #:  C-201
   Account Name:  Ace Secretarial Services

        Address:  5214 Main Street
                  Salem           OR   97201

Current Balance:  2,830.00
     Amount Due:    566.00
```

Fig. 8.48.

A sample report.

Fig. 8.49.

A mailmerge report.

```
                        INTEROFFICE MEMO


     Date:        December 31, 1988

     To:          James C. Smith

     From:        George T. Chou, President

     Subject:     Year-end Bonus and Personnel Record Update


     Dear Employee:

     It is a great pleasure for me to inform you that, because of your
     dedication to the company, our profits for the year of 1988 are the
     highest we have ever had since we began the business. As a token
     of appreciation, you will be awarded a bonus of $2,117.50,
     equivalent to one month of your salary. Thank you for your
     contribution to our success and let us work toward another great
     year ahead.

     In order to keep our personnel files up to date, please verify
     your home telephone number shown below and inform the personnel
     director of any changes:

          Home telephone Number:   206 123-4567
```

4. Enter the text of the memo in the Detail Band.

In the layout, enter the field template where you want the field to appear. For example, you can define the employee's name as a calculated field called FULL_NAME with this expression: TRIM(FIRST_NAME) + " " + LAST_NAME (see fig. 8.50).

Similarly, the amount of bonus is displayed with the value of the calculated field BONUS ($9,999.99) using the formula ANNUAL_PAY/12. (see fig. 8.51).

The template for showing the telephone number at the end of the memo consists of the AREA_CODE and PHONE_NO fields (see fig. 8.52).

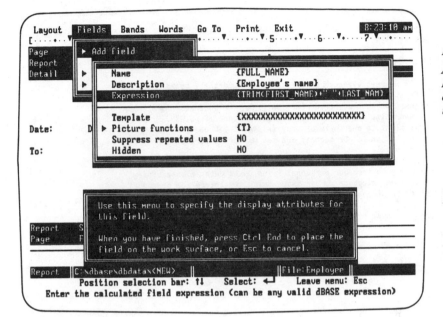

Fig. 8.50.

Adding the FULL_NAME calculated field to the memo.

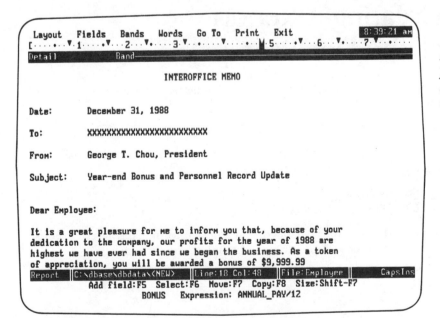

Fig. 8.51.

Adding the BONUS calculated field to the memo.

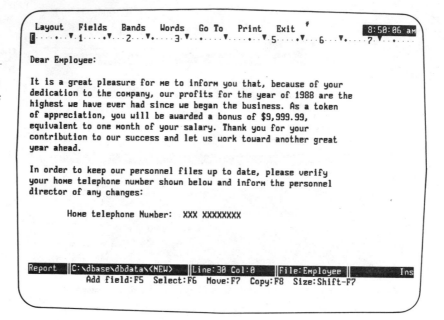

Fig. 8.52.

*Adding the
AREA_CODE and
PHONE_NO fields
to the memo.*

Creating a Report at the Dot Prompt

Command:

CREATE REPORT
*Brings up a new
report design
form.*

You can create a report in dot-prompt mode by using the CREATE REPORT command:

. CREATE REPORT < *name of report form file*>

For example, the following commands use the EXPENSES database file and create a report named COLUMN01:

. USE EXPENSES
. CREATE REPORT COLUMNØ1

The report generator is invoked, and a design form is displayed. You use the procedure described earlier to complete the form design.

Using a Report Form
at the Dot Prompt

In dot-prompt mode, you can produce a report by using an existing
report form:

> . REPORT FORM < *name of the report form file*>
> [filter conditions] [TO PRINT]

Command:
REPORT FORM
*Uses an existing
report design.*

In the following example, the REPORT FORM command produces a report
using the form saved in the COLUMN01.FRM. The report includes those
records whose values in the TYPE field are equal to "Foods". The TO
PRINT command instructs dBASE IV to print the report.

> . USE EXPENSES
> . REPORT FORM COLUMNØ1 FOR TYPE="FOODS" TO PRINT

If you group values in the report by a data field, you need to index the
records with the summary field before you issue the REPORT FORM
command. Use the SET ORDER TO command:

> . USE EXPENSES
> . SET ORDER TO TYPE
> . REPORT FORM COLUMNØ1

Modifying a Report Form
at the Dot Prompt

In dot-prompt mode, you modify an existing report form file by issuing
the MODIFY REPORT command:

> . MODIFY REPORT < *name of report form file*>

Command:
MODIFY REPORT
*Calls a report
design so that
you can make
changes.*

For example, you use the following command to modify the report
named COLUMN01:

> . USE EXPENSES
> . MODIFY REPORT COLUMNØ1

Once the existing report form COLUMN01.FRM is recalled and displayed
on-screen, use the procedure described earlier to make changes on the
form.

Chapter 8 QuickStart

In this chapter, you learn the procedure for creating mailing labels and reports. Let's bring up the QIKSTART.CAT file catalog and its files to practice these procedures. If you have problems, refer to the QuickStart in Chapter 4 for details.

Creating Mailing Labels

In the following exercise, use the records in ADDRESS.DBF to produce mailing labels. To design your mailing labels, invoke the label generator and then specify the dimensions and display attributes for the fields:

1. Put the ADDRESS database file into use in the Data panel.

2. Select < **create**> from the Labels panel and press Enter.

3. Invoke the Dimensions menu (press Alt-D) and press Enter to view the predefined size options for the labels.

4. Select the label size (for example, 15/16 × 3 1/2 by 1) and press Ctrl-End.

5. Specify label width (for example, 30 characters wide).

6. Specify label height (for example, 4 lines high).

7. Specify indentation (for example, 2 characters).

8. Specify lines between labels (for example, 2 lines).

   Your label dimensions should look like those in figure 8.53.

9. Press Ctrl-End to save the dimension specifications.

Now you can place the fields on the label with the following steps:

1. Invoke the Fields menu (press Alt-F) and choose the **Add field** option.

2. From the CALCULATED field list, select the < **create**> option to create the FULL_NAME field.

3. Select the **Name** option and enter FULL _ NAME.

4. Select the **Description** option and enter Full name.

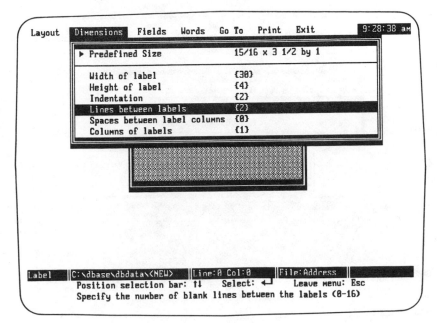

```
  Layout  Dimensions  Fields  Words  Go To  Print  Exit        9:28:38 am

          ▸ Predefined Size                15/16 x 3 1/2 by 1

            Width of label                 {30}
            Height of label                {4}
            Indentation                    {2}
            Lines between labels           {2}
            Spaces between label columns   {0}
            Columns of labels              {1}




  Label   C:\dbase\dbdata\<NEW>    Line:0 Col:0    File:Address
          Position selection bar: ↑↓    Select: ↵    Leave menu: Esc
          Specify the number of blank lines between the labels (0-16)
```

Fig. 8.53.

Specifying label dimensions.

5. Select the **Expression** option and enter the character expression TRIM(FIRST _ NAME) + " " + LAST _ NAME (see fig. 8.54).

6. Press Ctrl-End to place the field on the label.

7. Invoke the Fields menu again (press Alt-F), select the **Add field** option, and choose the ADDRESS field from the field list.

8. Press Enter and specify the display attributes for this field. Press Ctrl-End to accept the default setting.

9. Follow Steps 7 and 8 to place the CITY, STATE, and ZIP fields on the label form (see fig. 8.55).

Viewing Mailing Labels On-Screen

You can preview the mailing labels on-screen before you print them:

1. Invoke the Print menu (press Alt-P).

2. Select the **View labels on screen** option.

The mailing labels should look like those shown in figure 8.56. To view the next screen of labels, press the space bar.

Fig. 8.54.

Specifying the character expression for FULL_NAME.

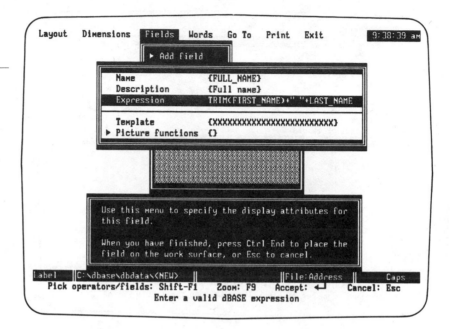

Fig. 8.55.

A sample mailing label layout.

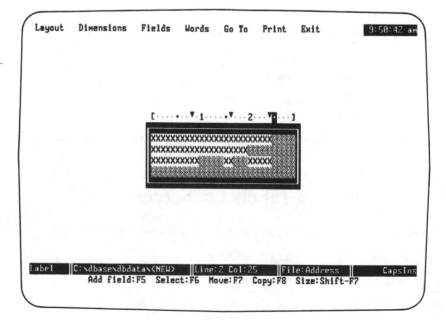

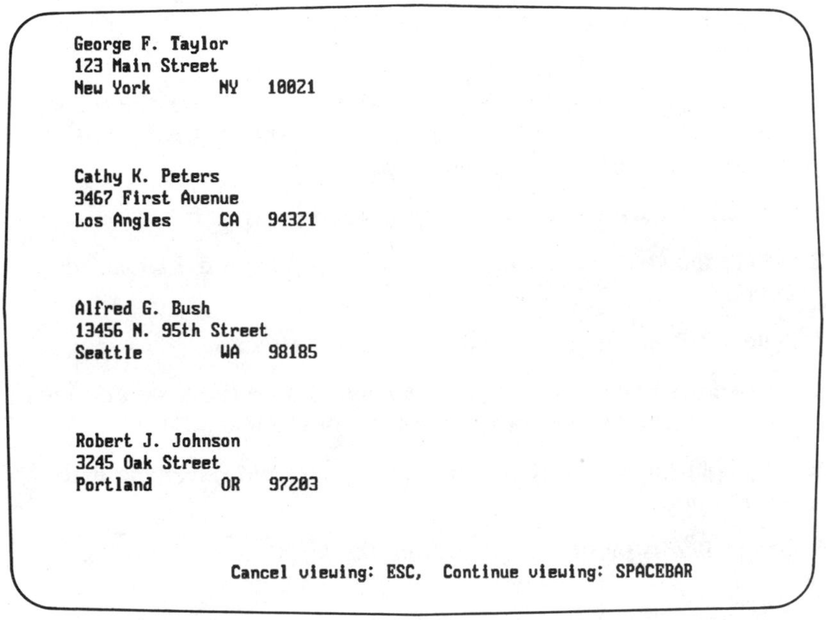

```
George F. Taylor
123 Main Street
New York        NY    10021


Cathy K. Peters
3467 First Avenue
Los Angles      CA    94321


Alfred G. Bush
13456 N. 95th Street
Seattle         WA    98185


Robert J. Johnson
3245 Oak Street
Portland        OR    97203



              Cancel viewing: ESC,  Continue viewing: SPACEBAR
```

Fig. 8.56.

Previewing the mailing labels.

Printing Labels

After you preview the labels on-screen, you can print them:

1. Invoke the Print menu (press Alt-P).

2. Select the **Begin printing** option.

After you print the labels, you return to the label design screen.

Saving the Label Design

To save the label form, follow these steps:

1. Press Ctrl-End.

2. Type the name of the label form file (for example, MAILABEL.LBL) at the Save as: prompt and press Enter.

Sorting Labels

To sort mailing labels by their ZIP codes, you need to index the records in the ADDRESS.DBF database file before you use the MAILABEL.LBL label form. To sort the labels, follow these steps:

1. Highlight ADDRESS in the Data panel and press Shift-F2.

2. Select the **Order records by index** option from the Organize menu.

3. Select ZIP as the index tag for ordering the records.

4. Invoke the Exit menu (press Alt-E) and choose the **Save changes and exit** option to return to the Control Center.

5. Highlight the MAILABEL in the Labels panel and select the **Print label** option.

6. Select **Begin printing** option from the Print menu and press Enter.

The mailing labels printed are arranged by their ZIP codes (see fig. 8.57).

Designing Reports

To design a report, use some of the data fields in ADDRESS.DBF to produce a listing of addresses. The report is summarized by the values in the STATE field (see fig. 8.58).

To design the report shown in figure 8.58, invoke the report generator and then design the report layout using these steps:

1. Put the ADDRESS database into use in the Data panel.

2. Select < **create**> from the Reports panel and press Enter.

3. Choose the **Quick layouts** option.

4. Select the **Column layout** option to display the standard columnar report design (see fig. 8.59).

```
George F. Taylor
123 Main Street
New York        NY    10021



Steven W. King
2771 Plaza Drive
Pittsburgh      PA    15230



Janet Peterson
3098 Oceanview Road
San Diego       CA    92121



Linda K. Swanson
1345 Bayview Drive
San Meteo       CA    94105



Cathy K. Peters
3467 First Avenue
Los Angles      CA    94321



Peter T. Morrow
2046 Skyline Drive
Fremont         CA    94538



Thomas Ball
9440 Rockcreek Road
Beaverton       OR    97201



James L. Watson
3891 S.W. Powell St.
Portland        OR    97201



Albert C. Morgan
1354 S. 78th Avenue
Portland        OR    97202



Robert J. Johnson
3245 Oak Street
Portland        OR    97203



Alfred G. Bush
13456 N. 95th Street
Seattle         WA    98185
```

Fig. 8.57.

Mailing labels sorted by ZIP codes.

Fig. 8.58.

A sample report.

```
Page No.    1
12/10/88
                         LISTING ADDRESSES BY STATE
Last Name    First Name  Address               City         Zip    Wealth
---------    ----------  --------------------  ----------   -----  -------
State:   WA
Harvey       Jane W.     9709 Broadway         Vancouver    98665  75,000
Bush         Alfred G.   13456 N. 95th Street  Seattle      98185  50,000
                                                                   --------
                                               Subtotal            125,000

State:   PA
King         Steven W.   2771 Plaza Drive      Pittsburgh   15230  25,000
                                                                   --------
                                               Subtotal            25,000
State:   OR
Watson       James L.    3891 S.W. Powell St.  Portland     97201  39,000
Ball         Thomas      9440 Rockcreek Road   Beaverton    97201  45,000
Morgan       Albert C.   1354 S. 78th Avenue   Portland     97202  90,000
Johnson      Robert J.   3245 Oak Street       Portland     97203  105,000
                                                                   --------
                                               Subtotal            279,000
State:   NY
Taylor       George F.   123 Main Street       New York     10021  185,000
                                                                   --------
                                               Subtotal            185,000
State:   CA
Swanson      Linda K.    1345 Bayview Drive    San Meteo    94105  65,000
Peterson     Janet       3098 Oceanview Road   San Diego    92121  82,000
Morrow       Peter T.    2046 Skyline Drive    Fremont.     94538  150,000
Peters       Cathy K.    3467 First Avenue     Los Angles   94321  125,000
                                                                   --------
                                               Subtotal            422,000
                                                                   ---------
                                                  TOTAL            1,036,000
                                                                   =========
```

Modifying the Standard Report Layout

You can modify the standard report design by deleting the unwanted fields.

1. Move the cursor to the beginning of the line below the Detail Band and press the Tab key several times.

2. Use the left and right arrow keys to position the cursor on the field template (XXXXX) for the STATE field.

3. Press Ctrl-T to remove the field from the report.

4. Move the cursor to the STATE label and press Ctrl-T to delete it.

5. Move the cursor two spaces after the field template (XXXXX) for the ZIP field and press Ctrl-T.

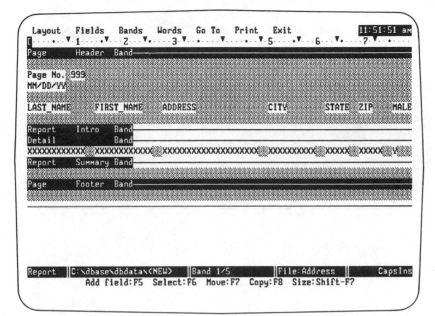

Fig. 8.59.

A standard columnar report layout.

6. Press Ctrl-T to remove the MALE field.

7. Press Ctrl-T again to remove the field template MM/DD/YY for the BIRTH_DATE field.

8. Position the cursor to the field label line above the field label 99999999 and press Ctrl-T to remove the MALE label.

9. Press Ctrl-T to remove the BIRTH_DATE label. (See figure 8.60 for the resulting screen.)

Adding the Report Heading and Field Labels

You now can edit the field labels and add a report heading:

1. Move the cursor to the beginning of the line below the system date template (MM/DD/YY).

2. Press Enter to insert a new line. (Turn on Insert mode by pressing the Ins key).

3. Type the report heading (LISTING ADDRESSES BY STATE) at the center of the line and press Enter.

4. Edit the field labels and add dashes below the labels (see fig. 8.61).

Fig. 8.60.

A modified report layout.

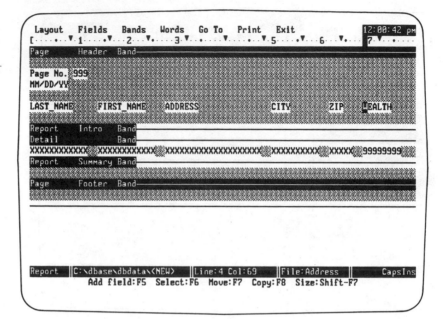

Fig. 8.61.

Modified field labels and report heading.

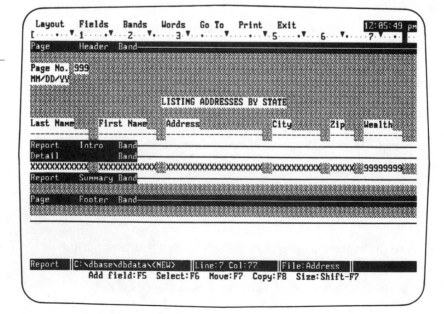

Reformatting a Field

Next reformat the field template for the WEALTH field so that the values are displayed in a business convention format (for example, 999,999):

1. Move the cursor to the field template (99999999) for the WEALTH field and invoke the Fields menu (press Alt-F).

2. Select the **Modify field** option.

3. Move the cursor to the **Template** option and press Enter.

4. Change the template to 999,999 and press Enter (see fig. 8.62).

5. Press Ctrl-End to return to the report layout.

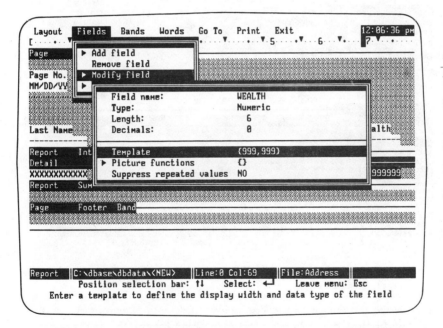

Fig. 8.62.

Modifying the WEALTH field template.

Adding a Group Band

To group the addresses in the report by state, you need to add a group band and the necessary summary field (total) for the numeric field:

1. Move the cursor to the beginning of the line labeled Report Intro Band and invoke the Bands menu (press Alt-B).

2. Select the **Add a group band** option and press Enter.

3. Select the **Field value** option and press Enter.

4. Choose the STATE field from the field list and press Enter.

5. Enter the label State: in the line below the Group 1 Intro Band.

6. Invoke the Fields menu and select the **Add field** option.

7. Select STATE from the field list and press Enter.

8. Press Ctrl-End to return to the report layout (see fig. 8.63).

Fig. 8.63.

Adding a group band to the report layout.

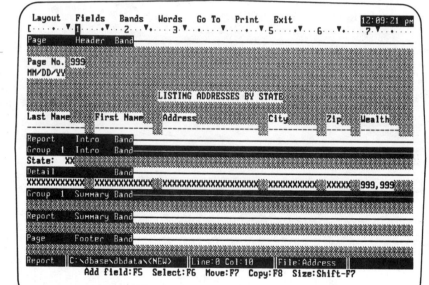

9. Move the cursor to the line below the Group 1 Summary band and below the field template (999,999) for the WEALTH field.

10. Invoke the Fields menu (press Alt-F) and select the **Add field** option.

11. From the SUMMARY fields column, select Sum operator.

12. Specify the display attributes for the summary ST_TOTAL field as shown in figure 8.64.

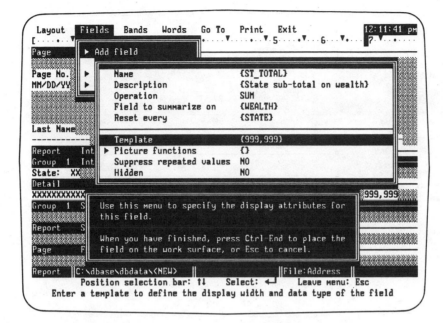

Fig. 8.64.

Placing a summary field on the report.

13. Press Ctrl-End to return to the report layout.

14. Type Subtotal for the summary field ST_TOTAL.

15. Move the cursor to the field template (99999999) for the SUM(WEALTH) field. (Press the Tab key several times to see it.)

16. Press F6 and Enter to select the field.

17. Press F7, use the left arrow key to move the template under the ST_TOTAL field template, and press Enter.

18. Change the field template to 999,999.

19. Enter the label TOTAL in the summary field and add dashes above the summary field templates.

Figure 8.65 displays the final report layout produced by this procedure.

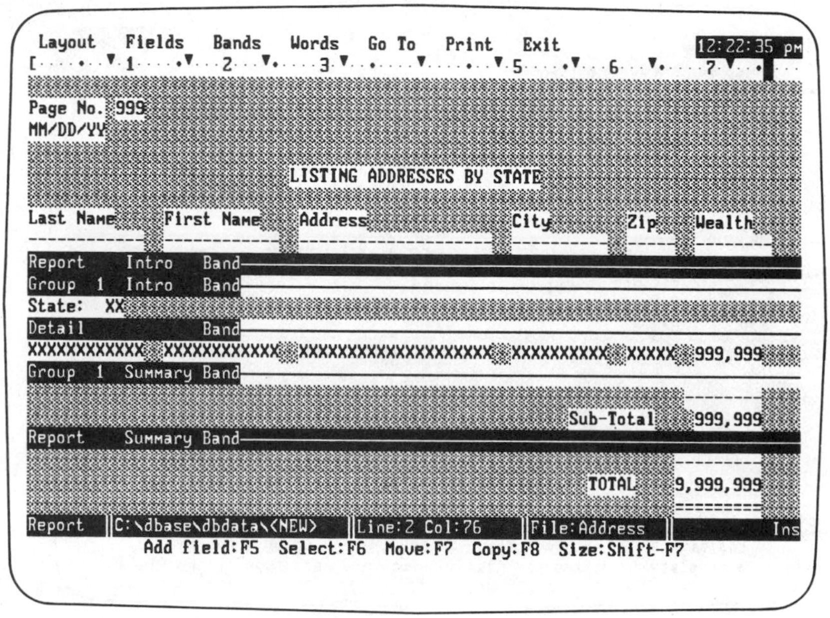

Fig. 8.65.

The final report layout.

Saving the Report Layout

To save the report layout, follow these steps:

1. Press Ctrl-End.

2. Type a name for the report form file (for example, ADDRESS1.FRM) and press Enter.

Sorting Records

Because the report is summarized by state, you need to index the records in ADDRESS.DBF. Before you use the report form, you must use the STATE index tag. To do so, follow these steps:

1. Highlight ADDRESS in the Data panel and press Shift-F2.

2. Select the **Order records by index** option from the Organize menu.

3. Select STATE as the index tag for ordering the records.

4. Invoke the Exit menu (press Alt-E) and choose the **Save changes and exit** option to return to the Control Center.

5. Highlight the ADDRESS1 in the Reports panel and select the **Print report** option.

6. Select the **Begin printing** option from the Print menu and press Enter.

Chapter Summary

This chapter discussed using the label and report generator. With the label generator, you can design a label form and create mailing labels. With the report generator, you can design a complete report form, including text labels and data field contents. You can save label and report designs on disk so that you can make changes and use them again.

Part II

Command-File Programming

Includes

Fundamentals of Command-File Programming

Programming Input and Output Operations

Conditional Branching and Program Loops

9

Fundamentals of
Command-File
Programming

O nce you become comfortable with using dBASE IV commands in
interactive mode, you are ready to explore new possibilities—
writing programs. Remember that a batch file in DOS is nothing more
than a standard text file that contains DOS commands; the commands are
processed one after the other when you invoke the batch file. A dBASE IV
program is also just a standard text file that contains the commands you
want executed. dBASE IV, unlike DOS, is a true programming language.
Commands and functions included in dBASE IV allow you to control the
program's actions. For repetitive operations and complex database
management tasks, using program files is more efficient than issuing
commands at the dot prompt.

A dBASE IV program can be as simple or as complex as you choose. A
program can be as simple as automating five or six commands you type at
the dot prompt (saving you from retyping the commands each time you
want to perform a certain action). Or a program can be as complex as an
entire application from the main menu down to the last report. Because
the scope of the dBASE programming language is broad, this chapter
begins by introducing the fundamentals of creating and processing a
dBASE program. This chapter also explains how to create, edit, and save a
program file.

This chapter discusses the following dBASE IV commands:

```
MODIFY COMMAND
DO
TYPE
TYPE TO PRINT
COPY FILE
ERASE
SET TALK ON/OFF
```

Defining a Program

A dBASE IV program is a set of commands designed to perform a particular task or tasks. The advantages of creating dBASE IV programs over using interactive mode include increased speed of execution, elimination of typing errors, and the ability to create applications for users who are not trained in dBASE IV. Once you write and test a dBASE IV program, you can run it over and over again to perform daily database management tasks.

In dBASE II and dBASE III, program files were executed by an interpreter. An interpreter takes each line of a program, checks for syntax errors, translates the command into machine language, and then performs the command—similar to the way BASIC operates.

This method of program execution has built-in inefficiencies. Once you test a program, it is redundant to check command syntax and translate that command into machine language every time you run the program. dBASE IV solves this problem by creating a compiled object file (with the extension .DBO) whenever you alter the program. This file eliminates two of the three steps an interpreter executes each time a program is run. Once a dBASE program is compiled into a .DBO file, the syntax has been checked, and the program code has been translated into machine language. All dBASE IV has to do is execute the commands in the program. This method of execution results in increased efficiency and speed.

A Sample Program

In interactive mode, you can enter commands to search for and display records on-screen. Figure 9.1 shows a typical interactive session.

```
. USE CUSTOMER
. LOCATE FOR acct _ no="12345"
RECORD 7
. ?"Customer Name:",co _ name
Customer Name: Ralph's Pizzeria
```

Fig. 9.1.

Commands entered in interactive mode.

You can place the same set of commands in a program file, as shown in figure 9.2.

```
SET TALK OFF            && Suppresses  screen display
USE CUSTOMER            && Open the customer file
LOCATE FOR acct _ no = "12345"  && Search for an individual
                        && record
? "Customer Name: ",co _ name
RETURN                  && End program
```

Fig. 9.2.

A sample program file.

Figure 9.3 shows the result of the program's execution.

```
. DO SAMPLE
Customer Name: Ralph's Pizzeria
```

Fig. 9.3.

The output from SAMPLE.PRG.

Program Format

A program file consists of lines that contain dBASE IV commands—functions and expressions that instruct the computer to perform specific operations. The operation may be as simple as displaying data or as complicated as providing a menu from which the user can perform one of several different tasks or mathematical computations.

The instructions given by the programmer must be "understood" by the computer. To avoid errors, each command must follow the syntax rules that govern the command—just as if you typed it at the dot prompt. The syntax rules for dBASE IV commands are discussed in the preceding chapters. In most cases, the rules for using those commands are the same in a program as they are in interactive mode. However, a number of commands are useful only in a program.

Program Lines

Tip:
You must end
every program
line with a hard
return.

Unlike many other programming languages, dBASE IV has few restrictions for the format of a command line. For instance, you can use any number of spaces to separate words within a command. However, dBASE IV has one important requirement: You must end every command line with a hard return.

Tip:
Use comment
lines to
document your
program.

A dBASE IV program contains two types of lines—comment lines and command lines. *Comment lines* are remarks that describe the program and the logic behind the commands. Using comments to document the program makes program maintenance easier.

You can use two methods to include comments in your dBASE IV programs. If the entire line is a comment, place an asterisk at the beginning of the line, such as

```
* These are comment lines
* These lines will not be executed when you run the
* program
```

Or you can include a comment line by separating the command from the comment with a double ampersand (&&), as in the following example:

```
USE NEWFILE    && Text to the right of the double ampersand
               && is a comment and is ignored by the program
```

Command lines, the other type of line contained in a program, instruct the computer to carry out specific operations. The syntax rules of dBASE IV require that each command line begin with a command verb. The command verb can be a word such as USE or SEEK or a symbol such as the question mark. The following lines are examples of command lines:

```
USE EMPLOYEE
LOCATE FOR emp_no="1234"
?"Employee Name: ", TRIM(first_nam)+last_name
```

You can begin the command verb at the first position on the line or indent the verb for easier reading. You can use both upper- and lowercase letters in a program line; dBASE IV is not case-sensitive. In this book, all command words and function names appear in uppercase. Variable and array names appear in lowercase.

Creating and Executing a dBASE IV Program

To write a dBASE IV program, you type into a standard ASCII (DOS text) file the commands and functions you want executed. You can use either the text editor supplied with dBASE IV or a text editor of your choice.

Using dBASE's Text Editor

To create a program with the text editor provided by dBASE IV, use MODIFY COMMAND. Type the command and the program file name at the dot prompt, as in

. MODIFY COMMAND < *name of program*>

The file extension .PRG is assigned automatically when you use MODIFY COMMAND. For example, to create a new file named SAMPLE.PRG invoke the editor by typing the following:

. MODIFY COMMAND sample

In the text editor, type the command lines. Be sure to press Enter at the end of each line. When you press Enter, the cursor moves to the beginning of the next line, and a less than symbol (<) is displayed.

If a program line is longer than 80 characters, you can keep typing (lines longer than 80 characters "wrap" to the next line). Even though the wrapped text may not look neat, the content of the line is not affected. The maximum number of characters you can place on a command line is

Tip:
To create a program that can be run by dBASE IV, use MODIFY COMMAND *to invoke the text editor.*

1024. To make the program more readable, you can use the semicolon to break a program line into two or more lines. Placing a semicolon (;) at the end of a line indicates that the next line is part of the same command.

Pressing Ins toggles between insert and overstrike modes. As you type in insert mode, characters are inserted on-screen, and previous text is pushed right. When insert mode is turned off, typed characters overwrite the characters at the cursor location. To delete a character at the cursor position, use the Del key.

While you create and edit a program file, you can use the arrow keys to move the cursor on-screen. You can scroll the screen up and down with the PgUp and PgDn keys. Table 9.1 lists the keys you can use for cursor movement and screen editing.

Table 9.1
Keystrokes Used for Editing with MODIFY COMMAND

Keystroke	Function
Left arrow (←)	Moves cursor left one character
Right arrow (→)	Moves cursor right one character
Up arrow (↑)	Moves cursor up one line
Down arrow (↓)	Moves cursor down one line
Home	Moves cursor to previous word
End	Moves cursor to next word
Ins	Toggles insert and overwrite modes
Ctrl-N	Inserts a line at cursor
Backspace	Deletes character to left of cursor
Del	Deletes character at cursor
Ctrl-Y	Deletes line at cursor
Ctrl-T	Deletes from cursor to next word
PgUp	Scrolls screen down one screenful
PgDn	Scrolls screen up one screenful

Keystroke	Function
Esc	Aborts text editor without saving file
Ctrl-W	Writes file to disk and exits editor
Ctrl-KR	Reads another text file into file at cursor position
Ctrl-KW	Writes file to another file name

Note from the preceding table that you can control dBASE IV by using many of the classic WordStar cursor-movement and editing commands.

Using a Different Text Editor

If you prefer to use a text editor other than the one supplied with dBASE IV, you can use any text editor that is capable of producing pure ASCII files. The file editor you use makes no difference in the way your program runs. You will find, however, that much of your time is spent using the editor, so choose the editor with which you are most comfortable. Simply specify the necessary dot prompt command in your CONFIG.DB file to start the text editor. For example, if you use WordStar, add the following line to your CONFIG.DB file:

```
TEDIT=WS
```

After you modify your file, exit dBASE IV and restart the program to activate the changes. When you use MODIFY COMMAND, the text editor you selected will be invoked. When you exit your text editor, you return immediately to the dBASE IV dot prompt.

When you use an external editor, you use a special variation of the SET command, called SET DEVELOPMENT. When you edit with the internal dBASE IV editor, the .DBO file is deleted and re-created automatically. Alternate text editors do not automatically delete the .DBO file. To set development on, just type SET DEVELOPMENT ON at the dot prompt.

If SET DEVELOPMENT is ON, each time you ask dBASE IV to execute your program, dBASE IV first looks at the date and time stamp of the .PRG file and compares this stamp with the date/time stamp of the .DBO file. If

Tip:
You can use any text editor that produces pure ASCII files.

changes have been made to the .PRG file (the date/time stamp of the program is more recent than the stamp on the object file), dBASE IV automatically recompiles your program.

Saving a Program

▶
Tip:
Press Ctrl-W or Ctrl-E to save the modified program.

After you enter your program lines, press Ctrl-W or Ctrl-End to save the file. The program is saved under the name you specified in the MODIFY COMMAND line. If you are using an alternative text editor, use the appropriate commands to save and exit the editor and return to the dot prompt.

Executing a Program

▶
Tip:
Use DO to execute a program.

To execute a program, use the DO command. The DO command instructs dBASE IV to perform the operations specified in a program file. The file you specify must be a program file. Because the DO command is reserved for program files, you do not need to include the .PRG file extension.

. DO < *name of program file*>

For example, to execute the program named SAMPLE, enter the following command:

.DO SAMPLE

The first time you run the program, dBASE IV automatically compiles your .PRG file into an object file. The object file has the same file name as your program file, but has the extension .DBO. This .DBO file is the file actually processed and executed when dBASE IV runs your program. Because the .DBO file has already been checked for correct syntax and has been translated into machine language, compiling your program into an object file eliminates two of the three steps an interpreter follows.

Correcting Program Errors

No matter how good you get at writing dBASE IV programs, you still may make typing errors or use a command incorrectly. These unexpected mistakes are called "bugs." Because the compiler spots most of the bugs for you, debugging your programs is fairly easy. When you use DO to run a program and your source code contains an error, the compiler displays a message similar to the one shown in figure 9.4.

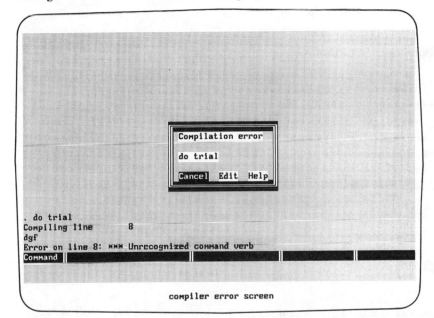

Fig. 9.4.

A compiler error.

Notice that the error message tells you which program line contains the problem. Use this error message to pinpoint the problem; then use MODIFY COMMAND to correct the program's source code before you run the program again. For instance, in figure 9.4, you see that the error message is an unrecognized command verb in line 8. Use MODIFY COMMAND to check and correct the verb in line 8. Then run the program again.

Once you make the needed corrections, use DO to execute the program again. If the line has been fixed properly, it no longer causes an error. If the line is still not correct, edit the file and use DO again.

Displaying the Contents of a Program

After you write and save a program, you may want to examine the contents of the program file in order to see the code structure or find a section of code that isn't working properly. As one way to display and edit the contents, you can use MODIFY COMMAND. You also can display the contents of a program file with the dBASE IV TYPE command. Note that you cannot edit the file. You enter the TYPE command at the dot prompt in the following format:

. TYPE < *name of program*>

As shown in figure 9.5, the TYPE command produces on-screen the contents of SAMPLE.PRG.

```
***** Program: SAMPLE.PRG *****
* This is a sample program.
* Activate the database file.
USE EMPLOYEE
* Search for the employee with "2Ø6" as his/her area code.
LOCATE FOR AREA_CODE="2Ø6"
* Display the first record found.
? "Employee's Name ........ ", FIRST_NAME, LAST_NAME
? "Area code, Phone Number: ", AREA_CODE, PHONE_NO
* Exit to the dot prompt.
RETURN
```

Just like the DOS TYPE command, the contents of the file scroll across the screen when you use TYPE. Pressing Ctrl-S or Ctrl-NumLock freezes the display so that you can read the contents. Pressing any other key restarts scrolling.

Printing a Program

Having a printed copy of your program allows you to follow along as the program executes. You can obtain a printed copy of the program in several ways. If all the program lines fit on-screen at one time, you can press Shift-PrtSc (or Shift-Print Screen on an Enhanced Keyboard). Or you can use the TYPE TO PRINT command to print your program file. For example, to print SAMPLE.PRG, issue the following command:

. TYPE sample TO PRINT

If your text editor can print your file, use it to produce a printout. Or you may want to investigate public domain and commercial programs that print and format your program file; some even add line numbers to the printout for easier reference. LP, which is supplied as part of the Norton Utilities, prints program files and adds line numbers.

Copying a Program

You can modify and save a program with MODIFY COMMAND; however, the original program is lost when you save the new version with the same file name. If you need to retain a copy of the original version, you need a different approach. Suppose that, for instance, you need a second program module that is close to one you already have. You can create a duplicate copy of the program under a new file name. Then, without disturbing the contents of the original program, you simply can edit the file to make the program perform a different task.

To copy a program file to another file with a new name, you can use the COPY FILE command, as in

. COPY FILE <*existing program name*> TO <*new program name*>

With the COPY FILE command, you must include the file extension (.PRG). dBASE IV treats the new program as though you created it in the text editor. You can examine or modify the new program with MODIFY COMMAND.

Deleting a Program

Often, you will find it useful to try techniques in a small test program that can be discarded once you have figured out how to solve a problem. You can delete a program file you no longer need by using the ERASE command:

. ERASE < *name of program*>

For example, the following command deletes the program file named SAMPLE1:

. ERASE SAMPLE1.PRG

Controlling Program Output

When you use some dBASE IV commands from the dot prompt, information is displayed on-screen. You may want to suppress this display so that your program executes smoothly without cluttering the screen with unwanted verbiage. You can use the SET TALK OFF command to suppress these interactive messages. Most of the time you will want to control these messages, showing users only what you want them to see.

The program instructions in figure 9.6 produce two kinds of screen activity: message responses from dBASE IV and results generated by commands that display information.

Fig. 9.6.

Program instructions.

```
CLEAR
? DATE( )
balance = 25
cust = "John Doe"
credit = .T.
@15,30 SAY cust
@16,30 SAY balance
```

Figure 9.7 shows the screen after the program is run with SET TALK ON.

Fig. 9.7.

The effect of SET TALK ON.

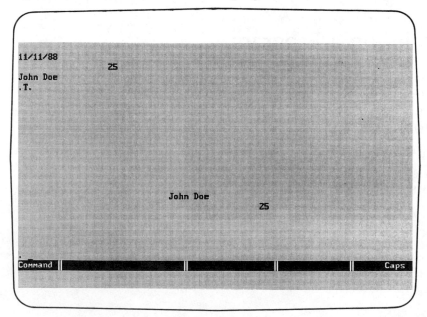

Figure 9.8 shows the screen after the same program is executed with SET TALK OFF.

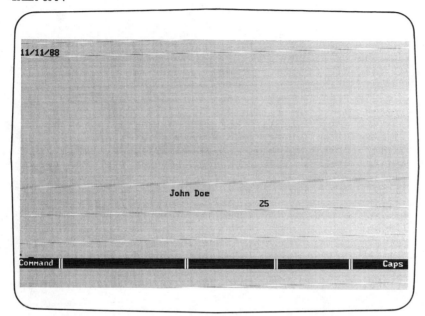

Fig. 9.8.

The effect of SET TALK OFF.

The SET TALK OFF command eliminates all the interactive messages during processing. Only the results produced by display commands such as DISPLAY, LIST, ?, and @. . . SAY display information on-screen. You can SET TALK OFF at the dot prompt or include the command as an instruction line within the program. (Note that SET TALK ON instructs the computer to display all the interactive messages during processing.)

Chapter Summary

This chapter introduced another approach to data manipulation with dBASE IV. Instead of using interactive mode, you can perform data processing tasks by collecting all the necessary commands to form a command (or program) file. Then you can execute the commands in the program file with the DO command. This chapter also explained how to create, save, run, copy, delete, and edit a program file. In addition, this chapter presented ways you can display and print program files, and control the display of messages during program execution. In the next chapter, you learn to program input and output operations.

10

Programming Input and Output Operations

This chapter explains how to use input commands to enter and modify data, and output commands to place data on-screen or on a printed page. The following commands are covered in this chapter:

```
STORE/=
DECLARE
ACCEPT TO
INPUT TO
WAIT TO
APPEND BLANK
@...SAY...GET
READ
CLEAR GETS
?/??/???
@...SAY
PRINTJOB...ENDPRINTJOB
```

This chapter also introduces you to printing System Variables. System Variables are used to keep track of many different conditions (such as line, column, and page numbers) during print operations.

Defining Memory Variables

Memory variables provide a way to control dBASE IV programs. You use variables to communicate values between modules of a program, to store data for later use, and to provide a place to store input received from the program user or the application.

Memory variables also can store data that will replace the contents of other data. For example, you can use a set of memory variables to replace field values in either an existing record or a newly appended one.

Tip:

Use STORE or = to store data in one specific memory variable.

You assign values to memory variables in two different ways. You can use the STORE command to assign a particular value to one or more memory variables, or you can use the equal sign (=) to store data into one specific memory variable. Memory variables have the same attributes as fields, but you cannot define a memo variable type.

Look at the following examples:

```
STORE Ø TO var1, var2, var3    && Stores Ø to all three
                               && variables
STORE .T. TO varL              && Stores TRUE to a logical
                               && variable
STORE "abcdef" TO var_char     && Stores a character string to
                                  && a variable
var2 = 244.35                  && Stores 244.35 to a numeric
                                  && variable
sumdat = CTOD(" / / ")         && Stores a blank date to a date
                                  && variable
```

In a program, when you assign a variable with the STORE or = command, the command line must contain the value. For example, when AREACODE.PRG, shown in figure 10.1, is executed, the alphanumeric string 2Ø6 is assigned to the memory variable AREACODE. Figure 10.2 shows the output from this program.

To search for a data record with the area code 415, you change the command line that assigns the alphanumeric string to the memory variable AREACODE. To enter the change, use the text editor to modify the program line to the following one:

```
AREACODE="415"
```

```
. TYPE AREACODE.PRG
***** Program: AREACODE.PRG *****
* Find the first record with area code of "206".
SET TALK OFF
SET ECHO OFF
* Specify the area code to be located.
AREACODE="206"
* Select the database file.
USE EMPLOYEE
* Search for such an area code.
LOCATE FOR AREA_CODE=AREACODE
* Show the data record found.
DISPLAY
RETURN

.
```

Fig. 10.1.

A program using memory variables.

```
. DO AREACODE
Record#  FIRST_NAME LAST_NAME AREA_CODE PHONE_NO MALE  BIRTH_DATE ANNUAL_PAY
     1   James C.   Smith       206      123-4567 .T.   07/04/60   22000.00
```

Fig. 10.2.

The output generated by the memory variable program.

As in this case, you often will have memory variables that need to change values as the program executes. Changing the alphanumeric string whenever you want to search for a new value (like a new area code, in this example) is inefficient. Later in this chapter, you learn several methods for pausing program execution to wait for input from the keyboard.

Arrays as Memory Variables

An array is a special type of memory variable. You can think of this variable as a grid or a table in which groups of memory variables can be stored together. To best illustrate an array, think of a wall of post office boxes. Usually, post office boxes are arranged in rows and columns, much like a grid. Each individual mail box in any of the rows or columns can be empty or can contain letters. Each of the mailboxes can contain different types of letters; one may contain a bill, while another may contain a letter from home.

Tip:

An array stores information in rows and columns.

In this same way, arrays are used to store information in rows and columns. Each individual intersection of a row and column is called an *element*. Each array you declare counts as one memory variable, but the individual elements of an array do not count as individual memory variables.

To create an array called SAMPLE that contains three rows of seven elements, place the following command in your program:

```
DECLARE sample[3,7]
```

This array contains 21 elements.

The DECLARE command initializes each element of the array as a logical false. Array elements do not take on any other value until data of a particular type is STOREd into an element. For example, the following command places the number 256 into the third element in row one of the array named SAMPLE:

```
STORE 256 to sample[1,3]
sample[1,3] = 256
```

The array type is numeric. You can mix and match data types within the elements of an array.

To retrieve the contents of an element, you can use the following command:

```
? sample[1,3]    && The result is 256
```

PUBLIC versus PRIVATE Variables

Tip:

Memory variables and arrays are initialized as PRIVATE by default.

When you initialize a memory variable or an array, it is by default PRIVATE. This means that only that program or any program module that the program may call can read the variable and its value. When the program ceases operation and returns to any other program that may have called it, the memory variable is released from memory, and its value cannot be read by the original calling program.

Tip:

Initializing a memory variable or an array as PUBLIC makes the item and its values available globally.

Declaring a memory variable or an array PUBLIC before assigning values makes this memory variable/array and its values available globally to any program or procedure within an application; that is, the values are not released when the program terminates, and they can be read by any other module.

You use PRIVATE to protect the integrity of memory variables that are part of a program that calls another program, PROCEDURE, or function. (User-defined functions and PROCEDURES are explained in Chapter 12.)

If, for example, PROGRAM A (PROGA.PRG) has a memory variable called var1 and a command that says DO PROGB (PROGB.PRG), a conflict could arise if PROGB uses a memory variable with the name var1.

In this case, because the variable name is already initialized, any changes made by PROGB to var1 affects the variable's value in PROGA. This factor becomes important when you design subroutines and functions you can "plug in" to any program you write. To protect the integrity of the original memory variable, the subroutine or function must declare the variable as PRIVATE.

```
***PROGA
**The code for program A
var1 = 123
DO PROGB
? var1

***PROGB
**The code for program B
var1 = 456
RETURN
```

In the preceding example, PROGA calls PROGB. PROGB changes var1 to 456 and returns to PROGA. When PROGA executes the ? var1 command, the result is 456, not 123. By adding one line of code to PROGB, the value of var1 is protected when PROGA executes the ? line:

```
***PROGB
**The amended code for program B
PRIVATE var1  && This line creates a second variable called
              && var1 and protects the same variable in PROGA.
              && When RETURN is executed, this variable is
              && released, and the original var1 is restored
              && to active status.
var1 = 456
RETURN
```

With the amended lines in PROGB, PROGA executes the ? command, and the result is 123.

You also use the PRIVATE command to isolate variables created in subroutines so that they do not change the value of variables already in existence. You can write pieces of program code you can add to any application without fear of a conflict if the subroutine uses a variable name that is already initialized.

Entering Data in Memory Variables

As stated earlier, the main use of memory variables is transferring information from one program module to another or temporarily storing information that the user enters. You can use one of several methods for creating a point in your program where the program will stop and prompt the user for an entry.

Entering Alphanumeric Strings with ACCEPT TO

Tip:
Use ACCEPT TO *to assign alphanumeric strings to a memory variable.*

You use the ACCEPT TO command to assign alphanumeric strings to a memory variable. ACCEPT TO enters the string in a character variable; you can use this command with or without a prompting message. If you include a prompt, it must be enclosed in quotation marks.

The ACCEPT TO command allows the user to enter an unspecified number of characters up to the maximum of 254. To use the ACCEPT TO command in a program, include something similar to the following line:

```
ACCEPT "Enter information here: " TO var1
```

Or you can exclude the prompt and use the following form:

```
ACCEPT TO var1
```

The preceding command pauses program execution and waits for the user to enter a character string, but it does not display a prompt. The wait state created by the ACCEPT TO command ends when the user presses the Enter key.

The values of the ROW( ) and COL( ) functions determine the placement on-screen where the ACCEPT TO command will be placed.

Figure 10.3 shows the use of the ACCEPT TO command in a program. This program produces the output shown in figure 10.4. When the program is executed, the prompt and a blinking cursor appear on-screen, and the execution of the program pauses, waiting for your input. After you type an answer to the prompt and press Enter, the data you typed is assigned as the variable AREACODE; the program then uses this variable as a search key for the LOCATE command.

```
. TYPE PROMPT.PRG
*****   Program: PROMPT.PRG *****
* Find the first record with an area code keyed in.
SET TALK OFF
SET ECHO OFF
* Prompt for the area code to be located.
ACCEPT "Enter the area code to be searched .... " TO AREACODE
USE EMPLOYEE
LOCATE FOR AREA_CODE=AREACODE
DISPLAY
RETURN
```

Fig. 10.3.

A program using the ACCEPT *command.*

With this program, you don't have to change the program each time you want to search for a new area code. Instead, you can specify the area code as the program executes.

You can assign only a character string with ACCEPT; you cannot assign values to numeric, date, or logical variables. However, you can use a string of numbers with the command and then transform the numbers into a numeric value by using the VAL( ) function (see fig. 10.5). Similar functions are available to transform characters into date and logical type variables.

Tip:
To use numbers with ACCEPT, *enter a string of numbers and then convert the string to values by using the* VAL( ) *function.*

In the program in figure 10.5, the user is prompted for values for X and Y. The VAL function then converts the alphanumeric strings to numeric values, assigns those values to the variables X and Y, and sums the two variables (123 + 234 = 357).

Fig. 10.4.

*The output from
PROMPT.PRG.*

```
. DO PROMPT
Enter the area code to be located .... 415
Record#  FIRST_NAME   LAST_NAME   AREA_CODE  PHONE_NO MALE  BIRTH_DATE  ANNUAL_PAY
      5  Tina B.      Baker       415        567-7777 .F.   10/12/56      27195.00
. DO PROMPT
Enter the area code to be located .... 212
Record#  FIRST_NAME   LAST_NAME   AREA_CODE  PHONE_NO MALE  BIRTH_DATE  ANNUAL_PAY
      2  Albert K.    Zeller      212        457-9801 .T.   10/10/59      29347.50
. DO PROMPT
Enter the area code to be located .... 513
Record#  FIRST_NAME   LAST_NAME   AREA_CODE  PHONE_NO MALE  BIRTH_DATE  ANNUAL_PAY
      3  Doris A.     Gregory     513        204-8567 .F.   07/04/62      17745.00
```

Fig. 10.5.

*Converting a
string to a
numeric variable.*

```
. TYPE XPLUSY.PRG
*****  Program:  XPLUSY.PRG   *****
* A program to add X and Y.
* Prompt for values of variables X and Y.
ACCEPT "Enter value for X =" TO X
ACCEPT "       value for 6 =" TO Y
* Convert strings X and Y to numeric values.
X=VAL(X)
Y_VAL(Y)
? "Sum of X and Y =",X+Y
RETURN

. DO XPLUSY
Enter value for X =123
       value for Y =234
Sum of X and Y =              357
.
```

Figure 10.6 illustrates another example of using the VAL function. This program shows that the VAL function retains the decimal digits in the variable, even though the decimal point and the digits to the right of the decimal point are not shown.

The first ? command displays the contents of the alphanumeric string X. This and the second command show that the value returned by the VAL( ) function is 124 (123.85 rounded to the nearest integer). The third ?

```
. TYPE VALUEOFX.PRG
***** Program: VALUEOFX.PRG *****
* Illustrate the effects of VAL function.
X="123.85"
* X is an alphanumeric string
? VAL(X)
? VAL(X)+200
? VAL(X)*100
RETURN

. DO VALUEOFX
        124
          324
            12385
```

Fig. 10.6.

The results of the VAL function.

command, which displays the result of multiplying VAL(X) by 100, shows that the decimal digits are retained.

With the help of the VAL( ) function, you can use the ACCEPT command to assign a decimal value to a numeric variable. For instance, you can use the following lines to assign the value of 123.85 to the numeric variable X:

```
ACCEPT "Enter a value for X . . . " TO X
X=VAL(X)*100/100
```

The value of VAL(X)*100 is 12385; this value is then divided by 100. The result (123.85) is entered in the variable X.

The drawback to using the ACCEPT command is determining what type of entry the user typed, and then translating, if necessary, that data into the proper memory variable type. Also, because the character string that is ACCEPTed can vary in length, the user may enter more characters than you intend. If so, the user's entry may be cut off if the entry is placed into a field.

Entering Values with INPUT TO

The INPUT TO command allows the user to enter any type of value into a memory variable. The form of the command follows:

Tip:
Use INPUT TO to allow any type of value to be entered into a memory variable.

INPUT *"Prompt"* TO <*name of variable*>

For example, the following command prompts the user for the number of units on hand and then assigns this value to the variable onhand:

```
INPUT "Enter number of units on hand: " TO onhand
```

The type of variable is determined when you enter the data element. Character strings must be surrounded by quotation marks. Date memory variables must be surrounded by curly braces. Because of these requirements, you should seldom, if ever, incorporate the INPUT command as part of one of your programs. Better, safer methods exist for reading user input. (See @...SAY...GET later in this chapter.)

Entering a Single Keystroke with WAIT TO

Tip:
Use WAIT TO *when the input is a single keystroke.*

The WAIT TO command is similar to the ACCEPT command except for one minor difference: The WAIT TO command is terminated by the first keystroke. Use the WAIT TO command when you want only a single keystroke from the user. The user does not have to press Enter.

You often use WAIT TO in programs that prompt for the answer to a decision variable. The answer is applied to conditional commands such as IF...ENDIF and DO CASE...ENDCASE to determine how the program should proceed, as in the following example:

```
WAIT "Do you want to continue (Y/N) " TO  confirm
IF UPPER(confirm) = "Y"
     DO nextprog
ENDIF
```

Receiving Input with @...SAY...GET

@...SAY...GET is the most powerful and flexible method for pausing and accepting input into memory variables. By initializing memory variables and then using the @...SAY...GET command to receive input, you can use a number of arguments in the @...SAY...GET command to format and validate input, check the range of numeric input, change screen colors, display messages or instructions on-screen, and other purposes.

The @...SAY...GET command gives you control over what you will and will not allow the user to enter into the memory variables.

Follow these three basic steps to use the @...SAY...GET command for input:

1. Initialize memory variables of the type and length required.

2. Use the @...SAY...GET command to mark the spots on-screen where the user will be asked to input information.

3. Issue the READ command to activate the @...SAY...GET commands in the order they were issued.

The READ command is the command that actually stops and waits for input. For example, the program shown in figure 10.7 clears the screen and takes information for a typical mailing label.

Tip:
Use
@...SAY...GET *in your program to pause operation and accept input for memory variables.*

```
CLEAR
STORE SPACE(3Ø) TO nam,addr     && Create memory variables and
                                && fill them with blank spaces
cit= SPACE(17)                  && of the correct length; this
st= SPACE(2)                    && procedure correctly sizes the
zip= SPACE(5)                   && GET boxes.

@ 1Ø,1Ø SAY "      NAME: " GET nam
@ 12,1Ø SAY "   ADDRESS: " GET addr
@ 14,1Ø SAY "      CITY: " GET cit
@ 16,1Ø SAY "GET STATE: " GET st
@ 18,1Ø SAY "ENTER ZIP: " GET zip
READ
```

Fig. 10.7.

A program using the READ *command.*

Figure 10.8 shows the screen that is produced by the program in figure 10.7.

When you use the @...SAY...GET command, you have almost unlimited flexibility about how you want the screen to appear.

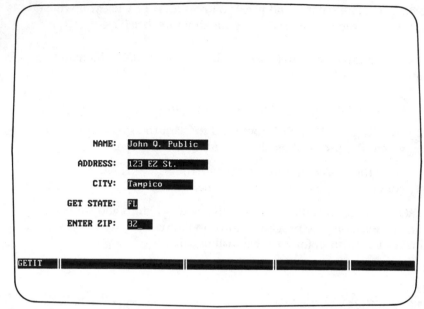

Entering Data into a Data File

Once you create a data structure, you will add new records, edit existing records, and delete records you no longer need. You can use one of two different methods for entering and editing data in the data file.

As one method, you can use the @...SAY...GET command to manipulate the fields directly. As the second method, you can create a set of memory variables that have the exact same structure as the fields and then accept input into the memory variables. The program can check, verify, accept, or reject the values of the memory variables. If the input is valid, you can use the REPLACE command to place the value of the memory variable into the field within a record.

To simplify things, the examples in this chapter show you how to manipulate fields directly; however, the same rules apply to using memory variables.

Using Formats

As you have seen in previous chapters, you can create custom entry screens with the CREATE SCREEN command. You can use the output of this command to help you write better dBASE IV programs in one of two ways.

As one way, you can use the CREATE SCREEN command. When you use this command to make a custom screen, three files are written to the disk when you SAVE and EXIT. Each file has the basic file name that you specified in the CREATE SCREEN command, but the extensions differ. One file uses .FMT, one uses .FMO, and one uses .SCR. To specify the custom screen, use the SET FORMAT TO command.

The second method involves using the contents of the .FMT file as a template by importing the .FMT file into your program file. You can use the @...SAY...GET commands that are a part of your .FMT file as the basis for your program.

Adding a New Record with APPEND

You can use a program to add new data records to a database file. For example, the program in figure 10.9 uses the APPEND command to add a new data record to EMPLOYEE.DBF.

Tip:
Use APPEND in a program to add new data records.

```
. TYPE APENDIT.PRG
***** Program: APENDIT.PRG  *****
*  Program to append an employee's record.
SET TALK OFF
SET ECHO OFF
*  Clear the screen.
CLEAR
*  Select the database file.
USE EMPLOYEE
*  Append the new record to active database file.
APPEND
RETURN

.
```

Fig. 10.9.

A program to append records.

When you execute the program, the data-entry form is displayed so that you can enter a new set of data items (see fig. 10.10). As soon as the data record is added, you can press Ctrl-End to save the new record and exit the program.

```
  Record No.          11
  FIRST _NAME
  LAST _NAME
  AREA _CODE
  PHONE _NO
  MALE
  BIRTH _DATE
  ANNUAL _PAY
```

Adding a New Record with APPEND BLANK

Tip:
Use APPEND BLANK *to add a blank data-entry form for data entry.*

You can place new information in the data file by creating a blank record at the end of the file and then filling the fields with data. To create a new data record, use the APPEND BLANK command. When you issue this command in a program, a new record is appended to the data file. Spaces fill in the character fields; numeric fields have a value of zero; logical fields have a value of FALSE (.F.); and date fields have an initial value of CTOD(" / / ").

Suppose that, for instance, you create a mailing list database. When the program executes the APPEND BLANK command, the fields are assigned the initial values you assigned when you created the data file. For example, the name and address are filled with 30 spaces; city has 17, state 2, and zip code 5.

To accept input directly into a new record, you can use the program shown in figure 10.11.

The program in figure 10.11 opens the data file, pegs a blank record onto the end of the file, and then takes your entry. Once you finish the entry, the record is added; the file is closed; and the program ends.

```
***** Program: APPEN.PRG *****
SET TALK OFF
USE EMPLOYEE

APPEND BLANK
@ 10,10 SAY "     NAME: " GET nam
@ 12,10 SAY "  ADDRESS: " GET addr
@ 14,10 SAY "     CITY: " GET cit
@ 16,10 SAY "GET STATE: " GET st
@ 18,10 SAY "ENTER ZIP: " GET zip
READ
CLOSE DATABASES
RETURN
```

Fig. 10.11.

Using APPEND BLANK *to add a new record.*

Editing Data Records

When you want to change the contents of a record in the data file, you first must move the record pointer to that record. You easily can accomplish this task using LOCATE, FIND, or SEEK.

Tip:
Move the record pointer to the record to be edited by using the LOCATE, FIND, *or* SEEK *commands.*

(*Note:* You should avoid the LOCATE command when there are more than 10 to 20 records in the database because as the database gets larger, the LOCATE command gets slower. Both the FIND and SEEK commands use the active index to position the record pointer. Even on large databases that contain thousands of records, positioning the record pointer is almost instantaneous with FIND and SEEK.)

The best method for locating the record pointer is to create a memory variable that is a duplicate of the key field. Accept keyboard input into that variable and then use the SEEK or FIND command to position the record pointer. For example, the program in figure 10.12 illustrates positioning the record pointer.

The program in figure 10.12 opens a data file, asks the user for the search item, performs the search, and then allows editing if the program finds a matching record.

```
***** Program: EDIT.PRG *****

SET TALK OFF
USE mail                    && Open the mailing list file
SET INDEX TO name           && Open the name index

CLEAR                       && Erase the screen
v_name= (30)                && Initialize a variable of the same type as
                            && the key field in the index

@ 10,10 SAY "ENTER NAME: "GET v_name
READ                        && Accept user input
SEEK v_name                 && Look for a matching record

IF EOF()                    && Check if end of file function is true.
                            && IF is covered in the next chapter
   RETURN                   && If SEEK does not find a record,
                            && position pointer at end of file,
                            && terminate the edit, and return to the menu
                            && or calling program.

ENDIF

@ 10,10 SAY "     NAME: " GET nam     && Each of the boxes on-
@ 12,10 SAY "  ADDRESS: " GET addr    && screen will have the
@ 14,10 SAY "     CITY: " GET cit     && value in the fields
@ 16,10 SAY "GET STATE: " GET st      && displayed for editing.
@ 18,10 SAY "ENTER ZIP: " GET zip
READ

CLOSE DATABASES             && Store the data file on disk
RETURN                      && Return to dot prompt or to program
                            && that called this one.
```

Deleting Data Records

With one simple twist and the CLEAR GETS command, you can modify the program for editing a record to allow a user to delete a record. The program in figure 10.13 takes the information, just like the program in figure 10.12, but this time the code displays only the entry screen.

In DELET.PRG, the user is prompted to enter a name; the program then searches for a record with that name. If the program reaches the end of

```
***** Program: DELET.PRG *****

SET TALK OFF
USE mail              && Open the mailing list file
SET INDEX TO name     && Open the name index

CLEAR                 && Erase the screen
v_name= (30)          && Initialize a variable of the same type as
                      && the key field in the index

@ 10,10 SAY "ENTER NAME: "GET v_name
READ                  && Accept user input
SEEK v_name           && Look for a matching record

IF EOF()
   RETURN             && If SEEK does not find a record,
                      && position the pointer at end of file,
                      && terminate the edit, and return to the menu
                      && or calling program.
ENDIF

@ 10,10 SAY "     NAME: " GET nam    && Each of the boxes on-
@ 12,10 SAY " ADDRESS: " GET addr    && screen will have the
@ 14,10 SAY "     CITY: " GET cit    && field values displayed
@ 16,10 SAY "GET STATE: " GET st
@ 18,10 SAY "ENTER ZIP: " GET zip

CLEAR GETS
WAIT "Delete this record? (Y/N)" TO confirm    && Pause to ask
                                               && for confirmation

IF UPPER(confirm) = "Y"   && If the user presses Y,
   DELETE                 && mark the record for deletion
ENDIF
CLOSE DATABASES           && Put away the data file on disk.
RETURN                    && Return to dot prompt or
                          && calling program.
```

Fig. 10.13.

A program to delete records.

the file (no matching record was found), it terminates. Otherwise, the program displays the matching record in a screen that looks like the original entry form.

The fields in the record contain the values on-screen that they do in the file. The user then is asked to confirm the deletion. If the user presses Y, the record is marked for deletion. Any other keystroke answers no, and the record is not marked for deletion.

The command CLEAR GETS displays the @...SAY...GET commands on-screen, but does not pause to allow for input. This command is useful when you want to use @...SAY...GET to retrieve and display the values of fields within the data records. Once you display the information on-screen, the user needs only to confirm the deletion.

Controlling the Screen Display

When you write dBASE IV programs, you take on the responsibility of creating screen output that is balanced and easy to use. When designing screens, try to imagine yourself using that screen four or five hours a day. Are the prompts and GET boxes balanced so that the screen is easy to read? If not, you need to make changes.

A well-designed screen is not only more productive, but it also affects how your work will be judged by users and clients. Screen design determines your program's first impression. dBASE IV gives you a number of different ways to control the appearances of your screen.

Displaying User Entry with GETs

Tip:
To control screen display, use SET INTENSITY, SET DELIMITERS TO, *and* SET DELIMITERS ON/ OFF.

Because you often can omit the SAY portion of an @...SAY...GET command, dBASE programmers frequently refer to the action of receiving user input as *GETs*. Sometimes you may not want GETs to be displayed on-screen as reverse video or colored boxes. You can set dBASE IV to display GETs on-screen bounded or delimited with characters rather than in reverse video. This variety is handy when designing screens for older computers with monochrome video cards. To control the display, you can use the following commands: SET INTENSITY, SET DELIMITERS TO, and SET DELIMITERS ON/OFF.

SET INTENSITY toggles the screen output of GETs between reverse video and the normal colors/attributes selected with the SET COLOR command.

SET DELIMITERS TO specifies the width of the data field. This command places the characters you specify before and after the area where the GET takes place. If you specify only one character, the character is used both before and after the GET area. Specifying two characters places the first in front of and the second behind the GET areas. SET DELIMITERS ON turns on the display of delimiters; SET DELIMITERS OFF turns off the display.

Figure 10.14 shows a program that uses delimiters to change the
appearance of GETs.

Figure 10.15 shows what the GETs look like on-screen.

```
***** Program: DELIM.PRG *****

SET TALK OFF
STORE SPACE(5) TO var1,var2    && Initialize two variables as
                               && character types
CLEAR                          && Blank the screen
SET INTENSITY OFF              && Turn off reverse video for GETs
SET DELIMITERS TO "[]"         && Declare front and back
                               && delimiters
SET DELIMITERS ON              && Turn on the delimiters

@10,10 SAY " ENTER FIRST DATA: " GET var1
@12,10 SAY "ENTER SECOND DATA: " GET var2
READ                           && Accept the entry
```

Fig. 10.14.

*Using delimiters
for screen display.*

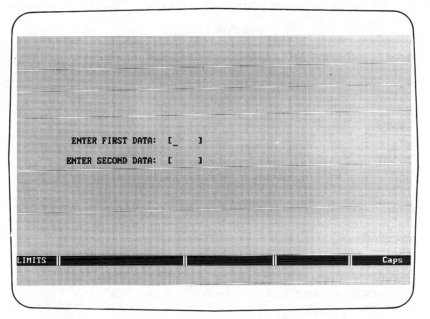

Fig. 10.15.

*The results of
DELIM.PRG.*

Setting Color Attributes

Tip:
To set the color
of the display,
use SET COLOR ON/
OFF, SET COLOR TO,
and SET COLOR OF.

With the SET COLOR command, you can change screen color settings.
(Remember that many personal computers have a color graphics card
that changes colors into shades of gray on a monochrome monitor.) You
can use the following commands to set the color: SET COLOR ON/OFF, SET
COLOR TO, and SET COLOR OF.

SET COLOR ON/OFF toggles between monochrome and color displays on
systems equipped with both.

With the SET COLOR TO command, you can change color settings for
normal foreground/background, enhanced areas of the screen (for
example, entry boxes created with the @...SAY...GET command), border
color, and background color.

For instance, if you want to paint the screen with white letters on a blue
background for normal text and to have GET boxes painted in black on
cyan, you issue the following command:

SET COLOR TO w+/b,n/bg

Table 10.1 shows the values you can use in the SET COLOR commands.

Table 10.1
Values for SET COLOR commands

Color	Value
BLACK	N
BLUE	B
GREEN	G
CYAN	BG
BLANK	X
GRAY	N+
RED	R
MAGENTA	RB
BROWN	GR
YELLOW	GR+
WHITE	W
BLINKING	*
HIGH INTENSITY COLOR	+ (Bright White = W+)

Note that most video cards do not allow you to specify high intensity colors as the background.

The SET COLOR OF command controls special case screen paintings. Menu highlights, alerts, titles, boxes, and messages are examples of screen parts you can change with the SET COLOR OF command.

If you want boxes drawn on-screen in a different color combination than the enhanced color setting, you use the SET COLOR TO command. For example, to display all boxes in bright yellow on a blue background, issue the following command:

```
SET COLOR OF BOXES TO GR+/B
```

Displaying and Printing Output

The dBASE IV commands ?, ??, ???, and @...SAY give you control over how data is displayed and printed. While the ? and ?? commands are primarily intended for use at the dot prompt, they are often useful in writing dBASE IV programs. The @...SAY command is the most powerful of the display commands when used properly. Various arguments for the @...SAY command allow you to display data in a different color and allow you to format and place output.

Printing with the ?/?? Command

The ?/?? command displays on-screen and prints output depending on the status of SET PRINT. (If you SET PRINT ON, the result is displayed on-screen and sent to the printer.) For example, when the following command is used in a program, the contents of var1 are displayed on-screen:

Tip:
Use ? and ?? to display and print output.

```
?var1
```

The value of the ROW() function determines the placement of the variable. The ? command places the result on the next row (ROW() +1) against the left margin of either the screen or printed page, assuming that you have not used the AT clause of the ?/?? command.

You can display/print several items at a time by placing a list of the items (separated by commas) after the ?/?? command, as in the following example:

    ? TRIM(fir_name),last_name,phone

This command displays the following line:

    Mike Zerega   555-1111

The only difference between the ? and the ?? commands is that the ?? command places the output at the current ROW() and COL() positions. Suppose that, for example, you enter the following commands:

    ?"Hello "
    ??"There"

The following line is displayed on-screen:

    Hello There

The ? and ?? commands have been expanded in dBASE IV to include a PICTURE clause for formatting expressions and the AT clause that allows you to include the column number where you want the output placed. The following lines show an example of specifying placement:

    var1 = 34.45
    ?"Value: " AT 12,var1 PICTURE '99.99' AT 20

The preceding lines result in a screen line that looks like the following:

    Value: 34.45

The ? command displays the output elements from left to right on a new display line. The display position of an output element depends on the type of the element. Figure 10.16 shows a program that uses the ? command. Note the output of the program in figure 10.17.

As you can see, the contents of the alphanumeric string on the second ? command line, ABCDE, is displayed on the far left position of the display line. The comma used to separate the alphanumeric strings inserts a blank space between the strings ABCDE and XYZ. The comma separating a date variable and a logical variable in the fourth ? command also inserts a blank space.

```
. TYPE PRINT1.PRG
***** Program: PRINT1.PRG *****
* A program to show the printing positions.
SET TALK OFF
SET ECHO OFF
ASTRING="ABCDE"
BSTRING="XYZ"
VALUEX=-123.45
VALUEY=Ø.6789
VALUEZ=98765
DATE1=CTOD("Ø3/Ø8/85")
LOGIC=.T.
* Display a ruler.
?"123456789Ø123456789Ø123456789Ø123456789Ø123457890"
?ASTRING,BSTRING
?VALUEX,VALUEY,VALUEZ
?DATE1,LOGIC
RETURN
```

Fig. 10.16.

A program for demonstrating display positions.

```
. DO PRINT1
123456789Ø123456789Ø123456789Ø123456789Ø123456789Ø
ABCDE XYZ
        -123.45         Ø.6789         98765
Ø3/Ø8/85 .T.
.
```

Fig. 10.17.

The output of PRINT1.PRG.

However, the same spacing rules do not apply to numeric output. Figure 10.18 shows a program for positioning numeric values. When you execute the program, the results shown in figure 10.19 are displayed.

The output of this program shows some interesting results. With a ? command, the decimal point of the first numeric variable always is displayed at the eleventh column. Commas do not provide the same consistent spacing with the ? command, and, as a result, positioning numeric values can be difficult.

To solve the spacing problem, you can convert the output elements to alphanumeric strings with the STR function. For example, to convert the value of VALUEX (-123.45) to an alphanumeric string, you enter

```
. TYPE PRINT2.PRG
***** Program: PRINT2.PRG *****
* Show printing position of numeric variables.
SET TALK OFF
SET ECHO OFF
VALUEX=-123.45
VALUEY=Ø.6789
VALUEZ=98765
* Display a ruler.
?"1234567890123456789012345678901234567890123456789Ø"
?VALUEX
?VALUEY
?VALUEZ
?VALUEX,VALUEY,VALUEZ
?VALUEY,VALUEX,VALUEZ
?VALUEZ,VALUEX,VALUEY
RETURN
```

```
. DO PRINT2.PRG
1234567890123456789012345678901234567890123456789Ø
      -123.45
         Ø.6789
   98765
      -123.45            Ø.6789     98765
         Ø.6789       -123.45       98765
   98765            -123.45            Ø.6789
```

STR(VALUEX,7,2). The result is a string of 7 characters with 2 decimal places. Figure 10.20 shows a program that sets equal lengths for numeric values and positions numeric output. The decimal points are aligned vertically because you set the length of the return strings to 15 characters (see fig. 10.21).

As you have seen, a comma separating alphanumeric strings inserts a blank space between elements. But what if you do not want a space? To solve that problem, you can use arithmetic operators between elements

```
.TYPE PRINT3.PRG
***** Program: PRINT3.PRG *****
* Show effect of STR on printing position.
SET TALK OFF
SET ECHO OFF
VALUEX=-123.45
VALUEY=Ø.6789
VALUEZ=98765
* Display a ruler.
?"123456789Ø123456789Ø123456789Ø123456789Ø123456789Ø"
?STR(VALUEX,15,4),STR(VALUEY,15,4),STR(VALUEZ,15,4)
?STR(VALUEY,15,4),STR(VALUEX,15,4),STR(VALUEZ,15,4)
?STR(VALUEZ,15,4),STR(VALUEX,15,4),STR(VALUEY,15,4)
RETURN

.
```

Fig. 10.20.

A program using the STR( ) *function.*

```
. DO PRINT3
123456789Ø123456789Ø123456789Ø123456789Ø123456789Ø123456789Ø
    -123.45ØØ          Ø.6789       98765.ØØØØ
        Ø.6789      -123.45ØØ       98765.ØØØØ
    98765.ØØØØ      -123.45ØØ           Ø.6789
.
```

Fig. 10.21.

The results of STR( ).

and specify the string as an expression. For example, to display the contents of the strings ASTRING and BSTRING without a space between them, use a plus sign, such as

    . ?ASTRING+BSTRING

Because of erratic spacing, you may want to avoid placing commas in the ? command line. The program in figure 10.22 converts data fields to alphanumeric strings and then displays the strings as alphanumeric expressions. Commas are not used. The output produced by the program is shown in figure 10.23.

To print a copy of the program output, add the SET PRINT ON command to the beginning of the program. After printing the report, you can use SET PRINT OFF to deactivate the printer and return the display to the screen.

```
. TYPE PRINT4.PRG
***** Program: PRINT4.PRG *****
* A program to display an employee's record.
USE EMPLOYEE
CLEAR
?"Employee's Name: "+TRIM(FIRST_NAME)+" "+LAST_NAME
?"Telephone No:    ("+AREA_CODE+") "+PHONE_NO
?"Birth Date:      "+DTOC(BIRTH_DATE)
?"Annual Salary:   "+STR(ANNUAL_PAY,8,2)
RETURN
```

```
Employee's Name: James C. Smith
Telephone No:    (206) 123-4567
Birth Date:      07/04/60
Annual Salary:   22000.00
```

Sending Printer Control Sequences with the ??? Command

The ??? command, new to dBASE IV, is used to send control sequences directly to the printer without changing ROW( ) or COL( ) and without requiring SET PRINT ON. The sequences bypass any installed printer driver.

In earlier versions of dBASE, you had to enter a special code to set a printer to compressed print, such as

```
SET PRINT ON
? CHR(15)        && This line assumes that the printer
                 && responds to the ASCII Shift In command
SET PRINT OFF
```

To send the command directly to the printer in dBASE IV, you simply include the following line:

```
??? CHR(15)
```

Controlling Screen and Printer Output with @...SAY

The @. . .SAY command gives you complete control over both screen and printer output. With the @. . .SAY command, you can place the output exactly where you want it, format the output with a PICTURE clause, and change the color of that item if the output is sent to the screen.

To place output on a printed page, use SET DEVICE TO PRINT. The SET DEVICE command allows you to direct the results of @. . .SAYs to either the printer, the screen, or a file.

Screen Output with @...SAY

Displaying field contents and memory variables on-screen is a simple job if you're using the @. . .SAY command. Take a minute to study the program in figure 10.24.

```
var1 = "Hi! How are you?"      && Initialize a character variable
var2 = 234.09                  && Initialize a numeric variable
CLEAR                          && Blank the screen
@5,20 SAY var1                 && Display a character string at line
                               && 5, column 20
@7,20 SAY var2                 && Display the numeric value without
                               && any formatting
@8,20 SAY var2 PICTURE '999.99' COLOR R/W   && Format the value
                                            && and paint it red
                                            && on white
@10,20 SAY DATE()              && Display the current date
@12,20 SAY "Please Pay: $" + LTRIM(STR(var2,6,2)) COLOR W*/G
* The preceding line converts the numeric to a string, combines
* the strings, and paints the strings blinking white on green
RETURN
```

Fig. 10.24.

Using the @. . .SAY command.

Running this program produces the screen shown in figure 10.25.

Notice how the formatting affects the numeric variable. By specifying a PICTURE, you trim off the leading blanks (the blanks are caused by the default length of numbers—10 integer digits in dBASE IV).

Fig. 10.25.

*The output from
the program using
@. . .SAY.*

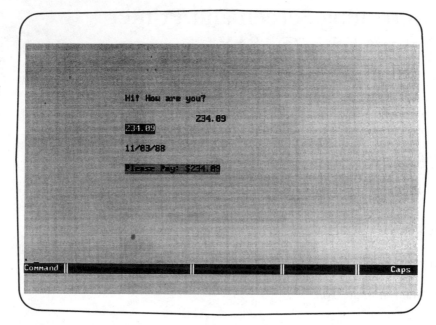

Fig. 10.25.

The output from the program using @. . .SAY.

Printer Output with @...SAY

You can use the @. . .SAY command to send output to the printer as well as to the screen. To control where data is printed, you can use a memory variable to keep track of the current line number of the page, or you can use the PROW() function to do the same function.

The SET DEVICE TO PRINT command directs the output from @. . .SAYs to the printer; the SET DEVICE TO SCREEN ends the printer output.

The only caution in using @. . .SAYs to format printing is to make sure that you do not try to print on a line above the current line. If PROW() = 12 and your program tells the printer to print a line on row 10, the page is ejected, and the line is printed on line 10 of the next page. With some printers, a similar problem can occur if you try to print a column to the left of a previously printed one.

A sample program showing @. . .SAYs that control printing is shown in figure 10.26.

```
var1 = 55.25
SET DEVICE TO PRINT    && Direct @...SAYs to the printer
@PROW()+4,1Ø SAY "This is the first line."  && PROW() = Ø This
                                            && line causes the
                                            && first line to
                                            && print on line 4
@PROW()+1,1Ø SAY "This is the second line." && PROW() now = 5
@PROW()+1,1Ø SAY "This is the third line."  && PROW() = 6
@PROW()+1,1Ø SAY "Today's date is: " + DTOC(DATE()+1)
@PROW()+1,1Ø SAY "The average age is: " + STR(var1,5,2)
SET DEVICE TO SCREEN      && Redirect @...SAYs to the screen
EJECT                     && Advance to next page--releases last
                          && @...SAY from print buffer

RETURN
```

Fig. 10.26.

A program to control printing.

This program produces the printout shown in figure 10.27.

```
This is the first line.
This is the second line.
This is the third line.
Today's date is: 11/Ø4/88
The average age is: 55.25
```

Fig. 10.27.

The output from the program to control printing.

In the preceding code, the EJECT command is used to dislodge the last line from the printer buffer and to advance to the top of the next page. When you use @...SAYs to print, the last line sent to the printer stays in a buffer until the next line is sent. You should always conclude print jobs with the EJECT command. If you do not want to advance the paper to the next page, end by printing a single word space so that the last line prints.

Tip:
When you use @...SAYs to print, include the EJECT command to advance the paper to the next page.

Comparing the ? and @...SAY Commands

Most of the time you can use either the ? or the @...SAY command to provide both screen and printed output. The ? and ?? commands require that you SET CONSOLE OFF, unless you want the output echoed to the screen. On the other hand, @...SAYs require you to convert all the values you want to print with one command into the same data type.

The answer to the question of which form of output command to use is really a matter of what you are comfortable with. In most complex applications, the use of the two commands is fairly evenly split.

Using PRINTJOB To Set System Variables

With the PRINTJOB...ENDPRINTJOB command, you can take advantage of the printing system variables. You can use the PRINTJOB...ENDPRINTJOB command only in a program; you cannot use this command in interactive mode.

Tip:

Use system variables to control print jobs.

You can use a number of system variables (for example, _plineno, _peject, and so on) to help automate printing chores. Each of these variables begins with the underscore (_) symbol to mark the variables as ones that are initialized by dBASE IV.

Before you begin printing, issue the PRINTJOB command to initialize the system variables for the job. You then can use the variables as needed to help format your output. These variables add a great deal of power to the ?/?? command. Table 10.2 lists the system variables and provides a brief description of what they control.

Table 10.2
System Variables

Variable	Use
_alignment	Controls left, right, center justification
_box	Determines if boxes print
_indent	Controls paragraph indentation when printing long fields
_lmargin	Specifies left margin
_padvance	Advances paper using line feeds instead of form feeds
_pageno	Stores current page number

Variable	Use
_pbpage	Stores beginning page number
_pcolno	Stores current column number
_pcopies	Specifies number of copies to print
_pdriver	Specifies current printer driver
_pecode	Specifies code to be sent to printer at the end of a print job
_peject	Specifies page eject to occur before or after the print job or both
_pepage	Stores ending page number
_pform	Stores current printer form file
_plength	Stores length of page
_plineno	Stores current line number of current page
_ploffset	Stores current page offset
_ppitch	Stores current printer-pitch setting
_pquality	Stores current print-quality setting
_pscode	Specifies code to be sent to printer at the start of a print job
_pspacing	Stores current line-spacing setting
_pwait	Stores current wait for paper-change setting
_pwidth	Stores current line-width setting
_rmargin	Stores current right margin
_tabs	Specifies one or more tabs to be set
_wrap	Stores current word-wrap setting

Figure 10.28 shows a simple example of a PRINTJOB.

```
***** Program: PRINTIT.PRG *****

SET TALK OFF
USE LIST
_peject = 'AFTER'      && Set for eject after the job
SET PRINT ON           && Direct output to the printer

PRINTJOB               && Begin the print job
   ?"LISTING OF BALANCES DUE       ","PAGE: ",STR( _pageno,2,Ø)
   ?
   ?"NAME" AT Ø,"BALANCE" AT 32, "LAST PAYMENT" AT 42
   ?
   ?
   DO WHILE .NOT. EOF()
      ?TRIM(first)+' '+last AT Ø,BALANCE AT 32, LASTPAYDAT AT 42
      ?
      SKIP
   ENDDO
ENDPRINTJOB
CLOSE DATABASES
SET PRINT OFF
RETURN
```

The program in figure 10.28 produces the output shown in figure 10.29.

```
LISTING OF BALANCES DUE       PAGE:   1

NAME                          BALANCE   LAST PAYMENT

Bill Jackson                   5Ø.99    12/15/88

John Waters                    23.32    Ø3/Ø3/89

Jane Fowler                    43.43    Ø2/Ø3/89

Paco Rodriguez                 34.23    Ø1/Ø4/89

Martha Gross                  642.45    12/12/88

Sheldon Musgart                23.33    Ø2/Ø2/89
```

Chapter Summary

In this chapter, the ACCEPT, WAIT, INPUT, and @...SAY...GET commands were introduced. You learned how to use these commands to receive user entries and store them into memory variables and fields. The ACCEPT command takes character strings; the INPUT command requires the user to specify the type of input; and the WAIT command pauses for just one keystroke from the user. You can use the @...SAY...GET command to control what you will and will not allow the user to enter. In addition, this chapter shows you how to use memory variable to add, edit, and delete records and explains how you can control screen display and output. In the next chapter, you learn about conditional branching and program loops.

11

Conditional Branching and Program Loops

U p to this point, the program examples in this book have been processed in logical sequence: processing started at the first instruction line and continued until the last command executed.

This chapter shows how to change the normal processing sequence by using conditional branching and program loops. Conditional branching is one of dBASE IV's most powerful tools. The dBASE IV commands (commonly called *constructs*) that you can use in conditional branching include the following:

```
IF...ENDIF
IF...ELSE...ENDIF
DO CASE...ENDCASE
DO CASE...OTHERWISE...ENDCASE
```

Program loops also are explained in this chapter. Instead of entering the same program lines to perform repetitive tasks in several places in a program, you can use a program loop to repeat the segment of the program efficiently. For example, you can use a loop to process each data record in a database file. The following dBASE IV commands are used in program loop operations:

```
DO WHILE...ENDDO
LOOP
EXIT
```

451

Conditional Branching

So far the programming examples in this book have been little more than dBASE IV batch files. The programs perform a series of commands in sequence, without variations. One of the fundamental differences between a batch file and a true computer program is the capability to evaluate the condition of data, make a comparison, and choose the appropriate actions to take based on the data's value.

The nineteenth century Englishman, Charles Babbage, put forth the theory that all problems could be solved if they were reduced to a series of yes or no questions taken in turn. His mechanical computer is today renowned and respected as a breakthrough in logic and human thought. Much of the power of today's computer is based partly on Babbage's early work, laying a foundation for binary problem solving.

dBASE IV has several groups of commands or constructs that allow you to provide a framework for conditional branching. *Conditional branching* is simply the capability of the program to decide which portions of the program code should be executed and which portions should not be executed based on an evaluation of some piece of data.

A typical example of conditional branching is computing wages in a payroll program. If the employee has put in more than 40 hours, you need to calculate overtime pay.

For example, in a normal work week, the following formula calculates the wages:

Regular pay = Hours × Wage Rate
Overtime = 0

But, for overtime, you need another formula:

Regular pay = 40 × Wage Rate
Overtime = (Hours–40) × Wage Rate × 1.5

The condition you need to evaluate is whether the number of hours totals more than 40. In a dBASE program, you can use constructs to test conditions.

Evaluating Conditions with IF...ENDIF

The IF...ENDIF command is the simplest of the dBASE IV program constructs. This command allows you to evaluate a condition (the value of data or environment) to determine whether a set of commands should be executed. You use the IF...ENDIF command whenever you want commands to be executed only when a condition is true. For example, if a 10 percent discount is in order for sales over $500, you could use the following construct to apply the discount to the appropriate sales:

```
IF TOTAL > 500
    DISC = 10
ENDIF
```

The first statement contains the word IF and defines the condition. If the condition is true, the program executes the segment between the IF and ENDIF statements. If the condition is false, the program skips the segment between the IF and ENDIF. Typically, an IF...ENDIF construct takes the following form:

```
IF <condition>
    <section executed when the condition is true>
ENDIF
```

For example, the following lines figure overtime pay:

```
IF HOURS>40
    REGULARPAY=40*RATE
    OVERTIME=(HOURS-40)*RATE*1.5
ENDIF
```

If the condition is true (IF HOURS > 40), the program executes the section between IF and ENDIF. If the condition is false, the section is skipped.

The condition in the IF clause can be any valid dBASE IV expression:

Numeric

```
IF balance >5000
    @10,10 SAY "Over limit"
ENDIF
```

Character

```
IF name = "Smith"
    @10,10 SAY "Customer Name is not Jones"
ENDIF
```

Logical

```
IF EOF()  && EOF() returns a value of .T. or .F.
    @10,10 SAY "End of File encountered"
ENDIF
```

Date

```
IF birthdate = DATE()
      @10,10 SAY "Today is your birthday"
ENDIF
```

You can create an IF...ENDIF construct that evaluates multiple conditions by including the .AND., .OR., and .NOT. comparators. When you join two conditions by the .AND. comparator, both conditions must be true for the IF clause to be evaluated as true. If you join the conditions by the .OR. comparator, either of the conditions can be true for the program to evaluate the IF clause as true.

You use the .NOT. comparator to reverse logical conditions. For example, the end-of-file function EOF() returns a logical true (.T.) or false (.F.) value. The expression IF .NOT. EOF() evaluates .T. if the expression EOF() is .F.

The following examples illustrate multiple comparisons:

```
IF f_name = "TOM" .AND. l_name = "Smith"
    @10,10 SAY "The name is Tom Smith"
ENDIF

IF balance > 500 .AND. .NOT. paid
    @10,10 SAY "You owe us money"
ENDIF

IF balance > 0 .AND. due_date >= DATE()
   @10,10 SAY "Your payment is past due"
ENDIF
```

In all the preceding examples, if the condition is true, the message is displayed on-screen. If the condition is false, the message is not displayed.

To illustrate conditional branching, look at the program created from the hourly wage example (see fig. 11.1). When you execute this program, you see the output shown in figure 11.2.

```
***** Program: PAYROLL.PRG *****
* A simplified payroll program.
SET TALK OFF
SET ECHO OFF
* Get hours and rate.
?
?
INPUT "     Enter Number of Hours Worked .... " TO HOURS
INPUT "               Hourly Wage Rate .... " TO RATE
* Start computing wage.
REGULARPAY=HOURS*RATE
OVERTIME=Ø
IF HOURS>4Ø
   REGULARPAY=4Ø*RATE
   OVERTIME=(HOURS-4Ø)*RATE*1.5
ENDIF
?
?
? "          Regular Pay ........ " +STR(REGULARPAY,7,2)
? "          Overtime Pay ........ " +STR(OVERTIME,7,2)
? "          Total Gross Pay ..... " +STR(REGULARPAY+OVERTIME,7,2)
?
?
RETURN
```

Fig. 11.1.

A program using IF...ENDIF.

The program calculates the wage by using the numbers entered in the variables HOURS and RATE. The value stored in HOURS determines whether overtime pay is calculated.

You also can use conditional branching to process data records. For example, look at a new database file, named WAGES.DBF. The structure of WAGES.DBF is shown in figure 11.3, and figure 11.4 displays the data records in WAGES.DBF.

Fig. 11.2.

*The output from
the program using
IF...ENDIF.*

```
. DO PAYROLL

          Enter Number of Hours Worked .... 38
                    Hourly Wage Rate .... 7.5Ø


          Regular Pay ........  285.ØØ
          Overtime Pay ........    Ø.ØØ
          Total Gross Pay .....  285.ØØ
```

Fig. 11.2.

*The output from
the program using
IF...ENDIF.*

Fig. 11.3.

*The structure of
WAGES.DBF.*

```
. USE WAGES
. DISPLAY STRUCTURE
Structure for database : B:WAGES.DBF
Number of data records :     16
Date of last update    : 12/Ø4/88
```

Field	Field name	.Type	Width	Dec	Index
1	FIRST _ NAME	Character	1Ø		N
2	LAST _ NAME	Character	8		Y
3	DEPT	Character	1		Y
4	HOURS	Numeric	2		N
5	RATE	Numeric	5	2	N
6	GROSS _ PAY	Numeric	6	2	N
7	DEDUCTIONS	Numeric	6	2	N
8	NET _ PAY	Numeric	6	2	N
** Total **			45		

Each data record contains the worker's name and wage information
(hours worked, wage, and so on). You can use a program similar to
PAYROLL.PRG to calculate the wage. You can modify PAYROLL.PRG so
that it locates an employee's record according to the contents of a data
field (see fig. 11.5). Figure 11.6 shows the output of PAYROLL1.PRG.

Fig. 11.4.

The data records in WAGES.DBF.

```
. USE WAGES
. LIST
```

Record#	FIRST_NAME	LAST_NAME	DEPT	HOURS	RATE	GROSS_PAY	DEDUCTIONS	NET_PAY
1	Cindy T.	Baker	B	38	7.50	0.00	0.00	0.00
2	William B.	Davison	A	41	11.50	0.00	0.00	0.00
3	Floyd C.	Fuller	C	40	7.50	0.00	0.00	0.00
4	Bob R.	Hill	A	42	7.75	0.00	0.00	0.00
5	Mike D.	James	B	38	6.50	0.00	0.00	0.00
6	David F.	Larson	C	38	11.00	0.00	0.00	0.00
7	Alice G.	Miller	A	45	8.50	0.00	0.00	0.00
8	Peter A.	Morrison	A	48	8.25	0.00	0.00	0.00
9	Ellen F.	Norton	B	58	7.50	0.00	0.00	0.00
10	Charlic H.	Olson	A	36	9.25	0.00	0.00	0.00
11	Tony W.	Palmer	A	37	7.25	0.00	0.00	0.00
12	Grace S.	Porter	B	40	12.25	0.00	0.00	0.00
13	Howard G.	Rosen	C	36	8.00	0.00	0.00	0.00
14	George D.	Stan	A	39	10.95	0.00	0.00	0.00
15	Tamie K.	Tower	C	36	9.50	0.00	0.00	0.00
16	Albert L.	Williams	B	43	8.50	0.00	0.00	0.00

Although the program has calculated the wages correctly, the logic of the conditional branching is inefficient. Regular pay and overtime pay are computed twice when the number of hours is greater than 40. For example, when the condition HOURS > 40 is true, the regular pay is first computed with the following command:

```
REGULARPAY = HOURS*RATE
```

Then the result of the following command replaces the preceding total:

```
REGULARPAY = 40*RATE
```

To avoid repetition and increase execution speed, you can revise the logic:

If hours worked is less than or equal to 40,

> Regular Pay = Hours × Wage Rate
> Overtime Pay = 0

Fig. 11.5.

A program to process WAGES.DBF.

```
***** Program: PAYROLL1.PRG *****
* A payroll program for processing the WAGES.DBF.
SET TALK OFF
SET ECHO OFF
* Get worker's name.
?
ACCEPT "     Enter Worker's First Name .... " TO FIRSTNAME
ACCEPT "                    Last Name ..... " TO LASTNAME
USE WAGES
LOCATE FOR LAST_NAME=LASTNAME.AND.FIRST_NAME=FIRSTNAME
* Start computing wage.
REGULARPAY=HOURS*RATE
OVERTIME=Ø
IF HOURS>4Ø
   REGULARPAY=4Ø*RATE
   OVERTIME=(HOURS-4Ø)*RATE*1.5
ENDIF
?
? "     Worker's name : " +TRIM(FIRST_NAME) +"   " +TRIM(LAST_NAME)
?
? "          REGULAR PAY ........ " +STR(REGULARPAY,7,2)
? "          OVERTIME PAY ....... " +STR(OVERTIME,7,2)
? "          TOTAL GROSS PAY ..... " +STR(REGULARPAY+OVERTIME,7,2)
?
RETURN
```

Fig. 11.6.

The output of PAYROLL1.PRG.

```
. DO PAYROLL1
        Enter Worker's First Name .... Cindy
                    Last Name ..... Baker

     Worker's Name : Cindy T. Baker

             Regular Pay ........  285.ØØ
             Overtime Pay ........    Ø.ØØ
             Total Gross Pay ....  285.ØØ
```

If hours worked is more than 40,

> Regular Pay = 40 × Wage Rate
> Overtime Pay = (Hours−40) × (Wage Rate × 1.5)

In this way, the program performs only one calculation, depending on the condition of the data. By introducing the phrase ELSE in the IF...ENDIF command, you can convert the new logic in a program.

Conditional Execution with IF...ELSE...ENDIF

The ELSE phrase in the IF...ENDIF command adds a second section of program code that directs the computer to execute one section of code if the condition is evaluated as true and the other section if the condition is false. When the condition in the IF clause is false, the program executes the segment enclosed between the ELSE and ENDIF commands:

```
IF <condition>
     <section executed when the condition is true>
ELSE
     <section executed when the condition is false>
ENDIF
```

For example, the following lines illustrate using ELSE to calculate wages:

```
IF HOURS <= 40
   REGULARPAY=HOURS*RATE
   OVERTIME=0
ELSE
   REGULARPAY=40*RATE
   OVERTIME=(HOURS-40)*RATE*1.5
ENDIF
```

You can use these program lines in PAYROLL2.PRG (see fig. 11.7) to accomplish the task performed by PAYROLL1.PRG. The programs are identical, but PAYROLL2.PRG requires fewer steps than PAYROLL1.PRG.

In the PAYROLL2.PRG program, the wage is processed in two different ways: one way when HOURS <=40 and another way when HOURS>40.

In the program in figure 11.7, the program code inside the IF evaluation is indented. Although you don't have to indent your IF commands,

Fig. 11.7.

A program using
IF...ELSE...
ENDIF.

```
***** Program: PAYROLL2.PRG *****
* Another payroll program for processing the WAGES.DBF.
SET TALK OFF
SET ECHO OFF
* Get worker's name.
?
ACCEPT "    Enter Worker's First name .... " TO FIRSTNAME
ACCEPT "                    Last name ..... " TO LASTNAME
USE WAGES
LOCATE FOR LAST_NAME=LASTNAME.AND.FIRST_NAME=FIRSTNAME
* Start computing wage.
IF HOURS <=40
  REGULARPAY=HOURS*RATE
  OVERTIME=0
ELSE
   REGULARPAY=40*RATE
   OVERTIME=(HOURS-40)*RATE*1.5
ENDIF
?
? "    Worker's Name : " +TRIM(FIRST_NAME) +" " +TRIM(LAST_NAME)
?
? "          Regular Pay ........ " +STR(REGULARPAY,7,2)
? "          Overtime Pay ........ " +STR(OVERTIME,7,2)
? "          Total Gross Pay ..... " +STR(REGULARPAY+OVERTIME,7,2)
?
RETURN
```

▶

Tip:
You must follow
an IF *command*
with an ENDIF.

indenting makes the logic of your program easier to read and follow. If your code is indented and you need to change an IF command, you can more easily go back and see the logic of the program.

When you issue an IF command, you must follow it with an ENDIF. The ENDIF ends the construct.

Using Nested IF...ELSE...ENDIF Commands

Occasionally, you must make comparisons within another comparison. For example, you might have to make a second comparison only if

a first comparison is true (.T.). To do this, you can nest one
IF...ELSE...ENDIF inside another. This process can be compared to the
children's toy in which a series of progressively smaller plastic barrels fit
inside each other. Look at the following constructs:

```
IF name="Smith"
    IF sex="Male"
        @10,10 SAY "Boy Smith"
    ELSE
        @10,10 SAY "Girl Smith"
    ENDIF
ELSE
    @10,10 SAY "Child's name is not Smith"
ENDIF
```

The preceding example first tests the condition to see if the name
variable is equal to the character string "Smith". If the name is not equal
to "Smith", the program displays a message that states that the child's
name is not Smith. If this comparison is true, the program makes a
subcomparison to determine if the child named Smith is a boy or a girl. If
the child is a boy (the statement is true), the program displays Boy
Smith. If the child is a girl (the statement is false), the program displays
Girl Smith.

In the PAYROLL2.PRG program, the wage is processed in two different
ways: one way when HOURS <=40 and another way when HOURS>40. Many
times, however, you need to handle more than two conditions. For
example, to calculate personal income taxes, you need a formula for each
income bracket. Because you need a set of discount factors for different
quantity levels, calculating quantity discount is another example of
multiple conditions. To manage these applications, you can use nested
IF...ENDIF commands to check data ranges. To nest IF...ENDIF
commands, enclose one IF...ENDIF program segment within another, as
in the following example:

```
IF <condition>
   . . .
   . . .
    IF <condition>
       . . .
       . . .
        IF <condition>
```

```
          . . .
          . . .
        ENDIF
          . . .
          . . .
      ENDIF
       . . .
       . . .
    ENDIF
```

You can write the program segment for calculating the amount of withholding tax (which is stored in the variable WITHHOLD) with nested IF...ENDIF commands as follows (the variable GROSSWAGE contains the weekly gross pay):

```
IF GROSSWAGE >27
   WITHHOLD=.12*(GROSSWAGE-27)
      IF GROSSWAGE > 79
         WITHHOLD=6.24 +.15*(GROSSWAGE-79)
            IF GROSSWAGE > 183
               WITHHOLD=21.84 +.19*(GROSSWAGE-183)
                  IF GROSSWAGE > 277
                     WITHHOLD=39.7 +.25*(GROSSWAGE-277)
                  ENDIF
            ENDIF
      ENDIF
ENDIF
```

Each evaluation is listed in ascending order. If the GROSSWAGE is 307, all the evaluations will be true. Because of the way the evaluations are stated, the result will be accurate.

Figure 11.8 shows a program that uses nested IF...ENDIF commands to calculate the weekly withholding tax for workers with records in WAGES.DBF. When you execute NESTEDIF.PRG, you see the output shown in figure 11.9.

If the gross wage is greater than 277, the amount of withholding tax (WITHHOLD) is calculated and replaced repeatedly. Because the two-branch IF...ENDIF command is inefficient for this type of problem, you may want to use the multiple-branch DO CASE...ENDCASE command.

```
***** Program: NESTEDIF.PRG *****
* Computing withholding using nested IF commands.
SET TALK OFF
SET ECHO OFF
* Get worker's name.
?
ACCEPT "    Enter Worker's First Name .... " TO FIRSTNAME
ACCEPT "                    Last Name ..... " TO LASTNAME
USE WAGES
LOCATE FOR LAST_NAME=LASTNAME.AND.FIRST_NAME=FIRSTNAME
* Start computing wage.
IF HOURS <=40
  REGULARPAY=HOURS*RATE
  OVERTIME=0
ELSE
   REGULARPAY=40*RATE
   OVERTIME=(HOURS-40)*RATE*1.5
ENDIF
GROSSWAGE=REGULARPAY+OVERTIME
* Determine withholding taxes.
WITHHOLD=0
IF GROSSWAGE >27
  WITHHOLD=.12*(GROSSWAGE-27)
     IF GROSSWAGE > 79
        WITHHOLD=6.24+.15*(GROSSWAGE)
           IF GROSSWAGE > 183
              WITHHOLD=21.84+.19*(GROSSWAGE-183)
                 IF GROSSWAGE > 277
                    WITHHOLD=39.7+.25*(GROSSWAGE-277)
                 ENDIF
              ENDIF
           ENDIF
     ENDIF
ENDIF
NETWAGE=GROSSWAGE-WITHHOLD
?
? "    Worker's Name : " +TRIM(FIRST_NAME) +" " +TRIM(LAST_NAME)
?
? "          Regular Pay ........ " +STR(REGULARPAY,7,2)
? "          Overtime Pay ........ " +STR(OVERTIME,7,2)
? "          Total Gross Pay ..... " +STR(REGULARPAY+OVERTIME,7,2)
? "          Tax Withheld ........ " +STR(WITHHOLD,7,2)
? "          Net Pay ............. " +STR(NETWAGE,7,2)
RETURN
```

Fig. 11.8.

A program using nested IF...ENDIF *commands.*

Fig. 11.9.

*The output from
NESTEDIF.PRG.*

```
. DO NESTEDIF

        Enter Worker's First Name .... Albert
                        Last Name ..... Williams

Worker's Name : Albert L. Williams

        Regular Pay ......... 340.00
        Overtime Pay ........  38.25
        Total Gross Pay ..... 378.25
        Tax Withheld ........  65.01
        Net Pay ............. 313.24

.
```

Using Multiple Conditions with DO CASE...ENDCASE

You occasionally need nested IF...ENDIF constructs. But, in cases where more than two possible segments of program might be executed, the DO CASE...ENDCASE construct is valuable. The DO CASE...ENDCASE construct defines multiple conditions and multiple program sections. When one of the conditions is evaluated as true, the corresponding program section is executed.

You use a CASE clause to define each possible condition. Then you can use as many conditions as necessary to define the potential branchings of the program. The DO CASE and ENDCASE enclose all the CASE clauses used, as in the following example:

```
DO CASE
   CASE < condition 1>
      < program section for condition 1 being true>
   CASE <condition 2>
      < program section for condition 2 being true>
   CASE <condition 3>
      < program section for condition 3 being true>
   ...
   ...
ENDCASE
```

The program evaluates each of the CASE clauses between the DO CASE and ENDCASE statements in turn until one is evaluated as true. Then the program executes the section of program code between the CASE clause and the following CASE clause. Only one of the program code segments is executed even if more than one of the CASE statements is evaluated as true. Only the program segment following the first CASE statement evaluated as true is performed. Once that section of program code has been executed, the DO CASE...ENDCASE construct ends.

For example, look at the following sample CASE structure:

```
CLEAR
? "Enter A to Add new customers to the file."
? "Enter E to Edit the customers on file."
? "Enter D to Delete customers from the file."
WAIT "Choose here: " TO action

DO CASE
    CASE action = UPPER('A')
         DO addcust
    CASE action = UPPER('E')
         DO editcust
    CASE action = UPPER('D')
         DO delcust
ENDCASE
```

In this example, the user can press A to add new customers, E to edit customers on file, or D to delete customers from the file. Depending on what the user selects, the program calls the appropriate subroutine.

The program in figure 11.10 makes the same evaluations as the nested IFs in the preceding example, but is more efficient. Because only one of the CASE statements can be true, the wage is computed only once. As figure 11.11 illustrates, the output of the program is unchanged.

For every DO CASE there must be a matching and terminating ENDCASE. Also, notice that because the DO CASE construct evaluates lines of code and executes only some, the program lines are indented.

Tip:
For every DO CASE there must be a matching and terminating ENDCASE.

Fig. 11.10.

Replacing
IF...ENDIF *with*
CASE *conditions.*

```
***** Program: DOCASES.PRG *****
* Computing withholding using DOCASE commands.
SET TALK OFF
SET ECHO OFF
* Get worker's name.
?
ACCEPT "     Enter Worker's First Name .... " TO FIRSTNAME
ACCEPT "                    Last Name ..... " TO LASTNAME
USE WAGES
LOCATE FOR LAST_NAME=LASTNAME.AND.FIRST_NAME=FIRSTNAME
* Computing gross wage.
DO CASE
   CASE HOURS <=40
       REGULARPAY=HOURS*RATE
       OVERTIME=0
   CASE HOURS>40
       REGULARPAY=40*RATE
       OVERTIME=(HOURS-40)*RATE*1.5
ENDCASE
GROSSWAGE=REGULARPAY+OVERTIME
* Determine amount of tax withholding.
DO CASE
   CASE GROSSWAGE <27
       WITHHOLD=0
   CASE GROSSWAGE>=27 .AND. GROSSWAGE <79
       WITHHOLD=.12*(GROSSWAGE-27)
   CASE GROSSWAGE>=79 .AND. GROSSWAGE <183
       WITHHOLD=6.24+.15*(GROSSWAGE-79)
   CASE GROSSWAGE>=183 .AND. GROSSWAGE <277
       WITHHOLD=21.84+.19*(GROSSWAGE-183)
   CASE GROSSWAGE>=277
       WITHHOLD=39.7+.25*(GROSSWAGE-277)
ENDCASE
NETWAGE=GROSSWAGE-WITHHOLD
?
? "    Worker's Name : " +TRIM(FIRST_NAME) +" " +TRIM(LAST_NAME)
?
? "          Regular Pay ........ " +STR(REGULARPAY,7,2)
? "          Overtime Pay ........ " +STR(OVERTIME,7,2)
? "          Total Gross Pay ..... " +STR(REGULARPAY+OVERTIME,7,2)
? "          Tax Withheld ........ " +STR(WITHHOLD,7,2)
? "          Net Pay ............. " +STR(NETWAGE,7,2)
RETURN
```

```
. DO DOCASES

        Enter Worker's First Name .... Albert
                      Last Name ..... Williams

Worker's Name : Albert L. Williams

        Regular Pay ........ 340.00
        Overtime Pay ........  38.25
        Total Gross Pay .....  378.25
        Tax Withheld ........   65.01
        Net Pay ............  313.24
```

Fig. 11.11.

*The results of
DOCASES.PRG.*

Specifying Multiple Conditions with DO CASE...OTHERWISE...ENDCASE

The DO CASE construct has an additional tool to use when none of the CASE statements are true. The OTHERWISE clause can be used to provide a branch that will be executed when none of the CASE statements is true. OTHERWISE can be used to trap error conditions; for example,

```
DO CASE
    CASE <condition 1>
        <program section for condition 1 being true>
    CASE <condition 2>
        <program section for condition 2 being true>
    CASE <condition 3>
        <program section for condition 3 being true>
    OTHERWISE
        <program section for no condition being true>
ENDCASE
```

The OTHERWISE clause in the DO CASE...ENDCASE construct is similar to the ELSE statement in the IF...ELSE...ENDIF construct. If none of the statements is evaluated as true, the program executes the code between the OTHERWISE and the ENDCASE.

Using Program Loops

Although the conditional branching commands or constructs are powerful tools for data manipulation, they can process only one record at a time. The examples presented so far in this chapter have a limited scope in that they act only on whatever record or variable is current at the time you run the program.

Often, you must manipulate all the records in a file or a sequence of records within the file rather than a single record. You can accomplish this task by establishing a program loop. A loop does exactly what it sounds like it does. A loop begins data manipulation, circles back up, and begins processing those commands again. You can control how a program loop operates within your own program.

Beginning Program Loops with DO WHILE...ENDDO

The DO WHILE statement in a program signals the beginning of a program loop. You use program loops to repeat sections of program code for as long as necessary to accomplish a particular task. For example, a loop can be used to process all of the records in a file without having to know how many records are in the file.

For example, if you want to update all the records in a file, you can build a program loop that starts with the first record, performs whatever data manipulation is necessary, SKIPs to the next record, and repeats the loop. This skip/repeat action continues as long as or until the condition is false. A typical DO WHILE construct might look like the following:

```
DO WHILE .NOT. EOF()
    ... <the program section to be repeated>
ENDDO
```

The condition following DO WHILE determines whether the program section in the loop is executed. If the condition is true, the program section is executed; otherwise, the program section is skipped, and execution begins again at the program line following the ENDDO statement.

When the program reaches the ENDDO, the program automatically returns to the command line that follows the DO WHILE statement and begins processing again. The processing continues as long as the condition is true.

The DO WHILE condition statement is similar to the condition portion of the IF statement. For example, consider the following commands:

```
DO WHILE balance > 5ØØ
DO WHILE AREA _ CODE="216"
DO WHILE AREA _ CODE="216".OR.AREA _ CODE="5Ø3"
DO WHILE UNITS _ SOLD <=3 .AND. price = "low"
DO WHILE .NOT. EOF()
```

In the first example, the program will continue to loop as long as the balance is greater than 500. In the second, the program loops as long as the area code is 216; in the third, the program loops as long as the area code is 216 or 503. If the units sold is less than or equal to 3 and the price is low, the fourth example continues to loop. And in the last example, the program continues as long as it does not reach the end of the file.

The program in figure 11.12 uses DO WHILE to loop; this program prints the name and address of every customer in the file.

```
*****PROGRAM: PRINTALL.PRG *****
*This program processes each record in the file.
USE cust
SET TALK OFF
SET PRINTER ON
? "Listing of all companies in the file. As of: " + DTOC(DATE())
DO WHILE .NOT. EOF()
    ? "Company: " + co _ name
    ? "Address: " + co _ addr
    ? "          " + TRIM(co _cit) + ", " + co _st + " " + co _zip
    ?
    ?
    SKIP
ENDDO
SET PRINTER OFF
CLOSE DATABASES
RETURN
```

Fig. 11.12.

An infinite loop program.

Creating a Program Loop Counter

You can design program loops so that they process themselves a specific number of times. You use a counter variable to record the number of passes through the loop that the program makes. When the specified number is reached, the loop ends. Figure 11.13 shows a DO WHILE loop that is controlled by evaluating a variable.

Fig. 11.13.

A program using a counter to control loops.

```
*****PROGRAM: KOUNT.PRG *****

* This program repeats five times
KOUNT = 1
DO WHILE KOUNT  < 6
    ? "PASS #: " + LTRIM(STR(kount,1,Ø)
    WAIT "PRESS ANY KEY TO GO THROUGH THE LOOP AGAIN"
    KOUNT = KOUNT  + 1
ENDDO
```

Each time the commands within the program loop are processed, the value of the counter variable is increased by one (see fig. 11.13). As long as the value of count is less than six, the program loop is repeated. When the value exceeds five, the condition in DO WHILE is no longer true, and the loop ends. The command line following the ENDDO is processed.

In the preceding program, each of the following three commands affect the number of passes made through the loop:

```
KOUNT=1
DO WHILE KOUNT  <= 5
KOUNT=KOUNT +1
```

To alter the number of passes through the program loop, you can change one or more of these commands. In fact, your program can assign a value to count even as the program is running. This way you can control dynamically the number of loop repetitions.

Using EOF( ) To Control Loop Execution

Using the value of the EOF( ) function is one useful way to make sure that a loop is repeated once for every record in a data file. Consider the following example structure:

```
USE datafile          && The record pointer is on the first
                      && record in the file.
DO WHILE .NOT. EOF()
    ...
    ... <the program section to be repeated>
    ...
ENDDO
```

The EOF( ) function returns a value of .F. as long as the record pointer is not positioned at the end of the data file. Once the record pointer is moved past the last valid record, EOF( ) becomes .T., and the program ends.

Remember that you use the comparator .NOT. to invert a logical value. If the EOF( ) = .F., then .NOT. EOF( ) = .T., which is illegal in dBASE. By using this logic, you can create a program loop in which the condition stated in the DO WHILE statement is evaluated as .T. as long as the record pointer is not positioned at the EOF( ). Figure 11.14 illustrates this concept.

Using Conditionals inside a Loop

You can control the action of a program and include or eliminate records from the process based on a comparison. Certain conditions would call for a record not to be processed, and other conditions would signal the need to end the loop entirely. Consider the following example:

```
?
?" Employee name      Telephone number"
?

DO WHILE .NOT. EOF()
      && The program loop repeats until the record pointer
      && reaches the end of file.
```

```
              IF fulltime     && The conditions set forth in the IF
                              && statement are evaluated as .T. only
                              && if the value of the logical field
                              && fulltime is = to .T.
                   ? Last name, first name, phone
              ENDIF
              SKIP            && Move record pointer to next record
         ENDDO
         RETURN
```

In the preceding program, only those records with .T. in the fulltime
field are displayed on-screen. Regardless of whether the IF section of
code is executed, the next command (SKIP) positions the record pointer
to the next record in the data file, and the loop is repeated.

Fig. 11.14.

A program using
EOF().

```
*****PROGRAM: EMPLIST.PRG *****
* Produce directory of employees and their phone numbers

SET TALK OFF
USE EMP  && Open the employee datafile
*The record pointer by default is positioned to the first
*record at the top of the file.
?
?" Employee name       telephone number"
?
* The program loop repeats until the record pointer reaches
* the end of the file.

DO WHILE .NOT. EOF()
    ? last_name, first_name, phone
    SKIP       && Position the record pointer to the next record
               && in the file.
ENDDO
RETURN
```

Setting an Infinite Loop
with DO WHILE .T.

One of the most useful variations of the DO WHILE command is the DO
WHILE .T. command. DO WHILE .T. sets up an infinite program loop. The

condition evaluated in the DO WHILE statement will always be true; therefore, the loop theoretically will continue executing forever:

```
DO WHILE .T.
    . . .
    . . .
ENDDO
```

Because the condition is always true, the loop will repeat indefinitely unless you include a way to terminate the process. For example, the phrases in the following code are displayed on-screen over and over again.

```
DO WHILE .T.
        ?"An infinite loop"
        ?"Will repeat and repeat"
        ?"OVER and OVER."
ENDDO
RETURN
```

The only way out of an infinite loop program, short of rebooting, is to press the Esc key. (Depending on the status of SET ESCAPE, you can use the Esc key to terminate a program.) Pressing Esc cancels the operation of this program.

The RETURN statement in the preceding code will never be executed because the loop will never voluntarily break. A conditional branching operation that falls into an infinite loop such as the preceding one is generally considered a bug caused by the programmer.

You can use one of several different methods for terminating a DO WHILE...ENDDO construct. As one method, you can use an external condition such as using EOF() to close the loop. Another method is to set up a variable that acts as a counter, which is either incremented or decremented each time the loop is processed. The third method for terminating a loop is to use an IF statement to evaluate a condition.

Controlling Loops with LOOP and EXIT

To make the DO WHILE .T. useful, you can add two commands, LOOP and EXIT, to provide maximum control over the execution of a loop.

Whenever the program encounters the LOOP command within a DO
WHILE. . .ENDDO construct, the program ignores the code between LOOP
and ENDDO. The next program line that is executed is the program line
following the DO WHILE statement. Generally, you use this command to
eliminate a portion of the loop's processing.

You can use the EXIT command as a method for terminating the loop
based on the evaluation of a condition. If the EXIT command is executed,
program flow falls to the first command line following the ENDDO
statement. The sample program in figure 11.15 uses both the LOOP and
EXIT commands to regulate the actions performed within the loop.

Fig. 11.15.

*Using EXIT to end
a program loop.*

```
USE EMP
DO WHILE .T.   && This command opens an infinite command loop that
                && can be terminated only by the EXIT command.
    IF EOF
        EXIT
    ENDIF
    IF .NOT. Fulltime
        SKIP
        LOOP
    ENDIF
    ? Last name, first name, department
ENDDO
CLOSE DATABASES
RETURN
```

In the program in figure 11.15, an infinite loop is opened up.
Immediately, the record pointer is tested for its EOF() condition. If the
program reaches the end of file, control of the program is passed to the
command following the ENDDO, in this case CLOSE DATABASES. Otherwise,
the fulltime field is tested for its value. If fulltime is not .T., the record
pointer is positioned to the next record, and the LOOP is repeated. If
fulltime is .T., the LOOP command is ignored, and the information is
displayed on the next line.

When the program flow reaches the ENDDO, the record pointer is moved
to the next record, and the LOOP is repeated automatically. If, after

moving the record pointer, the value of EOF becomes .T., the program executes the EXIT command and passes control to the command line following the ENDDO.

Creating Nested Loops

Although you can nest loops one inside the other, just as you can nest IF...ENDIF constructs, don't attempt this operation if you are a new programmer. Generally, if a procedure inside of a loop requires another loop (when printing the items on an invoice, for example), call the second loop as a subroutine. This method of programming makes debugging your program easier.

Chapter Summary

This chapter has introduced two of the most powerful programming features of dBASE IV: conditional branching and program loops. With conditional branching, you can change the normal processing path according to specified conditions. Conditional branching operations use the IF...ENDIF and DO CASE...ENDCASE procedures. With the ELSE and OTHERWISE options, you can meet any data condition and direct the program the way you choose. Program loops repeat a portion of a program until the program encounters an EXIT condition. By setting up a counter variable within a program loop, you can control the number of passes the program makes. Or you can use the EOF() function to exit a program loop. The next chapter explains the important role that conditional branching and program loops play in modular programming and menu design.

Part III

Advanced dBASE IV Programming

Includes

Modular Programming

An Integrated Database System

dBASE IV SQL

12

Modular Programming

Y ou use the technique of *modular programming* to create an application by using small program modules as the building blocks. This approach to programming has several advantages.

Because the modules are small, they are easier to create and maintain. Long program files that perform a multitude of tasks can frustrate the programmer. Problem areas are harder to pinpoint. If each module performs one major task, you can more easily keep track of the elements of your program. You also can find and correct programming errors quickly with this system.

After testing the modules, you can link them to form a complete system. When a new application arises, you can reorganize the appropriate program modules to create another database management system. Remember that all database management programs consist of three distinct functions:

❑ Accept user input and/or store data to disk.

❑ Manipulate or compute data on the basis of its relationship to other data. (For example, you can multiply the tax rate by the subtotal of an invoice to derive the amount of tax owed.)

❑ Create the output of the results.

No matter what the application is used for, these three elements are present. How you arrange them into program modules will determine the success or failure of your program.

Five main points make up a successful modular program design. First, the data files that hold the information must be well thought out so that you can control the record pointer in each of several open files. Second, you should break the functions of the application into small, manageable routines that each do one job. Third, you should be able to move data and variables from one module to the other easily to increase speed and efficiency. Ways to meet these three requirements are discussed in this chapter.

The fourth element of modular programming deals with the methods you use to process information. This is the area of program writing where you can best express creativity. Often you can use one of several ways to compute the same result. How you choose to manipulate data is determined by the data structures you create and by how imaginative you are at finding the simplest, most efficient way of computing the result you need.

Because modular programming breaks the application into small pieces to perform data management tasks, you need to learn different ways to pass information between modules. You use memory variables and the dBASE IV commands that are used to control memory variables. You also use the PUBLIC and PRIVATE commands along with the PARAMETERS command to pass data and variables within your applications modules. In addition, you need to handle several open database files at the same time; you can do this with the SELECT command. And you need to manipulate data with the UPDATE and APPEND FROM commands. All these commands are covered in this chapter.

The fifth element of modular programming is tying all the modules into a cohesive menu structure. This structure should make it easy for you to perform the task needed to get the proper results from the application. A sample menu is presented in this chapter.

Designing Program Modules

Using dBASE IV is not difficult. The small program examples presented in previous chapters can form the basis of a more sophisticated database management system. A real database management program may be large and complicated, and you will soon see the advantages in structuring the system in simple program modules.

You easily can create and maintain a small program module. After you design each module, you can test it for errors in syntax and logic before linking the modules to form a complete application.

You use three different building blocks in modular programming: program files (.PRG), procedures, and functions.

The PROCEDURE and FUNCTION commands are at the heart of multilevel modular program designs. Both of these commands signal the beginning of a section of program code that is called as the main program executes. Procedures are usually thought of as subroutines. You can think of user-defined functions (UDFs, for short) as any of the native dBASE IV functions. However, because you can design UDFs to execute commands, a UDF could be used as a subroutine as well. Remember, you cannot place a UDF (or any native dBASE IV function) on a line by itself to be used as a command.

dBASE IV programs are compiled from their .PRG form into a compiled .DBO file before you run them. There is no real difference between a program, a procedure, or a function (user-defined or dBASE native functions). All three are simply pieces of program code that fit together to create the whole application. Programs, procedures, and functions are differentiated by the way you use them and the syntax you use to call them.

Programs and procedures are so closely related that you use the same command to start both. You invoke each in programs with the DO command. But you cannot use the DO command at the dot prompt to execute the code in a procedure. You can call on the procedures and functions only while a program is running.

From the dot prompt, you can execute only .DBO files. A .DBO file, however, can be made up of many procedures and functions that can be called from any other procedure or function in the program. In fact, when a program is compiled, all the programs that it calls are compiled into procedures. Once an application is running, any procedure or function can call into service any other procedure or function at any time (provided it is in a file that is available to the compiler at compile time).

Using Procedures

A *procedure* is a section of code you can call to perform some task. Because dBASE IV programs are compiled into .DBO files, any procedure can be called by any other procedure, user-defined function, or program.

The following commands illustrate a sample procedure:

```
PROCEDURE ADDCUST

USE CUST
CLEAR                        && Clear the screen.
SET FORMAT TO custscreen     && Make a format file active.
APPEND                       && Display format and take entry.
SET FORMAT TO                && Deactivate format without
                             && activating any other.
USE                          && Close data file.
CLEAR
RETURN          && Terminate and go back up one level toward
                && the "first called" program/procedure.
```

Tip:

To include a procedure in your program, place it at the bottom of the file or between two other procedures.

You can use this procedure to add customers to the file. This procedure can be called by any other program/procedure that is part of the application.

You do not have to place a procedure in a separate .PRG file. To include a procedure in your program, place it at the bottom of the file or between two other procedures. Don't place the procedure in the middle of another section of code. When the dBASE IV compiler encounters the PROCEDURE command, it compiles everything from that point up to the next occurrence of the RETURN command.

Creating User-Defined Functions

User-defined functions are like native dBASE IV functions with two exceptions. First, you create user-defined functions yourself. Second, you can make the functions perform tasks that native dBASE functions cannot perform, such as display messages on-screen, move record pointers, and so on. The main purpose of a user-defined function is to accept data and send it the program to be evaluated and then returned in usable form. For example, dBASE IV includes DTOC(DATE()), a native function.

When you invoke the DATE( ) function, dBASE looks at the system clock and returns the correct date as an expression in the same format as a date field in a .DBF file. You use the DTOC( ) function to turn that expression into a character string.

You use the FUNCTION command to create your own functions; then you can use them anywhere in the program. Native dBASE functions can only return values, but UDFs are not limited to just this function. There are many commands you cannot use inside a UDF, but despite this limitation, you can use UDFs to position record pointers, provide default values to variables, and so on. UDFs are useful for validating entries into GETS as well as performing small utilities.

Tip:
Use functions to position record pointers, provide default values to variables, and validate entries into GETs.

Transforming Data

The most common type of UDF is one that transforms data. You feed the function data, and the function returns the data in another form. For example, the following UDF translates Celsius degrees into Fahrenheit:

```
FUNCTION CTOF   && Everything from this command until a
                && RETURN command is defined as a function
                && called CTOF().

PARAMETERS cel_no    && Accept the number to transform.
PRIVATE ret_val      && Create a variable to hold the
                     && return value.
ret_val = (9/5)cel_no  + 32    && Compute value.
RETURN ret_val                 && Pass value back and  end.
```

The variable is declared PRIVATE so that it does not interfere with a variable of the same name in another part of the program. This makes the function generic so that you can use it anywhere. For instance, you can use this function in a program just as you use any other function:

```
degrees = 10
? CTOF(degrees)    && The result is 50 degrees Fahrenheit.
```

You do not have to place a function in a separate .PRG file. To include a function in your program, place it at the bottom of the file or between two other procedures or functions. Don't place the function in the middle of another section of code. When the dBASE IV compiler encounters the FUNCTION command, it compiles everything from that point up to the next occurrence of the RETURN command.

It is useful to put UDFs that are used in other programs in a separate file. These UDFs need to be available to the compiler at compile time.

Displaying an Error Message

You can create user-defined functions to perform a variety of tasks. For example, the program in figure 12.1 displays an error message on-screen.

Fig. 12.1.

A program to display an error message.

```
***** Program: TRIAL.PRG  *****

* A test program with a UDF that displays an error message.
* This code is part of a larger program that SEEKs a record.
IF EOF()
   er_1 = "ERROR. No record in the data file"
   er_2 = "matches the search string you entered."
   er_3 = "PRESS ANY KEY to go back to the menu."
   var1 = USERDEF()
   RETURN
ENDIF

* Somewhere later in the program a function is defined.

FUNCTION USERDEF

CLEAR
@8,12 TO 17, 68 DOUBLE
@10,15 SAY er_1
@12,15 SAY er_2
@14,15 SAY er_3
WAIT ' '
CLEAR
CLOSE DATABASES
RETURN .T.        && A UDF must always return a value of some type.
```

If you reach the end of the file (the search is unsuccessful), the function USERDEF() uses the @...SAY command to display an error message. The error message is determined by the three variables (er_1, er_2, and er_3) in the program.

Two things stand out in the program shown in figure 12.1. First, the program uses the line var1 = USERDEF() to invoke the UDF. A user-defined function always must return a value, but you do not have to do anything with that returned value. In the example, the value of var1 is of no consequence. The variable will always be .T., and because the variable never changes, there's no point in using it as the basis for a comparison. For example, the command IF USERDEF() makes no sense. But by having the UDF return a value to the variable, you use the UDF as a command that displays the contents of three variables (the error message).

Second, the tasks that the UDF performs are not dependent on the data structure, open files, and so on. The successful operation depends only on the values in the three message variables. This function is universal: you can use this function in any application if the application assigns values to the three variables before calling the function.

Validating Data in @...SAY...GETs

You also can use functions to validate your input during a read. You create a user-defined function that evaluates the data entered by the user, and then returns a value that is either True or False (.T. or .F.). If the return value is True, the input is accepted. Otherwise, a message is displayed which states that the input is not acceptable, and the GET is not terminated. The user must type an acceptable entry to move the cursor out of the GET box.

You can include user-defined functions in the @...SAY...GET as part of the VALID clause. You use the VALID clause to determine whether the input for the GET is acceptable. If the GET is acceptable, you can end the GET; otherwise, the GET will not end if it still contains an invalid entry.

One of the best uses for a VALID clause in an @...SAY...GET command is to make sure that a particular record is found or to make sure that a record does not already exist. For example, before you add a new record to the customer database, you want to make sure that the account number is not already used. The sample program in figure 12.2 assumes that the file CUST is indexed by the ACTNO field and uses the SEEK command to see whether the account number already exists. If the number is already used, the program displays a message and lets the user try again. If the number is not used, the program calls another procedure to perform the task. The function named ISTHERE() does the actual looking.

Tip:
Include functions in the VALID clause of @...SAY...GET commands to determine whether the input is acceptable.

```
SET TALK OFF          && Turn off screen messages from dBASE IV.
SET ESCAPE OFF        && Do not allow the Esc key to quit to
                      && the dot prompt.
STORE SPACE(6) TO vcust  && Initialize a variable to hold the
                          && customer account number.
CLEAR                 && Erase the screen.

* The next command does four things:
* 1. Displays the prompt on-screen on row 7 col 12.
* 2. Takes entry into a GET box.
* 3. Checks the validity of the GET.
* 4. Sets the error message displayed if VALID is False.

@ 7,12 SAY "ENTER CUSTOMER ID NUMBER: " GET vcust VALID ISTHERE() ;
          ERROR 'That account number is already used.'
READ                  && Activates the GET

IF LASTKEY() = 27     && If the user presses Esc, the function
RETURN                && returns .T. This evaluation checks to see
ELSE                  && if the procedure needs to be terminated.
                      && If so, RETURN is executed; ELSE
   DO CUSTOMER        && the Customer program is executed.
ENDIF

* Somewhere else in the application, the following lines of
* code define the function ISTHERE().

FUNCTION ISTHERE

IF LASTKEY() = 27     && If the user presses Esc, let it
   RETURN .T.         && pass. The calling program decides
ENDIF                 && how to handle the key press.
USE cust              && Open the customer data and .MDX files.
SET ORDER TO acct     && Activate the proper index TAG.
SEEK vcust            && Take the entry and see if it matches
                      && any of the other index entries.
IF EOF()              && If the record pointer is at the end of
RETURN .T.            && the file, you can use the number
                      && for a new account number.
ELSE
   RETURN .F.         && If the pointer didn't get to the end of
ENDIF                 && the file, the number is already used
                      && in another record.
```

The program in figure 12.2 illustrates how you can use a user-defined function to validate data when you use the @...SAY...GET command for user input. Before the GET can terminate, the UDF must return a value of True.

The return value of a UDF used in a VALID clause must be logical. The value should return True (.T.) if the entry is acceptable, or False (.F.) if the entry is not acceptable. You control the value using the RETURN command. RETURN .T. causes the @...SAY...GET to terminate successfully.

Controlling Program Flow

Little distinction exists between programs and procedures in dBASE IV. When the compiler is activated, it begins compiling the main program file. As it compiles the main program file, the compiler also includes all the program files, procedures, and user-defined functions that can be called from within the application. If any of the programs or procedures call other programs or procedures, these programs or procedures are included automatically in the application.

Every dBASE IV application contains a main or MASTER program file—the program you execute with DO at the dot prompt. Most of the time this MASTER program contains a menu which you can use to choose the tasks that need to be performed. When you choose a task, the program calls the proper procedure.

With modular programming, you easily can reorganize the program modules whenever necessary. Reorganizing a modular system involves modifying only some of the program modules and is often a simple task.

Figure 12.3 shows a program with three modules. Each program module is an individual program file (.PRG), such as PROGA.PRG, PROGB.PRG, and PROGC.PRG.

Each module is a program file that ends with a RETURN command, which transfers execution back to the main program:

```
***** Program: PROGA.PRG *****
* A program module
  . . .
  . . .
  . . .
RETURN
```

When the user executes MAINPROG.PRG and the program encounters the command DO PROGA, execution transfers to the module PROGA. After the program processes PROGA.PRG, the RETURN command in the module returns program control to the main program. Execution then continues with the command line that follows DO PROGA in the main program.

```
***** Program: MAINPROG.PRG *****
* This is the main program.
. . .
. . .
* Go do module A.
   DO PROGA
   RETURN
   * Return from module A.
. . .
. . .
* Go do module B.
   DO PROGB
   RETURN
   * Return from module B.
. . .
. . .
* Go do module C.
   DO PROGC
   RETURN
   * Return from module C.
. . .
. . .
RETURN
```

To understand how execution passes from the main program to the program module, examine MAINPROG.PRG (see fig. 12.4). The program modules PROGA.PRG (see fig. 12.5) and PROGB.PRG (see fig. 12.6) are shown also.

```
***** Program: MAINPROG.PRG *****
* The main program
?"***   We are now in the Main Program."
* Go to PROGA.PRG.
  DO PROGA
  ?
  ?"We have returned from PROGA.PRG."
?
* Go to PROGB.PRG.
  DO PROGB
  ?
  ?"We have returned from PROGB.PRG."
RETURN
```

Fig. 12.4.

A main program module.

```
***** Program: PROGA.PRG *****
* Program Module A
SET TALK OFF
SET ECHO OFF
?
?"          We have entered PROGA.PRG."
* Return to main program.
RETURN
```

Fig. 12.5.

Program module A.

```
***** Program: PROGB.PRG *****
* Program Module B
?
?"          We have entered PROGB.PRG."
* Return to main program.
RETURN
```

Fig. 12.6.

Program module B.

The output of MAINPROG.PRG shows that execution passes from the main program to the modules and back again (see fig. 12.7). When the main program encounters the command DO PROGA, execution transfers to the module PROGA.PRG. At RETURN, the execution returns to the main program, starting with the line immediately following the DO PROGA command line.

Fig. 12.7.

The output of the modular program.

```
. DO MAINPROG
***  We are now in the Main Program.

             We have entered PROGA.PRG.

We have returned from PROGA.PRG.


             We have entered PROGB.PRG.

We have returned from PROGB.PRG.
```

The structures you have seen are two-level modular designs. In other words, execution changes from the first level (main program) to the second level (PROGA.PRG or PROGB.PRG) and then back to the main program. If necessary, you can increase the number of levels to accommodate more sophisticated database management applications. For example, the structure in figure 12.8 shows a three-level modular design.

When you run SAMPLE.PRG, the program displays a message and calls PROCESS1. This procedure displays a message and calls PROCESS2, which displays a message and returns to PROCESS1. The second message in PROCESS1 is displayed, and the program returns to SAMPLE.PRG. Three more messages from SAMPLE.PRG are then displayed. Program execution has moved through three levels of program modules.

In a multilevel modular design, the first called program (MASTER program) is the highest level. When execution transfers to a lower-level module, the execution starts at the first program line of the lower-level module. (Transferring execution to a lower-level module is sometimes termed *calling* the module.) When the program executes the RETURN command in the lower-level module, control returns to the higher-level module and resumes execution at the next line—the line that follows the one that called the module.

```
***** Program: SAMPLE.PRG *****

CLEAR
? "This message is brought to you by SAMPLE.PRG"
DO PROCESS1
? "This message is brought to you by SAMPLE.PRG again."
?
?
? "See how the messages show you the way control is passed."
WAIT "Press a key to return to the dot prompt with a clean slate."
CLEAR
RETURN

PROCEDURE PROCESS1
? "This message is brought to you by PROCESS1"
DO PROCESS2
? "This message is brought to you by PROCESS1 again."
RETURN

PROCESS2
? "This message is RIGHT IN THE MIDDLE"
?   " and is brought to you by PROCESS2."
RETURN
```

Fig. 12.8.

A three-level modular design.

Passing Memory Variables between Program Modules

You can easily pass program control by using DO and RETURN. Variables present a different situation. Variables that are created by a program module are released when the program terminates—unless they are declared PUBLIC. You can control variables using PUBLIC, PRIVATE, and PARAMETERS. You can declare variables PRIVATE in lower-level modules to keep the variables from overwriting data that may have been created in a higher-level module. You also can use the PARAMETERS command to send data to a lower-level module that uses different names for the variables.

Remember from the discussion in Chapter 10 that PRIVATE variables are released when the program module that creates them passes control back to a higher-level module. PUBLIC variables, on the other hand, are not released when the module terminates.

Variables are PRIVATE by default, unless you declare them PUBLIC. This section illustrates how the PRIVATE command can be used to protect variables initialized by higher-level modules from being changed. This enables you to write UDFs and subroutines that are universal (that is, they can be used in any future programs) even if they use variable names that are already in use in higher-level modules. The PARAMETERS command lets you pass values to these UDFs and subroutines without worrying about what the variable names are in the lower module.

With dBASE IV, you can pass only higher-level module data to lower-level modules. The programs in figures 12.9, 12.10, and 12.11 show how variable data elements are transferred among different program modules.

Fig. 12.9.

A main program using memory variables.

```
***** Program: MAIN.PRG *****
* The main program
SET TALK OFF
SET ECHO OFF
?
INPUT "Enter Value of A ... " TO A
INPUT "      Value of B ... " TO B
?
? "In Main Program:"
? "A=",A
? "B=",B
* Go to ADDAB.PRG.
DO SUMA&B
?
? "We have returned to MAIN.PRG from SUMA&B.PRG."
RETURN
```

```
***** Program: SUMA&B.PRG *****
* Program module to add A and B
?
?"          We have entered SUMA&B.PRG."
* Do not use the reserved word SUM for the variable name.
SUMAB=A +B
? "                    A = ",A
? "                    B = ",B
? "          SUM OF A, B = ",SUMAB
* Go to PRINTA&B.PRG
DO PRINTA&B
?
?"          We have returned to SUMA&B.PRG from PRINTA&B.PRG."
* Return to main program.
RETURN
```

```
***** Program: PRINTA&B.PRG *****
* Module to print results from SUMA&B.PRG
?
? "                              We have entered PRINTA&B.PRG."
? "                                        A = ",A
? "                                        B = ",B
? "                              SUM OF A, B = ",SUMAB
* Return to SUMA&B.PRG.
RETURN
```

When you execute the main program in figure 12.9, you see the output shown in figure 12.12.

Variables A and B are created in the main program and then passed to the second-level module SUMA&B.PRG. The program creates variable SUMAB in the second level and passes the variable to the third-level module PRINTA&B.PRG. Passing the variables occurs automatically, and the values in the variables are available to the lower-level modules.

Data elements created in lower-level modules, however, are not passed to higher-level modules. Instead, when the lower level procedure/module terminates, all the nonpublic memory variables and arrays created in that module are released from memory: they no longer exist. The program

```
. DO MAIN
Enter Value of A ...   123
       Value of B ...   456

In Main Program:
A=        123
B=        456

          We have entered SUMA&B.PRG.
                        A =         123
                        B =         456
              SUM OF A, B =         579

                        We have entered PRINTA&B.PRG.
                                A =         123
                                B =         456
                    SUM OF A, B =         579

          We have returned to SUMA&B.PRG from PRINTA&B.PRG.

We have returned to MAIN.PRG from SUMA&B.PRG.

.
```

Fig. 12.12.

The output of MAIN.PRG.

TEST.PRG illustrates this concept (see fig. 12.13). The output of TEST.PRG is shown in figure 12.14.

The variable var is initialized in PROC1. When the program executes RETURN, the variable ("yes") is released from memory. The variable can be used only while the procedure PROC1 is active. When TEST.PRG tries to use the variable, the error message shown in figure 12.14 is displayed on-screen.

Fig. 12.13.

The program module TEST.PRG.

```
***** Program: TEST.PRG *****
SET TALK OFF
SET ESCAPE OFF
DO PROC1
? var
RETURN

PROCEDURE PROC1

var = "yes"
RETURN
```

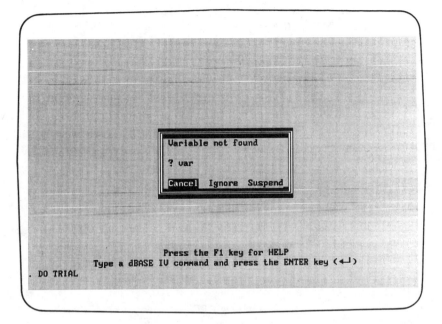

Fig. 12.14.

The output from TEST.PRG.

Initializing the Variable

To pass information back from lower-level modules, you must declare the variable PUBLIC, or you must initialize the variable before you pass control to the lower-level module.

The amended program in figure 12.15 does not cause an error because the code in PROC1 just changes a variable that already existed. Because var is created in a higher-level module, when PROC1 ends, the variable is not released from memory.

Declaring a Variable PUBLIC

You also can write the program as shown in figure 12.16 and avoid the error message. The variable is declared PUBLIC before the procedure terminates.

Tip:
To pass information back from lower-level modules, declare the variable PUBLIC.

Fig. 12.15.

*Amended
TEST.PRG.*

```
***** Program: TEST.PRG *****
SET TALK OFF
SET ESCAPE OFF
var = "Yard"
DO PROC1
? var                  && Even though PROC1 ends, var = "yes".
RETURN

PROCEDURE PROC1

var = "yes"
RETURN
```

Fig. 12.16.

*Making a variable
PUBLIC.*

```
***** Program: TEST.PRG *****
SET TALK OFF
SET ESCAPE OFF
DO PROC1
? var                  && Even though PROC1 ends, var = "yes".
RETURN

PROCEDURE PROC1

PUBLIC var
var = "yes"
RETURN
```

Using PARAMETERS

Command:

PARAMETERS
*Passes variables
from one module
to another.*

Using the PARAMETERS command is another way to pass variables from
one module to another. The PARAMETERS command is part of the toolbox
for designing modular programs.

When you pass variables as PARAMETERS, it does not matter whether they
are declared PUBLIC or PRIVATE, nor does it matter what the lower-level
module wants to call those variables. You can design procedures that are
universally applicable. You can include procedures in any future program
you write because you don't have to worry about matching variable
names.

As an example, take a short procedure that calculates the sales tax (at present, five percent). Instead of having a module for each time you need to calculate the tax, use a small module that calculates for all the other modules. When the rate changes, you have to change only one place in the program.

When you need the sales tax calculated, use the following command:

```
DO TAX_FIND WITH total,tax_amt
```

total and tax_amt are the names of two variables that must be initialized before they are passed to the lower-level module. In this case, one holds the amount on which to compute the tax, and the other holds the amount of the computed tax after TAX_FIND terminates.

Somewhere else in the application, include the following procedure:

```
PROCEDURE tax_find

PARAMETERS a,b
PRIVATE a,b
b = a * .05
RETURN
```

Even though the procedure uses the names a and b to manipulate the data, when the procedure terminates and control is passed to the calling program, the value of total will not have changed. tax_amt, however, will be equal to five percent of the total variable's value.

In the preceding example, you can see that the TAX_FIND procedure does not have to be rewritten whenever you want to compute sales tax. Because the procedure uses its own names to manipulate the data, you can include this procedure in any program where you want to calculate a sales tax.

User-defined functions that use the PARAMETERS command to accept data from the calling module are as universally applicable as procedures. In fact, you can rewrite the TAX_FIND procedure as a user-defined function. The program in figure 12.17 does exactly the same thing as the procedure TAX_FIND.

```
STORE 5Ø TO total
STORE Ø TO tax_amt    && Initialize variables.
? TAX_FIND(total)     && Give the function the amount to use
                      && in the computation.
RETURN                && Terminate the program after the function
                      && displays the value of the tax on-screen.

* Beginning of UDF
FUNCTION tax_find     && Name the function.

PARAMETERS a          && Accept data for the computation.
PRIVATE a,b           && Keep the function from changing data
                      && in higher-level modules unintentionally.
b = a * .Ø5           && Compute.
RETURN b              && Change the variable and end the function.
```

Building Your Own Library of Modules

It is sometimes a good idea to place procedures and functions into separate files. As you write programs, you will develop a few modules that you will want to use in every program you write. You can put these "core" modules into one file; then you can include this file as part of your application.

To do this, use the SET PROCEDURE command in your application's master program file. This command makes the compiler look on the disk for the program (.PRG) file you name in the command. The compiler then compiles each of the procedures and functions in that file and includes them in the application.

Figures 12.18 and 12.19 demonstrate how to use the SET PROCEDURE command.

In figure 12.19, several procedures and functions are placed together in a file so that they form a "library" of procedures. These procedures can be called on from any other module in an application. By announcing this file to the compiler with the SET PROCEDURE command, you include all the functions and procedures in the file in the application.

```
* Main Program file

SET TALK OFF
SET DECIMALS TO 3
SET ALTERNATE OFF
SET PROCEDURE TO toolbox   && This command has the compiler look
                           && for TOOLBOX.PRG and compile all
                           && the procedures and functions in
                           && the file into the application.
```

Fig. 12.18.

Using the SET PROCEDURE *command.*

```
***** Program: TOOLBOX.PRG *****
* This toolkit includes functions and procedures used in this
* application.

FUNCTION tax_find
PARAMETERS a
PRIVATE a,b
b = a * .Ø5
RETURN b

PROCEDURE PROCESS1
? "This message is brought to you by PROCESS1"
DO PROCESS2
? "This message is brought to you by PROCESS1 again."
RETURN

FUNCTION CTOF

PARAMETERS cel_no
PRIVATE ret_val        ret_val = (9/5)cel_no + 32
RETURN ret_val

PROCESS2
? "This message is RIGHT IN THE MIDDLE"
?  " and is brought to you by PROCESS2"
RETURN
```

Fig. 12.19.

The toolbox program.

Whenever you want to add the functions and procedures you have built into a new application, you need only to refer to the file with a SET PROCEDURE command. All the parts in the file can be used by any other module in the application.

Passing Data Records between Program Modules

Unlike memory variables, data records are always PUBLIC and can be shared by every module in the program structure. You can use a database file in a program module. Lower-level procedures/modules have the same level of access to the file as the module that opened it.

In the program MAINGET.PRG (see fig. 12.20), the module GETFILE.PRG (see fig. 12.21) accesses the database file EMPLOYEE.DBF. That module calls another module, GETRECRD.PRG (see fig. 12.22), which positions the record pointer at the fifth data record. The output of these program modules is shown in figure 12.23.

Fig. 12.20.

A main program using modules.

```
***** Program: MAINGET.PRG *****
* The main program to get records
SET TALK OFF
SET ECHO OFF
* Go get a file from GETFILE.PRG module.
DO GETFILE
* Display the record returned from GETRECRD.PRG.
?
? "Data record retrieved from GETFILE.PRG and GETRECRD.PRG"
?
DISPLAY
* Look at the next data record.
SKIP
?
? "Returned from GETFILE.PRG."
?
DISPLAY
RETURN
```

```
***** Program: GETFILE.PRG *****
* Open a database file.
USE EMPLOYEE
RECORDNO=5
* Go to get No.5 data record.
DO GETRECRD
* Return to main program.
RETURN
```

Fig. 12.21.

The program module GETFILE.PRG.

```
***** Program: GETRECRD.PRG *****
* Set record pointer at record no. RECORDNO set by GETFILE.PRG.
GOTO RECORDNO
RETURN
```

Fig. 12.22.

The program module GETRECRD.PRG.

```
. DO MAINGET
Data record retrieved via GETFILE.PRG and GETRECRD.PRG

Record# FIRST_NAME LAST_NAME AREA_CODE PHONE_NO MALE BIRTH_DATE ANNUAL_PAY
      5 Kirk D.    Chapman   618       625-7845 .T.  08/04/61   20737.50

Returned from GETFILE.PRG!

Record# FIRST_NAME LAST_NAME AREA_CODE PHONE_NO MALE BIRTH_DATE ANNUAL_PAY
      6 Mary W.    Thompson  213       432-6782 .F.  06/18/55   25725.00
.
```

Fig. 12.23.

The output of MAINGET.PRG.

When execution returns to the main program after calling the modules GETFILE.PRG and GETRECRD.PRG, the record pointer is still positioned at data record 5. The fields of the data record can be accessed by any module or by the main program.

Accessing Multiple Database Files

Up to this point, you have used only one database file at a time, and the record pointer has been positioned at the current active record. You have been able to access the current data record at any time, in any program module, and at any level.

If, however, you open another database file with the USE command, the current active database file is replaced, and the data record pointer is repositioned. As a result, you cannot return to a data record of the original database file. This limitation can present a problem if you need to access more than one database file at a time. To solve this problem, use the SELECT command.

Using the SELECT Command

Command:

SELECT *Selects and stores a database in an active work area.*

You use the SELECT command to choose and store a database file in an active work area. dBASE IV supports the use of up to 10 different work areas. The following shows the format of the SELECT command:

    . SELECT <*work area*>

You can designate the work area by a number (1 through 10) or a letter (A through J):

    . SELECT 1
    . SELECT A

For instance, to put EMPLOYEE.DBF in the first work area, enter the following commands:

    . SELECT 1
    . USE EMPLOYEE

When you assign a database file to a work area, you can activate the file with the SELECT command without entering the database name:

    . SELECT 1

Although you can use 10 different work areas, only one database file is active at a time. The last database file you use with the SELECT command is the active file, and the other files remain in the background work area.

You can bring another file to the foreground again by using the SELECT command. When you call another file, the record pointer of the previous database file marks the current data record location in that file.

When the previous file is brought back to the foreground, the data record marked is the active data record for that database file. In figure 12.24, the program GETFILES.PRG alternates between the EMPLOYEE.DBF and QTYSOLD.DBF databases.

```
***** Program: GETFILES.PRG *****
* Accessing different database files in the same program
SET TALK OFF
SET ECHO OFF
* Put EMPLOYEE.DBF in work area 1.
SELECT 1
USE EMPLOYEE
GOTO 5
DISPLAY
* Put QTYSOLD.DBF in work area 2.
SELECT 2
USE QTYSOLD
DISPLAY
* Switch back to EMPLOYEE.DBF.
SELECT 1
* Go to the next data record.
SKIP
DISPLAY
RETURN
```

Fig. 12.24.

Accessing different database files

The output from the program is shown in figure 12.25. The program displays record 5 from work area 1 (EMPLOYEE). Then the program moves to work area 2. When the program returns to work area 1, it displays the next record—record 6. As you can see, the record pointers remain in place.

When you open a file with the USE command, the file's name is recorded automatically as the ALIAS for the SELECT command. An ALIAS is simply a name or label for the file. You can use the ALIAS rather than the work area number or letter to refer to the file. If you open a data file called CUST in work area 2, you can switch to the file by using any of the following variations:

Fig. 12.25.

*The output of
GETFILES.PRG.*

```
. DO GETFILES
Record# FIRST_NAME LAST_NAME AREA_CODE PHONE_NO MALE BIRTH_DATE ANNUAL_PA
      5 Kirk D.     Chapman     618       625-7845 .T.  Ø8/Ø4/61   2Ø737.5Ø
Record# DATE      MODEL      UNITS_SOLD
      1 12/Ø7/84 RCA-XA1ØØ       2
Record# FIRST_NAME LAST_NAME AREA_CODE PHONE_NO MALE BIRTH_DATE ANNUAL_PA
      6 Mary W.     Thompson    213       432-6782 .F.  Ø6/18/55   25725.ØØ
  .
```

```
SELECT 2
SELECT B
SELECT CUST
```

You can use this capability in a file in the following way:

```
SELECT 1
USE EMPLOYEE

   . . .

   . . .
SELECT 2
USE CUSTOMER

   . . .

   . . .
SELECT EMPLOYEE
```

You now have two data files open in different work areas. You can move between these work areas with the SELECT command.

Processing Multiple Database Files

An inventory evaluation program demonstrates the use of the SELECT command to switch between two database files. The database file structures and data are shown in figures 12.26 through 12.29. The database STOCKS.DBF stores the inventory items. Each data record contains the description of an inventory item and the quantities on hand and on order. The costs of the inventory items are stored in the database file COSTS.DBF.

```
Structure for database : B:STOCKS.DBF
Number of data records :   11
Date of last update    : Ø1/2Ø/89
Field  Field name   Type        Width    Dec     Index
   1   STOCK_NO     Character    12               Y
   2   MODEL_NO     Character    1Ø               N
   3   MFG          Character     9               N
   4   OPTIONS      Character    25               N
   5   ON_HAND      Numeric       3               N
   6   ON_ORDER     Numeric       3               N
** Total **                      63
```

Fig. 12.26.

The structure of STOCKS.DBF.

```
Record# STOCK_NO     MODEL_NO    MFG       OPTIONS                    ON_HAND ON_ORDER
   1 ST-Ø1-19P-Ø1 RCA-XA1ØØ    RCA       Standard                      5        2
   2 ST-Ø1-25C-Ø2 RCA-XA2ØØ    RCA       Stereo, Wireless Remote      1Ø        5
   3 ST-Ø2-19P-Ø1 ZENITH-19P   ZENITH    Standard, Portable            7        3
   4 ST-Ø2-21C-Ø2 ZENITH-21C   ZENITH    Standard, Wire Remote         3        2
   5 ST-Ø2-25C-Ø3 ZENITH-25C   ZENITH    Stereo, Wireless Remote       5        5
   6 ST-Ø3-17P-Ø1 SONY17ØØP    SONY      Standard                      4        4
   7 ST-Ø3-26C-Ø2 SONY26ØØXT   SONY      Stereo, Wireless Remote       5        5
   8 ST-Ø3-19P-Ø1 PANAVØ19PT   PANASONIC Monitor, Wireless Remote      3        2
   9 ST-Ø3-25C-Ø2 PANAV25CTX   PANASONIC Monitor, Wireless Remote      4        5
  1Ø ST-Ø4-19P-Ø1 SANYO-19-P   SANYO     Standard                      3        2
  11 ST-Ø4-21C-Ø2 SANYO-21-C   SANYO     Table Model, Wire Remote      5        4
```

Fig. 12.27.

The data for inventory evaluation.

```
Structure for database : B:COSTS.DBF
Number of data records :   11
Date of last update    : Ø1/2Ø/89
Field  Field name  Type        Width    Dec     Index
   1   STOCK_NO    Character    12               Y
   2   MODEL_NO    Character    1Ø               N
   3   LIST_PRICE  Numeric       7       2        N
   4   OUR_COST    Numeric       7       2        N
   5   DLR_COST    Numeric       7       2        N
** Total **                     44
```

Fig. 12.28.

The structure of COSTS.DBF.

Record#	STOCK_NO	MODEL_NO	LIST_PRICE	OUR_COST	DLR_COST
1	ST-Ø1-19P-Ø1	RCA-XA1ØØ	349.95	229.50	259.95
2	ST-Ø1-25C-Ø2	RCA-XA2ØØ	595.ØØ	389.ØØ	459.ØØ
3	ST-Ø2-19P-Ø1	ZENITH-19P	385.ØØ	255.ØØ	325.ØØ
4	ST-Ø2-21C-Ø2	ZENITH-21C	449.95	339.ØØ	389.5Ø
5	ST-Ø2-25C-Ø3	ZENITH-25C	759.95	589.ØØ	669.5Ø
6	ST-Ø3-17P-Ø1	SONY17ØØP	45Ø.95	33Ø.ØØ	38Ø.5Ø
7	ST-Ø3-26C-Ø2	SONY26ØØXT	139Ø.95	85Ø.ØØ	1Ø95.ØØ
8	ST-Ø3-19P-Ø1	PANAVØ19PT	579.95	395.ØØ	425.ØØ
9	ST-Ø3-25C-Ø2	PANAV25CTX	1Ø95.95	795.ØØ	885.ØØ
1Ø	ST-Ø4-19P-Ø1	SANYO-19-P	369.ØØ	249.ØØ	319.ØØ
11	ST-Ø4-21C-Ø2	SANYO-21-C	525.95	365.5Ø	425.5Ø

Fig. 12.29.

The contents of COSTS.DBF.

The program in figure 12.30 calculates the value of each inventory item. To calculate the inventory value, the DO WHILE...ENDDO loop accesses records for each of the items in STOCKS.DBF. Then the corresponding costs and stock numbers of the items are located in COSTS.DBF. The output of VALUES.PRG is shown in figure 12.31.

VALUES.PRG stores the stock number (STOCK_NO from the records in STOCKS.DBF) in a memory variable named STOCKNO. Then the program uses the contents of the memory variable as a search key to find the cost in COSTS.DBF with the following command:

```
LOCATE FOR STOCK_NO=STOCKNO
```

Controlling the Record Pointer

You use the LOCATE command when the data file contains only a few records or when you cannot conduct the search by using an index. When you deal with large data files, use the indexing capability to position the record pointer quickly.

By making slight alterations to the program in figure 12.30, you can enhance greatly the efficiency of the program. Note that the example in figure 12.32 uses the SEEK command rather than the LOCATE command. This program is faster than the one with the LOCATE command, which must process each record individually until it finds a record that meets the searching criteria. That process creates a tremendous amount of disk activity as each record is read in turn.

```
***** Program: VALUES.PRG *****
* A program to compute value of each stock item
SET TALK OFF
SET ECHO OFF
?
?"                        Value of Stock Items"
?
?" Stock No.        Model     Quantity    Unit Cost    Total Value"
* Put database files to work areas.
SELECT 1
USE STOCKS
SELECT 2
USE COSTS
* Get stock items sequentially from STOCKS.DBF.
DO WHILE .NOT. EOF()
SELECT 1
STOCKNO=STOCK_NO
* Get its cost from COSTS.DBF.
SELECT 2
LOCATE FOR STOCK_NO=STOCKNO
* Store cost in memory variable.
COST=OUR_COST
* Return to STOCKS.DBF.
SELECT 1
VALUE=COST*ON_HAND
? STOCK_NO +"   " +MODEL_NO +"   " +STR(ON_HAND,5,Ø);
   +STR(COST,14,2) +STR(VALUE,13,2)
* Process next stock item.
SKIP
ENDDO
```

Fig. 12.30.

A program to calculate the value of inventory items.

The SEEK command uses a different method to find the same record. The SEEK command uses the index to perform the search. By using the index, the SEEK command can find one of thousands of records in less than a second; the LOCATE command can take minutes to find the same record.

The program in figure 12.32 assumes that the COSTS data file has been indexed on the STOCK_NO field. Because an index maintains the sort order in memory, you can more quickly position the record pointer using the index order.

```
. DO VALUES
```

Fig. 12.31.

The output of VALUES.PRG.

```
                              Value of Stock Items
    Stock No.        Model      Quantity   Unit Cost    Total Value
    ST-Ø1-19P-Ø1   RCA-XA1ØØ        5        229.5Ø       1147.5Ø
    ST-Ø1-25C-Ø2   RCA-XA2ØØ       1Ø        389.ØØ       389Ø.ØØ
    ST-Ø2-19P-Ø1   ZENITH-19P       7        255.ØØ       1785.ØØ
    ST-Ø2-21C-Ø2   ZENITH-21C       3        339.ØØ       1Ø17.ØØ
    ST-Ø2-25C-Ø3   ZENITH-25C       5        589.ØØ       2945.ØØ
    ST-Ø3-17P-Ø1   SONY17ØØP        4        33Ø.ØØ       132Ø.ØØ
    ST-Ø3-26C-Ø2   SONY26ØØXT       5        895.ØØ       4475.ØØ
    ST-Ø3-19P-Ø1   PANAVØ19PT       3        395.ØØ       1185.ØØ
    ST-Ø3-25C-Ø2   PANAV25CTX       4        795.ØØ       318Ø.ØØ
    ST-Ø4-19P-Ø1   SANYO-19-P       3        249.ØØ        747.ØØ
    ST-Ø4-21C-Ø2   SANYO-21-C       5        365.5Ø       1827.5Ø
```

Joining Database Files

Data in files seldom remains unchanged for long. Often you will need to alter data in a file to conform to data in another file. You use the UPDATE command to change the data records in the active file, using data values from another database file. With APPEND FROM, you can add records from the source file to the active file.

Using UPDATE

Command:

UPDATE
Replaces key fields in the active file with key fields in the source file.

The UPDATE command uses data from a source file to change records in the active database file. To update a file, you match the records in two databases on a specified key field, using the following format:

. UPDATE ON <*key field*> FROM <*source file*> REPLACE <*existing field*> WITH <*expression*>

You can use the UPDATE command to update only the active file; the source file must be in a background work area. Make sure that both the source file and the file to be updated have been sorted or indexed on the key field to be matched. If you have not sorted the files, you must add the word RANDOM to the end of the command.

```
***** Program: VALUES.PRG *****
* A program to compute value of each stock item
SET TALK OFF
SET ECHO OFF
?
?"                          Value of Stock Items"
?
?" Stock No.      Model       Quantity    Unit Cost    Total Value"
* Put database files to work areas.
SELECT 1
USE STOCKS INDEX STOCK_NO
SELECT 2
USE COSTS
* Get stock items sequentially from STOCKS.DBF.
DO WHILE .NOT. EOF()
SELECT 1
STOCKNO=STOCK_NO
* Get its cost from COSTS.DBF.
SELECT 2
SEEK STOCKNO
* Store cost in memory variable.
COST=OUR_COST
* Return to STOCKS.DBF.
SELECT 1
VALUE=COST*ON_HAND
? STOCK_NO +"   " +MODEL_NO +"   " STR(ON_HAND,5,Ø) +STR(COST,14,2) +STR(VALUE,13,2)
* Process next stock item.
SKIP
ENDDO
```

Fig. 12.32.

VALUES.PRG amended to use the SEEK *command.*

For example, suppose that the database file NEWCOSTS.DBF contains new cost information on the stock items. The contents of the database file are shown in figure 12.33.

The data records in NEWCOSTS.DBF contain the revised costs for the stock items. Instead of returning to COSTS.DBF to update each of the new cost items, you can use an UPDATE command. UPDACOST.PRG, the program used for the updating operation, is shown in figure 12.34.

Fig. 12.33.

The structure and contents of NEWCOSTS.DBF.

```
. USE NEWCOSTS
. DISPLAY STRUCTURE
Structure for database : B:NEWCOSTS.DBF
Number of data records :      3
Date of last update    : Ø1/26/89
Field  Field name  Type       Width    Dec     Index
    1  STOCK_NO    Character    12                Y
    2  MODEL_NO    Character    1Ø                N
    3  OUR_COST    Numeric       7      2         N
** Total **                    3Ø

. LIST
Record#  STOCK_NO      MODEL_NO    OUR_COST
      1  ST-Ø3-26C-Ø2  SONY26ØØXT    85Ø.ØØ
      2  ST-Ø1-25C-Ø2  RCA-XA2ØØ     369.ØØ
      3  ST-Ø2-21C-Ø2  ZENITH-25C    559.ØØ
```

Fig. 12.34.

A program using the UPDATE *command.*

```
***** Program: UPDACOST.PRG *****
* Use data in NEWCOSTS.DBF to update COSTS.DBF.
SET TALK OFF
SET ECHO OFF
SELECT B
USE NEWCOSTS
INDEX ON STOCK_NO TO SORT1
SELECT A
USE COSTS
INDEX ON STOCK_NO TO SORT2
UPDATE ON STOCK_NO FROM NEWCOSTS REPLACE OUR_COST WITH B->OUR_COST
RETURN
```

The following UPDATE command is used in UPDACOST.PRG:

```
. UPDATE ON STOCK_NO FROM NEWCOSTS REPLACE OUR_COST
  WITH B->OUR_COST
```

The symbol B-> designates the work area in which the data field is found. When you execute UPDACOST.PRG, the costs of the items in COSTS.DBF are updated. For example, the cost of ST-03-26C-02 is now $850.00 instead of the original $895.00 (see fig. 12.35).

```
. DO UPDACOST
. USE COSTS
. LIST
Record#   STOCK_NO     MODEL_NO     LIST_PRICE  OUR_COST  DLR_COST
      1   ST-Ø1-19P-Ø1  RCA-XA1ØØ      349.95     229.5Ø    259.95
      2   ST-Ø1-25C-Ø2  RCA-XA2ØØ      595.ØØ     369.ØØ    459.ØØ
      3   ST-Ø2-19P-Ø1  ZENITH-19P     385.ØØ     255.ØØ    325.ØØ
      4   ST-Ø2-21C-Ø2  ZENITH-21C     449.95     559.ØØ    389.5Ø
      5   ST-Ø2-25C-Ø3  ZENITH-25C     759.95     589.ØØ    669.5Ø
      6   ST-Ø3-17P-Ø1  SONY17ØØP      45Ø.95     33Ø.ØØ    38Ø.5Ø
      7   ST-Ø3-26C-Ø2  SONY26ØØXT    139Ø.95     85Ø.ØØ   1Ø95.ØØ
      8   ST-Ø3-19P-Ø1  PANAVØ19PT     579.95     395.ØØ    425.ØØ
      9   ST-Ø3-25C-Ø2  PANAV25CTX    1Ø95.95     795.ØØ    885.ØØ
     1Ø   ST-Ø4-19P-Ø1  SANYO-19-P     369.ØØ     249.ØØ    319.ØØ
     11   ST-Ø4-21C-Ø2  SANYO-21-C     525.95     365.5Ø    425.5Ø
```

Fig. 12.35.

*The results of
UPDACOST.PRG.*

You also can use the UPDATE command to add the contents of the records
in a source file to the corresponding records in the master file. For
example, RESTOCK.PRG updates the items in the master file
STOCKS.DBF, using the data records in the source file RECEIVED.DBF
(see fig. 12.36).

```
***** Program: RESTOCK.PRG *****
* Use data in NEWITEMS.DBF to update STOCKS.DBF
SET TALK OFF
SET ECHO OFF
SELECT B
USE RECEIVED
INDEX ON STOCK_NO TO SORT1
SELECT A
USE STOCKS
INDEX ON STOCK_NO TO SORT2
UPDATE ON STOCK_NO FROM RECEIVED REPLACE ON_HAND WITH ON_HAND +B->ON-HAND
RETURN
```

Fig. 12.36.

*Using new data to
update
STOCKS.DBF.*

Figure 12.37 shows the contents of the master file STOCKS.DBF before you perform the updating operation. The structure and contents of the source file RECEIVED.DBF are displayed in figure 12.38. You can see in figure 12.39 that after you execute RESTOCK.PRG, the on-hand quantities are updated.

```
. USE STOCKS
. LIST STOCK_NO,MODEL_NO,ON_HAND,ON_ORDER
Record#   STOCK_NO       MODEL_NO      ON_HAND ON_ORDER
      1   ST-Ø1-19P-Ø1   RCA-XA100        5        2
      2   ST-Ø1-25C-Ø2   RCA-XA2ØØ       1Ø        5
      3   ST-Ø2-19P-Ø1   ZENITH-19P       7        3
      4   ST-Ø2-21C-Ø2   ZENITH-21C       3        2
      5   ST-Ø2-25C-Ø3   ZENITH-25C       5        5
      6   ST-Ø3-17P-Ø1   SONY17ØØP        4        4
      7   ST-Ø3-26C-Ø2   SONY26ØØXT       5        5
      8   ST-Ø3-19P-Ø1   PANAVØ19PT       3        2
      9   ST-Ø3-25C-Ø2   PANAV25CTX       4        5
     1Ø   ST-Ø4-19P-Ø1   SANYO-19-P       3        2
     11   ST-Ø4-21C-Ø2   SANYO-21-C       5        4
```

```
. USE RECEIVED
. DISPLAY STRUCTURE
Structure for database : e:RECEIVED.DBF
Number of data records :      3
Date of last update    : Ø1/3Ø/89
Field  Field name  Type        Width    Dec     Index
    1  STOCK_NO    Character     12               Y
    2  MODEL_NO    Character     1Ø               N
    3  ON_HAND     Numeric        3               N
** Total **                      26

. LIST
Record#   STOCK_NO       MODEL_NO      ON_HAND
      1   ST-Ø3-26C-Ø2   SONY26ØØXT       2
      2   ST-Ø1-25C-Ø2   RCA-XA2ØØ        1
      3   ST-Ø2-21C-Ø2   ZENITH-21C       2
```

```
. DO RESTOCK
SORT1.NDX already exists, overwrite it? (Y/N) Yes
SORT2.NDX already exists, overwrite it? (Y/N) yes
. USE STOCKS
. LIST STOCK_NO,MODEL_NO,ON_HAND.ON_ORDER
Record#   STOCK_NO      MODEL_NO     ON_HAND ON_ORDER
       1  ST-Ø1-19P-Ø1  RCA-XA1ØØ        5        2
       2  ST-Ø1-25C-Ø2  RCA-XA2ØØ       11        5
       3  ST-Ø2-19P-Ø1  ZENITH-19P       7        3
       4  ST-Ø2-21C-Ø2  ZENITH-21C       5        2
       5  ST-Ø2-25C-Ø3  ZENITH-25C       5        5
       6  ST-Ø3-17P-Ø1  SONY17ØØP        4        4
       7  ST-Ø3-26C-Ø2  SONY26ØØXT       7        5
       8  ST-Ø3-19P-Ø1  PANAVØ19PT       3        2
       9  ST-Ø3-25C-Ø2  PANAV25CTX       4        5
      1Ø  ST-Ø4-19P-Ø1  SANYO-19-P       3        2
      11  ST-Ø4-21C-Ø2  SANYO-21-C       5        4
```

Fig. 12.39.

The results of RESTOCK.PRG.

Using APPEND FROM

The APPEND FROM command adds records to the file. With this command, you can take data records from the source file and add the records to the active database file, with or without a qualifier. Use the following form of the command:

Command:
APPEND FROM
Adds new records.

. APPEND FROM <*name of source file*> <*a qualifier, if needed*>

The source file may or may not have the same data structure as the active database file. The APPEND FROM command appends only the data fields common to both files. To append NEWITEMS.DBF to STOCKS.DBF, enter the following commands:

```
USE STOCKS
APPEND FROM NEWITEMS
```

To append only selected records (those with model number RCA-XA200, for example), you can add a qualifier to APPEND FROM:

```
APPEND FROM NEWITEMS FOR  MODEL_NO="RCA-XA2ØØ"
```

A program to append the records of NEWITEMS.DBF to the STOCKS.DBF database is shown in figure 12.40. The structure and contents of the source file NEWITEMS.DBF are displayed in figure 12.41.

```
***** Program: ADDITEMS.PRG *****
* Append data records of NEWITEMS.DBF to STOCKS.DBF
SET TALK OFF
SET ECHO OFF
USE STOCKS
APPEND FROM NEWITEMS
RETURN
```

```
Structure for database : B:NEWITEMS.DBF
Number of data records :       2
Date of last update    : Ø1/26/89
Field  Field name  Type       Width  Dec      Index
    1  STOCK_NO    Character     12            Y
    2  MODEL_NO    Character     1Ø            N
    3  MFG         Character      9            N
    4  OPTIONS     Character     25            N
    5  ON_HAND     Numeric        3            N
    6  ON_ORDER    Numeric        3            N
** Total **                     63
```

Record#	STOCK_NO	MODEL_NO	MFG	OPTIONS	ON_HAND	ON_ORDER
1	ST-Ø5-19P-Ø1	PHILCO-19X	PHILCO	Standard	5	0
2	ST-Ø5-25C-Ø1	GE-25ØØ-ST	GE	Stereo, Wireless Remote	3	1

After the appending operation, you see the contents of STOCKS.DBF, as shown in figure 12.42. The records from NEWITEMS.DBF are appended to STOCKS.DBF.

In short, you use the APPEND FROM command to bring new data records into the data file from outside files in batch mode. This capability is especially convenient when you want to share data with someone who uses the same data structure and you are not connected to a multiuser system.

Record#	STOCK_NO	MODEL_NO	MFG	OPTIONS	ON_HAND	ON_ORDER
1	ST-Ø1-19P-Ø1	RCA-XA2ØØ	RCA	Standard	5	2
2	ST-Ø1-25C-Ø2	RCA-XA2ØØ	RCA	Stereo, Wireless Remote	11	5
3	ST-Ø2-19P-Ø1	ZENITH-19P	ZENITH	Standard, Portable	7	3
4	ST-Ø2-21C-Ø2	ZENITH-21C	ZENITH	Standard, Wire Remote	5	2
5	ST-Ø2-25C-Ø3	ZENITH-25C	ZENITH	Stereo, Wireless Remote	5	5
6	ST-Ø3-17P-Ø1	SONY17ØØP	SONY	Standard	4	4
7	ST-Ø3-26C-Ø2	SONY26ØØXT	SONY	Stereo, Wireless Remote	7	5
8	ST-Ø3-19P-Ø1	PANAVØ19PT	PANASONIC	Monitor, Wireless Remote	3	2
9	ST-Ø3-25C-Ø2	PANAV25CTX	PANASONIC	Monitor, Wireless Remote	4	5
1Ø	ST-Ø4-19P-Ø1	SANYO-19-P	SANYO	Standard	3	2
11	ST-Ø4-21C-Ø2	SANYO-21-C	SANYO	Table Model, Wire Remote	5	4
12	ST-Ø5-19P-Ø1	PHILCO-19X	PHILCO	Standard	5	Ø
13	ST-Ø5-25C-Ø1	GE-25ØØ-ST	GE	Stereo, Wireless Remote	3	1

Fig. 12.42.

The results of appending new records.

Using the Macro Function

Up to this point, you have used a fixed field name in the conditional qualifier of a LOCATE command, such as FOR STOCK_NO=. You also have specified a fixed database file name in a USE command, such as USE EMPLOYEE or USE QTYSOLD. You can use a program with fixed field names and database file names to process only those fields and files. If you want the program to process a different database file, you must change the file name in the USE command line.

With a more flexible program, you could process different data files (that have the same structure) by simply entering their names. The macro function was created for that purpose. By placing the & symbol before a memory variable name, you can use the contents of the variable as a data field or database file name. Suppose, for example, that you use the following command to store the string EMPLOYEE in a memory variable file name:

    STORE "EMPLOYEE" TO <filename>

or

    <filename>="EMPLOYEE"

You then can activate the database file by entering the following command:

USE & <*filename*>

By changing the contents of the variable <*filename*>, you can activate different database files without changing the USE command in the program. The program GETDATA.PRG (see fig. 12.43) shows how to find the data record that contains a given key data item (KEYITEM) in a key field (KEYFIELD) of a key database file (KEYFILE). The results of the program are shown in figure 12.44.

Fig. 12.43.

The program module GETDATA.PRG.

```
***** Program: GETDATA.PRG *****
* Search a key data item in a key field of a key file
SET TALK OFF
SET ECHO OFF
?
ACCEPT "      Enter Name of Database File .... " TO KEYFILE
ACCEPT "                      Data Field ....... " TO KEYFIELD
ACCEPT "                      The Search Key ... " TO KEYITEM
* Activate the key file.
USE &KEYFILE
* Locate the key item.
LOCATE FOR &KEYFIELD=KEYITEM
* Display the data record found.
?
? "The Data Record Found:"
DISPLAY
?
RETURN
```

Macro substitution is a powerful tool that lets you place a variable's data into a command. This capability provides you with the flexibility to let the environment (date, time, conditional comparisons, and so on) or user input direct the way a program operates.

```
. DO GETDATA

        Enter Name of Database File .... EMPLOYEE
                     Data Field ....... LAST_NAME
                     The Search Key ... Nelson

The Data Record Found:
Record# FIRST_NAME LAST_NAME AREA_CODE PHONE_NO MALE BIRTH_DATE ANNUAL_PAY
      3 Harry M.    Nelson       315     576-0235 .T.  02/15/58   30450.00
. DO GETDATA

        Enter Name of Database File .... COSTS
                     Data Field ....... STOCK_NO
                     The Search Key ... ST_03-26C-02

The Data Record Found:
Record#   STOCK_NO      MODEL_NO    LIST_PRICE OUR_COST  DLR_COST
      7  ST-03-26C-02  SONY2600XT    1390.95    850.00   1095.00
.
```

Fig. 12.44.

The results of GETDATA.PRG.

Building Menus

One of the benefits of writing dBASE programs is the capability to create menu-driven applications that people with little or no knowledge of dBASE IV can use. A noncomputer user should be able to learn a properly constructed data management application in less than an hour—no matter how complex that application is.

dBASE IV provides an arsenal of tools for building light-bar menus and for screen handling. One of the most powerful sets of these commands is the set that creates POPUPs. As you see in the next chapter, you can use POPUPs to create the entire menu structure for an application.

You follow four basic steps to create and use a POPUP menu:

1. Define the name of the menu.

2. Define the bar information.

3. Declare what action to take when the user makes a choice.

4. Activate the menu.

By introducing the steps for creating a menu structure, you have a head start on the next chapter. The main menu of an integrated application is presented in the next chapter. This chapter shows you how to design a modular application that does everything you want from one main menu.

The program in figure 12.45 shows how to build a POPUP menu you can use for the main menu of an application.

```
***** Program: MAINMENU.PRG *****

* Set up the environment the way you want it to be.

SET TALK OFF          && Turn off messages from dBASE IV.
SET STATUS OFF        && Turn off the status line.
SET SCOREBOARD OFF    && Turn off row Ø messages from dBASE IV.
IF ISCOLOR()          && If there is a color card, set colors to
    SET COLOR TO GR+/B,N/BG   && yellow on blue and black on cyan.
    SET COLOR OF BOX TO GR+/B && Menu boxes also.
ENDIF

CLEAR                 && Erase the screen.

* This command initializes a POPUP menu called main. The menu
* is surrounded by a box from 4,2Ø to 2Ø,6Ø.

DEFINE POPUP main FROM 4,2Ø TO 2Ø,6Ø

* The BAR positions are relative to the top line of the menu.
* BAR 2 is two lines under line 4 where the menu starts.
* The SKIP at the end of the first two lines keeps the
* light bar from stopping on those two lines.
* MESSAGE centers a description of the choice on line 24.
* Remember the semicolon (;). The semicolon breaks one long
* command into two or more lines.
* The function CENT_STR() is user-defined. The code, placed at
* the bottom of the file, centers a character string within
* however many spaces you choose. This makes it easy to center
* menu prompts.

DEFINE BAR 2 OF main PROMPT CENT_STR("Main Menu",39) SKIP
DEFINE BAR 3 OF main PROMPT REPLICATE(CHR(2Ø5),39) SKIP
* CHR(2Ø5) is the ASCII character for the double line.
DEFINE BAR 5 OF main PROMPT CENT_STR("Account Billing",37) ;
    MESSAGE "ADD, EDIT and DELETE Customer Accounts, PRINT mailing list"
```

Fig. 12.45—continued

```
DEFINE BAR 7 OF main PROMPT CENT_STR("Prepare Billing",37) ;
   MESSAGE "Prepare invoices, and perform BILLING tasks"
DEFINE BAR 9 OF main PROMPT CENT_STR("Cost Maintenance",37)  ;
   MESSAGE "Perform maintenance of wholesale costs lists and files"
DEFINE BAR 11 OF main PROMPT CENT_STR("Inventory Control",37) ;
   MESSAGE "Perform tasks to keep inventory information accurate"
DEFINE BAR 13 OF main PROMPT CENT_STR("Personnel file Control",37) ;
   MESSAGE "Perform tasks to keep the Personnel records up to date"
DEFINE BAR 15 OF main PROMPT CENT_STR("Quit",37) ;
   MESSAGE "Terminate this program and go back to the DOT prompt"

* The following line determines what happens when the user makes
* a selection. In this case, the program calls PROCEDURE M_CASES.

ON SELECTION POPUP main DO M_CASES

* The next four lines set everything into motion. Once you
* activate the POPUP menu, it stays active until the user
* chooses Quit. The program then clears the screen, memory, and
* returns to the dot prompt.

ACTIVATE POPUP main
CLEAR
CLEAR ALL
RETURN

PROCEDURE M_CASES  && This procedure is called by a selection
                   && from the POPUP menu named main.
DO CASE
   CASE BAR() = 5
      ACTIVATE POPUP acct      && POP window over this one.
   CASE BAR() = 7
      DO BILLING               && Do procedure or program called
                               && BILLING.
   CASE BAR() = 9
      DO COSTMENU
   CASE BAR() = 11
      DO INVMENU
   CASE BAR() = 13
      DO EMPLMENU
   CASE BAR() = 15
      DEACTIVATE POPUP    && This command terminates POPUP main.
                          && Until this command is given, POPUP
                          && is active.
```

Fig. 12.45—concluded

```
        RETURN
ENDCASE

FUNCTION CENT_STR
PARAMETERS string, stlen        && Accept the string to be padded
                                && and the width of the area to
                                && display the string.
PRIVATE ret_val, lpad, tpad     && Isolate these variables from
                                && others even if they have the
                                && same name.
lpad = INT((stlen - LEN(LTRIM(TRIM(string))))/2)
tpad = stlen - lpad - LEN(LTRIM(TRIM(string)))
                                && Trailing pad is the number
                                && of spaces left.
                                && Assemble the return value.
ret_val = SPACE(lpad) + LTRIM(TRIM(string)) + SPACE(tpad)
RETURN ret_val                  && Send value to calling module.

* END OF MAINMENU.PRG
```

Figure 12.46 shows the menu that MAINMENU.PRG creates. To choose an item from the menu, the user can highlight the choice with the up- and down-arrow keys and then press Enter, or the user can type the first letter of the choice. When the user makes a choice, the procedure M_CASE is performed. M_CASE is a simple DO CASE construct that uses the BAR( ) function to determine which of the choices was engaged. The CASE statements direct the flow of the program.

Fig. 12.46.

The menu from MAINMENU.PRG.

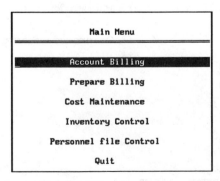

```
┌─────────────────────────────────────┐
│              Main Menu               │
├─────────────────────────────────────┤
│ ████████Account Billing████████████ │
│                                      │
│           Prepare Billing            │
│                                      │
│           Cost Maintenance           │
│                                      │
│           Inventory Control          │
│                                      │
│         Personnel file Control       │
│                                      │
│                 Quit                 │
└─────────────────────────────────────┘
```

ADD, EDIT and DELETE Customer Accounts, PRINT mailing list

Please note that you must define the POPUP called acct before you activate it. Remember that you can call another POPUP to sit over the top of this one. You can use this method to present submenus.

Chapter Summary

This chapter introduced modular programming. The examples showed you how to use the PROCEDURE and FUNCTION commands to create program structures that function on multiple levels and to create modules that you can include in any application you write. This chapter also showed you how to use two or more database files with the SELECT command and how to update and append records. Finally, this chapter introduced building menus. In the next chapter, you learn more about using menus to create a fully integrated database system.

13

An Integrated
Database System

You attain the full realization of dBASE IV's power when you can put that power into the hands of users who wouldn't know a dot prompt from an apostrophe.

It takes a great deal of time to learn the capabilities of a program as large and complex as dBASE IV. The average office worker simply can't spare the time away from other duties to adequately learn an intricate piece of software. This chapter introduces you to simple methods of putting the power of dBASE IV into users' hands.

This chapter presents a multiple-level, menu-driven application that consists of several modules for billing, controlling inventory, and maintaining customers' accounts. These modules have been deliberately kept simple so that the user can easily understand them. Comments in the code provide a "blow-by-blow account" of the action. For your convenience, all the code is included at the end of the chapter. Seeing the printouts of the program code helps you to understand how the three main building blocks (programs, procedures, and functions) are cemented together to build the whole application program.

This chapter also presents program code that handles several data files at the same time, automatically evaluates user input, and prints reports using multiple files.

The last and final module is left for you to complete. You can use the examples in the other modules as your guide.

Creating an Integrated Database Management Program

Modular programming divides a complex database management system into simple program modules. Program modules can include program (.PRG) files, procedures, and functions. Each module performs a specific task. Using modular programming, you can design a large database management system by creating several small program modules. After you design and test the modules, you can use menus to bind the modules together into a complete program.

This chapter uses as an example a simple database management system for Super Stereo and Television Distributors, Inc., a television wholesaler. The company currently performs five basic data management functions:

❏ Maintaining business accounts for each retailer

❏ Billing customers for purchases made during a specified period

❏ Maintaining stock information, including descriptions and costs

❏ Monitoring and controlling inventory level

❏ Maintaining personnel files

The logical design of the overall application is shown in figure 13.1. Notice that all the program's functions are tied back to the MAINMENU module.

Designing the Main Menu

The main menu presents five basic database management functions. This presentation is one of the elements of a successful modular program: the main menu is a mirror that reflects the organizational structure of the application.

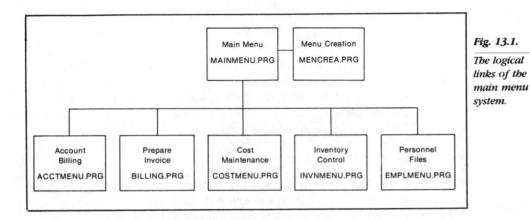

Fig. 13.1.

*The logical
links of the
main menu
system.*

The user invokes the main program, MAINMENU.PRG, from the dot
prompt with the following command:

   .DO MAINMENU

The menu in figure 13.2 is displayed. The user can make a selection by
moving the highlight bar with the up and down arrow keys or pressing
the first letter of the appropriate choice.

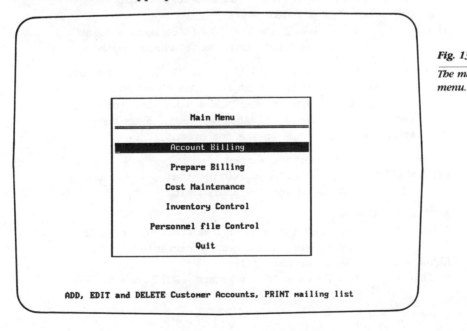

Fig. 13.2.

*The main
menu.*

Two parts of the program produce the main menu. MAINMENU.PRG sets up the structure for the application. MAINMENU.PRG then calls MEN_CREA.PRG to define the menus for the entire application. Because one file contains all the code, you easily can edit and reorganize the menu programs, if necessary. MAINMENU.PRG is shown in figure 13.3. This program activates a POPUP that provides the branches to other modules and menus.

Fig. 13.3.

MAINMENU.PRG.

```
***** Program: MAINMENU.PRG *****

* This is the top level program. All other functions and
* procedures in this application are a branch off this tree.
* As each command takes place a comment explains what the
* command does. When you type the program code for yourself,
* you can leave out the comments.

* Set up the environment the way you want it.

SET TALK OFF          && Turn off dBASE messages.
SET STATUS OFF        && Turn off the STATUS bar.
SET SCOREBOARD OFF    && Turn off line Ø at top of screen.
IF ISCOLOR()          && If the user has a color monitor,
    SET COLOR TO GR+/B,N/BG    && set screen colors.
    SET COLOR OF BOX TO GR+/B
ENDIF                 && If the user does not have a color
                      && video card, don't change anything.

* These next few lines are all that the MASTER program does.
* You activate a POPUP menu that provides the branches to
* everything else. When the user makes a choice, the CASE
* statement in M_CASES deactivates the menu. From there, the
* program terminates back to the dot prompt.

CLEAR           && Clear the screen.
DO MEN_CREA     && Perform a subroutine that defines all the
                && menus for the application.

ACTIVATE POPUP main
CLEAR           && Once the menu is deactivated, erase the
                && screen, clear memory variables, and
CLEAR ALL       && close data files.
RETURN          && Go back to dot prompt; QUIT goes to DOS.
```

Fig. 13.3 —continued

```
PROCEDURE M_CASES
                && When the program says DO M_CASES, all the
                && commands from here to the end are compiled and
                && executed.
DO CASE         && Begin comparison CASE by CASE.
    CASE BAR() = 5          && If the chosen BAR is 5,
        ACTIVATE POPUP acct && pop the acct menu into place.
    CASE BAR() = 7          && If the chosen BAR is 7,
        DO INVOICE          && do the invoicing routine.
    CASE BAR() = 9
        ACTIVATE POPUP cost
    CASE BAR() = 11
        ACTIVATE POPUP STOK
    CASE BAR() = 13
        DO EMPLMENU
    CASE BAR() = 15
        DEACTIVATE POPUP    && Deactivate main menu.
        RETURN
ENDCASE

FUNCTION CENT_STR   && This user-defined function centers
                *   a character string across a specified
                *   number of spaces.
PARAMETERS string, stlen    && Accept the string to be padded,
                            && and the width of the area into
                            && which the string goes.
PRIVATE ret_val, lpad, tpad && Isolate these variables from
                            && others even if they have
                            && the same name.
lpad = INT((stlen - LEN(LTRIM(TRIM(string))))/2)

* The preceding command trims all the blanks in front of and behind
* a string and subtracts that many spaces from the total width.
* You know how many spaces to pad the front.

tpad = stlen - lpad - LEN(LTRIM(TRIM(string)))
* Trailing pad (tpad) is the number of spaces left.
* Now assemble the return value.
ret_val = SPACE(lpad) + LTRIM(TRIM(string)) + SPACE(tpad)
RETURN ret_val
* Send the value back to the calling module.
```

Figure 13.4 shows the code to define the menus. This part of the program designs and defines the main menu as well as other menus that appear when the user makes a selection. Notice that the program code is basically the same for the menus; only the placement and prompt names are changed. The CASE statement uses input from the user to determine branching.

Fig. 13.4.

The program to define the menus.

```
***** Program: MEN_CREA.PRG *****

* This part of the program designs and defines each of the menus.
* Remember that BAR numbers are relative to the top line of the
* menu.

* Initialize a POPUP menu with a box around it from 4,20 to
* 20,60 for the main menu area.

DEFINE POPUP main FROM 4,20 TO 20,60

* The following commands center a string inside the box on
* lines relative to the top line of the menu.
* The SKIP argument tells the POPUP to display the lines
* in the box, but don't let the light bar stop there.

DEFINE BAR 2 OF main PROMPT CENT_STR("Main Menu",39) SKIP
DEFINE BAR 3 OF main PROMPT REPLICATE(CHR(205),39) SKIP
* CHR(205) is the ASCII double line character.

* The following message commands are divided with a semicolon.
* The MESSAGE is displayed whenever the light bar is positioned
* on that PROMPT.

DEFINE BAR 5 OF main PROMPT CENT_STR("Account Billing",37) ;
   MESSAGE "ADD, EDIT and DELETE Customer Accounts, PRINT mailing list"
DEFINE BAR 7 OF main PROMPT CENT_STR("Prepare Invoice",37) ;
   MESSAGE "Prepare and print an invoice"
DEFINE BAR 9 OF main PROMPT CENT_STR("Cost Maintenance",37) ;
   MESSAGE "Perform maintenance of wholesale costs, lists and files"
DEFINE BAR 11 OF main PROMPT CENT_STR("Inventory Control",37) ;
   MESSAGE "Perform tasks to keep inventory information accurate"
DEFINE BAR 13 OF main PROMPT CENT_STR("Personnel File Control",37) ;
   MESSAGE "This module is for you to build based on the other modules"
```

Fig. 13.4—continued

```
DEFINE BAR 15 OF main PROMPT CENT_STR("Quit",37) ;
   MESSAGE "Terminate this program and go back to the DOT prompt"

* Define the Account Billing menu.
* Same commands as the preceding ones, but different names and
* prompts. Notice that the POPUP frame is 6,5Ø to 18,7Ø
* and that the frame is centered over the side of the main menu
* frame. When the user chooses Account Billing from the main menu,
* this menu pops up over the other. When the user deactivates the
* POPUP, this menu disappears, and the main menu is reactivated.

DEFINE POPUP acct FROM 6,5Ø TO 18,7Ø
DEFINE BAR  2 OF acct PROMPT CENT_STR("Add a new Account",19) ;
   MESSAGE "ADD Customer Accounts"
DEFINE BAR  4 OF acct PROMPT CENT_STR("Delete an Account",19) ;
   MESSAGE "DELETE a customer from the file"
DEFINE BAR  6 OF acct PROMPT CENT_STR("Edit an Account",19) ;
   MESSAGE "EDIT a customer Account"
DEFINE BAR  8 OF acct PROMPT CENT_STR("Print Account list",19) ;
   MESSAGE "PRINT a list of accounts sorted the way you want them"
DEFINE BAR 1Ø OF acct PROMPT CENT_STR("Return",19) ;
   MESSAGE "RETURN to the main menu"

* Define the Account Mailing List menu.
* This menu pops up over the Account Billing menu when the user
* chooses to print the mailing list.

DEFINE POPUP acml FROM 8,4Ø TO 16,6Ø
DEFINE BAR  1 OF acml PROMPT CENT_STR("Sorted by ",19) SKIP
DEFINE BAR  3 OF acml PROMPT CENT_STR("Account #",19)
DEFINE BAR  5 OF acml PROMPT CENT_STR("State",19)
DEFINE BAR  7 OF acml PROMPT CENT_STR("Zipcode",19)

* Define the Costs menu.
DEFINE POPUP cost FROM 6,1Ø TO 16,3Ø
DEFINE BAR  2 OF cost PROMPT CENT_STR("Add a Cost Item",19) ;
   MESSAGE "ADD Cost Items to the file"
DEFINE BAR  4 OF cost PROMPT CENT_STR("Delete a Cost Item",19) ;
   MESSAGE "DELETE a Cost item from the file"
DEFINE BAR  6 OF cost PROMPT CENT_STR("Edit a Cost Item",19) ;
   MESSAGE "EDIT a Cost Item in the file"
```

Fig. 13.4—concluded

```
DEFINE BAR 8 OF cost PROMPT CENT_STR("Return",19) ;
   MESSAGE "RETURN to the main menu"

* Define the Inventory menu.
DEFINE POPUP stok FROM 6,10 TO 18,30
DEFINE BAR  2 OF stok PROMPT CENT_STR("Add a Stock Item",19) ;
   MESSAGE "ADD Stock Items to the file"
DEFINE BAR  4 OF stok PROMPT CENT_STR("Delete a Stock Item",19) ;
   MESSAGE "DELETE a Stock item from the file"
DEFINE BAR  6 OF stok PROMPT CENT_STR("Edit a Stock Item",19) ;
   MESSAGE "EDIT a Cost Item in the file"
DEFINE BAR  8 OF stok PROMPT CENT_STR("Stock Report",19) ;
   MESSAGE "PRINT a Stock Inventory Report"
DEFINE BAR 10 OF stok PROMPT CENT_STR("Return",19) ;
   MESSAGE "RETURN to the main menu"

* Define the selections that will trigger the actions.
* When the user makes a choice from a POPUP menu, the
* following commands specify what should be done. The first
* command specifies what happens when the user makes the initial
* choice at the main menu. M_CASES is a CASE construct
* that activates one of the other menus. Each of the menus
* in turn calls a different program module that evaluates which
* choice was made. Each of the programs has a CASE construct
* similar to M_CASES that it uses to determine branching.

ON SELECTION POPUP main DO M_CASES
ON SELECTION POPUP acct DO ACCTMENU
ON SELECTION POPUP acml DO MAILLIST
ON SELECTION POPUP cost DO COSTMENU
ON SELECTION POPUP stok DO INVNMENU

* Define a window to cover menus while entry takes place.
* When POPUPs are active, the screen becomes property of the POPUP.
* You need a window where you can display things on-screen.
* When you deactivate the window, the menus are again visible,
* and nothing you have displayed is visible. You also can create
* windows that pop in and cover only part of the screen.
* NONE means no border

DEFINE WINDOW cover FROM 0,0 TO 24,79 NONE
```

When the user highlights a choice, a message on the bottom of the screen tells the user what that choice does. When the user makes a selection, the ON SELECTION commands in MEN_CREA determine how the program branches. The design of the light bar menu makes it easy to build applications that take little or no training for a user to find the tasks they need to perform.

When the user chooses the Account Billing bar, another panel on-screen pops up into a menu (see fig. 13.5).

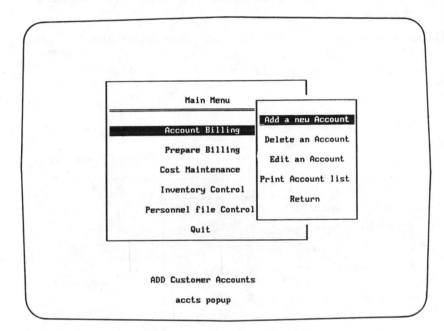

Fig. 13.5.

The menu for Account Billing.

Creating the Account Billing Submenu

Each choice on the main menu defines a branching possibility; each branch represents different data management functions. Each of the branches then breaks down into a number of subtasks. A second-level submenu defines each task. For example, the program module ACCTMENU.PRG defines the tasks required to maintain accounts. This structure is the core of the modular programming concept—breaking each of these tasks into a small manageable program. The tasks in ACCTMENU.PRG include four modules:

- ☐ Adding a new retailer's account
- ☐ Deleting an existing account
- ☐ Editing the contents of an existing account
- ☐ Preparing and printing a mailing list of all existing accounts, using various sort orders

The database file ACCOUNTS.DBF contains information about the existing accounts. The structure of the file is shown in figure 13.6. The file contains data records for 10 retailers. These records are shown in figure 13.7.

Fig. 13.6.

The structure of ACCOUNTS.DBF.

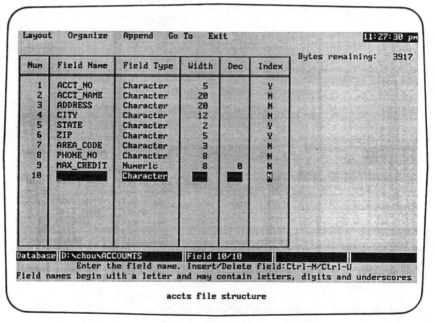

Figure 13.8 shows the logical structure of the Account Billing module. Each of these functions is a procedure found in ACCTMENU.PRG.

Record#	ACCT_NO	ACCT_NAME	ADDRESS	CITY	STATE	ZIP	AREA_CODE	PHONE_NO	MAX_CREDIT
1	10001	SUPER SOUNDS	123 Main Street	Portland	OR	97201	503	224-6890	25000
2	10002	ABC T.V. STORE	3459 Fifth Avenue	Portland	OR	97203	503	246-5687	20000
3	10003	ACE SUPERVISION	2345 Columbia St.	Vancouver	WA	98664	206	892-4569	12000
4	10004	DYNAVISION T.V. SHOP	13560 S.W. Division	Portland	OR	97201	503	287-8754	22000
5	10005	Tower Stereo & TV	7865 Highway 99	Vancouver	WA	98665	206	574-7892	10000
6	10006	REDDING SUPER TV	1245 Lakeview Drive	Redding	CA	94313	432	877-6543	20000
7	10007	National TV & Stereo	4567 Oak Street	Portland	OR	97204	503	289-6832	25000
8	10008	Superior TV & Sound	5789 S.W. Broadway	Portland	OR	97202	503	224-6541	5000
9	10009	Electronic Mart	2568 Evergreen Blvd.	Vancouver	WA	98662	503	256-4578	15000
10	10010	Stereo Super Store	10000 S. Division	Portland	OR	97206	503	224-7275	20000

Fig. 13.7.

The data records in ACCOUNTS.DBF.

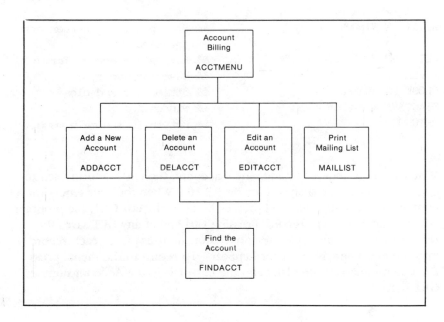

Fig. 13.8.

The logical links of the Account Billing submenu.

You can see how the flow of the modules is accomplished, using the menu as a home base. The program returns to the home base whenever a task is completed.

Adding New Customer Records

The procedure to add new accounts to the file is shown in figure 13.9. This program code activates a format file and appends new data records to the database file ACCOUNTS.DBF. This procedure uses the custom format file ACCOUNT.FMT to label the record fields (see fig. 13.10).

Fig. 13.9.

The procedure to add new accounts.

```
PROCEDURE ADDACCT                  && Add customers to the file.
USE ACCOUNTS ORDER TAG ACCT_NO     && Open account file and set
                                   && the index order to acct_no
                                   && TAG.
ACTIVATE WINDOW cover              && Pop up a blank screen over
                                   && the menu.
SET FORMAT TO ACCOUNT.FMT          && Activate a screen format.
APPEND                             && Take user entry.
CLOSE DATABASES                    && Store date and close
DEACTIVATE WINDOW cover            && window.
RETURN                             && Return to the main menu.
```

When the user chooses to add a new account, the custom form used to append a record is displayed (see fig. 13.10). When the user enters the contents of the data fields and presses Enter in the last GET, the program automatically saves the record. Pressing Ctrl-End at any GET saves the record to the file and ends the entry. After the user places each record into the file, a new blank record appears. To return to the menu, press Esc when the boxes are blank and the cursor is in the Account number GET box.

Deleting Customer Records

The DELTACCT procedure removes a data record from the database file ACCOUNTS.DBF (see fig. 13.11).

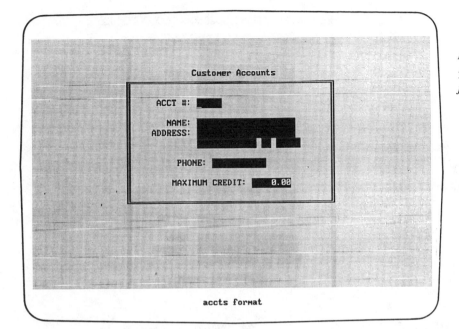

Fig. 13.10.

The custom format file.

```
PROCEDURE DELTACCT
STORE ' ' TO conf     && Create a variable to confirm deletion.
USE ACCOUNTS ORDER TAG ACCT_NO        && Open the data indexed for
                                      && the SEEK.
ACTIVATE WINDOW cover                 && Pop up a blank screen.

* See the following section to learn how FINDACCT works. FOUND()
* is logical function that will be .T. if the record is found.

DO FINDACCT
IF FOUND()
* If the record is located, use the @...SAY...GETS to display a
* copy of the record on-screen in the same format.
      @ 3,31 SAY " Customer Accounts"
      @ 4,19 TO 16,6Ø DOUBLE
      @ 6,24 SAY " ACCT #: "
      @ 6,33 GET acct_no PICTURE "XXXXX"
      @ 8,26 SAY " NAME: "
      @ 8,33 GET acct_name PICTURE "XXXXXXXXXXXXXXXXXXXXX"
      @ 9,24 SAY "ADDRESS:"
```

Fig. 13.11.

The procedure to delete accounts.

Fig. 13.11—continued

```
    @ 9,33 GET address PICTURE "XXXXXXXXXXXXXXXXXXXXXX"
    @ 10,33 GET city PICTURE "XXXXXXXXXXXXX"
    @ 10,46 GET state PICTURE "XX"
    @ 10,49 GET zip PICTURE "XXXXX"
    @ 12,24 SAY "     PHONE: "
    @ 12,36 GET area_code PICTURE "XXX"
    @ 12,39 GET phone_no PICTURE "XXXXXXXX"
    @ 14,28 SAY "MAXIMUM CREDIT: "
    @ 14,44 GET max_credit PICTURE "99999.99"
    CLEAR GETS
* This command cancels all the GETS so that the program does not
* stop for entry.
    @20, 24 SAY "DELETE THIS RECORD? " GET CONF
* Confirm deletion.
    READ
    IF UPPER(conf) = 'Y'        && If last key pressed is Y,
        DELETE                  && delete the record.
        PACK
    ENDIF
ENDIF                           && Return to main menu.
DEACTIVATE WINDOW cover
CLOSE DATABASES
RETURN
```

Before the user can delete an account, the account must be located. The FINDACCT procedure accomplishes that task. If the procedure finds a record with the needed account number, the dBASE IV function FOUND( ) is set to .T., and the @...SAY...GETs display the record on-screen. The command CLEAR GETS releases the GETs so that the program will not pause to let the user edit those fields. The user is then prompted to confirm the deletion. If the user presses Y, the record is deleted.

If the program does not find the record in FINDACCT, FOUND( ) is set to .F., and the program does not execute the lines that display the screen.

Finding a Customer Record

FINDACCT is a procedure that locates an account by the account number (ACCT_NO). The procedure is written so that both the Edit and Delete modules can use it. By placing code that can be accessed from more than one module in a module by itself, you avoid repeating the code. This method keeps the program smaller and contributes to speedier execution. A listing of FINDACCT is shown in figure 13.12.

Fig. 13.12.

The procedure to find a record.

```
PROCEDURE FINDACCT
* Both the edit and delete modules use this same code to set the
* record pointer on a chosen record.
STORE SPACE(5) TO v_acct
* Initialize a variable to hold the search key. GET the variable
* in the same place as the format on-screen. When the format
* file takes over the screen, changes look smoother because the
* user's entry never leaves the screen or moves.

@ 6,24 SAY " ACCT #: " GET v_acct PICTURE "XXXXX"
READ
SEEK v_acct
* Remember that the file was opened in the calling module.
IF EOF()
* If the record is not in the file, inform reader.
     @8,24 SAY "SORRY THAT ACCOUNT NOT FOUND"
     WAIT SPACE(24)+ "PRESS ANY KEY TO CONTINUE"
ENDIF
RETURN
* Notice that if a record is found, nothing is displayed
* on-screen. But the record pointer is located on the record
* whose key (acct_no) matched what the user typed.
```

When FINDACCT is called, the user is prompted to enter an account number. The procedure assigns the number entered to the memory variable v _ acct. The SEEK command then searches the index TAG to find a matching entry in the file. If a match is found, the record pointer is positioned on that record's data. If no match is found, the record pointer falls to the end of file, and a message is displayed that states the record does not exist.

Editing Customer Records

The module EDITACCT is shown in figure 13.13. This procedure also uses the FINDACCT procedure to find the record the user wants to edit. (Notice that FINDACCT is called both by EDITACCT and by DELTACCT.) When the account is found, the procedure uses the format file ACCOUNT.FMT to display the data fields. The READ command makes the program pause so that the user can make changes to the record's information. When the user finishes the edit and saves the record to the file, the procedure passes control back to the menu.

Fig. 13.13.

The procedure to edit a record.

```
PROCEDURE EDITACCT
USE ACCOUNTS ORDER TAG ACCT_NO
ACTIVATE WINDOW cover
DO FINDACCT
IF FOUND()
    SET FORMAT TO ACCOUNT.FMT
* You can't use CLEAR GETS with a format file, but you can use
* READ.
    READ
    CLOSE DATABASES
ENDIF
DEACTIVATE WINDOW cover
RETURN
```

To modify the record, use the editing keystrokes described in previous chapters. When you finish editing, press Ctrl-End or Enter in the last field to return to the menu. If you do not need to modify the record, press Esc to return to the menu.

Printing a Customer List

The MAILLIST program module prints a mailing list of all the addresses in ACCOUNTS.DBF. You can construct and order the mailing list by one of three search keys: account number, state, or zip code. A third POPUP menu is displayed so that the user can make a choice (see fig. 13.14).

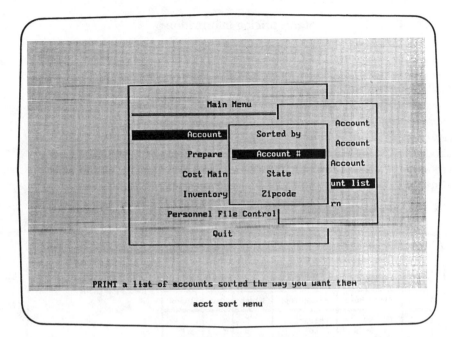

Fig. 13.14.
The sorting
menu for the
mailing list
program.

Once the user makes a choice, the DO CASE construct changes the order of the file. This command picks the appropriate index tag to make active. Each of the records in the data file is then printed in turn.

Creating and Printing an Invoice

The second major data management function—billing—includes preparing and printing invoices for sales. Invoicing requires using multiple files and defining relationships between those files by indexing.

In this particular case, you need five files to create an invoice:

INVOICE.DBF	Holds the base information of the invoice
SALE.DBF	Holds the individual items purchased
STOCKS.DBF	Stores inventory information

COSTS.DBF   Stores pricing information

ACCOUNTS.DBF   Stores customer information

In order to use this application, you will need to create the
INVOICE.DBF and SALE.DBF databases to store the information for the
invoices. The database structures for INVOICE.DBF and SALE.DBF are
shown in figures 13.15 and 13.16, respectively. The structure of
ACCOUNTS.DBF is shown in figure 13.6. The structures of STOCKS. DBF
and COSTS.DBF were shown in Chapter 12. The first function of the
module is to open the files and request an account number and an
invoice number from the user. The screen appears as shown in
figure 13.17.

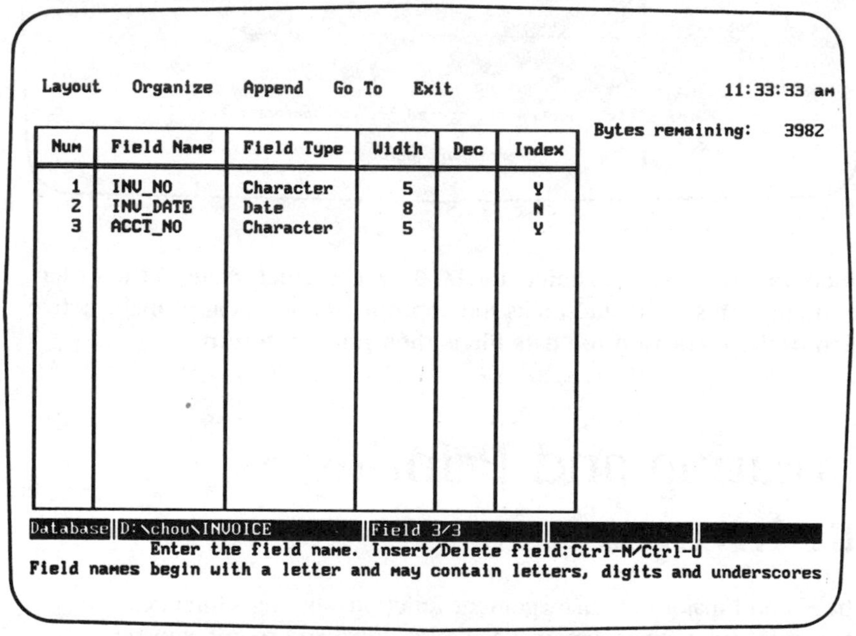

Fig. 13.15.

*The database
structure for
INVOICE.DBF.*

| Layout | Organize | Append | Go To | Exit | | | 11:33:33 am |

Bytes remaining: 3982

Num	Field Name	Field Type	Width	Dec	Index
1	INV_NO	Character	5		Y
2	INV_DATE	Date	8		N
3	ACCT_NO	Character	5		Y

Database D:\chou\INVOICE   Field 3/3
            Enter the field name. Insert/Delete field:Ctrl-N/Ctrl-U
Field names begin with a letter and may contain letters, digits and underscores

Once the program verifies that the account number exists, the program
accepts entries for the items being sold. After the user enters each item,
a prompt asks whether the user will enter other items (see fig. 13.18).
INVOICE.PRG performs these tasks (see fig. 13.19).

```
 Layout   Organize   Append   Go To   Exit                    11:36:05 am

                                              Bytes remaining:     3951

   ┌─────┬──────────────┬──────────────┬───────┬─────┬───────┐
   │ Num │ Field Name   │ Field Type   │ Width │ Dec │ Index │
   ├─────┼──────────────┼──────────────┼───────┼─────┼───────┤
   │  1  │ INV_NO       │ Character    │   5   │     │   Y   │
   │  2  │ STOCK_NO     │ Character    │  12   │     │   N   │
   │  3  │ MODEL_NO     │ Character    │  10   │     │   N   │
   │  4  │ QTY_ORDERD   │ Numeric      │   5   │  0  │   N   │
   │  5  │ QTY_SHIPED   │ Numeric      │   5   │  0  │   N   │
   │  6  │ QTY_BO       │ Numeric      │   5   │  0  │   N   │
   │  7  │ UNIT_PRICE   │ Numeric      │   7   │  2  │   N   │
   │     │              │              │       │     │       │
   │     │              │              │       │     │       │
   │     │              │              │       │     │       │
   │     │              │              │       │     │       │
   └─────┴──────────────┴──────────────┴───────┴─────┴───────┘
 Database D:\chou\SALE                    Field 7/7
           Enter the field name.  Insert/Delete field:Ctrl-N/Ctrl-U
 Field names begin with a letter and may contain letters, digits and underscores
```

Fig. 13.16.

The database structure for SALE.DBF.

```
             >>>>>>>>>> INVOICE <<<<<<<<<<

             Invoice what account?   ▭

             Use what invoice number?  ▭
```

Fig. 13.17.

The prompts for the invoice program.

```
                                         Caps

             >>>>>>>>>> INVOICE <<<<<<<<<<

   Account #: 1003
        Name: ACE SUPERVISION
     Address: 2345 COLUMBIA ST.
              VANCOUVER, WA  98664

                                  Invoice #: 21354
                                  Sales Date: 06/02/89
 ==========================================================================
        Enter stock nuber of item to sell:  ST-A1-19P-A1

        Enter the Quantity needed:    2

        WOULD YOU LIKE TO ENTER ANOTHER ITEM?  ▮
```

Fig. 13.18.

Completing an invoice.

```
* invoice.prg
ACTIVATE WINDOW cover
USE INVOICE ORDER inv_no
* Open five files, each in their own area.
SELECT 2
USE SALE ORDER inv_no
SELECT 3
USE STOCKS ORDER stock_no
SELECT 4
USE COSTS ORDER stock_no
SELECT 5
USE ACCOUNTS ORDER acct_no

SELECT 1
* Go to the first work area.
STORE SPACE(5) TO v_acct,v_invno
* Set up holding variables.
@2,Ø SAY CENT_STR(">>>>>>>>>> INVOICE  <<<<<<<<<<<",8Ø)
@5,25 SAY "Invoice what account? " GET v_acct
@7,25 SAY "Use what invoice number? " GET v_invno
READ
* Display the screen and accept entry for variables.
SELECT 5
* Go to accounts and look for this entry.
SEEK v_acct
IF EOF()
* If entries don't exist, state why the program ends.
   @12,25 SAY "That account is not on file."
   WAIT SPACE(25)+"Press any key to continue..."
   CLOSE DATABASES
   CLEAR
   DEACTIVATE WINDOW cover
   RETURN
ENDIF
@4,Ø CLEAR      && If the account exists, display the information
                && on-screen in a header.
@5,1Ø SAY "Account #: " +ACCOUNTS->ACCT_NO
@6,1Ø SAY "     Name: " +ACCOUNTS->ACCT_NAME
@7,1Ø SAY "  Address: " +ACCOUNTS->ADDRESS
@8,1Ø SAY "          " +TRIM(ACCOUNTS->CITY)+ ", " + STATE +;
   " "+ ZIP
```

Fig. 13.19—continued

```
@10,50 SAY "Invoice #: " + v_invno
@11,50 SAY "Sale Date: " + DTOC(DATE())
@12,3 SAY REPLICATE("=",70)
SELECT 1                        && Go to the invoice file and
APPEND BLANK                    && create a new record. Fill the
REPLACE INV_NO WITH v_invno     && record with some of the needed
                                && information.

REPLACE INV_DATE WITH DATE()
REPLACE ACCT_NO WITH v_acct     && This record is the anchor
                                && whenever you want to print or
                                && re-create the invoice.

SELECT 2                        && Select the invoice items file.
DO WHILE .T.                    && Start a loop to enter all the
                                && sale items.
    STORE SPACE(12) TO v_stock     && Clear variable.
    @ 14, 15 SAY "Enter stock number of item to sell: " ;
      GET v_stock
    READ            && Accept entry and see if it's a stock
    SELECT 4        && item. Then find the cost.
    SEEK v_stock    && You should add error messages to
                    && this procedure.
    SELECT 3
    SEEK v_stock
    SELECT 2
    APPEND BLANK
* Create a new item record and fill it with stock and cost
* information.
    REPLACE SALE->STOCK_NO WITH STOCKS->STOCK_NO
    REPLACE SALE->MODEL_NO WITH STOCKS->MODEL_NO
    REPLACE SALE->UNIT_PRICE WITH COSTS->DLR_COST
    REPLACE SALE->INV_NO WITH v_invno
    @ 16, 15 SAY "Enter the Quantity needed: " GET SALE->QTY_ORDERD
    READ
    DO CASE
* If the number ordered is more that what's on hand, change the
* backorder and ordering information to put more on order.
        CASE QTY_ORDERD > STOCKS->ON_HAND
            REPLACE QTY_SHIPED WITH STOCKS->ON_HAND
            REPLACE STOCKS->ON_HAND WITH 0
```

Fig. 13.19—concluded

```
                REPLACE QTY_BO WITH (SALE->QTY_ORDERD - SALE->QTY_SHIPED)
                REPLACE STOCKS->ON_ORDER WITH ;
                (STOCKS->ON_ORDER + (SALE->QTY_ORDERD - SALE->QTY_SHIPED))
* If there are enough on hand, do these calculations.
            CASE QTY_ORDERD <= STOCKS->ON_HAND
                REPLACE SALE->QTY_SHIPED WITH SALE->QTY_ORDERD
                REPLACE STOCKS->ON_HAND WITH STOCKS->ON_HAND - SALE->QTY_ORDERD
                REPLACE QTY_BO WITH Ø
        ENDCASE
        STORE ' ' TO conf          && Determine whether more
                                   && items exist.
        @ 18, 15 SAY "WOULD YOU LIKE TO ENTER ANOTHER ITEM? " GET conf
        READ
        IF UPPER(conf) = 'Y'       && If so, clear the bottom of the
            @14,Ø CLEAR            && screen and repeat the code.
            LOOP
        ELSE
            DO PRINTINV            && If there are no more items,
                                   && print the invoice.

            EXIT                   && Leave the loop, clean up, and
                                   && end.

        ENDIF
ENDDO
CLOSE DATABASES
EJECT
SET DEVICE TO SCREEN
DEACTIVATE WINDOW cover
RETURN
```

Notice that a PROCEDURE command is not included at the top of the file—the DO command that calls the program specifies a file name. When the application is compiled, dBASE IV automatically converts this code into a procedure.

After the user enters all the items and answers No to the prompt WOULD YOU LIKE TO ENTER ANOTHER ITEM?, the next step is to print the invoice.

Because all the items in the invoice are indexed by the invoice number, the items are grouped together in the file. Printing all the invoice items is a simple matter of putting the record pointer on the first one and printing the information. When the information is printed, skip to the next record and test to see that the invoice number is still the same in the new record. If so, repeat the process. If you have processed all the items, print the total and return to the calling module. The procedure that prints the invoice is shown in figure 13.20.

Fig. 13.20.

The procedure to print invoices.

```
PROCEDURE PRINTINV
* Remember that the record pointer is still positioned on the
* base invoice record and on the account information.
STORE Ø TO LINE, total
SET DEVICE TO PRINT
* Initialize variables and turn on printing.
@LINE+1,1Ø SAY "Account #:  " +ACCOUNTS->ACCT_NO
* Print the header.
@LINE+2,1Ø SAY "     Name:  " +ACCOUNTS->ACCT_NAME
@LINE+3,1Ø SAY "  Address:  " +ACCOUNTS->ADDRESS
@LINE+4,1Ø SAY "            " +TRIM(ACCOUNTS->CITY) + ;
                   ", " + ACCOUNTS->STATE + "  " + ACCOUNTS->ZIP
@LINE+6,5Ø SAY "Invoice #:  " + v_invno
@LINE+7,5Ø SAY "Sale Date:  " + DTOC(DATE())
@LINE+8,3 SAY REPLICATE("=",7Ø)
@LINE+9,3 SAY "STOCK NUMBER    MODEL #   ORDERED    SHIPPED    R/ORDER    "+;
              "UNIT PRICE   TOTAL"
STORE LINE +1Ø TO LINE
SELECT 2      && Make the items file active.
SEEK v_invno  && V_invno holds the current invoice number.
              && Find the first item.
IF EOF()      && If you reach the end of the file, you have a
   RETURN     && BIG problem. System may crash.
ENDIF

DO WHILE .T.
* You should have at least one record. Open a loop to handle all
* the items you may have.
    @LINE+1,3 SAY STOCK_NO
    @LINE+1,18 SAY MODEL_NO
    @LINE+1,3Ø SAY STR(QTY_ORDERD,3,Ø)
    @LINE+1,4Ø SAY STR(QTY_SHIPED,3,Ø)
    @LINE+1,5Ø SAY STR(QTY_BO,3,Ø)
```

Fig. 13.20—continued

```
     @LINE+1,57 SAY STR(UNIT_PRICE,7,2)
     @LINE+1,67 SAY STR(UNIT_PRICE*QTY_ORDERD,7,2)
     STORE  total + (QTY_ORDERD * UNIT_PRICE) TO total
* Update the total and the line number.
     STORE LINE + 1 TO LINE
     SKIP
* Move the record pointer.
     IF EOF() .OR. INV_NO <> v_invno
* If the invoice number is not the same and the program reaches
* the end of the file, print the total.
        @LINE+2,53 SAY "GRAND TOTAL: " + STR(total,8,2)
        EXIT
     ENDIF
ENDDO
RETURN    && Return to calling module.
```

Once the invoice is printed, the module returns to the main menu.

Creating the Cost Maintenance Submenu

When the user selects **Cost Maintenance** from the main menu, a POPUP menu appears, allowing the user to add, delete, or edit the information on the costs of items. The menu is shown in figure 13.21.

Essentially, this module is the same as the Account Billing module. Only the names of the data files and the FORMAT file change. Otherwise, the module is nearly an exact copy, using the same logic as the Account Billing module. See the program listing at the end of the chapter for the exact code. Compare the listing with the Account Billing code to see the similarities between the modules.

Duplicating the code shows you how you can apply code you have already written to other modules or applications just by changing the files that the module uses.

The one change made in this module is the EDIT command found in the EDITCOST procedure. In the Account Billing module, the READ command

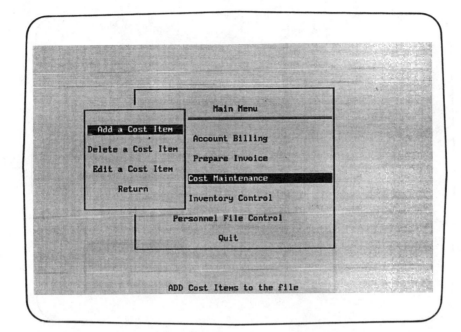

Fig. 13.21.

*The Cost
Maintenance
menu.*

performs this task. The difference in the way the two modules work is simply that the EDIT command skips the record pointer to the next record in the index. To terminate the edit, the user needs to press Esc.

Creating the Inventory Submenu

The inventory control module allows a user to add, delete, and edit items in the inventory file (STOCKS.DBF). The menu that appears when the user chooses **Inventory Control** from the main menu is shown in figure 13.22.

Two of the modules, ADDITEM and PRINTITM, are especially worth noting. The other two follow the same basic construction as their companion procedures in **Account Billing** and **Cost Maintenance**.

Fig. 13.22.

*The Inventory
Control menu.*

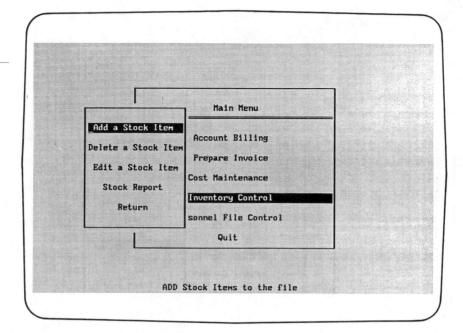

```
                         Main Menu

 ┌──────────────────────┐
 │ Add a Stock Item     │  Account Billing
 │ Delete a Stock Item  │
 │                      │  Prepare Invoice
 │ Edit a Stock Item    │
 │                      │  Cost Maintenance
 │ Stock Report         │
 │                      │  Inventory Control
 │ Return               │
 └──────────────────────┘  sonnel File Control

                           Quit


             ADD Stock Items to the file
```

Adding Inventory Items

ADDITEM.PRG uses the @...SAY...GET commands to append a new data
record to the database file STOCKS.DBF. The program checks the
existing records to see if the stock number entered by the user is a
duplicate of one already on file. Data management applications that deal
with customer or inventory listings usually require this check. Just as you
do not want two customers to have the same account number, you do
not want an item number to be duplicated.

ADDITEM uses a user-defined function as a part of the VALID clause of the
GET. The GET accepts the stock number from the user (see fig. 13.23).

When ADDITEM is called, it initializes a variable that "stands in" for the
stock number, opens the STOCKS data file, and prompts the user to enter
a stock number. The stock number controls the new item being added to
the inventory. The STK_CHK( ) function compares that number against the
other stock numbers on file (see fig. 13.24).

```
PROCEDURE ADDITEM
v_stock = SPACE(12)              && Initialize a search key as
                                 && a variable.
USE STOCKS ORDER TAG STOCK_NO && Open indexed file.
ACTIVATE WINDOW cover
@ 2,16 TO 16,60 DOUBLE           && Set the screen and do a GET on
                                 && the variable.

@ 4,26 SAY "STOCK #:"
@ 4,36 GET v_stock PICTURE "XXXXXXXXXXXX"  VALID STK_CHK() ;
     ERROR "That number is already used."
READ
* The error message is displayed if the VALID function
* returns .F.

IF v_stock = SPACE(12)           && These lines allow the user to
     CLOSE DATABASES             && quit if the user decides not to
                                 && add a record.
     DEACTIVATE WINDOW cover     && Delete the bad entry.
     RETURN
ENDIF

@ 6,26 SAY "MODEL #:"
@ 6,36 GET model_no PICTURE "XXXXXXXXXX"
@ 8,21 SAY "MANUFACTURER: "
@ 8,35 GET mfg PICTURE "XXXXXXXXX"
@ 10,22 SAY "OPTIONS:"
@ 10,32 GET options PICTURE "XXXXXXXXXXXXXXXXXXXXXXXXXX"
@ 12,22 SAY "ON HAND:"
@ 12,32 GET on_hand PICTURE "999"
@ 14,22 SAY "ON ORDER:"
@ 14,32 GET on_order PICTURE "999"
READ
* The record pointer is on the new record, and the key field has
* been replaced. Accept entry.
CLOSE DATABASES
DEACTIVATE WINDOW cover
RETURN
```

Fig. 13.23.

The procedure to add a stock item.

Fig. 13.24.

*A function to
check for
duplicate stock
numbers.*

```
FUNCTION stk_chk
* If the key is unique, append a blank record, fill in the stock
* number, and let the calling module take the rest of the
* information.
PRIVATE ret_val        && Initialize a variable to hold the
                       && return value.
ret_val = .F.          && Set the value.
IF v_stock = SPACE(12)
* If the entry is spaces, accept it.
    ret_val = .T.      && The calling module terminates on this
ENDIF                  && condition.
SEEK v_stock           && Look for a match.
IF EOF()               && If no match, accept the entry.
    APPEND BLANK       && Append a new record and fill in stock_no.
    REPLACE STOCK_NO WITH v_stock
    ret_val = .T.
ENDIF
RETURN ret_val         && Return the value.

PROCEDURE DELTITEM
STORE ' ' TO conf
USE STOCKS ORDER TAG STOCK_NO
ACTIVATE WINDOW cover
DO FINDITEM
IF FOUND()
    @ 2,16 TO 16,60 DOUBLE
    @ 4,26 SAY "STOCK #:"
    @ 4,36 GET stock_no PICTURE "XXXXXXXXXXXX"
    @ 6,26 SAY "MODEL #:"
    @ 6,36 GET model_no PICTURE "XXXXXXXXXX"
    @ 8,21 SAY "MANUFACTURER: "
    @ 8,35 GET mfg PICTURE "XXXXXXXXX"
    @ 10,22 SAY "OPTIONS:"
    @ 10,32 GET options PICTURE "XXXXXXXXXXXXXXXXXXXXXXXXXX"
    @ 12,22 SAY "ON HAND:"
    @ 12,32 GET on_hand PICTURE "999"
    @ 14,22 SAY "ON ORDER:"
    @ 14,32 GET on_order PICTURE "999"
    CLEAR GETS
    @20, 24 SAY "DELETE THIS RECORD? " GET CONF
```

Fig. 13.24—continued

```
      READ
      IF UPPER(conf) = 'Y'
            DELETE
            PACK
      ENDIF
ENDIF
DEACTIVATE WINDOW cover
CLOSE DATABASES
RETURN
```

The function first creates a private variable to hold the return value of the function. This return value determines if the GET can terminate. If the value returned is False (.F.), the error message is displayed, and the entry is not accepted.

The next line is included to show you how to change the value of a variable, but in reality is unneeded. Creating variables with the PRIVATE command automatically gives the variable a value of .F.

You need to leave the user a way out of the procedure; therefore, the STK_CHK() function lets a value of 12 spaces go through successfully, knowing that the code in the calling module looks for that value and terminates without adding a record if the value of v_stock is all spaces.

Next, the function does a seek to see if another stock item has a matching stock number. If one exists, the return value remains False (.F.); this triggers the ERROR clause in the @...SAY...GET command, and the user is prompted for a different entry.

If, however, the record pointer falls to the end of the file (no other record has the same value in the stock number field), a new record is added to the file, and the stock number is replaced with the entered value (v_stock). The return value of the function is set to True (.T.), and the function ends.

If the return value of the function is True (.T.), the ADDITEM module must check for one of two possible conditions. If the value of the entry is all spaces, the module terminates without adding a record to the file. If the user types an entry with a unique stock number, a record is added. The function next takes the entry from the user for the other fields in the record, closes the file, and returns to the menu.

Because the user-defined function appends the record and puts the entry value into the stock number field, the user cannot edit the stock number. If the user is allowed to edit the stock number field, an error can be introduced into the data because the new number would not be checked, and duplicates could be included.

With the STOCKS.FMT file, the user can introduce an error into the data file. Because each of these modules allows the user to edit the STOCK _ NO field, a duplicate entry can slip into the data file by accident (see fig. 13.25).

Fig. 13.25.

The stocks format file.

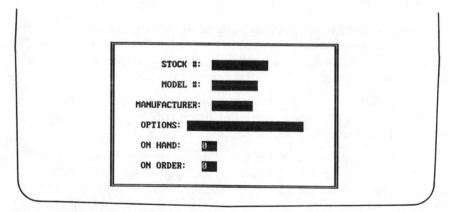

One of the best ways to combat duplicate entries is to use @...SAY...GET commands as the only method for taking keyboard entry. Have the user enter a value into a variable, and design a user-defined function that returns an error (a False return value) if the record pointer falls to the end of the file when the entry is used in a SEEK command.

Once you have established that a record exists, do not allow entry on the stock number field with an @...SAY...GET command. Usually, you should leave the earlier entry on-screen while the other fields are being edited, just in case the user is distracted. The user can look on-screen and see which item was being edited.

Printing a List of Inventory Items

The final procedure in the INVNMENU module is a procedure that prints a report. This report details the amount of each item in stock and the worth of those items. This report shows you how to handle reports that might take more than one page.

Figure 13.26 shows the procedure that produces the report.

Fig. 13.26.

The procedure to print a report.

```
PROCEDURE PRINTITM
* This procedure shows how to coordinate reports using more than
* one file.

USE STOCKS ORDER TAG STOCK_NO && Open the files with the
                               && proper indexing.
SELECT 2
USE COSTS ORDER TAG STOCK_NO
SELECT 1                       && Return to original work area.
ACTIVATE WINDOW cover
CLEAR
@12,10 SAY "Make sure printer is on and ready..........."
WAIT ' '
@12,10 CLEAR TO 13,78
@12,10 SAY "PRINTING the inventory report........."
STORE 0 TO total,line
* Initialize variables to hold the numeric total and line and
* page numbers.
page = 1
SET DEVICE TO PRINT        && Redirect @...SAYs to printer.

* This set of commands prints a page header.
@line+1,5 SAY CENT_STR("CURRENT INVENTORY REPORT    PAGE:    "+STR(page,2,0),75)
@line+2,5 SAY CENT_STR("AS OF: "+ DTOC(DATE()),75)
@line+4,5 SAY "   STOCK #    MODEL #      ON HAND   UNIT COST      VALUE"
@line+5,5 SAY REPLICATE("=",75)
STORE line+6 TO line       && Keep an eye on the counter.
                           && Begin the loop.
DO WHILE .T.
    IF line > 55           && This code determines page breaks.
        EJECT              && If needed, insert a new sheet of,
        STORE 0 TO line    && paper, reset line number,
        page = page + 1    && increment page number, and
                           && print a new header.
        @line+1,5 SAY CENT_STR("CURRENT INVENTORY REPORT            "+;
                   "PAGE: "+STR(page,2,0),75)
```

Fig. 13.26—continued

```
            @line+2,5 SAY CENT_STR("AS OF: "+ DTOC(DATE()),75)
            @line+4,5 SAY "   STOCK #    MODEL #     ON HAND          "+;
                      "UNIT COST    VALUE"
            @line+5,5 SAY REPLICATE("=",75)
            STORE line+6 TO line
        ENDIF
        STORE STOCK_NO TO lk        && Set the stock_no for this
                                    && record in memory.
        @line+1,3 SAY STOCK_NO      && Print the base information.
        @line+1,17 SAY STOCK_NO
        @line+1,31 SAY STR(ON_HAND,4,0)
        SELECT 2                    && Move to the other work area
        SEEK lk                     && and search for record.
        IF EOF()                    && If the record doesn't exist,
                                    && print a message.
            @line+1,45 SAY "NO COST RECORD FOUND"
        ELSE                        && If the record does exist, print
                                    && information and update total.
            @line+1,44 SAY STR(OUR_COST,7,2)
            @line+1,54 SAY STR(OUR_COST * A->ON_HAND,8,2)
            STORE total + (OUR_COST * A->ON_HAND) TO total
        ENDIF
        STORE line +1 TO line
* Placed here this command works for both sides of the IF.
        SELECT 1                    && Return to original work area
        SKIP                        && and move record pointer.
        IF EOF()                    && If you reach the end of file,
                                    && print the total.
            @line+3,54 SAY " ======="
            @line+4,28 SAY "Total value of inventory: "+ STR(total,8,2)
            EXIT            && Exit loop.
        ENDIF
ENDDO       && If you don't reach EOF(), the loop is automatic.
EJECT       && Once you hit the end of file, quit.
SET DEVICE TO SCREEN
CLOSE DATABASES
DEACTIVATE WINDOW cover
RETURN
```

This report requires information out of the COSTS and STOCKS data files. The program opens the files and displays a prompt on-screen that tells the user to make sure that the printer is ready. This reminder is a good idea because a printer-not-ready error can cause unexpected things to happen to the screen and the report when the user chooses retry.

The report initializes three variables to hold the line number, the total for the end of the report, and the page number. A header is printed on the first page, and a loop starts that makes each item in the STOCKS file print a line in the report.

An IF construct at the top of this loop determines how many lines of text are printed on the current page. If there are more than 55 lines, the sheet is ejected; the line is reset to 0; the page number is incremented; and a header is printed on the new page. Again, this printing occurs only when a page break occurs.

Before printing the information about the current item, the procedure places the stock number into a variable called lk (short for look). The procedure uses this variable as the argument for the SEEK command.

The next section of code illustrates a weakness in the design of the data structures used in this application. You must position the record pointer in another file to find the cost of the item. A better structure would be to include the cost information in the STOCKS data file. At least, in terms of this report, the structure makes printing the data easier. STOCKS and COSTS share the same keys and a one-to-one relationship. For every record in the STOCKS file, there should be a corresponding entry in the COSTS file with the same stock and model numbers. It is more efficient to have both the cost and inventory information in one data file.

Once the program has done the seek, a test determines the existence of an entry in the COSTS data file that corresponds with the current record in STOCKS. If there is no matching record, an error message is printed. This message alerts the user that a record is missing. The program does not update totals. The program counts items in the inventory but does not assign them any worth, making the grand total inaccurate.

If a matching record is found, the pricing information is printed along with a calculation that multiplies the cost by the number of the item on hand. (A-> is an alias that means the file is open in work area 1.) After the calculation is printed, the running total is updated.

The procedure selects the first work area again, and the record pointer advances to the next record. If the program reaches the end of file, the total is printed, and the procedure is terminated. If, however, another record needs to be printed, the ENDDO loops the program and repeats the process for every record in the STOCKS data file.

Developing the Employee Tracking Modules

This part of the program has been left for you to finish on your own. You need to include four procedures as part of this module: adding new employees, deleting employee records, editing employee information, and printing a list of current employees.

The structure of the employee file is shown in figure 13.27.

Fig. 13.27.

The structure of the employee file.

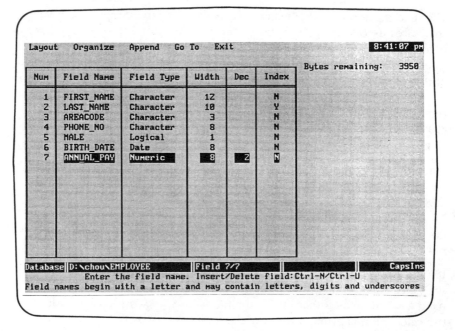

Num	Field Name	Field Type	Width	Dec	Index
1	FIRST_NAME	Character	12		N
2	LAST_NAME	Character	10		Y
3	AREACODE	Character	3		N
4	PHONE_NO	Character	8		N
5	MALE	Logical	1		N
6	BIRTH_DATE	Date	8		N
7	ANNUAL_PAY	Numeric	8	2	N

Layout   Organize   Append   Go To   Exit   8:41:07 pm

Bytes remaining: 3950

Database D:\chou\EMPLOYEE   Field 7/7   CapsIns
Enter the field name. Insert/Delete field:Ctrl-N/Ctrl-U
Field names begin with a letter and may contain letters, digits and underscores

Using this structure and the procedures you have seen in the other modules, construct a menu that pops up when the user chooses the Employee bar from the main menu. Create the modules for adding, deleting, and editing employee records; then attach those procedures to the menu using a DO CASE construct.

To learn one last way of getting information to the printer quickly and easily, create a report format similar to the one shown in figure 13.28.

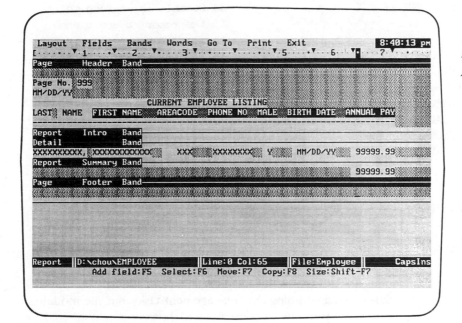

Fig. 13.28.

A report format.

Sending output to the printer is simple when you have a .FRM file. The example in figure 13.29 is fairly general; you can use this example in almost any situation, changing only the name of the report form.

By using the procedures and programs in previous modules and the code for printing standard dBASE IV report forms, you should be able to complete the application quickly.

Fig. 13.29.

Printing the report.

```
ACTIVATE WINDOW cover
CLEAR
@1Ø,1Ø SAY "Make sure that the printer is on and ready......."
WAIT SPACE(1Ø)+"Press any key to begin printing."
CLEAR
@1Ø,1Ø SAY " Printing the employee list....."
USE EMPLOYEE ORDER TAG LAST_NAME    && Open the data file and
                                    && set the index.
SET CONSOLE OFF                     && Disable the screen so that
                                    && the report doesn't echo
                                    && on-screen.
REPORT FORM EMPLOYEE TO PRINT       && Set the report into motion.
SET CONSOLE ON                      && Restore normal screen
                                    && handling.
EJECT                               && Push printer to new page.
DEACTIVATE WINDOW cover
CLOSE DATABASES
RETURN
```

Chapter Summary

This chapter has presented an integrated database management system. The example includes five major data management functions. The program modules presented in this chapter are not necessarily the most efficient means of accomplishing data management tasks, but the modules are designed to show you how to construct and execute a menu-driven data management system made up of single-task modules. Remember that programming is an art rather than a science: you should apply your talent to designing a system more suitable to your needs. The next chapter explores the Structured Query Language (SQL) capability of dBASE IV.

Program Listings

MAINMENU.PRG

```
***** Program: MAINMENU.PRG *****

* This is the top level program. All other functions and
* procedures in this application are a branch off this tree.
* As each command takes place a comment explains what the
* command does. When you type the program code for yourself,
* you can leave out the comments.

* Set up the environment the way you want it.

SET TALK OFF         && Turn off dBASE messages.
SET STATUS OFF       && Turn off the STATUS bar.
SET SCOREBOARD OFF   && Turn off line Ø at top of screen.
IF ISCOLOR()         && If the user has a color monitor,
     SET COLOR TO GR+/B,N/BG      && set screen colors.
     SET COLOR OF BOX TO GR+/B
ENDIF                && If the user does not have a color
                     && video card, don't change anything.

* These next few lines are all that the MASTER program does.
* You activate a POPUP menu that provides the branches to
* everything else. When the user makes a choice, the CASE
* statement in M_CASES deactivates the menu. From there, the
* program terminates back to the dot prompt.

CLEAR           && Clear the screen.
DO MEN_CREA     && Perform a subroutine that defines all the
                && menus for the application.

ACTIVATE POPUP main
CLEAR           && Once the menu is deactivated, erase the
                && screen, clear memory variables, and
CLEAR ALL       && close data files.
RETURN          && Go back to dot prompt; QUIT goes to DOS.

PROCEDURE M_CASES
                && When the program says DO M_CASES, all the
                && commands from here to the end are compiled and
                && executed.
```

MAINMENU.PRG—*continues*

```
DO CASE          && Begin comparison CASE by CASE.
     CASE BAR() = 5               && If the chosen BAR is 5,
          ACTIVATE POPUP acct && pop the acct menu into place.
     CASE BAR() = 7               && If the chosen BAR is 7,
          DO INVOICE               && do the invoicing routine.
     CASE BAR() = 9
          ACTIVATE POPUP cost
     CASE BAR() = 11
          ACTIVATE POPUP STOK
     CASE BAR() = 13
          DO EMPLMENU
     CASE BAR() = 15
          DEACTIVATE POPUP      && Deactivate the main menu.
          RETURN
ENDCASE

FUNCTION CENT_STR   && This user-defined function centers
                      *   a character string across a specified
                      *   number of spaces.
PARAMETERS string, stlen      && Accept the string to be padded,
                               && and the width of the area into
                               && which the string goes.
PRIVATE ret_val, lpad, tpad   && Isolate these variables from
                               && any others even if they have
                               && the same name.
lpad = INT((stlen - LEN(LTRIM(TRIM(string))))/2)

* The preceding command trims all the blanks in front of and behind
* a string and subtracts that many spaces from the total width.
* You know how many spaces to pad the front.

tpad = stlen - lpad - LEN(LTRIM(TRIM(string)))
* Trailing pad (tpad) is the number of spaces left.
* Now assemble the return value.
ret_val = SPACE(lpad) + LTRIM(TRIM(string)) + SPACE(tpad)
RETURN ret_val
* Send the value back to the calling module.

* End of MAINMENU.PRG
```

MAINMENU.PRG—*concluded*

MEN_CREA.PRG

```
***** Program: MEN_CREA.PRG *****

* This part of the program designs and defines each of the menus.
* Remember that BAR numbers are relative to the top line of the
* menu.

* Define the opening menu.
* Initialize a POPUP menu with a box around it from 4,20 to
* 20,60 for the main menu area.

DEFINE POPUP main FROM 4,20 TO 20,60

* The following commands center a string inside the box on
* lines relative to the top line of the menu.
* The SKIP argument tells the POPUP to display the lines
* in the box, but don't let the light bar stop there.

DEFINE BAR 2 OF main PROMPT CENT_STR("Main Menu",39) SKIP
DEFINE BAR 3 OF main PROMPT REPLICATE(CHR(205),39) SKIP
* CHR(205) is the ASCII double line character.

* The following message commands are divided with the semicolon.
* The MESSAGE is displayed whenever the light bar is positioned
* on that PROMPT.

DEFINE BAR 5 OF main PROMPT CENT_STR("Account Billing",37) ;
   MESSAGE "ADD, EDIT and DELETE Customer Accounts, PRINT mailing list"
DEFINE BAR 7 OF main PROMPT CENT_STR("Prepare Invoice",37) ;
   MESSAGE "Prepare and print an invoice"
DEFINE BAR 9 OF main PROMPT CENT_STR("Cost Maintenance",37) ;
   MESSAGE "Perform maintenance of wholesale costs, lists and files"
DEFINE BAR 11 OF main PROMPT CENT_STR("Inventory Control",37) ;
   MESSAGE "Perform tasks to keep inventory information accurate"
DEFINE BAR 13 OF main PROMPT CENT_STR("Personnel File Control",37) ;
   MESSAGE "This module is for you to build based on the other modules"
DEFINE BAR 15 OF main PROMPT CENT_STR("Quit",37) ;
   MESSAGE "Terminate this program and go back to the DOT prompt"

* Define the Account Billing menu.
* Same commands as the preceding ones, but different names and
* prompts. Notice that the POPUP frame is 6,50 to 18,70
* and that the frame is centered over the side of the main menu
* frame.  When you choose Account Billing from the main menu,
```

MEN_CREA.PRG—*continues*

```
* this menu pops up over the other. When you deactivate the
* POPUP, this menu disappears, and the main menu is reactivated.
DEFINE POPUP acct FROM 6,50 TO 18,70
DEFINE BAR  2 OF acct PROMPT CENT_STR("Add a new Account",19) ;
  MESSAGE "ADD Customer Accounts"
DEFINE BAR  4 OF acct PROMPT CENT_STR("Delete an Account",19) ;
  MESSAGE "DELETE a customer from the file"
DEFINE BAR  6 OF acct PROMPT CENT_STR("Edit an Account",19) ;
  MESSAGE "EDIT a customer Account"
DEFINE BAR  8 OF acct PROMPT CENT_STR("Print Account list",19) ;
  MESSAGE "PRINT a list of accounts sorted the way you want them"
DEFINE BAR 10 OF acct PROMPT CENT_STR("Return",19) ;
  MESSAGE "RETURN to the main menu"

* Define the Account Mailing List menu.
* This menu pops up over the Account Billing menu when you
* choose to print the mailing list.

DEFINE POPUP acml FROM 8,40 TO 16,60
DEFINE BAR  1 OF acml PROMPT CENT_STR("Sorted by ",19) SKIP
DEFINE BAR  3 OF acml PROMPT CENT_STR("Account #",19)
DEFINE BAR  5 OF acml PROMPT CENT_STR("State",19)
DEFINE BAR  7 OF acml PROMPT CENT_STR("Zipcode",19)

* Define the Costs menu.
DEFINE POPUP cost FROM 6,10 TO 16,30
DEFINE BAR  2 OF cost PROMPT CENT_STR("Add a Cost Item",19) ;
  MESSAGE "ADD Cost Items to the file"
DEFINE BAR  4 OF cost PROMPT CENT_STR("Delete a Cost Item",19) ;
  MESSAGE "DELETE a Cost item from the file"
DEFINE BAR  6 OF cost PROMPT CENT_STR("Edit a Cost Item",19) ;
  MESSAGE "EDIT a Cost Item in the file"
DEFINE BAR 8 OF cost PROMPT CENT_STR("Return",19) ;
  MESSAGE "RETURN to the main menu"

* Define the Inventory menu.
DEFINE POPUP stok FROM 6,10 TO 18,30
DEFINE BAR  2 OF stok PROMPT CENT_STR("Add a Stock Item",19) ;
  MESSAGE "ADD Stock Items to the file"
DEFINE BAR  4 OF stok PROMPT CENT_STR("Delete a Stock Item",19) ;
  MESSAGE "DELETE a Stock item from the file"
DEFINE BAR  6 OF stok PROMPT CENT_STR("Edit a Stock Item",19) ;
  MESSAGE "EDIT a Cost Item in the file"
```

MEN_CREA.PRG—*continues*

```
DEFINE BAR  8 OF stok PROMPT CENT_STR("Stock Report",19) ;
   MESSAGE "PRINT a Stock Inventory Report"
DEFINE BAR 10 OF stok PROMPT CENT_STR("Return",19) ;
   MESSAGE "RETURN to the main menu"

* Define the selections that will trigger the actions.
* When the user makes a choice from a POPUP menu, the
* following commands specify what should be done. The first
* command specifies what happens when the user makes the initial
* choice at the main menu. M_CASES is a CASE construct
* that activates one of the other menus. Each of the menus
* in turn calls a different program module that evaluates which
* choice was made. Each of the programs has a CASE construct
* similar to M_CASES that it uses to determine branching.

ON SELECTION POPUP main DO M_CASES
ON SELECTION POPUP acct DO ACCTMENU
ON SELECTION POPUP acml DO MAILLIST
ON SELECTION POPUP cost DO COSTMENU
ON SELECTION POPUP stok DO INVNMENU

* Define a window to cover menus while entry takes place.
* When POPUPs are active, the screen becomes property of the POPUP.
* You need a window where you can display things on-screen.
* When you DEACTIVATE the window, the menus are again visible,
* and nothing you have painted is visible any more.
* You also can create windows that pop in and cover only part
* of the screen.
* NONE means no border

DEFINE WINDOW cover FROM 0,0 TO 24,79 NONE

* END OF MEN_CREA.PRG
```

ACCTMENU.PRG

```
***** Program: ACCTMENU.PRG *****

* Making a choice from the acct menu calls this module
* whose first task is to decide which option was taken.
DO CASE
     CASE BAR() = 2 && BAR() is a function that remembers the
                    && number of the last chosen light-bar.
```

ACCTMENU.PRG—continues

```
            DO ADDACCT        && If it's 2, DO this procedure.
      CASE BAR() = 4
            DO DELTACCT
      CASE BAR() = 6
            DO EDITACCT
      CASE BAR() = 8              && If the user chooses this
            ACTIVATE POPUP acml && selection, display a menu
                                 && to choose sort order.
      CASE BAR() = 1Ø            && If the choice is return, this
                                 && command erases the last
            DEACTIVATE POPUP     && activated POPUP and returns
            RETURN               && to the calling module.
ENDCASE

PROCEDURE ADDACCT                       && Add customers to the file.
USE ACCOUNTS ORDER TAG ACCT_NO          && Open account file and set
                                        && the index order to acct_no
                                        && TAG.
ACTIVATE WINDOW cover                   && Pop up a blank screen over
                                        && the menu.
SET FORMAT TO ACCOUNT.FMT               && Activate a screen format.
APPEND                                  && Take user entry.
CLOSE DATABASES                         && Store date and close
DEACTIVATE WINDOW cover                 && window.
RETURN                                  && Return to the main menu.

PROCEDURE DELTACCT
STORE ' ' TO conf     && Create a variable to confirm deletion.
USE ACCOUNTS ORDER TAG ACCT_NO          && Open the data indexed for
                                        && the SEEK.
ACTIVATE WINDOW cover                   && Pop up a blank screen.

* See the following code to see how FINDACCT works. FOUND() is a
* logical function that will be .T. if the record is found.

DO FINDACCT
IF FOUND()
* If the record is located, use the @...SAY...GETS to display a
* copy of the record on-screen in the same format.
      @ 3,31 SAY " Customer Accounts"
      @ 4,19 TO 16,6Ø DOUBLE
      @ 6,24 SAY " ACCT #: "
      @ 6,33 GET acct_no PICTURE "XXXXX"
```

ACCTMENU.PRG—*continues*

```
    @ 8,26 SAY " NAME: "
    @ 8,33 GET acct_name PICTURE "XXXXXXXXXXXXXXXXXXXXX"
    @ 9,24 SAY "ADDRESS:"
    @ 9,33 GET address PICTURE "XXXXXXXXXXXXXXXXXXXXX"
    @ 10,33 GET city PICTURE "XXXXXXXXXXXX"
    @ 10,46 GET state PICTURE "XX"
    @ 10,49 GET zip PICTURE "XXXXX"
    @ 12,24 SAY "     PHONE: "
    @ 12,36 GET area_code PICTURE "XXX"
    @ 12,39 GET phone_no PICTURE "XXXXXXXX"
    @ 14,28 SAY "MAXIMUM CREDIT: "
    @ 14,44 GET max_credit PICTURE "99999.99"
    CLEAR GETS
* This command cancels all the GETS so that the program does not
* stop for entry.
    @20, 24 SAY "DELETE THIS RECORD? " GET CONF
* Confirm deletion.
    READ
    IF UPPER(conf) = 'Y'      && If last key pressed is Y,
        DELETE                && delete the record.
        PACK
    ENDIF
ENDIF                         && Return to main menu.
DEACTIVATE WINDOW cover
CLOSE DATABASES
RETURN

PROCEDURE EDITACCT
USE ACCOUNTS ORDER TAG ACCT_NO
ACTIVATE WINDOW cover
DO FINDACCT
IF FOUND()
    SET FORMAT TO ACCOUNT.FMT
* You can't use CLEAR GETS with a format file, but you can use
* READ.
    READ
    CLOSE DATABASES
ENDIF
DEACTIVATE WINDOW cover
RETURN
```

ACCTMENU.PRG—*continues*

```
PROCEDURE FINDACCT
* Both the edit and delete modules use this same code to set the
* record pointer on a chosen record.
STORE SPACE(5) TO v_acct
* Initialize a variable to hold the search key. GET the variable
* in the same place as the format on-screen. When the format
* file takes over the screen, changes look smoother because the
* user's entry never leaves the screen or moves.

@ 6,24 SAY " ACCT #: " GET v_acct PICTURE "XXXXX"
READ
SEEK v_acct
* Remember that the file was opened in the calling module.
IF EOF()
* If the record is not in the file, inform reader.
     @8,24 SAY "SORRY THAT ACCOUNT NOT FOUND"
     WAIT SPACE(24)+ "PRESS ANY KEY TO CONTINUE"
ENDIF
RETURN
* Notice that if a record is found, nothing is displayed
* on-screen. But the record pointer is located on the record
* whose key (acct_no) matched what the user typed.

PROCEDURE MAILLIST
USE ACCOUNTS
DO CASE          && Depending on the selection, choose the
                 && appropriate TAG from the .MDX file.
    CASE BAR() = 3
         SET ORDER TO ACCT_NO
    CASE BAR() = 5
         SET ORDER TO STATE
    CASE BAR() = 7
         SET ORDER TO ZIP
ENDCASE
ACTIVATE WINDOW cover
@12,10 SAY "Make sure printer is on and ready.........."
WAIT ' '
@12,10 CLEAR         && Clear lines 12 to 24.  Get rid of prompt.
@12,10 SAY "PRINTING the mailing list.........."
SET PRINT ON         && Send ?'s to the printer.
? CENT_STR("COMPANY MAILING LIST",80)
                     && Center a header at top of page.
```

ACCTMENU.PRG—continues

```
DO WHILE .NOT. EOF()          && Start a LOOP that prints each
     ? SPACE(5)+ACCT_NAME      && record's information until the
     ? SPACE(5)+ADDRESS        && record pointer reaches the end
                               && the file.
     ? SPACE(5)+TRIM(CITY) +", "+ STATE +" "+ ZIP
     ?
     ?                 && ? with no argument skips blank lines.
     SKIP              && Position record pointer to next record.
ENDDO                  && As long as the DO WHILE's condition remains
                       && .T., the LOOP is automatic.
SET PRINT OFF   && When EOF(), turn off the printing.
EJECT           && Push to next sheet in printer.
DEACTIVATE WINDOW cover
DEACTIVATE POPUP
RETURN

* END OF ACCTMENU.PRG
```

INVOICE.PRG

```
***** Program: INVOICE.PRG *****

ACTIVATE WINDOW cover
USE INVOICE ORDER inv_no
* Open five files, each in their own area.
SELECT 2
USE SALE ORDER inv_no
SELECT 3
USE STOCKS ORDER stock_no
SELECT 4
USE COSTS ORDER stock_no
SELECT 5
USE ACCOUNTS ORDER acct_no

SELECT 1
* Go to the first work area.
STORE SPACE(5) TO v_acct,v_invno
* Set up holding variables.
@2,0 SAY CENT_STR(">>>>>>>>>> INVOICE  < < < < < < < < < <",80)
@5,25 SAY "Invoice what account? " GET v_acct
@7,25 SAY "Use what invoice number? " GET v_invno
READ
* Display the screen and accept entry for variables.
```

INVOICE.PRG—*continues*

```
SELECT 5
* Go to accounts and look for this entry.
SEEK v_acct
IF EOF()
* If entries don't exist, state why the program ends.
   @12,25 SAY "That account is not on file."
   WAIT SPACE(25)+"Press any key to continue..."
   CLOSE DATABASES
   CLEAR
   DEACTIVATE WINDOW cover
   RETURN
ENDIF
@4,0 CLEAR        && If the account exists, display the information
                  && on-screen in a header.
@5,10 SAY "Account #: " +ACCOUNTS->ACCT_NO
@6,10 SAY "      Name: " +ACCOUNTS->ACCT_NAME
@7,10 SAY "   Address: " +ACCOUNTS->ADDRESS
@8,10 SAY "            " +TRIM(ACCOUNTS->CITY)+ ", " + STATE +;
   " "+ ZIP
@10,50 SAY "Invoice #: " + v_invno
@11,50 SAY "Sale Date: " + DTOC(DATE())
@12,3 SAY REPLICATE("=",70)
SELECT 1                    && Go to the invoice file and
APPEND BLANK                && create a new record. Fill the
REPLACE INV_NO WITH v_invno && record with some of the needed
                            && information.
REPLACE INV_DATE WITH DATE()
REPLACE ACCT_NO WITH v_acct  && This record is the anchor
                             && whenever you want to print or
                             && re-create the invoice.

SELECT 2                     && Select the invoice items file.
DO WHILE .T.                 && Start a loop to enter all the
                             && sale items.
      STORE SPACE(12) TO v_stock   && Clear variable.
      @ 14, 15 SAY "Enter stock number of item to sell: " ;
       GET v_stock
      READ          && Accept entry and see if it's a stock
      SELECT 4      && item. Then find the cost.
      SEEK v_stock  && You should add error messages to
                    && this procedure.
```

INVOICE.PRG—*continues*

```
      SELECT 3
      SEEK v_stock
      SELECT 2
      APPEND BLANK
* Create a new item record and fill it with stock and cost
* information.
      REPLACE SALE->STOCK_NO WITH STOCKS->STOCK_NO
      REPLACE SALE->MODEL_NO WITH STOCKS->MODEL_NO
      REPLACE SALE->UNIT_PRICE WITH COSTS->DLR_COST
      REPLACE SALE->INV_NO WITH v_invno
      @ 16, 15 SAY "Enter the Quantity needed: " GET SALE->QTY_ORDERD
      READ
      DO CASE
* If the number ordered is more that what's on hand, change the
* backorder and ordering information to put more on order.
         CASE QTY_ORDERD > STOCKS->ON_HAND
              REPLACE QTY_SHIPED WITH STOCKS->ON_HAND
              REPLACE STOCKS->ON_HAND WITH Ø
              REPLACE QTY_BO WITH (SALE->QTY_ORDERD - SALE->QTY_SHIPED)
              REPLACE STOCKS->ON_ORDER WITH ;
              (STOCKS->ON_ORDER + (SALE->QTY_ORDERD - SALE->QTY_SHIPED))
* If there are enough on hand, do these calculations.
         CASE QTY_ORDERD <= STOCKS->ON_HAND
              REPLACE SALE->QTY_SHIPED WITH SALE->QTY_ORDERD
              REPLACE STOCKS->ON_HAND WITH STOCKS->ON_HAND - SALE->QTY_ORDERD
              REPLACE QTY_BO WITH Ø
      ENDCASE
      STORE ' ' TO conf          && Determine whether more
                                 && items exist.
      @ 18, 15 SAY "WOULD YOU LIKE TO ENTER ANOTHER ITEM? " GET conf
      READ
      IF UPPER(conf) = 'Y'       && If so, clear the bottom of the
          @14,Ø CLEAR            && screen and repeat the code.
          LOOP
      ELSE
          DO PRINTINV            && If there are no more items,
                                 &&  print the invoice.
          EXIT                   && Leave the loop, clean up, and
                                 && end.
      ENDIF
```

INVOICE.PRG—*continues*

```
ENDDO
CLOSE DATABASES
EJECT
SET DEVICE TO SCREEN
DEACTIVATE WINDOW cover
RETURN

PROCEDURE PRINTINV
* This is the code to print the invoice. Remember that the
* record pointer is still positioned on the base invoice record
* and on the account information.
STORE Ø TO LINE, total
SET DEVICE TO PRINT
* Initialize variables and turn on printing.
@LINE+1,1Ø SAY "Account #: " +ACCOUNTS->ACCT_NO
* Print the header.
@LINE+2,1Ø SAY "      Name: " +ACCOUNTS->ACCT_NAME
@LINE+3,1Ø SAY "   Address: " +ACCOUNTS->ADDRESS
@LINE+4,1Ø SAY "           " +TRIM(ACCOUNTS->CITY) + ;
                    ", " + ACCOUNTS->STATE + "  " + ACCOUNTS->ZIP
@LINE+6,5Ø SAY "Invoice #: " + v_invno
@LINE+7,5Ø SAY "Sale Date: " + DTOC(DATE())
@LINE+8,3 SAY REPLICATE("=",7Ø)
@LINE+9,3 SAY "STOCK NUMBER   MODEL #   ORDERED   SHIPPED   "+;
               "R/ORDER   UNIT PRICE   TOTAL"
STORE LINE +1Ø TO LINE
SELECT 2       && Make the items file active.
SEEK v_invno   && V_invno holds the current invoice number.
               && Find the first item.
IF EOF()       && If you reach the end of the file, you have a
   RETURN      && BIG problem. System may crash.
ENDIF

DO WHILE .T.
* You should have at least one record. Open a loop to handle all
* the items you may have.
     @LINE+1,3 SAY STOCK_NO
     @LINE+1,18 SAY MODEL_NO
     @LINE+1,3Ø SAY STR(QTY_ORDERD,3,Ø)
     @LINE+1,4Ø SAY STR(QTY_SHIPED,3,Ø)
     @LINE+1,5Ø SAY STR(QTY_BO,3,Ø)
     @LINE+1,57 SAY STR(UNIT_PRICE,7,2)
```

INVOICE.PRG—*continues*

```
    @LINE+1,67 SAY STR(UNIT_PRICE*QTY_ORDERD,7,2)
    STORE  total + (QTY_ORDERD * UNIT_PRICE) TO total
* Update the total and the line number.
    STORE LINE + 1 TO LINE
    SKIP
* Move the record pointer.
    IF EOF() .OR. INV_NO <> v_invno
* If the invoice number is not the same and the program reaches
* the end of the file, print the total.
        @LINE+2,53 SAY "GRAND TOTAL: " + STR(total,8,2)
        EXIT
    ENDIF
ENDDO
RETURN    && Return to calling module.

*   END OF INVOICE.PRG
```

COSTMENU.PRG

```
***** Program: COSTMENU.PRG *****

* When the cost menu is active and the user makes a choice, this
* CASE is executed just as it was in ACCTMENU.PRG. Only the
* procedure names are changed.

DO CASE
    CASE BAR() = 2
        DO ADDCOST
    CASE BAR() = 4
        DO DELTCOST
    CASE BAR() = 6
        DO EDITCOST
    CASE BAR() = 8
        DEACTIVATE POPUP
        RETURN
ENDCASE

PROCEDURE ADDCOST            && Just like adding accounts.
USE COSTS ORDER STOCK_NO
ACTIVATE WINDOW cover
SET FORMAT TO COSTS.FMT
APPEND
CLOSE DATABASES
```

COSTMENU.PRG—*continues*

```
DEACTIVATE WINDOW cover
RETURN

PROCEDURE DELTCOST
STORE ' ' TO conf
USE COSTS ORDER STOCK_NO
ACTIVATE WINDOW cover
DO FINDCOST
IF FOUND()
     @ 4,33 SAY "Cost Information"
     @ 5,18 TO 17,62 DOUBLE
     @ 7,34 SAY "STOCK #:"
     @ 7,43 GET stock_no PICTURE "XXXXXXXXXXXX"
     @ 9,34 SAY "MODEL #:"
     @ 9,43 GET model_no PICTURE "XXXXXXXXXX"
     @ 11,31 SAY "LIST PRICE:"
     @ 11,43 GET list_price PICTURE "9999.99"
     @ 13,32 SAY "OUR PRICE: "
     @ 13,43 GET our_price PICTURE "9999.99"
     @ 15,30 SAY "DEALER COST:"
     @ 15,43 GET dlr_cost PICTURE "9999.99"
     CLEAR GETS
     @20, 24 SAY "DELETE THIS RECORD? " GET CONF
     READ
     IF UPPER(conf) = 'Y'
          DELETE
          PACK
     ENDIF
ENDIF
DEACTIVATE WINDOW cover
CLOSE DATABASES
RETURN

PROCEDURE EDITCOST
USE COSTS ORDER STOCK_NO
ACTIVATE WINDOW cover
DO FINDCOST
IF FOUND()
     SET FORMAT TO COSTS.FMT
     EDIT
     CLOSE DATABASES
ENDIF
```

COSTMENU.PRG—*continues*

```
DEACTIVATE WINDOW cover
RETURN

PROCEDURE FINDCOST
STORE SPACE(12) TO v_stok
@ 7,26 SAY "Enter a STOCK #:"
@ 7,43 GET v_stok PICTURE "XXXXXXXXXXXX"
READ
SEEK v_stok
IF EOF( )
    @8,24 SAY "SORRY THAT STOCK # NOT FOUND"
    WAIT SPACE(24)+ "PRESS ANY KEY TO CONTINUE"
ENDIF
RETURN

* From this program, you can see that you can use code you've
* already written code as a template. Then you can vary only the
* data and the user prompts. Besides cutting down on development
* time, using prefabricated modules makes for a more consistent
* user interface.

* END OF COSTMENU.PRG
```

INVNMENU.PRG

```
***** Program: INVNMENU.PRG *****
* The highlights of this program include the add feature which
* uses a user_defined function to prevent duplicate entries,
* and the report section which uses two files simultaneously.

DO CASE                 && No changes here except the names.
    CASE BAR( ) = 2
        DO ADDITEM
    CASE BAR( ) = 4
        DO DELTITEM
    CASE BAR( ) = 6
        DO EDITITEM
    CASE BAR( ) = 8
        DO PRINTITM
    CASE BAR( ) = 10
        DEACTIVATE POPUP
        RETURN
ENDCASE
```

INVNMENU.PRG—*continues*

```
PROCEDURE ADDITEM
v_stock = SPACE(12)                 && Initialize a search key as
                                    && a variable.
USE STOCKS ORDER TAG STOCK_NO && Open indexed file.
ACTIVATE WINDOW cover
@ 2,16 TO 16,60 DOUBLE              && Set the screen and do a GET on
                                    && the variable.

@ 4,26 SAY "STOCK #:"
@ 4,36 GET v_stock PICTURE "XXXXXXXXXXX"  VALID STK_CHK() ;
       ERROR "That number is already used."
READ
* The error message is displayed if the VALID function
* returns .F.

IF v_stock = SPACE(12)             && These lines allow the user to
     CLOSE DATABASES               && quit if the user decides not to
                                    && add a record.
     DEACTIVATE WINDOW cover       && Delete the bad entry.
     RETURN
ENDIF

@ 6,26 SAY "MODEL #:"
@ 6,36 GET model_no PICTURE "XXXXXXXXXX"
@ 8,21 SAY "MANUFACTURER: "
@ 8,35 GET mfg PICTURE "XXXXXXXXX"
@ 10,22 SAY "OPTIONS:"
@ 10,32 GET options PICTURE "XXXXXXXXXXXXXXXXXXXXXXXXXX"
@ 12,22 SAY "ON HAND:"
@ 12,32 GET on_hand PICTURE "999"
@ 14,22 SAY "ON ORDER:"
@ 14,32 GET on_order PICTURE "999"
READ
* The record pointer is on the new record, and the key field has
* been replaced. Accept entry.
CLOSE DATABASES
DEACTIVATE WINDOW cover
RETURN

FUNCTION stk_chk
* If the key is unique, append a blank record, fill in the stock
* number, and let the calling module take the rest of the
* information.
```

```
PRIVATE ret_val        && Initialize a variable to hold the
                       && return value.
ret_val = .F.          && Set the value.
IF v_stock = SPACE(12)
* If the entry is spaces, accept it.
     ret_val = .T.   && The calling module terminates on this
ENDIF                  && condition.
SEEK v_stock           && Look for a match.
IF EOF()               && If no match, accept the entry.
     APPEND BLANK    && Append a new record and fill in stock_no.
     REPLACE STOCK_NO WITH v_stock
     ret_val = .T.
ENDIF
RETURN ret_val         && Return the value.

PROCEDURE DELTITEM
STORE ' ' TO conf
USE STOCKS ORDER TAG STOCK_NO
ACTIVATE WINDOW cover
DO FINDITEM
IF FOUND()
     @ 2,16 TO 16,60 DOUBLE
     @ 4,26 SAY "STOCK #:"
     @ 4,36 GET stock_no PICTURE "XXXXXXXXXXXX"
     @ 6,26 SAY "MODEL #:"
     @ 6,36 GET model_no PICTURE "XXXXXXXXXX"
     @ 8,21 SAY "MANUFACTURER: "
     @ 8,35 GET mfg PICTURE "XXXXXXXXX"
     @ 10,22 SAY "OPTIONS:"
     @ 10,32 GET options PICTURE "XXXXXXXXXXXXXXXXXXXXXXXXXX"
     @ 12,22 SAY "ON HAND:"
     @ 12,32 GET on_hand PICTURE "999"
     @ 14,22 SAY "ON ORDER:"
     @ 14,32 GET on_order PICTURE "999"
     CLEAR GETS
     @20, 24 SAY "DELETE THIS RECORD? " GET CONF
     READ
     IF UPPER(conf) = 'Y'
          DELETE
          PACK
     ENDIF
```

INVNMENU.PRG—continues

```
ENDIF
DEACTIVATE WINDOW cover
CLOSE DATABASES
RETURN

PROCEDURE EDITITEM
USE STOCKS ORDER TAG STOCK_NO
ACTIVATE WINDOW cover
DO FINDITEM
IF FOUND( )
     SET FORMAT TO STOCKS.FMT
     READ
     CLOSE DATABASES
ENDIF
DEACTIVATE WINDOW cover
RETURN

PROCEDURE FINDITEM
STORE SPACE(12) TO v_stok
@ 4,16 SAY "Enter the STOCK #:" GET v_stok PICTURE "XXXXXXXXXXXX"
READ
SEEK v_stok
IF EOF( )
     @8,24 SAY "SORRY THAT ITEM NOT FOUND"
     WAIT SPACE(24)+ "PRESS ANY KEY TO CONTINUE"
ENDIF
RETURN

PROCEDURE PRINTITM
* This procedure shows how to coordinate reports using more than
* one file.

USE STOCKS ORDER TAG STOCK_NO && Open the files with the
                                 && proper indexing.
SELECT 2
USE COSTS ORDER TAG STOCK_NO
SELECT 1                        && Return to original work area.
ACTIVATE WINDOW cover
CLEAR
@12,1Ø SAY "Make sure printer is on and ready..........."
WAIT ' '
@12,1Ø CLEAR TO 13,78
@12,1Ø SAY "PRINTING the inventory report........."
```

INVNMENU.PRG—*continues*

```
STORE Ø TO total,line
* Initialize variables to hold the numeric total and line and
* page numbers.
page = 1
SET DEVICE TO PRINT        && Redirect @...SAYs to printer.

* This set of commands prints a page header.
@line+1,5 SAY CENT_STR("CURRENT INVENTORY REPORT      PAGE:    "+STR(page,2,Ø),75)
@line+2,5 SAY CENT_STR("AS OF: "+ DTOC(DATE()),75)
@line+4,5 SAY "   STOCK #     MODEL #       ON HAND   UNIT COST     VALUE"
@line+5,5 SAY REPLICATE("=",75)
STORE line+6 TO line        && Keep an eye on the counter.
                            && Begin the loop.
DO WHILE .T.
    IF line > 55            && This code determines page breaks.
        EJECT              && If needed, insert a new sheet of,
        STORE Ø TO line     && paper, reset line number,
        page = page + 1     && increment page number, and
                            && print a new header.
        @line+1,5 SAY CENT_STR("CURRENT INVENTORY REPORT              PAGE: "+;
                +STR(page,2,Ø),75)
        @line+2,5 SAY CENT_STR("AS OF: "+ DTOC(DATE()),75)
        @line+4,5 SAY "   STOCK #     MODEL #       ON HAND            UNIT COST"+;
                "VALUE"
        @line+5,5 SAY REPLICATE("=",75)
        STORE line+6 TO line
    ENDIF
    STORE STOCK_NO TO lk    && Set the stock_no for this
                            && record in memory.
    @line+1,3 SAY STOCK_NO   && Print the base information.
    @line+1,17 SAY STOCK_NO
    @line+1,31 SAY STR(ON_HAND,4,Ø)
    SELECT 2                && Move to the other work area
    SEEK lk                 && and search for record.
    IF EOF()                && If the record doesn't exist,
                            && print a message.
        @line+1,45 SAY "NO COST RECORD FOUND"
```

INVNMENU.PRG—*continues*

```
        ELSE                    && If the record does exist, print
                                && information and update total.
            @line+1,44 SAY STR(OUR_PRICE,7,2)
            @line+1,54 SAY STR(OUR_PRICE * A->ON_HAND,8,2)
            STORE total + (OUR_PRICE * A->ON_HAND) TO total
        ENDIF
        STORE line +1 TO line
* Placed here this command works for both sides of the IF.
        SELECT 1                && Return to original work area
        SKIP                    && and move record pointer.
        IF EOF()                && If you reach the end of file,
                                && print the total.
            @line+3,54 SAY " ======="
            @line+4,28 SAY "Total value of inventory: "+ STR(total,8,2)
            EXIT                && Exit loop.
        ENDIF
    ENDDO   && If you don't reach EOF(), the loop is automatic.
    EJECT   && Once you hit the end of file, end.
    SET DEVICE TO SCREEN
    CLOSE DATABASES
    DEACTIVATE WINDOW cover
    RETURN

    * END OF INVNMENU.PRG
```

14

dBASE IV SQL

In the past decade, personal computers have become an integral part of the American work place. To a certain extent, however, these machines have existed in a vacuum; the data that is collected and created on these machines often is trapped on the hard drive or on floppy disks, unavailable to anyone else in the organization. Local area networks have done much to improve communications within work groups of personal computers, but have only just begun to open the door to information stored on larger computer systems.

Structured Query Language (SQL), a database management language developed by IBM in the 1970s, is primarily intended for use on mainframe and minicomputers. Much of the success of SQL lies in the fact that, unlike most database management languages, a user only describes the needed data, and SQL develops the required procedures to deliver the data.

dBASE IV SQL is a link between individual, stand-alone personal computers; local area networks; minicomputers; and mainframes. Over the next few years, a number of products will be introduced that form a bridge between personal computers and their larger cousins. Ashton-Tate and Microsoft jointly have developed a database server that provides advantages for running data management programs on local area networks.

This chapter looks into the future—a time when personal computers will become extensions of larger computer systems. dBASE IV SQL is one of the first steps in that direction.

This chapter is not meant as a comprehensive discussion of SQL. Instead, this chapter is an introduction to a complex subject. An overview of the different parts of SQL is presented so that you can understand the concepts involved. The chapter also offers a foundation of information you can use to integrate SQL into your dBASE programs.

Accessing SQL

You can follow two modes of operation for dBASE IV SQL: interactive mode (you type commands one at a time at the SQL dot prompt) or program mode (SQL commands are "embedded" within a program).

Using SQL from the SQL Prompt

Command:

SET SQL ON
Allows you to access SQL commands in interactive mode.

To access SQL commands in interactive mode, you must use the dBASE IV SET command to SET SQL ON. Then the dot prompt becomes an SQL dot prompt (see fig. 14.1).

Fig. 14.1.

The SQL dot prompt.

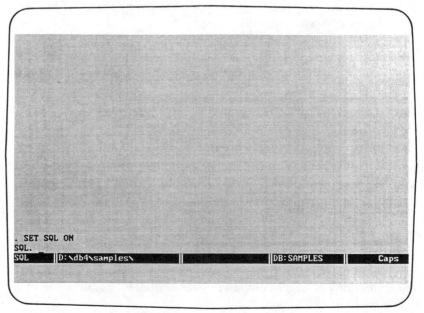

```
. SET SQL ON
SQL.
SQL    ||D:\db4\samples\              ||          ||DB:SAMPLES ||      Caps
```

Once you SET SQL ON and are at the SQL dot prompt, you can enter SQL commands. One difference between SQL commands and native dBASE IV commands (most of which are available in SQL mode) is that you must terminate or follow SQL commands with a semicolon (;).

Using SQL in Programs

Programs that use SQL commands are similar to program files that do not contain SQL commands. You create both with the MODIFY COMMAND command, but program files that contain SQL components must have the extension .PRS rather than the extension .PRG. When you use MODIFY COMMAND, you must specify the .PRS extension on the command line.

The following creates a .PRS file called SAMPLE:

```
MODIFY COMMAND SAMPLE.PRS
```

Programs do not use the command SET SQL ON. When the compiler sees a program file with the extension .PRS, the compiler assumes that SQL commands are present and automatically turns on SQL.

All SQL commands must be terminated with a semicolon. Non-SQL program files use the semicolon to indicate that a long command has been broken into two lines. You can continue to use this convention in SQL program files; the dBASE compiler recognizes the difference between a native dBASE IV command and a dBASE IV SQL command.

Command:
MODIFY COMMAND
Creates SQL programs when used with a .PRS extensioin.

Defining SQL Objects

An SQL database application consists of many different types of objects that combine to define the structure of the data. Among these SQL objects are database tables, views, synonyms, indexes, and so on. Each of these objects plays a different part in maintaining the integrity and structure of an SQL database application.

Creating SQL Databases

Command:
CREATE DATABASE
Creates a new SQL database.

SQL uses databases as the overall shell; this shell is built around all the information related to an SQL application. When you use the CREATE DATABASE command to create a new database, a new subdirectory is created on your hard drive to store all the objects within the database. Figure 14.2 shows the command to create a new database called NEW_INFO. Figure 14.3 shows a file listing of the system tables created in the new subdirectory.

Each of these newly created files controls some aspect of an SQL database and its objects. You can use several commands to manipulate databases:

CREATE DATABASE	Creates new SQL databases.
START DATABASE	Opens SQL databases that already exist.
STOP DATABASE	Closes and writes to disk an open SQL database.
DROP DATABASE	Erases an SQL database from the disk.
SHOW DATABASE	Provides a listing of all the available SQL databases.

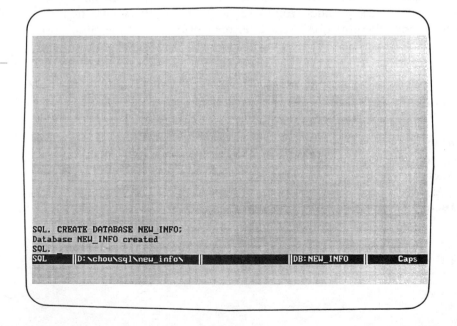

Fig. 14.2.

Creating a new database.

```
SQL. CREATE DATABASE NEW_INFO;
Database NEW_INFO created
SQL. _
SQL     ||D:\chou\sql\new_info\ ||              ||DB:NEW_INFO ||        Caps
```

```
D:\CHOU\SQL>DIR NEW_INFO

 Volume in drive D is DATA_TRAIN
 Directory of  D:\CHOU\SQL\NEW_INFO

 .            <DIR>      11-19-88    2:28p
 ..           <DIR>      11-19-88    2:28p
 SYSTABLS DBF     1094   11-19-88    2:28p
 SYSCOLS  DBF     5586   11-19-88    2:28p
 SYSIDXS  DBF      418   11-19-88    2:28p
 SYSKEYS  DBF      226   11-19-88    2:28p
 SYSVIEWS DBF      258   11-19-88    2:28p
 SYSVDEPS DBF      270   11-19-88    2:28p
 SYSSYNS  DBF      163   11-19-88    2:20p
 SYSAUTH  DBF     1156   11-19-88    2:28p
 SYSCOLAU DBF      226   11-19-88    2:28p
 SYSTIMES DBF      427   11-19-88    2:28p
 SYSTIME  MEM       41   11-19-88    2:28p
        13 File(s)   7641088 bytes free

D:\CHOU\SQL>_
```

Fig. 14.3.

The system tables for a new SQL database.

Defining SQL Data Tables

In SQL, a table is the basic structure used to store data. In this respect, a table is similar to a .DBF file. You use different terminology, however, to refer to an SQL table. What dBASE IV users think of as a record is called a row in an SQL table; each of the fields is called a column. An SQL table can contain as many as 255 columns (fields) and up to 1 billion rows (records). The maximum size of the row is 4,000 bytes.

You use the CREATE TABLE command to define a data structure within an SQL database. Several different data types, not part of the normal dBASE IV .DBF file structure, are available to you in SQL. These data types, numeric in nature, emulate number types normally used in assembly language and certain other programming languages. SQL data types include the following:

Command:
CREATE TABLE
Defines a table in an SQL database.

SMALLINT   Small integer. This data type can hold up to 6 digits. Legal data values range from –99,999 to 99,999.

INTEGER	Large integer. This data type can hold a number up to 16 digits long with no digits to the right of the decimal point. Legal values range from $-999,999,999,999,999$ to $9,999,999,999,999,999$.
DECIMAL(x,y)	Use this data type for fixed decimal point numbers with x digits to the left of and y digits to the right of the decimal point. Legal values for x range from 1 to 19; legal values for y range from 0 to 18. The value of y cannot be larger than $x-1$.
NUMERIC(x,y)	This data type holds a fixed decimal point with x total digits to the left of and y digits to the right of the decimal point. This data type differs from decimal only in that y cannot be more than $x-2$.
FLOAT(x,y)	Floating point number. This data type holds a floating point number with x digits to the left of and y digits to the right of the decimal point. Legal values for x range from 1 to 19; legal values for y range from 0 to 18. y cannot be more than $x-2$.
	Using this data type, you can store numbers as small as 1×10^{-308} or as large as $9 \times 10^{+307}$. You enter floating number data types using scientific notation—for example, $-1.85E +35$.
CHAR(n)	Use this data type to store character strings up to 254 characters in length. (n) specifies the length of CHAR.
DATE	Use this data type to hold dates in the format specified by SET DATE and SET CENTURY. The default is the same as the normal dBASE IV native date format, mm/dd/yy.
LOGICAL	Use this data type to store Boolean values (true or false). Legal values for this field include .T., .t., .Y., .y., .F., .f., .N., and .n.

Table 14.1 shows the structure of a data table to hold information about customers on file.

Table 14.1
Structure of a Data Table

Column	Data Type	Width
ACCT	Character	5
NAME	Character	20
ADDRESS	Character	20
CITY	Character	12
STATE	Character	2
ZIP	Character	5
BEG_DAT	Date	8

Figure 14.4 shows the CREATE TABLE command used to create this table. Because the command creates a new storage unit for data, it is similar to the CREATE command in native dBASE IV.

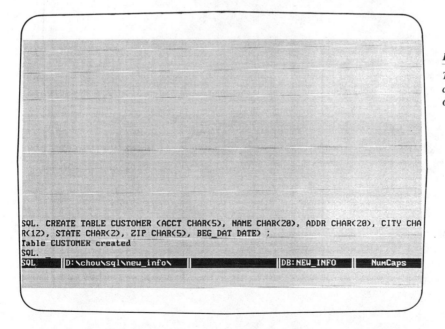

Fig. 14.4.

The commands to create the CUSTOMER table.

```
SQL. CREATE TABLE CUSTOMER (ACCT CHAR(5), NAME CHAR(20), ADDR CHAR(20), CITY CHA
R(12), STATE CHAR(2), ZIP CHAR(5), BEG_DAT DATE) ;
Table CUSTOMER created
SQL.
SQL      D:\chou\sql\new_info\              DB:NEW_INFO        NumCaps
```

Creating SQL Views

A view is a special type of table and is sometimes called a "virtual table" because it exists only in memory. A view is based on the data contained in one or more tables and is basically a subset of that data.

▶

Command:
CREATE VIEW
Defines a view that includes only the columns you want.

Suppose that, for example, you have a table with a large number of columns and often perform tasks that need to include only information from five of the columns. You can create a view that allows you to extract just the information you need. The view treats the information as if it were a full-fledged table. Figure 14.5 shows the CREATE VIEW command, which is used to define a view of the CUSTOMER table that includes only the name, state, and beginning date of customer account status.

Fig. 14.5.

Creating a view of the CUSTOMER table.

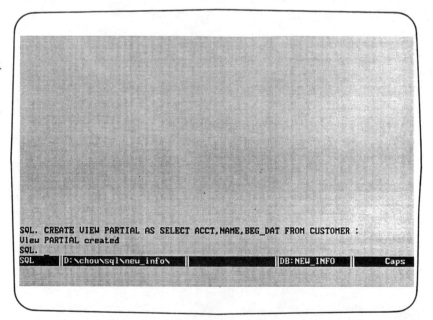

```
SQL. CREATE VIEW PARTIAL AS SELECT ACCT,NAME,BEG_DAT FROM CUSTOMER ;
View PARTIAL created
SQL.
```
```
SQL    ||D:\chou\sql\new_info\ ||              ||DB:NEW_INFO ||    Caps
```

In the CREATE VIEW command in figure 14.5, the SELECT command chooses the three columns of the CUSTOMER table and defines the view called PARTIAL. You now can use this view as if it were a table. Any changes to the data in the CUSTOMER table are reflected in the view.

Using SQL Synonyms

A synonym in SQL is used like an alias in dBASE IV. You use two commands, CREATE SYNONYM and DROP SYNONYM, to manage the use of synonyms. You name a synonym according to the same rules used for naming tables and views.

The following shows the syntax for the SYNONYM commands:

    CREATE SYNONYM <*name*>
        FOR <*table name*>;

    DROP SYNONYM <*name*>;

You would use a synonym whenever you wanted to call someone by a nickname. The following creates a synonym for James:

    CREATE SYNONYM Jim FOR James

Indexing SQL Data

You can index SQL tables in much the same way you index .DBF files. Figure 14.6 illustrates how to create an index that orders the table by the account number in the CUSTOMER table.

The commands in figure 14.6 create an index called ACT_NO. This index orders the CUSTOMER table by the account number. The argument, ASC, which appears in parentheses with the key field, specifies to sort the index in ascending order. To create an index in descending order, use the argument DESC.

Any index you create should match the way you normally work with the data in a table. When you use dBASE IV SQL, you do not specify which index to use. SQL selects what it considers to be the most efficient index to use when you retrieve data.

While you can create as many as 47 index tags per table, remember that the execution speed of many commands deteriorates as the number of indexes grows.

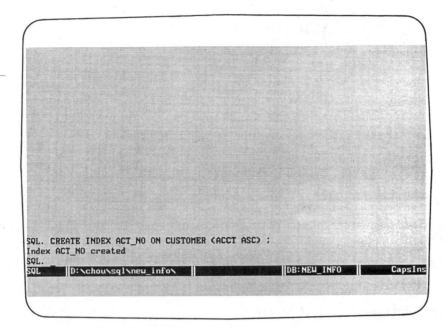

Fig. 14.6.

Indexing the CUSTOMER table.

```
SQL. CREATE INDEX ACT_NO ON CUSTOMER (ACCT ASC) ;
Index ACT_NO created
SQL. _
SQL      D:\chou\sql\new_info\              DB: NEW_INFO        CapsIns
```

Manipulating Data

SQL provides three primary commands for manipulating data in a table. You use the INSERT command to create new rows of information; you use LOAD DATA to import information from non-SQL file types; and you use UNLOAD DATA to import information from dBASE IV SQL to other data file types, including the .DBF file.

Inserting New Rows into the Table

Command:

INSERT
Places new rows into a table or view.

The INSERT command places new rows into tables and views. The syntax of the command follows:

    INSERT INTO <*Table*>
        [(<*Column List*>)]
        VALUES (<*Value List*>);

An alternative syntax allows you to substitute the values into the rows with a SELECT statement. (For more information, see the section in this chapter on the SELECT command.)

For example, to insert a row of information into the CUSTOMER table, you use the following command:

```
INSERT INTO customer
    VALUES
    ("23232","Ross Common Acres","123 Easy Street",
    "Walla Walla","Washington","98712",CTOD("03/04/89"));
```

As you can see, you must surround character values in quotation marks. To insert a date into an SQL table, use the dBASE CTOD( ) function. You can insert multiple rows into a table (usually from another table) by using a SELECT command in place of the VALUES clause.

Importing Non-SQL Data into Tables

With the LOAD DATA command, you can import non-SQL files by translating them into rows that can be added to a previously created table. The syntax for this command follows:

```
LOAD DATA FROM [path]<filename>INTO TABLE <table name>
    [[TYPE]SDF/DIF/SYLK/FW2/RPD/dBASEII/
    DELIMITED [WITH /<delimiter>];
```

LOAD DATA can read the same file formats as the dBASE IV APPEND FROM command. The supported file types are shown in table 14.2.

Command:
LOAD DATA
Imports non-SQL tables.

Table 14.2
Supported File Types

Type	Description
dBASE II	Files created with dBASE II
dBASE III, dBASE III PLUS, and dBASE IV	Data files created by other dBASE versions
RPD	Data files created in RapidFile
FWII	Files created with Framework II
SDF	System Data Format
DIF	VisiCalc data files
SYLK	Multiplan spreadsheet files
WKS	Lotus 1-2-3 spreadsheet files
DELIMITED	Delimited ASCII files

If the non-SQL file is not in the current subdirectory, you must specify the PATH. If you do not include a TYPE clause in the command, SQL assumes that you are importing data from a dBASE III or dBASE IV file.

If, for example, a .DBF file called CO_CUST has the same field structure as the columns in your SQL table, you can import the data from your .DBF file into the SQL table with the following command:

```
LOAD DATA FROM CO_CUST
     INTO TABLE customer;
```

All the records within the file CO_CUST are copied into the CUSTOMER table.

Exporting Data from Tables

Command:
UNLOAD DATA
Exports data from a table or view into a non-SQL format.

The opposite of the LOAD DATA command is the UNLOAD DATA command; this command enables you to export data from a table or view into a non-SQL format. All the file types supported by the LOAD DATA command are supported by the UNLOAD DATA command. For example, to unload the rows in the CUSTOMER table into the CO_CUST data file, you use the following command:

```
UNLOAD DATA TO CO_CUST
     FROM TABLE customer;
```

All the rows in the table are appended to the .DBF file called CO_CUST.

Selecting Data from SQL Tables

Command:
SELECT
Extracts data from one or more tables or views and creates a resu table.

The SELECT command is far and away the most powerful and potentially complex command in dBASE IV SQL. You can use the SELECT command to extract data from one or more tables or views and assemble that data into what is called a "result table," using the following syntax:

```
SELECT [ALL/DISTINCT] <column list>
     FROM <table/alias list>
     [INTO <variable list>]
     [WHERE <condition>]
     [GROUP BY <column list>]
     [HAVING <condition>]
     [UNION <additional SELECT>]
```

```
[ORDER BY <column list>]
[FOR UPDATE OF <column list>]
[SAVE TO TEMP <table> [KEEP]];
```

The individual parts of the SELECT command can be broken down in the following manner.

[ALL/DISTINCT]<column list>

The column list refers to the columns in the table you want transferred to the result table. The default condition, ALL, selects all the rows that satisfy the WHERE condition. DISTINCT, however, filters out duplicate records, providing you with a result table in which each row is unique.

FROM<table/alias list>

This clause specifies the tables and views to be used to supply the information being requested by the SELECT command.

[INTO<variable list>]

You can use this part of the SELECT command only in program files. This command specifies memory variables that will hold the selected information. The result table should be designed to have exactly one row.

[WHERE<condition>]

The WHERE clause in a SELECT command is similar to the FOR clause in the dBASE LOCATE command. This command specifies a logical condition that must be true for the row to be selected and placed in the result table.

[GROUP BY<column list>]

The GROUP BY clause allows you to arrange the rows in the result table, grouping together those rows with a common value in the column or columns specified by the GROUP BY clause. Suppose that, for example, you include the following clause in your SELECT command:

```
GROUP BY sales_per
```

The result table groups each sales person's transactions together in the result table.

[HAVING<condition>]

The HAVING clause specifies search conditions; these conditions are used to restrict row groupings in the result table. The search condition in the HAVING clause must contain an SQL aggregate function—AVG(), MAX(),

MIN( ), COUNT( ), or SUM( ). If you include a GROUP BY clause in the SELECT command, you must specify each column mentioned in the HAVING clause in the GROUP BY clause.

[UNION <*additional SELECT*>]

The UNION clause of the SELECT command allows you to nest an additional SELECT command so that the result table is a combination of two or more tables.

[ORDER BY <*column list*>]

You use the ORDER BY clause to provide a sort order for the rows in the result table.

[FOR UPDATE OF <*column list*>]

You use the FOR UPDATE OF clause only in program mode to specify columns that can be accessed later using the UPDATE WHERE CURRENT OF command. You cannot use this clause in the SELECT command if you also use the INTO, ORDER BY, or SAVE TO TEMP clauses.

[SAVE TO TEMP <*table*>[KEEP]];

You use the SAVE TO TEMP clause of the SELECT command to store the result table temporarily to a location in memory. With this command, you do not lose the data in that result table when you issue the next SELECT command.

Using SELECT To View Data

You use the SELECT command to create a result table and to display the results of the SELECT command on-screen. The most basic SELECT command displays all the rows in a table:

This command displays only those rows that are unique; duplicate rows are ignored.

You can pick and choose the columns you want to select. For instance, the following SELECT command displays the data stored in all the rows in the table, but displays only the specified columns:

```
SELECT ACCT,NAME,ZIP
     FROM customer;
```

This command is similar to the LIST and DISPLAY commands native to dBASE IV.

You also can use the SELECT command to combine two tables into one result table and display the information on-screen, as in the following example:

```
SELECT *
     FROM customer,sal_staff;
```

The result table from this command can be large. The result table contains the row from the CUSTOMER table combined with each of the rows in SAL_ STAFF. If 5 sales people are listed in sal_ staff and there are 100 customers in the CUSTOMER table, the resulting table has 500 rows—1 row for each sales person and for each customer.

Using the WHERE Clause

You use the WHERE clause in a SELECT command to include (or reject) rows in the table that do (or do not match) a specified condition. The following command selects from the SALES table all rows whose total is greater than 25.50:

```
SELECT *
     FROM sales
     WHERE total > 25.50;
```

The WHERE clause in a SELECT command is similar to the FOR clause in the dBASE LOCATE command. This clause initializes a condition that must be met in order for a row in the table to be selected and placed in the result table. You can specify multiple conditions.

You should follow most of the rules used in the IF command in native dBASE programs. Additionally, you can use the BETWEEN...AND...

optional clause to specify an acceptable range of values. Unlike native dBASE IV commands, the operators AND, OR, and NOT are not bound by periods.

For example, if you want to find the invoice number of the sales ticket where item A37-24y was sold to account number 12127, you enter the following command:

```
SELECT INV_NO
    FROM sales
    WHERE ACCT="12127" AND ITEM_NO = A37-24y;
```

In the preceding example, the result table consists of only those sales where the account number and the item number matched those specified in the WHERE clause. Unless this customer purchases large quantities of this item, the result table probably has only one row.

Combining SQL and dBASE IV Programs

You can use most dBASE IV functions in SQL mode; however, you cannot use some functions within SQL commands. Most of the dBASE IV commands will be recognized while running a program in SQL mode. Note, however, certain exceptions—for example, the USE command. You cannot use a .DBF file while executing commands in SQL mode.

You still can build applications that use SQL commands even though the application may contain commands that cannot be run in SQL mode. Any commands contained in a program file with the extension .PRS are run in SQL mode.

Those SQL program modules, however, legally can call a subroutine or other module that is saved to the disk in a .PRG program file. The DO command is recognized within SQL mode; therefore, you can use this command to call a .PRG module. Within that .PRG module, you can use any dBASE commands whether or not they are recognized in SQL mode.

Figure 14.7 displays the structure of a database file called DB4_CUST. This native dBASE file has the same structure as the CUSTOMER table in the NEW_INFO SQL database.

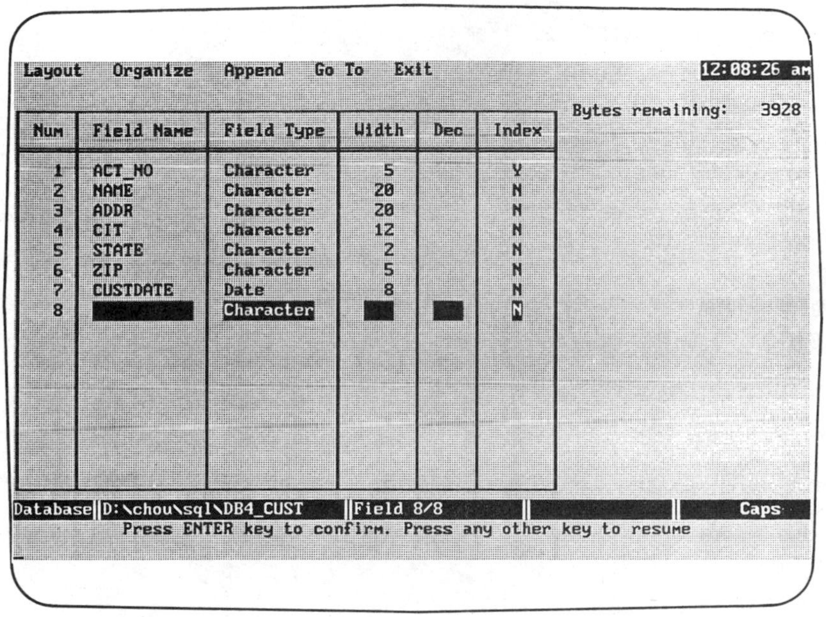

Fig. 14.7.

The structure of DB4_CUST.DBF.

A common task you encounter when writing SQL embedded commands within dBASE programs is to convert SQL data—appending the data to a dBASE IV .DBF file. Figure 14.8 shows a simple program to accomplish this task.

The programs shown in figure 14.8 are a mixture of dBASE and SQL commands. However, the USE and BROWSE commands are not supported in SQL mode. To open the data file to see what data has been written to the file, you must run CON_SUB, which is stored in a .PRG file.

As long as program control transfers to code stored in a .PRG file, these commands are acceptable. When these commands are executed, control returns back to the .PRS file, which continues in SQL mode from that point to the RETURN command.

Note one caution: The .DBF file that receives the data from the SQL table contains only those records that were in the result set of the UNLOAD DATA command. Any data stored in the receiving file before the UNLOAD DATA command is lost.

If you need to append the rows from the SQL table into a data file without erasing the file's previous content, unload the data into a temporary file that contains the same structure as the target .DBF file.

Fig. 14.8.

*A program to
convert SQL data.*

```
***** Program: CONVERT.PRS *****
* This code is saved to disk with the extension .PRS.
* This program converts SQL data to dBASE IV format.

START DATABASE NEW_INFO ;
UNLOAD DATA TO db4_cust
   FROM TABLE customer;
DO CON_SUB
STOP DATABASE ;
CLEAR
RETURN

* End of CONVERT.PRS

***** Program: CON_SUB.PRG *****

* This file has the extension .PRG.

USE db4_cust
BROWSE
RETURN
* Even though the BROWSE and USE commands are not allowed in
* SQL programs, you can place them in a .PRG file and call them
* by a .PRS file.

* End of file CON_SUB.PRG
```

Then use APPEND FROM to add the records in the temporary file to the
permanent .DBF file.

Bringing dBASE IV Data into SQL Tables

Command:
DBDEFINE
*Creates SQL
tables from .DBF
files.*

dBASE IV provides two commands, DBDEFINE and DBCHECK, to take data
from .DBF files created in dBASE native mode and place the files as tables
within a database.

The DBDEFINE command creates tables in the current SQL database with the same structure and contents as the original .DBF files. Remember that when you create an SQL database, a subdirectory is created where that SQL database resides. You must copy the .DBF files into that SQL database subdirectory so that the DBDEFINE command can find and act on those files. The DBDEFINE command takes a data file name as an argument:

    DBDEFINE EMPLOYEE;

With the preceding command, only one table is created in the SQL database—the EMPLOYEE table. This table contains both the structure and the data found in EMPLOYEE.DBF. Remember that the database file must reside in the same subdirectory as the SQL database.

If, on the other hand, you want all the .DBF files in the subdirectory to become tables in the SQL database, do not include an argument with the DBDEFINE command. The following command creates tables for all the .DBF files in the subdirectory:

    DBDEFINE;

SQL indexes are created automatically for any .MDX index files that are a part of the .DBF file structure.

Because you cannot have an open .DBF file at the same time you are working in an SQL database, the contents of the two files may get out of sync. You can use the DBCHECK command to determine whether the catalog entries in the SQL database are consistent with the .DBF and the .MDX file structures. For example, the following command checks to see that the EMPLOYEE table and the EMPLOYEE.DBF file agree:

Command:
DBCHECK
Makes sure that the SQL table and the database file are in sync.

    DBCHECK EMPLOYEE;

If the table and database file are not in sync, this command makes them so.

If you want to check all the data files in the directory, use DBCHECK without an argument. The following command evaluates all the SQL tables and their underlying .DBF and .MDX files:

    DBCHECK;

Chapter Summary

In this chapter, you have seen the basic aspects of SQL. You have seen how to create SQL databases with the CREATE DATABASE command and tables or views with the CREATE TABLE and CREATE VIEW commands. To move data in and out of SQL databases, use the INSERT, LOAD DATA, and UNLOAD DATA COMMANDS. DBDEFINE and DBCHECK automate moving data into SQL tables. To extract data and display it on-screen, use the SELECT command.

Part IV

Command Summary and Functions Summary

Includes

dBASE IV Command Summary

dBASE IV Functions Summary

dBASE IV Command Summary

T he commands used in interactive processing and batch processing are summarized in this section. Although most of these commands are discussed in this book, you may find a few commands that have not been introduced. In many cases, you can use several different commands to perform the same task. This book introduces the easiest commands that yield the best results. Use the information in this section to explore any unfamiliar commands.

Symbol Conventions

Text in capital letters represents key words of the command.

File names, texts, values, or expressions are enclosed in angle brackets < >. Don't type the brackets when you enter this information.

Contents in square brackets [ ] are optional. If you include these optional elements, don't type the brackets.

Omitted portions of a command are represented by a series of periods (...).

Consider, for example, the following commands:

```
USE < name of database>
DISPLAY [ALL][FOR < filter condition> ][TO PRINT]
```

601

The second command can take one of the following forms:

```
DISPLAY
DISPLAY ALL
DISPLAY ALL TO PRINT
DISPLAY FOR AREA_CODE="2Ø6"
DISPLAY FOR AREA_CODE="2Ø6" TO PRINT
```

Definition of Terms

The following special terms are used in this appendix.

< file name>

A string of up to 8 characters (including the underscore) and a file extension (for example, .DBF, .DBT, .FMT, .FRM, .LBL, .MEM, .NDX, .PRG, and .TXT). A sample file name is EMPLOYEE.DBF.

< data field name>

A string of up to 10 characters, including the underscore:

```
LAST_NAME
```

< data field list>

A series of data field names separated by commas:

```
LAST_NAME, FIRST_NAME, AREA_CODE, PHONE_NO
```

< variable name>

A string of up to 10 characters, including the underscore:

```
TOTALPRICE
```

< variable list>

A series of variable names separated by commas:

```
Hours, PayRate, GrossWage, TotalSale
```

< expression>

A formula that consists of fields, memory variables, constants, functions, and operators.

< character expression>

A collection of character data joined with plus signs:

```
"Employee's Name: "+TRIM(FIRST_NAME)+" "+LAST_NAME
```

< date expression>

A date:

```
{12/1/89}
```

< numeric expression>

A collection of numeric data joined with arithmetic operators (+, –, *, /, ^):

```
40*PAYRATE+(HOURS-40)*PAYRATE*1.5
```

< expression list>

A series of expressions separated by commas:

```
30*PAYRATE+(HOURS-30)*PAYRATE*1.5,
    40*PAYRATE+(HOURS-40)*PAYRATE*1.5
```

< filter conditions>

A clause that begins with FOR and is followed by one or more conditions. In most cases, you also can add the WHILE clause to the filter conditions.

```
FOR AREA_CODE="206"
FOR ANNUAL_PAY> =25000
FOR LAST_NAME="Smith" .AND. FIRST_NAME="James C."
WHILE .NOT. EOF()
```

dBASE IV Commands Listed by Function

To create, modify, and manipulate files:

APPEND FROM
CLOSE ALTERNATE
CLOSE DATABASES
CLOSE FORMAT
CLOSE INDEX
CLOSE PROCEDURE
CONVERT
COPY TO
COPY TAG
COPY FILE
COPY INDEXES
COPY MEMO
COPY STRUCTURE TO
COPY STRUCTURE EXTENDED
CREATE
CREATE FROM
CREATE LABEL
CREATE QUERY
CREATE REPORT
CREATE SCREEN
CREATE VIEW
CREATE VIEW FROM ENVIRONMENT
DELETE
EXPORT
IMPORT
JOIN
MODIFY COMMAND
MODIFY LABEL
MODIFY QUERY
MODIFY REPORT
MODIFY SCREEN
MODIFY STRUCTURE
MODIFY VIEW
RENAME

```
SAVE TO
SELECT
SET BLOCKSIZE
SET EXCLUSIVE
SET LOCK
SET MARK
SET MEMOWIDTH
SET REFRESH
SET SKIP
USE
```

To edit data in a database file:

```
@...GET APPEND
APPEND FROM
APPEND FROM ARRAY
APPEND MEMO
BROWSE
CHANGE
DELETE
EDIT
ERASE
INSERT
PACK
READ
RECALL
REPLACE
UPDATE
ZAP
```

To display data:

```
@
@...CLEAR
@...TO
@...SAY
?
??
???
BROWSE
DIR
DISPLAY
DISPLAY FILE
```

```
DISPLAY HISTORY
DISPLAY STRUCTURE
LABEL FORM
LIST
LIST FILE
ON PAGE
PRINTJOB...ENDPRINTJOB
REPORT FORM
SET SPACE
```

To control the record pointer:

```
CONTINUE
FIND
GO BOTTOM
GOTO
GO TOP
LOCATE
SEEK
SET NEAR
SET ODOMETER
SKIP
```

To index and sort data records:

```
DELETE TAG
INDEX ON...TO
INDEX ON...TAG...OF
REINDEX
SET INDEX TO
SORT ON...TO
```

To protect data:

```
PROTECT
SET AUTOSAVE
SET ENCRYPTION
UNLOCK
```

To use memory variables/arrays:

```
ACCEPT TO
CLEAR ALL
CLEAR GETS
CLEAR MEMORY
```

```
    COPY TO ARRAY
    DECLARE
    DISPLAY MEMORY
    INPUT
    LIST MEMORY
    PARAMETERS
    PRIVATE
    PUBLIC
    READ
    RELEASE
    RESTORE FROM
    SAVE TO
    STORE
    WAIT
```

To process files and macro commands:

```
    BEGIN TRANSACTION
    END TRANSACTION
    PLAY MACRO
    RESET
    RESTORE MACRO
    ROLLBACK
    SAVE MACRO
```

To perform mathematical and statistical operations:

```
    AVERAGE
    CALCULATE
    COUNT
    SUM
    TOTAL
```

To work with menu operations:

```
    ACTIVATE MENU
    ACTIVATE POPUP
    ACTIVATE WINDOW
    DEACTIVATE MENU
    DEACTIVATE POPUP
    DEACTIVATE WINDOW
    DEFINE BAR
    DEFINE BOX
    DEFINE MENU
```

```
DEFINE PAD
DEFINE POPUP
DEFINE WINDOW
MOVE WINDOW
ON PAD
ON SELECTION PAD
ON SELECTION POPUP
RESTORE WINDOW
SAVE WINDOW
SHOW MENU
SHOW POPUP
```

To control media/display*:

```
@...FILL
CLEAR
EJECT
EJECT PAGE
SET COLOR TO
SET CONFIRM on/OFF
SET CONSOLE ON/off
SET INTENSITY ON/off
SET PRINTER on/OFF
SET DEVICE TO
SET MARGIN TO
SET VIEW
SET WINDOW
```

To specify control parameters*:

```
SET ALTERNATE TO
SET ALTERNATE on/OFF
SET BELL ON/off
SET BORDER
SET CARRY on/OFF
SET CATALOG ON/off
SET CATALOG TO
SET CENTURY
SET CLOCK
SET CURRENCY
SET DATE
```

---

* Uppercase indicates default settings.

```
SET  DEBUG
SET  DECIMALS  TO
SET  DEFAULT  TO
SET  DELETED  on/OFF
SET  DELIMITERS  on/OFF
SET  DOHISTORY  on/OFF
SET  DOHISTORY  TO
SET  ECHO  on/OFF
SET  ESCAPE  ON/off
SET  EXACT  on/OFF
SET  FIELDS  on/OFF
SET  FIELDS  TO
SET  FILTER  TO
SET  FIXED  on/OFF
SET  FORMAT  TO
SET  FULLPATH
SET  FUNCTION  TO
SET  HEADING  ON/off
SET  HELP  ON/off
SET  HISTORY  ON/off
SET  HOURS
SET  INDEX  TO
SET  INSTRUCT
SET  MARGIN  TO
SET  MENUS  ON/off
SET  MESSAGE  TO
SET  ORDER  TO
SET  PATH  TO
SET  POINT
SET  PRECISION
SET  PROCEDURE  TO
SET  RELATION  TO
SET  SAFETY  ON/off
SET  SCOREBOARD  ON/off
SET  SEPARATOR
SET  STATUS  ON/off
SET  STEP  on/OFF
SET  TALK  ON/off
SET  TITLE  ON/off
SET  TYPEAHEAD  TO
SET  UNIQUE  on/OFF
```

For programming (general):

```
*
&&
COMPILE
CREATE APPLICATION
FUNCTION
MODIFY COMMAND
MODIFY APPLICATION
NOTE
SET DEVELOPMENT
TEXT
```

For programming (error handling):

```
CANCEL
DEBUG
ON ERROR
ON ESCAPE
ON KEY
ON READERROR
RESUME
RETRY
SET TRAP
SUSPEND
```

For programming (procedures):

```
CALL
LOAD
PROCEDURE
RETURN
```

For programming (branching, loops):

```
CASE
DO
DO WHILE...ENDDO
DO CASE...ENDCASE
EXIT
IF...ENDIF
IF...ELSE...ENDIF
GO
GO TO
LOOP
```

QUIT
SCAN...ENDSCAN
SKIP

For other purposes:

HELP
LIST/DISPLAY STATUS
LIST/DISPLAY USERS
LOGOUT
QUIT
RUN/!
SET DESIGN
SET DISPLAY
SET REPROCESS

Summary of Commands

?

Syntax: ? [< *character or numeric expression*>]
      [PICTURE < *picture template*>]
      [FUNCTION < *function list*>]
      [AT < *numeric expression*>]
      [STYLE < *font #*>]

Displays the contents of a character or numeric expression on a
new display line:

```
? "Employee's name . . . "+FIRST_NAME+ LAST_NAME
? Hours*PayRate
? "Gross Pay . . . "+STR(GrossPay,7,2)
? LAST_NAME PICTURE "!XXXXXXXXXXXXXXXX"
```

??

Syntax: ?? [< *character or numeric expression*>]
               [PICTURE < *picture template*>]
               [FUNCTION < *function list*>]
               [AT < *numeric expression*>]
               [STYLE < *font #*>],
               [< *character or numeric expression*>] . . .

Displays output on the same display line:

```
?? "Invoice number: "+INVNO
```

???

Syntax: ??? < *character string*>

Sends a character string (as a control code) directly to the printer:

```
??? CHR(27) + CHR(15)     &&Condense EPSON print
```

@

Syntax: @ < *row,column*>
               [SAY < *character or numeric expression*>]
               [PICTURE < *picture template*>]
               [FUNCTION < *function list*>]
               [GET < *memory variable*>]
               [[OPEN]WINDOW < *name of window*>]
               [PICTURE < *picture template*>]
               [FUNCTION < *function list*>]
               [RANGE < *low value,high value*>]
               [VALID < *conditions*> [ERROR < *message*>]]
               [WHEN < *conditions*>]
               [DEFAULT < *character or numeric expression*>]
               [MESSAGE < *message*>]
               [COLOR [< *standard*>][, < *enhanced*>]]

Defines input and output data format, display attributes, and so on:

```
USE EMPLOYEE
@5,1Ø SAY "Employee name .... "+TRIM(FIRST_NAME);
     +" "+LAST_NAME PICTURE "!XXXXXXXXXXXXXXXXXX"
STORE Ø TO VariableA
@1Ø,5 SAY "Enter value to A " GET VariableA PICTURE "999"
```

@...CLEAR

Syntax: @ < *row,column*> CLEAR [TO < *row,column*>]
           [[OPEN] WINDOW < *name of window*>]

Clears a portion of the screen formed by the coordinates of the upper left corner and lower right corner:

```
@ 5,1Ø CLEAR TO 2Ø,6Ø
```

When you omit the lower right corner coordinates, the line beginning with the < *row,column*> is cleared to the end of the screen:

```
@ 1Ø,5 CLEAR
```

@...FILL

Syntax: @ < *row,column*> FILL TO < *row,column*>
           [COLOR < *attribute*>]

Changes the text color in the area between the two sets of coordinates:

```
@ 5,5 FILL TO 2Ø,5Ø COLOR B/W
```

If no color is specified, this command clears the area:

```
@ 5,5 FILL TO 2Ø,5Ø
```

@...GET

Syntax: @< *row,column*> GET
            [[OPEN] WINDOW < *name of window*>]
            [PICTURE < *picture template*>]
            [FUNCTION < *function list*>]
            [RANGE < *low value,high value*>]
            [VALID < *conditions*> [ERROR < *message*>]]
            [WHEN < *conditions*>]
            [DEFAULT < *character or numeric expression*>]
            [MESSAGE < *message*>]
            [COLOR [< *standard*>][, < *enhanced*>]]

Displays user-formatted data at the screen location specified in
< *row,column*> and allows editing:

```
@ 5,1Ø GET LAST_NAME
@ 8,1Ø GET SC_NO PICTURE "###--##--####"
```

@...SAY

Syntax: @ < *row,column*> SAY
            [[OPEN] WINDOW < *name of window*>]
            [PICTURE < *picture template*>]
            [FUNCTION < *function list*>]
            [RANGE < *low value,high value*>]
            [VALID < *conditions*> [ERROR < *message*>]]
            [WHEN < *conditions*>]
            [DEFAULT < *character or numeric expression*>]
            [MESSAGE < *message*>]
            [COLOR [< *standard*>][, < *enhanced*>]]

Displays or prints user-formatted data at the location specified in
< *row,column*>:

```
@ 5,1Ø SAY LAST_NAME
@ 5,1Ø SAY "Last name . . . " LAST_NAME
@ 1Ø,5 SAY "Annual salary:" ANNUAL_PAY PICTURE "$##,###.##"
```

@...SAY...GET

Syntax: @ < *row,column*> SAY...GET
            [[OPEN] WINDOW < *name of window*>]
            [PICTURE < *picture template*>]
            [FUNCTION < *function list*>]
            [RANGE < *low value,high value*>]
            [VALID < *conditions*> [ERROR < *message*>]]
            [WHEN < *conditions*>]
            [DEFAULT < *character or numeric expression*>]
            [MESSAGE < *message*>]
            [COLOR [< *standard*>][, < *enhanced*>]]

Displays user-formatted data on-screen at the location specified in
< *row,column*> ; use for appending or editing a data field:

```
@ 5,1Ø SAY "Last name : " GET LAST_NAME
```

@...TO

Syntax: @ < *row,column*> TO < *row,column*>
            [DOUBLE/PANEL/< *border definition string*>]
            [COLOR < *attribute*>]

Draws a single (by default) or double box in the specified color
between the two sets of coordinates:

```
@ 3,2 TO 22,78
@ 3,2 TO 22,78 DOUBLE
@ 5,5 TO 2Ø,5Ø DOUBLE COLOR N/BG
```

If no color is specified, the normal color is used.

ACCEPT

Syntax: ACCEPT [< *prompt*>] TO < *memory variable*>

Assigns a character string to a memory variable, with or without a
prompt:

```
ACCEPT "Enter your last name . . . " TO LastName
ACCEPT TO LastName
```

ACTIVATE MENU

Syntax: ACTIVATE MENU < *menu bar name*>
           [PAD< *menu pad name*>]

Activates an existing bar menu, with or without specifying a menu pad:

```
ACTIVATE MENU DataMenu PAD EditData
```

ACTIVATE POPUP

Syntax: ACTIVATE POPUP < *name of pop-up menu*>

Displays the pop-up menu created with the DEFINE POPUP and DEFINE BAR commands:

```
DEFINE POPUP DATAMENU FROM 5,5 TO 10,25
DEFINE BAR 1 OF DATAMENU PROMPT "Add data record"
DEFINE BAR 2 OF DATAMENU PROMPT "Edit data record"
DEFINE BAR 3 OF DATAMENU PROMPT "Delete data record"
ACTIVATE POPUP DATAMENU
```

ACTIVATE SCREEN

Syntax: ACTIVATE SCREEN

Restores access to the full screen and overshadows the active window. You can redisplay the contents of the window with the ACTIVATE WINDOW command.

ACTIVATE WINDOW

Syntax: ACTIVATE WINDOW < *window list*> /ALL

Activates the specified windows:

```
DEFINE WINDOW WindowA FROM 1,1 to 10,10
DEFINE WINDOW WindowB FROM 15,1 to 20,30
DEFINE WINDOW WindowA FROM 1,30 to 10,20
ACTIVATE WINDOW WindowA,WindowB,WindowC
```

APPEND

Syntax: APPEND [BLANK]

Adds a data record to the end of the active database file; displays an entry form:

```
USE EMPLOYEE
APPEND
APPEND BLANK
```

APPEND BLANK works like APPEND but does not display an entry form.

APPEND FROM

Syntax: APPEND FROM < *database file* > /?
            [TYPE < *file type* >][FOR < *filter conditions* >]

Adds data records from one database file (FILE1.DBF) to another database file (FILE2.DBF), with or without a qualifier:

```
USE FILE2
APPEND FROM FILE1
USE FILE2
APPEND FROM FILE1 FOR ACCT_NO < ="10123"
```

APPEND FROM ARRAY

Syntax: APPEND FROM ARRAY < *array name* >
            [FOR   < *filter conditions* >]

Adds data records to the database file from the values in an array:

```
DECLARE ArrayX[3]
ArrayX[1]=10
ArrayX[2]=20
ArrayX[3]=15
USE XVALUES
APPEND FROM ARRAY ArrayX
```

APPEND MEMO

Syntax: APPEND MEMO < *memo field*> FROM < *text file name*>
[OVERWRITE]

Adds the contents of a text file to a memo field:

```
USE ACCOUNTS
APPEND MEMO COMMENTS FROM REMARKS
```

Use OVERWRITE to erase the existing contents of the memo field:

```
APPEND MEMO COMMENTS FROM REMARKS OVERWRITE
```

ASSIST

Syntax: ASSIST

Calls the Control Center from the dot prompt. You also can press F2 at the dot prompt to issue the ASSIST command.

AVERAGE

Syntax: AVERAGE < *numeric expression*> [< *record scope*>]
[FOR < *filter conditions*>]
[WHILE < *filter conditions*>]
[TO < *memory variable*> /TO ARRAY < *name of array*>]

Computes the average of a numeric expression and assigns the value to a memory variable, with or without a condition:

```
AVERAGE ANNUAL_PAY TO AveragePay
AVERAGE QTY_SOLD TO AvgSale FOR MODEL_NO="XYZ"
AVERAGE HOURS*PAYRATE TO AveragePay FOR .NOT. MALE
```

BEGIN/END TRANSACTION

Syntax: BEGIN TRANSACTION[< *name of path*>]
  < *commands for transaction*> END TRANSACTION

Sets up processing so that you can revert to the state of the
database before the start of the transaction if changes are made
within the transaction:

```
BEGIN TRANSACTION
    USE EMPLOYEE
    . . .
    ACCEPT "Changes OK?" TO MOK
    IF UPPER(MOK)="N"
        ROLLBACK
    ENDIF
END TRANSACTION
```

BROWSE

Syntax: BROWSE [NOINIT][NOFOLLOW][NOAPPEND][NOMENU][NOEDIT]
  [NODELETE][NOCLEAR][COMPRESS][FORMAT]
  [LOCK < *numeric expression*>][WIDTH < *field width*>]
  [WINDOW < *name of window*>][FIELDS < *field list*> [/R]]
  [FREEZE < *field name*>]

Displays for review or modification up to 17 records from the active
database file:

```
USE EMPLOYEE
GO TOP
BROWSE
BROWSE FIELDS FIRST_NAME, LAST_NAME, PHONE_NO
BROWSE FIELDS FIRST_NAME,LAST_NAME,PHONE_NO FREEZE PHONE_NO
```

CALCULATE

Syntax: CALCULATE [< *record scope*>] < *function list*>
           [TO < *memory variables*> /TO ARRAY < *name of array*>]
           [FOR < *filter conditions*>]
           [WHILE < *filter conditions*>]

Computes financial and statistical functions and saves them to
memory variables, with or without filter conditions:

```
USE EMPLOYEE
CALCULATE AVG(ANNUAL_PAY) TO AveragePay
CALCULATE MAX(ANNUAL_PAY), MIN(ANNUAL_PAY) TO
HighestPay, LowestPay FOR MALE
```

The financial and statistical functions you can use include the
following: AVG (average), CNT (count), MAX (maximum), MIN
(minimum), NPV (net present value), STD (standard deviation), SUM
(sum), and VAR (variance).

CALL

Syntax: CALL < *name of binary file*>
           [WITH < *expression list*>]

Executes a binary file program module loaded in memory. You can
pass parameters or memory variables as an expression list by using
the WITH clause.

```
LOAD SUMAB
VariableA=1Ø
VariableB=2Ø
CALL SUMAB WITH VariableA, VariableB
```

CANCEL

Syntax: CANCEL

Terminates processing a program file and returns to the dot
prompt; does not close database or procedure files:

```
IF ErrorCond
     CANCEL
ENDIF
```

CHANGE

Syntax: CHANGE [NOINIT][NOFOLLOW][NOAPPEND][NOMENU][NOEDIT]
            [NODELETE][NOCLEAR][< *record #*>]
            [FIELDS < *field list*>][< *record scope*>]
            [FOR < *filter conditions*>]
            [WHILE < *filter conditions*>]

Displays for editing the data records in the active database file
sequentially, with or without a qualifier. This command performs
the same function as the EDIT command.

```
USE EMPLOYEE
GOTO 5
CHANGE
```

Use the FIELDS clause to change selective data fields sequentially,
with or without a qualifier:

```
USE EMPLOYEE
CHANGE FIELDS ANNUAL_PAY
CHANGE FIELDS AREA_CODE,PHONE_NO FOR AREA_CODE="2Ø6"
```

CLEAR

Syntax: CLEAR [ALL/FIELDS/GETS/MEMORY/MENUS/POPUPS/
           TYPEAHEAD /WINDOWS]

Clears the full screen:

    CLEAR

Closes all open database files (including .DBF, .NDX, .FMT, and
.DBT files) and releases all memory variables:

    CLEAR ALL

Releases the data fields that have been created by the SET FIELDS TO
command:

    CLEAR FIELDS

Clears all data displayed by @...SAY...GET commands issued before
the CLEAR GETS command:

    CLEAR GETS
    @5,1Ø SAY "Account number : " GET ACCT_NO
    @7,1Ø Say "Account name : " GET ACCT_NAME
    READ

Releases or erases all memory variables:

    CLEAR MEMORY

Clears and removes all user-defined menus from memory:

    CLEAR MENUS

Clears and removes all pop-up menus from memory:

    CLEAR POPUPS

Empties the type-ahead buffer:

    CLEAR TYPEAHEAD

Clears and removes all windows from memory:

    CLEAR WINDOWS

CLOSE

Syntax: CLOSE [ALL/ALTERNATE/DATABASES/FORMAT/INDEX/
            PROCEDURE]

Closes all files:

> CLOSE ALL

Closes the ALTERNATE file in use:

> CLOSE ALTERNATE

Closes all database files and their associated format (.FMT) and index (.NDX, .MDX) files:

> CLOSE DATABASES

Closes all format (.FMT) files in use:

> CLOSE FORMAT

Closes all index (.NDX, .MDX) files in use:

> CLOSE INDEX

Closes all procedure files in use:

> CLOSE PROCEDURE

COMPILE

Syntax: COMPILE < *name of file*>

Converts a file that contains dBASE IV source code to executable object code. This step is done the first time you DO a program.

CONTINUE

Syntax: `CONTINUE`

Resumes the search started with the LOCATE command:

```
USE EMPLOYEE
LOCATE FOR AREA_CODE="206"
DISPLAY
CONTINUE
DISPLAY
```

CONVERT

Syntax: CONVERT [TO < *numeric expression*>]

Adds an extra field to the database file to track lock detection for use in a multiuser system.

COPY

Syntax: COPY TO < *file name*> [[TYPE] < *file type*>]
            [FIELDS < *field list*>][< *record scope*>]
            [FOR < *filter conditions*>]
            [WHILE < *filter conditions*>]

Copies contents of the current database file to another database file:

```
USE EMPLOYEE
COPY TO BACKUP
```

Copies selected fields of a source database file to a new file, with or without filter conditions:

```
USE EMPLOYEE
COPY TO ROSTER.DBF FIELDS FIRST_NAME, LAST_NAME
COPY TO SALARY FIELDS LAST_NAME, ANNUAL_PAY FOR MALE
```

COPY FILE

Syntax: COPY FILE *< source file>* TO *< target file>*

Duplicates an existing file of any type:

```
COPY FILE MAINPROG.PRG TO MAIN.PRG
COPY FILE COST.FMT TO NEWCOST.FMT
COPY FILE ROSTER.FRM TO NAMELIST.FRM
```

COPY INDEXES

Syntax: COPY INDEXES *< .ndx files>* [TO *< .mdx file>*]

Converts individual index (.NDX) files to index tags in the multiple index (.MDX) file. If you omit the .MDX file, the current production multiple index file is assumed.

```
SET INDEX TO BY_LAST
COPY INDEXES BY_LAST
```

COPY MEMO

Syntax: COPY MEMO *< memo field name>* TO *< text file name>*
            [ADDITIVE]

Copies the contents of a memo field to a text file:

```
USE ACCOUNTS
COPY COMMENTS TO B:NOTES.TXT
```

To append the contents of the memo fields to an existing text file, use the ADDITIVE clause:

```
COPY COMMENTS TO B:NOTES.TXT ADDITIVE
```

COPY STRUCTURE

Syntax: COPY STRUCTURE TO < *target .dbf file*>
                 [FIELDS < *field list*>]

Copies the data structure of one database file to another database file:

```
USE COST
COPY STRUCTURE TO NEWCOST.DBF
```

Use the FIELDS clause to copy only selective fields to the new database file:

```
USE EMPLOYEE
COPY STRUCTURE TO ROSTER.DBF FIELDS LAST_NAME,FIRST_NAME
```

COPY STRUCTURE EXTENDED

Syntax: COPY TO < *new database file name*>
                 STRUCTURE EXTENDED

Creates a new database file with records that contain the field attributes of the database structure:

```
USE EMPLOYEE
COPY TO DBFSTRUC STRUCTURE EXTENDED
```

COPY TAG

Syntax: COPY TAG < *index tag name*> [OF < *.mdx file*>]
                 TO < *.ndx file*>

Converts an index tag in a multiple index (.MDX) file to an individual index (.NDX) file:

```
USE EMPLOYEE
COPY TAG LAST_NAME TO BY_LAST
```

If you omit the name of the .MDX file, the current production multiple index file is assumed.

COPY TO ARRAY

Syntax: COPY TO ARRAY < *array name*> [FIELDS < *field list*>]
           [< *record scope*>][FOR < *filter conditions*>]
           [WHILE < *filter conditions*>]

Copies the contents of data records in the current database file to
the declared array:

    USE EMPLOYEE
    DECLARE MalePay[2Ø]
    COPY TO ARRAY MalePay FIELDS ANNUAL_PAY FOR MALE

COUNT

Syntax: COUNT [TO < *memory variable*>][< *record scope*>]
           [FOR < *filter conditions*>]
           [WHILE < *filter conditions*>]

Counts the number of records in the active database file and assigns
the number to a memory variable:

    USE EMPLOYEE
    COUNT TO NRecords
    COUNT FOR NEXT 1ØØ ANNUAL_PAY> ="5ØØØØ" .AND. MALE TO NRichMen

CREATE

Syntax: CREATE < *database file name*>

Sets up a new file structure and adds data records:

    CREATE EMPLOYEE

CREATE FROM

Syntax: CREATE < *.dbf file name*> FROM
           < *structure extended file name*>

Creates a database file by using the database structure information contained in the records of the structure extended file:

```
USE EMPLOYEE
COPY TO DBFSTRUC STRUCTURE EXTENDED
USE DBFSTRUC
CREATE NEWFILE FROM DBFSTRUC
```

CREATE VIEW FROM ENVIRONMENT

Syntax: CREATE VIEW < *.vue file name*> FROM ENVIRONMENT

Creates a dBASE III PLUS view (.VUE) file that remains compatible with dBASE III PLUS applications.

CREATE/MODIFY APPLICATION

Syntax: CREATE/MODIFY APPLICATION < *application file name*>
           /?

Starts the dBASE IV applications generator.

CREATE LABEL

Syntax: CREATE LABEL < *.lbl file name*>

Displays a design form so that you can create custom labels (.LBL file):

```
CREATE LABEL MAILLIST
```

CREATE QUERY/VIEW

Syntax: CREATE QUERY/VIEW < *.qbe file name*>

Displays the query design screen so that you can create a new query file (.QBE):

```
USE EMPLOYEE
CREATE QUERY FINDEMPL
```

CREATE REPORT

Syntax: CREATE REPORT < *.frm file name*>

Displays a design form so that you can create a report form file (.FRM):

```
USE EXPENSES
CREATE REPORT COLUMNØ1
```

CREATE SCREEN

Syntax: CREATE SCREEN < *.fmt file name*>

Displays the screen design so that you can create a custom screen (.FMT) file:

```
USE EMPLOYEE
CREATE SCREEN DATAFORM
```

DEACTIVATE MENU

Syntax: DEACTIVATE MENU

Deactivates and clears the active bar menu from the screen. If you do not erase the menu from memory, you can activate it with the ACTIVATE MENU command.

DEACTIVATE POPUP

Syntax: DEACTIVATE POPUP

Deletes the pop-up menu from the screen without removing it from memory. You can reactivate the menu with the ACTIVATE POPUP command.

DEACTIVATE WINDOW

Syntax: DEACTIVATE WINDOW < *list of window name*> /ALL

Erases the windows from the screen without removing them from memory. You can redisplay the window with the ACTIVATE WINDOW command.

DEBUG

Syntax: DEBUG < *name of program or procedure*>
            [WITH < *parameters*>]

Executes the program or procedure and invokes the dBASE IV debugger.

DECLARE

Syntax: DECLARE < *array dimension list*>

Specifies the dimensions for each of the array variables, separated with commas. An array variable can be one- or two-dimensional. For a single-dimensional array, specify the number of rows in a pair of square brackets:

    DECLARE ArrayA[1Ø], ArrayB[2Ø]

Specify the number of rows and columns in a pair of square brackets for a two-dimensional array:

    DECLARE ArrayC[1Ø,1Ø]

DEFINE BAR

Syntax: DEFINE BAR < *line #*> OF < *pop-up name*>
PROMPT < *character expression*>
[MESSAGE < *character expression*>]
[SKIP [FOR < *filter conditions*>]]

Defines a single menu option in a pop-up menu box:

```
DEFINE POPUP DataPopup FROM 5,5 TO 10,25;
     MESSAGE "Pop-up Menu for Data Maintenance"
DEFINE BAR 1 OF DataPopup PROMPT "Add data record";
     MESSAGE "Adding new data records to .DBF file"
DEFINE BAR 2 OF DataPopup PROMPT "Edit data record";
     MESSAGE "Editing contents of a data record"
DEFINE BAR 3 OF DataPopup PROMPT "Delete data record";
     MESSAGE "Deleting data records from .DBF file"
ACTIVATE POPUP DataPopup
```

DEFINE BOX

Syntax: DEFINE BOX FROM < *left-most column*> TO
< *right-most column*> HEIGHT < *box height*>
[AT LINE < *print line*>]
[SINGLE/DOUBLE/< *border definition string*>]

Displays a single- or double-line box of a specified height (in lines)
at the defined print line between the left-most and right-most
column:

```
DEFINE BOX FROM 5 TO 40 HEIGHT 10 AT 3 DOUBLE
```

DEFINE MENU

Syntax: DEFINE MENU < *menu name*>
[MESSAGE < *character expression*>]

Creates a bar menu, assigns a menu name, and displays a message at
the bottom of the screen:

```
DEFINE MENU DataMenu MESSAGE "Data Maintenance Menu"
```

DEFINE PAD

Syntax: DEFINE PAD < *pad name* > OF < *menu name* >
PROMPT < *character expression* >
[AT < *row,column* >]
[MESSAGE < *character expression* >]

Defines a menu pad in a bar menu at a given location on-screen and displays its corresponding prompt (with or without messages) at the bottom of the screen:

```
DEFINE MENU DataMenu
DEFINE PAD ViewData of DataMenu PROMPT "View a record";
    AT 3,1
DEFINE PAD EditData of DataMenu PROMPT "Edit a record";
    AT 3,20


ON PAD ViewData of DataMenu ACTIVATE POPUP ViewMenu
ON PAD EditData of DataMenu ACTIVATE POPUP EditMenu
```

DEFINE POPUP

Syntax: DEFINE POPUP < *pop-up menu name* >
FROM < *row,column* > TO < *row,column* >
[PROMPT FIELD < *field name* > /PROMPT FILES
[LIKE < *skeleton* >]/PROMPT STRUCTURE]
[MESSAGE< *character expression* >]

Defines a pop-up menu in the specified area on-screen, with or without a message at the bottom of the screen:

```
DEFINE POPUP DataPopup FROM 5,5 TO 10,25;
    MESSAGE "Pop-up Menu for Data Maintenance"
DEFINE BAR 1 OF DataPopup PROMPT "Add data record";
    MESSAGE "Adding new data records to .DBF file"
DEFINE BAR 2 OF DataPopup PROMPT "Edit data record";
    MESSAGE "Editing contents of a data record"
DEFINE BAR 3 OF DataPopup PROMPT "Delete data record";
    MESSAGE "Deleting data records from .DBF file"
ACTIVATE POPUP DataPopup
```

DEFINE WINDOW

Syntax: DEFINE WINDOW < *window name*>
            FROM < *row,column*>
            TO < *row,column*> [DOUBLE/PANEL/NONE/
            < *character string for the window frame*>]
            [COLOR < *attributes*>]

Defines the window between two sets of coordinates; specifies
color and appearance of window frame (for example, double-line,
panel, special characters, and so on):

```
DEFINE WINDOW WindowA FROM 5,5 TO 20,30 DOUBLE
ACTIVATE WINDOW WindowA
```

DELETE

Syntax: DELETE [< *record scope*>][FOR < *filter conditions*>]
            [WHILE < *filter conditions*>]

Marks the records in the active database file for deletion, with or
without filter conditions:

```
USE EMPLOYEE
DELETE
DELETE RECORD 5
DELETE NEXT 3
DELETE FOR AREA_CODE="503"
```

DELETE TAG

Syntax: DELETE TAG < *name of index tag*>
            [OF < *.mdx file*> /< *.ndx file*>]

Deletes the specified index tag from the multiple index (.MDX) file.
If you omit the .MDX file name, the production multiple index file
is assumed:

```
USE EMPLOYEE
DELETE TAG LAST_NAME
DELETE TAG ACCOUNT_NO OF ACCOUNTS
```

DIR

Syntax: DIR

Displays .DBF files:

    DIR

Displays all files:

    DIR *.*

Displays program files:

    DIR *.PRG

Displays .DBF file names beginning with C:

    DIR C*.DBF

Displays .PRG file names with six letters and P as the third character:

    DIR ??P???.PRG

DISPLAY

Syntax: DISPLAY [< *record scope*>][< *field list*>][OFF]
          [FOR < *filter conditions*>]
          [WHILE < *filter conditions*>]
          [TO PRINT/FILE < *name of text file*>]

Displays, prints, or sends to the specified text file the contents of all or selective fields of all or selective records in the current database file:

    USE EMPLOYEE
    DISPLAY
    DISPLAY RECORD 3 TO PRINT
    DISPLAY NEXT 2
    DISPLAY LAST_NAME,FIRST_NAME TO ROSTER.TXT
    DISPLAY AREA_CODE,PHONE_NO FOR AREA_CODE="2Ø6"

Use the OFF clause to suppress the record numbers:

    DISPLAY NEXT 5 OFF

DISPLAY FILES

Syntax: DISPLAY FILES [LIKE < *skeleton*>]
                  [TO PRINT/FILE < *name of text file*>]

Displays, prints, or sends to a text file all files in the file directory:

```
DISPLAY FILES
DISPLAY FILES *.DBF
DISPLAY FILES *.FRM TO PRINT
DISPLAY FILES TO FILESDIR.TXT
```

DISPLAY HISTORY

Syntax: DISPLAY HISTORY [LAST < *numeric expression*>]
                  [TO PRINT/FILE < *name of text file*>]

Displays on-screen, prints, or sends to the specified text file the commands in the history:

```
DISPLAY HISTORY
DISPLAY HISTORY TO PRINT
DISPLAY HISTORY TO FILE COMMANDS.TXT
```

DISPLAY MEMORY

Syntax: DISPLAY MEMORY [TO PRINT/FILE < *name of text file*>]

Displays, prints, or sends to the specified text file the name, type, and size of each active memory variable:

```
DISPLAY MEMORY
DISPLAY MEMORY TO PRINT
DISPLAY MEMORY TO MEMVARS.TXT
```

DISPLAY STATUS

Syntax: DISPLAY STATUS [TO PRINT/FILE < *name of text file*>]

Displays, prints, or sends to the specified text file the current processing situation, including the names of active files, work area number, and so on:

```
DISPLAY STATUS
DISPLAY STATUS TO PRINT
DISPLAY STATUS TO TEXTFILE.TXT
```

DISPLAY STRUCTURE

Syntax: DISPLAY STRUCTURE [IN < *alias file name*>]
            [TO PRINT/FILE < *name of text file*>]

Displays on-screen, prints, or sends to the specified text file the data structure of the active database file:

```
USE EMPLOYEE
DISPLAY STRUCTURE
DISPLAY STRUCTURE TO PRINT
DISPLAY STRUCTURE TO DBFSTRUC.TXT
```

DO

Syntax: DO < *name of program or procedure file*>
            [WITH < *parameters*>]

Executes a program or procedure file, with or without passing the parameters:

```
DO MAINPROG
DO SUMAB WITH ValueA, ValueB
```

DO CASE

Syntax: DO CASE
        CASE *< condition>*
         ...
        [CASE *< condition>*
         ...]
        [OTHERWISE
         ...]
      ENDCASE

Provides multiple avenues for branching:

```
DO CASE
     CASE ANSWER="Y"
        ...
     CASE ANSWER="N"
        ...
     OTHERWISE
        RETURN
ENDCASE
```

DO WHILE

Syntax: DO WHILE *< condition>*
        ...
        ...
        [LOOP]
         [EXIT]
      ENDDO

Loops a program:

```
DO WHILE .NOT. EOF()
     ...
     ...
     IF ...
        LOOP
     ELSE
        EXIT
     ENDIF
ENDDO
```

EDIT

Syntax: EDIT [NOINIT][NOFOLLOW][NOAPPEND][NOMENU][NOEDIT]
           [NODELETE][NOCLEAR] < *record #*>
           [FIELDS < *field list*>][< *record scope*>]
           [FOR < *filter conditions*>]
           [WHILE < *filter conditions*>]

Displays for editing the data records in the active database file
sequentially, with or without a qualifier. This command performs
the same function as the CHANGE command.

```
USE EMPLOYEE
GOTO 5
EDIT
EDIT 10
```

Use the FIELDS clause to change selective data fields sequentially,
with or without filter conditions:

```
USE EMPLOYEE
EDIT FIELDS ANNUAL_PAY
EDIT FIELDS AREA_CODE,PHONE_NO FOR AREA_CODE="206"
```

EJECT

Syntax: EJECT

Advances the paper to the top of the next page.

EJECT PAGE

Syntax: EJECT PAGE

Advances the printer to the defined ON PAGE line. If no ON PAGE line
is defined, advances the paper to the top of the next page.

ERASE

Syntax: ERASE < *file name*>

Removes a file from the directory (the file must be closed):

```
ERASE SALE.DBF
ERASE SAMPLE.PRG
```

EXIT

Syntax: EXIT

Allows a DO...WHILE loop to be abandoned. Processing continues after the ENDDO.

```
DO WHILE .T.
     ...
     ...
     IF EOF()
          EXIT
     ENDIF
     ...
ENDDO
```

EXPORT

Syntax: EXPORT TO < *file name*> [TYPE PFS/DBASEII/FW2/RPD]
                       [FIELDS < *field list*>][< *record scope*>]
                       [FOR < *filter conditions*>]
                       [WHILE < *filter conditions*>]

Copies contents of all or selective records in the current database file to a different type of file:

```
USE EMPLOYEE
EXPORT TO NAMES TYPE PFS FIELDS LAST_NAME, FIRST_NAME;
     FOR MALE
```

FIND

Syntax: FIND < *search key*>

Searches for the first data record in an indexed file with the specified search key:

```
USE EMPLOYEE
INDEX ON AREA_CODE TO AREAS
FIND "206"
DISPLAY
```

FUNCTION

Syntax: FUNCTION < *name of user-defined function*>

Specifies a user-defined function:

```
FUNCTION SumAB
PARAMETER A,B
SumAB=A+B
RETURN(SumAB)
?SumAB(10,20)
        30
```

GO

Syntax: GO BOTTOM/TOP [IN < *alias file name*>]

            Or

            GO [RECORD] < *record #*> [IN < *alias file name*>]

Positions the record pointer at the last, first, or specified record in the database file:

```
USE EMPLOYEE
GO BOTTOM
GO TOP
GO RECORD 12
```

GOTO

Syntax: GOTO < *record #*>

Or

GO BOTTOM/TOP [IN < *alias file name*>]

Positions the record pointer at a specified record:

```
USE EMPLOYEE
GOTO 4
GOTO BOTTOM
GOTO TOP
```

HELP

Syntax: HELP < *keyword*>

Calls the help screens. You can use this command with a keyword to specify the subject:

```
HELP
HELP CREATE
HELP RUN
```

IF

Syntax: IF < *condition*>

      . . .
      . . .
[ELSE]
      . . .
      . . .
ENDIF

Provides conditional branching:

```
WAIT "Enter your choice ([Q] to quit) " TO Choice
IF Choice="Q"
     RETURN
ELSE
   . . .
   . . .
ENDIF
```

IMPORT

Syntax: IMPORT FROM < *file name*> TYPE PFS/DBASEII/FW2/RPD/WK1

Converts the contents of a given file type to a dBASE IV database file:

```
IMPORT FROM NAMES TYPE PFS
```

The dBASE IV file is assigned the same name as the imported file.

INDEX

Syntax: INDEX ON < *key fields*>
              TO < *.ndx file*> /TAG < *index tag*>
              [OF < *.mdx file*>][UNIQUE][DESCENDING]

Creates an individual index (.NDX) file in which all records are ordered according to the contents of the specified key field. You can arrange the records in alphabetical, chronological, or numerical order:

```
USE EMPLOYEE
INDEX ON AREA_CODE TO AREACODE DESCENDING
INDEX ON AREA_CODE+PHONE_NO TO PHONES
```

Sets up the index tag and saves it to a multiple index (.MDX) file:

```
USE EMPLOYEE
INDEX ON LAST_NAME TAG LAST_NAME
INDEX ON ANNUAL_PAY TAG ANNUAL_PAY DESCENDING
```

If you omit the name of the .MDX file, the production multiple index file is assumed. Use the UNIQUE command to ignore duplicate records with the same value in the index key.

INPUT

Syntax: INPUT [<*prompt*>] TO <*memory variable*>

Assigns a data element to a memory variable, with or without a prompt:

```
INPUT PayRate
INPUT "Enter units sold :" TO UnitSold
```

INSERT

Syntax: INSERT [BEFORE][BLANK]

Adds a new record to the database file at the current record location:

```
USE EMPLOYEE
GOTO 4
INSERT
```

Adds a new record to the database file before the current record:

```
USE EMPLOYEE
GOTO 6
INSERT BEFORE
```

Adds a blank record at the current record position:

```
USE EMPLOYEE
GOTO 5
INSERT BLANK
```

JOIN

Syntax: JOIN WITH < *alias of joining file*>
            TO < *new file name*>
            FOR < *filter conditions*> [FIELDS < *field list*>]

Creates a new database file by merging specified data records from
two open database files:

```
SELECT A
USE NEWSTOCKS
SELECT B
USE STOCKS
JOIN WITH NEWSTOCKS TO ALLSTOCK FOR;
     STOCK_NO=A--> STOCK_NO
JOIN WITH NEWSTOCKS TO ALLSTOCK FOR;
     STOCK_NO=A--> STOCK_NO FIELDS MODEL_NO, ON_HAND, ON_ORDER
```

LABEL FORM

Syntax: LABEL FORM < *.lbl file name*> < *record scope*>
            [FOR < *filter conditions*>]
            [WHILE < *filter conditions*>]
            [SAMPLE][TO PRINTER/FILE < *text file name*>]

Displays, prints, or sends to a text file all or selective data records
in a label file:

```
USE EMPLOYEE
LABEL FORM ROSTER
LABEL FORM ROSTER TO PRINT
LABEL FORM ROSTER TO A:FILE.TXT
LABEL FORM ROSTER FOR AREA_CODE="206" .AND. MALE
```

Use the SAMPLE clause to display a sample label layout:

```
LABEL FORM ROSTER SAMPLE
```

LIST

Syntax: LIST [< *record scope*>][[FIELDS] < *field list*>][OFF]
            [FOR < *filter conditions*>]
            [WHILE < *filter conditions*>]
            [TO PRINTER/FILE < *name of text file*>]

Displays, prints, or sends to a text file the contents of all or
selective fields of all or selective records in the current database
file:

```
USE EMPLOYEE
LIST
LIST RECORD 3 TO PRINT
LIST NEXT 2
LIST LAST_NAME,FIRST_NAME TO ROSTER.TXT
LIST AREA_CODE,PHONE_NO FOR AREA_CODE="206"
```

Use the OFF clause to suppress the record numbers:

```
LIST RECORD 5 OFF
```

LIST FILES

Syntax: LIST FILES [LIKE < *skeleton*>]
            [TO PRINT/FILE < *name of text file*>]

Displays, prints, or sends to a text file all the files in the file
directory:

```
LIST FILES
LIST FILES *.DBF
LIST FILES *.FRM TO PRINT
LIST FILES TO FILESDIR.TXT
```

LIST HISTORY

Syntax: LIST HISTORY [LAST < *numeric expression*>]
           [TO PRINT/FILE < *name of text file*>]

Displays, prints, or sends to a text file the commands in the history:

```
LIST HISTORY
LIST HISTORY LAST 4 TO PRINT
LIST HISTORY TO FILE COMMANDS.TXT
```

LIST MEMORY

Syntax: LIST MEMORY [TO PRINT/FILE < *name of text file*>]

Displays, prints, or sends to a text file the name, type, and size of each active memory variable:

```
LIST MEMORY
LIST MEMORY TO PRINT
LIST MEMORY TO MEMVARS.TXT
```

LIST STATUS

Syntax: LIST STATUS [IN < *alias file name*>]
           [TO PRINT/FILE < *name of text file*>]

Displays, prints, or sends to a text file the current processing situation, including the names of active files, work area number, and so on:

```
LIST STATUS
LIST STATUS TO PRINT
LIST STATUS TO TEXTFILE.TXT
```

LIST STRUCTURE

Syntax: LIST STRUCTURE [TO PRINT/FILE $<$ *name of text file*$>$]

Displays, prints, or sends to the specified text file the data structure
of the active database file:

```
USE EMPLOYEE
LIST STRUCTURE
LIST STRUCTURE TO PRINT
LIST STRUCTURE TO DBFSTRUC.TXT
```

LOAD

Syntax: LOAD $<$ *name of binary file*$>$

Loads a binary file to memory before calling the file:

```
LOAD ADDAB
A=1Ø
B=2Ø
CALL ADDAB WITH A,B
```

LOCATE

Syntax: LOCATE [FOR $<$ *filter conditions*$>$][$<$ *record scope*$>$]
                     [WHILE $<$ *filter conditions*$>$]

Sequentially searches data records in the active database file for a
record that satisfies the specified condition:

```
USE EMPLOYEE
LOCATE FOR LAST_NAME="Smith"
LOCATE FOR UPPER(FIRST_NAME)="JAMES"
LOCATE FOR FIRST_NAME="J" .AND. LAST_NAME="S"
```

LOGOUT

Syntax: LOGOUT

Releases the current user logged into the application and sets up a new log-in screen.

LOOP

Syntax: LOOP

Transfers execution from the middle of a program loop to the beginning of the loop:

```
DO WHILE .T.
    ...
    ...
    IF ...
         LOOP
    ENDIF
    ...
ENDDO
```

MODIFY APPLICATION

Syntax: MODIFY APPLICATION < *file name*>]

Starts the dBASE IV applications generator.

MODIFY COMMAND

Syntax: MODIFY COMMAND < *name of the program or text file*>
           [WINDOW < *window name*>]

Invokes the text editor to create or edit a program file (.PRG), a format file (.FMT), or a text file (.TXT). The default file extension is .PRG.

```
MODIFY COMMAND MAINPROG
MODIFY COMMAND BILLING.PRG
MODIFY COMMAND EMPLOYEE.FMT
MODIFY COMMAND TEXTFILE.TXT
```

MODIFY LABEL

Syntax: MODIFY LABEL < *.lbl file name*>

Displays an existing label form (.LBL file) for modifications:

```
USE ADDRESS
MODIFY LABEL MAILLIST
```

MODIFY QUERY

Syntax: MODIFY QUERY < *.qbe file name*>

Displays the query design screen for an existing query file (.QBE) for modifications:

```
USE EMPLOYEE
MODIFY QUERY FINDEMPL
```

MODIFY REPORT

Syntax: MODIFY REPORT < *.frm file name*>

Displays a report design form for an existing report form file (.FRM) for modifications:

```
USE EXPENSES
MODIFY REPORT COLUMNØ1
```

MODIFY SCREEN

Syntax: MODIFY SCREEN < *.fmt file name*>

Displays a screen design for an existing screen file (.FMT) for modifications:

```
USE EMPLOYEE
MODIFY SCREEN DATAFORM
```

MODIFY STRUCTURE

Syntax: MODIFY STRUCTURE

Displays the database structure of the current database file for modifications:

```
USE EMPLOYEE
MODIFY STRUCTURE
```

MODIFY VIEW

Syntax: MODIFY VIEW < *.vue file name*>

Displays the view skeleton of an existing query design for modifications:

```
USE EMPLOYEE
MODIFY VIEW SAMPLE.VUE
```

MOVE WINDOW

Syntax: MOVE WINDOW < *name of window*>
            TO< *row, column*> /
            BY < *delta row, delta column*>

Moves a window to a new location:

```
DEFINE WINDOW W1 FROM 1,50 TO 10,79
ACTIVATE WINDOW W1
DIR
MOVE WINDOW W1 TO 10,5
DIR
MOVE WINDOW W1 BY 10,10
DIR
```

NOTE

Syntax: NOTE < *text*>

Or

[< *command*>] && < *text*>

Marks the beginning of a remark line in a program. You may use *
or && in place of NOTE:

```
NOTE This is a sample program
* Enter hours worked and pay rate.
INPUT "Enter hours worked . . . " TO Hours
INPUT "  hourly rate . . . " TO PayRate
. . .
. . .
QUIT       && This is the end of the program.
```

ON ERROR

Syntax: ON ERROR < *command*>

Executes the specified command if an error occurs:

```
ON ERROR DO PROGA
```

ON ESCAPE

Syntax: ON ESCAPE < *command*>

Executes the specified command if the Esc key is pressed:

```
ON ESCAPE DO PROGB
```

ON KEY

Syntax: ON KEY [< *key name*>] < *command*>

Traps the specified key in EDIT, BROWSE, and READ operations. The command is executed when you press the specified key in those operations:

```
ON KEY Esc STOP
ON KEY Home DO NEWRECORD
```

If you omit the key, pressing any key executes the command.

ON PAD

Syntax: ON PAD < *name of menu pad*> OF < *menu name*>
            [ACTIVATE POPUP < *pop-up name*>]

Associates a pop-up menu with the specified menu pad of a given bar menu, with or without activating the pop-up menu:

```
DEFINE MENU DataMenu
DEFINE PAD ViewData of DataMenu PROMPT "View a record";
    AT 3,1
DEFINE PAD EditData of DataMenu PROMPT "Edit a record";
    AT 3,20

ON PAD ViewData of DataMenu ACTIVATE POPUP ViewMenu
ON PAD EditData of DataMenu ACTIVATE POPUP EditMenu
```

ON PAGE

Syntax: ON PAGE [AT LINE < *line #*> < *command*>]

Executes the specified command (usually for printing a header, a page break, or a footnote) when the specified line is encountered:

```
ON PAGE AT LINE 50 DO ShowHeader
```

ON READERROR

Syntax: ON READERROR [< *command*>]

Executes the specified command when an error occurs during data
entry:

    ON READERROR STOP
    ON READERROR DO ErrorMsg

ON SELECTION PAD

Syntax: ON SELECTION PAD < *name of menu pad*>
            OF< *menu name*>
            [< *command*>]

Defines the command (usually activates a pop-up menu) to be
executed when the specified menu pad is selected:

    ON SELECTION PAD EditData OF DataMenu;
        ACTIVATE POPUP EditMenu

ON SELECTION POPUP

Syntax: ON SELECTION POPUP < *name of pop-up option*> /ALL
            [< *command*>]

Defines the command to be executed when the specified pop-up
menu option is selected:

    ON SELECTION POPUP AddRecord DO NewRecord

PACK

Syntax: PACK

Removes data records marked for deletion with the DELETE
command:

```
USE EMPLOYEE
DELETE RECORD 5
PACK
```

After packing the records, all index tags are rebuilt automatically.

PARAMETERS

Syntax: PARAMETERS *< parameter list>*

Assigns local variable names to data items that are to be passed
from a calling program module to another program or procedure:

```
***** Program: MULTIPLY.PRG *****
* A program to multiply variable A by variable B
PARAMETERS A,B,C
C=A*B
RETURN
```

The MULTIPLY.PRG program is called from the following main
program:

```
* The main program
Hours=38
PayRate=8.5
DO MULTIPLY WITH Hours,PayRate,GrossPay
?"Gross Wage =",GrossPay
RETURN
```

PLAY MACRO

Syntax: PLAY MACRO *< name of macro>*

Plays an existing macro:

```
PLAY MACRO EditData
```

PRINTJOB

Syntax: PRINTJOB

                    . . .

            < *commands*>

                    . . .

            ENDPRINTJOB

Defines the commands that are associated with a print job:

```
SET PRINT ON
PRINTJOB
    . . .
    ON PAGE AT LINE 5Ø DO NEWPATE
    . . .
ENDPRINTJOB
```

PRIVATE

Syntax: PRIVATE < *memory variable list*> /ALL
            [LIKE/EXCEPT < *skeleton*>]

Declares all or some variables in a program module private:

```
PRIVATE VariableA, VariableB, VariableC
PRIVATE ALL
PRIVATE ALL EXCEPT Var????
```

PROCEDURE

Syntax: PROCEDURE < *program procedure name*>

Identifies the beginning of a procedure:

```
*** MAIN PROGRAM ***
A=1Ø
B=2Ø
DO ADDAB
RETURN

PROCEDURE ADDAB
SumAB=A +B
?"Sum of A and B is =",SumAB
RETURN
```

PROTECT

Syntax: PROTECT

Maintains security in a single- or multiuser system.

PUBLIC

Syntax: PUBLIC < *memory variable list*> /
            [ARRAY< *array element list*>]

Declares memory variables or elements in arrays public (can be shared by all program modules):

```
PUBLIC VariableA, VariableB
PUBLIC ARRAY ArrayA[5], ArrayB[1Ø,3]
```

QUIT

Syntax: QUIT

Closes all open files, terminates dBASE IV processing, and exits to DOS.

READ

Syntax: READ [SAVE]

Activates all @...SAY...GET commands issued since the last CLEAR
or CLEAR GETS command:

```
USE EMPLOYEE
@5,1Ø SAY "Last name  : " GET LAST_NAME
@6,1Ø SAY "First name : " GET FIRST_NAME
READ
```

RECALL

Syntax: RECALL [< *record scope*>][FOR < *filter conditions*>]
            [WHILE < *filter conditions*>]

Recovers all or selected data records marked for deletion:

```
RECALL
RECALL ALL
RECALL RECORD 5
RECALL FOR AREA_CODE="2Ø6"
RECALL FOR RECNO( ) > =5 .AND. RECNO( ) < =8
```

REINDEX

Syntax: REINDEX

Rebuilds all active individual index (.NDX) and multiple index
(.MDX) files in the current work area:

```
USE EMPLOYEE
SET INDEX TO AREACODE
REINDEX
```

RELEASE

Syntax: RELEASE < *memory variable list*> /
ALL [LIKE/EXCEPT < *skeleton*>]

Deletes all or selected memory variables:

```
RELEASE PO_NUM
RELEASE ALL
RELEASE ALL LIKE NET*
RELEASE ALL EXCEPT ???COST
```

RENAME

Syntax: RENAME < *old file name*> TO < *new file name*>

Changes the name of a disk file:

```
RENAME XYZ.DBF TO ABC.DBF
RENAME MAINPROG.PRG TO MAIN.PRG
RENAME MAILIST.LBL TO MAILLIST.LBL
```

REPLACE

Syntax: REPLACE < *field name*> WITH
< *new field value*> [ADDITIVE]
[< *field name*> WITH < *new field value*> ,...
[ADDITIVE]][< *record scope*>]
[FOR < *filter conditions*>]
[WHILE < *filter conditions*>]

Replaces the contents of specified data fields with all or selective
records in the current database file:

```
USE EMPLOYEE
REPLACE ALL ANNUAL_PAY WITH ANNUAL_PAY*1.Ø5
REPLACE FIRST_NAME WITH "James K." FOR FIRST_NAME="James C."
REPLACE ALL AREA_CODE WITH "2Ø6" FOR AREA_CODE="216"
```

REPORT FORM

Syntax: REPORT FORM < .frm file> /? [PLAIN]
           [HEADING < heading text>][NOEJECT][SUMMARY]
           [< record scope>][FOR < filter conditions>]
           [WHILE < filter conditions>]
           [TO PRINT/FILE < name of text file>]

Displays, prints, or sends to a text file information from the active
database file in the report form specified. Use the HEADING clause to
add an extra heading (in addition to any heading specified in the
report form layout). Use the NOEJECT clause to suppress the form
feed so that all the report pages are printed on a continuous form.
The SUMMARY clause displays only the contents of the summary
bands in the report; information in the detail bands is skipped.

```
USE QTYSOLD
REPORT FORM WEEKLY
REPORT FORM WEEKLY FOR RECNO()> =2 .AND. RECNO() < =1Ø
REPORT FORM WEEKLY HEADING "A Weekly Sale Report"
REPORT FORM WEEKLY FOR QTY> 1Ø
REPORT FORM WEEKLY TO PRINT
REPORT FORM WEEKLY TO TEXTFILE.TXT
```

RESTORE

Syntax: RESTORE FROM < .mem file> [ADDITIVE]

Retrieves all the memory variables from the specified memory
variable (.MEM) file and places them in memory. Use the ADDITIVE
clause to add the memory variables to those already in memory;
otherwise, all existing memory variables are cleared:

```
RESTORE FROM MemFile
RESTORE FROM MemFile ADDITIVE
```

RESTORE MACROS

Syntax: RESTORE MACROS FROM < *.key file name*>

Retrieves all macros from the specified macro key (.KEY) file and places them in memory:

```
RESTORE MACROS FROM MACFILE
```

RESTORE WINDOW

Syntax: RESTORE WINDOW < *window name list*> /
           ALL FROM< *.win file name*>

Restores all or selective window definitions from an existing window definition (.WIN) file:

```
DEFINE WINDOW WindowA FROM 1,1 TO 5,20
DEFINE WINDOW WindowB FROM 10,10 TO 20,50
SAVE WINDOW ALL TO WINFILE
...
...
RESTORE WINDOW WindowA FROM WINFILE
RESTORE WINDOW WindowB FROM WINFILE
```

RESUME

Syntax: RESUME

Causes a program to continue processing after it has been suspended.

RETRY

Syntax: RETRY

Reexecutes a section of the program that caused an error.

RETURN

Syntax: RETURN [< *expression*> /TO MASTER/
                  TO < *name of procedure*>]

Passes program control among program modules and to the dot prompt:

   RETURN

Passes program control with parameters from a module or line to the calling program:

   RETURN Mnum

Passes program control from within a program module to the main program:

   RETURN TO MASTER

Passes program control from within a procedure to the specified procedure:

   RETURN TO ProgA

ROLLBACK

Syntax: ROLLBACK [< *database file name*>]

Undoes all changes that were made in a transaction declared by BEGIN TRANSACTION/END TRANSACTION:

   BEGIN TRANSACTION
      . . .
      ROLLBACK
   END TRANSACTION

RUN/!

Syntax: RUN/! *< DOS command>*

Executes a DOS command from within dBASE IV:

```
RUN TIME
RUN DIR B:*.MDX
RUN COPY ABC.DBF XYZ.DBF
RUN ERASE *.BAK
```

Brings up a DOS shell (type EXIT and press Enter to return to dBASE IV):

```
.RUN COMMAND
C:\EXIT
```

SAVE

Syntax: SAVE TO *< .mem file name>*
            [ALL LIKE/EXCEPT *< skeleton>*]

Stores all or selective memory variables currently in memory to the specified memory variable (.MEM) file:

```
SAVE TO ALLVARS
SAVE TO VARLIST ALL EXCEPT NET*
SAVE TO VARLIST ALL LIKE COST????
```

SAVE MACROS

Syntax: SAVE MACROS TO *< .key file name>*

Stores all the macros currently in memory to the specified macro key (.KEY) file:

```
SAVE MACROS TO MACFILE
```

SAVE WINDOW

Syntax: SAVE WINDOW < *window name list*> /
            ALL TO < *.win file name*>

Stores all or selective window definitions to the specified window
definition (.WIN) file:

```
DEFINE WINDOW WindowA FROM 1,1 TO 5,20
DEFINE WINDOW WindowB FROM 10,10 TO 20,50
SAVE WINDOW ALL TO WINFILE
```

SCAN

Syntax: SCAN < *record scope*> [FOR < *filter conditions*>]
            [WHILE < *filter conditions*>]

                . . .
            < *commands*>
                . . .
            [LOOP]
            [EXIT]
            ENDSCAN

Scans and processes the records within the record scope that meet
the filter conditions:

```
USE EMPLOYEE
SCAN ALL FOR AREA_CODE="503"

        . . .
    IF ANNUAL_PAY > =20000

            . . .
    ELSE
            LOOP
    ENDIF
        . . .
        . . .
ENDSCAN
```

SEEK

Syntax: SEEK < *searching key value*>

Finds the first record with a value in the indexed field that matches the specified key value:

```
USE EMPLOYEE
SET ORDER TO LAST_NAME
SEEK "Gregory"
IF FOUND()
     EDIT
ENDIF
```

SELECT

Syntax: SELECT < *work area #/alias*>

Places a database file in a specified work area; or defines an alias for an active database file:

```
SELECT 1
USE EMPLOYEE
SELECT B
USE COSTS
```

SET

Syntax: SET

Sets control parameters for processing. The default settings (indicated by uppercase letters) are appropriate for most purposes.

SET ALTERNATE

Syntax: SET ALTERNATE on/OFF

Or

SET ALTERNATE TO
[< *name of text file*> [ADDITIVE]]

Creates a text file to record processing activities:

```
SET ALTERNATE TO LISTING.TXT
SET ALTERNATE ON
```

Use the ADDITIVE clause to add processing activities to an existing text file; otherwise, the contents of the text file are cleared.

SET AUTOSAVE

Syntax: SET AUTOSAVE on/OFF

Saves each data record to the disk file after you make any changes.

SET BELL

Syntax: SET BELL ON/off

Or

SET BELL TO [< *frequency, duration*>]

Turns on and off the bell that sounds when you reach the end of a data field.

SET BLOCKSIZE

Syntax: SET BLOCKSIZE < *blocks of memo files*>

Specifies the size of the memo file blocks (1–31) in multiples of 512 bytes.

SET BORDER

Syntax: SET BORDER TO [SINGLE/DOUBLE/PANEL/NONE/
            < *border definition string*>]

Defines the default border for menus and windows as single-,
double-line, or special character boxes.

SET CARRY

Syntax: SET CARRY on/OFF

            Or

            SET CARRY TO [< *field list*> [ADDITIVE]]

Carries the contents of the previous record into an appended
record.

SET CATALOG

Syntax: SET CATALOG ON/off

            Or

            SET CATALOG TO [< *.cat file name*>]

Selects or creates a catalog (.CAT) file and adds files to the open
catalog:

    SET CATALOG TO EMPLOYEE
    SET CATALOG ON

SET CENTURY

Syntax: SET CENTURY on/OFF

Shows the century in date displays:

```
?Date( )
12/25/88
SET CENTURY ON
?Date( )
12/25/1988
```

SET CLOCK

Syntax: SET CLOCK on/OFF

          Or

          SET CLOCK TO [< *row,column*>]

Turns on and off the display of the system clock and determines
where to display the system time. The default is at row 0, column
69 (0,69).

```
SET CLOCK ON
SET CLOCK TO 1,1Ø
```

SET COLOR

Syntax: SET COLOR ON/OFF

Sets the output display to a color or monochrome monitor. The
default is the mode from which dBASE IV is started.

SET COLOR TO

Syntax: SET COLOR TO [[< *standard* >][, < *enhanced* >]
            [, < *perimeter or border* >][, < *background* >]]

Sets screen color attributes. Available colors and their codes include
the following:

Color	Letter
Black	N
Blue	B
Green	G
Cyan	BG
Blank	X
Red	R
Magenta	RB
Brown	GR
White	W

Use an asterisk (*) to indicate blinking characters and a plus sign
(+) to indicate high intensity.

The following command sets a standard video to yellow characters
on a red background, and an enhanced video to white letters on a
red background with a yellow (GR +) screen border:

```
SET COLOR TO GR+/R,W/R,GR
```

SET CONFIRM

Syntax: SET CONFIRM on/OFF

Controls the cursor movement from one variable to the next when
the first variable is filled.

SET CONSOLE

Syntax: SET CONSOLE ON/off

Turns on and off the video display.

SET CURRENCY

Syntax: SET CURRENCY TO < *currency symbol*>

Or

SET CURRENCY LEFT/right

Specifies the currency symbol (up to nine characters) used to display monetary values. Use the LEFT or RIGHT clause to display the currency symbol to the left or right of the value:

```
SET CURRENCY TO "HK$"
SET CURRENCY LEFT
SET CURRENCY TO "DM"
SET CURRENCY RIGHT
```

You also can use the SET POINT TO command to define the symbol for the decimal point and the SET SEPARATOR command to specify the symbol for the digits separators (for example, DM12.345,67):

```
SET CURRENCY TO "DM"
SET POINT TO ","
SET SEPARATOR TO "."
```

SET DATE

Syntax: SET DATE AMERICAN/ansi/british/french/
          german/italian/japan/usa/mdy/dmy/ymd

Specifies the format for date expressions:

SET DATE AMERICAN	(mm/dd/yy)
SET DATE ANSI	(yy.mm.dd)
SET DATE BRITISH	(dd/mm/yy)
SET DATE FRENCH	(dd/mm/yy)
SET DATE GERMAN	(dd.mm.yy)
SET DATE ITALIAN	(dd-mm-yy)
SET DATE JAPAN	(yy/mm/dd)
SET DATE USA	(mm-dd-yy)
SET DATE MDY	(mm/dd/yy)
SET DATE DMY	(dd/mm/yy)
SET DATE YMD	(yy/mm/dd)

SET DEBUG

Syntax: SET DEBUG on/OFF

Traces the command errors during processing. When DEBUG is on,
messages from the SET ECHO ON command are routed to the printer.

SET DECIMALS

Syntax: SET DECIMALS TO < *decimal places*>

Sets the number of decimal places for values:

    SET DECIMALS TO 4

SET DEFAULT TO

Syntax: SET DEFAULT TO < *disk drive*> [:]

Designates the default disk drive:

    SET DEFAULT TO D:
    SET DEFAULT TO C

SET DELETED

Syntax: SET DELETED on/OFF

Determines whether data records marked for deletion are ignored.

SET DELIMITERS

Syntax: SET DELIMITERS on/OFF

Or

SET DELIMITERS TO
   < character expression> /DEFAULT

Marks field widths with the delimiter defined with the SET
DELIMITERS TO command:

```
SET DELIMITERS TO '[]'
SET DELIMITERS ON
```

SET DESIGN

Syntax: SET DESIGN ON/off

Enables or disables transferring to design mode (for label, query,
report, data entry form, and so on) from the dot prompt or from
the Control Center.

SET DEVELOPMENT

Syntax: SET DEVELOPMENT ON/off

Checks the development or creation date of the object code
(.DBO) file with the source (.PRG) file to ensure that the object
code reflects the changes made in the source file.

SET DEVICE

Syntax: SET DEVICE TO SCREEN/printer/file
   < name of text file>

Selects the display medium for @. . .SAY commands.

SET DISPLAY

Syntax: SET DISPLAY TO MONO/COLOR/EGA25/EGA43/MONO43

Selects the display monitor mode and number of lines displayed on-screen.

SET DOHISTORY

Syntax: SET DOHISTORY on/OFF

Remains for dBASE III PLUS compatibility; not used.

SET ECHO

Syntax: SET ECHO on/OFF

Displays instructions during execution.

SET ENCRYPTION

Syntax: SET ENCRYPTION on/OFF

If used with PROTECT, establishes whether a database file is encrypted.

SET ESCAPE

Syntax: SET ESCAPE ON/off

Controls capability of aborting execution with the Esc key. When ESCAPE is on, pressing Esc aborts the execution of a program.

SET EXACT

Syntax: SET EXACT on/OFF

Determines how two character strings are compared.

SET EXCLUSIVE

Syntax: SET EXCLUSIVE on/OFF

On a multiuser system, allows a database to be open for exclusive use only.

SET FIELDS

Syntax: SET FIELDS on/OFF

Or

SET FIELDS TO [< *fields list* > [/R]]

Or

SET FIELDS TO ALL [LIKE/EXCEPT < *skeleton* >]

Activates the selection of data fields named with the SET FIELDS TO command. SET FIELDS TO selects a set of data fields to be used in one or more files:

```
USE EMPLOYEE
SET FIELDS TO LAST_NAME, FIRST_NAME
SET FIELDS ON
```

SET FILTER TO

Syntax: SET FILTER TO [FILE < *.dbf file name* > /?]
           [< *filter conditions* >]

Defines the filter conditions:

```
USE EMPLOYEE
SET FILTER TO AREA_CODE="216"
```

SET FIXED

Syntax: SET FIXED on/OFF

Sets all numeric output to the fixed number of decimal places defined by SET DECIMALS TO.

SET FORMAT

Syntax: SET FORMAT TO $<$ *.fmt file name* $>$

Selects the custom format defined in a format (.FMT) file.

SET FULLPATH

Syntax: SET FULLPATH on/OFF

Returns the full file name and its directory path for those functions that return file names—MDX( ), NDX( ), DBF( ), and so on.

SET FUNCTION

Syntax: SET FUNCTION $<$ *function key* # $>$
           TO $<$ *character expression* $>$

Redefines a function key for a specific command:

    SET FUNCTION 1Ø TO "QUIT"

SET HEADING

Syntax: SET HEADING ON/off

Uses field names as column titles for displaying data records with the DISPLAY, LIST, SUM, and AVERAGE commands.

SET HELP

Syntax: SET HELP ON/off

Determines whether the Help screen is displayed.

SET HISTORY

Syntax: SET HISTORY ON/off

OR

SET HISTORY TO < *number of executed commands*>

Turns on and off the history feature. SET HISTORY TO specifies the number of executed commands saved in the history.

    SET HISTORY TO 1Ø

SET HOURS

Syntax: SET HOURS TO [12/24]

Sets system time to either a 12- (default) or 24-hour clock.

SET INDEX

Syntax: SET INDEX TO ?/< *.ndx or .mdx file name*>
              [ORDER < *.ndx file name*> /
              ORDER TAG < *index tag*>
              [OF < *.mdx file name*>]]

Assigns a controlling index with an individual index (.NDX) file or an index tag from a multiple index (.MDX) file:

    USE EMPLOYEE
    SET INDEX TO BYLAST
    SET ORDER TO LAST_NAME
    SET INDEX TO STAFF.MDX ORDER TAG LAST_NAME

SET INSTRUCT

Syntax: SET INSTRUCT ON/off

Displays prompts for input operations such as APPEND, BROWSE, and EDIT.

SET INTENSITY

Syntax: SET INTENSITY ON/off

Displays data fields in reverse video with the EDIT and APPEND commands.

SET LOCK

Syntax: SET LOCK ON/off

Determines whether records in a multiuser database should be locked.

SET MARGIN

Syntax: SET MARGIN TO < *left margin in characters*>

Adjusts the left margin for all printed output:

SET MARGIN TO 1Ø

SET MARK

Syntax: SET MARK TO [< *character expression*>]

Determines the character used to separate the month, day, and year in date display.

SET MEMOWIDTH

Syntax: SET MEMOWIDTH TO
            < *width of memo field output in characters*>

Defines the width of memo field output (default width is 50).

SET MEMOWIDTH TO 3Ø

SET MESSAGE

Syntax: SET MESSAGE TO [< *character string for the message*>]

Displays a character string (up to 79 characters) in the message window:

```
SET MESSAGE TO "Hello!"
```

SET NEAR

Syntax: SET NEAR on/OFF

Positions the record pointer to the record nearest the searching key value (when the value was not found in the search).

SET ODOMETER

Syntax: SET ODOMETER TO < *record number*>

Defines the interval (up to 200 records, default is 1) at which the record counter is updated.

SET ORDER

Syntax: SET ORDER TO [< *number of open .ndx files*>]

            Or

            SET ORDER TO < *.ndx file*>

            Or

            SET ORDER TO TAG < *index tag*>
            [OF < *.mdx file name*>]

Designates the controlling index by using an individual index (.NDX) file or an index tag of a multiple index (.MDX) file:

```
USE EMPLOYEE INDEX LASTNAME,PAYRANK,AREACODE
SET ORDER TO 3
SET ORDER TO TAG FIRST_NAME
```

SET PATH

Syntax: SET PATH TO < *path list*>

Defines the search directory path:

    SET PATH TO C:\DBASE\DBDATA\SALES

SET PAUSE

Syntax: SET PAUSE on/OFF

Controls the display of the SQL SELECT command. When PAUSE is on, the SELECT command works with DISPLAY; otherwise, it works with LIST.

SET POINT

Syntax: SET POINT [< *symbol for the decimal point*>]

Specifies the symbol (default is a period) for the decimal point for displaying foreign monetary values:

    SET POINT TO ","

SET PRECISION

Syntax: SET PRECISION TO [< *number of precision digits*>]

Specifies the number of precision digits (10–20, default is 16) used in computations:

    SET PRECISION TO 20

SET PRINTER

Syntax: SET PRINTER on/OFF

Or

SET PRINTER TO < *DOS device*>

Or

SET PRINTER TO \\< *computer name*> \
      < *printer name*> =< *destination*>

Or

SET PRINTER TO \\SPOOLER

Or

SET PRINTER TO \\CAPTURE

Or

SET PRINTER TO FILE < *file name*>

Directs output generated with @. . .SAY commands to the printer, screen, or other device.

SET PROCEDURE

Syntax: SET PROCEDURE TO [< *procedure file name*>]

Opens a specified procedure program file.

SET REFRESH

Syntax: SET REFRESH TO < *numeric expression*>

Specifies the interval of time that a file is checked for changes in a multiuser system (default is 0).

SET RELATION

Syntax: SET RELATION TO [< *linking key expression*>]
            [INTO < *alias of the linking .dbf file*>]

Links two open database files according to a common key expression:

```
SELECT 1
USE ACCOUNTS ORDER TAG ACCT_NO
SELECT 2
USE BALANCE ORDER TAG ACCT_NO
SET RELATION TO ACCT_NO INTO ACCOUNTS
```

SET REPROCESS

Syntax: SET REPROCESS TO < *numeric expression*>

Defines the number of times to try a network file or locked record before an error message is displayed.

SET SAFETY

Syntax: SET SAFETY ON/off

Displays a warning message before you overwrite an existing file or use a command that destroys data (ZAP, for instance).

SET SCOREBOARD

Syntax: SET SCOREBOARD ON/off

Displays or hides dBASE messages on the status line.

SET SEPARATOR

Syntax: SET SEPARATOR TO [< *separator symbol*>]

Specifies the symbol (default is a comma) for separating digits in foreign monetary values (for example, 1.234,56):

    SET SEPARATOR TO "."

SET SKIP

Syntax: SET SKIP TO [< *alias file name*>]

In conjunction with the SET RELATION TO command, determines the sequence of updates on the database files.

SET SPACE

Syntax: SET SPACE ON/off

Displays a space between the expression value printed with ? and ?? commands.

SET SQL

Syntax: SET SQL on/OFF

Invokes Structure Query Language (SQL) mode within dBASE IV.

SET STATUS

Syntax: SET STATUS ON/off

Displays or hides the status bar at the bottom of the screen.

SET STEP

Syntax: SET STEP on/OFF

Pauses execution after each command.

SET TALK

Syntax: SET TALK ON/off

Displays interactive messages during processing.

SET TITLE

Syntax: SET TITLE ON/off

Displays the catalog file title prompt.

SET TRAP

Syntax: SET TRAP on/OFF

Activates the debugger for tracing errors in a program.

SET TYPEAHEAD

Syntax: SET TYPEAHEAD TO < *number of characters*>

Specifies the size of the type-ahead buffer (0–32,000 characters; default is 20 characters):

    SET TYPEAHEAD TO 3Ø

SET UNIQUE

Syntax: SET UNIQUE on/OFF

When on, prepares an ordered list with the INDEX command, displaying only the first record with identical keys.

SET VIEW

Syntax: SET VIEW TO < *.qbe file name* > /?

Selects an existing query (.QBE) file.

```
SET VIEW TO EMPLOYEE
```

SET WINDOW

Syntax: SET WINDOW OF MEMO TO < *window name* >

Selects the window to display the memo field:

```
DEFINE WINDOW UPPERWIN FROM 1,1 to 10,30
SET WINDOW OF MEMO TO UPPERWIN
```

SHOW MENU

Syntax: SHOW MENU < *name of bar menu* >
            [PAD < *name of menu pad* >]

Displays over the existing contents the specified bar menu:

```
SHOW MENU DataMenu PAD AddData
```

SHOW POPUP

Syntax: SHOW POPUP < *name of pop-up menu* >

Displays the specified pop-up menu:

```
SHOW POPUP ViewData
```

SKIP

Syntax: SKIP [< *number of records*>]
           [IN< *alias file name*>]

Skips the specified number of records in the current database file:

```
USE BALANCE
GOTO 3
DISPLAY
SKIP 2
DISPLAY
USE ACCOUNTS IN 2
GO BOTTOM
SKIP 3 IN ACCOUNTS
```

SORT

Syntax: SORT TO < *.dbf file name*> ON < *sorting key field #1*>
           [/A][/C][/D][, < *sorting key field #2*> [/A][/C]
           [/D]...][ASCENDING]/[DESCENDING]
           < *record scope*> [FOR < *filter conditions*>]
           [WHILE < *filter conditions*>]

Rearranges data records on one or more key fields in ascending or
descending order (the default is ascending order):

```
USE EMPLOYEE
SORT TO AREACODE ON AREA_CODE
SORT TO SORTED ON AREA_CODE, PHONE_NO DESCENDING
SORT ON ANNUAL_PAY/D TO RANKED FOR MALE
SORT ON AREA_CODE, LAST_NAME/D TO PHONLIST FOR
   AREA_CODE="206"
```

STORE

Syntax: STORE < *expression*> TO < *memory variable list*> /
            < *array element list*>

Assigns the value of the expression (numeric or character) to one
or more memory variables or array elements:

```
DECLARE Name[5]
STORE 1 TO Count
STORE "James" TO FirstName
STORE Ø TO Sum1, Sum2, Sum3
STORE SPACE(1Ø) TO Name[1],Name[2],Name[3]
```

SUM

Syntax: SUM [< *numeric expression list*>]
            [TO< *memory variable list*> /
            TO ARRAY< *name of array*>]
            [< *record scope*>][FOR < *filter conditions*>]
            [WHILE < *filter conditions*>]

Totals and stores the value of a numeric expression in one or more
memory variables or array elements:

```
DECLARE SumPay[2]
USE EMPLOYEE
SUM ANNUAL_PAY TO TotalPay
SUM ANNUAL_PAY, ANNUAL_PAY*Ø.1 TO ARRAY SumPay FOR MALE
```

SUSPEND

Syntax: SUSPEND

Suspends the execution of a program or procedure.

TEXT

Syntax: TEXT

　　　　　　. . .

　　　　　　< *text*>

　　　　　　. . .

　　　　　　ENDTEXT

Displays or prints a block of text; used in a program:

```
*****    Program: BULLETIN.PRG    *****
SET PRINT ON
TEXT
This is a sample message to be displayed on the printer
when this program is executed.
ENDTEXT
```

TOTAL

Syntax: TOTAL ON < *key field*> TO < *.dbf file*>
　　　　　　[FIELDS < *fields list*>][< *record scope*>]
　　　　　　[FOR < *filter conditions*>]
　　　　　　[WHILE < *filter conditions*>]

Sums the numeric values of the active database file on a key field
and stores the results to another database file:

```
USE STOCKS
TOTAL ON MODEL_NO TO BYMODEL
TOTAL ON STOCK_NO TO BYSTOCNO FOR ON_HAND> ="2"
```

TYPE

Syntax: TYPE < *name of text file*>
　　　　　　[TO PRINT/TO FILE < *name of text file*>]

Displays, prints, or sends to another text file the contents of a text
or program (.PRG) file:

```
TYPE MAINPROG.PRG
TYPE EMPLOYEE.FMT TO PRINT
TYPE MAINPROG.PRG TO FILE PRGTEXT.TXT
```

UNLOCK

Syntax: UNLOCK [ALL/IN < *alias file name*>]

Releases records or files that have been locked in selected or all
data areas.

UPDATE

Syntax: UPDATE ON < *key field*> FROM < *alias file name*>
REPLACE < *field name #1*> WITH < *new field value*>
[, < *field name #2*> WITH < *new field value*> ...]
[RANDOM]

Uses records in one database file to update records in another file:

```
SELECT A
USE RECEIVED
SELECT B
USE STOCKS
UPDATE ON STOCK_NO FROM RECEIVED REPLACE ON_HAND WITH;
    ON_HAND +A--> ON_HAND
```

USE

Syntax: USE [< *.dbf file name*> /?][IN < *work area #*>]
[[INDEX < *.ndx or .mdx file list*>]
[ORDER [TAG] < *.ndx file name*> /
< *.mdx index tag*>] [OF < *.mdx file name*>]]
[ALIAS < *alias file name*>][EXCLUSIVE][NOUPDATE]

Opens an existing database file, with or without assigning the
controlling index (.NDX) file or index tag of the multiple index
(.MDX) file:

```
USE EMPLOYEE
USE EMPLOYEE INDEX BYLAST
USE EMPLOYEE INDEX TAG AREA_CODE
USE EMPLOYEE INDEX TAB ANNUAL_PAY OF PAYINDEX
USE EMPLOYEE ORDER TAB FIRST_NAME IN 2
```

WAIT

Syntax: WAIT [< *prompt*>][TO < *memory variable*>]

Pauses execution until a key is pressed, with or without displaying a prompt:

```
WAIT
WAIT TO MenuChoice
WAIT "Enter your answer (Y/N)? " TO Answer
```

ZAP

Syntax: ZAP

Removes all data records from the database file without deleting the data structure:

```
USE EMPLOYEE
ZAP
```

dBASE IV Functions Summary

Built-In Functions Listed by Purpose

To manipulate time and date data:

CDOW( )
CMONTH( )
DATE( )
DAY( )
DOW( )
MONTH( )
TIME( )
YEAR( )

To convert contents of data fields or memory variables:

CTOD( )
DMY( )
DTOC( )
DTOS( )
MDY( )
STR( )
VAL( )

To convert character strings:

```
ASC( )
CHR( )
LOWER( )
UPPER( )
```

To manipulate character strings:

```
AT( )
DIFFERENCE( )
LEFT( )
LEN( )
LIKE( )
LOOKUP( )
LTRIM( )
REPLICATE( )
RIGHT( )
RTRIM( )
SOUNDEX( )
SPACE( )
STUFF( )
SUBSTR( )
TRANSFORM( )
TRIM( )
```

To perform mathematical operations:

```
ABS( )
ACOS( )
ASIN( )
ATAN( )
ATN2( )
CEILING( )
COS( )
DTOR( )
EXP( )
FIXED( )
FLOAT( )
FLOOR( )
INT( )
LOG( )
LOG10( )
MAX( )
```

```
MIN( )
MOD( )
PI( )
RAND( )
ROUND( )
RTOD( )
SIGN( )
SIN( )
SQRT( )
TAN( )
```

To perform statistical and financial computations:

```
FV( )
PAYMENT( )
PV( )
```

To perform operations related to memo fields:

```
MEMLINES( )
MLINE( )
```

To track the record pointer:

```
RECCOUNT( )
RECNO( )
RECSIZE( )
```

To identify the location of the cursor and print head:

```
COL( )
PCOL( )
PROW( )
ROW( )
```

To check file attributes, error conditions, and data-element types:

```
ALIAS( )
BOF( )
COMPLETED( )
DELETED( )
DISKSPACE( )
EOF( )
ERROR( )
FIELD( )
FILE( )
```

```
FOUND( )
IIF( )
ISALPHA( )
ISCOLOR( )
ISLOWER( )
ISUPPER( )
LINENO( )
LKSYS( )
LUPDATE( )
MEMORY( )
MESSAGE( )
NETWORK( )
PRINTSTATUS( )
PROGRAM( )
ROLLBACK( )
SELECT( )
SET( )
TYPE( )
VARREAD( )
```

To use the macro function:

```
&
```

To identify and use index files and tags:

```
KEY( )
MDX( )
NDX( )
ORDER( )
SEEK( )
TAG( )
```

To identify and use menus:

```
BAR( )
MENU( )
PAD( )
POPUP( )
PROMPT( )
```

To check keyboard input:

```
INKEY( )
LASTKEY( )
READKEY( )
```

To identify attributes of database and DOS files:

```
ALIAS( )
CHANGE( )
DBF( )
FIELD( )
FKLABEL( )
FKMAX( )
FLOCK( )
GETENV( )
ISMARKED( )
NDX( )
OS( )
RLOCK( )/LOCK( )
VERSION( )
```

To execute a subprogram or procedure:

```
CALL( )
```

Summary of Built-In Functions

 &

Syntax: &< *character memory variable*>

Substitutes the contents of a character memory variable for the
variable name:

```
STORE "ACCOUNTS.DBF" TO FileName
STORE "ACCT_NO" TO FieldName
USE &FileName
LOCATE FOR &FieldName="10005"
```

ABS( )

Syntax: ABS(< *numeric expression* >)

Returns the absolute value of a numeric argument:

```
A=1Ø
B=2Ø
?ABS(A-B)
      1Ø
```

ACCESS( )

Syntax: ACCESS( )

Returns the access level of the current user as specified with PROTECT:

```
IF ACCESS() < 2
      DO REPORTS
ELSE
      ? "Unauthorized Access"
      WAIT
      RETURN
END IF
```

ACOS( )

Syntax: ACOS(< *numeric expression* >)

Returns the arccosine value in angle size in radians:

```
A=3
B=1Ø
?ACOS(A/B)
      1.27
SET DECIMALS TO 5
?ACOS(A/B)
      1.266lØ
```

ALIAS( )

Syntax: ALIAS([< *numeric expression* >])

Returns the alias name of the .DBF file in the specified work area:

```
?ALIAS(2)
EMPLOYEE
```

ASC( )

Syntax: ASC(< *character expression* >)

Returns the ASCII code (a numeric value) for the leftmost character of the character argument:

```
?ASC("Smith")
83
```

ASIN( )

Syntax: ASIN(< *numeric expression* >)

Returns the arcsine value in angle size in radians:

```
A=3
B=10
?ASIN(A/B)
    0.30
```

AT( )

Syntax: AT(< *character expression* > , < *character expression* > / *name of memo field* >)

Returns the starting position of the first character argument within the second character argument:

```
?AT("ABC","XYZABC")
4
```

ATAN()

Syntax: ATAN($<$ *numeric expression*$>$)

Returns the arctangent value in angle size in radians:

```
A=3
B=1Ø
?ASIN(A/B)
     Ø.29
```

ATN2()

Syntax: ATN2($<$ *numeric expression*$>$, $<$ *numeric expression*$>$)

Returns the arctangent value in angle size in radians; calculated with
the sine and cosine values of the same angle specified:

```
X=SIN(DTOR(3Ø))
     Ø.5Ø
Y=COS(DTOR(3Ø))
     Ø.87
?ATN2(X,Y)
     Ø.52
?RTOD(ATN2(X,Y))
     3Ø.ØØ
```

BAR()

Syntax: BAR()

Returns the bar number of the menu bar from a pop-up menu:

```
DO CASE
     CASE BAR()=1
          DO RPT1
     CASE BAR()=2
          DO RPT2
     CASE BAR()=3
          DEACTIVATE POPUP
ENDCASE
```

BOF( )

Syntax: BOF([< *alias of the database file*>])

Returns the logical value .T. if the record pointer is at the beginning of the file:

```
DO WHILE ... .NOT. EOF()
    IF BOF()
        ....
        ....
    ENDIF
ENDDO
```

CALL( )

Syntax: CALL(< *character expression*> ,< *character expression*> /< *memory variable name*>)

Executes the specified binary program that has been placed in memory with the LOAD command.

CDOW( )

Syntax: CDOW(< *date expression*>)

Returns the name of the day of the week for the specified date expression:

```
?CDOW({12/25/88})
Sunday
```

CEILING( )

Syntax: CEILING(< *numeric expression* >)

Returns the smallest integer that is greater than or equal to the value of the numeric expression:

```
A=100
B=30
?A/B
        3.33
?CEILING(A/B)
        4
```

CHANGE( )

Syntax: CHANGE( )

Returns a logical value that indicates whether a record has been changed since it was opened in a multiuser environment:

```
USE DATAFILE
?CHANGE( )
.F.
```

CHR( )

Syntax: CHR(< *numeric expression* >)

Returns the ASCII character that corresponds to the numeric value supplied as an argument:

```
?CHR(85)
U
```

CMONTH( )

Syntax: CMONTH(< *date expression*>)

Returns the name of the month from the date expression supplied
as an argument:

```
?CMONTH({1Ø/1Ø/88})
October
```

COL( )

Syntax: COL( )

Returns the current column location of the cursor:

```
?COL( )
5
```

COMPLETED( )

Syntax: COMPLETED( )

Indicates whether the transactions in BEGIN TRANSACTION/END
TRANSACTION have been completed:

```
BEGIN TRANSACTION
     ...
END TRANSACTION
IF .NOT. COMPLETED
     ? "Transaction was not successful."
     ? "Rollback in progress."
     ROLLBACK
     ? "Rollback completed."
ENDIF
```

COS( )

Syntax: COS(< *numeric expression* >)

Returns the cosine value for the specified angle in radians:

```
?COS(.80)
      0.70
SET DECIMALS TO 5
?COS(.80)
      0.69671
```

CTOD( )

Syntax: CTOD(< *date expressed as a character string* >)

Converts a character string to a date memory variable:

```
STORE CTOD("12/25/88") TO Christmas
NewYearsDay=CTOD("01/01/89")
```

DATE( )

Syntax: DATE( )

Returns the system date:

```
?DATE()
01/03/89
```

DAY( )

Syntax: DAY(< *date expression* >)

Returns the numeric value of the day of the month from a date
expression supplied as an argument:

```
?DAY({12/25/88})
25
?DAY(DATE())
15
```

DBF( )

Syntax: DBF([< *alias of the database file* >])

Returns the name of the current database file:

```
USE EMPLOYEE
?DBF( )
C:EMPLOYEE.DBF
SET FULLPATH ON
?DBF( )
C:\DBASE\DBDATA\EMPLOYEE.DBF
```

DELETED( )

Syntax: DELETED([< *alias of the database file* >])

Returns the logical value .T. if the current data record has been marked for deletion:

```
USE EMPLOYEE
GOTO 10
DELETED( )
.T.
```

DIFFERENCE( )

Syntax: DIFFERENCE(< *character expression* > , < *character expression* >)

Returns the difference in SOUNDEX( ) codes (0–4) between the two specified character expressions:

```
?DIFFERENCE("Jane","Jan")
    4
?DIFFERENCE("Jane","Janet")
    3
?DIFFERENCE("Jane","Bob")
    2
```

DISKSPACE( )

Syntax: DISKSPACE( )

Returns an integer that represents the number of bytes available on the default disk drive:

```
?DISKSPACE( )
9Ø9248
```

DMY( )

Syntax: DMY(< *date expression*>)

Converts the specified date expression to a date in the Day/Month /Year format:

```
?DMY({12/25/88})
25 December 88
```

DOW( )

Syntax: DOW(< *date expression*>)

Returns the numeric code for the day of week from the date expression supplied as an argument:

```
?DOW(DATE( ))
7
```

DTOC( )

Syntax: DTOC(< *date expression*>)

Converts a date to a character string:

```
?"Today's date is "+DTOC(DATE( ))
Today's date is 12/25/88
```

DTOR( )

Syntax: DTOR(< *numeric expression*>)

Returns the degrees of the specified angle expressed in radians:

```
?DTOR(18Ø)
      3.14
SET DECIMAL TO 5
?DTOR(18Ø)
      3.14159
```

DTOS( )

Syntax: DTOS(< *date expression*>)

Converts a date to a string; useful for indexing:

```
CUSTOMER
INDEX ON DTOS(PO-DATE)+PO-NUM TO PO-DATE
```

EOF( )

Syntax: EOF([< *alias of the database file*>])

Returns the logical value .T. if the record pointer is at the end of file:

```
USE EMPLOYEE
GO BOTTOM
?EOF( )
.F.
SKIP
?EOF( )
.T.
```

ERROR( )

Syntax: ERROR( )

Use with the ON ERROR command to trap programming errors. When an error occurs in the program, this function returns the error number. You can use this number with a conditional command (such as IF or CASE) to take corrective action if recovery from the error is possible.

EXP( )

Syntax: EXP(< *numeric expression*>)

Returns the exponential value of the numeric argument:

```
SET DECIMALS TO 8
?EXP(1.0)
2.71828183
```

FILE( )

Syntax: FILE(< *character expression*>)

Returns the logical value .T. if a file in the current directory has
the name specified in the character argument:

```
?FILE("EMPLOYEE.DBF")
.T.
```

FIXED( )

Syntax: FIXED(< *numeric expression*>)

Returns the binary-coded decimal number for the specified long,
real floating value:

```
?FIXED(1.23456E+35)
.123456ØØØØØØØØØE+36
```

FKLABEL( )

Syntax: FKLABEL(< *numeric expression*>)

Returns the name of the function key whose number corresponds
to the numeric argument:

```
?FKLABEL(3)
F4
```

FKMAX( )

Syntax: FKMAX( )

Returns an integer that represents the maximum number of
programmable function keys available:

```
?FKMAX( )
9
```

FLOAT( )

Syntax: FLOAT(< *numeric expression* >)

Returns the long, real floating value for the specified binary-coded
decimal value:

```
?FLOAT( .123456E1Ø)
1234560000
```

FLOCK( )

Syntax: FLOCK([< *alias of the database* >])

Allows a file to be locked from access by other users in a multiuser
environment:

```
IF FLOCK( )
     ? "File in use."
ENDIF
```

FLOOR( )

Syntax: FLOOR(< *numeric expression* >)

Returns the largest integer that is less than or equal to the specified
value:

```
A=1ØØ
B=3Ø
?A/B
      3.33
?FLOOR(A/B)
      3
```

FOUND( )

Syntax: FOUND([< *alias of the database file* >])

Returns the logical value .T. if the previous FIND, SEEK, or CONTINUE operation was successful; otherwise, returns .F.:

```
USE EMPLOYEE
LOCATE FOR LAST_NAME="Smith"
Record = 1
?FOUND( )
 .T.
```

FV( )

Syntax: FV(< *payment* > , < *interest rate* > , < *periods* >)

Returns the compounded future values for the specified payment, interest rate (per period in decimal value), and number of payment periods. The following command shows the future value at the end of 10 years (120 months) if you deposit 100 dollars each month at 10 percent interest rate per year (0.10/12 per month):

```
?FV(100,0.10/12,120)
  20484.50
```

GETENV( )

Syntax: GETENV(< *character expression* >)

Returns a character string that describes the contents of a specific DOS environmental variable:

```
?GETENV("PATH")
C:\BIN;C:\DBASE4;C:\
```

IIF( )

Syntax: IIF(< *condition*> ,< *expression #1*> ,< *expression #2*>)

Evaluates the specified condition and returns the first expression if the condition is true. Otherwise, the second expression is returned:

```
MALE=.T.
.T.
LAST_NAME="Smith"
Smith
TITLE = IIF(MALE, "Mr. ", "Ms. ") + LAST_NAME
Mr. Smith
```

INKEY( )

Syntax: INKEY( )

Returns the numeric code of the key most recently pressed. Consult the dBASE IV manual for these key codes.

INT( )

Syntax: INT(< *numeric expression*>)

Converts a numeric value to an integer:

```
?INT(3.568)
3
```

ISALPHA( )

Syntax: ISALPHA(< *character expression*>)

Returns a logical .T. if the specified character expression begins with an alpha character; otherwise, returns .F.:

```
?ISALPHA("ABC-123")
.T.
?ISALPHA("123-abc")
.F.
```

ISCOLOR( )

Syntax: ISCOLOR( )

Returns the logical value .T. if the program is running in color mode:

```
?ISCOLOR( )
.T.
```

ISLOWER( )

Syntax: ISLOWER(< *character expression*>)

Returns a logical .T. if the leftmost character of the character argument is a lowercase letter; otherwise, returns .F.:

```
?ISLOWER("aBC-234")
.T.
?ISLOWER("Abc-234")
.F.
```

ISMARKED( )

Syntax: ISMARKED([< *alias of the database*>])

Returns a logical .T. if the file is being changed in a multiuser environment.

ISUPPER( )

Syntax: ISUPPER(< *character expression*>)

Returns a logical .T. if the leftmost character of the character argument is an uppercase letter:

```
?ISUPPER("aBC-234")
.F.
?ISUPPER("Abc-234")
.T.
```

KEY( )

Syntax: KEY([< *.mdx file* > ,] < *numeric expression* >
            [, < *alias of the database file* >]

Returns the index key expression for the specified index file:

```
USE EMPLOYEE
?KEY(1)
LAST _ NAME
?KEY(2)
AREA _ CODE
?KEY(3)
BIRTH _ DATE
```

LASTKEY( )

Syntax: LASTKEY( )

Returns the ASCII value of the last key pressed.

LEFT( )

Syntax: LEFT(< *character expression* > / < *memo field* > ,
            < *numeric expression* >)

Returns the specified number of characters from the left of the
character string or the specified memo field:

```
?LEFT("John J. Smith", 6)
John J
?"Dear "+LEFT("John J. Smith",4)+":"
Dear John:
```

LEN( )

Syntax: LEN(< *character expression* > / < *memo field* >)

Returns the number of characters in the expression or the specified memo field:

```
?LEN("James Smith")
11
```

LIKE( )

Syntax: LIKE(< *pattern* > , < *character expression* >)

Compares the specified string pattern with the character expression; returns .T. (agree) or .F (disagree):

```
?LIKE("J*","John")
.T.
?LIKE("J??","John")
.F.
```

LINENO( )

Syntax: LINENO( )

Returns to and executes the specified line number in the program.

LKSYS( )

Syntax: LKSYS(< *numeric expression* >)

Returns the log-in name of the user who locked a file or record and the date the file or record was locked.

LOG( )

Syntax: LOG(< *numeric expression* >)

Returns the natural (base-e) logarithm of the numeric argument:

```
?LOG(2.71828183)
      1.ØØ
SET DECIMAL TO 8
?LOG(2.7128183)
1.ØØØØØØØØ
```

LOG10( )

Syntax: LOG1Ø(< *numeric expression* >)

Returns the common (base-10) logarithm of the numeric argument:

```
?LOG1Ø(1ØØ)
      2
?LOG1Ø(1ØØØ)
      3
SET DECIMAL TO 8
?LOG1Ø(2ØØ)
      2.3Ø1Ø3ØØØ
```

LOOKUP( )

Syntax: LOOKUP(< *return field* > , < *search expression* > ,
          < *searching field* >)

Searches for the specified expression in the searching field and
returns the value in the return field:

```
USE EMPLOYEE
?LOOKUP(LAST_NAME,"415",AREA_CODE)
```

LOWER( )

Syntax: LOWER(< *character expression*>)

Converts any uppercase characters in the expression to lowercase characters:

    ?LOWER("James Smith")
    james smith

LTRIM( )

Syntax: LTRIM(< *character expression*>)

Trims leading blanks from the character argument; useful with the STR function:

    ? '"'+STR(3.145,1Ø,2)+'"'
    "   3.15"
    ? '"'+LTRIM(STR(3.145,1Ø,2))+'"'
     "3.15"

LUPDATE( )

Syntax: LUPDATE([< *alias of the database file*>])

Returns the date of the last update of the current database file:

    USE ACCOUNTS
    ?LUPDATE( )
    Ø1/1Ø/89

MAX( )

Syntax: MAX(< *numeric expression> / < date expression>* ,
             < *numeric expression> / < date expression>*)

Returns the larger value of the two numeric expressions or date
expressions:

```
A=3.45
B=6.78
?MAX(A,B)
6.78
?MAX({Ø1/Ø1/89},{12/24/88})
Ø1/Ø1/89
```

MDX( )

Syntax: MDX(< *numeric expression>* [, < *alias of the database
             file>*])

Returns the name of the multiple index (.MDX) file of the specified
index order number in the expression:

```
USE EMPLOYEE
?MDX(1)
C:EMPLOYEE.MDX
SET FULLPATH ON
?MDX(1)
C:\DBASE\DBDATA\EMPLOYEE.MDX
```

MDY( )

Syntax: MDY(< *date expression>*)

Returns the date in the Month Day, Year format:

```
?MDY({12/25/88})
December 25, 88
SET CENTURY ON
?MDY({12/25/88})
December 25, 1988
?MDY(CTOD("Ø1/Ø1/89")
January Ø1, 1989
```

MEMLINES( )

Syntax: MEMLINES(< *name of the memo field* >)

Returns the number of lines in the specified memo field.

MEMORY( )

Syntax: MEMORY( )

Returns the amount of free RAM in kilobytes:

```
?MEMORY( )
    116
```

MENU( )

Syntax: MENU( )

Returns the name of the menu in use:

```
?MENU( )
ORDER _ MENU
```

MESSAGE( )

Syntax: MESSAGE( )

Returns the error message for the error encountered in the
ON ERROR condition.

MIN( )

Syntax: MIN(< *numeric expression*> /< *date expression*> ,
              < *numeric expression*> /< *date expression*>)

Returns the smaller value of the two numeric arguments or date expressions:

```
A=3.45
B=6.78
?MIN(A,B)
3.45
?MIN({Ø1/Ø1/89},{12/25/88})
12/25/88
```

MLINE( )

Syntax: MLINE(< *name of memo field*> ,< *numeric
              expression*>)

Returns the specified line in the named memo field.

MOD( )

Syntax: MOD(< *numeric expression*> ,< *numeric expression*>)

Returns the remainder that results from dividing the first numeric value by the second numeric value:

```
A=1Ø
B=3
?MOD(A,B)
1
```

MONTH( )

Syntax: MONTH(< *date expression* >)

Returns the numeric code for the month from the date expression
supplied as an argument:

```
Christmas={12/25/88}
?MONTH(Christmas)
      12
```

NDX( )

Syntax: NDX(< *.ndx file number* > [, < *alias of the database
            file* >])

Returns the name of the current active index file in the selected
work area:

```
USE EMPLOYEE
SET INDEX TO BYLAST,BYFIRST
?NDX(1)
C:BYLAST.NDX
?NDX(2)
C:BYFIRST
```

NETWORK( )

Syntax: NETWORK( )

Returns .T. if the program is operating on a network; otherwise,
returns .F.

ORDER( )

Syntax: ORDER([< *alias of the database file>*])

Returns the the name of the controlling individual index (.NDX) or
the index tag of the multiple index (.MDX) file:

```
USE EMPLOYEE
SET ORDER TO TAG LAST_NAME
Master index: LAST_NAME
?ORDER()
LAST_NAME
```

OS( )

Syntax: OS( )

Returns the version of DOS under which the program is running:

```
?OS()
DOS 3.3
```

PAD( )

Syntax: PAD( )

Returns the name of the menu pad last selected.

PAYMENT( )

Syntax: PAYMENT(< *loan amount>* , < *interest rate>* ,
               < *payment periods>*)

Returns the period payment for a given amount of loan at a
specified interest rate (in decimal per period). The following
example shows the monthly mortgage payment for a $100,000 loan
at an annual rate of 10.5 percent (0.105/12 for monthly rate) for
360 months:

```
?PAYMENT(100000,0.105/12,360)
     914.74
```

PCOL( )

Syntax: PCOL( )

Determines the current column position of the print head:

```
?PCOL( )
10
```

PI( )

Syntax: PI( )

Returns the value of pi, the irrational number:

```
?PI( )
      3.14
SET DECIMALS TO 10
      3.1415926536
```

POPUP( )

Syntax: POPUP( )

Returns the name of the active pop-up menu:

```
?POPUP( )
POPMENU1
```

PRINTSTATUS( )

Syntax: PRINTSTATUS( )

Returns .T. if the printer is ready to print; otherwise, returns .F:

```
IF .NOT. PRINTSTATUS( )
     ?"Printer not ready! Please set up printer!"
     WAIT
ENDIF
```

PROGRAM( )

Syntax: PROGRAM( )

Returns the name of program being executed when an error was encountered.

PROMPT( )

Syntax: PROMPT( )

Returns the prompt of the most recently chosen menu option from the pop-up menu.

PROW( )

Syntax: PROW( )

Determines the current row position of the print head:

```
?PROW( )
5
```

PV( )

Syntax: PV(<*payment amount*> , < *interest rate*> , < *periods*>)

Returns the present value of a specified number of payment periods at a given interest or discount rate (per period, in decimal):

```
?PV(100,0.10,10)
614.46
```

RAND( )

Syntax: RAND(< *a numeric seed for generating random numbers* >)

Returns a random number (0–999999) which is generated with the default seed (using the system time) or with the specified numeric seed:

```
?RAND( )
      0.47
?RAND(10)
      0.06
?INT(RAND(10)*1000)
      55
SET DECIMALS TO 10
?RAND(10)
      0.0558793478
```

READKEY( )

Syntax: READKEY( )

Returns the numeric key code for the key pressed in order to exit from a full-screen command.

RECCOUNT( )

Syntax: RECCOUNT([< *alias of the database file* >])

Returns the number of records in the current database file:

```
USE EMPLOYEE
?RECCOUNT( )
      10
```

RECNO( )

Syntax: RECNO([< *alias of the database file* >])

Returns the number of the active data record:

```
USE EMPLOYEE
GOTO 4
SKIP 2
?RECNO( )
      6
```

RECSIZE( )

Syntax: RECSIZE([< *alias of the database file* >])

Returns the total width of each record in the active database file:

```
USE EMPLOYEE
?RECSIZE( )
      51
```

REPLICATE( )

Syntax: REPLICATE(< *character expression* > , < *numeric expression* >)

Repeats the first argument the number of times specified in the second argument:

```
?REPLICATE("Hello! ",3)
Hello! Hello! Hello!
```

RIGHT( )

Syntax: RIGHT(< *character expression*> / < *memory variable*> , < *numeric expression*>)

Returns the number of characters specified in the second argument from the right of first argument:

```
?RIGHT("John J. Smith", 5)
Smith
?"Dear Mr. "+RIGHT("John J. Smith",5)+":"
Dear Mr. Smith:
```

RLOCK( )/LOCK( )

Syntax: RLOCK([< *character expression list*> , < *alias of the database*>]/[< *alias of the database*>])

Locks multiple records.

ROLLBACK( )

Syntax: ROLLBACK( )

Returns a logical value .T. if the last ROLLBACK command was successful.

ROUND( )

Syntax: ROUND(< *numeric expression*> , < *number of decimal places*>)

Rounds the first numeric argument to the number of decimal places specified in the second numeric argument:

```
?ROUND(3.71689,2)
      3.72
SET DECIMALS TO 4
?ROUND(3.71689,2)
      3.7200
```

ROW( )

Syntax: ROW( )

Returns the current row location of the cursor:

```
?ROW( )
      15
```

RTOD( )

Syntax: RTOD(< *numeric expression* >)

Returns the degrees for the specified angle expressed in radians:

```
SET DECIMALS TO 4
?RTOD(Ø.75)
      42.9718
?RTOD(PI( ))
      18Ø
```

RTRIM( )

Syntax: RTRIM(< *character expression* >)

Trims the trailing blanks from a character expression (effect is
identical to that of the TRIM function):

```
FIRST_NAME="John    "
LAST_NAME="SMITH    "
?FIRST_NAME+LAST_NAME+"."
JOHN    SMITH    .
?RTRIM(FIRST_NAME)+" "+RTRIM(LAST_NAME)+"."
JOHN SMITH.
```

SEEK( )

Syntax: SEEK(< *searching expression* > [, < *alias of the database file* >])

Finds the specified searching expression in the indexed database files:

```
USE EMPLOYEE
SET ORDER TO LAST_NAME
SEEK("Gregory")
EDIT
```

SELECT( )

Syntax: SELECT( )

Returns the number of the highest unused work area:

```
?SELECT( )
        10
```

SET( )

Syntax: SET(< *name of the SET command* >)

Displays the current status of the SET command:

```
?SET("CENTURY")
OFF
?SET("DECIMALS")
        4
?SET("TALK")
ON
```

SIGN( )

Syntax: SIGN(< *numeric expression* >)

Displays the numeric code for the sign of the specified value (1 for positive, –1 for negative, and 0 for zero):

```
?SIGN(12.34)
       1
?SIGN(-12.34)
       -1
?SIGN(Ø)
       Ø
```

SIN( )

Syntax: SIN(< *numeric expression* >)

Returns the sine value of the specified angle expressed in radians:

```
?SIN(1.Ø)
       Ø.8415
?SIN(PI())
       Ø
```

SOUNDEX( )

Syntax: SOUNDEX(< *character expression* >)

Returns a four-character SOUNDEX code when analyzing the character expression with the SOUNDEX rules:

```
SOUNDEX("HELLO WORLD")
H4ØØ
```

SPACE( )

Syntax: SPACE(< *numeric expression* >)

Creates a character string of the specified number of blanks:

```
?SPACE(1Ø) +LAST _ NAME+SPACE(5) +AREA _ CODE+PHONE _ NO
```

SQRT( )

Syntax: SQRT(< *numeric expression* >)

Returns the square root of the numeric expression:

```
?SQRT(1Ø)
      3.16
SET DECIMALS TO 1Ø
?SQRT(1Ø)
      3.16227766Ø2
```

STR( )

Syntax: STR(< *numeric expression* > [, < *length of character string* >][, < *decimal places* >])

Converts the numeric argument to a character string (default length is 10; default decimal is 0):

```
AnnualPay=2595Ø.5Ø95
?"Annual salary = "+STR(AnnualPay,8,2)
Annual salary = 2595Ø.51
```

STUFF( )

Syntax: STUFF(< *1st string* > , < *beginning position* > , < *number of characters* > , < *2nd string* >)

Replaces a portion of the first character argument with the second character argument, beginning at the character position specified and continuing for the number of characters specified:

```
?STUFF("Mary Jane Smith",6,4,"Kay")
Mary Kay Smith
```

SUBSTR( )

Syntax: SUBSTR(< *character expression*> / < *memo field*> ,
< *beginning position*> [, < *number of characters*>])

Returns characters from the first character argument. The second argument specifies the starting position, and the third argument specifies the number of characters to be returned:

```
?SUBSTR("ABCDEFG",4,3)
DEF
```

TAG( )

Syntax: TAG([< *.mdx file name*> ,] < *index tag* #>
[< *alias of the database file*>])

Returns the name of the specified index tag of the multiple index (.MDX) file:

```
USE EMPLOYEE
?TAG(1)
LAST_NAME
?TAG(2)
AREA_CODE
```

TAN( )

Syntax: TAN(< *numeric expression*>)

Returns the value of the tangent for the specified angle expressed in radians:

```
SET DECIMALS TO 5
?TAN(Ø.8)
      1.Ø2964
?TAN(PI())
      Ø
```

TIME( )

Syntax: TIME( )

Returns the current system time:

```
?TIME( )
22:15:35
```

TRANSFORM( )

Syntax: TRANSFORM(< *expression* > , < *character expression* >)

Use with ?, ??, DISPLAY, LABEL, LIST, and REPORT to display a
character expression with the specified picture format:

```
USE EMPLOYEE
GOTO 5
DISPLAY TRANSFORM(LAST _ NAME, "@R X X X X X X X X X X X")
Record#  TRANSFORM(LAST _ NAME, "@R X X X X X X X X X X X")
     5 B a k e r
```

TRIM( )

Syntax: TRIM(< *character expression* >)

Removes trailing blanks from a character string. See the example for
RTRIM( ).

TYPE( )

Syntax: TYPE(< *character expression*>)

Returns the data type of the memory variable or data fields in the character expression:

```
USE EMPLOYEE
?TYPE("LAST_NAME")
C
?TYPE("ANNUAL_PAY")
N
?TYPE("MALE")
L
Christmas={12/25/88}
?TYPE(Christmas)
D
```

UPPER( )

Syntax: UPPER(< *character expression*>)

Converts lowercase letters in the character string to uppercase letters:

```
?UPPER("James Smith")
JAMES SMITH

IF UPPER(ANSWER)="Y"
    . . .
    . . .
ENDIF
```

USER( )

Syntax: USER( )

Returns the log-in name of the user currently logged onto a protected system.

VAL( )

Syntax: VAL(< *character expression* >)

Converts a character string to a numeric value, based on the value
of SET DECIMALS TO:

```
?VAL("34.56789")
34.57
SET DECIMALS TO 5
?VAL("34.56789")
34.56789
```

VARREAD( )

Syntax: VARREAD( )

Used to create context sensitive help.

VERSION( )

Syntax: VERSION( )

Returns the version number of the dBASE IV program:

```
?VERSION()
dBASE IV version 1.Ø
```

YEAR( )

Syntax: YEAR(< *date expression* >)

Returns a four-digit value of the year from a date expression
supplied as an argument:

```
?YEAR(DATE())
1988
NewYearDay={Ø1/Ø1/89}
?YEAR(NewYearDay)
     1989
```

ASCII Character Set

The table lists the ASCII characters and their codes in decimal notation. Characters can be displayed with

? CHR(n)

where *n* is the decimal ASCII value. You can enter characters that do not appear on the keyboard by holding down the Alt key while you enter the ASCII value, using the numeric keypad. The standard interpretations of ASCII codes 0 to 31 are presented in the Control Character column.

Hex	Dec	Screen	Ctrl	Key	Hex	Dec	Screen	Ctrl	Key
00h	0		NUL	^@	1Ah	26	→	SUB	^Z
01h	1	☺	SOH	^A	1Bh	27	←	ESC	^[
02h	2	●	STX	^B	1Ch	28	∟	FS	^\
03h	3	♥	ETX	^C	1Dh	29	↔	GS	^]
04h	4	♦	EOT	^D	1Eh	30	▲	RS	^^
05h	5	♣	ENQ	^E	1Fh	31	▼	US	^_
06h	6	♠	ACK	^F	20h	32			
07h	7	•	BEL	^G	21h	33	!		
08h	8	◘	BS	^H	22h	34	"		
09h	9	○	HT	^I	23h	35	#		
0Ah	10	◙	LF	^J	24h	36	$		
0Bh	11	♂	VT	^K	25h	37	%		
0Ch	12	♀	FF	^L	26h	38	&		
0Dh	13	♪	CR	^M	27h	39	'		
0Eh	14	♫	SO	^N	28h	40	(		
0Fh	15	☼	SI	^O	29h	41	)		
10h	16	►	DLE	^P	2Ah	42	*		
11h	17	◄	DC1	^Q	2Bh	43	+		
12h	18	↕	DC2	^R	2Ch	44	,		
13h	19	‼	DC3	^S	2Dh	45	–		
14h	20	¶	DC4	^T	2Eh	46	.		
15h	21	§	NAK	^U	2Fh	47	/		
16h	22	▬	SYN	^V	30h	48	0		
17h	23	↨	ETB	^W	31h	49	1		
18h	24	↑	CAN	^X	32h	50	2		
19h	25	↓	EM	^Y	33h	51	3		

Hex	Dec	Screen	Hex	Dec	Screen	Hex	Dec	Screen
34h	52	4	62h	98	b	90h	144	É
35h	53	5	63h	99	c	91h	145	æ
36h	54	6	64h	100	d	92h	146	Æ
37h	55	7	65h	101	e	93h	147	ô
38h	56	8	66h	102	f	94h	148	ö
39h	57	9	67h	103	g	95h	149	ò
3Ah	58	:	68h	104	h	96h	150	û
3Bh	59	;	69h	105	i	97h	151	ù
3Ch	60	<	6Ah	106	j	98h	152	ÿ
3Dh	61	=	6Bh	107	k	99h	153	Ö
3Eh	62	>	6Ch	108	l	9Ah	154	Ü
3Fh	63	?	6Dh	109	m	9Bh	155	¢
40h	64	@	6Eh	110	n	9Ch	156	£
41h	65	A	6Fh	111	o	9Dh	157	¥
42h	66	B	70h	112	p	9Eh	158	₧
43h	67	C	71h	113	q	9Fh	159	ƒ
44h	68	D	72h	114	r	A0h	160	á
45h	69	E	73h	115	s	A1h	161	í
46h	70	F	74h	116	t	A2h	162	ó
47h	71	G	75h	117	u	A3h	163	ú
48h	72	H	76h	118	v	A4h	164	ñ
49h	73	I	77h	119	w	A5h	165	Ñ
4Ah	74	J	78h	120	x	A6h	166	ª
4Bh	75	K	79h	121	y	A7h	167	º
4Ch	76	L	7Ah	122	z	A8h	168	¿
4Dh	77	M	7Bh	123	{	A9h	169	⌐
4Eh	78	N	7Ch	124	|	AAh	170	¬
4Fh	79	O	7Dh	125	}	ABh	171	½
50h	80	P	7Eh	126	~	ACh	172	¼
51h	81	Q	7Fh	127	Δ	ADh	173	¡
52h	82	R	80h	128	Ç	AEh	174	«
53h	83	S	81h	129	ü	AFh	175	»
54h	84	T	82h	130	é	B0h	176	░
55h	85	U	83h	131	â	B1h	177	▒
56h	86	V	84h	132	ä	B2h	178	▓
57h	87	W	85h	133	à	B3h	179	│
58h	88	X	86h	134	å	B4h	180	┤
59h	89	Y	87h	135	ç	B5h	181	╡
5Ah	90	Z	88h	136	ê	B6h	182	╢
5Bh	91	[	89h	137	ë	B7h	183	╖
5Ch	92	\	8Ah	138	è	B8h	184	╕
5Dh	93	]	8Bh	139	ï	B9h	185	╣
5Eh	94	^	8Ch	140	î	BAh	186	║
5Fh	95	_	8Dh	141	ì	BBh	187	╗
60h	96	`	8Eh	142	Ä	BCh	188	╝
61h	97	a	8Fh	143	Å	BDh	189	╜

Hex	Dec	Screen	Hex	Dec	Screen	Hex	Dec	Screen
BEh	190	┘	D4h	212	╘	EAh	234	Ω
BFh	191	┐	D5h	213	╒	EBh	235	δ
C0h	192	└	D6h	214	╓	ECh	236	∞
C1h	193	┴	D7h	215	╫	EDh	237	φ
C2h	194	┬	D8h	216	╪	EEh	238	∈
C3h	195	├	D9h	217	┘	EFh	239	∩
C4h	196	─	DAh	218	┌	F0h	240	≡
C5h	197	┼	DBh	219	█	F1h	241	±
C6h	198	╞	DCh	220	▄	F2h	242	≥
C7h	199	╟	DDh	221	▌	F3h	243	≤
C8h	200	╚	DEh	222	▐	F4h	244	⌠
C9h	201	╔	DFh	223	▄	F5h	245	⌡
CAh	202	╩	E0h	224	α	F6h	246	÷
CBh	203	╦	E1h	225	β	F7h	247	≈
CCh	204	╠	E2h	226	Γ	F8h	248	°
CDh	205	═	E3h	227	π	F9h	249	•
CEh	206	╬	E4h	228	Σ	FAh	250	·
CFh	207	╧	E5h	229	σ	FBh	251	√
D0h	208	╨	E6h	230	μ	FCh	252	n
D1h	209	╤	E7h	231	τ	FDh	253	²
D2h	210	╥	E8h	232	Φ	FEh	254	■
D3h	211	╙	E9h	233	θ	FFh	255	

Major Differences between dBASE III Plus and dBASE IV

dBASE III Plus and dBASE IV differ in six major areas: general working environment, capacity, numeric data types, file types, built-in functions, and processing commands. Each of these areas is explored in this appendix.

General Working Environment

dBASE III Plus provides the Assistant to help users who need an easier method of using the program than is provided at the dot prompt. dBASE IV builds on the Assistant's ease of use and adds the Control Center, which provides additional integration of convenient management and productivity features. Even for power users, the Control Center represents an attractive alternative to dot prompt operations.

dBASE IV adds a powerful query by example (QBE) capability. With QBE, you can search and retrieve data from selective records by defining filter conditions. You can link files effortlessly by specifying their relationships with queries. Records generated from query operations can be saved to a database file.

dBASE IV adds DOS utilities to its program so that you can execute DOS commands without using the RUN command at the dot prompt or leaving dBASE IV. It also provides useful tools for managing disk files.

dBASE IV implements the Structured Query Language (SQL). You can issue SQL commands at the dot prompt for accessing the database created in dBASE IV.

dBASE IV incorporates an Application Generator so that you can create programs by choosing the menu options from the generator instead of writing your own commands in an editor.

dBASE IV implements new label and report generators by using the "what you see is what you get" (WYSIWYG) approach. Labels and reports can be designed with the enhanced screen painter. Using the screen painter, you can place data fields on the design forms together with the necessary descriptive text.

After designing label and report forms, dBASE IV automatically generates the program listing for the forms and saves it as a program (.LBG or .FRG) file. The program files are compiled when they are put to use, and object codes are produced (saved as .LBO or .FRO files).

In dBASE IV, you can produce reports and labels by using records from multiple database files that are linked or joined by means of a query operation. Records produced by the query can be saved as a database file or a view file. Reports and labels can be produced by using these records from the database file or from the query view.

dBASE III Plus uses individual index (.NDX) files for ordering records in a database file. Although these index files can still be used, in dBASE IV you can use a set of index tags in one or more multiple index (.MDX) files for arranging records. You need to reindex and rebuild individual index (.NDX) files yourself; index tags in a multiple index (.MDX) file are automatically updated whenever the contents of its database file are changed.

In dBASE IV, you must group your data files in file catalogs when you are in the Control Center. Once a file catalog is in use, all the data files subsequently created are automatically included in that file catalog.

dBASE IV supports multiple-child and multiple-file relationships in the database design. A database file can be linked to several database files simultaneously.

dBASE III Plus can be executed on a dual floppy system or a system with a hard disk; dBASE IV requires a hard disk to run the program once the program systems are installed. In dBASE IV, you are advised to organize your disk files in separate directories and subdirectories.

In dBASE IV, you can switch from edit mode (displaying one record at a time) to browse mode (displaying a set of records on-screen) by pressing a single keystroke (F2).

dBASE IV allows you to display the contents of a database file on the printer by using the quick report (Shift-F9) keystrokes.

dBASE IV provides a more powerful help screen system. Most help messages are context-sensitive—help messages are related to the operation being performed.

dBASE IV adds a macro capability, which allows you to save a series of keystrokes as a macro that can be played back later.

dBASE IV enhances the error-handling capability in dot prompt commands. When an error occurs, you can choose to re-edit the last command entered without retyping it.

dBASE IV allows you to encrypt your data for data security purposes. In addition, you can flag read-only files so that unintended deletions can be avoided.

dBASE IV supports Extended and Expanded memory that meets the Lotus/Intel/Microsoft 4.0 specification. You can therefore use more than 640K of conventional RAM.

dBASE IV allows you to use windows (up to 20) on the screen for displaying your output, menus, and messages.

Capacity

	dBASE III Plus	*dBASE IV*
Open data files allowed	10	99
Data fields per record	128	255
Command line length	256	1,024
Windows	N/A	20

Numeric Data Types

dBASE III used floating point numeric data type only (type N). dBASE IV supports floating point numeric data as type F. In addition, dBASE IV supports Binary Coded Decimal (BCD) as the default numeric data type (type N). Unlike floating point results, BCD results do not reflect rounding errors. BCD data type gives dBASE IV better handling of financial calculations where rounding errors would cause problems.

File Types

The following file types, not available in dBASE III Plus, are available in dBASE IV:

File Type	Description
.LBG	Program files for label form (.LBL)
.LBO	Object code files for label form (.LBL)
.FRG	Program files for report form (.FRM)
.FRO	Object code files for report form (.FRM)
.MDX	Multiple index files for holding index tags
.QBE	Query by Example files
.QBO	Object code files for query files

Built-In Functions

The dBASE IV functions that are either not available or different from those in dBASE III Plus are the following:

Mathematical and trigonometric functions:

ACOS( )	COS( )	RAND( )
ASIN( )	DTOR( )	RTOD( )
ATAN( )	FLOOR( )	SIGN( )
ATN2( )	LOG10( )	SIN( )
CEILING( )	PI( )	TAN( )

Financial functions:

FV( )	PAYMENT( )	PV( )

Memo field functions:

AT( )	MEMLINES( )	RIGHT( )
LEFT( )	MLINE( )	SUBSTR( )
LEN( )		

Index file or tag functions:

KEY( )	NDX( )	SEEK( )
MDX( )	ORDER( )	TAG( )

Pop-up or bar-menu functions:

BAR( )	PAD( )	PROMPT( )
MENU( )	POPUP( )	

Error-tracing and debugging functions:

LINENO( )	PROGRAM( )

Date conversion functions:

DMY( )	MDY( )

Other dBASE IV enhanced functions:

BOF( )	FIELD( )	LUPDATE( )
CHANGE( )	FOUND( )	RECCOUNT( )
DBF( )	INKEY( )	RECNO( )
DELETED( )	ISMARKED( )	RECSIZE( )
EOF( )	LOOKUP( )	

Other dBASE IV new functions:

ACCESS( )	LASTKEY( )	RLOCK( )
ALIAS( )	LIKE( )	ROLLBACK( )
CALL( )	LKSYS( )	SELECT( )
COMPLETED( )	LOCK( )	SET( )
DIFFERENCE( )	MEMORY( )	SOUNDEX( )
DTOS( )	NETWORK( )	USER( )
FIXED( )	PICTURE( )	VARREAD( )
FLOAT( )	PRINTSTATUS( )	

Processing Commands

The dBASE IV commands that are either not available or different from those in dBASE III Plus are the following:

Commands for handling memo fields:

APPEND MEMO	SET BLOCKSIZE TO
COPY MEMO	SET WINDOW OF MEMO TO
REPLACE	

Commands for processing memory variables or arrays:

APPEND FROM ARRAY	DECLARE
COPY TO ARRAY	

Commands for performing index operations:

COPY TAG	INDEX...ON TO TAG
DELETE TAG	SET ORDER TO TAG

Commands for processing macros:

BEGIN TRANSACTION	RESTORE MACROS FROM
PLAY MACRO	ROLLBACK
RESET	SAVE MACRO TO

Commands for displaying data:

???	PRINTJOB...ENDPRINTJOB
ON PAGE	SET DESIGN

Commands for using pop-up or bar menus:

ACTIVATE MENU	DEFINE POPUP
ACTIVATE POPUP	ON PAD
DEACTIVATE MENU	ON SELECTION PAD
DEACTIVATE POPUP	ON SELECTION POPUP
DEFINE BAR	RELEASE POPUPS
DEFINE BOX	SHOW POPUP
DEFINE MENU	SHOW MENU
DEFINE PAD	

Commands for using windows:

ACTIVATE WINDOW	RELEASE WINDOWS
DEACTIVATE WINDOW	RESTORE WINDOW
DEFINE WINDOW	SAVE WINDOW

Commands for displaying foreign monetary values:

SET CURRENCY LEFT/RIGHT   SET POINT TO
SET CURRENCY TO   SET SEPARATOR TO

Commands for manipulating and displaying the date and time:

SET CLOCK ON   SET HOURS TO
SET CLOCK TO   SET MARK TO
SET DATE TO

Other enhanced dBASE IV commands:

?   ON KEY LABEL
??   PUBLIC ARRAY
@   REINDEX
AVERAGE   REPORT FORM
BROWSE   RETURN TO MASTER
CALL   SET ALTERNATE TO
CHANGE   SET BELL TO
COPY TO   SET CARRY TO
CREATE   SET COLOR OF
DISPLAY   SET DEVICE TO
DISPLAY FILES   SET DO HISTORY
DISPLAY HISTORY   SET FIELDS TO
DISPLAY MEMORY   SET FIXED
DISPLAY STATUS   SET FUNCTION
DO   SET INDEX TO
EDIT   SET MENUS ON
EXPORT TO   SET PRINTER TO
IMPORT FROM   SET RELATION TO
LABEL FORM   SET VIEW TO
LIST   SKIP
LIST MEMORY   SORT TO
MODIFY COMMAND/FILE   SUM
MODIFY COMMAND   TYPE
MODIFY STRUCTURE

Other new dBASE IV commands:

ACTIVATE SCREEN	MOVE WINDOW
BUILD	ON READERROR
CLEAR MENUS	PROTECT
CLEAR POPUPS	RELEASE MENUS
CLEAR WINDOWS	SET AUTOSAVE
COMPILE	SET BORDER TO
CONVERT TO	SET DISPLAY TO
COPY INDEXES/TAG	SET EXCLUSIVE
CREATE APPLICATION	SET LOCK ON
CREATE FROM	SET REFRESH TO
DEBUG	SET REPROCESS TO
EJECT PAGE	SET SKIP TO
FUNCTION	SET SPACE ON
LOGOUT	SET TRAP
MODIFY APPLICATION	UNLOCK

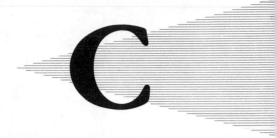

Summary of Function and Control Keys

Default Settings for the Function Keys

From the Control Center or menu:

Key	Function(s)
F1	Display on-screen help
F2	Display data in edit or browse format; toggle between edit and browse format in data
F3	Move to previous field in edit or browse mode; move to previous screen in query design; move to previous help screen
F4	Move to next field in edit or browse mode; move to next screen in query design; move to next help screen
F5	Add or modify field on form, report, and label layouts; add or remove field from view skeleton

Key	Function(s)
F6	Select text or field in form, report, and label layouts
F7	Move the text or field selected with F6
F8	Copy the text or field selected with F6
F9	Zoom (enlarge or shrink) the display box for memo fields, condition boxes, and file skeletons in query design; show or hide files in DOS utilities directory tree
F10	Access menu options

Key	Function
Shift-F1	Display fill-in items
Shift-F2	Bring up database structure, query, form, label, and report design for viewing and modifications
Shift-F3	Find previous occurrence of search string
Shift-F4	Find next occurrence of search string
Shift-F5	Find specified search string
Shift-F6	Replace search string with another string
Shift-F7	Resize display column width in browse
Shift-F8	Replicate field value of previous record
Shift-F9	Produce a quick report of data being displayed
Shift-F10	Access macros prompt box

From the dot prompt:

Key	Equivalent dBASE IV Command*
F1	HELP
F2	ASSIST (to Control Center)
F3	LIST
F4	DIR
F5	DISPLAY STRUCTURE
F6	DISPLAY STATUS
F7	DISPLAY MEMORY

Key	Equivalent dBASE IV Command*
F8	DISPLAY
F9	APPEND
F10	EDIT

*Different commands can be assigned to these keys with the SET FUNCTION commands.

Keystrokes for Cursor Movement and Screen Editing

Keystroke	Function
Enter (↵)	Move the cursor to the next data field or line
	In APPEND: Exit and save the contents of a file when issued from the first character of a blank data record
	In EDIT: Exit and save the file contents when issued from the last field of the last data record
	In text editor: insert a new line in Insert mode
Up arrow (↑)	Move the cursor up one line or one data field
Down arrow (↓)	Move the cursor down one line or one data field
Left arrow (←)	Move the cursor left one space
Right arrow (→)	Move the cursor right one space
Ctrl-left arrow (^ ←)	In BROWSE: Pan one data field to the left
	In MODIFY STRUCTURE: Scroll down the file structure display
	In MODIFY COMMAND: Move the cursor to the beginning of the line

Keystroke	Function
Ctrl-right arrow (^ →)	In BROWSE: Pan one data field to the right
	In MODIFY REPORT: Scroll up the file structure display
	In MODIFY COMMAND: Move the cursor to the end of the line
Backspace (←)	Erase the character to the left of the cursor
Delete (Del)	Erase the character above the cursor
End	Move to end of field, last field, or column
Home .	Move to beginning of field, record, left margin, or column
Insert (Ins)	Toggle insert mode on and off
Page Up (PgUp)	Move back to previous data record or screen
Page Down (PgDn)	Move to next data record or screen
Tab	Move to next field or column
Shift-Tab	Move to previous field or column
Ctrl-End (^End)	Exit and save modified data items
Escape (Esc)	Exit without saving modified data items
Ctrl-KW (^KW)	In text editor: Write the file to another file
Ctrl-KR (^KR)	In text editor: Reads another file into the current text at the cursor position
Ctrl-N (^N)	In MODIFY STRUCTURE: Insert a new line or data field
Ctrl-T (^T)	Erase one word to the right of the cursor
Ctrl-U (^U)	In BROWSE or EDIT: Mark a record for deletion
	In MODIFY REPORT or MODIFY STRUCTURE: Delete a data field
Ctrl-Y (^Y)	Erase the entire line at the cursor

Keystrokes for Control Processing

Keystroke	Function
Ctrl-P (^P)	Toggle printer on and off
Ctrl-S (^S)	Start and stop the screen scroll
Ctrl-X (^X)	Erase the command line in interactive processing mode

Keystrokes for Selecting Menus

To select menus from the Control Center, press Alt in combination with the first letter of the menu name. For example,

Keystroke	Control Center Menu Selected
Alt-C	Catalog menu
Alt-T	Tools menu
Alt-E	Exit menu

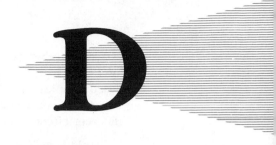

Installing dBASE IV on a
Hard Disk System

To install dBASE IV on a hard disk, you must have at least 4M of hard disk storage space. The Developers Edition of dBASE IV requires at least 5.2M of hard disk space. However, because you also need disk space for storing data tables and their related disk files, a minimum of about 6M to 7M of disk space is highly recommended. To determine the amount of free disk space on your hard disk, you can use the DOS command CHKDSK:

```
C>CHKDSK
```

Before you type CHKDSK at the C> prompt, make sure that the DOS file CHKDSK.COM is located on the hard disk. If the file is not in the current directory or in the path given by the latest path specifier, the following error message appears:

```
Bad command or file name
```

You must install dBASE IV from a floppy disk, which will normally be drive A:. During installation, the installation program interacts with you by issuing prompt messages that tell you what action the installation program is taking and what you need to do next. Since dBASE IV requires a hard disk, you will normally install dBASE IV to drive C:. Drive C: is also normally the start-up drive because most users boot from drive C:. In some cases, users boot from a floppy if they need to start DOS when their hard disk is configured to boot OS/2 or some other operating system. In other cases, users may have their hard disk partitioned into additional logical drives such as D: and E:. If you are booting from DOS-based floppies on an OS/2 system or have logical drives configured beyond C:, you will need to modify the installation steps where your different circumstances become apparent.

To begin installing dBASE IV, have ready all the system disks from the dBASE IV package. Then follow these steps:

1. Start the system with either a cold boot or a warm boot and wait for the DOS system prompt to appear.

2. Insert the dBASE IV Installation Disk in drive A:.

    If you are starting the system from drive C:, you can switch to drive A: by typing A: at the C> prompt:

    ```
    C>A:
    ```

    With this step you make the floppy disk drive A: the current active drive. Unless specified otherwise, drive A: remains the default disk drive.

3. Type Install at the A> prompt and then press Enter:

    ```
    A>Install
    ```

4. Follow the prompts that appear on-screen during the installation process.

Software Registration

The first time you install the dBASE IV program files on the hard disk, you are prompted to enter your name, your company name, and the serial number (which can be found on System Disk #1). After these items are entered, they are saved on a system disk file and are displayed on subsequent use of the program. You must be careful not to make a mistake in entering these items; after they are saved, they cannot be altered. If you type the wrong serial number, you will need to start the installation again.

The DBASE Directory

During the installation process, in addition to software registration, a number of important tasks are accomplished. First, the installation process creates a directory named DBASE on drive C: if it has not already been created. The disk space within the directory will be used to store all the dBASE IV program and configuration files.

System Configuration

After creating the DBASE directory, the installation process copies all the dBASE IV program files onto the hard disk in that directory. In addition, two configuration files are created. The first one, named CONFIG.SYS, is a system configuration file that will be saved on the disk (drive A: or drive C:) from which you start the computer.

dBASE IV is a program that instructs the computer to perform the tasks required for managing a database. The computer program consists of a set of commands that are coded and stored on the dBASE IV system files. Before dBASE IV is loaded into memory, the computer must be informed about the environment in which the program is to be operated. For example, the number of files to be used by the program and the amount of memory to be reserved for data storage must be specified before the program is loaded. The default disk drive for data storage also must be designated so that the disk operating system can locate the data files when they are needed. You provide this information in a procedure called *system configuration*.

System configuration involves specifying necessary parameters, such as the number of files and the size of reserved memory. Booting the computer begins the execution of instructions stored in ROM. The computer is instructed to initialize the input and output devices and to allocate memory space for normal processing. By default, DOS sets at 8 the number of files that can be open at one time; however, 5 files are used by DOS, leaving only 3 for the user's programs. Because dBASE IV can accommodate many more files, the number of files is set to 40 during system configuration.

The processor sets aside a certain amount of computer memory as temporary working space for manipulation of disk data. This temporary working space is reserved in blocks of RAM that are called *buffers*. The more buffers you reserve, the faster processing is achieved. The total number of buffers is restricted by the amount of RAM available on the computer system. Because the dBASE IV program itself and the active data files used in the program compete with buffers for memory space, the number of buffers should not be set too high. Otherwise, you will not have enough memory for storing your database files during processing. With a minimum of 640K RAM in the computer, it is safe to designate 15 memory buffers—the number recommended by the dBASE IV developers.

The CONFIG.SYS file, which is created by the installation process, will contain at least the following two lines:

```
FILES=4Ø

BUFFERS=15
```

If a CONFIG.SYS file is already present on the boot disk, these two lines will be added to the current contents of the file during the installation process. To verify the contents of the CONFIG.SYS file, you can enter TYPE CONFIG.SYS at the root directory of the boot disk, as in the following examples:

```
A>TYPE CONFIG.SYS
```

or

```
C>TYPE CONFIG.SYS
```

You also can modify the contents of the CONFIG.SYS file by using a line editor (such as the EDLIN.COM program in the DOS disk) or a text processor.

dBASE IV Configuration

In addition to the system configuration CONFIG.SYS file, a dBASE IV configuration file named CONFIG.DB is created and saved in the \DBASE directory at the root level during the installation process. The CONFIG.DB configuration file contains processing commands that initiate certain operations when the program is first activated.

The CONFIG.DB file later can be used to set up all the parameters and commands for starting dBASE IV when it is invoked. The contents of the

CONFIG.DB file created by the installation process may look like that shown in figure D.1.

```
C:\DBASE>type config.db

*
*          dBASE IV Configuration File
*          Tuesday August 23, 1988
*

COLOR OF NORMAL       = W+/B
COLOR OF HIGHLIGHT    = GR+/BG
COLOR OF MESSAGES     = W/N
COLOR OF TITLES       = W/B
COLOR OF BOX          = GR+/BG
COLOR OF INFORMATION  = B/W
COLOR OF FIELDS       = N/BG
COMMAND               = ASSIST
DISPLAY               = EGA25
SQLDATABASE           = SAMPLES
SQLHOME               = C:\DBASE\SQLHOME
STATUS                = ON

C:\DBASE>
```

Fig. D.1.

The contents of the CONFIG.DB file.

You can change the contents of the CONFIG.DB file by using a line editor or a text processor.

dBASE IV is designed to be used on a system with a hard disk. During processing, the program assumes that drive C: is the working hard disk. If you want to designate a different hard disk for your storage space, you can specify it in the CONFIG.DB configuration file by modifying the CONFIG.DB file to include the following command:

DEFAULT=< *default disk drive*>

You enter the drive letter in place of < *default disk drive*>.

Hardware Setup

During the installation process, you also will be prompted to specify the hardware configuration for use in dBASE IV. The hardware configuration can include, among other elements, the type of monitor, printer, and printer port. Information on such hardware configuration is stored in an appropriated file in the DBASE directory as well.

You can specify as many as four custom printers with dBASE IV. To set up these printers, you enter the printer port (such as LPT1 or LPT2), the name of the printer, and its driver during the hardware setup process. Figure D.2 shows the setup for the EPSON® LX-80 and HP® LaserJet™.

Fig. D.2.

The setup for the EPSON LX-80 and HP LaserJet.

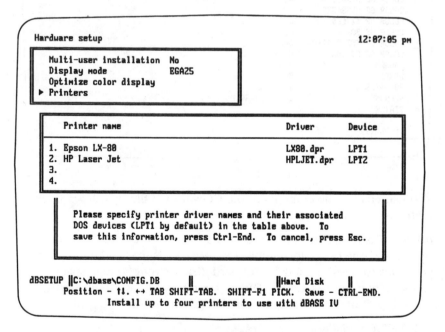

Uninstalling dBASE IV from the Hard Disk

The process of uninstalling dBASE IV involves removing all the program files that are copied from the program disks during the installation process. To uninstall dBASE IV from your hard disk, you need to specify the disk directory in which the program files are stored. To perform the uninstalling operation, you use a program called DBSETUP.EXE, which normally is saved in the DBASE directory. To execute DBSETUP.EXE, you first change your working directory to the dBASE directory by using the CD (Change Directory) command at the C> prompt:

C>CD \DBASE

From the DBASE directory, you can execute the DBSETUP program by typing the program name at the prompt:

C>DBSETUP

In response to the program name, you will be presented with the menu from which you can select the **Uninstall dBASE IV** option, as shown in figure D.3. You will then be prompted to enter the drive and directory from which to uninstall the dBASE IV files. After the uninstalling process, all the program files of dBASE IV will be removed from the hard disk.

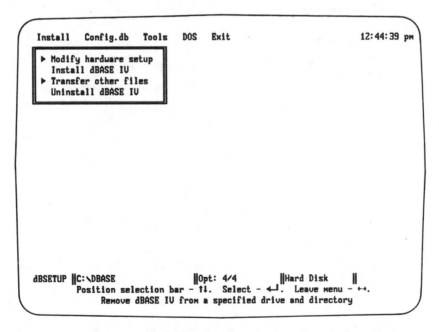

Fig. D.3.

The **Uninstall dBASE IV** *option in the DBSETUP program.*

Because dBASE IV is not copy protected and can be installed as many times as you want, you can also uninstall the program from your hard disk simply by erasing all the files from the \DBASE directory. To use this method to erase all the files from the directory, you first change your current directory to \DBASE by using the CD \DBASE command. From that directory, you can then issue the ERASE *.* command to remove the files permanently from the directory. Once all the files in the directory are erased, you can delete the directory by using the RD (Remove Directory) command:

```
C>CD \DBASE
C>ERASE *.*
Are you sure (Y/N)?Y
C>CD \
C>RD DBASE
```

If you have any subdirectories within the \DBASE directory, you must erase all those files and subdirectories before you can remove the \DBASE directory. For example, if you have a DBDATA subdirectory within the \DBASE directory, you need to follow these steps before removing the directory from the hard disk:

```
C>CD \DBASE\DBDATA
C>ERASE *.*
Are you sure (Y/N)?Y
C>CD \DBASE
C>RD DBDATA
```

Index

S

More Computer Knowledge from Que

SELECT QUE BOOKS TO INCREASE
YOUR PERSONAL COMPUTER PRODUCTIVITY

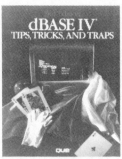

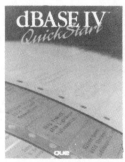

ORDER FROM QUE TODAY

Item	Title	Price	Quantity	Extension
854	dBASE IV Tips, Tricks, and Traps, 2nd Edition	$21.95		
873	dBASE IV QuickStart	21.95		
867	dBASE IV Quick Reference	6.95		
75	dBASE IV QueCards	21.95		

Book Subtotal

Shipping & Handling ($2.50 per item)

Indiana Residents Add 5% Sales Tax

GRAND TOTAL

Method of Payment

☐ Check ☐ VISA ☐ MasterCard ☐ American Express

Card Number _____ Exp. Date _____

Cardholder's Name _____

Ship to _____

Address _____

City _____ State _____ ZIP _____

If you can't wait, call **1-800-428-5331** and order TODAY.
All prices subject to change without notice.

FOLD HERE

Place
Stamp
Here

Que Corporation
P.O. Box 90
Carmel, IN 46032

REGISTRATION CARD

Register your copy of *dBASE IV Handbook*, 3rd Edition, and receive information about Que's newest products. Complete this registration card and return it to Que Corporation, P.O. Box 90, Carmel, IN 46032.

Name _____ Phone _____

Company _____ Title _____

Address _____

City _____ State _____ ZIP _____

Please check the appropriate answers:

Where did you buy *dBASE IV Handbook*, 3rd Edition?
- ☐ Bookstore (name: _____)
- ☐ Computer store (name: _____)
- ☐ Catalog (name: _____)
- ☐ Direct from Que _____
- ☐ Other: _____

How many computer books do you buy a year?
- ☐ 1 or less
- ☐ 2–5
- ☐ 6–10
- ☐ More than 10

How many Que books do you own?
- ☐ 1
- ☐ 2–5
- ☐ 6–10
- ☐ More than 10

How long have you been using dBASE software?
- ☐ Less than 6 months
- ☐ 6 months to 1 year
- ☐ 1–3 years
- ☐ More than 3 years

What influenced your purchase of *dBASE IV Handbook*, 3rd Edition?
- ☐ Personal recommendation
- ☐ Advertisement
- ☐ In-store display
- ☐ Price
- ☐ Other: _____
- ☐ Que catalog
- ☐ Que mailing
- ☐ Que's reputation

How would you rate the overall content of *dBASE IV Handbook*, 3rd Edition?
- ☐ Very good
- ☐ Good
- ☐ Satisfactory
- ☐ Poor

How would you rate the *Command Summary and Functions Summary*?
- ☐ Very good
- ☐ Good
- ☐ Satisfactory
- ☐ Poor

How would you rate the *Quick Start tutorials*?
- ☐ Very good
- ☐ Good
- ☐ Satisfactory
- ☐ Poor

How would you rate *Chapter 13: An Integrated Database System*?
- ☐ Very good
- ☐ Good
- ☐ Satisfactory
- ☐ Poor

What do you like *best* about *dBASE IV Handbook*, 3rd Edition?

What do you like *least* about *dBASE IV Handbook*, 3rd Edition?

How do you use *dBASE IV Handbook*, 3rd Edition?

What other Que products do you own?

For what other programs would a Que book be helpful?

Please feel free to list any other comments you may have about *dBASE IV Handbook*, 3rd Edition.

_____

_____

_____

_____

_____

_____

FOLD HERE

_____

_____

_____

_____

Que Corporation
P.O. Box 90
Carmel, IN 46032